Where to wat[ch]

Britain

Simon Harrap and Nigel Redman

Christopher Helm
London

Published 2003 by Christopher Helm, an imprint of
A & C Black Publishers Ltd.,
37 Soho Square, London W1D 3QZ

Reprinted with corrections 2004

Copyright © 2003 text and maps
by Simon Harrap and Nigel Redman
Copyright © 2003 illustrations by Dan Powell,
John Wright and Ren Hathway

ISBN 0-7136-4137-1

A CIP catalogue record for this book is available from
the British Library

A & C Black uses paper produced with elemental chlorine-
free pulp, harvested from managed sustainable forests.

www.acblack.com

Typeset and designed by Susan McIntyre

Printed and bound in Spain by Printek

10 9 8 7 6 5 4 3 2

CONTENTS

ACKNOWLEDGEMENTS

The compilation of a birding site guide inevitably involves tapping into many sources of information. We have trawled the literature (regional and local site guides, county bird reports, magazine articles, reserves information leaflets, websites etc), as well as seeking the priceless knowledge and assistance of a great many people. The considerable number of people and organisations who helped provide and check information for our original guide need to be thanked again. In addition, many others kindly helped us by checking final drafts of this new book. We are very grateful for all their comments and advice, and hope that no names have been omitted from the following list: Annette Adams (Abberton Reservoir), Peter Alker (Pennington Flash), Mike Bailey (Dyfi Estuary), Dawn Balmer (Thetford), Bill Boyd (Holme and Hunstanton), Bob Bullock (Northamptonshire), P. Burns (Pagham Harbour), Dave Bromwich (Gibraltar Point), Jo Calvert (Grafham Water), Phil Chantler (Kent), Nick Collinson (Walberswick), Simon Cox (Essex), Paul Culyer (Cors Caron), Mark Dennis (Trent Valley Pits, Bleasby and Hoveringham Pits), Paul Doyle (Cruden Bay), Bob Elliot (Threave Estate), Pete Ellis (Shetland), Peter Exley (Exe Estuary, Hayle and Sedgemoor), Richard Fairbank (Sussex), Brian Fellows (Thorney Island), Paul Fisher (Snettisham and Titchwell), Laurie Forsyth (Fingringhoe Wick), Nick Gardiner, Andrew Grieve (Blacktoft), Ren Hathway (Scilly and Cornwall), Ray Hawley (Ken–Dee Marshes), Norman Holton (Campfield Marsh, Hodbarrow and St Bees Head), Tony How (Paxton Pits), Michael Hughes (Oxwich, Gower Coast, Worms Head and Burry Inlet), Martin Humphreys (Cwm Clydach), Colin Jakes (Lackford Wildfowl Reserve), Pete Jennings (Elan Valley), Stephen John (Welsh Wildlife Centre), Russell Jones (Ynyshir), Bill Kenmir (Haweswater), Charlie Kitchin (Nene Washes), Paul Laurie (St Margaret's Bay), Russell Leavett (Stour Estuary), Martin Lester (Wicken Fen), Ian Lewington (Oxfordshire), Eddie Maguire (Machrihanish Seabird Observatory), Pete Marsh (Heysham and Morecambe Bay), Trevor Maynard (Aber), Eric Meek (Orkney), Richard Millington (Norfolk), Carl Mitchell (Welney), Steve Moon (Kenfig, Eglwys Nunydd Reservoir and Ogmore Estuary), Derek Moore (Suffolk), Pete Naylor (Staines Reservoirs), Malcolm Ogilvie (Islay), Scott Paterson (Lochwinnoch), Richard Porter (Grafham Water), Geoff Proffitt (Penclacwydd), Doug Radford (Fowlmere), Mick Rogers (Portland), Mike Rogers (county recorders), Roger Riddington (Fair Isle), Peter Robinson (Scilly), Bill Rutherford (Holme), David Saunders (Pembrokeshire), J. N. Sears (Cotswold Water Park), Charlie Self (Coll), Julia Sheehan (Lake Vyrnwy), Brian Small (Suffolk), Graham Smith (Bradwell), Andy Tasker (Brandon Marsh), Chris Tyas (Old Hall Marshes), Steve Whitehouse (Worcestershire), John Wilson (Leighton Moss and Morecambe Bay), Patrick Wisniewski (Martin Mere) and W. Wright (Caerlaverock).

We are also very grateful to our successive editors, Robert Kirk and Mike Unwin, for their patience and understanding over the long gestation of this book, to Marianne Taylor for much help with figure captions, indexing and mapping, to Brian Southern for producing some of the maps (the rest were prepared by SH), to Dan Powell, John Wright and Ren Hathway for the delightful illustrations, to Guy Kirwan for the copy-editing, to Tony Thorn and Sue Paine for preparing the indexes, and to Susan McIntyre for designing and laying out the book, and for dealing with a seemingly endless number of last-minute corrections.

Last but not least we owe a huge debt of gratitude to our families, Anne and Eleanor Harrap, Cheryle Sifontes and Emily Redman, for their unswerving support and love while we spent considerable periods of time researching and writing. We dedicate this book to them.

INTRODUCTION

A bird-finding guide is now a recognised part of any birder's kit – to be kept in the car alongside field guide, map and pub guide. Most birdwatchers are hungry to see as much as possible, and the majority will wish to visit new sites in search of new or unusual birds. *Where to Watch Birds in Britain* is intended to provide an efficient guide for today's mobile birder who wants to visit Britain's best birding areas. This is a book for every birdwatcher, but primarily for those not 'in the know' about all those special places for birds.

Only 35 years ago, there was no comprehensive guide to the best birding sites in Britain. Since then, there have been several, each with a different emphasis, and a series of 14 guides covering each region of Britain in depth. In addition, other local guides cover specific sites or areas, and many nature reserves produce their own leaflets and have their own websites. Indeed, we have witnessed a positive explosion of information in the last three decades.

Our own guide to the best sites in Britain, *Birdwatching in Britain: a site by site guide*, was published in 1987 and has been long overdue for revision. It treated 115 sites or groups of sites of national interest, arranged on a regional basis, as well as a further 88 subsidiary sites. *Where to Watch Birds in Britain* is its successor and, at over 600 pages, it is a considerably expanded volume. In this book, all the 'subsidiary' sites have been expanded into full entries, and many new places have been included. Thus, we now have almost 440 'sites' in the book, but even this is a misleading figure, as in some cases a whole island or a long stretch of coastline is a single site. All the information has been fully revised and expanded, and all the maps have been re-drawn. There are now over 240 maps - but more than 240 sites are mapped, as some maps feature more than one site.

The aims of *Where to Watch Birds in Britain* are very simple, and remain much as in the original guide. Our purpose is simply to provide a single-volume reference to the very best birding sites in Britain, covering as wide a range of habitats and species as possible. It will, we hope, be equally useful for resident birders visiting unfamiliar parts of the country as well as to visitors from overseas who wish to identify and visit the best areas that Britain has to offer. With this guide, we hope that birders will be able to see almost all of the British breeding species, most of the scarce migrants to the country, and even find a few rarities at key migration sites.

It is inevitable that a site guide such as this will become out of date as soon as it is published. In order to help us prepare future editions, we would welcome any corrections or further information. Please write to the authors at Christopher Helm Publishers, 37 Soho Square, London W1D 3QZ.

HOW TO USE THIS BOOK

SITE SELECTION

The choice of sites in a guide such as this is obviously highly subjective. We have tried to select sites that cover a full range of habitats and species, and which provide something that you might not find at your local patch (unless your local patch is one of the sites listed). The principles for site selection remain unchanged from the previous edition:

1. Quality. Does the area provide good birding, whether for a few hours or several days?
2. Species range. Can you see some of the more localised and uncommon species? A few sites have been included which have just one or two of these, but most will have a range of interesting birds, be they regional specialities, important concentrations at certain seasons, or passage migrants.
3. Accessibility. Is it possible to visit the area without making special arrangements? For some sites this can take weeks, which rules out a casual trip. We have made an exception in the case of offshore islands, which usually require advance planning, because their attractions often easily outweigh any inconvenience.

Our choices have been made irrespective of scenic considerations or the possibility of good walking, and there is inevitably a bias towards coastal areas. Most birdwatchers live inland, but the coast offers the most interesting variety of habitats and birds, as well as being the best area to see migrants. The first edition had a bias towards certain regions, for example East Anglia, but this book now has a full range of sites for each region. There is still an emphasis on wetland areas, and reservoirs in particular, as these are more likely to provide a greater variety of species than, say, just another piece of mature woodland. We have not tried to give equal weight to each county, and if any county has few sites with the necessary qualifications, then there are few entries for it in this book. This does not mean that there are no good places for birds in these places, but that they may be inaccessible to the casual visitor or of a local, rather than national, interest. In the end, however, the final selection has been a personal one, based on our own experience and the advice of others.

For reasons of space and practicality, we could not include every site, and some readers may complain that their own particular favourites have been excluded (as a few did after the first edition was published). In some cases they may be justified. However, we have now included many sites that were previously omitted, having had some of these brought to our attention by readers and reviewers, and have tried to strike a reasonable balance overall. We hope that birders will write to us with their views and comments, and that the content will continue to evolve and improve in subsequent editions.

SITE ACCOUNTS

Sites have been grouped into seven regions. The book begins with the Southwest and ends with Scotland. Each regional section commences with an overview map on which each site (or group of sites) is marked with a number that corresponds to the key below it and to the main text entry. County boundaries are marked on the overview maps to help determine the approximate locations of sites. A few sites that are close together and share similar birds are given a slightly different treatment: there is a general introduction to such 'site clusters' and a habitat section covering all the sites in the group. Under the Access heading, the different sites within a cluster are given their own sections, followed by general Birds and Information sections that cover all the sites together. Examples of site clusters include the Isles of Scilly, New Forest, Outer Hebrides, Orkney, and Shetland.

After the site name, the county recorder to whom records should be sent is given in parentheses. This broadly equates to the county in which the site is located, but recording regions are not always the same as counties. In the last 30 years some county boundaries have changed several times and, in a few cases, local bird groups have elected to use the old county boundaries for recording purposes. The 'counties' largely affected by these changes are Avon (now subsumed into North Somerset), Cleveland (still retained even though it does not officially exist), Tyne & Wear (now divided between Northumberland and Durham), and much of Wales and Scotland. Names and addresses of county recorders can be found in *The Birdwatcher's Yearbook*, an annual compendium of invaluable information.

For each site, the relevant Ordnance Survey (OS) sheet number is given. These mostly refer to the OS Landranger series, at a scale of 1:50,000. In some cases, reference is also given to the OS Outdoor Leisure series, or the OS Explorer series; both of these are at a scale of 1:25,000. Whilst any good road atlas will guide birders to every site when used in conjunction with the access information in this book, it is recommended that an OS map is used to locate footpaths and other more precise topographical features, particularly in the case of large areas that are not nature reserves (e.g. Sutherland). Ordnance Survey maps are regarded as the ultimate authority when it comes to the spelling of place names and road numbers.

Each site account begins with a short introduction, highlighting a few key facts and the main points of ornithological interest. This may also include the existence of a reserve (and who owns it), and the most profitable period(s) for a visit. Sometimes, the approximate area of the reserve is given; we have consistently used acres rather than hectares in such cases.

This introductory paragraph is followed by several headed sections (sometimes combined for shorter site entries):

Habitat

The Habitat section briefly outlines the habitats represented and the general layout of the location. Where relevant, historical changes in the habitats may be mentioned and features of the surrounding area if they affect the sites concerned.

Access

The Access section is particularly important. For those sites where the use of the text in conjunction with any of the standard road atlases is sufficient, no map is provided. For the majority, however, a specially drawn map accompanies the text to illustrate the features described. They may help locate the reserve or show the position of trails and hides. The exceptions are very large sites, such as some areas in Scotland, where access away from roads and main tracks in such extensive and complicated areas is impossible for us to depict adequately. Reference to larger-scale Ordnance Survey maps is recommended in these cases. Some 240 maps are included in the book, with some maps covering more than one site.

Directions from the nearest town or main road are given to the point(s) where you can park and exploration on foot begins. Distances and other measurements are in imperial units to conform to current road signs and atlases. Thus we use miles not kilometres, and yards not metres. Take care to park in designated areas wherever possible, and if there are none use common sense and do not obstruct farm gates or private roads. It will be noted that directions invariably assume the use of a car. Most birders use cars to go birding, but it is still possible to use public transport to get to most sites and details can be obtained easily from rail and bus companies, tourist offices and websites. Many reserves have special access arrangements for the disabled and should be contacted for details. For offshore islands, brief details of ferries and flights are given.

Details of the best trails, vantage points, and hides are given, where appropriate, together with brief notes on any specialities to be found. Any restrictions on access and permit arrangements, if needed, are also specified. Prices have generally been excluded as they rarely remain valid for long.

Visiting arrangements for reserves vary a great deal and are frequently subject to changes. We have specified the most vital information but a few points apply to most reserves and have not been constantly repeated. You should assume that all reserves are closed on Christmas and Boxing Days, and that dogs are not allowed onto any reserve. Larger groups are normally required to make special arrangements with the warden prior to a visit. Where members of various organisations are allowed free entry (or reductions on permit prices), they should expect to produce their membership card (if issued). Non-members will be expected to purchase a permit. Remember also that information/visitor centres often have more restricted times of opening than the reserve itself. As a number of the sites are RSPB reserves it is worth noting that an annual summary of access arrangements is available (or check the RSPB website: www.rspb.org.uk).

Accommodation is outside the scope of this book (though such information is provided for bird observatories), but its availability on islands is indicated. Full details can be obtained from the relevant tourist office (see also Information sections).

Birding may take you into unfamiliar situations where there is an element of risk for the inexperienced. We hardly need to point out the dangers presented by cliffs, but saltmarshes and tidal flats are also potentially lethal. In some places the tide can advance extremely quickly and unless you have expert local knowledge it is best to leave these well before high water or to avoid them altogether.

Birds

In this section we have tried to highlight the more interesting species you may see, as well as mentioning some of the commoner ones; very common and widespread species are generally omitted. It should be stressed that you will not see all the birds listed on a single visit or even after several visits. At migration sites in particular, many days can be quite birdless if the weather conditions are wrong, and good 'falls' of migrants should be regarded as unusual. Scarce migrants are frequently specified where their occurrence is reasonably regular, although some may only be recorded once or twice a year. However, as a rule, rarities have only been mentioned if they have occurred in a more-or-less predictable pattern. In some instances, a few impressive rarities that have occurred in the past have been mentioned to whet the appetite.

The Birds section has been roughly divided into seasons, but the treatment has been kept flexible. Rather than give a bald list of species which may be found, we have attempted to provide more detail which will assist in locating particular birds, such as an indication of a species' abundance, as well as any specific locations within the site and, in some cases, tactics (such as timing) which may be helpful in tracking down the bird. Where relevant, general weather considerations are also mentioned.

Information

The final section of the site accounts is Information. For reserves, the name and address of the warden is usually given, but be aware that wardens do change jobs. In many instances telephone numbers and e-mail addresses have also been included, but please have consideration for the privacy of the warden where the address is clearly a private one. Many reserves nowadays have visitor centres, and these are only open during 'office hours'.

Sources of further information (such as wildlife trusts, local authorities and water companies) may also be given. Details on obtaining permits are mentioned where necessary but, with the exception of some reservoirs, most permits are available on site. Books or checklists devoted entirely to the site are sometimes listed but county avifaunas and local bird reports, both essential sources for anyone interested in a particular area, are not.

ENGLISH NAMES AND TAXONOMY

We have been conservative in our approach to the use of English names. Whilst we generally approve of the recent proposals to make all English names for species unique (but not necessarily for them to indicate taxonomic affinities), we have chosen to use simpler names in many cases. Thus, we have omitted the now familiar prefixes for many species listed in the site accounts. This is partly for simplicity (it takes up less space), but also because in practice these are the names in use in the field. So, we have Swallow, not Barn Swallow, and Redstart, not Common Redstart. One cannot deny that the majority of birders still use these names without the prefixes in the field, even if they do include them in their notebooks or in published work. We hope that visitors from overseas will not be confused by this, nor that they will accuse us of imperialism.

Taxonomy is not really an issue in a book such as this. We generally follow the British Ornithologists' Union in such matters, as they are keepers of the official British List. However, we do treat Yellow-legged Gull *Larus michahellis* and Caspian Gull *L. cachinnans* as separate species (from Herring Gull), even though the BOU does not recognise this yet. Both are mentioned in site accounts; the former is the more frequent visitor to Britain.

Other recent splits include Green-winged Teal *Anas carolinensis*, now separated from Common Teal, and Redpoll, which has been split into Lesser Redpoll *Carduelis cabaret* and Common Redpoll *Carduelis flammea*. In the former case, Green-winged Teal is only a vagrant and cannot be guaranteed at any site; it is, in fact, mentioned in passing for a couple of sites. In the case of the redpolls, the form that commonly breeds in Britain is Lesser Redpoll, whilst Common is a migrant. In the text, we have not distinguished between the forms involved. In most cases, reference to Redpoll will refer to the resident Lesser Redpoll, but Common may well be encountered on passage or in winter. We also include Balearic Shearwater (formerly united with Yelkouan Shearwater under the name Mediterranean Shearwater). However, we do sometimes use established English names for well-marked subspecies, e.g. Dark-bellied and Pale-bellied Brent Geese, and Black Brant.

ABBREVIATIONS

Abbreviations used throughout the book (without explanation) are: CCW (Countryside Council for Wales), EN (English Nature), FC (Forestry Commission, now called Forest Enterprise), LNR (Local Nature Reserve), NNR (National

Nature Reserve), NP (National Park), NR (Nature Reserve), NT (National Trust), NTS (National Trust for Scotland), OS (Ordnance Survey), RSNC (Royal Society for Nature Conservation), RSPB (Royal Society for the Protection of Birds), SNH (Scottish National Heritage), SPA (Special Protection Area), SSSI (Site of Special Scientific Interest), SWT (Scottish Wildlife Trust), and WWT (Wildfowl & Wetlands Trust). Other acronyms have only been employed on a site-by-site basis, and in each case the name is given in full at the first mention in the site account.

FURTHER INFORMATION

Probably the single most important additional source of information is the indispensable *Birdwatcher's Yearbook*. This is published annually by Buckingham Press and includes a full listing of county recorders, names and addresses of local bird clubs and national organisations, websites, tide tables and much more besides.

For more detailed site information, and for sites of more local interest rather than national interest, we recommend the excellent series of regional *Where to Watch* guides, also published by Christopher Helm. Fourteen guides cover the whole of Britain (plus another for Ireland), and these are listed opposite the title page at the front of this book.

There are many other sources of information for birders. Most counties publish county avifaunas and produce annual bird reports (these are all listed in the *Birdwatcher's Yearbook*). In addition, a number of reserves and local bird clubs publish their own reports (usually annually), and most reserves have free leaflets available. Almost all organisations and many reserves now have their own websites, and these are perhaps the best way to get up-to-date information on sites. For a useful summary of the status and population of Britain's resident and more regular migrant species, we can recommend Chris Mead's *The State of the Nation's Birds* (Whittet Books, 2000). This excellent book looks at the past fortunes of many of our birds and even gives predictions for the future.

Finally, for those that seek information about rarities there are various telephone hotlines, both for national and regional news, and also websites which give up-to-date bird news. If you must keep abreast of rare bird news as it happens, then a personal pager is the only solution.

INDEXES

Two indexes are provided. The first is an index to bird species mentioned in the site accounts, allowing the reader to locate all the best sites for a particular species. Every species in the text is indexed by site number; the site numbers in the index follow the sequence of the main text, with prefixes of SW, SE, EA, CE, W, NE and S to indicate where each region's index entries begin.

Secondly, the index of sites lists every site and many other places within a site. This is indexed by page number, and is designed to help locate unfamiliar places.

KEY TO THE MAPS

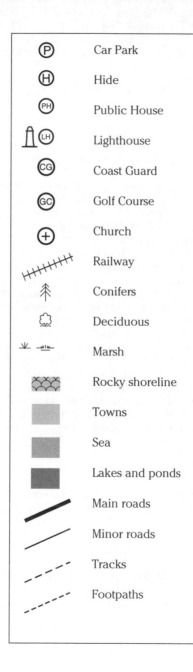

℗	Car Park
Ⓗ	Hide
⒫⒣	Public House
🗼 ⓛⒽ	Lighthouse
ⓒⒼ	Coast Guard
ⓖⒸ	Golf Course
⊕	Church
⊩⊩⊩⊩⊩⊩	Railway
🌲	Conifers
🌳	Deciduous
⊻	Marsh
▨	Rocky shoreline
▨	Towns
▨	Sea
▨	Lakes and ponds
╱	Main roads
╱	Minor roads
╱	Tracks
╱	Footpaths

14

SOUTHWEST ENGLAND

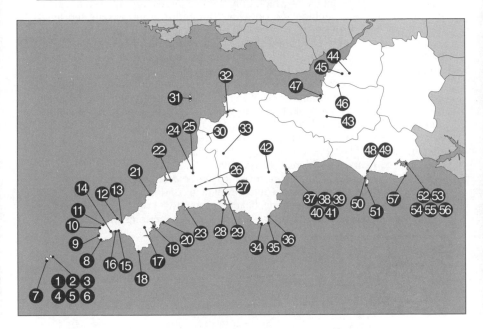

Isles of Scilly:
1 St Mary's
2 St Agnes
3 Tresco
4 Bryher
5 St Martin's
6 Uninhabited Islands
7 Pelagic Seabird Trips

8–10 Land's End
8 Porthgwarra
9 Sennen Cove
10 St Just
11 Pendeen Watch
12 St Ives
13 Hayle Estuary
14 Drift Reservoir
15 Marazion
16 Mount's Bay
17 Stithians Reservoir
18 The Lizard
19 Fal Estuary

20 Gerrans Bay
21 Newquay
22 Camel Estuary
23 Par Beach and Pool
24 Davidstow Airfield
25 Crowdy Reservoir
26 Colliford Reservoir
27 Siblyback Reservoir
28 Rame Head
29 Tamar Estuary
30 Tamar Lakes
31 Lundy
32 Taw-Torridge Estuary
33 Roadford Lake
34 Prawle Point
35 Start Point
36 Slapton Ley
37–41 Exe Estuary
37 Exminster Marshes
38 Bowling Green Marsh
39 Powderham
40 Dawlish Warren

41 Exmouth
42 Yarner Wood
43 West Sedgemoor
44 Chew Valley Lake
45 Blagdon Lake
46 Cheddar Reservoir
47 Bridgwater Bay
48 Radipole Lake
49 Lodmoor
50 Portland Harbour,
      Ferrybridge & Fleet
51 Portland Bill
52–57 Poole Harbour and
      Isle of Purbeck
52 Poole Harbour
53 Studland Heath
54 Shell and Studland Bays
55 Brownsea Island
56 Arne
57 Durlston Head–
      St Aldhelm's Head

ISLES OF SCILLY

Approximately 150 islands, of which only the five largest are inhabited, consti-
tute the picturesque archipelago of Scilly. The entire group is only ten miles
across and lies 28 miles off Land's End. The geographical position of Scilly
ensures a wide variety of migrants in spring and autumn, and many seabirds
breed in summer. The best times for migrants are mid-March to May and
August–October; breeding seabirds are best seen May–July.

Over the last 30 years the Isles of Scilly have established themselves as the premier site in Britain for rarities, even overtaking the legendary Fair Isle. Although
Nearctic species are particularly sought-after and are now an annual feature,
almost anything can and does turn up. October is the key month but late
September and early November can also be outstanding. In addition to true
vagrants, some of Britain's scarcer migrants, which occur only irregularly on the
mainland, can almost be guaranteed on Scilly.

Weather has a major influence on birding on Scilly. The conditions bringing
vagrants to the islands are complex and only partially understood. Light southerlies
are best for falls of migrants in spring. In autumn southwest winds prevail, and fast-
moving wave depressions originating off North America are sometimes responsible

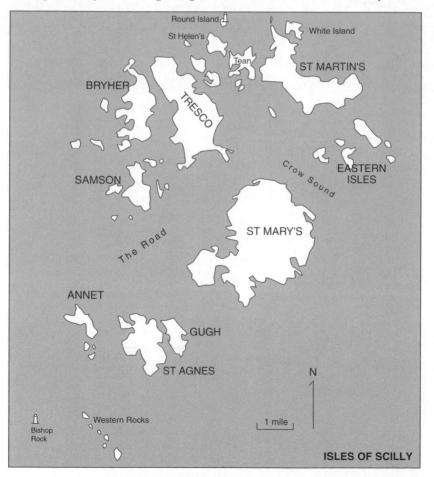

ISLES OF SCILLY

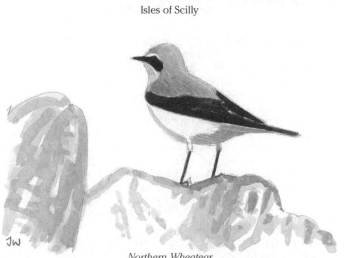

Northern Wheatear

for small falls of American landbirds, chiefly in late September to late October. American waders are less affected by such weather systems and tend to arrive somewhat earlier. Southeast winds in autumn may bring Asiatic birds but sometimes rarities appear in apparently unsuitable weather conditions. Strong SW–NW winds can be good for seawatching but this pursuit is rarely well rewarded on Scilly, although occasionally there is a good passage of large shearwaters in August.

Scilly is exceedingly popular with traditional holidaymakers during summer but by October they are replaced by legions of birdwatchers. Strangely, the islands are comparatively neglected by birders in spring.

Habitat

The smaller islands tend to be rocky and sparsely vegetated, while the larger ones, particularly those inhabited, possess a range of habitats. Around the coast are low granite cliffs, rocky shores, and sandy beaches. Exposed areas with poor soil remain as heaths or grassy downs, and on St Mary's the golf course and airfield have created an important habitat. The few freshwater pools and associated marshland with dense clumps of sallows are especially attractive, but there is little natural woodland. Cornish elms grow in more sheltered areas and stands of introduced pines occur in places. Tresco Abbey Gardens hold a broad variety of exotic trees and shrubs but are not very exciting ornithologically.

Large areas of the inhabited islands are farmed. This includes grazing land, but the dominant industry on Scilly, other than tourism, is flower farming. The tiny bulb fields are surrounded by tall hedges of introduced shrubs to protect them from the winds.

Access

By air: British International Helicopters operates between Penzance and St Mary's daily (except Sunday); April–October inclusive there are also daily flights to Tresco. The journey takes 20 minutes, and the number of flights per day is considerably reduced November–March. Penzance Heliport lies 1 mile east of Penzance by the A30, and parking is available (fee). The Isles of Scilly Skybus operates frequent flights throughout the year from Land's End Aerodrome, St Just, and from Newquay (except Sundays). A car park (fee) is available at St Just, and also a minibus connection to Penzance railway station. Between March and October, Skybus also offers flights from Southampton, Bournemouth, Bristol and Exeter. The eight-seater Skybus can also be chartered for urgent twitches.

By sea: the Scillonian III sails from Penzance to St Mary's. The voyage takes 2½ hours, but may be prolonged by rough weather. The usual departure times are 09.15 from Penzance, 16.30 from St Mary's but these times vary on Saturday sailings in summer. There are daily sailings (except Sundays) April–October, but no service November–March inclusive. Always check departure times in advance.

There is a wide variety of accommodation on the islands, with the greatest choice on St Mary's. Information and accommodation lists are available from the Tourist Information Centre, and early booking of all transport and accommodation is essential, especially for October.

Once on the islands it is easy to walk anywhere, but there are taxis and buses on St Mary's. Passenger launches leave St Mary's quay daily to the off-islands March–October inclusive, normally at 10.15 and 14.15, with extra sailings on demand. 'Seabird Specials' are organised in season for locally breeding seabirds. Full details are posted on the quay. For those staying on other islands, inter-island transport is more problematic and, apart from the regular services to St Mary's, ad hoc arrangements must be made.

Roads, footpaths and nature trails access most areas on the islands. Birders should keep out of fields and other private areas. In addition, the airport may only be viewed from the perimeter and the golf course should not be traversed when play is in progress.

1 ST MARY'S (Isles of Scilly)

OS Landranger 203
OS Explorer 101

This is the largest island and contains a wide variety of habitats. In addition to the sites detailed, it is worth checking all sheltered bushes and trees for migrants and the ploughed and grassy fields for larks, pipits and buntings.

The Garrison A choice of trails leads around this headland. Access is from Hugh Town, up a steep hill past Tregarthen's Hotel. There is a stand of pine trees next to the playing field (campsite nearby) and many sheltered spots for migrant passerines amid the more open areas. The Lower Walk, accessible via Sally Port, has attractive belts of elms and takes you to the main circular path.

Peninnis Head The fields and bushes are well worth checking on the way. Certain migrants favour the short turf around the headland and the Head itself is one of the best seawatching points on St Mary's. The elms in Old Town churchyard regularly attract migrants. There is a temporary trail in October.

Lower Moors A nature trail (From Rocky Hill via Rose Hill to Old Town Bay) crosses the marshes and reedbeds and there are two hides and a small scrape. Check the dense sallows carefully.

Airport Waders (including occasional Dotterel and Buff-breasted Sandpiper), pipits, and buntings occur occasionally. Check from the edges only. In October there is arranged access to an observation area by the windsock, accessed from the coastal path.

Salakee The fields around the farm have produced some outstanding rarities. Access from the airport is no longer allowed, but Salakee can still be reached from Porth Hellick or the road at Carn Friars Lane.

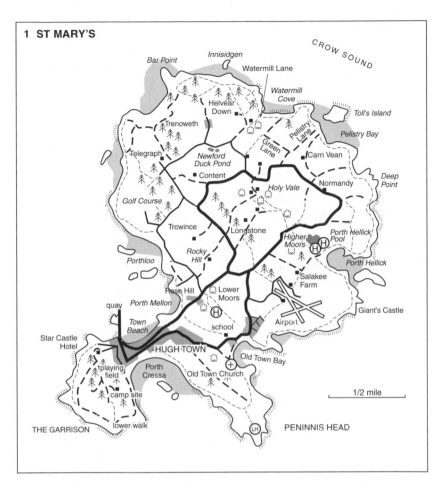

1 ST MARY'S

Porth Hellick Pool and Higher Moors A nature trail skirts the west side of the pool and continues through the marshland of Higher Moors. Two hides overlook the pool and reedbeds, which attract wildfowl and a few waders; migrant passerines favour the shallows.

Holy Vale This is one of the best areas and receives considerable attention. The trail from Higher Moors crosses the road and continues through sallows, brambles and marshland into a narrow trail through tall elms with dense undergrowth—a jungle by Scilly standards. The trail continues to Holy Vale Farm and the main road. Two temporary trails are opened in October at the discretion of the farmers.

Watermill Lane and Cove Newford Duck Pond, the elms alongside Watermill Lane, and the bushes near the Cove are worth checking. From the Cove, a coastal path heads south to Pelistry and north to Bar Point, passing through bracken-covered slopes and scattered clumps of pines.

Golf Course Dotterel and Buff-breasted Sandpiper are almost annual, and pipits and buntings turn up regularly. The surrounding fields may also hold the same species.

2 ST AGNES (Isles of Scilly)

OS Landranger 203
OS Explorer 101

The most southwesterly of the inhabited islands, facing directly into the Atlantic and therefore the first landfall for American vagrants. It is a little more than 1 mile in length with a very small population. The islet of Gugh is connected to St Agnes at low tide by a sand bar.

The Parsonage This secluded garden and small orchard surrounded by elms, hedges and dense vegetation is undoubtedly the best spot for migrant passerines and rarities on St Agnes. Unfortunately there is no access to the garden, but the trees of the Parsonage can be viewed from the lane outside.

Big Pool This pool, surrounded by sedges, usually appears devoid of birds but a number of unexpected species have turned up here over the years.

Periglis and Porth Killier The best bays for waders on St Agnes.

Chapel Fields and Troy Town Fields These small bulb fields, surrounded by brambles and hedges, are always worth checking in autumn.

Barnaby Lane A tree-lined lane favoured by warblers and Firecrest.

Covean A track leads to this sheltered bay from Covean Cottage in Higher Town. Tamarisks, brambles and hedges surround the bulb fields.

Wingletang Down This area of moorland with gorse bushes and granite boulders is often disappointing for birds but Lapland Bunting is fairly regular and several rarities have been found.

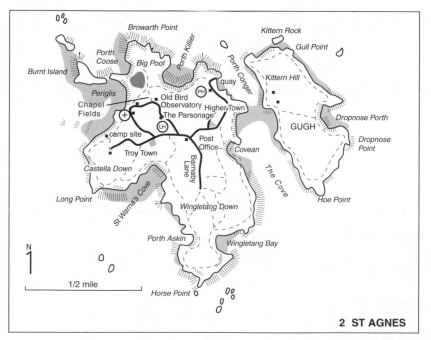

2 ST AGNES

Horse Point This is the best seawatching site on St Agnes.

Gugh The small overgrown fields in the middle of the island sometimes harbour migrants.

3 TRESCO (Isles of Scilly)

OS Landranger 203
OS Explorer 101

The island, dominated by Tresco Abbey and its gardens of exotic trees and plants, is a privately leased estate. Depending on the tides, boats land either at Carn Near or New Grimsby. Though private, access is generally unrestricted along footpaths and roads. Areas of woodland occur in many places but most are unproductive pine plantations. Tresco is a large island with a great potential for rarities. Most birders only make brief visits and to the same few areas— greater coverage would undoubtedly produce more.

Abbey Pool A small pool with sandy edges easily checked for waders.

Great Pool The largest area of fresh water on Scilly, surrounded by reeds and sallows. Not all of the pool is easily viewed; in particular try at each end and from certain points along the north side. Two hides provide good viewing opportunities for wildfowl and waders. Wildfowl are a notable feature and rarer species are found quite regularly. The sallows around the edges should be checked, and the fields on the north side often hold finches and buntings.

Borough Farm The fields and hedges around the farm have attracted several rarities in recent years. Access is limited to the main tracks through the farm.

4 BRYHER (Isles of Scilly)

OS Landranger 203
OS Explorer 101

Lying immediately west of Tresco, Bryher is surprisingly little visited by birders. The weedy fields in the centre of the island attract finches and buntings but there is little farming here now, and any area of bushes should be checked. The pool on the west side has produced some unusual waders though the commoner species prefer the coastal bays and Stinking Porth is one of the best.

5 ST MARTIN'S (Isles of Scilly)

OS Landranger 203
OS Explorer 101

This large island lies north of St Mary's. There are two widely separated landing points: Lower Town at high tide, Higher Town at other times. Much of the island is cultivated and the higher part is rather open. The most sheltered areas are the fields and hedges on the south side. One of the best areas is east of Higher Town: from the quay, walk towards Higher Town and bear right around the coast checking the bushes and trees on the left. After ½ mile turn left along a track to a farm where a short nature trail runs through fields; there are some mature elms here.

6 UNINHABITED ISLANDS (Isles of Scilly)

OS Landranger 203
OS Explorer 101

There are three main groups: Western Rocks, Northern Rocks and the Eastern Isles. The main interest is breeding seabirds. Several of the best islands have restricted access during the breeding season, but are easily viewed from the boats.

Birds

Over 400 species of birds have been recorded on Scilly including a remarkable number of rarities and numerous firsts for Britain.

Spring passage gets underway in March and the main passage continues into April–May, but numbers are rarely impressive. Spring overshoots are annual, the most frequent species being Hoopoe in March–April. A Woodchat Shrike or something rarer is a distinct possibility, with this period often producing records of the scarcer British herons, and small numbers of Golden Orioles are regular in May.

Summer is essentially for breeding seabirds. Most are present April–July, though some species can be seen around the islands all year. Shag and Kittiwake are common and Fulmar has increased recently. Razorbill is the most numerous auk but only c.200 pairs breed. Guillemot is rather less numerous. Most of the Puffins breed on Annet, which is also home to Manx Shearwater and Storm Petrel. The latter two, however, are rarely seen around the islands during the day and are best seen from the Scillonian. Common Tern breeds on the islands, but Roseate Tern no longer does so.

Since 1997 deep-sea fishing boats have provided sightings of Wilson's Petrel and large shearwaters, and even an occasional Fea's Petrel. Between July and September two boats (*Sapphire* and *Kingfisher*) regularly go up to 8 miles south or southwest off St Agnes (usually 17.00 to dark), giving extremely close views of petrels and shearwaters.

Autumn wader passage occurs July–October with a peak in September, but numbers are generally small. Commoner waders include Little Stint and Curlew Sandpiper. American vagrants (18 species recorded) are annual, mainly in September. American Golden Plover and Pectoral Sandpiper are among the more frequent but equally predictable is Buff-breasted Sandpiper, a grassland wader uncommon on the east coast of America but a near-annual visitor to the golf course and airfield in September. One or two Dotterel quite often share this habitat, occurring late August–October.

Seabird passage is rarely impressive and is usually best during or after southwest or northwest gales. The best seawatching points are Peninnis Head and Deep Point (St Mary's), Horse Point (St Agnes), and the north tip of Tresco. Seabirds are often better observed from the Scillonian. Great and Cory's Shearwaters can be expected in late July and August in the right conditions, from southern viewpoints. Manx and Sooty Shearwaters and Great and Arctic Skuas are quite regular in September. Later in the autumn, gales may bring Leach's Petrel or Grey Phalarope.

Passerine migration is most evident in September and includes Redstart, Ring Ouzel, Whinchat and Pied Flycatcher. Many of the scarcer migrants are annual on Scilly and sometimes outnumber their more familiar counterparts. Among the earlier arrivals are Icterine and Melodious Warblers and Red-backed and Woodchat Shrikes, which occur from late August to October. Other species recorded annually in variable numbers, mainly September–October, are Wryneck, Richard's and Tawny Pipits, Bluethroat, Barred Warbler, Common Rosefinch, and Lapland, Snow and Ortolan Buntings. Yellow-browed Warbler, Firecrest and Red-breasted Flycatcher are regular between late September and early November, sometimes in comparatively large numbers, and can almost be guaranteed in October. A number of rarities are now annual, or almost so, on Scilly. These include Short-toed Lark, Rose-coloured Starling, and Rustic and Little Buntings. Late September to the end of October is the best time for American landbirds; perhaps the most frequent is Red-eyed Vireo, but Grey-cheeked Thrush, Blackpoll Warbler, Rose-breasted Grosbeak and Bobolink have all put in a number of appearances, and a host of other Nearctic passerines has been recorded.

Asiatic visitors tend to arrive slightly later, mostly early October to early November: the most regular in the last decade have included Olive-backed Pipit and Booted, Radde's, Dusky and Pallas's Warblers. But extreme vagrants from this sector also occur with some frequency, with Pechora Pipit, Siberian and White's Thrushes and Yellow-browed Bunting all having occurred in recent years. Rarities from closer to home also make landfall; Red-throated Pipit and Subalpine, Greenish, Arctic and Bonelli's Warblers have each been recorded a number of times.

Raptors are not infrequent in autumn with Merlin and Peregrine seen almost daily from October. Rarer visitors include occasional Osprey, Honey Buzzard, harriers and Black Kite, and Scilly recently played host to Britain's first Short-toed Eagle. Late September and October usually produces a few Spotted Crakes and Corncrakes but their retiring habits cause them to be easily overlooked. By November, the birding scene is considerably quieter; migrant passerines include thrushes, finches, Blackcap, Chiffchaff and a few Firecrests, some of which winter in the archipelago. New arrivals include Woodcock, one or two Short-eared Owls, and perhaps a Long-eared Owl (the latter winters regularly on Tresco, but numbers fluctuate considerably). Black Redstarts sometimes arrive in considerable numbers at this time, frequenting the rocky coasts and bulb fields.

Winter is bleak and few birders visit the islands. Severe gales are frequent, though freezing conditions are rare. Several Great Northern Divers are usually present in the channels between the islands, Crow Sound being particularly favoured. Gannet and Kittiwake can usually be seen offshore and numbers of Purple Sandpipers frequent coasts. Geese are occasional visitors in very small numbers and a variety of duck winters on the Great Pool on Tresco. One or two sea duck and grebes (especially Slavonian) winter in The Roads. Visiting Water Rails greatly outnumber the few residents and a wintering Merlin could be seen anywhere.

Information

Accommodation: Tourist Information Centre, Hugh Street, Hugh Town, Isles of Scilly TR21 0LL. Tel: 01720 422536. E-mail: tic@scilly.gov.uk   Internet: www.simplyscilly.co.uk

British International Helicopters, The Heliport, Penzance, Cornwall TR18 3AP. Tel: 01736 363871. Scilly, Tel: 01720 422646. Internet: www.scillyhelicopter.co.uk

Isles of Scilly Travel (Isles of Scilly Steamship Group), Quay Street, Penzance, Cornwall TR18 4BZ. Tel: 0845 710 5555. Internet: www.ios-travel.co.uk (operates Skybus and Scillonian).

Isles of Scilly Bird Group, Membership Secretary: Katharine Sawyer, Alegria, High Lanes, St Mary's, Isles of Scilly.

In October, a bird log is called each evening at the Scillonian Club in Hugh Town. This is an excellent source of information, and an enjoyable occasion for all who participate. Temporary membership of the Scillonian Club is required for all visiting birders. In addition, a blackboard with indispensable bird information is located outside the back door of the Pilot's Gig Restaurant, opposite the Mermaid Inn. It also contains notices of the Isles of Scilly Bird Group (ISBG), and now remains here all year. A similar, less extensive, noticeboard is located outside St Agnes Post Office.

7 PELAGIC SEABIRD TRIPS

Pelagic trips into the rich waters of the Western Approaches to the English Channel often yield good views of species unlikely to be seen well from the mainland. A much sought-after speciality is Wilson's Storm Petrel, which is recorded regularly on pelagic trips but very seldom seen from land. Charter trips take place in late summer and early autumn, this being the peak period for seabirds. Birds are most numerous around trawlers and are often drawn in towards the charter vessel by using 'chum', a foul mixture of fish oil and offal that floats on the surface.

Birds

Storm Petrel is common while Wilson's Storm Petrel is reasonably regular, albeit usually in tiny numbers. Great Shearwaters can be fairly numerous but Cory's Shearwater is scarce. All of the commoner skuas occur with Long-tailed Skua being the rarest, and Sabine's Gull is another rarity that is seen regularly. There is always the possibility of an extreme rarity; for instance, a Fea's Petrel followed one boat for a considerable period in 2001, permitting all those on board to gain excellent views.

Information

The Isles of Scilly ferry, the *MV Scillonian* runs one pelagic per year (usually in mid-August) sailing from Penzance (16 hours return trip). Contact the Isles of Scilly Steamship Company, Penzance (tel: 0845 7105555) or look for advertisements in birdwatching magazines. Interest in these trips is usually high and it is therefore best to book well in advance. Private vessels can be chartered from large ports such as Penzance or Falmouth by arrangement. For pelagics out from the Isles of Scilly, see page 24.

8–10 LAND'S END (Cornwall)   OS Landranger 203

The Land's End area is famed for attracting migrants in spring and autumn and, in particular, rarities. Though overshadowed by Scilly, it has produced some outstanding rarities and is worthy of more extensive coverage, especially in late autumn. Seawatching off Porthgwarra can be rewarding especially in August–September.

Habitat

The exposed peninsula of Land's End comprises moorland and rough grazing fields surrounded by impressive granite cliffs. Trees and bushes only gain a foothold in the more sheltered valleys and hollows, and these are important refuges for migrants.

Access (see map)

All of the following sites are close together and several may be combined in a single visit.

8 PORTHGWARRA (Cornwall)   OS Landranger 203

The most famous valley in west Cornwall, its position at the southwest tip of the peninsula ensures a regular trickle of American landbirds. Leave Penzance west on the A30. At Catchall, turn left on the B3283 to St Buryan. Beyond St Buryan, join the B3315 and continue towards Land's End for 2 miles. At Polgigga, turn left to Porthgwarra. There is a car park in the village, just beyond the final hairpin at the end of the valley. Migrant passerines may use any suitable cover. In particular, check the dense bushes in the valley and gardens in the village. From the car park the road continues to the coastguard cottages and several paths lead to the cliffs and across the moorland to a small pool at the head of the valley. Seawatching is best from Gwennap Head, near the coastguard lookout. From Porthgwarra village a coastal footpath heads east to St Levan, which has more gardens and trees.

9 SENNEN COVE (Cornwall)

OS Landranger 203

This village lies at the south end of Whitesand Bay, 1 mile north of Land's End. Divers, grebes and various seabirds may be seen offshore in season. From Land's End, turn left off the A30 beyond Sennen on a minor road to Sennen Cove. There is a car park overlooking the bay. Walk the beach or seawatch from the coastguard lookout west of the village.

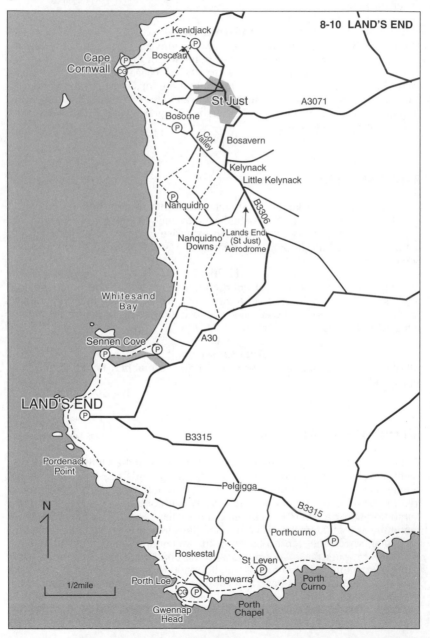

10 ST JUST (Cornwall)

There are several sites in the St Just area which are worthy of exploration:

St Just Airfield This small airfield 3 miles northeast of Land's End is not heavily used and attracts waders. From Land's End, turn left north on the B3306 towards St Just. The airfield is on the left after 1½ miles. The best views are from the minor road to Nanquidno along its north side.

Nanquidno This sheltered, well-vegetated valley west of St Just airfield is another excellent area for migrant passerines, and several American rarities have been found. Park at the end of the road and explore the dense bushes and trees in the valley bottom.

Cot Valley This valley lies north of Nanquidno and is also good for migrants. Leave St Just village on the road to Cape Cornwall and almost immediately turn left on a minor road signed Cot Valley. Parking is limited along the road. Check the gardens at the head of the valley and any other areas of cover. The road and a footpath continue alongside the valley to the coast.

Kenidjack This valley lies to the north of Cot Valley, and northwest of St Just. It is also good for migrants. Leave St Just northwards on the road to St Ives and take the first turning on the left at the bottom of the hill. There is limited parking here. Walk the valley towards the coast.

Birds

Spring migration commences early, in March, and a variety of migrants pass through in April–May, though generally in small numbers. Typical species include Turtle Dove, Cuckoo, Redstart, Whinchat, Ring Ouzel, Grasshopper Warbler, and Spotted and Pied Flycatchers. An unusual spring migrant or a rarity is most likely in May, though March–April can produce unexpected rarities such as a white-phase Gyrfalcon which graced the cliffs near St Just in 2000.

Seabird passage in spring is light, peaking April–May. All three divers may be seen as well as small numbers of Manx Shearwater, Common Scoter, Whimbrel, Sandwich and Common Terns, and the occasional skua. Numbers and diversity of seabirds increase from July. Balearic Shearwater and Great and Arctic Skuas are regular in small numbers. Much less frequent, and generally later in autumn, are Great and Sooty Shearwaters and Pomarine Skua. The best winds are usually SE–SW and not too strong. In recent years, Cory's Shearwater has regularly appeared off Porthgwarra in July–August, sometimes in large numbers. Fea's Petrel has also been claimed several times recently.

Passerine migrants reappear from August and a few scarce visitors, such as Melodious Warbler or Woodchat Shrike, are found annually. Later, light easterlies may bring Wryneck, Barred and Yellow-browed Warblers or Red-breasted Flycatcher. October–November sees movements of Skylarks, pipits, Robins, Goldcrests and finches, and a few Black Redstarts, Ring Ouzels and Firecrests. A sprinkling of raptors arrives at this time including Hen Harrier, Merlin, Peregrine and Short-eared Owl, but late autumn is most notable for rarities, including occasional Nearctic landbirds, especially after strong southwest winds. While the valleys are perhaps most famed for their attractiveness to North American migrants, just as on Scilly vagrants have appeared from most points of the compass. Be prepared (but never hope) for the unexpected. The short turf of St Just airfield attracts Golden Plovers and Lapwings in autumn, and species such as Ruff and Whimbrel may accompany them. Very small numbers of Dotterel are regular in autumn and occasionally also Buff-breasted Sandpiper. Richard's and Tawny Pipits, and Lapland and Snow Buntings occur infrequently, and most exceptionally both Blyth's and Pechora Pipits have been recorded. Some of the fields and grassy clifftops offer a similar habitat.

Winter is fairly quiet. A few seabirds such as Gannet can be seen and divers are sometimes offshore. Small numbers of Hen Harrier and other raptors winter on the moors and Chiffchaff and Firecrest in the sheltered valleys. Resident species are usually in evidence, including Buzzard, Sparrowhawk, Peregrine, Green Woodpecker, Rock Pipit and Raven.

11 PENDEEN WATCH (Cornwall)   OS Landranger 203

Pendeen Watch lies at the extreme northwestern tip of the Land's End peninsula and is an important seawatching site.

Habitat
The watchpoint is an open grassy clifftop, beside the lighthouse.

Access
The village of Pendeen lies on the B3306 between St Just and St Ives. From the village, a minor road is signed to the lighthouse. After 1 mile, park at the end of the road and descend the steps to the right of the lighthouse, to seek shelter from northwest winds at the base of the east-facing wall. This is better than watching from the car park.

Birds
Seawatching at Pendeen is rather similar to St Ives (see below), and indeed many of the same birds pass both sites within a short time of each other. The same weather conditions apply to both sites, although slightly more westerly winds can produce good numbers of birds at Pendeen. The passing seabirds can sometimes be a little distant compared to St Ives, but Pendeen is generally better for the larger shearwaters: Great, Cory's and Sooty are regular here in July - September. As for St Ives, it is vital to check the weather forecast to ensure a successful visit.

12 ST IVES (Cornwall)   OS Landranger 203

St Ives is well known as one of Britain's best seawatching points, if not the best, though in recent years it has been somewhat overshadowed by the advent of regular pelagic trips into the Southwest Approaches and greater attention having been paid to Porthgwarra due to the discovery of regular (sometimes large) movements of Cory's Shearwater off the latter. In appropriate weather in autumn the seabird passage can be truly spectacular, but if the winds are wrong you could see nothing. In addition to large numbers of birds, good days offer a chance of seeing species rarely seen from land. The main attractions in winter are divers and perhaps one of the rarer gulls.

Habitat
St Ives lies on the west side of St Ives Bay and north of the town is The Island, which is actually a rocky headland.

Access (see map)

At the north end of the town follow signs to the car park on The Island and walk to the top of the headland. Seawatching is best from the perimeter of the coastguard lookout. For gulls, check the harbour and (from the car park) the sewage outfall. Other parts of the bay can be viewed from various points in the town and it is possible to walk east along the shore to search for terns on Porth Kidney Sands.

Birds

Weather is critical for large movements of seabirds. Ideal winds are WNW–N, preferably preceded by a southwest gale. Such conditions may only occur a few times a year, and rather than visit on the off-chance you should ideally wait until the correct conditions are forecast. Good winds can produce seabirds at any season but the greatest number and diversity occur late August–November. In west winds seawatching can be better at Pendeen Watch (see p.28), c.10 miles west of St Ives, though the birds are generally more distant.

A few Great Northern Divers and Slavonian Grebes are regularly seen in St Ives Bay in winter. Black-throated Diver is less common and more likely in late winter or early spring. Sea duck (mainly Eider and Common Scoter) are not numerous. Gannet, Cormorant and Shag may occur offshore at any time. A few Purple Sandpipers winter on the headland. Gull flocks should always be checked; Glaucous is the most regular of the scarcer species and late winter is the best time. Iceland Gull is also frequent at this time.

In spring, Mediterranean and Little Gulls are occasional. There is a small passage of Sandwich Terns, with a few Common and Arctic. In appropriate weather there may be a movement of Manx Shearwaters and Kittiwakes, and perhaps the occasional Storm Petrel.

Early-autumn passage is dominated by Fulmar, Manx Shearwater, Arctic Skua, and Common and Sandwich Terns. Smaller numbers of Sooty and Balearic Shearwaters, Great Skua, Little Gull, and Roseate, Little and Black Terns are seen regularly. Storm Petrel occurs but in very variable numbers. Northwest winds in September are likely to bring in thousands of Gannets and Kittiwakes. Leach's Petrel and Sabine's Gull are two of St Ives' specialities and sometimes occur in quite large numbers though a few of each is more normal (beware of misidentifying young Kittiwake as Sabine's Gull—it happens frequently). Pomarine Skua is occasional and Long-tailed Skua rare. Auk passage almost exclusively consists of Razorbill and Guillemot, sometimes in huge numbers in late autumn.

Seabird passage peters out in November though Great Skua, Kittiwake and auks are still much in evidence. Two late species seen in variable numbers are Grey Phalarope and Little Auk. All three divers may be found, including Red-throated, normally the scarcest species in Cornwall. Rock Pipit occurs around the coast and one or two Black Redstarts or Snow Buntings may visit The Island.

13 HAYLE ESTUARY (Cornwall)   OS Landranger 203

The Hayle Estuary's compact size and easy access permit close views of a good variety of wildfowl, waders and gulls. The RSPB bought the estuary in 1992, and added Ryan's Field in 1995. It is best visited in autumn and winter, and American vagrants are a regular feature.

Habitat

The estuary is surrounded by urban development and is effectively divided into two sections, the main bay and Copperhouse Creek; the latter lies within the

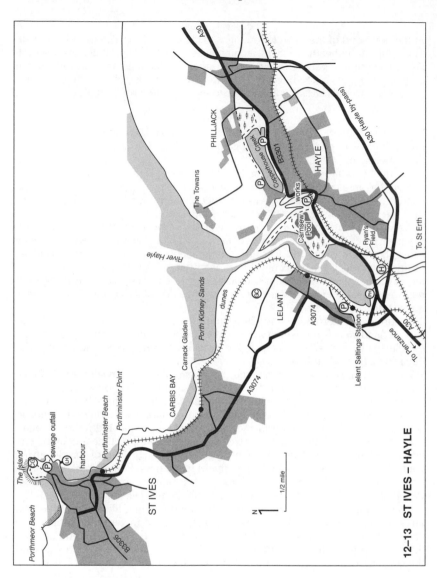

12–13 ST IVES – HAYLE

town of Hayle itself. At low tide, most of the estuary is mudflats with an area of saltmarsh in the southwest corner. Carnsew Pool is separated from the main part of the estuary by a narrow embankment; it is tidal but retains some open water even at low tide. Ryan's Field (RSPB) lies across the road at the southern end of the estuary. This is now being managed, and a lagoon and four islands have been constructed.

Access (see map)

The B3301 (formerly the A30) runs alongside the estuary offering good views from the roadside with several parking places. Waders are best seen within two hours of high tide. Carnsew Pool can be viewed from a public footpath which follows the embankment around the pool and also gives good views of the

Black-headed and Mediterranean Gulls

mudflats. Access is from the B3301 west of Hayle or from the town itself—through a small industrial area west of the viaduct. It may also be worth walking along the spit to the mouth of the estuary. Small numbers of waders roost on the spit and the Pool's embankments. Copperhouse Creek can be watched from the B3301 and the footpaths surrounding it. Ryan's Field lagoon has a hide overlooking it, and an adjacent car park. Waders roost on the lagoon at high tide. To the west of Hayle, Porth Kidney Sands is the best beach for terns in late summer and autumn, and for Sanderling; it can be reached from St Uny church in Lelant.

Birds

In winter Black-throated and Great Northern Divers and Slavonian Grebe are occasionally present on Carnsew Pool. A few Goldeneye and Red-breasted Merganser are regular. Most ducks on the estuary in winter are Teal and Wigeon with smaller numbers of Gadwall. A few Knot, Spotted Redshank, Greenshank and Common Sandpiper usually winter among the commoner waders. Large numbers of gulls are present; a few Mediterranean, Little and Glaucous are regularly seen, especially in late winter, and Ring-billed and Iceland Gulls are annual. Search for the former at Copperhouse Creek, a regular site in winter where the birds are often attracted to the car park by birders throwing food down for them. Peregrine is seen irregularly through the winter and Little Egrets may be seen on Ryan's Field.

Spring passage brings small flocks of Whimbrel, and a few Little Ringed Plovers and Wood Sandpipers are seen annually. Small numbers of terns pass through, and Roseate, Little and Black Terns may feature in these movements.

A greater variety of waders occurs in autumn and although the numbers of each are usually small, they may include Little Stint or Curlew Sandpiper. An American rarity is found almost annually, the most frequent being White-rumped and Pectoral Sandpipers and Long-billed Dowitcher. American Wigeon has been recorded more than once, with at least one multiple occurrence. Dedicated gull-watchers are likely to find Mediterranean and Little Gulls, and small numbers of terns are regularly seen.

Information

Dave Flumm, RSPB, The Manor Office, Marazion, Cornwall TR17 0EF. Tel: 01736 711682.

14 DRIFT RESERVOIR (Cornwall)

OS Landranger 203

This small reservoir lies just west of Penzance and is good for waders and gulls.

Habitat

Areas of mud are exposed around its edges when the water is low, usually in autumn. The surrounding area is largely fields, but there is some woodland at its north end.

Access

Leave Penzance southwest on the A30 and at Lower Drift turn right on a minor road to Sancreed. After a few hundred yards the road passes close to the south end of the reservoir. Part can be viewed from here (there is an unlocked hide) and you can walk around the sides (no permit required). For views of the north end, continue along the road and fork right towards Sellan.

Birds

Drift is noted for attracting gulls, particularly in winter, from the nearby seafront and Glaucous, Iceland, Ring-billed and even Bonaparte's Gulls have been seen there, though Mediterranean is more likely. Other winter/spring attractions include occasional scarce grebes and sea duck. In recent years vagrant Lesser Scaup has occasionally been found among small groups of Scaup.

In autumn attention is focused on passage waders such as Ruff, Curlew Sandpiper and Little Stint. Transatlantic vagrants have included Lesser Yellowlegs and Spotted Sandpiper.

Information

Graham Hobin, Lower Drift Farmhouse, Buryas Bridge, Drift. Penzance, Cornwall. Tel: 01736 362206.

15 MARAZION (Cornwall)

OS Landranger 203

Marazion Marsh is on the coast, east of Penzance. It attracts a number of interesting species, including rarities, in spring and autumn.

Habitat

Most of the marsh is dense reeds and sedges (the largest reedbed in Cornwall) with scattered clumps of bushes. A few open pools with muddy margins attract waders. A road runs along the seaward side, a railway crosses the marsh, and housing flanks another side, but despite this the area remains relatively undisturbed. The 132-acre site is now an RSPB reserve.

Access (see map)

Leaving Penzance on the A30 to Hayle, fork right at Longrock to follow the coast road to Marazion. The marsh is easily viewed from the road. There is a car park just beyond the railway bridge and another at the east end (Ropewalk car park) which is immediately opposite the reserve entrance. Trails lead to a hide and along the seaward side of the marsh.

Birds

Cetti's Warbler is resident and with patience may be seen at any time. Wintering birds include small numbers of the commoner ducks, Water Rail (mostly heard),

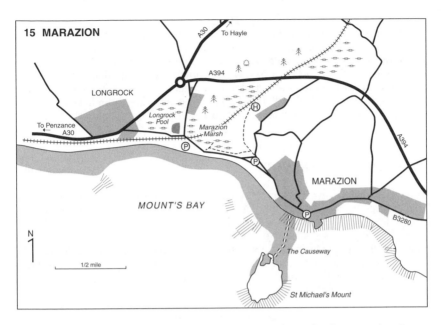

and occasionally Jack Snipe. Marazion also hosts a huge Starling roost in winter.

Spring sees a sprinkling of early passerine migrants and passage waders, and Garganey is regular in early spring. Later a scarce migrant or a rarity is almost inevitable; some of the more likely candidates are Little Egret, Spoonbill, Marsh Harrier and Hoopoe. Water Pipit is occasionally found on the drier edges.

Autumn waders include Little Stint, Curlew Sandpiper and Wood Sandpiper, and a North American wader such as Pectoral Sandpiper or Long-billed Dowitcher is found most years. Spotted Crake is fairly regular, especially in August–September. The passage of hirundines often attracts a Hobby in autumn and Little Gull and Black Tern are seen occasionally. A few Aquatic Warblers are seen each year, usually in mid–late August, and although this species is renowned for skulking in reedbeds Marazion probably offers the best chance of seeing one in Britain—but beware of young Sedge Warblers with crown-stripes.

Information

Dave Flumm, RSPB, The Manor Office, Marazion, Cornwall TR17 0EF. Tel: 01736 711682.

16 MOUNT'S BAY (Cornwall)   OS Landranger 203

This large south-facing bay encompasses the towns of Penzance and Newlyn, as well as St Michael's Mount. It is an important site for seabirds in winter.

Habitat

The undisturbed parts of the shoreline comprise sandy beaches with rocky areas.

Access

Part of this huge bay can be viewed from the beach at Marazion. There is unrestricted access to other areas from the coast road but much of it is disturbed.

Birds

Great Northern Diver is regular in winter and Black-throated Diver frequent but less common. Slavonian Grebe is also usually to be found. Sanderling is common on sandy beaches while Purple Sandpiper prefers rocky areas. Large numbers of gulls gather on the shore or at freshwater outflows when the tide is out. Scarce species such as Glaucous, Iceland, Mediterranean and Little Gulls are regular and rarities such as Ring-billed Gull, Baird's Sandpiper and King Eider have occurred. A small passage of terns occurs in spring and Kentish Plover is almost annual.

17 STITHIANS RESERVOIR   OS Landranger 203

This well-known reservoir lies south of Redruth and is best in autumn and winter for wildfowl and waders. Indeed, it holds an American wader almost every autumn.

Habitat

Much of the reservoir is shallow with natural banks and mud is frequently exposed when the water level drops, while marshy areas at either end provide variety. The surrounding area is largely open moorland. There is some disturbance by windsurfers at weekends.

Access (see map)

Leave Helston on the A394 towards Penryn. After 4½ miles turn left (north) on a minor road signed Stithians. After Carnkie the road crosses the south tip of the reservoir. Waders can be seen well from the road here and there is a marshy area south of the road. Two hides are available (key required, see below) though they are not really necessary on a casual visit. Continue along the road to the north of the reservoir. Beyond the Golden Lion pub, the road again crosses an arm of the reservoir giving views over exposed mud and open water. From here you can also walk along the west edge.

Birds

Waders are the prime interest. Spring passage is poor but autumn can be excellent. In 1994 a long-staying Pied-billed Grebe paired with a Little Grebe and produced several hybrid offspring. The most frequent species from July may include numbers of Little Stint, Curlew and Wood Sandpipers, and occasional Little Ringed Plover. Later in autumn, numbers of Golden Plover and Lapwing reach several thousand. The Golden Plover flock attracts an American Golden Plover almost every year, but the latter can be hard to find on the ground. Another American rarity of incredible regularity is Pectoral Sandpiper—sometimes several together. Other vagrants recorded several times are Long-billed Dowitcher and Lesser Yellowlegs. A variety of raptors has been seen, and in autumn Peregrine is not infrequent. A few Little Gulls and Black Terns occur each autumn. Ducks should not be ignored and Teal flocks should be checked for Garganey and Blue-winged Teal.

Most of the wildfowl arrive in November, a few Goldeneye winter and Scaup is occasional. Few of the waders, other than Golden Plover and Lapwing, remain during the winter, though there are usually a few Ruff.

Information

David Conway, Tregenna, Cooksland, Bodmin, Cornwall PL31 2AR. Tel: 01208 77686

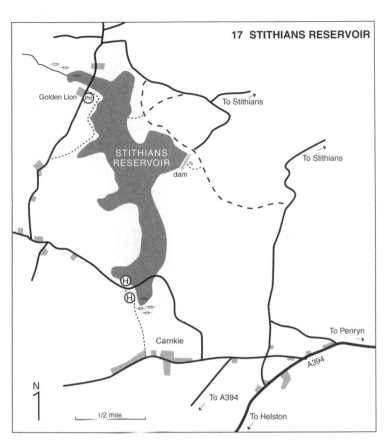

17 STITHIANS RESERVOIR

Golden Lion (PH)

To Stithians

STITHIANS
RESERVOIR

dam

To Stithians

To Penryn

A394

Carnkie

N

1/2 mile

To A394

To Helston

18 THE LIZARD (Cornwall)

OS Landranger 203/204

The Lizard Peninsula on the south coast of Cornwall possesses few trees or other cover for migrants but its southerly aspect makes it attractive to numerous and varied migrants, including rarities, although the area is not as frequently visited as it perhaps deserves.

Habitat

Habitat on the Lizard is extremely varied and includes cliffs and coves, gardens, fields and wet maritime heath, the latter being of European-level conservation importance.

Access

There are six major areas of interest to birders.

Lizard village and headland The peninsula is reached via the A3083 from Helston. Various public footpaths can be taken from Lizard village permitting coverage of the entire headland, and the village itself is a good area to search for migrants. Before entering the village a private toll road leads to Kynance Cove and within Lizard village a road on the left goes to Church Cove. Behind the church is a

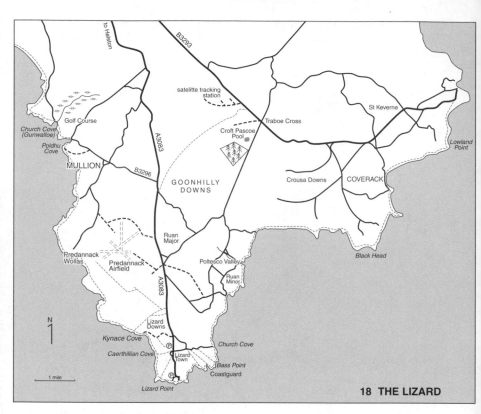

18 THE LIZARD

car park and the nearby sycamores have produced rarities such as Pallas's Warbler and Red-eyed Vireo.

Lizard Downs–Kynance to Predannack Wollas This walk takes in cliffs and moorland as well as Kynance Valley, which can hold migrants. Another good spot to search for migrants is on the north route from Kynance NT car park, which passes Predannack airfield. Here there are bushes and fields of rough grass.

Goonhilly Downs–Traboe Cross The moors can be viewed from Traboe cross-roads on the B3293 and should be searched for raptors, while small pools in this area can produce interesting waders.

Crousa Downs and Coverack Area Take the B3293 from the A3083 and continue until the B3294 to reach Coverack. Crousa Downs are accessed by taking a minor road from the B3293 at Zoar. Crousa Downs possess a variety of habitats that could hold migrants while the footpath east from the north end of Coverack village can also be worth checking.

Poltesco Valley This area is unusual on the Lizard in that it possesses extensive cover and tall trees, but it has not been intensively watched. To reach Poltesco take the road beside the church at Ruan Minor.

Gunwalloe and Poldhu Marsh Reeds in Gunwalloe Valley and around Poldhu Marsh attract unusual migrants such as Marsh Harrier and even rarities like

Purple Heron and Aquatic Warbler. Poldhu is signed off the B3296 at Mullion village. From the NT car park walk the road towards the beach and turn left over a stone bridge on a public track at the valley mouth.

Birds

Winter is the dullest season though raptors may include Peregrine, Merlin and Hen Harrier.

Spring migration can be strong involving common arrivals such as Chiffchaff, Whitethroat, Wheatear and Whinchat. Scarce migrants typical of more open areas include Black Redstart and Ring Ouzel, and rarities have included Alpine Swift, Subalpine Warbler and Woodchat Shrike.

Early autumn is probably the best time for seawatching and may produce shearwaters and skuas. Early-autumn rarities recorded most years include Wryneck, Icterine and Melodious Warblers. Subsequently passerine migration increases and many species are commoner than in spring, e.g. Spotted and Pied Flycatchers are more numerous in autumn, as is Tree Pipit. Several extreme rarities have been found late in the year, most notably Upland Sandpiper and Little Bustard. More likely are Chaffinch and Brambling, or perhaps a Lapland or Snow Bunting.

19 FAL ESTUARY (Cornwall) OS Landranger 204

The Carrick Roads waterway is formed by the confluence of the Truro and Fal Rivers between the headlands of St Antony and Pendennis. Deep water makes this a particularly good area for diving birds in winter.

Habitat

Even at low tide the water is deep and no sand or mud is exposed, making it ideal for diving birds. Creeks run away from both sides of the Roads but the largest of these, Restronguet, is heavily disturbed. Further north, to the east of Truro, a narrow tree-lined river, the Tresillian, is less disturbed.

Access

There are three major areas of interest.

Carrick Roads (see map) Drive to Mylor from the A39 at St Gluvias, and park in the village. Walk along the south side of the creek to Pencarrow Point, which affords a view over the Roads.

Restronguet Creek (see map) Devoran Creek, in the upper reaches of Restronguet Creek, is a good place to watch waders around high tide. It is reached by turning right from the direction of Carnon Downs on the A39 south of Truro. From Greenbank Road enter Quay Road and park carefully on the side of the road after a very sharp bend. From here walk the road by the creek.

Tresillian After leaving Truro on the A39 towards St Austell, follow the sign to Pencalenick. Park carefully at the side of the road as close as possible to the public footpath at Pencalenick, and take the path that follows the river to St Clement.

Birds

Diving duck such as Goldeneye and Red-breasted Merganser are regular in the Roads in winter. Rarer species include all three divers and the scarcer grebes, with Black-necked Grebe regularly occurring in significant numbers (over 30

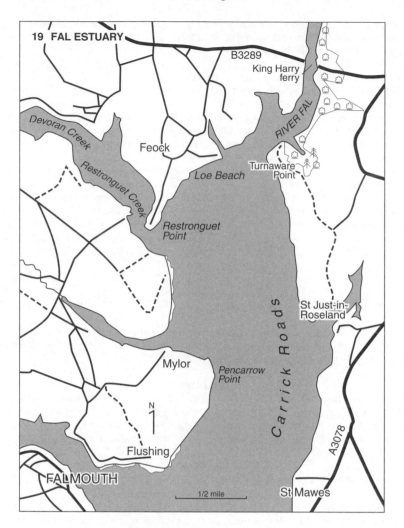

prior to roost in late afternoon). Sea duck, including occasional Velvet Scoter, and auks may also be present.

Small numbers of passage waders including Spotted Redshank and Greenshank join Dunlin and resident Redshank in spring and autumn. Shelduck, Grey Heron and Kingfisher are also resident.

20 GERRANS BAY (Cornwall)   OS Sheet No. 204

Gerrans Bay lies on the south Cornish coast east of the Fal estuary and is bounded by Portscatho and Nare Head. It is the best place in the southwest to see Black-throated Diver.

Habitat
The shoreline is rocky and unprotected from heavy seas.

Access

Viewing is best from Pendower Beach within the innermost part of the bay. Access is from the A3078 south of Tregony along a minor road signed Pendower Beach and Hotel. Park by the road near the hotel and view from the clifftop. Alternatively, look out from the point of Pednavadan (north of Portscatho) on the west of the bay.

Birds

Black-throated Diver normally occurs November–April, numbers peaking in early April, and late-staying individuals may attain summer plumage prior to departing. A few Great Northern Divers and Slavonian Grebes are usually evident and small numbers of sea ducks and auks may also be present.

21 NEWQUAY (Cornwall)   OS Landranger 200

Famous as a tourist resort, the town of Newquay and nearby areas can yield migrants and good seawatching. Nearby, the Gannel Estuary should be checked for gulls and Porthjoke Valley attracts migrant passerines.

Habitat

Newquay is well known for its cliffs and beaches, but a feature of particular interest to birdwatchers is the sewage outfall, though ironically it is now less attractive to seabirds as the sewage is treated prior to release. This outfall is particularly well known for gulls and in autumn Storm Petrel is regular on passage.

Access

Newquay is a popular tourist destination and is easily located. Follow signs north past the harbour towards Fistral Beach, turning right opposite Carnmarth Hotel for Towan Head. There is a small car park at the end, near the base of the head. The sewage outfall is directly in front of the head. For the Gannel Estuary take the A3075 towards Redruth and turn right at a mini-roundabout just beyond Trenance Park Lake (on the right). From the parking area ½ mile along this road (past the Medallion Court flats on the right) the river can be reached on foot. Porthjoke is reached by continuing from the mini-roundabout c.1 mile along the A3075 and

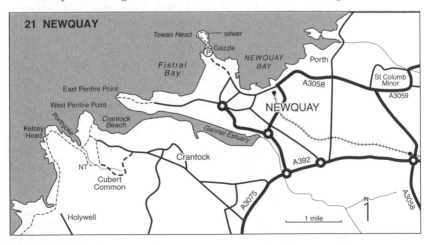

taking the right turn to Crantock. From here follow signs to West Pentire and turn left on the minor road past Treago Farm. Continue beyond the farm, through a gate (please shut this behind you) and past the NT Cubert Common sign, keeping left on the sandy track to a car park at the end. Walk to the valley from here and check bushes and any flooded areas along the track.

Birds

Winter gull flocks can contain scarcities such as Mediterranean, Little, Glaucous and Iceland Gulls. All three divers occur, Red-throated being the commonest. Grebes, sea duck and auks are all possible.

Manx Shearwater, Sandwich Tern and Whimbrel are regular in spring while typical passerine migrants could include Grasshopper Warbler and Lesser Whitethroat, with scarcer species always possible. West Pentire headland holds breeding Corn Buntings.

Late summer and early autumn sees the best seawatching. Storm Petrel is regular and other possibilities include Sooty Shearwater and Arctic and Pomarine Skuas. Later in autumn Leach's Petrel or Sabine's Gull could pass. Wheatears are common in autumn and rarities have included Firecrest and Red-breasted Flycatcher. From October, other scarce species that are possible are Grey Phalarope, Little Auk and Snow Bunting.

22 CAMEL ESTUARY (Cornwall)   OS Landranger 200

Situated on the north Cornish coast the Camel Estuary is productive for waders and waterfowl, including geese in winter.

Habitat

The upper estuary has marshy meadows and mudflats while the lower reaches are sandy.

Access

For the upper estuary take the A239 north from Wadebridge and turn left on the B3314 to Trewornan Bridge. From roadside parking at the bridge follow the footpath on the left, through a gate into a field near the bridge. This path leads to Burniere Point at Amble Dam where a Cornwall Bird Watching and Preservation Society (CBWPS) hide is located (key required). To access two other hides, in the restored Walmsley Sanctuary, use the narrow pedestrian gate on the right of the verge just beyond the bridge and follow the path diagonally across the field to a stile. Cross this and the next field to a second stile, which leads to a hide with a combination lock. A hide on stilts is reached by not crossing the second field but following the hedgerow right until the gated hide entrance. Another hide, at Tregunna, can be accessed by taking the minor road to Edmonton from the A39 at Wadebridge and then turning right to Tregunna. Park near the farm and follow a lane to the estuary and hide. A track runs along the entire length of the estuary to Padstow.

To reach the lower estuary continue from Trewornan Bridge to St Miniver and follow the signs to Rock where there is parking. The estuary can be viewed from the road.

Birds

In winter up to 100 White-fronted Geese formerly occurred on the upper estuary, but recently numbers have fallen to around 20, which are not present annually.

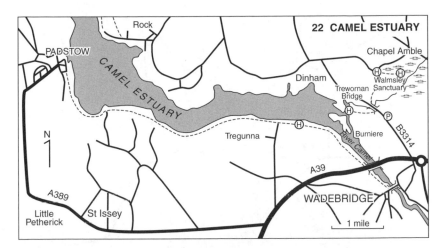

Other geese include Barnacle and Greenland White-fronted Geese, while Bewick's and Whooper Swans also occur infrequently. Surface-feeding duck such as Wigeon and Teal are present in significant numbers as are Golden Plover and Lapwing. Divers and grebes are best looked for lower down the estuary.

Ruff appear on spring passage and terns could include Sandwich or even possibly Roseate or Black.

Curlew and Wood Sandpipers and Little Stint pass through in autumn and Osprey is possible, although Peregrine is far more likely.

Information

For access to the hides contact the Cornwall Birdwatching and Preservation Society. Current secretary: Sara McMahon, 72 Underwood Road, Plympton PL7 1SZ.

23 PAR BEACH AND POOL (Cornwall)   OS Landranger 200

Par Sands Beach is part of St Austell Bay and, despite the harbour waterfront alongside having been developed, the area is still rich in birds. Migrants occur around the pool with gulls congregating on the beach, and the sheltered bay provides refuge for divers, grebes and sea duck.

Habitat

Par Pool is a freshwater pool that covers approximately 2½ acres. Though most of the banks are open there are some reed fringes. The sandy beach is broad and the water shallow, and offshore areas are partially sheltered.

Access

From the A3082 take the minor road signed to Par Sands Holiday Park. Immediately west of the Ship Inn there is parking overlooking the beach, beside the pool.

Birds

Migrants use the reedbeds around the pool and large numbers of Swallows and Yellow and Pied Wagtails gather there in autumn. Rare reedbed denizens passing through have included Bittern, Spotted Crake and Savi's Warbler.

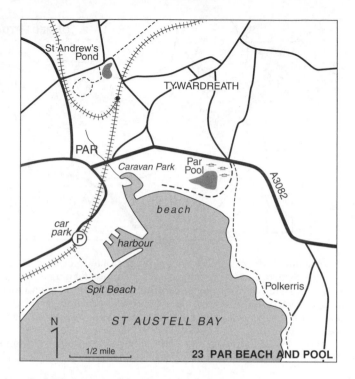

23 PAR BEACH AND POOL

In winter Reed Buntings and Starlings use the reeds. Large numbers of gulls gather on the beach and scarce species such as Mediterranean, Little, Glaucous or even Iceland may be located with skill, patience and luck. Common waders include Oystercatcher and Turnstone, although Sanderling is present in surprisingly low numbers. Purple Sandpiper, Grey and Ringed Plovers, and Dunlin are also possible. In the bay in winter Great Northern Diver may be joined by Red-throated and Black-throated Divers, Slavonian and Red-necked Grebes, Common Scoter and Eider.

Summer breeders and residents include Reed Warbler and at least one pair of Cetti's Warbler.

24 DAVIDSTOW AIRFIELD (Cornwall)   OS Landranger 201

A disused airfield on the north edge of Bodmin Moor, with the ruined control tower and runways still present. The short turf is grazed by sheep, and shallow pools occur after rain.

Access (see map)

Leave Camelford northeast on the A39. After 2 miles turn right onto a minor road running through the airfield. Pull off to the left and drive along the old runways scanning for birds. Stay in your vehicle: this does not scare the birds and enables more ground to be covered. The control tower area is often best for waders.

Birds

Large flocks of Golden Plover and Lapwing occur in autumn and winter and occasionally an American Golden Plover is with them. A few Ruff are usually

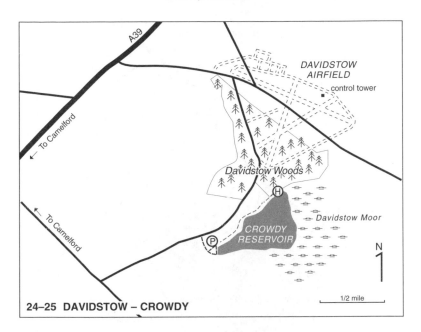

24–25 DAVIDSTOW – CROWDY

present and Buff-breasted Sandpiper now turns up annually. Very small numbers of Dotterel are reasonably regular in spring and autumn. Hen Harrier, Merlin and Peregrine are sometimes encountered in autumn and winter, and Goshawk has been claimed on a number of occasions.

25 CROWDY RESERVOIR (Cornwall)   OS Landranger 201

This reservoir is very close to Davidstow Airfield. Mud is exposed when the water is low and there are marshy areas on its east side.

Access (see map)
A signed road from the airfield leads to the reservoir. Alternatively it can be reached directly from Camelford: turn right (southeast) off the A39 at the north edge of the town and after 1 mile turn left to the airfield. The reservoir can be viewed from the road but for close views follow a track to the water's edge. A hide is sited at the north end (key and permit from South West Water Authority).

Birds
There are reasonable numbers of the commoner ducks in winter usually including a few Goldeneye. Raptors may also be seen (as at Davidstow). A variety of waders frequents the muddy margins in autumn and occasionally includes a rarity. Very small numbers of Black Terns are recorded annually in spring and autumn.

Information
Permits and keys to hides: Leisure Services Department, South West Water, Higher Coombe Park, Lewdown, Okehampton, EX20 4QT. Tel: 01837 871565.

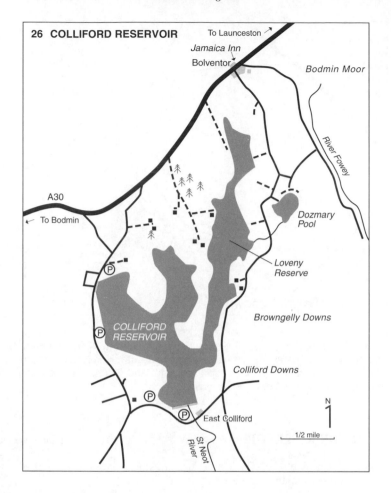

26 COLLIFORD RESERVOIR (Cornwall) OS Landranger 201

This new reservoir a few miles west of Siblyback is the largest in the county and well worth visiting, especially in autumn and winter, for ducks and waders. The northeast part is relatively shallow with grassy islands, and is now a reserve. At present disturbance is minimal at Colliford, unlike at Siblyback.

Access (see map)

Turn south off the A30 at Bolventor (virtually opposite Jamaica Inn) onto a road signed 'Dozmary Pool'. Follow this road for c.2 miles, passing Dozmary Pool to the left, and reasonable views may be had of the reservoir's northeast arm from the roadside. Continue south, turning west by the china-clay works, and pass below the dam (the dam area is poor for birds due to the deep water). Another road follows the reservoir's west side, affording reasonable views of the northwest arm before rejoining the A30. Footpaths exist around much of the reservoir, but a permit is required for the path covering the reserve area (available from the warden at Siblyback).

Birds

There is a significant autumn build-up of ducks, with a chance of Garganey, and the shallow margins have produced Pectoral Sandpiper and Spotted Crake as well as the commoner waders. In winter Smew and Goosander appear to be regular in very small numbers, and look also for the occasional Scaup and Ruddy Duck. Towards dusk both Hen Harrier and Merlin roost around the reservoir, and Short-eared Owl winters in small numbers. Particularly good vantage points for these are at the northwest and northeast corners of the reservoir. Dippers inhabit the nearby Fowey Valley.

Information

David Conway, Tregenna, Cooksland, Bodmin, Cornwall PL31 2AR. Tel: 01208 77686.

27 SIBLYBACK RESERVOIR (Cornwall)   OS Landranger 201

This reservoir lies on the southeast edge of Bodmin Moor, north of Liskeard, surrounded by moorland and grassland. Areas of mud are exposed on the north shore when the water is low.

Access (see map)

Leave Liskeard north on the B3254. After 1 mile fork left onto a minor road to St Cleer. Turn right immediately beyond the village and continue past the cross-

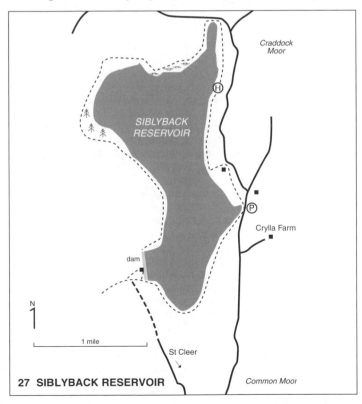

27 SIBLYBACK RESERVOIR

roads to the reservoir and car park overlooking it. You can walk in either direction but the north end is generally best and there is a hide here (permit from South West Water Authority).

Birds

There is a variety of ducks in winter, and a few Goosander and Smew are annual visitors. Jack Snipe can sometimes be found in the marshy edges and Golden Plover and Lapwing are common in the fields. Hen Harrier, Merlin and Peregrine are seen occasionally in winter. Autumn wader passage includes most of the usual species and a rarity is found most years. Small numbers of Little Gulls and Black Terns occur each autumn.

Information

Permits and keys to hides: Leisure Services Department, South West Water, Higher Coombe Park, Lewdown, Okehampton, EX20 4QT. Tel: 01837 871565.

28 RAME HEAD (Cornwall)   OS Landranger 201

Facing south on the southeast Cornish coast, Rame Head is a passerine-migrant trap and offers a good vantage point for seawatching.

Habitat

Cover for migrants can be found around Rame Church and Farm in the form of gardens, trees and hedgerows. The road to the old fortification at Penlee Point takes in a variety of habitats including a copse. Along the coast to the west is Whitsand Bay, and gorse and bracken slopes can be accessed in this direction, with fields on the tops.

Access

Take the A374 from Torpoint to Antony, then the B3247 to Tregantle and turn right on the coast road to Rame. There is a car park at the latter and public footpaths along the coast. One leads east to Penlee while another good route heads in the opposite direction to Polhawn, permitting coverage of the bushes by the old fort (private) before looping back to Rame Farm and Church.

Birds

Passerines tend to move quickly from the exposed headland to the cover of the trees and hedgerows, and early morning is the best time to search for recent arrivals, feeding up before heading inland. Warblers are sometimes present in large numbers and scarcer migrants can include Pied and Spotted Flycatchers, Whinchat, Redstart and Black Redstart. In autumn rarities such as Pallas's Warbler have been found alongside common migrants like Goldcrest. Fields should be checked for larks and pipits, while migrant raptors could also pass through.

Spring seawatching can produce divers, which are also present through the winter in Whitsand Bay. Scarce grebes, particularly Slavonian, and sea duck such as Common Scoter and Eider are often present offshore. Gannet and Manx Shearwater may pass in the hundreds with occasional skuas in spring and autumn. Terns, auks and waders also occur at both seasons though autumn seawatching is better when there is the possibility of scarcer species such as Sooty Shearwater.

Whinchat

29 TAMAR ESTUARY (Cornwall/Devon) OS Landranger 201

Situated on the Devon/Cornwall border, the Tamar Estuary is best known as a wintering site for Avocet.

Habitat

Extensive mudflats are located between the Tamar roadbridge and Kingsmill Lake. Further upstream the estuary narrows and is bordered by farmland and trees.

Access (see map)

Take the A388 from Saltash and turn right to Landulph. Park near the church and follow the narrow road to the left, passing through a wooden gate and stile, and then crossing a meadow to a public path that leads to an embankment affording views of Kingsmill Lake. At low tide walk the beach and check the saltmarsh. The nearby village of Cargreen is a regular Avocet feeding site and it is possible to observe the birds from a car if you park on the waterfront.

Birds

Avocets arrive from early winter with 100+ present mid-season and peak numbers reach in excess of 200. Duck, often including Goldeneye, are present during winter and all three sawbills have been recorded. Kingsmill Lake is actually a creek, which is good for waders such as Redshank and Curlew on the incoming tide. Passage waders in marshy areas may include Curlew and Wood Sandpipers, while Black Tern is possible in autumn. Osprey also occurs on autumn passage and sometimes lingers around the estuary.

Information

Stuart Hutchings, 5 Acres, Allet, Cornwall TR4 9DJ. Tel: 01827 273939. E-mail: stuart@cornwt.demon.co.uk

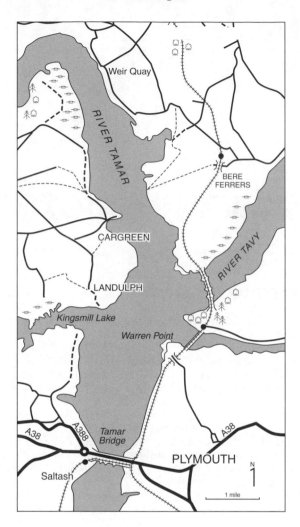

30 TAMAR LAKES (Cornwall/Devon)   OS Landranger 190

These two reservoirs with natural banks lie on the Cornwall/Devon border, amidst open farmland. The 80-acre Upper Lake is used for sailing, and the smaller 40-acre Lower Lake is used for recreation only.

Habitat
The Tamar Lakes have wooded edges with shallow marshy areas. The natural habitats are attractive to birds, although there is some disturbance from fishing and recreational activities.

Access
The lakes lie to the east of the A39 Bude-Bideford road. From Bude, heading north on the A39, turn right at Kilkhampton onto the B3254 to Launceston, and

after ½ mile turn left onto a minor road towards Bradworthy and Holsworthy. For the Upper Lake, turn left after 1 mile and left again to the car park. For the Lower Lake, continue towards Holsworthy and take the second left into the car park. The lakes are connected by a footpath. There is a hide overlooking the Lower Lake, part of which is maintained as a bird sanctuary from August to April. A permit is required for the hide and for the Upper Lake banks (available from the warden's office and information centre by the Upper Lake dam).

Birds

In winter, a good selection of wildfowl may be found, although not in huge numbers. Rare American species have been found here in the past. Occasionally, small parties of Bewick's Swans or White-fronted Geese may visit, and the edges may hold a few Snipe and the odd Jack Snipe. The surrounding area hosts the usual wintering raptors and it may be possible to see a Hen Harrier or a Peregrine in the area, or perhaps even a Merlin.

The spring will bring a variety of migrants to the lakes, and they can be numerous. Large flocks of hirundines and Swifts are a regular feature. Waders include Common and Green Sandpipers, Greenshank and Ruff. Breeding species include Kingfisher and Willow Tit (try the trees by the Lower Lake).

Wader species are more numerous and more varied in autumn, and are likely to include Little Stint and Spotted Redshank. A number of American species have been found here over the years. Black Tern is another regular visitor at this time.

31 LUNDY (Devon)   OS Landranger 180

The island of Lundy, c.3½ miles long, lies in the Bristol Channel 12 miles north of Hartland Point. The cliffs hold good numbers of breeding seabirds but the island is best known as a migration watchpoint; a bird observatory operated from the Old Lighthouse from 1947 to 1973.

Habitat

The cliffs rise to over 300 feet and are most impressive on the west and north sides. Much of the island is barren moorland that is damp in places, with a few small areas of standing water, notably at Pondsbury. The sole habitation on the island is a small village at the south end where there are some fields. The Eastern Sidelands and sheltered areas such as Millcombe Valley contain bushes and a few small areas of woodland.

Access (see map)

A regular supply ship operates from Ilfracombe and a steamer runs day trips in the summer (but these do not permit much time ashore). The *MV Oldenburg* sails to Lundy from Bideford; tickets should be obtained from Lundy Oldenburg Office, Bideford Quay, Devon (tel: 01237 470422). A variety of accommodation is available on Lundy but space is limited. For further information on transport and accommodation contact the Landmark Trust.

The gardens and bushes of Millcombe Valley are perhaps the best area for migrants in spring and autumn. Other suitable areas for warblers and flycatchers are largely confined to the Eastern Sidelands, and a walk along the east coast checking the bushes and disused quarries may be profitable. The main seabird colonies are at North Light and Battery Point. A track from the village leads north across the moors to North Light. Immediately east of the lighthouse, a series of steps descends into Kittiwake Gully offering good views of the breeding seabirds.

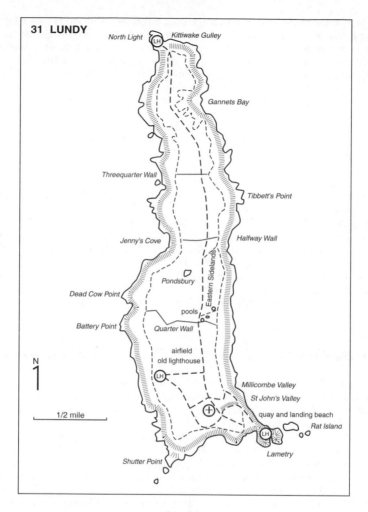

31 LUNDY
North Light — Kittiwake Gulley
Gannets Bay
Threequarter Wall
Tibbett's Point
Jenny's Cove
Halfway Wall
Eastern Sidelands
Pondsbury
Dead Cow Point
pools
Battery Point
Quarter Wall
airfield
old lighthouse
Millicombe Valley
St John's Valley
quay and landing beach
Rat Island
Lametry
Shutter Point

N

1/2 mile

Birds

Spring migration begins in March and usually includes a few Black Redstart and Firecrest. A steady stream of commoner summer visitors passes in April–May. East or southeast winds are generally best for falls of migrants. Small numbers of Redstarts, Ring Ouzels and Pied Flycatchers are recorded annually, and scarce migrants are a regular feature, especially following light southerly winds. Hoopoe is generally among the first, in late March or April, and a few Dotterel are seen each year in late April or May. Both species favour short turf. Late spring often brings a Golden Oriole, and migrant raptors may include Merlin and Short-eared Owl.

Though many of the seabirds, such as Gannet, are visible offshore all year, the breeding species mostly return to their ledges or burrows in spring. Hundreds of Guillemots and Razorbills nest alongside over 1,000 pairs of Kittiwakes and smaller numbers of Fulmar and Shag. Up to 100 pairs of Puffins breed, mostly at Battery Point. Gulls (mostly Herring) are also numerous. Manx Shearwater and Storm Petrel breed in small numbers, largely on the west side, but only return to their burrows at night and the best chance of seeing them is on the boat crossing. Rock Pipit and Raven are resident.

Autumn wader passage is relatively insignificant due to scarcity of habitat, but several American waders have been recorded, usually after west gales; Pectoral Sandpiper is almost annual. A few returning Dotterel occur each year. Passerine migrants filter through in August–September, sometimes accompanied by a scarcer species such as Melodious or Barred Warbler. Ortolan Bunting is annual from late August and a few Lapland Buntings usually appear later. In late autumn there are large movements of larks, pipits, finches and buntings. Rarities can be found at any time but are most likely from late September to early November. Lundy has an astonishingly long list of vagrants, despite having been largely neglected by rarity-hunters. No fewer than seven firsts for Britain have been found here, and the Ancient Murrelet, first found in June 1990 among the breeding auks, was the first and only Western Palearctic record.

Information
Lundy Field Society, Hon. Secretary, Chris Webster, 38 Greenway Avenue, Taunton, Somerset TA2 6HY. Tel: 01823 282889. E-mail: chris@webster5.demon.co.uk
Accommodation bookings, and travel information: The Landmark Trust, Shottesbrooke, Maidenhead, Berks SL6 3SW. Tel: 01628 825925. E-mail: bookings@landmarktrust.co.uk

32 TAW-TORRIDGE ESTUARY (Devon)   OS Landranger 180

The extensive estuaries of the Taw and the Torridge, between Bideford and Barnstaple, are the largest in North Devon, supporting the region's largest wader population after the Exe and the Tamar.

Habitat
In addition to typical estuarine habitats, the area is fringed by sand dunes and rough grazing marsh. To the north lies the well-known Braunton Burrows, famous for its high dunes and rare plants, and to the south the smaller Northam Burrows. Areas of saltmarsh occur at Skern, Isley Marsh (now an RSPB reserve) and Penhill Point.

Access (see map)
There are a number of access points in the area, and the following is based on Norman & Tucker (2001). The estuary is difficult to watch at low tide. An incoming tide is best, and a visit to a roost two hours up to high tide is recommended. There is a fair amount of disturbance at certain times from water sports, motorbike scrambling in the dunes and general public use, but this is mainly at weekends.

NORTH SIDE:
Braunton Burrows Leave Barnstaple on the A361 northwestwards towards Ilfracombe. In Braunton, turn left on the B3231 towards Saunton and Croyde, and after 1 mile turn left again onto a minor road to the Burrows. Park in car parks along the rough track to explore the dunes, or continue to the estuary mouth. After 2 miles, park and walk straight on to Crow Point for waders and views of the estuary, or right to the beach. To complete a circuit of the area, continue northeastwards around Braunton Marsh. It is worth making a number of stops to check for birds in this rich area. Eventually you will reach a tarmac road and a tollgate at Velator, before returning to the main road.

Sherpa Marsh This area of grazing marshes lies across the pill (creek) from

Braunton Marsh. From Wrafton village, a path follows the seawall alongside the east side of the pill. It is worth checking the fields for geese and the pond for rails or possibly Bittern.

Downend Continuing beyond Braunton and Saunton on the B3231, the road reaches a rocky headland overlooking Croyde Bay. This is Downend. Park on the left at the sharp corner, and check the sea for Common Scoter and Eider. Purple Sandpipers may be found on the rocks here.

Heanton Court Hotel The car park at this hotel, 5 miles west of Barnstaple on the A361, gives great views over the central part of the Taw estuary. Penhill Point lies across the river, but views are distant. Check for duck flocks and perhaps a wintering Spoonbill. For closer views, walk 300 yards east where a footpath (opposite the road to West Ashford) leads down to the disused railway embankment. A stone lookout provides a good vantage.

Pottington Just west of Barnstaple, turn off the A361 (left) to Pottington Industrial Estate. At the end of the road turn left into Riverside Road until it bends away from the river. Park here and follow a signed path to check the inner estuary, with views to Penhill Point.

SOUTH SIDE:

Penhill Point From Barnstaple head west along the B3233 (old A39). Between Bickington and Fremington, a rough track leads right towards the estuary. Park by the main road and walk down beside Fremington Pill (check for waders). Turn right along the estuary bank and after 1 mile you can view Penhill Point.

Isley Marsh RSPB reserve In Lower Yelland, turn off the B3233 northwards for 300 yards towards the oil depot. This is a major access point to the Tarka Trail. Park at the end of the lane and walk right (east). The marsh can be viewed from the path, or from a coastal footpath around the western edge of the bay.

Northam Burrows Northam Burrows lies opposite Braunton Burrows. From Bideford, head north on the A386 to Northam. To view Skern saltmarsh, turn right to Appledore and second left into Broad Lane. Continue straight for 1 mile, following signs to the recycling centre, with views of marshes on the right and freshwater pools on the left. Walking across the dunes gives great views of the estuary. Alternatively, access the pebble ridge, on the west side, by following signs for Westward Ho! Turn right past the holiday camps and golf course to Sandymere Pool.

Kenwith Valley This small reserve on the outskirts of Bideford has produced the occasional scarce migrant passerine and even an overwintering Dusky Warbler. From Bideford town centre, head towards Westward Ho! and turn left at Raleigh Garage. Park after 400 yards and walk back to the reserve. The entrance is across a stile over a low wall. There are public paths through the reserve and a public hide overlooking a lake.

Birds

Braunton Marshes hold large flocks of waders in winter, notably Lapwing and Golden Plover, with occasional Ruff. A Peregrine or Merlin may hunt in the area. High tide roosts of waders at Crow Point or Northam Burrows hold all the usual shore species including Dunlin, Oystercatcher, Curlew, Redshank and Grey Plover, and smaller numbers of other species. Bewick's and Whooper Swans or White-fronted Geese may visit in cold weather, and Brent Geese are now regular in small

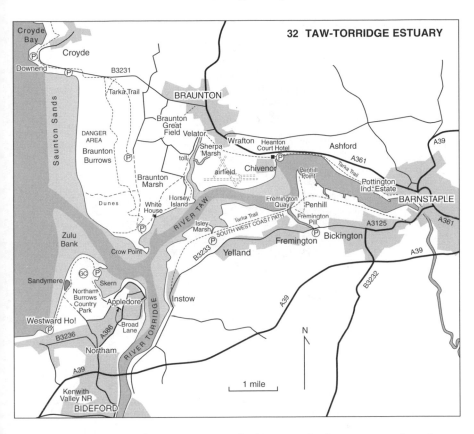

32 TAW-TORRIDGE ESTUARY

numbers. A variety of the commoner ducks occurs in the estuary and on the marshes. Wigeon predominate, and Common Scoter occur in Bideford Bay. A regular non-breeding flock of Eider in the estuary mouth is notable. Slavonian Grebes may occasionally be seen in the channel. Little Egrets are now present throughout the year, and Spoonbill is an occasional winter visitor, as is Greenshank and Spotted Redshank. Large numbers of gulls inhabit the estuary and rarer species such as Glaucous, Iceland and Ring-billed are almost annual.

Spring brings a notable passage of waders including Whimbrel and Common Sandpiper, as well as some warblers and other passerines. The Great Field at Braunton is a long established site for Quail although, as always, it is lucky even to hear one in Britain. Unusually, Wheatears breed in the dunes around the estuary mouth.

Autumn wader passage may produce an American vagrant, but Little Stint or Curlew Sandpiper is more likely. Greenshanks may be seen in small flocks in the lower estuary and small flocks of Common, Sandwich and Little Terns frequent the mouth. Later, a Short-eared Owl or Hen Harrier may hunt over the dunes, and the area is notable for regular wintering Snow Buntings (especially along Northam pebble ridge). Twite, Shore Lark and Lapland Bunting have occurred, but are not annual. A Grey Phalarope may drop in after northerly gales in autumn.

Information

RSPB Isley Marsh: c/o Unit 3, Lions Rest Estate, Station Road, Exminster, Exeter, Devon EX6 8DZ. Tel: 01392 824614.

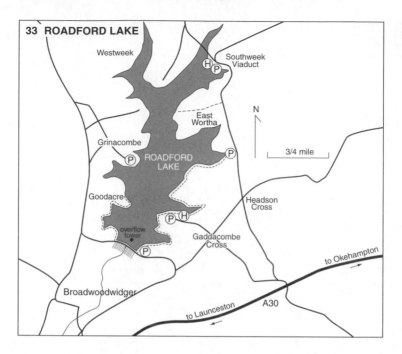

33 ROADFORD LAKE (Devon)

OS Landranger 190

At more than 700 acres when full, this reservoir is the largest in the region. Completed only in the early 1990s, this lake has still to reach its full potential.

Habitat

Roadford is the only reservoir in Devon that is not on acidic moorland. The two northern arms of the lake are designated as nature reserves.

Access (see map)

From the A30 Launceston-Okehampton road, turn left (north) onto a minor road to Broadwoodwidger (the lake is signed). After 2 miles turn right to a car park (fee) just before the dam – there is a shop and cafe here (open Easter to October, 11.00-17.00). Cross the dam and follow the footpath to Goodacre inlet and wood. On the east side, a network of trails follows the shoreline to Gaddacombe hide (public access). Further tracks lead to Wortha inlet where there is another car park. Alternatively, both these areas can be reached by road. Perhaps the best place for birds is the northeast arm of the lake, where there is another hide. Park on the left just before Southweek viaduct, and from here walk left through a gateway signed to the hide. The hide has open access and a logbook inside. After the viaduct, a 'no-through road' to the left leads down to the northwest arm of the lake (Westweek). The west side of the lake can be checked from the car park at Grinacombe, but there are no paths on this side. Sailing and fishing activities can disturb the birds at Roadford at weekends.

Birds

Good numbers of wildfowl use the lake in winter and, in addition to the usual dabbling duck, the lake is particularly attractive to diving duck. Goldeneye numbers can reach up to 100, and up to 50 Goosander may gather in winter roosts (try the dam end). Smew turn up from time to time but this species is scarce in the southwest. Other rarities include occasional Scaup or Long-tailed Duck, or even an American vagrant – a Bufflehead wintered one year, but its origin was unproven. Single divers or one of the rarer grebes occur occasionally, and the lake attracts good numbers of gulls. Raptors are not seen regularly, but Hen Harrier, Short-eared Owl, Peregrine and Merlin are all possible. A wintering Kingfisher or Stonechat is more likely.

Waders are not significant at Roadford; their variety increases at passage times, but as yet the lake has not attracted many rarer species. Other passage birds may include Gargeney, Green Sandpiper and Black Tern.

Resident breeding species are not especially notable. Redpolls and Willow Tits are quite numerous in the surrounding areas, and a Barn Owl may be seen from time to time (dusk at the Southweek hide is perhaps the best bet). A few Grasshopper Warblers and Tree Pipits breed around the edge of the lake and a Hobby may hunt in the area in summer.

Information

South West Water, Leisure Services Department, Higher Coombe Park, Lewdown, Okehampton, Devon EX20 4QT. Tel: 01837 871565.

34 PRAWLE POINT (Devon)   OS Landranger 202

This outstanding migration watchpoint is the most southerly point on the south Devon coast, and lies south of Kingsbridge. Though best in spring and autumn there is usually something to see at any season. Prawle is also one of the most reliable places in Britain to see Cirl Bunting.

Habitat

The cliffs along this coast are quite spectacular. The tops are covered with grass, bracken, gorse and boulders, and behind lie fields surrounded by stone walls and hedges. Sheltered hollows and valleys contain dense vegetation and bushes attractive to migrants. There is a small wood near East Prawle.

Access (see map)

Leave Kingsbridge east on the A379. Turn right at Frogmore or Chillington onto minor roads south to East Prawle. Continue through the village, down the no-through road, to the NT car park within a sheltered hollow surrounded by bushes. These bushes often harbour migrants and, indeed, are one of the best places to look. Several other places should also be checked.

Prawle Point Continue to the Point from the car park, past the coastguard cottages, checking for migrants on the way. Seawatching is best from the memorial seat below the west side of the Point.

Eastern Fields From the car park walk east along the coastal path, checking bushes and gullies. Beyond Langerstone Point a small wood lies on the left. After checking this you can return to the car park along the lane, via the top fields.

Pig's Nose Valley This deep, lush valley lies about 1 mile west of the point. It can be reached either by walking northwest along the coastal path via Gammon Head or from East Prawle village by taking the lane past the duck pond.

Early mornings are generally best for observing migrant passerines. If a fall has occurred, all suitable cover should be checked thoroughly, especially in sheltered areas. There is disturbance by non-birders at weekends. Seawatching is often best in hazy conditions or after strong, onshore gales.

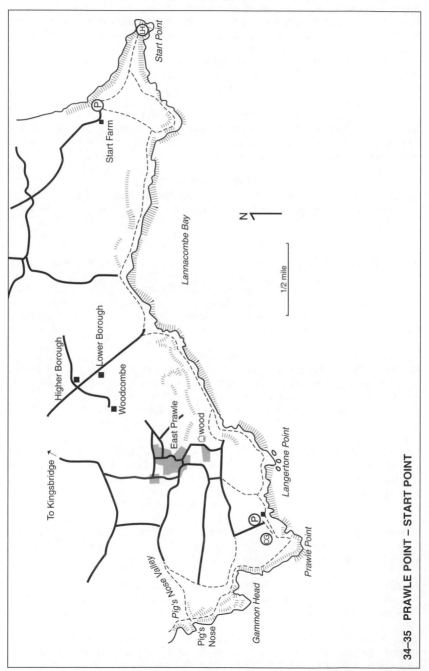

34–35 PRAWLE POINT – START POINT

Birds

Among residents, Cirl Bunting is Prawle's speciality: several pairs breed in hedgerows around Prawle and in winter small flocks may be found in the bushes around the car park. Little Owl is frequently seen and other residents include Buzzard, Sparrowhawk, Rock Pipit and Raven.

In winter, a few divers occur offshore – Great Northern is the most frequent. Small numbers of Shag and Common Scoter are usually to be seen as well as many Gannets, gulls and auks. Flocks of Golden Plover favour the short grassy fields and a few Purple Sandpipers winter below the cliffs. The bushes may hold the occasional wintering Chiffchaff or Firecrest, and more open areas should be checked for Black Redstart.

The first spring arrivals include Wheatear and Goldcrest. A few migrant Black Redstarts and Firecrests may be found from mid-March and Hoopoe is seen most years. A wide variety of migrant passerines occur, mostly in April–May, when a few raptors also pass through. Seawatching can be productive in spring: regular species include all three divers, Manx Shearwater, Fulmar, Eider, Common Scoter, Red-breasted Merganser, Whimbrel, Bar-tailed Godwit, skuas and terns; late April to early May is probably best. Scarce migrants and rarities are occasionally found, mostly in late spring.

Small numbers of Balearic Shearwaters tend to replace Manx from mid-July. They are sometimes accompanied by a Sooty Shearwater but the latter is more frequent in September. Arctic and Great Skuas are regular in autumn. Passerine migrants are mainly present August–September; the main species are Yellow Wagtail, Tree Pipit, Wheatear, Whinchat, Redstart, warblers and flycatchers. Late September and October bring large movements of hirundines, pipits and wagtails, and usually a few Ring Ouzels. A Merlin or Hobby is also often present at this time. Late autumn can produce the most exciting finds. A few Firecrests are usually present from late September into November, and Melodious, Icterine and Yellow-browed Warblers, and Red-breasted Flycatcher all occur most years, albeit in very small numbers. An American passerine is a possibility following west gales, with both Black-and-white and Chestnut-sided Warblers having been found in recent years, and an Asian vagrant such as Pallas's Warbler may turn up as late as November. Late autumn also brings a few Black Redstarts.

35 START POINT (Devon)   OS Landranger 202

This migration watchpoint lies just east of Prawle. However, cover is limited and passerine migrants tend to move through quite quickly. Cirl Bunting is an equally prominent feature of the local avifauna.

Habitat

Start Point is a rocky promontory with open farmland lying immediately inland. Start Farm Valley, behind the point, is sheltered and has trees and bushes providing cover for migrants.

Access (see map)

From Stokenham village, south of Slapton village, turn sharp left and drive to the car park at the top of the Point (passing Start Farm valley on the right). A gate leads to Start Lighthouse access lane and a footpath right into the valley where there is some cover. For the Point continue along the lighthouse lane. A side valley immediately east of the Point is reached by turning off the coast path beyond the sandy cove.

Birds

In winter attention is best focused on the sea where Great Northern Diver and Eider can occur. Resident Raven, Peregrine and Rock Pipit should also be evident.

Chiffchaff, Grasshopper Warbler, Wheatear and Goldcrest are typical spring migrants, but more unusual species could include Firecrest, Black Redstart and Hoopoe. This season is also a good time to search for migrant raptors such as returning Hobby and Honey Buzzard or even rare vagrants like Black Kite, which has been recorded at nearby Prawle.

Summer is a good time to search for resident Cirl Buntings and Dartford Warblers as they are holding territory and singing. Skuas and shearwaters may be observed offshore from late summer, but the best time for seawatching is early autumn.

Early-autumn migrants can include Spotted and Pied Flycatchers, Yellow Wagtail and Tree Pipit. The chance of an extreme rarity increases later in the season and Booted and Arctic Warblers have been recorded at Start. Wryneck, Red-backed Shrike and Ortolan Bunting are possible drift migrants at this time. In late autumn passage is characterised by movements of larks, pipits, finches and buntings.

36 SLAPTON LEY (Devon) OS Landranger 202

Slapton Ley is a nature reserve managed by the Field Studies Council. Its reedbeds and bushes attract a variety of migrants and some interesting breeding species, but the area is best known for wildfowl in winter.

Habitat

A series of freshwater pools lies behind a long shingle bank on the coast of Start Bay. The largest of these is Slapton Ley itself; 1½ miles long and fringed by reeds, especially in Ireland Bay. Wintering ducks occur on the open water, often favouring the Lower Ley. Dense bushes along the seaward edge provide habitat for migrant passerines. Immediately north of Slapton Ley, and separated from it by a narrow strip of land, is Higher Ley. This is now mainly an extensive reedbed with encroaching scrub. south of Torcross, the much smaller Beesands Ley consists of open water fringed with reeds. Further south still, Hallsands Ley is a semi-dry reedbed.

Access (see map)

Slapton is c.6 miles south of Dartmouth on the coastal A379. There are three car parks along the road, which runs along the seaward side of the lake (it was damaged by severe weather in early 2001 though was still passable on foot and repairs are planned). Slapton Ley is easily viewed from the car parks, and the sea is worth checking at various points along the beach. Further exploration may prove profitable. A ringing hut maintained by the Devon Birdwatching and Preservation Society is sited across the bridge from monument between Slapton and Higher Leys, and a logbook is kept in a tin under the left side for reporting sightings when the hut is unmanned. Opposite here a trail leads through a gate and gives good views over Ireland Bay. Continue until a gated track leading to France Wood appears on the left (permit required): dense bushes and an overgrown quarry should be checked for wintering Chiffchaff and Firecrest. Higher Ley may be viewed from the coast road (e.g. at Strete Gate) or along a path which leads north from the ringing hut. Beesands Ley can be reached by walking south along the

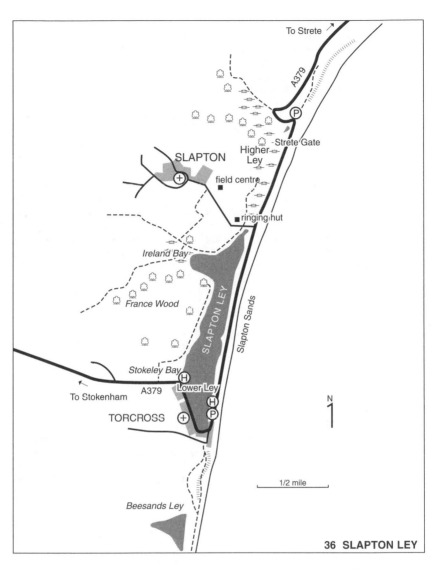

36 SLAPTON LEY

coast from Torcross or by driving south from Stokenham (on the A379) on minor roads to Beesands village; the Ley is immediately north of the village.

Birds

Divers and grebes occur on the sea in winter, Great Northern Diver and Slavonian Grebe being the most regular. Shag, Eider and Common Scoter are also frequent offshore. Slapton is particularly attractive to diving duck, and there are usually a few Gadwall. Small numbers of Ruddy Duck occasionally winter, and Long-tailed Duck turns up most years. In hard weather, Goosander and Smew may visit. There have been a number of records of Ring-necked and Ferruginous Ducks in recent years. Gull flocks on the beach at this season should be checked for rarer species such as Mediterranean or Glaucous Gulls. Several

Water Rails inhabit the reedbeds, and in hard weather Bittern and Bearded Tit may visit. A few Chiffchaffs and Firecrests usually winter in the surrounding bushes and a Black Redstart may use the beach.

In spring all three divers occur offshore and passage terns are noted in small numbers. Garganey is a regular visitor in early spring. Migrant passerines may be found in the bushes and Wheatears favour the shingle bank. Scarcer migrants include the occasional Marsh Harrier or Hoopoe.

In summer a few pairs of Great Crested Grebes breed and Sedge and Reed Warblers are common. Resident Buzzard, Sparrowhawk and Raven are all seen frequently, and the explosive song of Cetti's Warbler is a familiar sound year-round from the dense scrub and reeds. Cirl Bunting occurs in the sheltered valley leading inland; it often sings from high trees in summer, but in winter moves nearer the coast and favours hedgerows and low bushes. In late summer, light south winds can produce feeding flocks of Manx Shearwaters at sea as well as the more usual Gannets and Kittiwakes. Occasionally a Sooty Shearwater is seen.

Autumn sees large numbers of Swifts and hirundines gather over the lake and they are sometimes chased by a Hobby. Black Tern is regular and ringing has proven that the elusive Aquatic Warbler appears most years in small numbers following east winds, though the species is unlikely to be seen in the field. At sea Arctic Skuas chase the Sandwich Terns and, following severe gales in late autumn, oddities such as Grey Phalarope may shelter on the Ley.

Information
Slapton Ley Field Centre, Slapton, Kingsbridge, Devon TQ7 2QP. Tel: 01548 580466. E-mail: enquiries.sl@field-studies-council.org

37–41 EXE ESTUARY (Devon)   OS Landranger 192

The Exe, containing 6 miles of extensive tidal mudflats between Exeter and the sea, is the most important estuary for wildfowl and waders in the Southwest. A variety of habitats ensures a strong diversity of birds all year though it is best during migration seasons and in winter. It is noted in particular for wintering Brent Goose, Avocet and Black-tailed Godwit.

Habitat
The estuary is tidal as far as Countess Wear on the outskirts of Exeter and is over 1 mile wide in places, with considerable areas of mud and sand at low tide. Two sand spits lie at its mouth: Dawlish Warren extends for 1 mile into the estuary from the west and contains a series of dunes, a golf course and a small reedbed. Behind lies an area of saltmarsh; to the east the spit at Exmouth is much smaller and there are high cliffs east of the town. Between Exminster Marshes and Topsham is a tidal reedbed in the estuary's narrower inner section.

Access (see map)
The estuary can be observed from many points but the west side tends to be most profitable due to less development and restriction of shooting, though the light is inevitably unfavourable in the early morning. The waders can be very distant at low tide and are best seen 2–3 hours before high water. Alternatively, they may be observed at their high-tide roosts, notably at Dawlish Warren, Exminster Marshes or Topsham. The sea is best watched from Langstone Rock (southwest of Dawlish Warren) or from Exmouth. The latter and Dawlish Warren are tourist

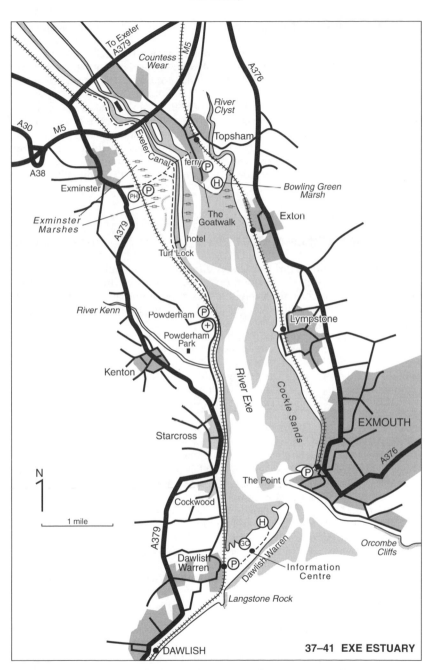

37–41 EXE ESTUARY

havens particularly in summer; weekdays or early mornings are therefore best for birding. One of the best ways to see the birds is to take one of the regular birding cruises which operate throughout the year. The boats leave from Exmouth Dock or Topsham Quay. Information and bookings can be made via the RSPB website or by contacting the RSPB South West Regional Office.

37 EXMINSTER MARSHES (Devon)

OS Landranger 192

These fresh marshes comprise rough grazing dissected by ditches and are subject to occasional flooding. They are situated on the estuary's upper west bank, separated from it by the disused Exeter Canal. The marshes form part of the RSPB's Exe Estuary reserve.

South of Exminster on the A379, park in the RSPB car park near the Swan's Nest Inn. Footpaths lead across the marshes to the estuary (where there is an occasional passenger ferry to Topsham). Continue south alongside the canal to Turf (about 1¼ miles). This track affords good views over the marshes, the tidal reedbed and the estuary. At Turf you can cross over the lock and walk a short way upstream to gain a better view of the estuary. Continuing south from Turf, an embankment follows the edge of the estuary.

38 BOWLING GREEN MARSH (Devon)

OS Landranger 192

The recent acquisition of Bowling Green Marsh by the RSPB is an important complement to their Exminster reserve on the other side of the estuary. Active management of the coastal grazing marsh is transforming the area into a valuable site for wildfowl and waders. A hide overlooking the marsh and a viewing platform overlooking the estuary are provided.

The reserve lies just south of Topsham, and is signposted from Holman Way car park in Topsham, close to the railway station (do not park in the lane by the reserve). Bowling Green Marsh is open at all times, but access is restricted to the public footpaths and hide. The Goatwalk, a path running alongside the estuary, is probably the best place to see the wintering Avocets at high tide.

39 POWDERHAM (Devon)

OS Landranger 192

The wooded parkland of Powderham Park lies on the estuary's west bank immediately south of Exminster marshes. A small river runs through the park, occasionally flooding certain areas. The park and adjacent meadows to the north are used by roosting waders at high tide.

Continue south on the A379 from Exminster, turn left at the first crossroads to Powderham, and park by the church. A track north leads to an embankment, which gives good views of the estuary and reaches Turf Lock after c.1½ miles. South from the church the road follows the edge of the estuary, and the park and its meres can be viewed from various points along here.

40 DAWLISH WARREN (Devon)

OS Landranger 192

This is a LNR managed by Teignbridge District Council. The central area comprises dunes, bushes and a reedbed. A golf course lies on the north side and the beach is popular with tourists. A public hide overlooks the estuary and offers close views of roosting waders at high tide. Access is unrestricted except for the golf course, which is private.

South of Starcross (off the A379) turn left onto a minor road leading to Dawlish Warren. Cross the railway under the bridge and walk northeast across the dunes, past the reedbed. The estuary can be viewed from the north side of the Warren and the hide is on this shore beyond the golf course. From Dawlish Warren station walk south to reach the coast and Langstone Rock.

41 EXMOUTH (Devon)

The seafront gives good views of the sea and the mudflats. Head east along the seafront to reach Orcombe Cliffs. A sheltered bay north of the spit is favoured by Brent Goose; this can be viewed from the Imperial Road car park west of the station.

Birds

Red-throated Diver and Slavonian Grebe are regular in winter, usually off Dawlish Warren or Langstone Rock but sometimes also off Exmouth. Small parties of Eider and Common Scoter are often on the sea and the latter may include a few Velvet Scoter. The regular wintering flock of Brent Geese numbers over 2,000 birds; the preferred feeding area is the bay north of Exmouth, though they are also seen off Dawlish Warren at high tide. Bewick's Swan and White-fronted Goose are only irregular at Exminster Marshes. Several thousand Wigeon winter, favouring the saltings behind Dawlish Warren or Exmouth. Other dabbling ducks include small numbers of Gadwall and Pintail. Goldeneye and Red-breasted Merganser prefer the deeper channels and a Long-tailed Duck is found most winters. Scaup is irregular, off Turf or on the sea. Peregrine is seen fairly regularly in winter while resident Buzzard and Sparrowhawk are more frequent. Over 100 Little Egrets can now be seen on the Exe in winter, and occasionally a few Spoonbills. Thousands of waders winter, including Grey Plover and Turnstone, a few Knot and Sanderling. Over 600 wintering Black-tailed Godwits are of national importance; they may be seen on the east shore or off Powderham and usually roost on Exminster Marshes (where they were briefly joined in winter 1981–2 by Britain's first Hudsonian Godwit), which also hold Golden Plover and several Ruff. Redshank roost in Powderham Park at high tide and should be checked for Spotted Redshank and Greenshank. The wintering Avocets, numbering 400–500 birds, form the third largest flock in Britain and are usually found off Turf or Bowling Green Marsh. On the coast a few Purple Sandpipers inhabit the rocks below Orcombe Cliffs and less frequently at Langstone Rock. The large gull roost on the marshes consists mainly of Black-headed Gulls but should be checked for the occasional Mediterranean Gull. Short-eared Owl is often seen over Exminster Marshes or at the east end of Dawlish Warren and a Kingfisher may be found along the canal. A few Chiffchaffs winter in the bushes on Dawlish Warren, occasionally accompanied by a Firecrest. Cirl Bunting should be looked for in low vegetation on the seafront at Dawlish and Black Redstart occasionally winters. Water Rails and Cetti's Warblers can be heard along the canal at Exminster.

Spring is heralded by the arrival of Wheatears and sometimes a Garganey on Exminster Marshes. One year there was a Great Spotted Cuckoo at Dawlish Warren. Terns are regularly observed offshore and roost on the Warren; Sandwich is commonest with smaller numbers of Common and Little and a few Arctic, while one or two Roseate are regular in May. Passage waders include Whimbrel and Green Sandpiper, and one of the few British records of Semipalmated Plover was found at this season.

In summer a few Shelduck and Lapwing breed on Exminster Marshes and the reedbeds hold Sedge and Reed Warblers and Reed Bunting. There is a small heronry in Powderham Park. Cirl Bunting breeds in hedges near Langstone and around Exminster; they are present all year.

Autumn wader passage begins in July and occasionally a Little Stint or Curlew

Sandpiper is found among the commoner species. Small numbers of Black Terns are regularly noted over the canal and Little Gull may also be seen. Osprey is almost annual in autumn and occasionally one stays several weeks. A Hobby sometimes chases the hirundines in late afternoon, particularly as they go to roost in the reedbeds. Gales in late autumn are likely to bring seabirds inshore. Gannet and Great and Arctic Skuas are often seen but seawatching is much better off more significant promontories such as Prawle. Scarce migrant passerines are found regularly at Dawlish Warren in autumn.

Information

Dawlish Warren (warden): c/o Countryside Management Section, Teignbridge District Council, Forde House, Brunel Road, Newton Abbot, Devon TQ12 4XX. Tel (visitor centre): 01626 863980. Teignbridge District Council: 01626 361101.

RSPB reserve office: Unit 3, Lions Rest Estate, Station Road, Exminster, Exeter, Devon EX6 8DZ. Tel: 01392 824614.

RSPB , South-West England Regional Office, Keble House, Southernhay Gardens, Exeter EX1 1NT. Tel: 01392 432691. Website: www.rspb.org.uk

42 YARNER WOOD (Devon)

OS Landranger 191
OS Outdoor Leisure 28

This small mixed woodland on the eastern edge of Dartmoor is a NNR, managed by English Nature. It is particularly rich in wildlife, harbouring a good variety of summer woodland birds and some unusual butterflies.

Habitat

Oak trees predominate in the woodland and there is a ground covering of bilberries.

Access

From the A38 Exeter-Plymouth road, turn right (north) onto the A382 to Bovey Tracey (left goes to Newton Abbot). At Bovey Tracey, turn left onto the B3387 to Haytor and Widecombe. After 1 mile fork right towards Manaton, and after 1½ miles turn left at a sharp right-hand bend, onto a tarmac lane into the wood. Park in the car park, beyond the warden's cottage. There are nature trails and a hide that overlooks several nestboxes. The wood is open from 08.30-20.00; access is free, but parties should book in advance.

Birds

Yarner Wood is a great place to see woodland birds. In summer, there is a colony of over 50 pairs of Pied Flycatchers, most of which use the nest boxes provided. Some 20 pairs of Redstarts also breed, as well as Spotted Flycatcher, Blackcap, Chiffchaff, Willow and Wood Warblers, and the commoner tit species. Lesser Spotted Woodpecker is relatively easy to find here, particularly in early spring before the leaves appear. The surrounding heathland holds a few pairs of Nightjars, as well as Grasshopper Warbler, Stonechat, Whinchat and Tree Pipit. A few pairs of Dartford Warbler inhabit Trendlebere Down, to the north of Yarner Wood. Overhead, Buzzard and Raven may be seen soaring, and a Hobby puts in an occasional appearance.

Information

Warden: Yarner Wood, Bovey Tracey, Devon TW13 9LJ. Tel: 01626 832330.

Bearded Tit

The sharp, pinging call of the resident Bearded Tit can be reliably heard in most of the more extensive reedbeds in England, although numbers may crash during harsh winters. They are less skulking than many reedbed species, and are often quite confiding provided the conditions are not too windy, so it is usually possible to obtain good clear views. When numbers are increasing Bearded Tits may begin to appear in smaller patches of suitable habitat.

Key sites: Lodmoor, Strumpshaw Fen, Minsmere, Cley, Blacktoft Sands, Leighton Moss.

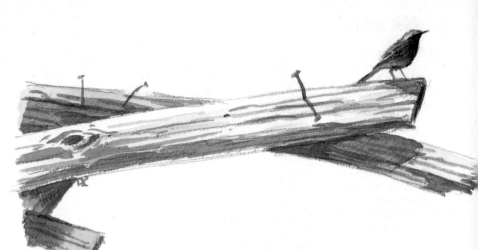

Black Redstart

Although common on the Continent, the Black Redstart remains a rarity in Britain. Most of the breeding birds are found in built-up areas, often exploiting derelict or abandoned buildings, but it also breeds on cliffs. Passage migrants appear regularly at almost all migration watchpoints, especially along the east coast, and a few birds overwinter, usually at coastal sites.

Key sites: Dungeness, Beachy Head, Prawle Point, Spurn Point, Flamborough Head.

Dartford Warbler

The extrovert and dainty Dartford Warbler is a resident species that depends on mild winter weather to survive and prosper, as it is at the northern limit of its range here. It occupies heathland with a good balance of gorse and heather, and is commonest in the south-west. This species almost became extinct in Britain after the harsh winter of 1962-63, but has recently spread north to Lincolnshire and east to Kent following a long succession of mild winters.

Key sites: Arne, Studland Peninsula, New Forest, Thursley Common.

43 WEST SEDGEMOOR (Somerset)

The Somerset Levels are one of England's largest remaining wet meadow systems. They hold internationally important numbers of waterfowl in winter, with up to 70,000 birds in some years, and important numbers of breeding waders in summer. Access is generally difficult, and the RSPB reserve of West Sedgemoor is probably the best bet.

Habitat
The RSPB manages 1,319 acres of hay meadows and pasture, and 104 acres of woodland. The 'moorland' comprises flat, low-lying fields which are cut for hay and grazed by cattle to provide good conditions for wildlife; in addition, the water levels are controlled. In winter, the fields are waterlogged and occasionally flooded, attracting thousands of ducks and waders. To the south of the levels, Swell Wood has the largest heronry in southwest England, as well as a good range of woodland species.

Access
The reserve car park is signed just off the A378 Taunton-Langport road, one mile east of Fivehead. There is a woodland trail from the car park with a hide to view the herons (March to June is best). Another trail leads to the Moorland Hide, overlooking the levels. There is an information board here.

Birds
Wigeon is the most numerous duck on the levels, exceptionally numbering in excess of 20,000 birds, and Teal numbers can reach 10,000 if conditions are right. Other duck species are less numerous, but recent counts of 1,000 Pintail are significant. Lapwing (up to 40,000 birds) and Golden Plover also winter in large numbers. Other waders include several hundred Snipe and Dunlin, as well as a few Ruff. Raptors are attracted to the area in winter, and Peregrine is frequently seen. Hen Harrier, Merlin and Short-eared Owl are also regular but less predictable.

West Sedgemoor is an important site for breeding waders in summer, mainly Lapwing, Snipe, Redshank and Curlew. A few pairs of Black-tailed Godwits may also breed. Hobbies are frequently seen in summer, and sometimes several at a time. Quail also occurs in the area, but are elusive as always. Amongst the passerines, Skylark, Yellow Wagtail, Whinchat, Sedge Warbler and Reed Bunting are the more typical species. Woodland species include the odd Nightingale and Buzzard.

Information
RSPB, South-West England Regional Office, Keble House, Southernhay Gardens, Exeter, Devon EX1 1NT. Tel: 01392 432691.

44 CHEW VALLEY LAKE (Avon/North Somerset)

This reservoir south of Bristol covers c.1,200 acres. Created in 1953, it has become one of the most important in Britain, noted for wintering wildfowl but also attracting an impressive passage of waders and other migrants. It is worth a visit at any time of year but is least productive in midsummer.

Habitat
Most of the lake is open water, part of which is set aside as a sailing area. The

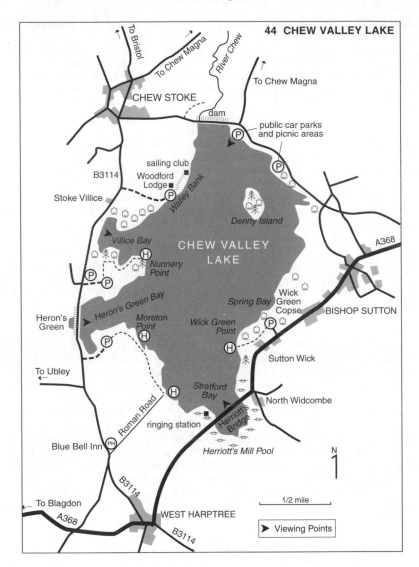

natural banks are attractive to waders, and in addition to exposed mud there are reedbeds, bushes and trees around the edge. A nature reserve has been established at Herriott's Bridge.

Access (see map)

The surrounding roads offer good views at the dam east of Chew Stoke, at Villice and Heron's Green Bays, and at Herriott's Bridge; the latter two are generally best. From Chew Magna on the B3130, take the B3114 to Chew Stoke. Continue on this road through the village and after 1 mile it runs alongside Villice Bay. Heron's Green is a little further on. Continue to West Harptree and join the A368 towards Bath. Herriott's Bridge is on this road c.1 mile northeast of the village. At Bishop Sutton turn left onto a minor road which completes the circuit back to Chew Stoke via the dam.

For a more thorough investigation five hides are sited around the edge with car parks off the roads. The hide at Nunnery Point is the best place for viewing gulls in the evening. Access to the shore is not allowed and a permit is required for the hides, obtained by post or personal application from Bristol Water at Woodford Lodge, which is north of Villice Bay (open 08.45–16.45 on weekdays, also at weekends from early April to mid-October). Permits cover access to Blagdon Lake and other local waters.

Birds

Bewick's Swan is regular in winter as well as a variety of ducks including Gadwall and Pintail. Small numbers of Goldeneye, Smew and Goosander are regular but the lake is perhaps best known for its Ruddy Ducks — this was the species' first breeding site in Britain. They are most numerous at the south end of the lake. Divers and the rarer grebes are not infrequent and many Dunlin remain through the winter. Water Rail and Bearded Tit are occasionally seen in the reeds and Golden Plover is found on the surrounding fields. There is a large gull roost in winter, mainly Common and Black-headed but a rarity such as Ring-billed is noted occasionally. A few Water Pipits are regular in winter.

A wide variety of waders occurs on passage, mainly in autumn, likely species including Curlew Sandpiper, Black-tailed Godwit, Spotted Redshank and Wood Sandpiper. There is a small passage of Black Terns in spring and autumn and a vagrant White-winged Black Tern is almost annual.

Summer is quiet. Garganey breeds but is only infrequently seen. Other breeding species include Gadwall, Ruddy Duck, and Reed and Sedge Warblers.

Information

Permits: Bristol Water, Recreation Dept., Woodford Lodge, Chew Stoke, Bristol BS18 8XH. Tel: 01275 332339.

45 BLAGDON LAKE (Avon/North Somerset)   OS Landranger 172 and 182

This 440-acre reservoir lies west of Chew and though generally less productive it can produce some interesting birds. The south and east sides of the lake are generally the best areas. It is possible to view from the road at the dam and at Rugmoor Bay, while along the south shore there are two hides (permits from Bristol Water at Woodford Lodge, Chew Valley Lake) and a footpath. At the north end of the dam there is public access to the reservoir's wooded north arm.

Habitat

There are some conifer plantations around the reservoir's shores as well as gardens and woodland near the dam. Mud is exposed when water levels drop, the best areas being at the east end.

Access

Blagdon Lake is situated between the villages of Blagdon and Ubley, north of the A368. A permit is required to access the reservoir enclosure (see above), but public roads allow reasonable coverage. For the west end follow signs for Butcombe from Blagdon village (Station Road) to the dam. A minor road at the south end of the dam affords views over the lake. A gated private road leads from where this road leaves the water and can be used by permit holders. Take the private road and turn left past the first bay, through trees to Home Bay hide. The road continues to the east end and another hide. For alternative access to

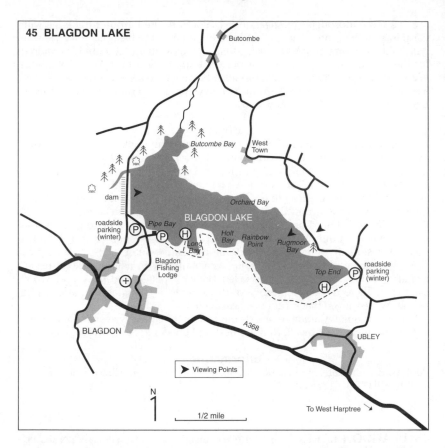

the east end take the A368 and the left fork to Ubley village. Turn left at the church and left again at the T-junction ½ mile further on. Entry to the reservoir is possible from the road where it crosses the River Yeo. There is a hide right of the track after c.½ mile.

Birds

In winter commoner ducks such as Wigeon, Gadwall, Goldeneye and Goosander may be joined by scarcer species such as Smew or Scaup. Divers and scarce grebes are also possible, while shoreline areas should be checked for Stonechat, Redpoll and Siskin.

Spring migrants include Common, Arctic and Black Terns as well as more regular species including Common Sandpiper.

Autumn wader passage is more interesting and could yield Spotted Redshank, Curlew Sandpiper, Little Stint and Ruff, while rare waders also occur, with Pectoral and Buff-breasted Sandpipers among those recorded. Autumn is also the best time to look for Hobby, and Osprey may also pass through on migration.

Information

Permits: Bristol Water, Recreation Dept., Woodford Lodge, Chew Stoke, Bristol BS18 8XH. Tel: 01275 332339.

46 CHEDDAR RESERVOIR (Somerset)   OS Landranger 182

This reservoir, between Cheddar and Axbridge, has man-made banks but nevertheless holds a number of wildfowl in winter, which can include unusual species such as Smew. In autumn exposed mud attracts waders and there is a good passage of terns. Several rarities have been found in recent years. There are no access restrictions.

Habitat
Though Cheddar Reservoir has concrete banks and no marginal vegetation, muddy banks and gravel islands are exposed when water levels drop. Some small reed-fringed pools and willows can be overlooked from the south end.

Access
There are two main entrances to Cheddar Reservoir. The north entrance is reached by taking the A371 bypass and then the gated road 200 yards along the road to Axbridge. From the car park at the end a perimeter track is reached, but is subject to restrictions detailed on information boards at the entrance. Alternatively, take the A371 west of Cheddar and then the B3151 to Wedmore. Turn right on Sharpham Road after the bridge over the disused railway and in 300 yards take the middle road at a three-way fork and continue to the car park.

Birds
In winter divers, grebes and sea duck can occasionally be found among more regular species on the open water, and the gull roost has produced Mediterranean, Yellow-legged and Ring-billed Gulls.

Common Sandpiper, Ringed and Little Ringed Plovers can occur in spring, as do Common, Arctic and Black Terns, and occasionally White Wagtail.

Waders and terns also pass through in autumn, when seabirds such as Grey Phalarope and Kittiwake have been recorded following strong gales.

47 BRIDGWATER BAY (Somerset)   OS Landranger 182

The vast mudflats and saltmarshes of Bridgwater Bay hold important concentrations of waders and waterfowl in winter and on passage. The bay extends from Minehead in the west to Burnham-on-Sea in the east, but the eastern part, around the estuary of the River Parrett, is the best area for birds. Some 8,800 acres are protected as a National Nature Reserve.

Habitat
The habitats of Bridgwater Bay range from extensive intertidal mudflats, salt-marsh and shingle shore to grazing marsh intersected by freshwater and brackish ditches. The River Parrett meanders north from Bridgwater across a low-lying plain, encircling Pawlett Hams before entering the bay between Stert and Berrow Flats. There are sand dunes at Berrow and Steart, and Stert Island, in the mouth of the Parrett, is mostly bare shingle and sand. There is a small reedbed west of Stert Point and several scrapes and pools have been excavated in front of the hides that overlook the estuary mouth.

Access
Junctions 23 and 24 on the M5 lead into Bridgwater. From here take the A39 westwards towards Minehead. In Cannington, turn right (north) onto a minor road to Combwich and Hinkley Point. About ½ mile after the turning to Combwich, turn

right on a road signed to Otterhampton and Steart. After 1 mile turn right again to Steart itself. Park in the car park on the left in Steart and continue for ½ mile to a tower hide and two other hides. The hides have free access and are open daily. Waders roost at the point at high tide (best to arrive up to an hour before), with the largest numbers just upriver on the west bank of the Parrett. The scrapes and pools can be viewed well from the tower hide.

Further west along the bay, waders can be seen for up to 2½ hours after high tide at Wall Common – park by the road 1 mile west of Steart and walk west along the seawall. Further west still, the bay can be viewed at Stolford and Hinkley Point. Park at Stolford and walk east to Catsford Common, or west to Hinkley Point. The nuclear power station's warm water outfall attracts gulls and terns (you can drive direct to the power station and park there).

It is essential to work Bridgwater Bay around high tide, as the mudflats are so extensive at low tide.

Birds

Over 10,000 Dunlin winter in the bay, with smaller numbers of Knot, Redshank, Curlew, Grey Plover and Oystercatcher. A few Spotted Redshanks also winter in the mouth of the Parrett, and occasionally Avocets. Wildfowl are mainly Wigeon with some Mallard and Teal. In hard weather, Lapwings and Golden Plover are numerous, and a few Brent Geese are regular. Raptors are a feature of winter and include small numbers of Hen Harriers, Peregrines, Merlins and Short-eared Owls.

Numbers and variety of waders increase during spring passage, and include Bar-tailed Godwits and Whimbrel; there is a spring roost of the latter on Stert Island.

Summer is quiet, but Nightingales are common in coastal copses, notably along the Hinkley Point nature trail. In late summer up to 2,000 Shelducks gather to moult, the major British site for them; smaller numbers are present throughout the year.

Autumn passage brings more waders, including Icelandic Black-tailed Godwits and occasional rarities. Yellow Wagtails are frequent and Aquatic Warblers have occasionally been found in the reedbed (but are more likely to be trapped than seen). Westerly gales may bring a wandering seabird to the estuary mouth.

Information

Robin Prowse, Dowells Farm, Steart, Bridgwater, Somerset TA5 2PX. Tel: 01278 652426.

48–49 RADIPOLE LAKE AND LODMOOR (Dorset)　　OS Landranger 194

Radipole Lake is an RSPB reserve of 192 acres in central Weymouth. Lodmoor is another RSPB reserve of 150 acres on the coast just east of town. Both are worth visiting at any season. Residents include Cetti's Warbler and Bearded Tit and both areas attract many migrants and wintering birds as well as regular rarities.

Habitat

Radipole Lake was formerly the estuary of the River Wey but since the completion of the Westham Bridge in 1921 has slowly become a freshwater lake. Extensive reedbeds cover much of the area but the remaining open water includes both shallow areas and deep channels. Dense scrub borders the trails and the perimeter while at the north end there are some water meadows. Lodmoor has pasture, shallow water, reedbeds and dykes, and is separated from Weymouth Bay by a seawall.

Access (see map)

Both reserves are within easy reach of Weymouth.

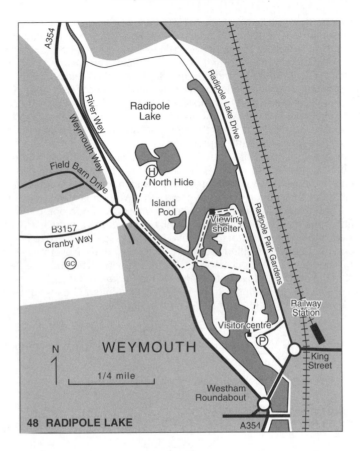

48 RADIPOLE LAKE

48 RADIPOLE LAKE (Dorset)

OS Landranger 194

The reserve lies close to Weymouth bus and railway stations. A large car park is available at the south end of the lake. A Visitor Centre sited here is open all year, 09.00–17.00 (16.00 in winter). Several raised trails transect the reedbeds, affording good views over the lagoons and reeds. The reserve is open at all times but the North Hide is only open 08.30–16.30, with a fee for non-members.

49 LODMOOR (Dorset)

OS Landranger 194

Leave Weymouth northwards on the coastal A353 to Wareham. The entrance to the Lodmoor reserve is at the public car park by the Sea Life Centre along this road. The reserve is open at all times and viewing areas are provided off the perimeter footpath.

Birds

Cetti's Warbler and Bearded Tit are resident at both sites, as are Kingfisher and a few Water Rails. During summer many Reed and Sedge Warblers breed as well several pairs of Grasshopper Warblers and Lesser Whitethroats in the areas of scrub.

A wide variety of migrants has occurred in spring and autumn, and there is always a chance of something unusual. Garganey is regular in spring and is one of the first-returning migrants. Waders are generally present in small numbers depending on water levels, and possibilities include Little Stint, Black-tailed Godwit and Wood Sandpiper. Little Gull and Black Tern occur but cannot be guaranteed. Thousands of hirundines, hundreds of Pied Wagtails and up to 3,000 Yellow Wagtails use the reeds for roosting during passage. Spotted Crake is found most years but is easily overlooked. Ringing at Radipole has demonstrated that small numbers of Aquatic Warblers pass through annually, but this denizen of dense reedbeds is rarely seen; 1–2 are found each year by a lucky few, usually in August or early September.

Winter sees the arrival of relatively small numbers of ducks including some Gadwall, Scaup and Goldeneye. Generally Lodmoor is more attractive to wildfowl than Radipole. A few Jack Snipe winter, and an influx of continental Water Rails increases the chance of seeing one. Cetti's Warbler is usually easier to see in winter and a few Water Pipits are regularly present at Lodmoor, often remaining until April by which time some will be in summer plumage. Gulls are prominent at both sites and an impressive list of rare species has been recorded; Mediterranean and Ring-billed Gulls are noted regularly November–May and Glaucous and Iceland are occasionally found in winter. The gulls are best seen at roost in the evening, close to the Information Centre at Radipole.

Extreme rarities at Radipole have included Pied-billed Grebe, Squacco and Purple Herons, Little Bittern and Red-rumped Swallow.

Information

Keith Ballard, RSPB Visitor Centre, The Swannery Car Park, Weymouth, Dorset DT4 7TZ. Tel: 01305 778313.

50 PORTLAND HARBOUR,
FERRYBRIDGE AND THE FLEET (Dorset)   OS Landranger 194

These areas are best in autumn and winter for a variety of waterfowl, waders and gulls, and can be conveniently combined with a visit to Radipole Lake and Portland Bill.

Habitat

Portland Harbour is a large, artificially enclosed harbour lying between Weymouth and the Isle of Portland – not actually an island as it is connected to the mainland by the unique Chesil Beach, a great 18-mile-long wall of shingle. Between the Beach and the coast is a narrow strip of tidal water known as The Fleet, which enters Portland Harbour at Ferrybridge.

Access (see maps)

1. The harbour is best viewed from Weymouth at the ruins of Sandsfoot Castle on Old Castle Road. It can also be seen from Ferrybridge but this area is often much disturbed by windsurfers.

2. The mudflats at the southeast end of The Fleet can be checked from Ferrybridge and there is a car park nearby which overlooks it. North of Ferrybridge a footpath follows the northeast edge of The Fleet to Langton Herring before turning inland.

3. The Fleet near Langton Herring is another good area for waders and wildfowl, and can be reached by leaving Weymouth northwest on the B3157: turn left at a mini-roundabout near Chickerell, park at a gate c.100 yards before Moonfleet Hotel, and follow the footpath to The Fleet. The bay north of Herbury Gore some-

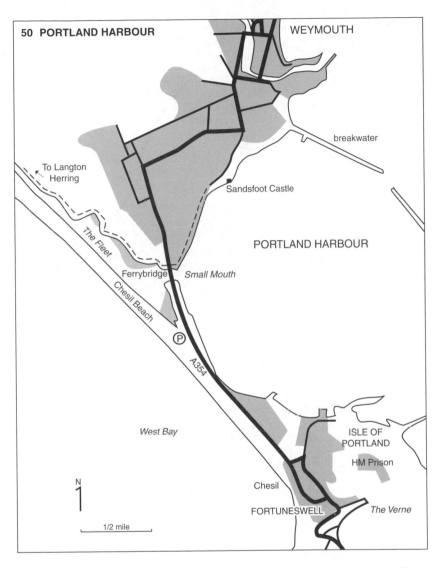

50 PORTLAND HARBOUR

WEYMOUTH

breakwater

To Langton Herring

Sandsfoot Castle

The Fleet

PORTLAND HARBOUR

Chesil Beach

Ferrybridge   Small Mouth

P

A354

West Bay

ISLE OF PORTLAND

HM Prison

N

Chesil

FORTUNESWELL   The Verne

1/2 mile

times holds a good variety of waders, and Rodden Hive can also be rewarding. **4.** At the northwest end of the Fleet is Abbotsbury Swannery, which is excellent for a wide variety of wildfowl besides Mute Swan. The Swannery lies ½ mile south of Abbotsbury village but is only open May–September. Outside these months the area can be viewed from Chesil Beach by taking a turning off the B3157 signed 'Subtropical Gardens' 100 yards west of Abbotsbury village. From the end of this road you can walk left along the beach to view the reedbeds and lagoons.

Birds

The harbour is best in calm weather, November–March. All three divers are regular in small numbers, Red-throated being least frequent. Black-necked Grebe haunts the vicinity of Sandsfoot Castle while Slavonian is more widespread. A variety of sea duck occurs including Red-breasted Merganser and Goldeneye

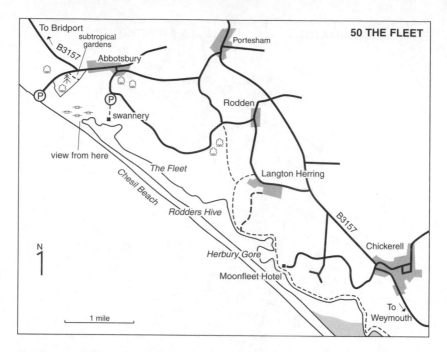

(both common) and a few Eider, Long-tailed Duck, and Common and Velvet Scoters. The bushes and gardens around Sandsfoot Castle usually hold small numbers of wintering Chiffchaff, Blackcap and Firecrest. Brent Geese are frequent at Ferrybridge, but the bulk of the flock winters further west on the Fleet. An interesting selection of waders occurs on the Fleet in autumn and winter including the occasional rarity such as Kentish Plover. Gulls and terns should always be checked as several of the rarer species have made appearances, and Mediterranean and Little Gulls are regular.

In spring and autumn the Subtropical Gardens and the bushes and reedbeds along the beach at Abbotsbury hold a good selection of migrants. In winter the lagoon here is a haven for large numbers of wildfowl, and Bearded Tit can frequently be seen in the reeds.

51 PORTLAND BILL (Dorset)   OS Landranger 194

The Isle of Portland protrudes c.6 miles into the English Channel from the Dorset coast, the south tip being known as Portland Bill. An active Bird Observatory is maintained at the Bill in recognition of its importance as a migration watchpoint for both landbirds and seabirds. The best times to visit are March–May and August–October.

Habitat

At first sight Portland appears uninviting being virtually treeless and heavily scarred by limestone quarries. Much of the north part of the island is settled or quarried but the south third is largely rural. This is the observatory's recording area, with the village of Southwell forming the north boundary. The various habitats include drystone-walled fields, clumps of bushes, hedgerows, grassy commons and disused quarries that have become overgrown with a rich variety of plants; all are attractive to migrants. The West Cliffs rise to over 200 feet and are used by breeding seabirds, but the East Cliffs are low and of little interest. There is virtually no wader habitat.

Access (see map)

Leave Weymouth south on the A354 signed to Portland and continue through Fortuneswell and Easton to Southwell. Turn left in Southwell to the Bill. The observatory is sited in the Old Lower Lighthouse beside the road c.½ mile before the Bill. There is parking at the Observatory for residents but casual visitors should use the large car park north of the new lighthouse (parking is not permitted beside the road between Southwell and the Bill).

Generally, the most productive birding areas are within the Observatory's recording area but much of this is common land and has become very popular with non-birders at weekends; on Bank Holidays it can be positively crowded. The best times to search for migrants are early morning and late afternoon when there is least human activity. Cover is fairly limited and any patch of bushes may hold migrants, but several areas deserve specific mention:

1. Observatory garden, containing a variety of cover and a small pond. Trapping and mist-netting are carried out here. (Residents and members only.)
2. The bushes around the Coastguard Cottages.
3. Culverwell, a dense area of bramble and elder.
4. Any of the overgrown quarries, especially the one behind the Eight Kings pub in Southwell (the latter is private property).

The Top Fields are noted for attracting migrants, especially finches and buntings (but be aware that much of this is private agricultural land – keep to footpaths). Certain species, such as pipits and wheatears, favour the short turf of the commons. Seawatching is best at the Bill beside the obelisk, which offers some protection to this hardy pursuit. In spring and summer the West Cliffs hold one of the south coast's few seabird colonies; a footpath runs along the clifftop. If time permits, the Verne, at the north end of Portland, should be checked for migrants. This scrub-covered plateau is situated above the dockyard and below Verne Prison (see Portland Harbour map, p.73).

Portland Bird Observatory is open all year. Comfortable self-catering accommodation is available for up to 20 in six bedrooms and for another four in a small self-contained flat, all at reasonable rates. Members of Portland Bird Observatory and Field Centre pay reduced charges – further details from the warden.

Birds

Winter can be dismal but a variety of divers, sea ducks and auks occur offshore. Gannets sometimes appear in large numbers in January and Purple Sandpipers winter on the rocks around the Bill. A few Black Redstarts may be present.

Spring seabird passage commences in March with divers, Gannet and Common Scoter heading east along the Channel. It continues throughout April into early May when Manx Shearwater, skuas and terns add to the variety. Many of the shearwaters are seen in the evenings. A small concentrated passage of Pomarine Skuas occurs in early May. Passerine migration also begins in March, and summer visitors arrive in force in April–May (Portland frequently hosts some of the earliest spring arrivals in Britain), frequently including a 'spring overshoot' such as Hoopoe; small numbers of Ring Ouzel and Firecrest are regular (as in autumn). Rarities are a feature of the late spring, with recent occurrences of Egyptian Nightjar and Lesser Short-toed Lark among the most outstanding.

Summer is fairly quiet but small numbers of Guillemot, Razorbill and Puffin

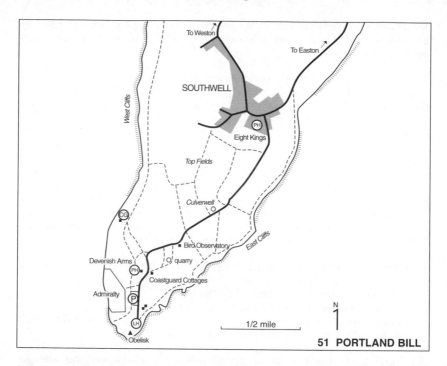

51 PORTLAND BILL

breed alongside Fulmar, Kittiwake and a few Shags. Rock Pipit is resident and Little Owl inhabits the quarries.

Autumn seabird passage is less predictable than spring, and the more pelagic species are only noted occasionally, usually when onshore winds prevail. Balearic Shearwater is annual in July–October but numbers vary. Sooty Shearwater, Grey Phalarope and Little Gull are recorded irregularly at this time, but Great and Arctic Skuas are more frequent. The bulk of the landbird passage is August–September when chats, warblers and flycatchers can be much in evidence. Migrants also include Turtle Dove, Swallow, House Martin, Yellow Wagtail, Whinchat and Pied Flycatcher. The chance of finding one of the scarcer migrants adds spice to Portland at this season. Melodious Warbler and Woodchat Shrike may appear after south winds and Tawny Pipit is annual in September. Ortolan Bunting is regularly found in the Top Fields, and anticyclonic conditions may bring one of the eastern drift migrants such as Wryneck, Bluethroat, Icterine and Barred Warblers or Red-breasted Flycatcher. A few of each are recorded most years and Portland's list includes many outstanding rarities from all compass points, including Alpine Swift, Pechora Pipit, Cliff Swallow, Booted and Orphean Warblers, and Northern Waterthrush.

In late autumn Portland witnesses large-scale movements of partial migrants such as Skylark, Meadow Pipit, Starling, Chaffinch, Goldfinch and Linnet. Spells of cold weather at the onset of winter frequently result in hard-weather movements of birds heading out to sea to the west or south. These typically comprise Lapwing, Redwing and Fieldfare, but Golden Plover and Skylark may also move on. Small numbers of some finches migrate throughout the winter.

Information

Warden (Martin Cade), Bird Observatory, Old Lower Light, Portland Bill, Dorset DT5 2JT. Tel: 01305 820553. E-mail: obs@btinternet.com.

52–57 POOLE HARBOUR AND ISLE OF PURBECK (Dorset)

Poole Harbour is the second largest natural harbour in the world. Its north and east shores have suffered considerable urbanisation at Poole and Bournemouth but the other sides are largely undeveloped. The harbour is good for wildfowl and waders in autumn and winter, and divers and grebes are often found in the coastal bays. To the south is the Isle of Purbeck (not actually an island), much of this being heathland and a stronghold for Dartford Warbler. Several areas are protected as nature reserves.

Habitat

Tidal mudflats and saltings surround the harbour, with the richest areas on the west and south shores. The open, dry heaths of the Isle of Purbeck are mainly heather and gorse with some bracken. There are small areas of both deciduous and coniferous woodland, carr and fresh marsh with reedbeds and small pools. The heaths have a particularly rich flora and fauna with many rare plants, all the British reptiles, and a host of insects.

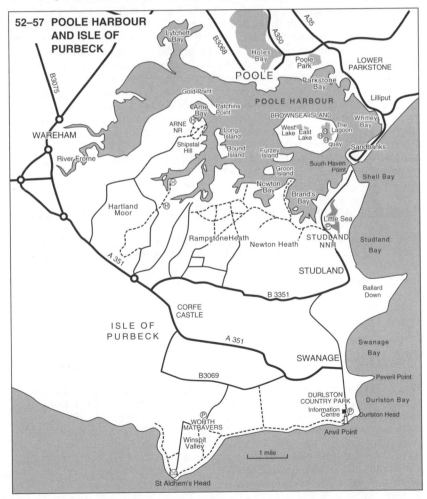

Access (see maps)

There are many places to birdwatch in this area. Six sites are detailed below:

52 POOLE HARBOUR (Dorset)   OS Landranger 195

The harbour itself can be viewed from Arne and also at South Haven Point on Studland where, with the changing tides, duck, waders and grebes fly in from and out to sea. Brand's Bay, which can also be viewed from Studland Heath, is probably the best area for wildfowl and waders. Gulls, waders and ducks frequent the northeast shore and the B3369 between Poole and Sandbanks can be excellent at low tide but it is very disturbed in summer.

53 STUDLAND HEATH (Dorset)   OS Landranger 195

Much of this heath is a NNR managed by EN. The habitats are essentially as at Arne. Leave Wareham on the A351 and turn left on the B3351 at Corfe Castle. On reaching Studland, Ferry Road heads north to South Haven Point. A toll is payable on this road but there is a car park before it on the seaward side. The road continues through prime heath that is excellent Dartford Warbler country. The reserve lies on both sides of the road and access is unrestricted, but visitors should observe the notices at the reserve entrances. There are two nature trails: the Dune Trail is open year-round and the Woodland Trail operates April–September. A large freshwater pool (Little Sea) east of the road is attractive to ducks in winter. There is an Information Centre and an observation hut that offers a good view over the pool. A hide at the north end is always open. Alternatively, you can reach Poole from Bournemouth by taking the B3369 to Sandbanks and catching the ferry to South Haven Point (runs at 20–30 minute intervals).

54 SHELL AND STUDLAND BAYS (Dorset)   OS Landranger 195

Both bays, north and east of Studland peninsula, are a favoured haunt of divers, grebes and sea duck in winter. Shell Bay is easily reached from the car park at South Haven Point. Studland Bay can be approached via the Knoll car park at the south end of Studland Bay or through Studland village; a minor road leads to the seafront where there is a car park. A bridleway from Studland village follows the clifftop to the Foreland. This gives good views over the bay and the two clumps of trees beside the path can harbour migrant passerines.

55 BROWNSEA ISLAND (Dorset)   OS Landranger 195

This 1½-mile-long island is the largest in Poole Harbour. It is owned by the NT, and the north part is managed as a reserve by Dorset Wildlife Trust. Its habitats include woodland, heath and freshwater pools and marshes. A hide overlooks the lagoon and marsh and is a good place to view wildfowl, waders and terns. Large numbers of waders roost on Brownsea at high tide and there is a heronry on the island. Boats to Brownsea Island go from Sandbanks (taking ten minutes) and Poole Quay (30 minutes); a landing fee is payable by non-NT members. The island is closed October–March.

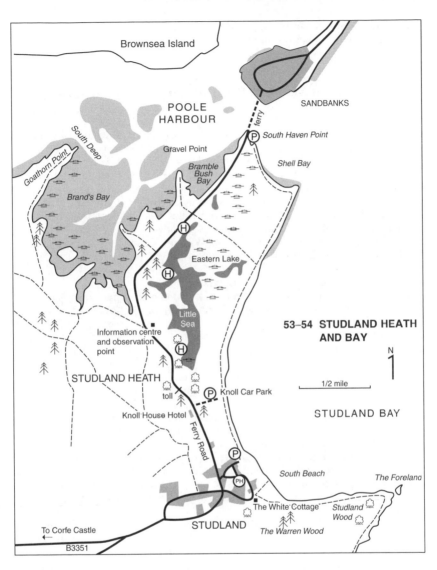

Brownsea Island

POOLE
HARBOUR

SANDBANKS

South Deep

Goathorn Point

Gravel Point

Ferry

South Haven Point

Shell Bay

Bramble
Bush
Bay

Brand's Bay

Eastern Lake

Little
Sea

53–54 **STUDLAND HEATH
AND BAY**

N

Information centre
and observation
point

1/2 mile

STUDLAND HEATH

toll

Knoll Car Park

STUDLAND BAY

Knoll House Hotel

Ferry Road

South Beach

The Foreland

PH

The White Cottage

Studland
Wood

To Corfe Castle

STUDLAND

The Warren Wood

B3351

56 ARNE (Dorset)

OS Landranger 195

This peninsula protrudes into the southwest corner of Poole Harbour. The RSPB
reserve of 1,307 acres consists mainly of heath but with some woodland and
freshwater reedbeds and marsh. Leave Wareham south on the A351 and after 1
mile turn left at Stoborough; in c.2 miles the Reception Centre (open late May to
early September) and car park are on the right. The reserve is open at all times
but visitors must keep to the footpaths. The ¾-mile Shipstal Trail is open from late
May to early September and takes in all the representative habitats, as well as giving fine views over the saltings and harbour; there is one hide. To reach the
nature trail continue beyond the Reception Centre to Arne village and park in
the car park; the trail begins opposite Arne church. The reserve is one of the best

places to see Dartford Warbler. It is present all year but often keeps hidden in the gorse, particularly in windy conditions.

57 DURLSTON HEAD–ST ALDHELM'S HEAD
(Dorset)

OS Landranger 195
OS Outdoor Leisure 15

There are some fine cliffs along this stretch of the coast. A variety of seabirds breed (March–July is best), and passerines occur on migration, especially in the sheltered valleys. The Heads can be good for seawatching. A minor road from Swanage leads south to Durlston Country Park, which is well signed, where there is a Visitor Centre. Durlston Head has held several rarities and is heavily vegetated with large stands of trees and bushy valleys. From here you can walk west along the cliff path to St Aldhelm's Head (c.5 miles), the main interest of the walk being breeding seabirds including Puffin. Alternatively, St Aldhelm's Head may be reached on foot from Worth Matravers. **Winspit Valley**, a well-vegetated valley running between Worth Matravers and Winspit, can be excellent for migrants.

Birds
Winter is a good time to visit, and with luck you can see three species of diver and five species of grebe. Black-necked and Slavonian Grebes are regularly present, sometimes in the harbour but more frequently in the coastal bays. Sea duck also winter, mainly Red-breasted Merganser and Common Scoter. Cormorant, Shag and a few auks are also usually present on the sea. Wildfowl in the harbour include Brent Goose, Pintail and, in the channels, Goldeneye. Avocet, Black-tailed Godwit, and Spotted Redshank winter (the former in good numbers), and Sanderling can be found on the shores of Studland Bay. Hen Harrier is occasional and Water Rail and Bearded Tit may be seen in the reedbeds at Arne or around Little Sea. Dartford Warbler is often silent and unobtrusive in winter. Black Redstart sometimes winters, usually on the coast, and in milder years one or two Firecrests and Chiffchaffs.

Spring and autumn bring a greater variety of waders to the harbour. Seawatching can be productive from the headlands, especially in spring, and the coastal bushes attract passerine migrants, including scarcities such as Wryneck, Icterine, Melodious and Yellow-browed Warblers, Red-breasted Flycatcher and Ortolan Bunting.

In summer Grey Heron, Little Egret, and Common and Sandwich Terns nest on Brownsea Island, and Yellow-legged Gulls may also be present. Breeding birds of the cliffs include Fulmar, Shag, Kittiwake, Guillemot, Razorbill and Puffin. Dartford Warbler is more in evidence on the heath and Nightjar should be looked for at dusk. The small areas of woodland hold Sparrowhawk, Green and Great Spotted Woodpeckers, and Marsh Tit.

Information
Arne (Senior Warden): Neil Gartshore, Syldata, Arne, Wareham, Dorset BH20 5BJ (enclose a SAE). Tel: 01929 553360. E-mail: neil.gartshore@rspb.org.uk
Durlston: The Ranger, Durlston Country Park, Swanage, Dorset BH19 2JL. Tel: 01929 424443.
Brownsea Island (Warden): Chris Thain, The Villa, Brownsea Island, Dorset BH13 7EE. Tel: 01202 709445. E-mail: dorsetwtisland@cix.co.uk
Studland Heath: English Nature, Slepe Farm, Arne, Wareham, Dorset BH19 3AX. Tel: 01929 450259.

SOUTHEAST ENGLAND

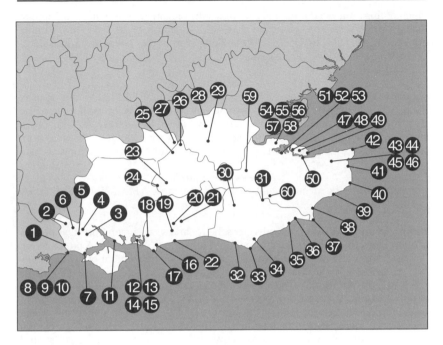

1 Hampshire Avon
2–6 New Forest
2 Ashley Walk and
  Hampton Ridge
3 Beaulieu Road
4 Acres Down
5 Bolderwood
6 Eyeworth Pond and
  Fritham
7 Keyhaven and
  Pennington Marshes
8 Christchurch Harbour
9 Stanpit Marsh
10 Hengistbury Head
11 Titchfield Haven
12–15 Langstone and
  Chichester Harbours
12 Farlington Marshes
13 Hayling Island
14 Chichester Harbour
15 Thorney Island
16 Pagham Harbour
17 Selsey Bill
18 Chichester Gravel Pits
19–21 Arun Valley
19 Arundel

20 Amberley Wild Brooks
21 Pulborough Brooks
22 Climping–Littlehampton
23 Thursley Common
24 Frensham Common
25 Virginia Water
26 Staines Reservoirs
27 Wraysbury Gravel Pits
28 Brent Reservoir
29 The Wetland Centre
  (Barn Elms)
30 Ashdown Forest
31 Bewl Water
32 Cuckmere and Seaford
33 Beachy Head
34 Pevensey Levels
35 Pett Level
36 Rye Harbour
37 Dungeness
38 Lade Sands and Lade
  Pit
39 Folkestone-Dover
40 St Margaret's Bay
41 Sandwich Bay
42 Thanet and North
  Foreland

43–46 Stour Valley
43 Stodmarsh
44 Grove Ferry
45 Westbere Marshes
46 Fordwich
47–49 Isle of Sheppey
47 Elmley
48 Capel Fleet and Harty
  Ferry
49 Swale NNR
50 Oare Marshes
51–53 Medway Estuary
51 Riverside Country Park
52 Ham Green and Lower
  Halstow
53 Funton Creek and
  Chetney
54–58 Hoo Peninsula
  (North Kent Marshes)
54 Cliffe Pools
55 Halstow Marshes
56 Northward Hill
57 Allhallows
58 Isle of Grain
59 Bough Beech Reservoir
60 Bedgebury Forest

81

1 HAMPSHIRE AVON (Hampshire/Dorset)

OS Landranger 195
OS Outdoor Leisure 22

Much of this area is a designated SSSI that supports an excellent flora and fauna. Rising in the Vale of Pewsey the river derives much of its water from chalk aquifers in the Salisbury Plain and the Hampshire Avon possesses a fine selection of riverine and wetland habitats.

Habitat

A broad floodplain is dominated by wet meadows that flood in winter. Marshy thickets of willows and alder, and in some places reedbeds, fringe the river. The Avon joins the Stour in Christchurch Harbour where there is an estuary. Gravel pits such as Blashford Lakes vary in age and support a broad variety of habitats from woodland and scrub to lakes with little vegetation and bare gravel shores.

Access (see maps)

Interesting birds occur at several locations, the most accessible of which are detailed below.

Lower Avon Meadows Footpaths cross the meadows between Christchurch and Burton. From the A35 Purewell roundabout take the B3347 north. A path may be accessed from a small stream almost 1 mile north of the roundabout while a second footpath starts at a lay-by north of the railway bridge. Coward's Marsh is reached from the B3073 (Fairmile Road) in Christchurch by turning east into Suffolk Avenue, about halfway between Fairmile Hospital and the Jumpers Ilford roundabout and then proceeding through the housing estate to Marsh Lane. From here walk north along the track to the stile by Marsh Cottage. Birds often include small numbers of waders and wildfowl during winter, with Lapwing and Redshank present in the breeding season. Cetti's Warbler frequents the riverside scrub, while Water Pipits may remain until early spring. Migrant waders can include Green, Wood and Common Sandpipers and Jack Snipe. Scarce and rare species have been recorded here with some regularity.

Bisterne and Ringwood Meadows Bisterne Meadows can be viewed from Matchams Viewing Point, which is accessible via the southern end of Hurn Lane south of Avon Castle and north off the A338. Meadows north of Ringwood can be observed from the small road to the electricity sub-station west of the A338 just north of the A31 roundabout. Flocks of Lapwing and Golden Plover occur here, while a small flock of White-fronted Geese is usually best viewed from Matchams Viewing Point. Flocks of Siskin and Redpoll frequent riverside alders in winter.

Blashford Lakes There is currently limited access to Ivy and Ellingham Lakes. Access points to this gravel pit complex may reached along the A338 between Ringwood and Ibsley.

Kingfisher, Linbrook and North Poulner Lakes: From the A338, ⅓ mile north of the A31 roundabout at Ringwood, follow Hurst Road east through the housing estate to the end of the road. Walk northeast and east along the Avon Valley Path to view the lakes.

Ivy, Snails, Spinnaker and Rockford Lakes: These waters may be viewed at various points along Ivy Lane, which is signposted to Rockford from the A338. Spinnaker, Snails and Linbrook Lakes are also viewable from the footpath starting south of the junction of Ivy Lane and Gorley Road and which follows the

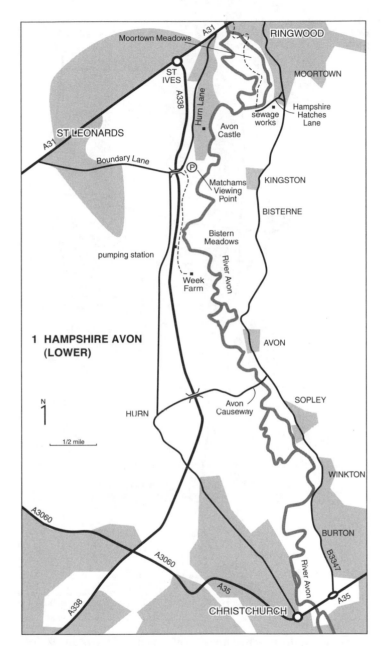

north shore of Spinnaker Lake southwest to Spinnaker Sailing Club. Continue south between Spinnaker and Snails Lakes to Snails Lane and then along the west shore of Linbrook Lake to the Avon Valley Path.

Mockbeggar Lake South: Accessed from the A338 by taking Ellingham Drove at Ellingham. Cross east towards Moyles Court. After ¾ mile the lake is viewable from the gate entrance along the embankment north of the road.

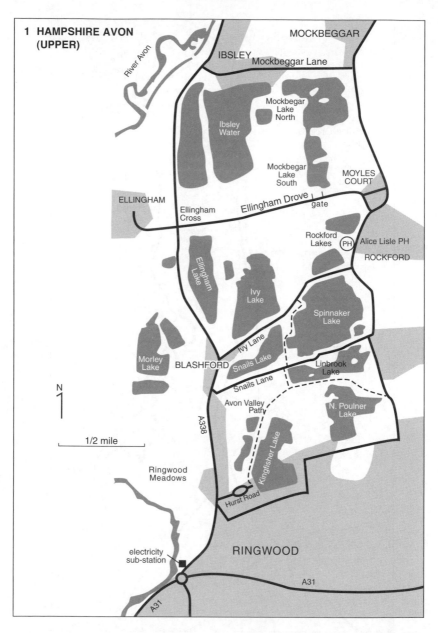

1 HAMPSHIRE AVON (UPPER)

MOCKBEGGAR

River Avon

IBSLEY
Mockbeggar Lane

Mockbegar Lake North

Ibsley Water

Mockbegar Lake South

MOYLES COURT

ELLINGHAM

Ellingham Cross

Ellingham Drove

gate

Rockford Lakes

PH — Alice Lisle PH

ROCKFORD

Ellingham Lake

Ivy Lake

Spinnaker Lake

Ivy Lane

Morley Lake

BLASHFORD

Snails Lake

Linbrook Lake

Snails Lane

N

Avon Valley Path

N. Poulner Lake

A338

1/2 mile

Kingfisher Lake

Ringwood Meadows

Hurst Road

electricity sub-station

RINGWOOD

A31

A31

Mockbeggar Lake North: Reached from the A338 at Ibsley and taking Mockbeggar Lane east to Mockbeggar and then the minor road south to Moyles Court. The lake can be viewed at several locations from both roads.

Ibsley Meadows and Bickton Mill The river and meadows are best viewed from the minor road between the A338 at Ibsley Bridge and Harbridge Church. The minor road north from Harbridge Church to Harbridge Green offers further views of the valley.

Birds

Winter wildfowl include small numbers of Bewick's Swans (best found near Ibsley Bridge) and White-fronted Geese (which have usually favoured the Bisterne area in recent years) and numbers of commoner ducks such as Wigeon, Teal and Shoveler. Small numbers of Goosander feed on the river and roost on Blashford Lakes, where Smew and Scaup may be present in cold weather. Riverside reeds may harbour a Bittern, while Little Egret can be found year-round. Large flocks of Lapwing and Golden Plover move around the valley, and Snipe is widespread. Green Sandpiper favours Blashford Lakes. Wet conditions may attract a greater variety of waders, with Jack Snipe, Redshank and Black-tailed Godwit sometimes present. Raptors can include Hen Harrier, Peregrine and Short-eared Owl. Water Pipits frequent the meadows near Christchurch, while almost any patch of alder and birch could produce flocks of Redpoll and Siskin.

Breeding species include small numbers of Lapwing, Redshank and Snipe. Reed and Sedge Warblers occur in the reedy fringes, and Cetti's Warbler is well established at a number of locations. Grey Wagtail and Kingfisher prefer smaller streams and tributaries.

The area is interesting for migrants with wildfowl and waders more prominent when the area is wet. Blashford Lakes is perhaps the most reliable area for a migrant waders, and Black Tern occurs with some regularity here. Garganey is frequent and a noticeable passage of raptors includes small numbers of Hobby and annual Osprey. Rarer raptors have included Montagu's and Marsh Harriers and Red Kite. Passerine migrants are not a major feature, but Wheatear and Whinchat are usually conspicuous.

2–6 NEW FOREST (Hampshire)

OS Landranger 195 and 196
OS Outdoor Leisure 22

This outstanding area of mixed woodland and heathland between Southampton and Bournemouth, is managed by Forest Enterprise and is popular with tourists in summer. A number of scarce species breed (though some are difficult to locate) and a fine variety of common woodland and heath birds can be seen. May–June is the best time to visit, with early mornings most profitable.

Habitat

The extensive woods are a mix of mature oak and beech with conifer planta-tions (mainly Scots pine). The conifers are generally less interesting ornithologically but can hold some unusual species, especially in the younger plantations. Heaths comprise heather, gorse and bracken with areas of rough grassland and scrub; parts are waterlogged. Though much of the area is com-mon land, some areas are permanently or temporarily enclosed with access forbidden or restricted.

Access (see map)

Birds can be found almost anywhere and there are many good sites; it is usually best to seek less-disturbed areas. Good areas include Beaulieu Road/Bishop's Dyke/Denny Lodge in the east, Acres Down and Bolderwood in the central area, and Ashley Walk/Pitts Wood/Black Gutter/Hampton Ridge and Eyeworth Pond/ Fritham in the northwest. Some of the best sites are detailed below and by visit-ing these most of the key species of the area can be found, but probably not all in a single visit.

2 ASHLEY WALK AND HAMPTON RIDGE (Hampshire)

Several important sites are situated in the northwest of the forest. In the past, Hampton Ridge was an essential component of a visit to the New Forest, as it was one of the best places for Dartford Warbler and other interesting species. Nowadays, it has largely been superseded. Dartford Warblers are now commoner elsewhere in south England and may be found in many heathland areas. Ashley Walk is more convenient for Pitts Wood and, more importantly, Black Gutter Bottom has achieved fame as a site for a pair of Montagu's Harrier in summer.

Hampton Ridge Leave Fordingbridge east on the B3078. After 1 mile turn right to Blissford. Hampton Ridge is reached by tracks east from Blissford or from Abbots Well to the south. The main track across the ridge passes through excellent heath with gorse favoured by Dartford Warbler. It also offers fine views over the distant forest with a chance of raptors including Honey Buzzard. After almost 2 miles the track reaches woodland (Pitts Wood Inclosure and Amberwood Inclosure). The elusive Woodlark may be found here, as well as Redstart, Crossbill and Siskin.

Ashley Walk/Pitts Wood Continue east on the B3078, and beyond Godshill stop in the Ashley Walk car park. A track leads across the valley to Cockley Hill and

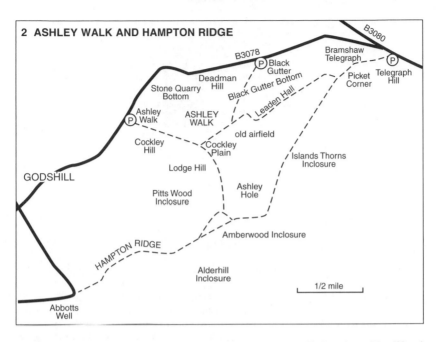

2 ASHLEY WALK AND HAMPTON RIDGE

Cockley Plain. Look for Hen Harrier in this area in winter. Fork right to Pitts Wood Inclosure. This is a good area for Hawfinch and other woodland species such as Crossbill and Siskin, as well as Tree Pipit in summer. Hawfinch is often elusive, but may be seen more easily in winter at the edge of the wood (right of the entrance gate) or in the holly bushes. Early mornings in spring are best to hear Woodlark.

Black Gutter Further east along the B3078 another car park is open in summer at Black Gutter, set within a clump of Scots pines. The area is wardened if Montagu's Harrier is present in Black Gutter Bottom. This species is one of Britain's rarest breeding birds and Black Gutter is one of the very few sites where it can be seen. Dartford Warbler is common here and Hobby is a frequent sight in summer. Sadly, Red-backed Shrike is here no more – this was its last breeding haunt in the New Forest, in 1984. In winter look for Hen Harrier, and if you are very fortunate Merlin and Great Grey Shrike can sometimes be seen.

3 BEAULIEU ROAD (Hampshire)

This is one of the best areas in the New Forest throughout the year. Leave Lyndhurst east on the A35. At the end of the town turn right on the B3056 to Beaulieu. After 3 miles pull off to the right into Shatterford car park, just before the road crosses the railway line at Beaulieu Road station. The small patch of pines beside the road is a picnic site and sometimes holds Crossbill during irruptions. There are several tracks in the area, but the best route is a clockwise circuit via Bishop's Dyke and Denny Wood. Head south from the car park, parallel to the railway line. Woodlark occurs between the track and railway line, and Dartford Warbler can be seen on the heath to the right. In winter it may be worth taking a small detour to cross the railway over the old bridge to Stephill Bottom. Hen Harrier is regular at this season and with luck Great Grey Shrike may be present.

Honey Buzzard

Continuing south on the original track, cross Bishop's Dyke and a boggy area. This is a favoured site for Hobby (especially in late afternoon) and Cuckoo, and it is worth scanning the wooded skyline (Denny Wood Inclosure) for Buzzard, Sparrowhawk and the occasional Honey Buzzard. Beyond the bog the track bears right to skirt Denny Lodge Inclosure. Tree Pipit occurs in summer and Woodcock rode here in spring. The track continues past Denny Wood, an excellent area of broadleaf woodland that holds all the expected woodland species, including Wood Warbler in summer and all three species of woodpecker. To complete the circuit, the track crosses the heath of Shatterford Bottom.

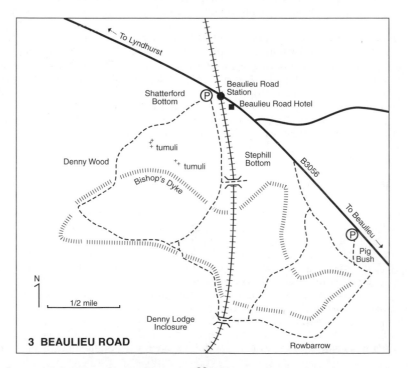

3 BEAULIEU ROAD

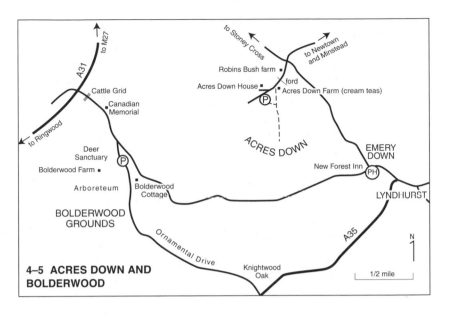

4-5 ACRES DOWN AND BOLDERWOOD

4 ACRES DOWN (Hampshire)

This is probably the best site in the New Forest for watching raptors. Take the A35 west from Lyndhurst. After c.1 mile turn right on a minor road to Emery Down and continue northwest towards Stoney Cross. Two miles beyond Emery Down, where there is a right turn to Newtown, turn left on a minor no-through road signed 'cream teas'. After crossing a ford and beyond Acres Down Farm (cream teas), there is a small gravel car park on the left. From here walk up a steep small hillock immediately in front of you. At the top follow the track left through some scrubby trees. The ridge provides a good vantage to overlook a large tract of woodland. Buzzard, Sparrowhawk and Hobby are regularly seen, but Honey Buzzard is the key species here. If a pair is breeding nearby, the birds may be seen here regularly, especially on mornings early in the season; it is best to be in position by 10.00. Goshawk is occasionally seen at this site but it does not breed here. Other raptors may also occur.

5 BOLDERWOOD (Hampshire)

Bolderwood provides forest walks and deer-viewing opportunities, and is thus popular with visitors. Some of the best woodland in the New Forest is found here. Bolderwood can be reached either along Bolderwood Ornamental Drive, c.2 miles southwest of Lyndhurst along the A35 or along a minor road west of the New Forest Inn at Emery Down. The car park lies by the north part of the Ornamental Drive. There are a number of good trails through the forest and most woodland species can be found in the area. Key species are Firecrest, Hawfinch and Crossbill. Firecrest can be found anywhere but the area between the car park and Bolderwood Cottage is often good; listen for their song from the treetops. Hawfinch sometimes favours the area around the Canadian Memorial, which is also good for Crossbill, or try the holly bushes at the north end of the deer sanctuary.

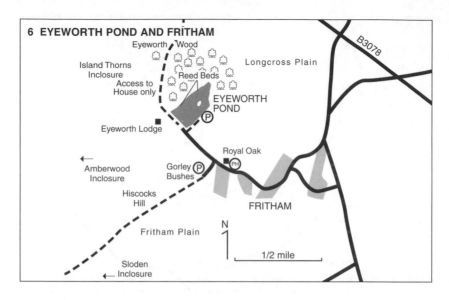

6 EYEWORTH POND AND FRITHAM

Eyeworth Wood

Island Thorns Inclosure

Access to House only

Eyeworth Lodge

Reed Beds

Longcross Plain

EYEWORTH POND

B3078

Royal Oak

Amberwood Inclosure

Gorley Bushes

Hiscocks Hill

FRITHAM

Fritham Plain

N

1/2 mile

Sloden Inclosure

6 EYEWORTH POND AND FRITHAM (Hampshire)

Excellent woodland, holding Lesser Spotted Woodpecker, Hawfinch, Redstart and Wood Warbler, is situated in the vicinity of Fritham. Added variety is provided by Eyeworth Pond, a good site for Mandarin, which nests in the adjacent woodland. Fritham is located between the east carriageway of the A31 at Stoney Cross and the B3078 at Longcross Plain, and is reached by taking the road signed 'Fritham and Eyeworth only'. Continue through the village to the Royal Oak pub and from here head northwest on the metalled road to Eyeworth Pond or southwest on the gravel track to Fritham car park. Open heath areas should be searched for Nightjar, Woodlark and Dartford Warbler.

Birds

Buzzard, Sparrowhawk and Hobby are widespread and frequently seen. Honey Buzzard is a New Forest speciality but requires a great deal of luck. Localised breeders with a marked preference for conifers are Siskin and Crossbill. Firecrest also favours these trees but not exclusively. It was first discovered as a British

Woodlark

breeding species in the New Forest, but is very elusive and numbers fluctuate widely. Recently planted conifers or woodland edges are favoured by the localised Woodlark and commoner Tree Pipit; Woodcock and Nightjar are sometimes found here, as well as on heaths, and dusk is the best time to look for both. Deciduous woodland harbours all three woodpeckers, Redstart, Wood Warbler, Marsh and Willow Tits, Nuthatch and Treecreeper. Hawfinch is much less widespread and unlikely to be seen on a single visit. The star bird of the heath is Dartford Warbler for which the New Forest is a major stronghold; other heathland birds include Curlew, Wheatear, Stonechat and Whinchat.

In winter, Hen Harrier and Great Grey Shrike may be encountered on some of the less disturbed heaths, and with luck Merlin.

Information
Birds of the New Forest: A Visitor's Guide by A.M. Snook (1998).

7 KEYHAVEN AND PENNINGTON MARSHES (Hampshire)

OS Landranger 196
OS Outdoor Leisure 22/29

An extensive area of marshes noted for wildfowl, waders and raptors, particularly in winter. The area is a well-known wintering site for Short-eared Owl. It also has good potential for rarities during migration periods with aquatic species most likely but occasional scarce passerines also show up.

Habitat
Keyhaven and Pennington are extensive marshes with muddy creeks and channels, shallow pools and lagoons separated from the saltings by a seawall.

Access
South of Lymington leave the A337 in Pennington on a minor road south to Lower Pennington and continue to the coast. The marshes can be viewed from the seawall. From Creek Cottage, Lower Pennington, the Solent Way footpath follows the seawall to Keyhaven Harbour. There is also a track between Keyhaven Harbour and Pennington Lane, and a footpath along Ridgeway Lane. Footpaths cross the marsh to the seawall from Ridgeway Lane and the rubbish tip.

Birds
Winter wildfowl numbers are impressive, with up to 4,000 Brent Geese accompanied by Shelduck, Gadwall, Wigeon, Teal, Shoveler and Pintail. Offshore scan for divers, grebes and sea duck. Waders include Black-tailed and Bar-tailed Godwits, and Ruff formerly overwintered in some numbers but are scarce now. Short-eared Owl, Peregrine, Merlin and Hen Harrier are sometimes present, and Snow Bunting is an occasional visitor.

Commoner spring migrants include Little Ringed Plover, Ruff and Greenshank, but Spotted Redshank and Whimbrel are also possible. Garganey, Marsh Harrier and Osprey have all been recorded at this season.

Waders such as Knot, Sanderling, Curlew and Wood Sandpipers, Little Stint and Greenshank occur in autumn. Rarer species including Grey Phalarope and Spoonbill may also appear and sometimes migrant passerines, typically Ring Ouzel or Black Redstart, both of which use more open areas.

Information
Hampshire County Council, Mottisfont Court, High Street, Winchester SO23 8ZF.

8–10 CHRISTCHURCH HARBOUR (Dorset)

OS Landranger 195
OS Outdoor Leisure 22

Formed by the River Stour and Hampshire Avon, Christchurch Harbour is well known for its wide variety of wintering and migrant populations of wildfowl and waders. On the north side of the harbour lies Stanpit Marsh, while Hengistbury Head on the south side is a noted migration watchpoint.

Habitat

Much of the harbour is dominated by typical estuarine habitats such as mudflats and a shingle island, with pasture and marshy areas dissected by muddy channels, some of which have extensive reeds and sedges. A series of semi-permanent pools flank the landward edge of the marsh, while scrubby areas are dominated by gorse.

Hengistbury Head comprises a low-lying area of grassland and gorse scrub, a steeply sloping hill covered by open heath and densely vegetated areas dominated by birch and sallow merging into oak woodland at the base of the hill. The seaward side of the head consists of some unstable cliffs, a shingle beach and a low sandy spit at the point.

Access (see map)

There are three main access points, with Stanpit and the north harbour both reached from Christchurch, and Hengistbury Head accessed via Southbourne.

8 CHRISTCHURCH HARBOUR (Dorset)

South of Christchurch, take Mudeford Lane and turn south into Chichester Way to reach Mudeford Quay. Alternatively take Argyle Road, which can be reached off Stanpit Lane to access Fisherman's Bank. Both will give access to the northern side of the harbour.

9 STANPIT MARSH (Dorset)

Accessed from the Recreation Ground car park, which is off Stanpit Lane south of the Ship in Distress pub. Alternatively park in the Christchurch Swimming Pool car park off Stony Lane South and follow the footpath south along the edge of the golf course to the marsh. The final option is to park in the Christchurch Civic Offices car park and follow the path south between the river and the golf course. Crouch Hill offers good views of the high-tide wader roost on Stanpit East Marsh.

10 HENGISTBURY HEAD (Dorset)

Hengistbury Head is reached from Southbourne. Park in the car park at the end of The Broadway. There is access to most of the headland. The woodland near the Old Nursery Garden is good for passerines. Seawatch from Warren Hill, and check the end of the spit opposite Mudeford for bird movements in and out of Christchurch Harbour. Wick Hams (a small marsh) and Wick Fields (rough pasture) are also worth checking.

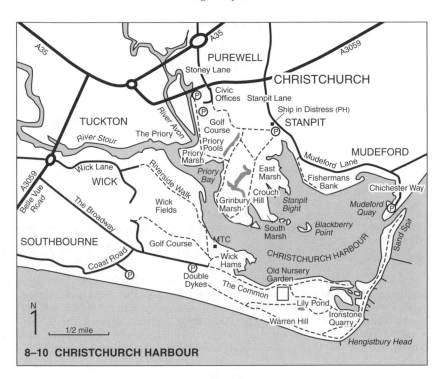

8–10 CHRISTCHURCH HARBOUR

Birds

In winter large numbers of wildfowl include Brent Goose, Wigeon and Teal with smaller numbers of Gadwall, Pintail, Shoveler and Goldeneye. Commoner waders include Black tailed Godwit, while up to 100 Snipe and a few Jack Snipe are present at Stanpit Marsh and Wick Hams. Purple Sandpiper frequents the breakwaters off Hengistbury Head. Large gull flocks host Mediterranean, Yellow-legged and Little Gulls on a regular basis. Reedbeds are home to Water Rail and the occasional Bittern. Good numbers of Little Egrets frequent the area throughout the year, while Rock Pipit, Stonechat and Cetti's and Dartford Warblers are also resident. Hengistbury Head may hold wintering Chiffchaff and Firecrest.

Migration periods bring numbers of waders in both spring and autumn. These include Little Ringed Plover, Ruff, Little Stint, Curlew Sandpiper, both godwits, Whimbrel, Spotted Redshank, Greenshank, and Green, Wood and Common Sandpipers. Kentish Plover is almost annual. Garganey sometimes join the flocks of ducks. Raptor passage includes small numbers of Hobby and occasional Marsh Harrier and Osprey. Seabird passage may occur during strong SE–SW winds and can include divers, Fulmar, Manx and Sooty Shearwaters (autumn), occasional Grey Phalarope, skuas, Little Gull, Black Tern and auks. Landbirds are most obvious at Hengistbury Head with Water Pipit, Black Redstart, Ring Ouzel, Pied Flycatcher, Firecrest and Wood Warbler all regular. Oddities include almost annual Spotted Crake, the occasional Spoonbill, Temminck's Stint, Hoopoe and Serin.

Breeding birds hold relatively little interest though good numbers of terns may be present and sometimes include Roseate. Reed and Sedge Warblers breed, while irregular offshore passage at sea in summer can include Manx Shearwater, Storm Petrel and Gannet.

Information
Stanpit Marsh: Peter Holloway, Christchurch Countryside Service, Steamer Point Woodland, Highcliffe, Christchurch, Dorset BH23 4XX. Tel: 01425 272479. E-mail: countrysideservice@christchurch.gov.uk

11 TITCHFIELD HAVEN (Hampshire)   OS Landranger 196

Titchfield Haven is a small, wetland NNR on The Solent, southwest of Fareham. It can provide good birding at any time of year, and is a stronghold for Cetti's Warblers.

Habitat
The 365-acre reserve comprises reedbeds, willow scrub, wet grazing meadows and freshwater scrapes.

Access
Leave the M27 at junction 9 onto the A27 to Fareham. After 2½ miles, turn right onto the B3334 to Stubbington. In Stubbington, turn right into Bells Lane (signed to Hill Head). Park in the car park on the left, adjacent to Hill Head Sailing Club. Haven House Visitor Centre is a large white house across the road. The reserve is open Wednesday-Sunday all year, plus Bank Holidays (except Christmas and Boxing Days), from 09.30-17.00 (09.30-16.00 in winter). There are five hides.

Birds
Large numbers of wildfowl visit the reserve in winter. Up to 1,500 Wigeon are present with good numbers of other species. Brent Geese feed in the surrounding fields, and occasionally grey geese also appear, most frequently White-fronted. Amongst many wintering waders, counts of over 1,000 Black-tailed Godwits are notable. Gulls are also in evidence, and may include Mediterranean. Bittern is a regular winter visitor, and Kingfishers are frequently seen.

Titchfield's most famous breeding inhabitant is Cetti's Warbler, and up to 50 singing males may be present. Bearded Tit also breeds in small numbers.

Spring and autumn are good for passage waders, terns, and a wide variety of other species. Titchfield's list of scarce migrants and rarities is surprisingly good.

Information
Barry Duffin, Haven House Visitor Centre, Cliff Road, Hill Head, Fareham, Hants PO14 3JT. Tel: 01329 662145.

12-15 LANGSTONE AND CHICHESTER HARBOURS (Hampshire/West Sussex)
OS Landranger 196 and 197
OS Explorer 119 and 120

This massive complex of tidal mudflats and saltings is one of the most important estuaries on the south coast and is of both national and international significance for wintering waders and wildfowl. Several areas are LNRs and 1,370 acres of Langstone Harbour are an RSPB reserve. The best times to visit are autumn and winter.

Habitat
The estuary is largely tidal mudflats and saltings. Much of the surrounding area

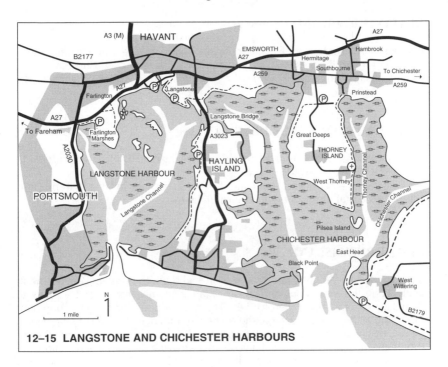

12–15 LANGSTONE AND CHICHESTER HARBOURS

has been built upon, especially at the west end, but the shoreline of Chichester Harbour is mostly undeveloped. There is some farmland on Hayling Island and at the east end of the complex. Farlington has some fresh marsh and lagoons.

Access (see map)

The harbours can be reached from many points though certain areas have restricted access, particularly much of Chichester Harbour. The major wader roosts are on Farlington Marshes and its offshore islands, west Hayling Island and Thorney Island. The mouths of the estuary can be viewed from East Head (West of West Wittering) and from both sides of Hayling Island. Views inside the estuary can be obtained from Hayling and Thorney Islands, and the north shore can be watched from a coastal footpath (park at Broadmarsh, southeast of A27/A3(M) junction). The following four routes are among the best.

12 FARLINGTON MARSHES (Hampshire)

Leave the A27 Chichester–Fareham road at the intersection with the A2030 immediately north of Portsmouth. A track leads off the roundabout between the A27 east and A2030 south exits and runs east below and parallel to the A27 towards Farlington Marshes. Follow the coast on foot around the west side of the marshes. A freshwater lagoon and associated marshland are worth checking en route. Continue around the peninsula. Areas of scrub at the north end attract migrants. Alternatively, access from Broadmarsh car park and walk west along the coast to the reserve.

13 HAYLING ISLAND (Hampshire)

Take the A3023 south from Havant, cross Langstone Bridge onto Hayling Island and walk around the west side of the island. The Black-necked Grebes are best seen at high tide from the NW corner of Hayling Island (now West Hayling LNR).

14 CHICHESTER HARBOUR (West Sussex)

To view the north shore: From the north side of Langstone Bridge walk east along the coastal footpath towards Emsworth.

Alternatively, explore East Head and the east shore: Park at West Wittering and follow the coastal footpath towards West Itchenor.

15 THORNEY ISLAND (West Sussex)

Leave the A259 at Southbourne on a minor road south to Prinsted. Park and walk south along the east shore of Thorney Island. Alternatively, from the A259 at Hermitage take the minor road to West Thorney and turn first left into Thornham Lane. Park at the end and explore the east coast from here. The area to the right is good for Short-eared Owl in winter and Osprey on passage. At the junction of Thornham Lane, park in the small pull-off area, cross the main road and explore the west coast and the Deeps from here – this is good for Bearded Tit and Cetti's Warbler. Pilsey Island off the south tip (an RSPB reserve) attracts roosting waders at high tide.

Birds

Up to 90,000 waders (mostly Dunlin) and 15,000 wildfowl winter on the huge complex of mudflats. Numbers of Grey Plover and Black-tailed Godwit are of national importance, and the largest flocks of Knot on the south coast are found here. Small numbers of Ruff, Spotted Redshank and Greenshank winter in the area. Brent Goose numbers have increased dramatically over the last few years to peak at 10,000; they can be seen in many places and are quite approachable at Farlington. The numbers of Shelduck, Wigeon, Teal and Pintail are important, and Goldeneye and Red-breasted Merganser frequent the channels. Up to 15 Black-necked Grebes and a few Slavonian Grebes favour the northwest part of Langstone Harbour. In the mid-1990s the largest roost in Britain of Little Egrets was at Thorney Great Deeps, but the birds appear to have relocated elsewhere in more recent years. As many as 20,000 gulls roost in the harbour, mostly Black-headed. Sparrowhawk and Short-eared Owl are occasionally seen hunting over the marshes.

A wider variety of waders occurs in spring and autumn, and may include Little Stint and Wood Sandpiper. September–October is a good time for passage waders.

Summer is the least interesting season ornithologically, but Sandwich, Common and Little Terns breed, as well as Oystercatcher, Ringed Plover and Redshank. A few pairs of Mediterranean Gulls also breed.

Information

Farlington Marshes: Bob Chapman, c/o Hampshire Wildlife Trust, Woodside House, Woodside Road, Eastleigh, Hants SO50 4ET. Tel: 01392 214683.

Langstone Harbour: RSPB Warden, Chris Cockburn, 20 Childe Square, Stamshaw, Portsmouth, Hants PO2 8PL. Tel: 023 9265 0672. E-mail: chris.cockburn @rspb.org.uk

Firecrest

This exquisite little bird is a scarce breeder and more frequent passage migrant and winter visitor in Britain. It is less closely associated with coniferous woodland than its commoner relative, the Goldcrest, and in winter and on passage it often frequents scrubland. Like all small, insectivorous birds that winter in Britain, it suffers greatly in harsh weather, and is then likely to be found on the coast where temperatures remain higher.

Key sites, breeding: Bedgebury Forest, New Forest; non-breeding: Isles of Scilly, Portland, Porthgwarra.

Nightjar

The soft, mesmeric churring of male Nightjars is part of the magic of a late summer evening on a quiet heathland. This species is quite widespread throughout much of England, Wales and southern Scotland, breeding on lowland heaths and also among young conifer plantations. It should be looked for at dusk, when the males begin to churr and perform their wing-clapping display flight.

Key sites: Arne, Fforest Fawr, New Forest, Ashdown Forest.

Hobby

This summer visitor requires a supply of large flying insects during the breeding season, so is most frequently found on heathland or wetland areas where dragonflies are abundant. In spring, passage birds may reach double figures at some sites. Family groups of adults and juveniles may be seen hawking for prey on summer evenings as they prepare to migrate. It tends to associate with hirundine flocks towards the end of the summer and when on passage.

Key sites: Thursley Common, New Forest, Stodmarsh, West Sedgemoor, Abberton Reservoir.

Smew

These attractive and extremely popular little sawbills are uncommon winter visitors, mainly occurring close to the southern and eastern coasts of England. They appear most often during very cold spells, when small parties will arrive at favoured lakes. The females and juveniles (collectively known as 'redheads') usually outnumber the stunning, mostly white males.

Key sites: Dungeness, Wraysbury Gravel Pits, Abberton Reservoir, Pitsford Reservoir, Eyebrook Reservoir.

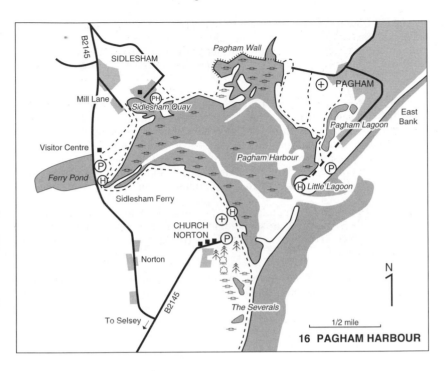

16 PAGHAM HARBOUR (West Sussex)

OS Landranger 197
OS Explorer 120

This site, south of Chichester, is one of the best on the south coast. Part of the area is a LNR managed by West Sussex County Council. Although primarily a major wintering area for wildfowl and waders it is also noted for migrants and is an important breeding site for several species.

Habitat
Eight hundred acres consist of relatively undisturbed tidal mudflats intersected by numerous channels, while shingle beaches flank either side of the harbour mouth. Patches of gorse and scrub occur around the perimeter alongside the harbour banks and seawalls, and are attractive to migrant passerines. Small areas of reeds grow around the non-tidal pools. The only woodland of note is at Church Norton and this can be productive for migrants. The harbour is surrounded by fields, which are frequently used by waders at high tide.

Access (see map)
There is a public footpath around the entire embankment enclosing the harbour, as well as a few other paths. Visitors should keep to these. Parts of the shingle are closed April–July to protect breeding birds. It is not practical to walk around the entire harbour but there are four good access points.

Sidlesham Ferry The B2145 from Chichester crosses the west arm of the harbour here. A Visitor Centre, manned principally at weekends, and a small hide are sited beside the road on the north side. A nature trail starts here following the seawall northeast towards Sidlesham Quay. Ferry Pond, west of the road and easily viewed from it, attracts many interesting waders in autumn and winter, and several rarities have been found. From Sidlesham Ferry, the walk along the seawall around the south edge of the harbour to Church Norton is recommended. This stretch offers some of the best views over the harbour, although at low tide waders tend to be well scattered and distant.

Church Norton Continue south from Sidlesham Ferry on the B2145, turn left to Church Norton after 1¼ miles, and park at the end of the road by the church. A short track leads to the harbour. The woodland and hedges should be checked for migrants and the harbour mouth can be viewed from here. Turn right to reach the shingle shore. Sea ducks and grebes are regularly seen offshore in winter. Just inland of the beach to the south there are some small freshwater pools and reedbeds (the Severals), which can hold interesting birds.

North Wall From the Crab and Lobster pub in Sidlesham Quay you can walk east around the seawall towards Pagham village. Pagham Wall (also known as North Wall) is a good place to view Little Egrets flying to roost, and to see waders, especially in autumn.

Pagham Lagoon From Chichester take the B2145 south. After 1½ miles turn left onto the B2166 and in 2½ miles turn right to Pagham village. The road west out of the village past the church leads to the harbour's northeast corner. Walking right along Pagham Wall leads to Sidlesham, and left takes you to the coast past the end of Pagham Lagoon. Alternatively, a road follows the coast past the lagoon to a car park on the spit. The end of the spit is a good place from which to see waders and duck at the mouth of the harbour, especially at high tide. Pagham Lagoon is best in winter and the scrub and gardens near the lagoon may hold migrants.

Birds

In winter Red-throated Diver, Slavonian Grebe, Eider, Common Scoter and Redbreasted Merganser are regular offshore and best viewed from Church Norton. Guillemot and Razorbill are less frequent. In the harbour a few thousand Brent Geese winter as well as many dabbling duck, including Pintail. Goldeneye favours the deeper channels and Smew is occasionally seen on Pagham Lagoon. Large numbers of waders use the harbour and a few Avocet, Ruff and Blacktailed Godwit are often seen on the Ferry Pond. Water Rail, Kingfisher and Bearded Tit frequent the Severals in small numbers in winter, Short-eared Owl sometimes hunts over the saltings, and Little Egret is now regularly seen.

In spring and (especially) autumn waders are more varied and regularly include Little Stint and Curlew Sandpiper, while Black-tailed Godwit sometimes occurs in large numbers. Sandwich and Common Terns are often present but Arctic and Black Terns are less frequent, and Little Gull only occasional. Rednecked Grebe is a rare autumn visitor, usually on the sea. Passerine migration is sometimes prominent, and typical species include Yellow Wagtail, Redstart, Whinchat, Wheatear, Spotted Flycatcher and a variety of warblers. Black Redstart and Pied Flycatcher are annual in small numbers. Firecrest is quite scarce, occurring mainly in spring, and Hoopoe is recorded most years. Wryneck and Melodious Warbler occur in autumn but are only occasional.

Summer brings up to 70 pairs of Little Terns, plus Oystercatcher and Ringed Plover, breeding on the shingle beaches and shingle island within the harbour. Shelduck nests in the adjoining fields and Reed and Sedge Warblers occupy the reedbeds. Barn Owl is often seen hunting in the Sidlesham Ferry area and breeds nearby. Though they may hunt by day, dawn and dusk offer the best chances of seeing one. Little Owl can sometimes be seen in the vicinity of Church Norton.

Information

Sarah Patton, Pagham Harbour LNR, Selsey Road, Sidlesham, Chichester PO20 7NE Tel: 01243 641508. E-mail: pagham.nr@westsussex.gov.uk

17 SELSEY BILL (West Sussex)

OS Landranger 197
OS Explorer 120

Although not in the same league as Dungeness or Portland, Selsey is one of the most important seawatching sites on the south coast. The area is also attractive to passerine migrants in both spring and autumn.

Habitat

Despite considerable development of the town of Selsey, the area still retains some large vegetated gardens and a small playing field, which are attractive to migrants. The old holiday camp was demolished in 1989 and subsequently areas of trees, scrub and patches of grass have developed. The shingle beach to the west of Selsey is bounded on the landward side by grassland, which gives way to cereals. This area is known as Selsey West Fields and is accessed through West Sands Caravan Park.

Access

To reach the Bill, continue south from Sidlesham Ferry on the B2145 and once in Selsey turn left at the mini-roundabout into Church Road. Follow this until you reach the coast and park next to Bill House. Seawatchers usually gather in front of the large concrete wall ahead of you to the right. Peak seabird movements occur in spring, especially between late April and early May, the most favourable winds being light southeast.

Birds

In winter Red-throated Diver, Great Crested and Slavonian Grebes, Red-breasted Merganser, Eider and auks are all regular offshore. Black Redstart can be found feeding along the beach among the breakwaters. Check gull flocks for Mediterranean Gull which is present year-round. The onset of freezing weather conditions may stimulate a westerly passage of Lapwing, Golden Plover, Skylark and winter thrushes.

In spring large numbers of Common Scoter migrate east, with the majority in late April, but Velvet Scoter is much less frequent. Other birds seen regularly with peak numbers in spring are divers, Eider, Red-breasted Merganser, Bar-tailed Godwit, terns and auks. A few Pomarine Skuas are recorded annually in early May, while Arctic Skua is not uncommon in both spring and autumn. Wheatears arrive in significant numbers during March, with a steady movement of other common spring migrants passing through.

Autumn witnesses regular arrivals of passerine migrants, with numbers usually exceeding those of spring. Warblers, Redstart and Pied Flycatcher frequent the scrubby areas, while Whinchat and Wheatear prefer the fields to the west. Easterly winds might produce something unusual, with Red-backed Shrike, Wryneck and Tawny Pipit possible. In October–November, the bushes may harbour a Firecrest among the larger numbers of Goldcrests, and perhaps a Ring Ouzel. Winter thrushes are a feature from late October. Visible migration can include Swifts and hirundines, Grey and Yellow Wagtails, and Tree Pipits. Strong southwest winds may produce seabirds, with numbers of Manx, a few Balearic and occasionally Sooty Shearwaters. Arctic, Pomarine and Great Skuas are also frequent in this period.

18 CHICHESTER GRAVEL PITS (West Sussex)

OS Landranger 197
OS Explorer 120

This is a series of gravel pits located by the A27 Chichester bypass. Despite occasionally intensive use of these pits for watersports and fishing, interesting birding is possible here.

Habitat

A complex of gravel pits with little marginal reed growth, but in some places covered with willows, sallows and bramble scrub. There are few muddy fringes, but there are sand washings on the Portfield North Pit.

Access (see map)

The pits are situated by the A27 Chichester bypass east and south of the town. Leave the A27 at the roundabout after Westhampnett and explore the northern pits. Most are viewable from roads. Rejoin the A27 southwards, and at the next roundabout take the minor road to Runcton. More pits are visible on the right and a footpath runs along their west side. Another pit can be seen from the B2145 immediately south of the A27. There have been many changes to the pits in recent years, with some being filled and others newly created.

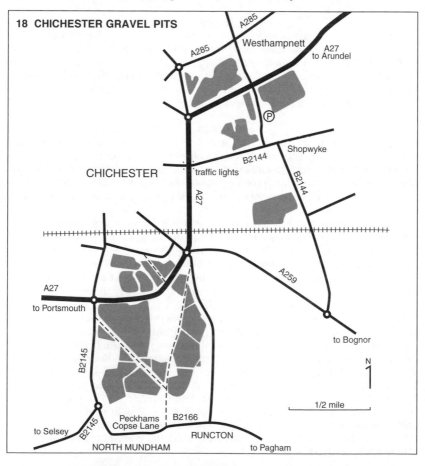

Birds

In winter a few Scaup and Goldeneye often occur among the rafts of more numerous Tufted Duck and Pochard. Dabbling duck are relatively scarce, though numbers of Shoveler and Teal occur. The pits are best in hard weather when Goosander, Smew and the occasional diver may appear. Cormorants roost on an island in Ivy Lake. Chiffchaffs winter in the waterside trees.

Easterly winds in spring can produce small numbers of Little Gulls and Black Terns over the pits, and Whimbrel and Bar-tailed Godwit sometimes pass overhead.

Breeders include Great Crested Grebe, Shelduck, Ruddy Duck, Pochard, Tufted Duck, Kingfisher and the commoner warblers. Common Tern breeds on rafts constructed by the Sussex Ornithological Society.

In autumn passage waders, including Greenshank, Little Stint and Ruff, frequent the muddy margins. Small numbers of Little Gulls and Black Terns are regular, and large numbers of hirundines roost at the pits.

19–21 ARUN VALLEY (West Sussex)

OS Landranger 197
OS Explorer 121

North of the A27 at Arundel, the beautiful valley of the River Arun is a winter home to 25,000–35,000 birds. Wildfowl are the predominant feature of this locality, but the patchwork of habitats offers some varied birding throughout the year.

Habitat

Though much of the valley has been drained, there is an interesting mosaic of lowland grazing meadows, patches of woodland and chalk escarpments. Arundel has one of the largest reedbeds in West Sussex. The RSPB reserve at Pulborough Brooks is characterised by grazing meadows managed with appropriate use of grazing animals and by varying water levels. It also features pasture, scrub and mixed woodland.

Access

A number of roads and footpaths permit fairly easy exploration of the valley. However three 'hotspots' provide the best birding opportunities.

19 ARUNDEL WWT (West Sussex)

In the town of Arundel take the minor road just east of the castle towards Offham. This leads to the WWT reserve (open 09.30–17.30 in summer, to 16.30 in winter; closed Christmas Day), where there is a large car park. Access to the bank of the River Arun is by walking south 200 yards from the WWT car park and then taking the path on the left bank of the mill stream for a further 200 yards. On reaching the river it is possible to walk the 1½ miles to South Stoke, but it will be necessary to retrace your steps. Just before the WWT car park, Swanbourne Lake lies to the left of the road, and a footpath goes round it. 'Wild' ducks include Mandarin and Ruddy Duck.

20 AMBERLEY WILD BROOKS (West Sussex)

These marshes in the valley of the River Arun are situated immediately north of

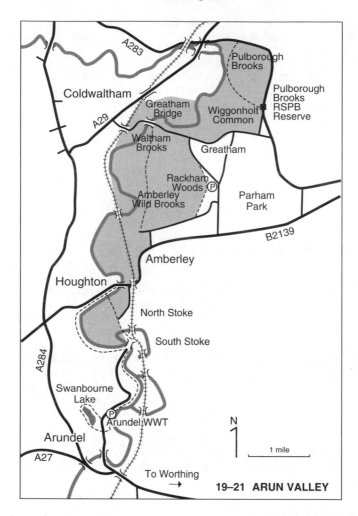

19–21 **ARUN VALLEY**

Amberley, c.8 miles north of Littlehampton. From Arundel take the A284 north and after 2½ miles turn right onto the B2139. Continue for 2½ miles and turn left into Amberley. A track leads north across the marshes from the village and it is possible to walk to Greatham Bridge, 2 miles distant. Alternatively, drive to Greatham Bridge on minor roads around the east side of Amberley Wild Brooks, via Rackham and Greatham. Waltham Brooks lie just south of Greatham Bridge and are viewable from the car park.

21 PULBOROUGH BROOKS (West Sussex)

Situated 2 miles southeast of the village of Pulborough, the entrance to the RSPB reserve is on the left side of the A283, c.2 miles north of Storrington village. The reserve is open 09.00–21.00 (or sunset if earlier), closed Christmas Day, and there is a visitor centre (10.00–17.00), tea room (closes earlier) and four well-positioned hides along a circular 2-mile nature trail.

Birds

Wintering wildfowl are the main attraction of the valley: significant numbers of the commoner ducks are usually present, with up to 100 Bewick's Swans, mainly at Waltham or Pulborough Brooks, and sometimes roosting at Arundel in cold weather. Geese, usually White-fronted, are only occasional, but Merlin, Hen Harrier and Short-eared Owl are often present. A small flock of Ruff usually winters at Pulborough, while Arundel supports one or two wintering Green Sandpipers and Jack Snipe.

Both Waltham and Pulborough Brooks attract passage waders, including Little Ringed Plover, Black-tailed Godwit and Ruff, along with impressive numbers of Whimbrel.

Breeders include Garganey, Shoveler, Teal, Lapwing, Redshank, Snipe and Yellow Wagtail, with most of these at Pulborough. The reedbeds at Arundel support large numbers of Reed and Sedge Warblers, and Reed Bunting. The woodland between Rackham and Greatham has all three woodpeckers, and Marsh and Willow Tits. Wiggonholt Common, close to Pulborough, supports Woodcock, Nightjar and Nightingale.

Information

Arundel WWT: James Sharpe, Mill Road, Arundel, West Sussex BN18 9PB. Tel: 01903 883355. E-mail: wwt.arundel@virgin.org.uk

Pulborough Brooks RSPB: Tim Callaway (Site Manager) Upperton's Barn, Wiggonholt, Pulborough, West Sussex RH20 2EL. Tel: 01798 875851. E-mail: pulborough.brooks@rspb.org.uk

22 CLIMPING–LITTLEHAMPTON (West Sussex)   OS Landranger 197
OS Explorer 121

West Beach lies on the coast between Littlehampton and Climping and is of greatest interest during passage periods when good numbers of migrants pass through the area, including a number of rarities in recent years.

Habitat

Low sand dunes separate the hinterland from a sand and vegetated shingle beach and the sea. At low water the relatively wide area of beach comprises a mix of sand, shingle and stony ground. A golf course occupies the southeast corner, but much of the rest of the area is dominated by arable land. Inside the seawall are patches of rough ground, hawthorn and blackthorn scrub, and small patches of private woodland.

Access

Leave Littlehampton west on the A259 and ½ mile after crossing the river turn sharp left to backtrack on the old road to Littlehampton. Continue for ¾ mile and just before the footbridge turn right towards the mouth of the Arun. Park after ¼ mile and walk southwest towards the coast along the north edge of the golf course, looking for migrants on the way. At the coast turn right and work the coastal bushes. Alternatively, a minor road leads to the coast from Climping, past the Black Horse pub. Check the trees and bushes in this area and continue east along the coast to the golf course.

Birds

In winter Purple Sandpiper occurs at the river mouth at high tide, while other waders include Oystercatcher, Grey Plover and Sanderling. Fields support sizeable flocks of Lapwing, while Snipe and sometimes Jack Snipe frequent marshier areas. Offshore, Red-throated Diver, Great Crested Grebe, Common Scoter, Eider and Red-breasted Merganser feed. Gull flocks may include occasional Mediterranean, Glaucous or Iceland.

A good variety of migrants occurs in spring and autumn including small numbers of Redstart, Black Redstart, Ring Ouzel, Firecrest and Pied Flycatcher. Hobby and Short-eared Owl are occasional and several rarities have been found in recent years. The golf course is particularly attractive to Wheatear and Whinchat, and has produced fairly regular records of Tawny Pipit.

Breeding species are unremarkable, but include most of the commoner warblers, Yellowhammer and Corn Bunting.

23 THURSLEY COMMON (Surrey)

OS Landranger 186
OS Explorer 145

This 800-acre NNR is an important part of the west Surrey heaths. Several specialities breed, notably Hobby, Woodlark, and Dartford Warbler.

Habitat

The principal habitats are wet and dry heath, woodland and bog. The dry heath is dominated by heather with some gorse, and invading birch scrub is cleared to maintain this habitat. Fire is a great hazard but controlled burning is carried out to assist the regeneration of heather. In addition, water levels are regulated to prevent the bogs and pools drying out.

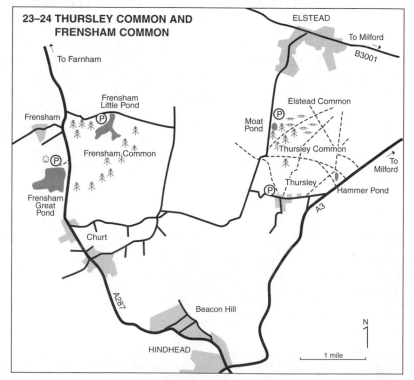

Access (see map)

The Common is adjacent to the A3, c.8 miles southwest of Guildford. Access is from Thursley village, the road along the common's south edge, or the Churt–Elstead road on the west side. There is a car park on the latter road. The Common is open to the public free of charge but you should keep to the paths.

Birds

This is one of the best places to see Hobby. A good time to look is late afternoon during summer as they hawk for insects or chase hirundines; find a good vantage point to watch from. Sparrowhawk also breeds and is regularly seen. Snipe and a few pairs of Curlew nest, the latter a scarce breeding bird in south England. The fluctuating population of Dartford Warbler is currently flourishing and favours areas of gorse but can be difficult to find. Woodlark is another speciality and may be found on the scrubby heath or woodland edge. Though resident they are often easiest to see when performing song flights in early spring. Commoner breeding species include all three woodpeckers, Tree Pipit, Redstart and Stonechat. Nightingale may also be seen but requires slightly more effort. Nightjars hawk for insects at dusk.

In winter, Hen Harrier and Great Grey Shrike are occasionally recorded.

Information

Simon Nobes, EN, Uplands Stud, Brook, Godalming, Surrey GU8 5LA. Tel: 01428 685878.

24 FRENSHAM COMMON (Surrey)

OS Landranger 186
OS Explorer 145

This area of heath and woodland, a few miles west of Thursley and straddling the A287, is owned and managed by Waverley Borough Council and the NT.

Habitat

An area of undulating heath, woodland and artificial ponds, created by the damming of several streams, with shallow shores and reeds at one end.

Access (see map on p.104)

Take the A287 south from Farnham and then the signed turning on the right to reach the car park (locked 21.00–09.00) at the north end of Frensham Great Pond. Here there is an information room, toilets and refreshments. Many paths cross the area but a walk through the woods and across the common to the Little Pond is probably the most profitable route.

Birds

In winter small numbers of wildfowl use the area, with Smew occasionally present. Bittern may winter in the reeds, while the area is a noted regular haunt for Great Grey Shrike.

Breeding birds include Buzzard, Hobby, all three woodpeckers, Woodlark, Tree Pipit, Nightingale, Redstart, Stonechat and Dartford Warbler.

Information

Mike Coates, Rangers Office, Bacon Lane, Churt, Surrey GU10 2QB. Tel: 01252 792416.

25 VIRGINIA WATER (Surrey)

OS Landranger 175
OS Explorer 160

Lying at the south end of Windsor Great Park, a few miles southwest of Staines, this is a well-known haunt of Mandarin and Hawfinch throughout the year.

Habitat
An area of sloping ground with stands of oak, sweet chestnut, beech, ash, pine and rhododendron surrounding the lake. There are some small patches of heath and wide lawns.

Access (see map on p.107)
Leave Staines on the A30 and beyond the Wheatsheaf Hotel turn right onto the A329, parking after 1 mile in the public car park on the right. Walk towards Virginia Water, bearing left to cross an arm of the lake over a small stone bridge. There are some hornbeams in this area, which are favoured by Hawfinch, though it is best to look for them in the early morning before the area becomes disturbed.

Birds
Mandarin can be found anywhere on the lake: the best areas are north of the car park and at the east end; in autumn flocks congregate on the Obelisk Pond. Common woodland species include all three woodpeckers, Nuthatch and Marsh Tit. Hawfinches can be hard to find here. Siskin, Redpoll and Brambling occur in winter.

26 STAINES RESERVOIRS (Surrey)

OS Landranger 176
OS Explorer 160

Of the many reservoirs in the London area, Staines is undoubtedly the best known and most accessible. It provides sanctuary for many wintering waterfowl and attracts a variety of migrants.

Habitat
Staines' 420 acres are divided by a narrow causeway. The edges are of sloping concrete but nevertheless attract a few waders during migration seasons. Occasionally the two sections have been drained (separately) for many months at a time, and the resulting mudflats and pools have offered a haven to waders, including several rarities.

Access (see map on p.107)
The A3044 runs north between King George VI and Staines Reservoirs and almost halfway along there is a building on the left. Park on the grass verge and on the opposite side go through a kissing gate to the causeway bisecting the reservoir. The iron railings here are useful for resting telescopes if you have no tripod—a telescope is usually essential. There is no restriction on access to the causeway, and at weekends it can become almost crowded, mainly with birders and dog-walkers. There is no facility to walk around the reservoir and access to King George VI Reservoir is totally restricted.

Birds
Large concentrations of waterfowl are present in winter. Black-necked Grebe is regular in small numbers and can be seen almost year-round, though rarely in winter; peak counts are usually March–April and August–October. Although almost

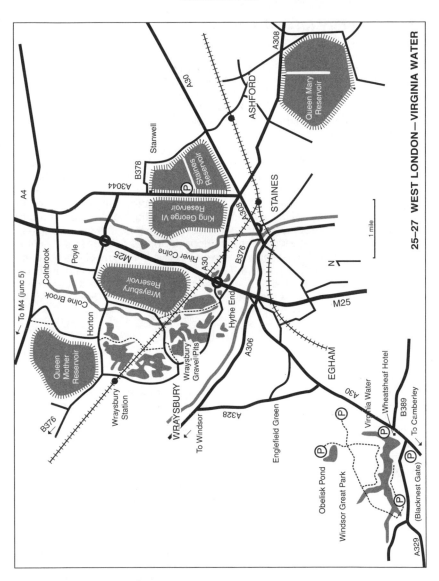

25–27 WEST LONDON—VIRGINIA WATER

annual, Slavonian and Red-necked Grebes should be regarded as unusual. The majority of duck are Tufted Duck and Pochard, but small numbers of Goldeneye and Goosander occur in winter. Smew are nowadays seen only infrequently.

A wide variety of migrants has occurred in spring and autumn. Common, Arctic, and Black Terns are regular, as is Little Gull. Black Tern in autumn should be checked for a vagrant White winged Black Tern (now almost annual in the London area). A sprinkling of waders use the concrete edges, though numbers and variety increase dramatically when the reservoir is drained. Migrant passerines often occur on the causeway, and include Wheatear, Yellow Wagtail and Whinchat. Hobby is regular in spring and autumn, often at dusk chasing hirundines.

Summer is usually quiet but some outstanding rarities have appeared in June–July, while Black-necked Grebe usually reappears from early July.

27 WRAYSBURY GRAVEL PITS (Berkshire)

OS Landranger 176
OS Explorer 160

These gravel pits lie west of Staines Reservoir in the Colne Valley and are a regular haunt of Smew in winter as well as a variety of other wildfowl.

Habitat

A complex of gravel pits surrounded by bushes and trees.

Access (see map on p.107)

Leave the A30 northwest of Staines on the B376 to Hythe End and Wraysbury. After ¼ mile there is a stile on the right just before a bridge over Colne Brook, and this leads onto a footpath that parallels the river. The pits on the right are a favoured haunt of Smew, particularly the end pit. Another pit is easily viewed from the B376 between Hythe End and Wraysbury. That immediately south of Wraysbury station is also good for Smew: leave Wraysbury towards the station and turn right to the latter before the humpback bridge; the pit on the right is viewable from the road. Wraysbury Reservoir lies east of the gravel pits but there is no access. To the north, Queen Mother Reservoir attracts grebes and the occasional diver: Access is limited to a small section of its northeast corner, which can be reached from the Colnbrook–Horton road. South of Horton, Horton Gravel pits can also be good; access from Park Lane.

Birds

In winter, waterfowl include Great Crested Grebe and Cormorant and most of the commoner dabbling and diving ducks, including Goldeneye and Goosander. Smew favour the pit immediately south of Wraysbury station and the pits to the right of Colne Brook. Wintering Chiffchaff and, less frequently, Blackcap are present in the bushes. Ring-necked Parakeet is regularly seen in this area and is resident.

28 BRENT RESERVOIR (Greater London)

OS Landranger 176

Situated next to the North Circular Road in northwest London, Brent Reservoir is one of the best birding sites within the metropolis.

Habitat

This 130-acre reservoir is fairly shallow with natural, well-vegetated edges. There are areas of willows bordering the Eastern Marsh and several stretches of oak woodland. A finger of the reservoir extending northwards is known as the Northern Marsh and is bordered by a reedbed. The water level rarely fluctuates, but occasionally areas of mud are exposed, often at the eastern end.

Access

The northern and eastern sections are recommended. The following is based on Mitchell (1997): Turn north off the A406 North Circular Road onto the A5 Edgware Road (signed to Edgware), and after ¾ mile turn left into Cool Oak Lane. Cross the northern arm of the reservoir (Cool Oak Bridge) and after ½ mile park in the free car park. Walk back towards Cool Oak Bridge and turn left onto a track just before the bridge to explore the Northern Marsh. To visit the Eastern Marsh, cross the bridge and a footpath around the back of the canoe club car park leads to the reservoir bank and on to the Eastern Marsh.

There is no restriction on access to the reservoir except the dam wall at the western end, but much of the southern edge is not visible from the well-wooded paths. Two hides overlook the Eastern Marsh, but a key is required to use them (one-off fee, from Welsh Harp Conservation Group).

Birds

The commoner ducks are present in winter, but Smew is now rare. A few Water Rails inhabit the Eastern Marsh between September and April, and Snipe (and occasionally Jack Snipe) are regular. Other waders are unpredictable. Large numbers of gulls are often present, sometimes including one of the less common species.

In summer, up to 50 pairs of Great Crested Grebes breed, as well as several pairs of Common Terns on rafts in front of the hides. Kingfishers occur throughout the year and the surrounding woodland holds a selection of the commoner warblers.

Spring and autumn offer the greatest variety of species and a number of unusual species have been found over the years.

Information

WHCG: Roy Beddard, 43 Kenerne Drive, Barnet, Herts. EN5 2NW. Tel:020 8447 1810. Website: www.brentres.com

29 THE WETLAND CENTRE (BARN ELMS)
(Greater London)

OS Landranger 176
OS Explorer 161

This former complex of four bleak, concrete, reservoirs has been ambitiously transformed into a new 105-acre Wildfowl and Wetlands Trust reserve, close to the heart of London.

Habitat

The site consists of a mosaic of natural-edge ponds and lagoons with islands and some grazing marsh, reedbeds and scrub. There is also a plush visitor centre, observatory and seven hides. As at most WWT centres, a collection of captive wildfowl is kept here.

Access

The Wetland Centre is reached by taking the Roehampton exit to Barnes from the South Circular, and then turning right off Rocks Lane by the Red Lion pub. The site is open 09.30–17.00 during winter, and 09.30–18.00 in summer. There is a charge for non-WWT members.

Birds

Wintering wildfowl include nationally important numbers of Gadwall and Shoveler. Water Rail is present in small numbers, Snipe in reasonable numbers and the occasional Jack Snipe occurs. Large numbers of gulls on the Main Lake infrequently include Yellow-legged Gull.

Breeding species include Pochard, Lapwing, Little Ringed Plover, Redshank, the commoner warblers and Reed Bunting.

Information

John Arbon (Grounds and Facilities Manager) or Stephanie Fudge (Manager), The Wetland Centre, Queen Elizabeth Walk, Barnes, London SW13 9WT. Tel: 020 8409 4400. E-mail: info@wetlandcentre.org.uk

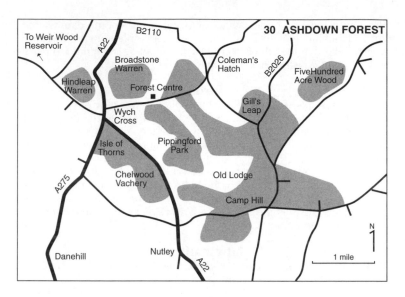

30 ASHDOWN FOREST (East Sussex)

OS Landranger 198
OS Explorer 135

The largest expanse of heathland in southeast England, this area is crossed by many paths and tracks that permit easy access.

Habitat

Extensive patches of heather-dominated heath have been invaded, in places, by bracken, gorse, birch and pine. Large tracts of oak and beech are present, but conifer plantations dominate other areas. Streams run off sandstone hills, cutting deep valleys and creating steep slopes where high humidity has encouraged the growth of woodland plant communities more typical of western Britain.

Access (see map)

The A22, A275 and B2026 are among the many roads which cross this large area. One of the best places to start is Ashdown Forest Centre situated ½-mile east of Wych Cross on the unclassified road to Colemans Hatch. Other large car parks are in the vicinity of Camp Hill, while many paths access the forest. Access is not permitted to the military training area near Pippingford Park.

Birds

In winter Hen Harrier may be seen quartering the heaths, and parties of Redpoll and Siskin frequent streamside alders, but otherwise this is usually a very quiet season. Formerly regular, Great Grey Shrike is now very irregular in its appearances.

Spring and summer visits should prove most productive. Breeders include all three woodpeckers, Tree Pipit, Stonechat, Redstart, Dartford Warbler, a few pairs of Wood Warbler and the other commoner warblers, Woodcock, Nightjar and Hawfinch.

31 BEWL WATER (East Sussex)

OS Landranger 199
OS Explorer 136

Bewl Water is one of the largest reservoirs in southern England. It was completed in 1975 and covers over 750 acres. Though much of the area is used for watersports, part of the lake is a designated nature reserve (Sussex Wildlife Trust).

Habitat

This large lake has natural margins around most of its 15-mile circumference, though there is usually little exposed mud suitable for waders. Woodlands border some areas of the shoreline, as well as arable, scrub and orchards.

Access (see map)

The main visitor centre and car park (small charge) are only accessible from the A21 between Lamberhurst and Flimwell. From here a good footpath circuits the entire reservoir (13 miles). Several minor roads access other parts of the water; in particular at Three Leg Cross (near The Bull pub), and at Ketley Pool where the road crosses the east arm of the reservoir.

Birds

In winter, moderate numbers of wildfowl use the reservoir, comprising the commoner dabbling species and including Wigeon. Smaller numbers of diving duck occur, usually including a few Goldeneye, and occasionally Smew or Goosander. Great Crested Grebe is resident and sometimes one of the rarer grebes, such as Red-necked, may be present. More severe weather often produces a diver or rarer grebe.

Spring is also a good time to visit. The woods and bushes are full of singing passerines and migration is in progress. Most of the commoner species are present. There may also be a few terns or waders passing through.

By July return wader passage has commenced, and Green and Common Sandpipers, Little Ringed Plover and Greenshank are regular. Look also for Common and Black Terns. Hobby is quite frequent and Osprey annual. Indeed, this is one of the most regular sites for the latter in the southeast.

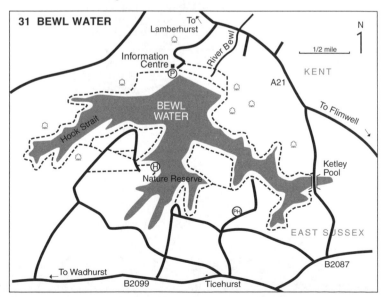

Information

Sussex Wildlife Trust, Woods Mill, Shoreham Road, Henfield, West Sussex BN5 9SD. Tel: 01273 492630. E-mail: sussexwt@cix.co.uk

32 CUCKMERE AND SEAFORD (East Sussex)

OS Landranger 199
OS Explorer 123

The valley of the Cuckmere River lies 3 miles west of East Dean, and is crossed by the A259. Seven Sisters Country Park lies immediately to the east (and reaches to Beachy Head), with Seaford Head to the west. Seaford is a well-known seawatching site.

Habitat

The lower reaches of the Cuckmere River comprise a series of grazing meadows and brackish marshes either side of the meanders of the old river, and the newer canalised river. A small scrape has been created close to the shore of Cuckmere Haven. Chalk downs lie to the east and west.

Access (see map)

Park in the large car park by the A259 (small charge). The Country Park's visitor centre north of the road has information and facilities. From here footpaths lead either side of the river to the Haven. A circular route east of the main river takes in both the old meanders and the scrape. To view the west side, walk along the road and cross the Exceat Bridge. From the pub, a footpath follows the river directly to the Haven. Alternatively, another path traverses an area of bushes west of the meadows before reaching the shore.

Seaford Head to the west is a 2-mile walk, but the best place to seawatch is Splash Point, which lies on the east side of Seaford (and is more conveniently reached from Seaford itself).

Birds

The Cuckmere Valley attracts wintering wildfowl, notably several hundred Wigeon. These can be wary and are easily disturbed. Smaller numbers of other

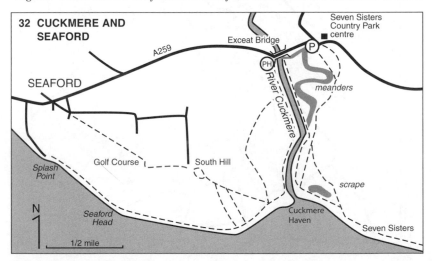

ducks may also be present, together with grebes and a few waders. Wildfowl numbers and variety increase in colder weather. Rock Pipit is regular by the river, and Twite occasionally overwinters. Kingfisher may be found (except summer) on the north oxbow and ditches west of the river. Peregrine is occasional and Little Egret is now a regular sight in the valley.

In spring and autumn migrants use the valley. Passerines are best seen in the bushes west of the river and waders favour the scrape. Check the smaller muddy pools (e.g. at Exceat Bridge) for Temminck's Stint in May. Rarities are occasionally found, especially in autumn.

Seaford Head attracts the usual downland species, while the cliffs have breeding Fulmar and Kittiwake. Unsurprisingly, the seawatching at Splash Point is similar to Birling Gap, a few miles to the east, with Pomarine Skua in early to mid-May being the speciality.

33 BEACHY HEAD (East Sussex)

OS Landranger 199
OS Explorer 123

The cliffs of Beachy Head, immediately southwest of Eastbourne, jut south into the English Channel and this prominent position has produced one of the best migration watchpoints on the south coast, both for seabirds and landbirds. Generally, it is only worth visiting in spring and autumn, and even then can be very quiet indeed if the winds are unfavourable.

Habitat

A narrow belt of coastal downs extends for c.4 miles between Eastbourne and Birling Gap, south of the minor road that connects the two. Areas of gorse and scrub occur on the downland and there is a small wood at Belle Tout. North of the road is farmland (mainly crops). The chalk cliffs vary from 50 feet at Birling Gap to over 500 feet opposite Beachy Head Hotel, and are constantly being eroded.

Access (see map)

There are three main areas to check, all accessible from the minor road which runs around the headland. The more energetic may wish to walk along the clifftop between each site in order to cover as much of the habitat as possible, particularly if it is a good day for migrants. Due to disturbance from non-birders, early mornings are always best.

Birling Gap From the car park, walk a short distance to the coast and turn right towards some beach huts. This is the best place to seawatch from. The area of bushes west of Birling is often good for migrants. Follow the track from the car park, which leads to the clifftop walk across the Seven Sisters. The bushes are just a few hundred yards from Birling.

Belle Tout Wood There is a small car park on the west side of the wood. Belle Tout is worth checking for passerine migrants, especially in autumn. Despite its small size, birds are often very hard to find here. The gorse and scrub on the slopes east of Belle Tout should also be explored for migrants.

Whitebread Hollow Park just east of the Beachy Head Hotel and walk along the cliff path to the top of the hollow, a large south-east-facing basin of scrub and woodland; the dense cover makes it a difficult area to work. Mist-netting is undertaken here by the Beachy Head Ringing Group (mainly at weekends, August–November).

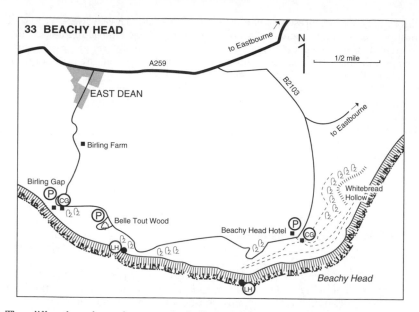

The cliff path and area between the hollow and the sea can also be rewarding.

Birds

Seabird passage is best in spring, between mid-March and mid-May. Light southeast winds are usually best. Good numbers of Red-throated and Black-throated Divers migrate east in early spring together with many Common Scoter. Brent Goose and a few Velvet Scoter can also be seen. From April, terns and Bar-tailed Godwit move in large numbers and skuas occur most days in the first half of May. Pomarine Skua is the key species here and is regularly seen in small groups, especially during southeast winds (from Birling Gap). A few Manx Shearwater, Mediterranean Gull, Roseate Tern and Puffin are seen each year and Little Gull and Black Tern are regular, sometimes in impressive numbers. Black Redstart and Firecrest occur from mid-March at Belle Tout and Birling Gap. The commoner migrants pass through in April–May and regularly include Nightingale, Redstart, and Ring Ouzel. Grasshopper and Wood Warblers and Pied Flycatcher are seen most years, and scarce migrants such as Hoopoe and Serin are occasional. Migrant raptors can sometimes be seen at this time; Osprey, Marsh Harrier and Hobby are recorded annually and with luck one of the rarer species may also put in an appearance.

In summer a few pairs of Fulmar nest and breeding passerines include Nightingale, Stonechat, Whitethroat and Lesser Whitethroat. Dartford Warbler formerly bred and is still occasionally seen in autumn.

There is little seabird passage in autumn. Migrant passerines, on the other hand, are usually present in good numbers, especially warblers and chats. August is the best month for the commoner species, notably *Sylvia* and Willow Warblers. In September, Chiffchaff and Blackcap predominate, with smaller numbers of Redstart, Whinchat and flycatchers. Scarce migrants are found almost annually; some of the more likely candidates are Dotterel, Wryneck, Tawny Pipit, Barred, Icterine and Melodious Warblers, Red-backed Shrike and Ortolan Bunting. Perhaps the most regular is Tawny Pipit—check the stubble fields in the second half of September. In October, flocks of finches and pipits arrive, and species such as Black Redstart, Ring Ouzel, and Firecrest are regular in late autumn. Yellow-browed Warbler is recorded annually and several rarities have occurred, one of the most frequent being Pallas's Warbler, which has been found several times in Belle Tout Wood in late October–early November.

There is little to see in winter, but movements of Gannet, auks, or divers are always possible and Peregrines regularly hunt the cliffs. On the headland, resident passerines include Stonechat, Yellowhammer and Corn Bunting.

34 PEVENSEY LEVELS (East Sussex)

OS Landranger 199
OS Explorer 124

Situated between Eastbourne and Bexhill, Pevensey Levels were formerly an important site for wintering wildfowl and waders. Although drainage and 'improvement' have taken their toll, some of the original habitat remains and interesting birds can still be found. Part of the area is managed by EN.

Habitat
Pevensey Levels originally comprised 10,000 acres of unimproved wet grassland, crisscrossed by a network of ditches. The latter hold some rare water plants and invertebrates. Large areas have now been converted to arable.

Access (see map)
Several minor roads cross the levels, providing good viewing. From the roundabout on the A259, just east of Pevensey, take the minor road to Normans Bay to view the south section of the levels (Pevensey Bridge Level). From the same roundabout, a minor road north goes to Herstmonceux via Wartling. This accesses Manxey Level South. Finally, another road to Herstmonceux via Rickney passes a range of habitats, including Horse Eye Level.

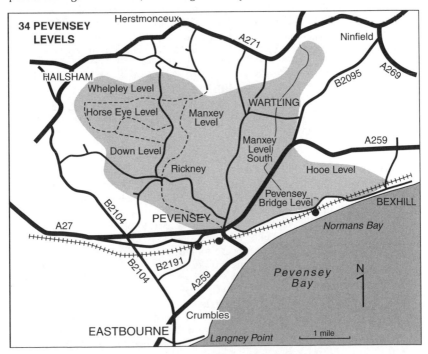

Birds

In winter, large flocks of Lapwing, Snipe and Golden Plover are present. Other waders are less frequent, and wildfowl also occur. Small numbers of swans include Bewick's and occasional Whooper. Hard weather often brings larger numbers of waders and wildfowl, and perhaps even a few geese. Raptors such as Hen Harrier, Merlin, Peregrine and Short-eared Owl are occasional. The coast at Pevensey Bay may be worth checking for gulls and waders (sometimes including Purple Sandpiper on rocks near Bexhill), and for sea duck and divers offshore.

In spring, migrants such as Yellow Wagtail are easily found, but Water Pipit and Garganey are much rarer. Several rarities have turned up over the years, including White Stork, Purple Heron, Great White Egret and Sociable Plover. Waders use the small pools on Pevensey Bridge Level, perhaps including Temminck's Stint or something rarer.

Breeding birds include Hobby, Lapwing, Redshank, Snipe, Yellow Wagtail, and Sedge and Reed Warblers.

Autumn migration is similar in extent and numbers to other coastal sites in the area, but a seawatch off Langney Point may be worthwhile. Skuas are regular and gulls favour the sewage outfall.

Information

Malcolm Emery, EN, Phoenix House, 32–33 North Street, Lewes, East Sussex BN7 2PH. Tel: 01273 476595. E-mail: sussex.surrey@english-nature.org.uk

35 PETT LEVEL (East Sussex)

OS Landranger 189
OS Explorer 125

This series of pools surrounded by damp meadows lies beside the coast road between Winchelsea Beach and Fairlight. The pools are easily viewed from the road, one of which is usually drained by Sussex Wildlife Trust in mid-July to attract a variety of waders. As this site is close to Rye Harbour, the two are easily combined in a day.

Habitat

Pett Level is a large area of pasture, heavily grazed by sheep and crisscrossed by a network of narrow dykes. Pett Pools, a series of small lagoons (some with reedbeds) lie close to the road.

Access (see map)

From Rye take the A259 to Hastings. After 2 miles (just before reaching Winchelsea), turn left beyond the River Brede onto a minor road to Winchelsea Beach. The road eventually follows the coast, behind a high seawall, with the levels on the right. The pools are easily viewed from the road, and there is no access other than a footpath along the back of the levels (alongside the Royal Military Canal). Rye Bay should be checked in winter for sea duck from the seawall. Slightly further west, the cliffs at Fairlight provide a higher elevation for seawatching, and Hastings Country Park, much favoured by dog-walkers, has some good areas of bushes and scrub that attract migrants.

Birds

In winter, the level holds large numbers of wildfowl and waders. Lapwing, Golden Plover, Curlew, and sometimes Brent Goose, use the grassland, while a few duck perhaps including Goldeneye and Smew visit the pools. Bearded Tit

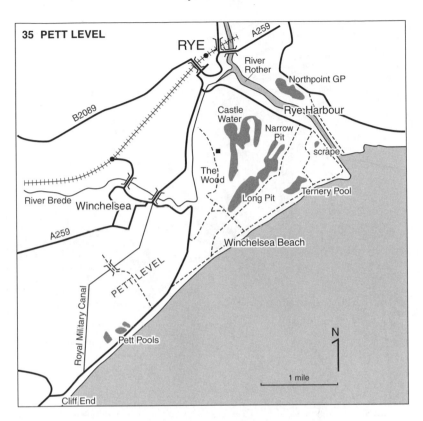

can occasionally be seen in the reedbeds. Offshore, flocks of Eider and Common Scoter can be seen; the latter should be checked for occasional Velvet Scoter (or even Surf). Red-throated Diver and Guillemot also occur, but are perhaps better seen from the cliffs at Fairlight.

From July, Pett Pools can attract a variety of waders, which can be viewed at close range. These often include Little Stint and Curlew Sandpiper, and sometimes a rarity such as Pectoral Sandpiper (September is best). The bushes at Hastings Country Park are good for migrant passerines, including the occasional rarity, and Dartford Warbler is regular.

Information

Sussex Wildlife Trust, Woods Mill, Shoreham Road, Henfield, West Sussex BN5 9SD. Tel: 01273 492630. E-mail: sussexwt@cix.co.uk

36 RYE HARBOUR (East Sussex)

OS Landranger 189
OS Explorer 125

Rye Harbour is best known for its terns, notably Little Tern. Almost every species of tern on the British list has been recorded there (but most are very rare!). The reserve boasts a variety of habitats and its position on the southeast coast ensures good numbers of birds year-round. In recent years Rye Harbour has become a reliable site for wintering Bitterns.

Habitat

This LNR chiefly comprises an important expanse of shingle, which hosts some rare plants. Past excavations of the shingle have created a series of pools that are now managed for birds. There are also saltings beside the River Rother and extensive mudflats at its estuary at low tide. Further inland, there are areas of grassland as well as arable and scrub.

Access (see map)

A minor road immediately south of Rye off the Winchelsea road (A259) follows the south side of the River Rother to Rye Harbour, with a car park and information centre at its end. Continue on foot but keep strictly to the footpaths. The concrete road to the Rother estuary (no vehicles) leads to Lime Kiln Cottage where there is a new information centre (open at peak times throughout the year). Continue to the scrape (overlooked by a hide) and the famous Ternery Pool (two hides). A choice of paths will take you back via the caravan site or (for a longer walk) via the Long and Narrow Pits. For the more energetic, another path leads around Castle Water (where there is another hide).

Birds

Rye Harbour is worth a visit at any time of year. Though particularly bleak in winter, it is at this season that many interesting species can be seen. A good variety of wildfowl is present in winter, including Goldeneye and Smew (regular, usually on the Long or Narrow Pits). Less frequent visitors include Long-tailed Duck and Scaup. Flocks of Eider and scoters, and sometimes divers, can often be found offshore in Rye Bay. All of the rarer grebes are recorded most years, particularly Black-necked and Slavonian. Numbers of waders use the mudflats at low tide, including many Sanderling. Merlin and Peregrine are regular over the reserve, and Hen Harrier often winters. Short-eared and Long-eared Owls occasionally put in an appearance, while Barn Owl is resident (Castle Water is best). Winter passerines include flocks of Linnets and Greenfinches, plus smaller numbers of Reed and Corn Buntings, and Tree Sparrow. Rock Pipit can be seen along the Rother, but Twite and Shore Lark are less frequent. A winter visit should not miss Castle Water at dawn or dusk. There is a Little Egret roost in a belt of trees also used by Cormorants, and Water Rail is common but as always more often heard than seen. Several immigrant Bitterns winter here and are almost guaranteed as they fly to and from their roost in the reedbeds. Conveniently, they can be viewed from a viewpoint near the road.

Rye Harbour is a good area to find early spring migrants such as Wheatear, Sand Martin and Sandwich Tern. The commoner warblers and Yellow Wagtail soon follow, while occasional Arctic Skua and Gannet occur offshore. Mediterranean Gull is frequent on the Ternery Pool at this time, often in full breeding plumage, and Hobby is regular in May. Particularly notable is a spring roost of Whimbrel in early May; up to 600 have been recorded, but you must arrive very early in the day to see them.

The most important breeding bird at Rye Harbour is Little Tern, with up to 70 pairs nesting on the shingle, heavily guarded by volunteers. Common Tern breeds on the Ternery Pool, but Sandwich Tern only nests infrequently. Roseate Tern does not breed, but singles make occasional visits to the colony. Among passerines, there are several pairs of Wheatear on the reserve.

July–August is a good time to visit Rye Harbour with numbers of returning waders usually including Little Ringed Plover, Green, Wood and Curlew Sandpipers, and Little Stint. Rare American waders have appeared on a number of occasions, the most frequent being Pectoral Sandpiper. Passerine migration comprises the usual warblers plus Spotted and Pied Flycatchers, Redstart and Whinchat. Hobby is often evident at this time and Marsh Harrier sometimes passes through. Later in autumn, Firecrest and Black Redstart may occur.

Information

Barry Yates (Manager), 2 Watch Cottages, Winchelsea, East Sussex TN36 4LU. Tel: 01797 223862. E-mail: yates@clara.net

37 DUNGENESS (Kent)

OS Landranger 189
OS Explorer 125

This unique peninsula, between Hastings and Folkestone, is famed for migrants in spring and autumn, and has an active Bird Observatory. In addition, the RSPB maintains a bird reserve with important gull and tern colonies on the flooded gravel pits.

Habitat

The area is a flat expanse of shingle with ridges and hollows. The flora is generally sparse, though in the deeper hollows and other sheltered areas a denser vegetation including gorse and broom has developed. The only natural fresh water on Dungeness is the Open Pits and these are surrounded by dense reeds, sedges, brambles and sallows. Recently, gravel workings have created more open water with islands, considerably improving the diversity of birds.

Access (see map)

From New Romney, turn left on the B2075 to Lydd c.1 mile west of the town centre (also signed Dungeness 6½). On entering Lydd, fork left beyond the airport and on reaching a roundabout take the first exit. A long road leads directly to Dungeness. Lydd can also be reached by a minor road from Rye via Camber. Dungeness is conveniently worked from two points.

RSPB Reserve About 1½ miles after the roundabout are the ARC pits on the left. Dungeness Reserve (RSPB) is signed to the right along a track with Boulderwall Farm on the corner. Follow the track to the Visitor Centre (open 10.00–17.00, until 16.00 in November–February) and park. The centre is sited at the edge of Burrowes Pit and there are five hides nearby affording good views of the pits and their islands. Most of the reserve's specialities can be seen from the hides although there is a trail of 1½ miles for the more energetic. The nearby ARC pits are always worth a look and can be viewed easily from the road. The RSPB reserve is open daily, 09.00–21.00 (or sunset if earlier).

Bird Observatory Continuing along the Lydd–Dungeness road, fork right c.½ mile after the ARC Pits and again shortly after (do not take the first right fork to the power station). Continue around the headland to Dungeness. Shortly after the Britannia pub the road reaches the old (black) lighthouse. Park opposite (if visiting the observatory you can drive along the private road to it on the seaward side of the old lighthouse). Dungeness Bird Observatory (DBO) is at the end of a row of coastguard cottages and is surrounded by a bush-filled moat. This and the various clumps of bushes scattered across the shingle attract migrants in spring and autumn. Access is largely unrestricted.

Dungeness is famed for seawatching and the best point to watch from is opposite 'The Patch'. This disturbed area of water, caused by the power station outflow, regularly attracts large numbers of gulls and terns, often including some uncommon species. There is a seawatching hide on the shingle for Observatory residents and Friends of DBO.

Hostel-type self-catering accommodation is available at the observatory for up to ten people throughout the year (bring own bedding/sleeping bag and toiletries). Bookings should be made in advance with the warden.

Two nearby areas are worthy of investigation:

Dengemarsh From Lydd, a minor road leads towards the Power Station, along the back of the RSPB reserve. In winter the fields here are worth checking for geese (especially Whitefronts and occasional Bean, amongst the usual Canadas and Greylags), Whooper and Bewick's Swans, and Red-legged Partridge.

Scotney Pit This large gravel pit straddles the Kent/Sussex border between Lydd and Camber. It can be viewed well from the road. In winter Whitefronts are frequently present at the back of the pit, and wildfowl regularly include Scaup, Goldeneye and Smew. Scotney is a favoured haunt for divers and grebes, and it is possible to see all the regular species here (but probably not on a single visit).

Birds

Spring migration gets underway in mid-March and the main passage commences in April and continues to mid-May. Most of the common migrants are well represent-

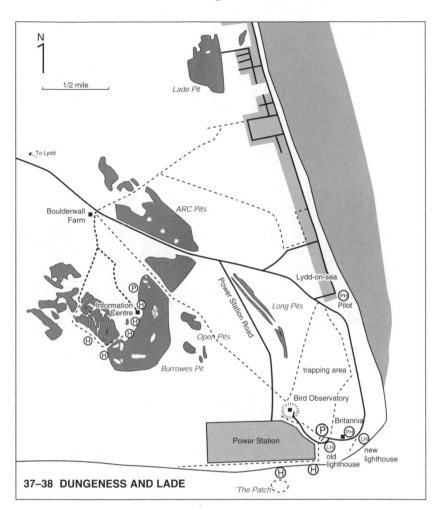

37–38 DUNGENESS AND LADE

ed, while Ring Ouzel and Firecrest are regular. South or southeast winds in late May and June are likely to produce a rarity, Hoopoe being one of the more likely, and Wryneck, Icterine Warbler, Red-backed Shrike and Serin are almost annual at this time. Seabird passage is particularly good in spring with the peak occurring April to mid-May. The bulk comprises Common Scoter, Bar-tailed Godwit and Common Tern, together with a broad variety of divers, grebes, ducks, waders, skuas, gulls and terns. A concentrated passage of Pomarine Skua is noted each spring, usually in the first half of May. Little Gull is sometimes numerous on the Patch, while Mediterranean Gull and Roseate Tern are regular in very small numbers.

In summer the islands in Burrowes and the ARC Pits hold impressive colonies of terns and gulls: mainly Common and Sandwich Terns and Black-headed and Herring Gulls, but a few pairs of Common Gull also nest (the only regular breeding site in south England). Recently, 1–2 pairs of Mediterranean Gull have attempted to breed and also a single pair of Roseate Terns, but much patience is usually required to find them. A few pairs of Little Terns breed on the coastal shingle and also on a specially created island on Burrowes Pit. Unfortunately, Kentish Plover and Stone Curlew are but a memory as breeders. Up to six pairs of Black Redstarts breed around the power station and can be seen along the perimeter fence.

In August, Gannet, Common Scoter and Sandwich Tern are likely to be the most obvious seabirds moving west, while Great Skua and Mediterranean Shearwater are occasional. The Patch is probably now at its best; a few Arctic Terns and Little Gulls are usually present amongst the commoner species, while Black Tern numbers peak from late August to early September and a vagrant White-winged Black Tern is usually found – although the Patch is the most likely place to look for one, all the pits in the area should be checked. Return wader migration commences in July and the commoner species may include small numbers of Little Stint and Curlew and Wood Sandpipers. A good variety of waders can be seen from the hides on the RSPB reserve.

The volume of autumn passerine migration is impressive and, from late August, east winds may bring Wryneck, Redstart and Pied Flycatcher. By September there is a chance of scarcer migrants from the continent. Tawny Pipit, Bluethroat, Icterine and Barred Warblers, Red-breasted Flycatcher, Red-backed Shrike and Ortolan Bunting are almost annual but usually very few of each. October is the most likely time for a major rarity. Good days are dependent on suitable weather such as east winds and early-morning precipitation; consequently, birdless days are not infrequent. By late September the bulk of migrants will be arriving from the continent to winter, including Skylark, Meadow Pipit, Robin, thrushes, finches and even tits, and these movements continue into November.

Winter is quieter, though large numbers of duck use the areas of open water. Among the commoner dabbling and diving ducks, a few Goldeneye, Smew and Goosander may be found, and sometimes a Long-tailed Duck. Rarer grebes are frequent in winter, especially Slavonian, and Dungeness is one of the few places where you may see all five regular grebes in one day, though probably not on a single pit. Offshore, a variety of divers, grebes and sea duck occurs.

Information

Dungeness RSPB Warden: Simon Busuttil, Boulderwall Farm, Dungeness Road, Lydd, Kent TN29 9PN. Tel: 01797 320588. E-mail: dungeness@ rspb.org.uk

Dungeness Bird Observatory: David Walker, Dungeness Bird Observatory, 11 RNSSS, Dungeness, Kent TN29 9NA. Tel: 01797 321309. E-mail: dungeness.obs @tinyonline.co.uk

38 LADE SANDS AND LADE PIT (Kent)   OS Landranger 189
OS Explorer 125

Lade Sands is an area of sandy mudflats between Dungeness and Greatstone-on-Sea with a gravel pit a short distance west of the coast road.

Habitat

The extensive mudflats of Lade Sands are exposed at low tide. Lade Pit is a flooded gravel pit, similar in character to the many other pits in the Dungeness area, with shallow edges and vegetation such as sallows, osiers and reeds.

Access (see map on p.121)

Follow the coast road for 1½ miles north of the Pilot pub. Turn left along Derville Road and park sensibly at the end of the road. From here walk across the shingle to view the pit. Lade Sands extend for c.4 miles north of the Pilot pub and may be viewed at a number of points from the coast road, with the Lade toilet block car park being perhaps the best.

Birds

Wintering waders include Oystercatcher, Ringed and Grey Plovers, Dunlin, Sanderling, Knot, Curlew and Bar-tailed Godwit. On the sea Red-throated Diver, Great Crested Grebe and possibly Common Scoter and Eider are often present. Check gull flocks for Mediterranean Gull. Lade Pit attracts some of the commoner dabbling and diving ducks, as well as a few Scaup, Goldeneye and Smew. A diver or one of the rarer grebes is often present, while a Bittern may also take up residence. A Chiffchaff sometimes frequents the sallow scrub at the north end of the pit, while Stonechat, Black Redstart and, in some winters, a Dartford Warbler may all be present.

On passage, waders such as Green and Common Sandpipers are likely but rarer species such as Pectoral Sandpiper, Red-necked or Grey Phalaropes appear only occasionally. Black Tern and Little Gull may also be seen.

39 FOLKESTONE—DOVER (Kent)

OS Landranger 179
OS Explorer 138

The sewage outfall at Copt Point, north of Folkestone harbour, is a particularly good spot for Mediterranean Gull. Samphire Hoe, southwest of Dover, is a convenient place to see some species which are local in southeast England.

Habitat

The area is dominated by the famous 'white cliffs'. Samphire Hoe is a new site, largely created from material excavated from the channel tunnel.

Access

Two sites are worth visiting:

Copt Point/Folkestone Warren From the harbour follow signs to East Cliffs and park on the clifftop beyond the East Cliff Pavilion. Either view from the clifftops or descend to the base of the cliffs by the path near the Pavilion, and walk along the shore to the Point. Walk east to explore the Warren, which may also be accessed from the clifftop cafe at Capel-le-Ferne.

Samphire Hoe From Dover, head towards Folkestone on the A20. Samphire Hoe is signed on the left, the minor road passing through a short tunnel to lead to the site. Park in the car park (fee) and walk to the west end of the complex alongside the railway.

Birds

Mediterranean Gull is regular at the sewage outfall throughout the year, with the largest numbers occurring in autumn and winter. Some regularly frequent the clifftop fields where they may be attracted by bread to offer superb views. At high tide many gulls roost in Folkestone harbour and Purple Sandpiper roosts on the harbour walls. The extensive scrub of Folkestone Warren attracts migrants in both spring and autumn, with Firecrest and Ring Ouzel regular. Though never in large numbers, southeast winds may produce movements of seabirds including divers, shearwaters, skuas and terns.

Shag is sometimes seen at the west end of Samphire Hoe and check the seawall and slopes for Stonechat, Black Redstart and Rock Pipit. Look out for Fulmar and Peregrine on the cliffs.

40 ST MARGARET'S BAY (Kent)

OS Landranger 179
OS Explorer 138

The coastline here is the closest point in Britain to France and consequently this can be an excellent place to observe visible passerine migration. Large falls of common migrants are not infrequent in autumn, especially October, and scarcer species are occasionally found. Weather conditions appear to be irrelevant and falls even occur in southwest winds when other migration watchpoints have few birds. An early-morning start is highly recommended as many birds move quickly through the area.

Habitat

While the coast faces southeast here, the main South Foreland valley runs north-east to southwest. Chalk cliffs reach a height of nearly 300 feet and have a rocky shoreline below. Scrub and copses are interspersed by grassy patches. North of the village is the NT-owned farm at Bockhill, which is surrounded by large trees and situated in a large area of arable land bisected by several paths and hedgerows.

Access

Leave Dover on the A258 to Deal and after c.2 miles turn right on the B2058 to St Margaret's at Cliffe. On entering the village turn right onto an unclassified road to the lighthouse and park before reaching it. Explore the valley in search of migrants. For Bockhill follow the road through the village and turn left onto Granville Road. Drive to the end and park by the monument. Visible migration can be observed here, and is at its best early morning. The farm is reached by walking along the path west from the clifftop.

Birds

This area is at its best in spring and, in particular, autumn when large numbers of pipits, commoner thrushes, warblers and finches pass through. Falls of night migrants can be very impressive. Grasshopper Warbler is regularly flushed from

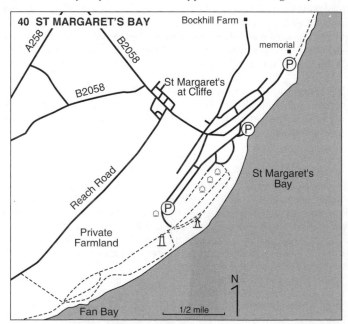

clifftop grass, while other frequently occurring scarcer species include Ring Ouzel, Firecrest, Tawny and Richard's Pipits, Yellow-browed and Pallas's Warblers, Golden Oriole and Ortolan Bunting. Major rarities are found most years and have recently included Alpine Accentor, Red-flanked Bluetail, Booted Warbler, Radde's Warbler and Nutcracker. Dotterel has become a regular feature of late August–early September, with flocks often found in the fields south of the South Foreland lighthouse and in the vicinity of Langdon Bay. Passage raptors include numbers of Sparrowhawk, Marsh and Hen Harriers and Hobby, with scarcer species such as Honey Buzzard, Rough-legged Buzzard and Osprey all recorded with some regularity. St Margaret's is not an ideal place to seawatch, but small numbers of skuas and shearwaters are recorded in most passage periods.

The cliffs are home to breeding colonies of Kittiwake and Fulmar. A few pairs of Rock Pipit also breed, but otherwise the area is rather quiet in summer.

41 SANDWICH BAY (Kent)

OS Landranger 179
OS Explorer 150

On the east coast of Kent south of Ramsgate, Sandwich is noted for migrants, including a sprinkling of scarce species and rarities. A Bird Observatory operates over an extensive area of privately owned dunes and marshland. The Observatory has recently undergone substantial redevelopment and now boasts much improved accommodation, a laboratory and educational facilities. The peak seasons are March–June and August–November. Pegwell Bay to the north and Sandwich Bay itself attract waders and wildfowl, especially in winter. Large areas of the mudflats, saltings and dunes around the mouth of the Stour estuary are protected as reserves and are maintained by the NT and Kent Wildlife Trust (KWT).

Habitat

The coast is dominated by a series of sand dunes, many of which have been converted into golf links. Inland, a large proportion of the area is farmed, and waders roost on these fields at high tide. Small areas of freshwater marsh, reedbeds, bushes and trees add diversity. To the north the River Stour enters the sea at Pegwell Bay and extensive areas of mud, sandflats and saltings surround the estuary.

Access (see map)

Leave Sandwich east along Sandown Road towards Sandwich Bay Estate. The observatory, at Old Downs Farm, is on the right shortly beyond the toll gate. Access to the main areas of interest is as follows.

Sandwich Bay Passerine migrants are mainly attracted to the bushes and gardens in the vicinity of the Estate. Access is from the toll road via the gate opposite the track to the Observatory. Cross the field to the stile and check the bushes around the Heligoland traps. There are no restrictions on visiting the Observatory but birders should not enter the enclosed trapping areas and should respect residents' privacy when watching birds in gardens.

Worth Marshes From the Observatory, continue south beyond the Estate on the Ancient Highway towards the Chequers pub. Footpaths cross Worth Marshes to North Stream and back to Old Downs Farm.

NT and KWT Reserves From the Observatory, continue through the Estate to the coast and drive north beside the beach to Prince's Golf Club car park. Walk north

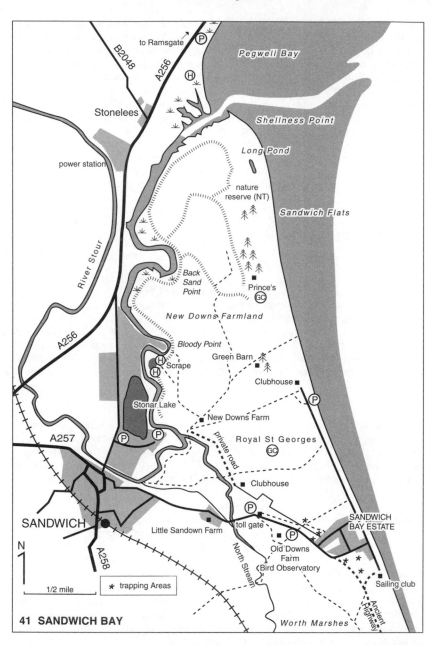

41 SANDWICH BAY

along the beach to the reserves. Access is largely unrestricted except to certain areas in the breeding season. It is possible either to return via the riverside footpath to New Downs Farm or cross the New Downs Farmland, checking the conifers at the north end of Prince's Golf Course en route. The entire area is privately owned and it is necessary to keep to roads and public footpaths at all times. Sandwich Bay Bird Observatory is open all year and provides hostel-type self-catering accommodation for up to 12 people. Further details are available from the honorary warden.

Birds

The first spring arrivals are in March and include Garganey, Black Redstart and Firecrest, and by the end of the month Sandwich Terns begin to appear. The bulk of the passage is April–May, when a number of scarce migrants are regularly recorded, including Kentish Plover and Golden Oriole.

Summer is quiet but up to 30 pairs of Little Tern breed in the area, and Kittiwakes, from their breeding cliffs at Dover, are frequently seen.

The autumn wader passage begins in mid-July and continues into September. Typical species include Curlew Sandpiper, Black-tailed Godwit and Wood Sandpiper. August brings return of passerine migrants, mainly chats, warblers and flycatchers. East winds encourage the occasional fall, which inevitably includes a scarce species or two. By late autumn the bulk consists of Goldcrest, Robin, thrushes, Starling and finches arriving from the continent to winter in Britain. Rarities can turn up at any time but late spring and particularly late autumn are the most likely periods. Sandwich Bay has recorded a number of outstanding species, and recently Pallas's Warblers have been almost annual in late October or early November, sometimes several at once.

Divers, grebes and sea duck may be seen offshore in winter and Hen Harrier and Short-eared Owl hunt the marshes. Golden Plover and Lapwing take up residence in the fields and a variety of the commoner waders inhabits the mudflats. Snow Bunting is regular on the shore and Twite can be found around the estuary.

Information

Gaynor Cross, Sandwich Bay Bird Observatory, Guildford Road, Sandwich Bay, Sandwich, Kent CT13 9PF. Tel: 01304 617341. E-mail: sbbot@talk21.com

Pete Forrest, Kent Wildlife Trust, Tyland Barn, Sandling, Maidstone, Kent ME14 3BD. Tel: 01622 662012. E-mail: kentwildlife@cix.co.uk

42 THANET AND NORTH FORELAND (Kent) OS Landranger 179
OS Explorer 150

Though heavily developed, the position of the Isle of Thanet in the extreme northeast corner of Kent, at the south end of the North Sea, makes it an obvious point for observing migration. It is a noted seawatching location and coastal scrub harbours a variety of passerine migrants.

Habitat

Chalk cliffs form the coastline from Ramsgate in the south to Margate. The rocky foreshore is interspersed by sandy bays. Grass covers most of the clifftop between Foreness Point and North Foreland, but more substantial cover occurs on the edge of North Foreland golf course and, 1 mile inland from Foreness Point, at the north end of Northdown Park.

Access (see map)

North Foreland can be reached by following the B2052 north from Broadstairs. There is a car park, from where you can seawatch, overlooking Joss Bay, just north of the lighthouse. The clifftop between Foreness Point and Botany Bay may be accessed by following the B2052 west past the Captain Digby pub for c.½ mile. Turn right into St George's Road and take the second right, Kingsgate Avenue. Follow this to its end and park. Walk northwest along the coast to Foreness Point. It is possible to drive to Foreness Point by proceeding north along Queen Elizabeth Avenue, turning sharp right and then left into Princess Margaret Avenue

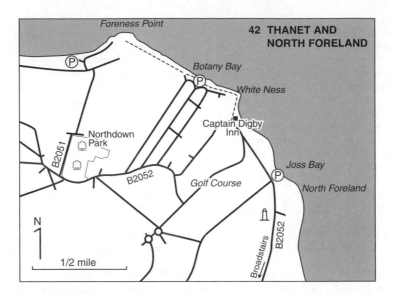

until you reach the pitch-and-putt golf course. Park in the spaces provided and walk to the Coastguard Station, which offers some shelter for seawatching.

Northdown Park is bordered by the B2052 to the south and the B2051 (Queen Elizabeth Avenue) to the west, where you can park.

Birds

In winter you can expect to find Red-throated Diver, Great Crested Grebe, Eider and large auks (mostly Guillemot) offshore. The rocky shoreline holds a variety of wintering waders, most notably substantial numbers of Sanderling and a regular group of Purple Sandpipers, which tend to roost in the sandy bays at White Ness. Small numbers of Rock Pipits and occasional Black Redstart are also present.

During passage substantial numbers of pipits, wagtails, chats, thrushes, warblers and finches pass through. Falls of the commoner night migrants are usually associated with east winds, with scarcer species such as Richard's Pipit, Icterine, Yellow-browed and Pallas's Warblers, and Red-breasted Flycatcher all regular in autumn. Autumn seawatching is most productive during north winds, with Gannet, Manx Shearwater, Arctic, Great and Pomarine Skuas, Kittiwake, terns and auks (including Little Auk in late October–November). Sparrowhawk, Merlin, Hen Harrier and Short-eared Owl all regularly arrive from the sea, with Osprey, Honey, Common and Rough-legged Buzzards, and Red Kite occasionally noted.

Breeding birds include colonies of Fulmar on the clifftops. Northdown Park has breeding Ring-necked Parakeet, which is easily found.

43–46 STOUR VALLEY (Kent)

OS Landranger 179
OS Explorer 150

The Stour Valley, lying northeast of Canterbury, contains some of the finest wetlands in southern England. Stodmarsh NNR is the best known site, but other areas are also good. They are notable for breeding Cetti's and Savi's Warblers, but are also worth a visit during migration periods and regularly produce uncommon birds. Much of the area is managed by EN.

Habitat

The large shallow lagoons, extensive reedbeds, and partially flooded riverside meadows have been created by a gradual subsidence of underground coal workings. Patches of woodland and scrub have developed in the drier areas. Water levels are carefully controlled and grazing is allowed on the damp meadows to produce suitable habitats; parts of the reedbed are cut annually to improve growth.

Access (see map)

Four sites in the Stour Valley are worthy of exploration. All except Stodmarsh are best reached from the A28 Canterbury–Margate road.

43 STODMARSH (Kent)

Leave Canterbury on the A257 towards Sandwich. After c.1½ miles, just past the golf course, take an inconspicuous left turn onto an unsigned minor road. This leads to the village of Stodmarsh, c.4 miles away. In the village, turn left immediately after the Red Lion pub into a narrow lane; the reserve car park is on the right after a short distance. Various leaflets are on sale here from a small hut. Access to the NNR is along the Lampen Wall (a flood protection barrier), which provides an excellent vantage point. From the car park continue on foot to the end of the lane, turning sharp right and onto the Lampen Wall (or take the short nature trail through woodland). The path runs alongside woodland and scrub, then past open water and reedbeds into a drier, scrubby area, and finally after c.1 mile reaches the River Stour. It continues along the south bank of the river, with reeds, wet meadows and pasture to the right. You can walk all the way to Grove Ferry (c.2 miles) and work the shallow pools and reedbeds in this area. A raised viewing area and hide overlooks this productive site. At Grove Ferry there is a pub, picnic site and cafe. You can return to Stodmarsh along the well-marked visitor trail via the Marsh Hide to the car park. If time is limited it is best to cover only a short stretch of the riverside path and then return to the car park

44 GROVE FERRY (Kent)

An alternative approach to the area is from Grove Ferry itself. A right turn 3½ miles after Sturry on the A28 leads to Grove Ferry down Grove Ferry Hill. Park in the car park by the pub and take the footpath leading to the recently created shallow pools and reedbeds. A riverside path to Stodmarsh offers alternative access.

45 WESTBERE MARSHES (Kent)

Leave the A28 west into the village of Westbere. Park at the west end of the village and cross the railway line. A footpath leads across the marshes to the river, which it then follows in both directions, alongside reedbeds and open water.

46 FORDWICH (Kent)

At Sturry, 2½ miles northeast of Canterbury, a minor road leads south to Fordwich village. Park in the village and walk east along the river.

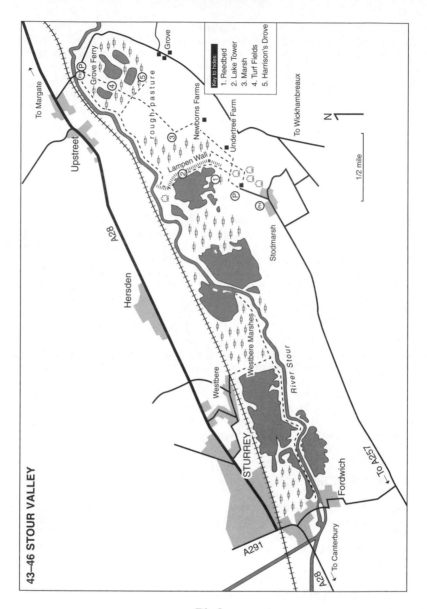

43–46 STOUR VALLEY

Key to hides:
1. Reedbed
2. Lake Tower
3. Marsh
4. Turf Fields
5. Harrison's Drove

Birds

Stodmarsh's position, in a major river valley only a few miles from the coast, ensures an impressive passage of migrants, especially in spring. It is one of the best places to see early arrivals before the main influx into Britain. A pair or two of Garganey may breed on the reserve, but the best chance is of migrants in spring and autumn. The pools at Grove Ferry or the wet meadows south of the riverside path are favoured. Marsh Harrier and Hobby are regular, with concentrations of up to 40 of the latter recorded in May during recent years. Osprey is uncommon. Passage waders include Green, Wood and Common Sandpipers, Whimbrel, Ruff and Black-tailed Godwit, while Little Egret and, less regularly,

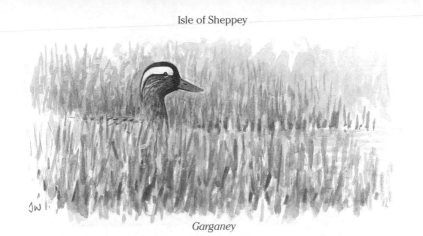

Garganey

Spoonbill are sometimes present. Recent autumns have seen regular appearances by Spotted Crake in August–September, with up to six noted on one day.

Although 1–2 pairs of Bittern probably nest, they are difficult to see. In spring and early summer one is more likely to hear the male's characteristic booming. Savi's Warbler is another speciality; one or two pairs formerly bred annually, but have been less reliable in recent summers. They can usually be heard and, with perseverance, seen in the reedbeds east of the Lampen Wall or at Grove Ferry from early May. Savi's are usually most vocal at dawn and dusk, but may sing briefly during the middle of the day. Stodmarsh's other warbler speciality, Cetti's Warbler, is commoner, more vocal and resident. It is not unusual to hear up to ten singing explosively from the dense thickets and scrub between the car park and the river. With patience they can be seen but are often reluctant to leave cover. Bearded Tit is not uncommon and small parties can usually be found in the reeds, particularly on still days. Grasshopper Warbler has declined as a breeding species in recent summers, while Reed and Sedge Warblers and Reed Bunting are very common. Yellow wagtail is frequently seen, but Water Rail is usually only heard. Lapwing, Redshank and Snipe breed on the wet meadows, as well as Shoveler and Teal. Patches of woodland hold the usual species (woodpeckers, warblers, tits), but look out for Lesser Spotted Woodpecker at Westbere.

Large numbers of wildfowl winter on the reserve, mainly the commoner dabbling and diving ducks. Hen Harrier is frequently seen and Golden Plover can be found in the surrounding fields. A few Water Pipits favour the riverside meadows and a Great Grey Shrike is occasionally present, while Cetti's Warbler is often easiest to see in winter.

Information

David Feast, English Nature, Coldharbour Farm, Wye, Ashford, Kent TN25 5DB. Tel: 01233 812525.

47–49 ISLE OF SHEPPEY (Kent)

OS Landranger 178
OS Explorer 149

The Isle of Sheppey lies on the south side of the Thames estuary, flanked by the Swale and Medway estuaries, and connected to the mainland by the Kingsferry Bridge. It is particularly productive in winter, harbouring significant numbers of wildfowl and waders in addition to several unusual species. A greater variety of waders, and sometimes impressive movements of seabirds, can be seen in autumn.

Habitat

The south half of the island is the most productive for birds. Much of this area comprises rough grazing and marshes intersected by dykes and creeks, as well as some arable, all protected from exceptionally high tides by long seawalls. At low tide, extensive mudflats are exposed on the Swale, bordered by saltings.

Access (see map on p.133)

Although interesting birds can be found in many places, three areas in particular are worthy of investigation.

47 ELMLEY RSPB RESERVE (Kent)

Part (the Spitend Marshes) has been successfully managed to become an important area for both breeding and wintering waterbirds. Three hides overlook the lagoons and marshes and two the Swale. After crossing the Kingsferry bridge continue on the A249 for c.1 mile. Turn right, following the RSPB signs, onto a rough track to reach the car park at Kingshill Farm after 2 miles. A walk of 1 mile is necessary to reach the hides. Keep to the main footpaths and walk below the seawall to avoid disturbing the birds. The reserve is open daily (except Tuesdays) 09.00–21.00 (or sunset if earlier).

48 CAPEL FLEET AND HARTY FERRY (Kent)

From Leysdown return west along the B2231 for c.2 miles. Before reaching Eastchurch turn left on a minor road signed 'Ferry Inn' towards the Isle of Harty. This crosses Capel Fleet (often worth a look) and eventually ends at the Swale, beyond the inn. In winter this is a good area for geese, swans and raptors.

49 SWALE NNR (Kent)

The small hamlet at Shell Ness lies at the east tip of Sheppey. Take the B2231 to Leysdown-on-Sea and continue along the seafront to Shell Ness. Park just before the hamlet and walk along the seawall to the coast. It is worth checking the sea as well as the marshes and mudflats. Continuing along the beach, the bay beyond the pill box holds considerable numbers of wintering waders at high tide. After checking this area return along the seawall a few hundred yards and turn left along the seawall which runs approximately parallel to the coast. Walk for up to 2 miles to view the extensive shallow floods of Swale NNR, overlooked by two hides.

Birds

Unless specifically mentioned for one site, the birds detailed below can be seen at any of the areas. Sheppey is particularly good in winter although it is often cold and windswept. Divers and grebes are regular off Shell Ness, the most frequent being Red-throated Diver and Great Crested Grebe; other species are occasional. Hen Harrier is a winter speciality, quartering the fields and marshes almost anywhere. Rough-legged Buzzard is only a rare visitor but Merlin and Peregrine are more frequent, though not often seen on a casual visit. White-fronted Goose is another winter speciality and all the fields should be checked. The Capel Fleet–Harty Ferry area is often favoured, and they sometimes roost at Elmley or the floods at Swale NNR. Small numbers of Bewick's Swans and the occasional Whooper sometimes frequent the Harty Ferry area while Brent Goose may be

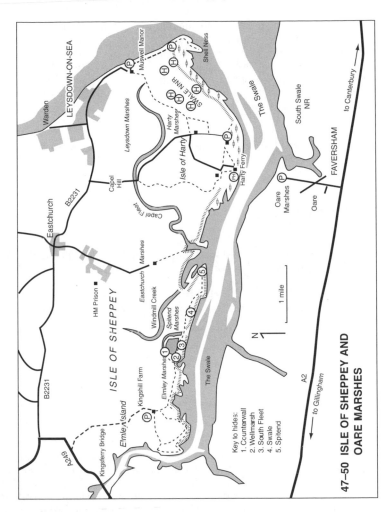

47–50 ISLE OF SHEPPEY AND OARE MARSHES

Key to hides:
1. Counterwall
2. Wellmarsh
3. South Fleet
4. Swale
5. Spitend

seen anywhere on the coast. Very large numbers of duck winter, the commonest being Wigeon, Teal, Mallard, Pintail and Shoveler. Large rafts of duck are often present offshore at Shell Ness and should be checked for Eider, Common Scoter, Goldeneye and Red-breasted Merganser. Velvet Scoter is less frequent. At low tide waders can be seen anywhere on the extensive mudflats and at high tide they roost at Shell Ness and Elmley. Knot and Dunlin are commonest, and other species include Sanderling. Short-eared Owl is present all year, though more numerous and most easily seen in winter. Twite and Lapland and Snow Buntings are sometimes seen on the beach at Shell Ness but Shore Lark is less frequent.

Species diversity increases in spring and autumn although the huge numbers of wildfowl and waders are absent. Marsh Harrier breeds and can be seen year-round. Garganey is regular at Elmley and the floods at Swale NNR in spring. The wide variety of waders may include Little Stint, Curlew Sandpiper and large numbers of Black-tailed Godwit, in addition to the wintering and breeding species, and rare waders are seen annually. Seawatching off Shell Ness can be productive in autumn, particularly after strong north winds. Gannet, Great and Arctic Skuas, Kittiwake, and Common, Little and Sandwich Terns are the most frequent species. Migrant passerines include Wheatear and Whinchat and occasionally something rarer. A number of recent records of Aquatic Warbler (including four at Elmley in August 1995) suggests this species may be overlooked in the reeds and rush-filled ditches.

In summer a variety of commoner ducks breed, occasionally including Garganey. Lapwing and Redshank are common and Common Tern nests on some of the saltmarsh islands at Elmley. Yellow Wagtail and Meadow Pipit are common breeding birds throughout.

Information
Bob Gomes, Elmley RSPB Reserve, Kingshill Farm, Elmley, Sheerness, Kent ME12 3RW. Tel: 01795 665969.

50 OARE MARSHES (Kent)

OS Landranger 178
OS Explorer 149

The Oare marshes LNR lies on the south bank of the Swale, immediately opposite Harty Ferry on the Isle of Sheppey.

Habitat
The reserve consists of 165 acres of grazing marsh with freshwater dykes, open water 'scrapes' and saltmarsh.

Access (see map on p.133)
The village of Oare lies just north of Faversham. From Oare, head north for 1½ miles and park opposite the Watch House, near the seawall at the end of Harty Ferry Road. Access is restricted to the public footpath and nature trail to minimise disturbance to the birds. The whole reserve may be viewed from the trails and hides.

Birds
The Oare Marshes are of importance for migratory, wintering and breeding birds. Suitable habitat is achieved through manipulation of water levels and grazing.

In winter the reserve hosts good numbers of wildfowl including Brent Goose and Wigeon, and many waders, notably Dunlin and Curlew. Like nearby Sheppey, raptors are often in evidence, and typical species include Hen Harrier, Merlin and Short-eared Owl. Other wintering species may include Bittern and Twite.

Diversity of waders increases during spring and autumn, and regular visitors include Little Stint, Curlew Sandpiper, Ruff, Black-tailed Godwit and Whimbrel. A rarity is a distinct possibility at the right time of year.

Breeding birds at Oare include Garganey, Water Rail, Avocet, Lapwing, Snipe, Redshank, Common Tern and Bearded Tit.

Information
Tony Swandale, Kent Wildlife Trust, Tyland Barn, Sandling, Maidstone, Kent ME14 3BD. Tel: 01622 662012. E-mail: kentwildlife@cix.co.uk

51–53 MEDWAY ESTUARY (Kent)

OS Landranger 178
OS Explorer 163

The maze of tidal creeks and extensive mudflats that form the Medway estuary are situated south of the Hoo Peninsula and immediately west of the Isle of

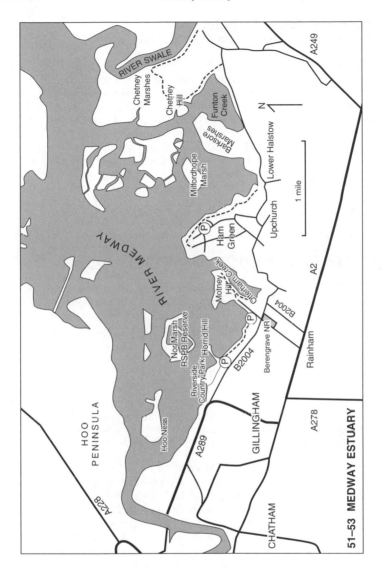

51–53 MEDWAY ESTUARY

Sheppey. Birds are similar to the estuaries of the Thames and Swale, and this area is at its best in autumn and winter.

Habitat

A large tidal basin with many saltmarsh islands and surrounded by mudflats at low tide. In the east the marshes of the Chetney peninsula are characterised by grazing marsh dissected by fleets and ditches. Further west, orchards, grazing and arable dominate the landward side of the seawalls around Ham Green. A small reedbed and extensive hawthorn and bramble scrub can be found at Riverside Country Park.

Access (see map)

Several areas are worthy of exploration.

51 RIVERSIDE COUNTRY PARK (Kent)
(Nor Marsh and Motney Hill RSPB reserve)

From Rainham take the B2004 north for 1 mile, turn left at the junction and travel for c.1 mile and park at the visitor centre car park. From here you can walk to Horrid Hill or west to Eastcourt Meadows. To access Motney Hill at the east end of the country park, you can use the small car park along Motney Hill Road, accessed from the B2004, ¼ mile west of the junction. From here you can walk north along the seawall to Motney Hill, viewing the estuary to the west and reedbed to the east. It is possible to walk along the shoreline and sewage works perimeter fence to view Rainham Creek and the saltmarsh that forms the RSPB reserves of Nor Marsh and Motney Hill. To view Otterham Creek walk to the sewage works gates and follow the path to the right, which runs along the edge of the field by the works fence. Berengrave Nature Reserve can be reached from a car park on the B2004, or alternatively from Berengrave Lane itself.

52 HAM GREEN AND LOWER HALSTOW (Kent)

From Upchurch follow the road northeast for 1 mile, where there is limited space for parking. The narrow lane on the right leads to the seawall. Walk right towards Lower Halstow in order to view the large expanse of mudflats in Twinney and Halstow Creeks. Walk left to view the deep Half Acre Creek.

53 FUNTON CREEK AND CHETNEY (Kent)

From Lower Halstow follow the road east for c.1 mile until the road runs alongside the estuary. There are several lay-bys where you can park and view the estuary. To reach Chetney follow the public footpath from the top of the hill across the fields to the seawall. Please keep strictly to the public footpath at this sensitive site.

Birds
The area is at its best in winter when huge numbers of wildfowl and waders use the estuary. Brent Goose, Shelduck, Wigeon, Teal, Shoveler, Pintail, Grey Plover, Dunlin, Knot, Redshank, Black-tailed Godwit, Curlew and Turnstone are all present in large numbers. Red-breasted Merganser and Goldeneye occur in the deeper channels, while sea duck and Scaup may move into the estuary in cold weather. One of the rarer grebes is usually present (often in Half Acre Creek or Otterham Creek) with all three sometimes present during hard weather. In most winters a diver is found, and there have been regular records of Great Northern Diver in recent seasons. Fields around Funton and Chetney are frequented by flocks of Lapwing and Golden Plover. Merlin, Marsh and Hen Harriers can be seen almost anywhere, but are perhaps most easily found on Chetney.

Shelduck, Lapwing and Redshank breed on Chetney, while the islands of the river support large colonies of Black-headed Gulls, along with smaller numbers of Common, Sandwich and Little Terns.

In autumn, the variety of waders increases. Chetney regularly attracts Little Ringed Plover, Ruff, Common, Green and the occasional Wood Sandpiper, and Little Stint. Spotted Redshank regularly roost on the saltmarsh at Motney Hill, while Curlew Sandpiper is recorded most autumns. Small numbers of Garganey also occur at Chetney in August–September. During southeast winds, Black Terns may appear at Motney Hill sewage outfall.

Information

Nor Marsh and Motney Hill RSPB, Michael Ellison, Bromhey Farm, Eastborough, Cooling, Rochester, Kent ME3 8DS. Tel: 01634 222480.

Riverside Country Park, Lower Rainham Road, Gillingham, Kent ME7 2XH. Tel: 01634 378987. E-mail: riversidecp@btinternet.com

54–58 HOO PENINSULA (NORTH KENT MARSHES)
(Kent)

OS Landranger 178
OS Explorer 163

These extensive marshes lie in the Thames estuary immediately west of the Isle of Sheppey, bordered by the Rivers Thames and Medway. Similar to Sheppey, they are best in winter or during migration.

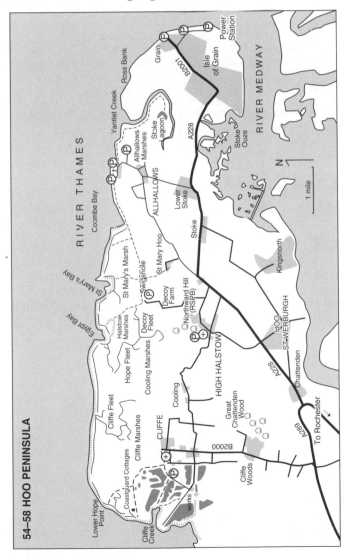

Habitat

Mainly grassland and saltmarsh dissected by dykes and seawalls, and surrounded by mudflats at low tide, much of the area has been drained for growing
wheat. Flooded pits at Cliffe are the result of clay extraction and this area has
recently been acquired by the RSPB. An area of deciduous woodland and scrub
near High Halstow is the RSPB reserve of Northward Hill.

Access (see map)

Several areas are worthy of exploration.

54 CLIFFE POOLS (Kent)

At the west end of the marshes, these flooded clay pits are perhaps the most
interesting area, attracting a variety of duck in winter and many waders on passage. The water level determines the best pits for waders. This is the newest RSPB
reserve in North Kent, but there are no visitor facilities as yet. Turn left off the
B2000 at the north end of Cliffe village and on reaching the first pool turn right.
This road passes around the perimeter of the pools (several of which can be seen
well) and continues to a gate. A short walk beyond this leads to the seawall.
Going north to Lower Hope Point may be profitable; alternatively walk south
back around the pits via Cliffe Creek. This is a long walk but if time is short much
of the area can be viewed from the roads. In addition, the road to the Works passes other pools and a track runs through the pits to Cliffe Creek.

55 HALSTOW MARSHES (Kent)

In the centre of the North Kent Marshes, these are excellent for wildfowl and waders,
especially at the coast. Egypt and St Mary's Bays are particularly notable for waders at
high tide. From High Halstow continue east towards the A228. After ½ mile turn left
(north) to Decoy Farm and park at Swigshole. Fork right across the marshes to St Mary's
Bay. Continue along the seawall west to Egypt Bay where another track leads back to
Swigshole. Some of this area is now managed by the RSPB, and is best viewed from
Bromhey Farm, reached by taking the road west from High Halstow towards Cooling for
c.1 mile and then turning right after the sharp south bend. Continue to the farm buildings
and park. The recently created flooded areas can be viewed from the nearby small hill.

56 NORTHWARD HILL (Kent)

This small reserve lies immediately north of High Halstow. The oaks hold Britain's
largest heronry; over 200 pairs are present February–July and a range of woodland
species can also be seen. High Halstow is north of the A228 in the centre of the
North Kent Marshes. Parking is available by the village hall and the entrance to the
reserve is north of Northwood Avenue. There is free access at all times but the
heronry may only be visited if escorted; apply in writing to the warden.

57 ALLHALLOWS (Kent)

Allhallows is reached by following the minor road off the A228 at Fenn Street for
3½ miles. Turn right along Avery Way to the British Pilot pub. Park here and follow the track across the marsh to the seawall. From here walk east to reach

Yantlet Creek and then south and subsequently west for 2 miles to Stoke Lagoon. Keep below the seawall to avoid disturbing the wildfowl and waders. Alternatively walk west to Coombe Bay.

58 ISLE OF GRAIN (Kent)

The Isle of Grain may be reached by following the A228 from Rochester. 1½ miles beyond Lower Stoke you can park and view the mudflats and saltings of Stoke Ouze. The adjacent fleet attracts duck. Follow the B2001 to Grain village, and follow Chapel Road until you are driving south and parallel to the seawall. View the mudflats from the seawall and work the bushes for migrants in autumn. The power station outflow can attract gulls and terns.

Birds

Bewick's Swan and White-fronted Goose regularly winter on the marshes and large numbers of dabbling duck include Pintail. Deeper pools attract diving duck, sometimes including Smew and Scaup. Waders are abundant and typical wintering species include a few Avocets at Cliffe pools. Hen Harrier and Short-eared Owl can usually be seen hunting the marshes and Merlin is regular. Snow Bunting can be rather elusive but Lapland Bunting is more frequent.

Garganey may appear in small numbers in spring and Black Tern is regular in both spring and autumn, but the main interest is the passage of waders. Species that may be found include Little Stint, Curlew Sandpiper and Wood Sandpiper, and something more unusual is a distinct possibility.

Summer is quiet. Shelduck, Lapwing and Redshank breed on the marshes and at Northward Hill the heronry and woodland species are the main attractions (though the reserve is best visited April–June when it can be combined with passage waders at Cliffe). Little Owl is common in the area and quite easy to see, but though Long-eared Owl breeds at Northward Hill it is rarely seen. Other species on the reserve include all three woodpeckers and Nightingale.

Information

Northward Hill RSPB: Michael Ellison, Bromhey Farm, Eastborough, Cooling, Rochester, Kent ME3 8DS. Tel: 01634 222480.

59 BOUGH BEECH RESERVOIR (Kent)

OS Landranger 188
OS Explorer 147

The largest area of fresh water in Kent, this man-made reservoir was first flooded in 1969–70. Bough Beech attracts a variety of wildfowl throughout the year as well as passage waders, and it regularly produces rarities.

Habitat

A large stretch of fresh water surrounded by a patchwork of woodland, fields and hedgerows. A sailing club uses the south section of the reservoir.

Access (see map)

From Riverhead the B2042 runs southwest towards Ide Hill. One mile south of Ide Hill take the minor road east to Winkhurst Green. There is a Kent Wildlife Trust Information Centre north of the reserve with car parking and toilet facilities. The road running through the north end of the reservoir affords excellent views, while woodland birds may be found by taking the path towards Bore Place.

Birds

Wintering wildfowl include Pochard, Tufted Duck, Goldeneye, Goosander and Ruddy Duck. Other waterbirds include Great Crested Grebe and Cormorant, and occasionally divers or rarer grebes.

In spring Little Ringed Plover usually appears in March and remains to breed in most years. Osprey is almost annual and one sometimes lingers for several days.

In autumn passage waders usually include Greenshank and Common and Green Sandpipers. Garganey occurs in most years.

Breeders include Grey Heron, Shelduck, Mandarin, Hobby, Sparrowhawk, Kingfisher, the three woodpeckers, a variety of warblers, Marsh Tit, Nuthatch and Treecreeper.

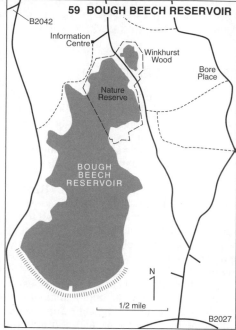

Information

Dave Hutton, Kent Wildlife Trust, Tyland Barn, Sandling, Maidstone, Kent ME14 3BD. Tel: 01622 662012. E-mail: kentwildife@cix.co.uk

60 BEDGEBURY FOREST (Kent)   OS Landranger 188 OS Explorer 136

This large area of forest south of Goudhurst is noted as a regular haunt of Crossbill and Hawfinch.

Habitat

Extensive coniferous plantations are mixed with small areas of sweet chestnut coppice. The Pinetum contains an excellent variety of conifers planted on grassy slopes, and a small lake.

Access

From Goudhurst take the B2079 south towards Flimwell. A car park, complete with refreshments and toilet facilities, is reached after c.3 miles. After paying a small entrance fee follow the path into the Pinetum and the cypress trees favoured by roosting finches are just beyond the sharp rise.

Birds

Noted as a regular winter site for Hawfinch, though numbers have declined in recent years; Siskin, Redpoll and Brambling are also usually present. This is one of the best sites in the county for Crossbill during irruptions.

Breeders include Woodcock, Nightjar, Great Spotted and Green Woodpeckers, Nightingale, a variety of warblers, Goldcrest, Firecrest, Siskin and Redpoll.

EAST ANGLIA

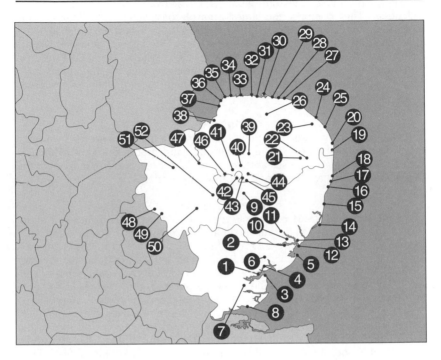

1 OLD HALL MARSHES AND TOLLESBURY (Essex)   OS Landranger 168

Old Hall Marshes lie on the north shore of the Blackwater estuary 8 miles south of Colchester. They comprise the largest area of coastal marsh in Essex and the fourth largest in England. A total of 1,134 acres is an RSPB reserve, which includes Great and Little Cob Islands, and in turn is part of the larger Blackwater Estuary NNR, which also includes the Tollesbury Wick Essex Wildlife Trust (EWT) reserve. A variety of waders and wildfowl breeds, including Avocet, but the primary interest is in winter and migration periods, when significant populations of wildfowl and waders are present.

Habitat
Three-quarters of the reserve is unimproved grazing marsh, dissected by numerous freshwater fleets, the rest is improved grassland, arable fields and saltmarsh, with a coastal lagoon and sizeable reedbed. Water levels are managed for the benefit of breeding and wintering wildfowl and waders.

Access (see map)
Old Hall Marshes RSPB reserve From Maldon, take the B1026 to Tolleshunt D'Arcy. Continue through the village on the B1026 towards Colchester and, after the B1023 turning to Tiptree, turn right (east) on the minor road towards Tollesbury. After 1¼ miles, the road bends sharply right and immediately after this turn left into Old Hall Lane (the track to Old Hall Farm, which itself if private), following this for c.⅔ mile to the reserve car park (which lies ¼ mile beyond the farm). Vehicle access to Old Hall Lane and the reserve car park is by permit only, available in advance from the warden, and the reserve is open daily except Tuesdays, 09.00–21.00 (or sunset when earlier). Access on foot to the public rights of way is possible at all times (non-permit holders should use the car park at Woodrolfe Green, off Woodrolfe Road in Tollesbury, TL964107). A public footpath follows the sea wall around the perimeter of the marshes for a total of 6½ miles and there is also a central public footpath across the marshes which allows a circuit of 3 miles.

Tollesbury Wick Marshes EWT reserve The whole of the north shore of the 10-mile-long Blackwater estuary is an excellent birdwatching area in winter, and Slavonian Grebe is a speciality of this river. The marshes are a reserve of the EWT and lie immediately east of Tollesbury village. They can be viewed from the surrounding seawall (which is continuous with that of Old Hall Marshes) and the birdlife is essentially the same. Enter Tollesbury on the B1023 and fork left (north) in the village centre to park at Woodrolfe Green, and then walk past the marina to the seawall. It is possible for the very energetic walker to continue along the seawall to Goldhanger or even Heybridge Basin, and there are several public footpaths from the seawall back to the B1023 near Tollesbury village.

Birds
Up to 10,000 Dark-bellied Brent Geese winter in the Blackwater area, with up to 6000 at Old Hall Marshes. They are often quite approachable, and it is worth checking at Old Hall for Pale-bellied Brent Geese and Black Brant among them. Duck are numerous, especially Wigeon, Teal and Shelduck. Eider, Goldeneye, Red-breasted Merganser and occasionally Long-tailed Duck frequent the various tidal waters. Red-throated Diver is common, and Great Crested, Little and Slavonian Grebes are all worth looking for. Great Northern and Black-throated Divers are occasional visitors. Hen Harrier, Merlin, and Barn and Short-eared Owls are quite frequent. The usual waders are numerous, with several thousand

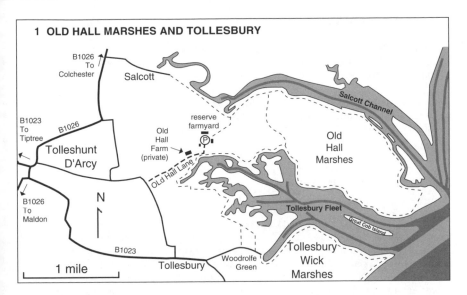

1 OLD HALL MARSHES AND TOLLESBURY

B1026 To Colchester

Salcott

Salcott Channel

B1023 To Tiptree

B1026

Tolleshunt D'Arcy

reserve farmyard

Old Hall Farm (private)

P

Old Hall Marshes

Old Hall Lane

B1026 To Maldon

N

Tollesbury Fleet

Great Cob Island

B1023

Tollesbury

Woodrolfe Green

Tollesbury Wick Marshes

1 mile

Lapwing and Golden Plover often present, as well as up to c.50 Ruff. Twite is the most interesting, regularly occurring passerine.

During migration seasons, waders likely to be encountered include Little Stint, Green, Wood and Curlew Sandpipers, Ruff, Spotted Redshank, Greenshank, godwits and Whimbrel.

The star breeding species is Avocet, but a range of other species nest, including Shelduck, Pochard, Shoveler, Gadwall, Lapwing, Redshank, Yellow Wagtail, Bearded Tit and Corn Bunting, and Common Tern may be viewed flying to and from Great Cob Island. Marsh Harrier and Garganey are not infrequently seen in summer.

Information

RSPB Old Hall Marshes (Site Manager): Paul Charlton, 1 Old Hall Lane, Tolleshunt D'Arcy, Maldon, Essex CM9 8TP. Tel: 01621 869015. E-mail: paul.charlton @rspb.org.uk

EWT: Jonathan Smith, Tollesbury, Maldon, Essex CM9 8RJ. Tel: 01621 868628. E-mail: jonathans@essexwt.org.uk

Brent Geese

143

2 STOUR ESTUARY (Essex)

Lying on the south shore of the Stour Estuary, this RSPB reserve offers the unusual combination of both woodland and estuarine species. The woodland is best in spring, however, while the estuary is most productive in autumn and winter.

Habitat

The reserve includes most of Copperas Bay on the south shore of the Stour Estuary, and extends east to near Parkeston. There are large areas of intertidal mud, with a little saltmarsh on the foreshore, and also small areas of estuarine reedbeds and bramble scrub. Stour Wood itself is mainly comprised of sweet chestnut, and after a lapse, coppicing has been reinstated over a 15-year rotation to provide a more varied habitat.

Access (see map)

The reserve is north of the B1352 between Harwich and Manningtree, c.7 miles east of its junction with the A137. The car park (signed) lies north of the road 1 mile east of Wrabness, c.600 yards after the wood appears on the left-hand side. There are two nature trails, 1 mile and 5 miles long, and three hides overlook the estuary east of Stour Wood. The reserve is open at all times, and for wildfowl and waders a rising tide, from 2 hours before high water until 2 hours after, is best.

Birds

The estuary attracts the usual range of wintering wildfowl and waders, including Dark-bellied Brent Goose, Shelduck, Wigeon, Teal, Pintail, Grey Plover, Curlew, Redshank and Dunlin, and good numbers of Black-tailed Godwit of the Icelandic race, with an average of 2,100 birds wintering on the Stour. Species present in smaller numbers include Turnstone, Oystercatcher and Ringed Plover, and

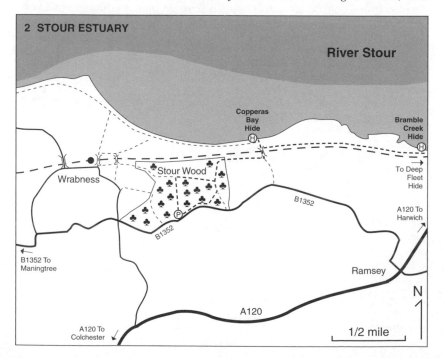

Goldeneye may be seen on the river channel. On passage a greater variety of waders may be found, with Greenshank, Spotted Redshank and, in autumn, Little Stint and Curlew Sandpiper possible, as well as Green and Common Sandpipers in the saltmarsh gutters.

Breeding birds in Stour Wood include Green, Great and Lesser Spotted Woodpeckers, Nightingale, Garden Warbler and Blackcap, with Shelduck, Reed Warbler and Common and Lesser Whitethroats along the estuary shore.

Information
RSPB Warden: Russell Leavett, 24 Orchard Close, Great Oakley, Harwich, Essex CO12 5AX. Tel: 01255 886043. E-mail: russell.leavett@rspb.org.uk

3 BRADWELL (Essex)
OS Landranger 168

Lying on the east shore of the Dengie Peninsula near the mouth of the Blackwater estuary, this bleakly attractive area is important for wintering wildfowl and waders, and attracts small numbers of passerine migrants in spring and autumn. The area around Sales Point is a reserve of the Essex Wildlife Trust, while a bird observatory has operated at Bradwell since the 1950s.

Habitat
A mixture of arable farmland, bounded by seawalls and their associated borrow-dykes, bordered by extensive areas of saltmarsh and the extensive mudflats of Dengie Flats. Near the Observatory there is a wooded thicket.

Access (see map)
Bradwell Leave Maldon southeast on the B1018 (and then B1010) for 5 miles to Latchingdon, and in the village, where the main road turns sharp right by the church, continue straight ahead on the minor road to Bradwell-on-Sea, a further c.8½ miles. Approaching Bradwell-on-Sea the minor road meets the B1021. Turn left (northeast) and after 600 yards turn right (east) on a minor road to the village. Follow this and turn right again (immediately before the church) towards St Peters Chapel, following the road for 1⅓ miles to the car park at Eastlands Farm. From here walk along the track for ½ mile to the seawall at St Peters Chapel (the observatory lies 100 yards south of here, and is manned every Sunday; it has dormitory accommodation for eight). From here you can either walk north for ½ mile to Sales Point, or south for 2½ miles to Marshhouse Outfall. Both directions offer good views of roosting waders, with the period before high water being best.

Alternatively, continue along the B1021 direct to Bradwell Waterside and follow the seawall in either direction (west leads to St Lawrence Bay and Ramsey Marsh).

Dengie Peninsula It is possible to ride a mountain bike along the seawall from Bradwell to the south end of the Dengie Peninsula near Holliwell Point. The dykes in this area are often good for migrant waders and wildfowl, and seabirds and sometimes passerine migrants are often commoner in this area. There is no access by car.

Birds
Wintering wildfowl include numbers of Dark-bellied Brent Geese, as well as Wigeon, Teal and Shoveler. Waders include all the common species, as well as Grey Plover, Knot and Bar-tailed Godwit. Raptors in the area can include Hen

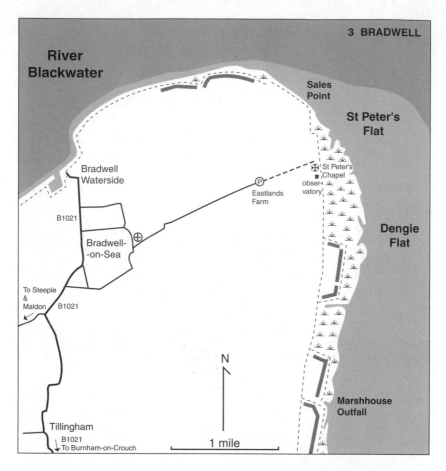

Harrier, Sparrowhawk, Peregrine, Merlin and sometimes Short-eared Owl. There may be a few Snow Buntings or even Shore Larks along the shore (but Twite is now extremely scarce). Offshore, Red-throated Diver and Slavonian Grebe may be present, and sometimes Great Northern or Black-throated Divers and Black-necked or Red-necked Grebes. There may also be sea duck, with Red-breasted Merganser, Eider and Common and Velvet Scoters possible.

On passage, Wheatear, Black Redstart and Firecrest are annual in spring and autumn, while Whinchat, Redstart, Pied Flycatcher and Ring Ouzel are largely confined to autumn. Scarce migrants such as Wryneck and Barred and Icterine Warblers have occurred on a few occasions, as have occasional rarities. Passage waders should include Sanderling (on the shell banks), and Green and Common Sandpipers in the dykes and saltmarsh gutters.

Breeders include Shelduck, small numbers of Little Tern (on Pewit Island), as well as Oystercatcher, Ringed Plover and Redshank, with Reed and Sedge Warblers in the dykes and Yellow Wagtail in some of the arable crops. In summer Marsh Harrier and Hobby are common visitors.

Information

Bradwell Bird Observatory: Graham Smith, 48 The Meads, Ingatestone, Essex CM4 0AE. Tel: 01277 354034.

4 ABBERTON RESERVOIR (Essex) OS Landranger 168

Lying c.5 miles south of Colchester, Abberton is the best-known reservoir in East Anglia. Noted for wildfowl, with nationally important concentrations of Mallard, Teal, Wigeon, Shoveler, Gadwall, Pochard, Tufted Duck and Goldeneye, its proximity to the coast also ensures a good variety of waders. A visit can be rewarding at any time of year.

Habitat

Covering 1,240 acres and 4 miles long, the reservoir is fed by Layer Brook at the west end, while the Roman River passes close to the dam at the north end. Most of the perimeter has concrete banks, but the west end has natural margins with lush vegetation and some bushes. A small area (9 acres) at the head of a sheltered bay adjacent to the B1026 is managed as a reserve by the Essex Wildlife Trust (EWT), and parts have been planted with a variety of native tree species.

Access (see map)

It is not permitted to walk around the reservoir's perimeter but most species can be seen from the reserve and two causeways across the west arm.

EWT reserve Leave Colchester south on the B1026 and after 4½ miles the reserve and visitor centre lie east of the road. The centre is open daily (except Mondays; closed Christmas Day and Boxing Day) 09.00–17.00. There is a loop nature trail, with five hides, providing views over the reservoir and passing through farmland and woodland.

Layer-de-la-Haye causeway Continuing south from the reserve on the B1026 for c.½ mile the road reaches the Layer-de-la-Haye causeway.

Layer Breton causeway Continue south on the B1026 for 1¼ miles to a T-junction and turn right onto a minor road north towards Layer Breton and Birch. After ½ mile the road reaches the causeway.

Birds

Abberton attracts large numbers of waterfowl throughout the year and peak counts over have included 550 Great Crested Grebe, 40,000 Wigeon, 5,000 Pochard, 1,000 Goldeneye, 113 Smew and almost 17,000 Coot. Indeed, Goldeneye often number several hundred and Abberton is the most important inland site for this species in Britain.

In winter there are large numbers of the commoner wildfowl, especially Teal and Wigeon, as well as Goldeneye, Goosander and sometimes a few Smew. Bewick's Swan and White-fronted Goose occur, especially in hard weather, grazing in the surrounding fields. Large numbers of Canada and Greylag Geese are resident and, depending on water levels, numbers of waders, especially Dunlin, may winter (up to c.3,000 Dunlin have been recorded), and large flocks of Golden Plover are regular in the surrounding farmland. Other visitors can include divers and sea duck, and occasionally Bittern.

In late summer there are large concentrations of moulting Mute Swan, Tufted Duck, Pochard and Coot. Gadwall, Shoveler and Pintail are also commonest in autumn, although they occur throughout the winter. Red-crested Pochard may occur at any season but is most likely in autumn. The origin of such birds is perhaps suspect and some may be escapes. Water Rail, Kingfisher and Water Pipit are other species that may occasionally be seen outside the breeding season.

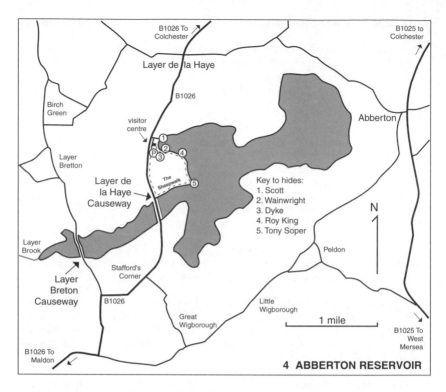

4 ABBERTON RESERVOIR

Key to hides:
1. Scott
2. Wainwright
3. Dyke
4. Roy King
5. Tony Soper

Many migrant waders pass through in spring and autumn, including Ringed and Little Ringed Plovers, Turnstone (mainly spring), Ruff, Black-tailed Godwit, Common Sandpiper and Little Stint (mainly autumn). The scarcer grebes, Marsh Harrier, Osprey, Garganey, Little Gull, and Arctic and Black Terns are recorded annually and there are sometimes huge flocks of Swift and hirundines.

Since 1981 Cormorant has nested in willows between the two causeways and the colony peaked at 551 pairs in 1996 (with only 407 in 1997). This is the largest tree-nesting colony in Britain, and most are of the form *sinensis*, which may be a distinct species. The colony is easily viewable from the Layer Breton causeway. Great Crested Grebe, Gadwall, Shoveler and Ruddy Ducks breed at the west end and Common Tern nests on specially constructed rafts. Other breeders include Yellow Wagtail, Nightingale, Reed and Sedge Warblers and Corn Bunting, and Garganey and Ringed Plover have bred.

Information

Annette Adams, Essex Wildlife Trust, Abberton Reservoir Visitor Centre, Layer-de-la-Haye, Colchester CO2 0EU. Tel: 01206 738172. E-mail: abberton@ essexwt.org.uk

5 WALTON-ON-THE-NAZE (Essex)   OS Landranger 169

The Naze forms the easternmost point of the large complex of marshes of Hamford Water. Between Harwich and Clacton, it forms an ideal habitat for wintering wildfowl and waders, as well as migrants.

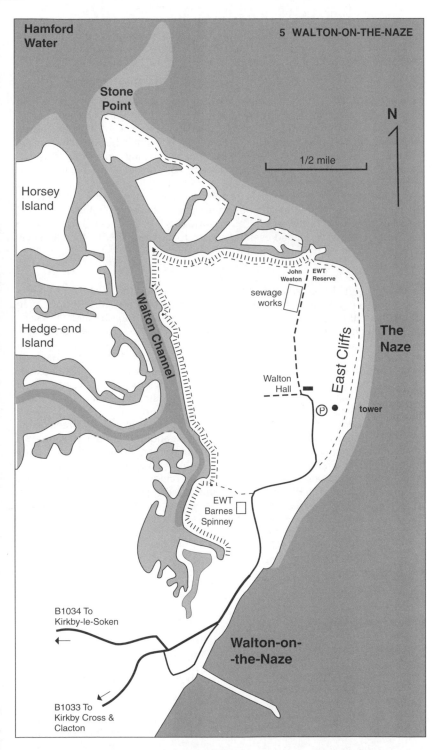

Hamford
Water

5 WALTON-ON-THE-NAZE

Stone
Point

N

1/2 mile

Horsey
Island

Hedge-end
Island

Walton Channel

John
Weston

EWT
Reserve

sewage
works

East Cliffs

The
Naze

Walton
Hall

P

tower

EWT
Barnes
Spinney

B1034 To
Kirkby-le-Soken

Walton-on-
-the-Naze

B1033 To
Kirkby Cross &
Clacton

Habitat

The area is mainly tidal flats and saltings with some rough grassland and pools, while bushes along the cliff path attract migrant passerines. A small area of grassland and thicket behind the seawall is a reserve of the Essex Wildlife Trust.

Access (see map)

On entering Walton, continue to the seafront and proceed north to the Naze, where there is a car park on the cliffs (by the tower). Walk north along the cliff path, checking areas of cover for migrants in season (note that the area east of the track from Walton Hall to the sewage works, to the East Cliffs, is the main birdwatching area at Walton). It is possible (and worthwhile) to continue, crossing various creeks as necessary, as far as Stone Point: note that in recent years the beach has been built up, permitting access to the latter area at all states of the tide. However, the situation may change and you are urged to seek up-to-date local advice, without which you should plan to be back at the seawall at least three hours before high water. On reaching the seawall turn west for c.¾ mile towards Walton Channel. The seawall follows the channel south and eventually back to the town; there is then a ½-mile walk north along the road back to the car park.

Birds

Several thousand Dark-bellied Brent Geese winter in Hamford Water and there is also a good chance of seeing Eider offshore, and Goldeneye and Red-breasted Merganser in the deeper waters off Stone Point or in Walton Channel. Other sea duck, including Long-tailed Duck, Velvet Scoter and Scaup, are occasional. Sanderling and the odd Purple Sandpiper frequent the shore, and the common waders are well represented, with Avocet and Black-tailed Godwit in backwaters. Hen Harrier, Merlin and occasionally Short-eared Owl hunt the saltmarshes. Snow Bunting is also usually present along the shingle beach, with numbers of Twite on the saltmarshes (especially along the strand line), and Rock Pipits favour the saltmarsh gutters.

In spring and autumn a variety of waders appear, including Greenshank, Spotted Redshank and, mostly in autumn, Curlew Sandpiper. Fulmar may be seen offshore in spring and summer, while in autumn passing Gannet and Arctic Skua are a possibility, and Manx Shearwater and Great Skua are sometimes seen in favourable seawatching conditions. The bushes on the clifftops are excellent for passerine migrants, with Black Redstart, Ring Ouzel and Firecrest possible in early spring. In autumn east winds during August to October are especially favourable. Ring Ouzel, Redstart, Whinchat, Garden Warbler and Pied Flycatcher are regular, and scarcer species such as Wryneck and Red-backed Shrike are occasional.

Shelduck, Oystercatcher, Ringed Plover and Little Tern nest along the beach towards Stone Point, but please respect signs restricting access to this area during the nesting period.

6 FINGRINGHOE WICK (Essex)   OS Landranger 168

Lying 5 miles southeast of Colchester, this reserve of the Essex Wildlife Trust (EWT) encompasses a very broad range of habitats in a relatively small area, and is worth visiting throughout the year (although midsummer is quietest).

Habitat

An area of former gravel workings, the resulting undulating hills and hollows have been transformed into a varied mosaic of habitats, including a freshwater

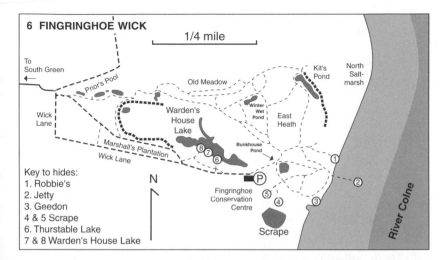

6 FINGRINGHOE WICK

1/4 mile

To South Green ←

Prior's Pool

Wick Lane

Old Meadow

Kit's Pond

North Salt-marsh

Warden's House Lake

Winter Wet Pond

East Heath

Marshall's Plantation

Wick Lane

Bunkhouse Pond

Fingringhoe Conservation Centre

P

N

Scrape

River Colne

Key to hides:
1. Robbie's
2. Jetty
3. Geedon
4 & 5 Scrape
6. Thurstable Lake
7 & 8 Warden's House Lake

lake, mature secondary woodland, planted conifers, scrub, stands of reeds and areas of heath. There is also a specially constructed scrape. Immediately to the east lies the River Colne with areas of saltmarsh and mudbanks along its margins, and to the south the extensive saltings of Geedon Marsh.

Access (see map)

Leave Colchester south on the B1025 towards Mersea, and after c.4½ miles turn east on a minor road towards Fingringhoe. After a further 1½ miles, turn right (east, signed to the reserve) on a minor road towards South Green, reaching the entrance to the reserve after a further 1½ miles. Follow this track for ½ mile to the car park. The Fingringhoe Conservation Centre is also the headquarters of the EWT, and there are two nature trails and eight hides. The reserve is open daily 09.00–19.00 in summer, 09.00–17.00 in winter. For waders on the estuary the period two hours either side of high water is best, but early morning can be problematic due to the east-facing aspect.

Birds

Wintering wildfowl include good numbers (2,000+) of Dark-bellied Brent Geese around the estuary, with Cormorant, Red-breasted Merganser, Goldeneye and occasionally Long-tailed Duck on the river channel. The complex of lakes holds Shoveler, Teal, Gadwall and Pochard and Goldeneye, as well as Water Rail. Little Egret has become increasingly regular, and is most often seen from the hides overlooking the scrape or the saltings. Waders include Grey and Ringed Plovers, Turnstone, Curlew, Black-tailed Godwit, Dunlin and Redshank, and a flock of c.100 Avocets is now regular along the Colne in autumn and winter, viewable from the hides. Winter raptors in the area may include Sparrowhawk, Hen Harrier, Merlin and Short-eared Owl, and Twite may be found on the saltings.

On autumn passage a variety of waders may occur, including Greenshank, Spotted Redshank, Green Sandpiper and Ruff.

Breeders include Little and Great Crested Grebes, Sparrowhawk, Barn Owl, Kingfisher, numbers of Nightingale (up to 30–40 pairs), Reed Warbler, and Common and Lesser Whitethroats.

Information

EWT: Laurie Forsyth, Fingringhoe Wick Nature Reserve, Wick Farm, South

151

Green Road, Fingringhoe, Colchester CO5 7DN. Tel: 01206 729678. E-mail: admin@essexwt.org.uk

7 HANNINGFIELD RESERVOIR (Essex)   OS Landranger 167

Lying 5 miles south of Chelmsford, this large reservoir attracts an excellent selection of waterbirds throughout the year. Around 100 acres along the south shore are a reserve of the Essex Wildlife Trust (EWT).

Habitat
Flooding the valley of the Sandon Brook between West and South Hanningfield, the reservoir was opened in 1957 and covers 870 acres impounded behind the longest dam in Europe. It has a mixture of concrete and natural banks, with some wooded areas. Depending on water levels, variable amounts of mud may be exposed.

Access (see map)
EWT Hanningfield Reservoir Visitor Centre Leave the A12 south on the A130 and, after 2½ miles, turn west on minor roads to West Hanningfield. In the village turn left (south) along Middle Mead, which follows the northern, embanked, perimeter of the reservoir. After 2 miles, at the first junction, turn right, after c.1 mile yards turn right again, and after a further c.¾ mile turn right following the reserve signs to the car park. Alternatively, turn off the B1007 (Billericay–Chelmsford road) on Downham Road and turn left on Hawkswood Road, with the visitor centre just beyond Fremnalls causeway. The reserve and visitor centre is open daily (except non-Bank Holiday Mondays) from 09.00–17.00. The trail to the four hides passes through woodland and thus, as well as waterbirds, a variety of common woodland species can be seen, sometimes including Crossbill.

Fishing Lodge When the reserve centre is closed, there is limited access to the reserve on weekdays only from the Fishing Lodge car park on Giffords Lane (turn opposite the Old Windmill pub).

Fremnalls Causeway This lies at the south end of the reservoir, and is formed by the minor road between Stock and Wickford. From here views can be had north over the reservoir.

Birds
Spring passage can be exciting, with movements of Arctic Tern in late April–May, and parties of Common Scoter occasionally pass through. Other migrants may include a variety of waders, and sometimes Osprey, Black Tern and Little Gull. On autumn passage a greater variety of waders may occur, including Greenshank, Ruff and Little Ringed Plover, and sometimes Little Stint, Curlew and Wood Sandpipers and Spotted Redshank.

In winter there is a sizeable gull roost, and Yellow-legged, Mediterranean, Iceland and Glaucous Gulls can occasionally be found with diligence. Wintering wildfowl include a notable concentration of Ruddy Duck and smaller numbers of Goldeneye, Shoveler and Pintail (the latter two peaking in autumn). Great Northern Diver and Red-necked, Slavonian and Black-necked Grebes are almost annual (and Black-necked Grebe and more rarely Red-necked Grebe may also turn up in summer and autumn).

Breeders include Great Crested and Little Grebes, Gadwall, Common Tern and Yellow Wagtail. Hobby is often seen in summer.

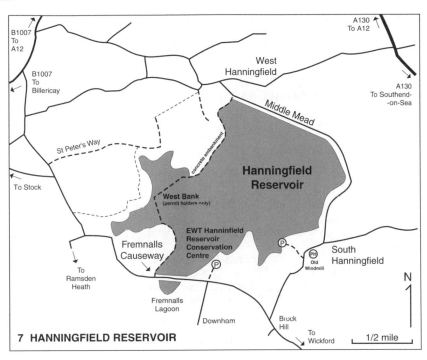

7 HANNINGFIELD RESERVOIR

Information

Chris Scott, Hanningfield Reservoir Visitor Centre, Hawkswood Road, Downham, Billericay, Essex CM11 1WT. Tel: 01268 711001. E-mail: chriss@essexwt.org.uk

8 THAMES SEAWATCHING STATIONS (Essex)   OS Landranger 178

In late summer and autumn strong to gale-force winds from an easterly direction (NE–SE) push seabirds into the Thames estuary, and in such conditions the Essex shore can provide exciting seawatching.

Access

East Tilbury Seawatch from the seawall immediately east of Coalhouse Fort, which is accessed via a minor road south from East Tilbury. There is a public car park nearby. The foreshore here is also attractive to waders.

Canvey seafront This lies on Canvey Island between Labworth Cafe and Canvey Point, with suitable viewpoints at the old lifeguard station near the amusement arcades, and Canvey Point itself, which is also good for waders.

Southend Pier This projects more than 1 mile into the river. The pier opens at 08.00. In Southend itself Gunners Park sometimes holds passerine migrants.

Birds

In the right conditions in autumn Fulmar, Manx Shearwater, Gannet, Arctic, Great and Pomarine Skuas, Little Gull, Kittiwake and good numbers of terns are recorded with some regularity, and Leach's Petrel, Sooty Shearwater, Long-tailed

Skua, Sabine's Gull and Little Auk (late winter only) have been recorded on several occasions. In winter, a mix of divers, grebes and sea ducks may be seen off Southend Pier and Mediterranean Gull is often seen throughout the area.

9 LACKFORD WILDFOWL RESERVE (Suffolk)   OS Landranger 155

This series of gravel pits lies in the Lark Valley between Mildenhall and Bury St Edmunds and attracts a variety of wildfowl throughout the year, as well as passage migrants, and has an excellent list of rarities to its credit.

Habitat
A complex of disused gravel pits, several of which have been specially landscaped to attract wildlife, while others are used for sailing and fishing; the site also includes areas of scrub, carr and meadow. To the north lies the King's Forest, a large area of conifer plantations (with Nightjar, Woodlark and Crossbill).

Access (see map)
The reserve lies just north of the A1101 between Bury St Edmunds and Mildenhall, with the entrance track signed 5 miles northwest of Bury, c.1 mile west of the minor road to West Stow. From the car park a footpath leads to eight hides.

Birds
Wintering wildfowl include Pochard, Goldeneye and Ruddy Duck, as well as significant numbers of Goosander, Gadwall and Shoveler; Red-crested Pochard and sea ducks are recorded occasionally. Other waterbirds include Cormorant, Great Crested and Little Grebes and occasionally divers or the rarer grebes. Kingfisher

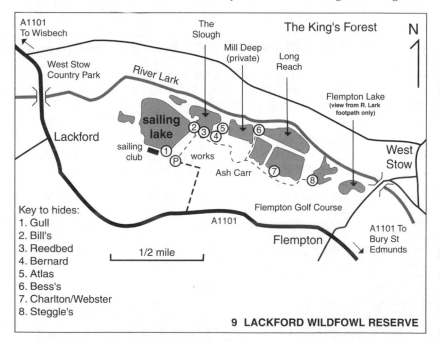

is frequent (especially from the hides overlooking The Slough). The large winter gull roost on the Sailing Lake (peaking at 10,000+ birds) regularly holds Mediterranean and Yellow legged Gulls, and the scarcer white-winged gulls are possible.

On passage Osprey is recorded annually, and a variety of waders may be seen, with Little and Temminck's Stints, Wood and Curlew Sandpipers, Black-tailed and Bar-tailed Godwits and Grey Plover joining more regular migrants. Terns may include Arctic and Black.

Breeders include Shelduck, Pochard, Water Rail, Redshank, Little Ringed Plover, Nightingale and Reed and Sedge Warblers, while Hobby is a regular visitor, hunting dragonflies and hirundines, and Sparrowhawk and, much more rarely, Goshawk visit throughout the year. Crossbill and Siskin may fly over en route to and from nearby plantations.

Information

Suffolk Wildlife Trust, Brooke House, The Green, Ashbocking, Ipswich, Suffolk IP6 9JY. Tel: 01473 890089. E-mail: info@suffolkwildlife.cix.co.uk

Joe Davis, Lackford Lakes Centre, Lackford, Bury St Edmunds, Suffolk. Tel: 01284 728541.

10 ALTON WATER (Suffolk)   OS Landranger 169

Just 5 miles south of Ipswich and close to the Stour estuary, Alton Water is an important area for waterbirds, best in winter or during passage periods.

Habitat

The reservoir was opened in 1987, has largely natural edges and its marshy fringes are attractive to waders. The surrounding area is farmed, with some woodland.

Access (see map)

Alton Water: north arm Leave the A14 dual carriageway immediately south of Ipswich south on the A137 towards Manningtree. After c.2 miles the road runs alongside the north tip of the reservoir. This is probably the best area and is easily viewed from the road.

Alton Water: Tattingstone Continuing south on the A137, after c.1 mile turn left (east) on a minor road to Tattingstone. In the village, footpaths lead to the reservoir banks (immediately north of Tattingstone Place), a good area for ducks and waders.

Alton Water: causeway Turning left (north) in Tattingstone, opposite the church, the road reaches a causeway across the north arm of the reservoir, affording further views, before continuing north to Tattingstone White Horse. It is possible to walk east or west from the causeway, on both the north and south banks (avoiding the marked conservation area on the northwest bank).

Alton Water: central section, south shore From Tattingstone take the minor road south towards Stutton, and after c.½ mile the road runs alongside the central section of the reservoir. At Tattingstone Wonder (a cottage that resembles a church), there is a car park and it is possible to walk east along the reservoir banks to a hide.

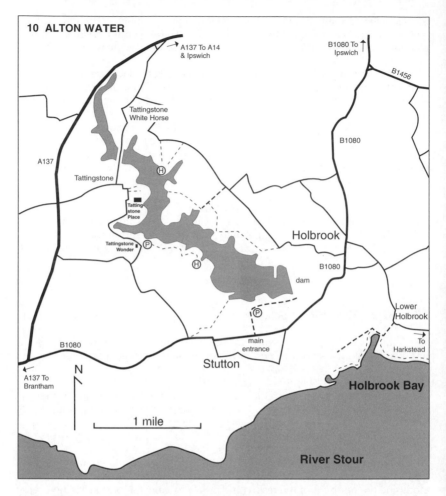

10 ALTON WATER

Alton Water: central section, north shore Turn off the A137 (c.1¼ miles south of the A14) on minor roads south to Tattingstone White Horse (also accessible from Tattingstone). Just north of the village take the minor road southeast towards Holbrook. The road makes two right-angle bends and, after c.300 yards and 600 yards, footpaths lead to the shore and a hide. For further access, after a further c.⅔ mile, turn right (southwest) on a track to the reservoir shore.

Alton Water: dam end Turn north off the B1080 between Stutton and Holbrook at the official Anglia Water gate and continue towards the dam to the car park with toilets and a cafe. The deeper water near the dam is usually best for any wintering divers.

Holbrook Bay On the north shore of the Stour estuary, southeast of Alton Water. Leave the B1080 at Holbrook on a minor road southeast to Harkstead. After 1 mile a track to the right (south) at the beginning of the hamlet of Lower Holbrook leads to the innermost part of the Bay. Walk in either direction along the seawall. In winter Dark-bellied Brent Goose regularly congregates in the Bay and there is a large wader roost at high tide.

Birds

The commoner ducks, such as Wigeon and Gadwall, reach several hundred in winter, with smaller numbers of Gadwall, Shoveler and Goldeneye. Scaup, Long-tailed Duck, Smew and Goosander are regular, as are divers and the rarer grebes. Feral Greylag and Canada Geese are often present in surrounding fields and Jack Snipe is sometimes found in the lakeside vegetation.

Passage brings a sprinkling of waders and terns of the more usual inland species, and Osprey is sometimes recorded. In summer Alton Water is an important breeding site for Great Crested Grebe (c.65 pairs).

Information

Anglian Water Warden. Tel: 01473 327398.

11 WOLVES WOOD (Suffolk)   OS Landranger 156

This small wood holds good numbers of Nightingale as well as many of the commoner woodland birds.

Habitat

Mixed broadleaf woodland with an area of coppiced scrub, surrounded by farmland.

Access

The reserve lies just north of the A1071 between Ipswich and Hadleigh, 2 miles east of Hadleigh, and is signed from the road. Open at all times, several trails lead from the car park and there is a small information centre.

Birds

Breeders include Woodcock, Lesser Spotted Woodpecker, Nightingale, a variety of warblers, six species of tit and Hawfinch.

Information

Russell Leavett, RSPB Warden, 24 Orchard Close, Great Oakley, Harwich CO12 5AX. Tel: 01255 886043.

12 LANDGUARD POINT (Suffolk)   OS Landranger 169

This site has an outstanding reputation for attracting interesting migrants in spring and autumn, including many major rarities. A Bird Observatory was established here in 1983, sited in a man-made shingle bank, which formerly held gun batteries, and part of the point comprises a LNR, managed by the Suffolk Wildlife Trust.

Habitat

Landguard Point is a shingle spit lying immediately south of Felixstowe at the mouth of the River Orwell. Behind the shingle beach lies Landguard Common, an area of compacted sand and gravel covered by very short, rabbit-cropped turf, with some stands of scrub that are attractive to migrants. Landguard was used by the military for nearly 200 years and many old fortifications remain. All around is the dockland sprawl of Felixstowe and Harwich.

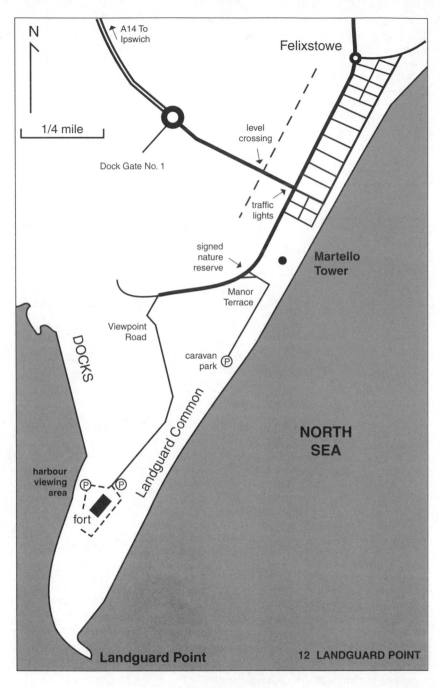

N

A14 To
Ipswich

Felixstowe

1/4 mile

Dock Gate No. 1

level
crossing

traffic
lights

signed
nature
reserve

Martello
Tower

Manor
Terrace

DOCKS

Viewpoint
Road

caravan
park (P)

Landguard Common

NORTH
SEA

harbour
viewing
area

(P) (P)

fort

Landguard Point

12 LANDGUARD POINT

Access (see map)

Follow the A14 towards Felixstowe Docks and, at the roundabout where the dual carriageway ends, continue straight ahead into Felixstowe. Pass over the level crossing and turn right at the first set of traffic lights. The first turning on the left,

Manor Terrace (signed Landguard), leads to a car park at the north end of Landguard Common. The second left turn (Viewpoint Road) leads to a car park at the south end of the Common, close to Landguard Fort, where an old gun emplacement houses Landguard Bird Observatory (no accommodation). Interesting migrants can be found anywhere on the Common, to which there is free access at all times. The fenced-off Bird Observatory ringing area holds the best and most extensive areas of cover, and though it is not open to the public, most of the birds can be seen from the footpath outside the fence—the west side of the compound can be accessed by walking around the large concrete building.

Birds
The Point is most active in spring and autumn when hundreds of the commoner thrushes, warblers and finches pass through, with plenty of Wheatear on the short turf and sometimes falls of night migrants or arrivals of Redwing, Fieldfare and Starling. Up to 10,000 birds are ringed annually at the Observatory. Some of the more regularly occurring scarce migrants include Wryneck, Bluethroat, Icterine and Barred Warblers, Firecrest, Red-breasted Flycatcher and Ortolan Bunting. Seawatching off Landguard is rarely notable but a few shearwaters and skuas are recorded each autumn, sometimes including Long-tailed Skua.

In summer, Ringed Plover and Little Tern breed on the shingle and Black Redstart nests around the docks and fort area, with Wheatear on the Common.

Information
Suffolk Wildlife Trust, Brooke House, The Green, Ashbocking, Ipswich, Suffolk IP6 9JY. Tel: 01473 890089. E-mail: info@suffolkwildlife.cix.co.uk
Malte Iden, Landguard Bird Observatory, View Point Road, Felixstowe, Suffolk IP11 8TW. Tel: 01394 673782.

13 TRIMLEY MARSHES (Suffolk)   OS Landranger 169

Immediately adjacent to Felixstowe Docks, this Suffolk Wildlife Trust reserve was created in 1989 to part-compensate for the loss of intertidal mudflats caused by an extension to the port. A variety of wetland habitats, re-created from arable farmland, attract a broad range of species, with year-round interest.

Habitat
The reserve comprises a complex of wet grazing meadows, a winter and a summer flood, a reedbed and two permanent freshwater lagoons, the larger acting as a reservoir for the reserve's water supplies, the smaller containing several shingle-covered islands that attract breeding waders and terns. Other habitats include a small area of saltmarsh along the estuary shore.

Access (see map)
Leave the A14 dual carriageway immediately west of Felixstowe at the exit for Trimley St Martin and Trimley St Mary. Proceed into Trimley St Mary, turn south over the railway, and park at the top of Cordy's Lane/end of Station Road. Walk down the lane and turn right past the warehouses; after 2 miles you reach the riverbank. There are five hides, open at all times. The first (Woodgate) overlooks a wet meadow, good for wildfowl and Snipe in winter. Continuing, the visitor centre and Hipkin hide overlook the large freshwater lagoon, favoured by diving ducks, the Longhurst hide looks over the permanent lagoon with islands for nesting waders and terns, while the Cobb hide affords views of the summer flood, which is a good area for passage waders,

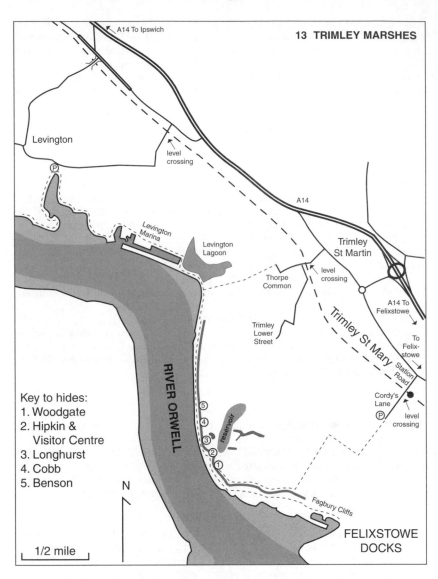

and the Benson hide the winter floods, good for wildfowl. The reserve is open all year, and the visitor centre at weekends, 10.00–16.00.

Access is also possible from Levington, walking east and south along the public footpath on the banks of the Orwell, past Levington Marina (check for interesting gulls) and Trimley Lake, and then following the seawall for c.2 miles to the reserve.

Birds

Wintering wildfowl include Dark-bellied Brent Goose, Wigeon, Teal, Gadwall, Shoveler, Pintail, Pochard and Goldeneye. Waders include Snipe and Redshank, with Grey Plover, Curlew, godwits, Knot and Dunlin on the Orwell estuary. Occasionally, Snow Bunting may be found on the shingle bund bordering the docks.

On passage a variety of waders has been recorded, unsurprisingly including some of the more uncommon species such as Spotted Redshank, Wood and Curlew Sandpipers, and Little and Temminck's Stints. Little Egret is regular, and several rarities have occurred.

Breeding birds include Avocet, Oystercatcher, Ringed Plover and Little and Common Terns on the specially constructed shingle islands, as well as Tufted Duck, Gadwall, Shoveler, Shelduck, Lapwing, Redshank and Sand Martin, with Yellow Wagtail and Corn Bunting in nearby fields.

Information

Suffolk Wildlife Trust, Brooke House, The Green, Ashbocking, Ipswich, Suffolk IP6 9JY. Tel: 01473 890089. E-mail: info@suffolkwildlife.cix.co.uk

Mick Wright, Warden, 15 Avondale Road, Ipswich 1P3 9JT. Tel: 01473 710032. E-mail: mickwright@btinternet.com

14 HAVERGATE ISLAND AND BOYTON MARSHES (Suffolk)

OS Landranger 169

Flooded as part of wartime defence measures, Havergate Island was the jump-off point for the Avocet's recolonisation of Britain in 1947, and the colony now numbers up to 120 pairs, with several other interesting breeding species. On passage and in winter a variety of waders and wildfowl can be found.

Habitat

Havergate Island is a low embanked island in the River Ore, with some saline lagoons, complete with islands. It is bounded by shingle beaches and surrounded by saltmarsh. Boyton Marshes lie west of the River Ore, in the angle formed by its confluence with the River Butley. They comprise grazing marshes divided by a network of ditches and bordered by extensive areas of saltmarsh along the Butley.

Access

Havergate Island RSPB reserve Boat trips run from Orford Quay (on the B1084) to Havergate Island April–August on the first and third Sunday of the month, and also every Thursday, departing at 10.00 and 11.30. In winter, September–March, boats run on the first Saturday of each month. Entrance is only by advance permit, available by post from the warden; there is a charge for both members and non-members of the RSPB. Facilities on the island include toilets and eight hides.

Boyton Marshes RSPB reserve These overlook Havergate Island and share a similar range of wildfowl, waders and raptors. Leave the A1152 just north of Woodbridge on the B1083 southeast towards Bawdsey. After ⅔ mile turn left (east) on a minor road to Hollesley and Boyton. After c.4 miles turn left to Boyton and continue over the crossroads to the village. Just past the pub turn right towards Boyton Hall Farm and follow the footpath to the River Ore, where it meets the coastal path (which follows the riverbank in both directions). Turn left (northeast) and follow the riverbank to the Butley River as far as the jetty; it is possible to return to Butley along the footpath towards Dock Farm, a circuit of c.3 miles.

Birds

Breeding birds on Havergate Island include Shelduck, Oystercatcher, Ringed Plover, Redshank, Common and usually Sandwich Terns, a handful of Arctic

Terns, Black-headed Gull and Short-eared Owl, as well as Avocet. Little Tern breeds on the shingle spit of Orford Ness, which separates the River Ore from the sea, and often visit Havergate. Boyton Marshes additionally support Reed and Sedge Warblers, and sometimes Grasshopper Warbler and Nightingale.

Many waders are present on passage, such as Black-tailed Godwit, Ruff and Greenshank in spring, with Turnstone, Little Stint and Curlew Sandpiper possible in autumn. Winter wildfowl include Wigeon, Teal, Pintail, Shoveler, Gadwall and occasionally Bewick's Swan, with Goldeneye and Red-breasted Merganser on the river channel. Grey Plover, Knot, Dunlin, Redshank, Bar-tailed Godwit and Curlew winter, as well as numbers of Avocet. Raptors may include Hen or Marsh Harriers and Short-eared Owl, and sometimes Rough-legged Buzzard.

Information
John Partridge, RSPB Site Manager, 30 Mundays Lane, Orford, Woodbridge IP12 2LX. Tel: 01394 450732.

15 ALDE ESTUARY, NORTH WARREN AND SIZEWELL (Suffolk)
OS Landranger 156

This small estuary on the Suffolk coast attracts nationally important numbers of wintering Black-tailed Godwit and Avocet, and to the north and south lie areas of coastal grazing marshes, some of which flood in winter, attracting wildfowl, waders and raptors. Nearby, the RSPB's North Warren has a range of heathland breeding species, best seen in early summer.

Habitat
Intertidal mudflats and saltings, with extensive areas of coastal grazing marsh on the north side of the river at Hazelwood Marshes; these, and the mudflats along the south shore, are reserves of the Suffolk Wildlife Trust (SWT). To the north, the shingle beach at Thorpeness holds an important flora and occasionally attracts Shore Lark, and just inland the RSPB's North Warren Reserve comprises an area of the Suffolk 'Sandlings', with acid grassy heath on sandy soils and areas of gorse and birch, as well as areas of 'fresh' marsh. This coast faces east and regularly attracts scarce migrants wherever there is cover, while a little to the north the warm-water outflow at Sizewell power station acts as a magnet for passing gulls and terns.

Access (see map)
Alde mudflats Leave the A12 at Wickham Market east on the B1078, and in Tunstall turn north on the B1069, turning right after 1 mile on a minor road to Iken, parking after a further 1 mile at Iken cliff car park. From here walk east along the shore of the Alde for c.½ mile to view the mudflats along the south shore of the estuary (a good area for Avocet; it is possible to continue further, to just north of the church). An incoming tide is best.

Hazelwood Marshes Leave the A12 on the A1094 east towards Aldeburgh. Just before Aldeburgh golf club, turn north into the SWT car park. From here follow the track past a reedbed, over an iron bridge and left over a stile. The right-hand fork leads to the Eric Hosking hide on the seawall, giving views south over the estuary. The left fork leads to grazing marshes, where a hide is planned. The reserve is open dawn to dusk.

Aldeburgh Marshes Lying immediately southwest of Aldeburgh, these may

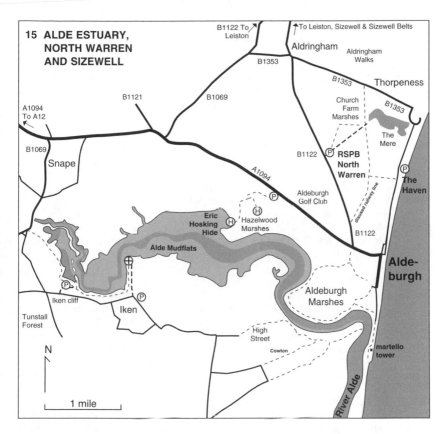

15 ALDE ESTUARY, NORTH WARREN AND SIZEWELL

attract wintering raptors (sometimes including Rough-legged Buzzard). Follow the A1094 to its end at Fort Green, and then take the track south to Slaughden Quay, from where a public footpath follows the seawall to circumnavigate the marshes.

The Haven, Thorpeness This SWT reserve comprises the shingle beach and adjacent areas of scrub and marsh inland of the coast road. From Aldeburgh take the minor road north towards Thorpeness, parking carefully after 1⅓ miles by the road to explore the beach.

RSPB Church Farm Marshes Under the remit of North Warren reserve, this area of coastal grazing marshes is prone to flood in winter, with some small reedbeds, the reserve attracts a range of wildfowl and waders in winter and on passage. As wildfowl, especially geese and swans, are liable to be mobile, the first step is a circuit of the Aldeburgh–Thorpeness–Aldringham triangle, via the coast roads, the B1353 and B1122. The area can be accessed on foot via the footpath which runs E–W midway between Thorpeness and Aldeburgh.

RSPB North Warren A typical range of heathland birds is present. Leave Aldeburgh northwest on the B1122 towards Leiston and, after c.1 mile, turn right at the RSPB sign on the track between the houses to the reserve car park. The reserve is crossed by several public footpaths and there is a nature trail. Access at all times.

RSPB Aldringham Walks Also under the remit of North Warren, this is another area of 'Sandlings' heath, lying north of the B1353 Aldringham– Thorpeness road. Access is via a maze of public footpaths that crisscross the area.

Sizewell Belts This extensive (600-acre) area is managed as a reserve by the SWT on behalf of British Energy. The mosaic of habitats includes heath, grazing marsh, fen and woodland. Leave Leiston north on the B1122 and, after c.¾ mile turn right (east) on a minor road (Lover's Lane), parking on the left after ½ mile where the road bends south. From here a network of nature trails radiate through the area.

Sizewell power stations The warm-water outflow offshore regularly attracts gulls and terns. A minor road east from Leiston leads directly to the power stations. From the seafront car park walk a short way north along the beach. Alternatively, you can walk c.2 miles south along the beach from the sluice at Minsmere; this is most profitable in spring and autumn when passerine migrants may be present in the coastal bushes. Scarcer species occasionally include Wryneck, Barred Warbler and Red-backed Shrike. The power stations hold breeding Black Redstart, which should be looked for in spring or summer around the perimeter fences. And, notably, nearly 100 pairs of Kittiwake breed on the offshore rigs.

Birds
Wintering wildfowl include numbers of Wigeon, Pintail, Shoveler and Teal, and sometimes Bewick's Swan, White-fronted and occasionally Tundra Bean Geese (especially on the grazing marshes around North Warren). Waders include Oystercatcher, Grey Plover, Turnstone, Dunlin and Curlew, as well as Avocet (e.g. 884 on the Alde in December 1977) and up to 800 Black-tailed Godwits also winter on the Alde. Numbers of Ruff usually overwinter at Church Farm Marshes. Raptors may include Hen Harrier and Sparrowhawk, and sometimes a Rough-legged Buzzard may take up residence for a season.

Breeders include Grey Heron, Shelduck, Gadwall, Teal, Shoveler, Marsh Harrier, Oystercatcher, Avocet, Lapwing, Snipe, Redshank and Barn Owl. At North Warren there are also Kingfisher, Woodlark (favouring heathland areas, with 18 territories in 1997), Yellow Wagtail, Nightingale (in woodland scrub), Grasshopper, Reed and Sedge Warblers, and Whitethroat, while Black Redstart breeds at Sizewell.

On passage Garganey and Ruff are often present in spring at Church Farm Marshes, making prolonged stays, and Spotted Redshank, Greenshank and Wood Sandpiper are fairly regular at both seasons. A variety of passerines may occur along the coast, especially in east or southeast winds.

Information
RSPB North Warren/Church Farm Marshes Warden, Rob Macklin, Racewalk, Priory Road, Snape, Suffolk IP17 1SD. Tel: 01728 688481. E-mail: rob.macklin@tesco.net
Rodney West, Hazelwood Marshes Warden, Flint Cottage, Stone Common, Blaxhall, Woodbridge, Suffolk. Tel: 01728 689171. E-mail:rodwest@ndirect.co.uk
Suffolk Wildlife Trust, Brooke House, The Green, Ashbocking, Ipswich, Suffolk IP6 9JY. Tel: 01473 890089. E-mail: info@suffolkwildlife.cix.co.uk

16 MINSMERE (Suffolk)   OS Landranger 156

Minsmere is one of Britain's finest reserves. Situated on the Suffolk coast between Southwold and Aldeburgh, it is owned by the RSPB. The diversity of habitats within its 2,300 acres ensures a wide variety of birds at all seasons,

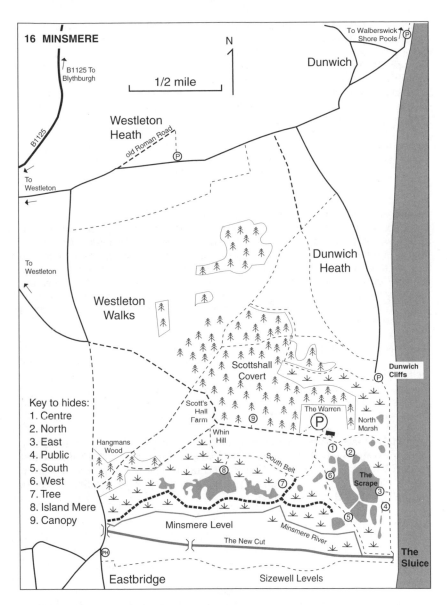

16 MINSMERE

B1125 To Blythburgh

1/2 mile

N

To Walberswick
Shore Pools

Dunwich

To Westleton

B1125

Westleton Heath

old Roman Road

To Westleton

Dunwich Heath

Westleton Walks

Scottshall Covert

Dunwich Cliffs

Key to hides:
1. Centre
2. North
3. East
4. Public
5. South
6. West
7. Tree
8. Island Mere
9. Canopy

Scott's Hall Farm

The Warren

North Marsh

Hangmans Wood

Whin Hill

South Belt

The Scrape

Minsmere Level

Minsmere River

The New Cut

Eastbridge

Sizewell Levels

The Sluice

although it is perhaps best in May when over 100 species can be seen in a day. Several rare breeding birds occur and many interesting migrants are possible in spring and autumn.

Habitat

Originally rough coastal grazing, Minsmere was flooded in the Second World War as part of the local coastal defences. The resultant habitat proved attractive to Avocet, and this initiated its career as a reserve. There are now extensive areas of freshwater marshes, with a large reedbed and several open meres. Management has produced Minsmere's most famous habitat, The Scrape, an area of shallow, brackish water and mud, with scattered small islands. Water levels and salinity are controlled by sluices to maintain optimum conditions at any given season, but the Scrape is best April–September (though successional changes have resulted in it becoming rather less attractive in recent years). The reserve is bordered to seaward by a small area of dunes, and although the beach is rather disturbed, the bushes by the main sluice can be attractive to migrant passerines. Over 600 acres of the reserve comprise mixed woodland; the most accessible area is the South Belt, a narrow strip bordering the reedbeds. There is also extensive heathland, including a large area of farmland bought with the specific purpose of reverting it to heath. To the north of the reserve, Dunwich and Westleton Heaths hold a similar range of heathland species. Finally, to the south of the reserve, Minsmere Level is an area of rough grazing drained by the New Cut.

Access (see map)

Minsmere RSPB reserve Two routes are available: via Eastbridge (cars only); from Leiston take the B1122 north and turn right to Eastbridge, thereafter cross the New Cut, from where the reserve is signed; and via Westleton; at the north end of Westleton leave the B1125 on a minor road to Dunwich, after ½ mile turn right and follow signs to the reserve. Both routes lead to the large car park and Visitor Centre. The reserve is open daily except Tuesday (and Christmas and Boxing Days), 09.00–21.00 or dusk when earlier, and the visitor centre is open 09.00–17.00 (to 16.00 in winter in November–January). There are two nature trails, c.2 miles long, accessing nine hides.

The beach and public hide From Westleton take a minor road east towards Dunwich. After 1¼ miles turn right, signed Dunwich Heath and Minsmere. Park in the NT Dunwich Cliffs car park at the end of the road, overlooking the reserve. A footpath leads down the cliffs to the beach. Continue south towards the sluice bushes and a track to the right goes to the visitor centre. Further along the beach there is a public hide on the seawall giving excellent views over the Scrape.

Dunwich Heath Holds a range of heathland species, most notably including Dartford Warbler which, following a long absence, returned to the Suffolk coast in 1997 when three pairs were present (and up to nine in 1998). Access is from the NT car park at Dunwich Cliffs, and a walk west from here should, in season, produce singing Dartford Warbler.

Westleton Heath This NNR is owned by EN and covers c.100 acres straddling the Westleton–Dunwich road. It holds a range of heathland birds. Only the area north of the road, as far as the old Roman Road, is open to the public (see map), with a car park at the southeast corner; otherwise access is limited to public footpaths.

Birds

Around 100 species of birds breed at Minsmere annually. The Scrape holds c.20 breeding species, many of which are present in large numbers. Common Tern nests on the islands, alongside Black-headed Gull, and Sandwich Tern is also regularly present but no longer breeds. The best-known inhabitant of the Scrape, however, is Avocet, of which c.100 pairs breed annually and are present mid-March to September. Several of Minsmere's other specialities occur in the reeds. A few pairs of Bitterns breed (just three booming males in 1997) but are difficult to see; midsummer is the best time for a sighting, when they are feeding young and can be seen flying to and from the best feeding areas. On the other hand, Marsh Harrier is hard to miss in summer and is best seen from the Island Mere hide (12 nesting females in 1996 is the record). Hobby also now breeds and up to 12 may be seen hunting over the reeds from West or Island Mere hides. Bearded Tit is common and in autumn may number over 1,000 birds. Water Rail also breeds but this is another shy species, which is heard more than seen. Sedge and Reed Warblers are both common. Savi's Warbler has bred on a number of occasions (but has become increasingly erratic) and the song of the Grasshopper Warbler is a familiar sound of the drier edges of the reedbeds. A few Cetti's Warbler are resident, the area near Island Mere hide being favoured. Small numbers of Grey Herons nest in the reeds (despite there being no shortage of trees) and Kingfisher is present throughout the year around the meres. Little Tern nests on the beach (where an area is cordoned-off in summer to protect them). The woodlands hold all three woodpeckers, Nightingale (an astonishing 40–60 pairs) and Redstart. Common birds of the heaths are Tree Pipit, Stonechat and Yellowhammer, and after an absence Woodlark has returned as a breeding species (13 pairs in 1998). At dusk look for Woodcock and Nightjar, both of which are regularly seen in small numbers.

A wide variety of migrants occurs in spring and autumn. Large numbers of waders visit the Scrape, the peak periods being May and July–August. Species regularly present include Knot, Little Stint, Curlew Sandpiper, Ruff, Black-tailed and Bar-tailed Godwits, Whimbrel, Spotted Redshank, Greenshank, and Green, Wood and Common Sandpipers. Temminck's Stint is recorded annually, usually in spring, and rarities can appear at any time. Over 20 species of wader are regularly present in autumn. Spoonbill is a speciality of Minsmere and individuals may stay many weeks. Purple Heron is less frequent but is one of Minsmere's most regular rarities. A few Little Gulls often remain through the summer and there may be large post-breeding concentrations of this species in July, but Black Tern is more frequent in autumn. Falls of migrant passerines occur and it is worth checking any patch of cover on the coast.

In winter, the Scrape is quieter. A few waders remain but wildfowl are more in evidence, with significant numbers of the commoner species. Goosander and Goldeneye are regular on Island Mere. Offshore, small parties of Common Scoter and Eider are not unusual and large numbers of Red-throated Diver are present (e.g. 1,200 in January 1999). Small numbers of Bewick's Swan and wild geese sometimes graze the meadows of Sizewell Levels. Greylag and White-fronted Geese are most likely but Bean and Barnacle Geese have also occurred. Marsh Harrier over-winters and is joined by Hen Harrier; both species roost in the reedbeds. Up to 20 Water Pipits winter and, infrequently, Twite is found on drier parts of the Scrape. Snow Bunting may occur on the beach and Siskin is partial to the alders of the South Belt. Scarcer and irregular winter visitors include Buzzard and Rough-legged Buzzard, Jack Snipe, Great Grey Shrike and Shore Lark.

Information

Geoff Welch, RSPB Manager, Minsmere Reserve, Westleton, Saxmundham, Suffolk IP17 3BY. Tel: 01728 648281. Internet: www.rspb.org.uk

EN, Suffolk Team: Regent House, 110 Northgate Street, Bury St Edmunds, Suffolk IP33 1HP. Tel: 01284 762218. E-mail: suffolk@english-nature.org.uk

17 WALBERSWICK AND BLYTH ESTUARY (Suffolk) OS Landranger 156

Walberswick NNR covers 1,600 acres on the coast south of Southwold. It includes Westwood Marshes, which extend inland for c.2½ miles, and the mudflats and saltings on the south side of the Blyth estuary. The variety of habitats guarantees an impressive list of breeding species and the coastal location ensures a variety of migrants. However, Walberswick is probably best in winter, particularly for raptors.

Habitat

The coast south of Walberswick village is bordered by shingle banks and a series of brackish pools. Further inland Westwood Marshes (at 450 acres) form the largest single block of freshwater reeds in Britain. The marshes were reclaimed to form grazing meadows in the 18th century but, like Minsmere to the south, were flooded in the Second World War for defence purposes, and reverted to marshland. Now, invading scrub of sallow, alder and birch is controlled to protect the reedbeds while the reeds themselves must be checked to prevent their encroaching the open pools. The higher ground surrounding the marshes is dominated by heath and areas of woodland, mainly oak, birch and Scots pine. north of the marshes lie one of the best-preserved remnants of the Suffolk 'Sandlings', and to the southwest the shady expanse of Dunwich Forest. The River Blyth forms the north boundary of the reserve, and due to breaches in the riverbank in 1921, 1926 and 1943 the river now broadens, 2 miles inland, into a large tidal estuary, important for wildfowl and waders.

Access (see map)

Access to the NNR is restricted to public rights of way, of which there are over 20 miles.

Walberswick Shore Pools and Dingle Marshes Enter Walberswick village on the B1387. Near the far end of the village turn right at the sharp bend to the beach car park. From here walk south along the beach, looking for birds on the sea as well as inland on Corporation Marshes. The shore pools are reached after c.1½ miles and have held a resident Little Egret in recent years, as well as being good for passage waders. Alternatively, park at Dunwich Beach car park and walk north. The 636 acres of Dingle Marshes were recently purchased by the RSPB and Suffolk Wildlife Trust (SWT).

Westwood Marshes Walking south along the beach as above, there are two banks close together on the right after c.1¼ miles. Take the second one to the derelict wind pump; this trail offers good views over the reeds and lagoons, and the bushy slopes of Dingle Hill on the left can produce migrant passerines. Bearing right at the wind pump eventually brings you back to the car park. There are other tracks across the marshes for the energetic but it is essential to keep to the paths.

Tinker's Marshes In Walberswick village take the track to the Bailey Bridge over the River Blyth. Do not cross the bridge, rather walk west along the south bank of the river to view the fresh grazing marshes.

Southwold Town Marshes Proceed as above, but cross the Bailey Bridge and walk southeast along the north bank of the river, for views north over the marsh. The area is also accessible from Southwold by following the minor road south along the coast and then inland, along the north bank of the river, to the Harbour Inn. This route gives views over the marshes, as does the footpath running northeast from the inn to Southwold.

Southwold This is the best site for seawatching on the Suffolk coast. Watch from the seafront shelter, c.200 yards south of the pier.

Southwold Boating Lake May hold odd sea ducks or grebes, especially after bad weather.

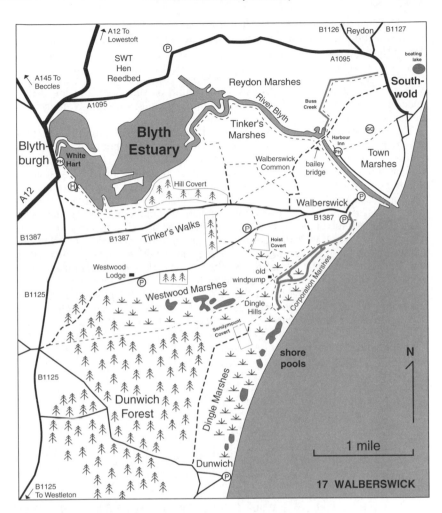

Westwood Lodge From Walberswick village take the B1387 west. Shortly before leaving the village fork left on a minor road and follow it for 2 miles to Westwood Lodge. Park nearby. From here there is a magnificent view over the marshes. This is the best place to see raptors in winter, and late afternoon is the best time to look.

Blyth Estuary The A12 crosses the west end of the Blyth estuary just north of Blythburgh. There is a lay-by on the west side of the road and the estuary can be viewed from the embankment opposite. In Blythburgh, the White Hart pub lies at the junction of the A12 and B1125. A footpath from here leads along the south edge of the estuary to a public hide (and continues for c.1 mile to join the B1387). The estuary is best viewed on a rising tide (at low tide the waders may be distant but at high tide they will have departed).

SWT Hen Reedbed (Norman Gwatkin reserve) This area of wet woodland and marsh lies north of the Blyth estuary, and following recent enlargement of the reserve, substantial reedbed creation is taking place. Turn east off the A12 on the A1095 towards Southwold. After c.1 mile the A1095 passes through the reedbeds and the car park is on the left as they end. Breeding species include Marsh Harrier.

Birds

Walberswick attracts many of the species found at Minsmere and the list of species below is far from exhaustive. The main differences are that Walberswick lacks the Scrape and is considerably less watched.

The reedbeds hold breeding Marsh Harrier, Water Rail and Bearded Tit, and two pairs of Bitterns bred in 1999. Avocet breeds around the shore pools and Snipe and Redshank on the grazing marshes. A few pairs of Common Terns breed, and Garganey occasionally does so. Barn Owl is resident, with Marsh Tit and smaller numbers of Willow Tit in the wetter woodlands. Reed and Sedge Warblers are common, and Nightingale and Grasshopper Warbler are not uncommon in summer. Areas of heath hold breeding Nightjar, Woodlark and Stonechat, and Dunwich Forest has Siskin and Crossbill. Hobby regularly visits in summer.

Waders are much in evidence in spring and autumn, with the greatest concentration on the Blyth estuary. Species may include Grey Plover, Black-tailed and Bar-tailed Godwits, Whimbrel, Spotted Redshank and Greenshank. Other migrants can include Osprey, Black Tern and Little Gull. For several years a Little Egret has been resident in the Shore Pools. Migrant passerines can be interesting, especially in autumn, when falls of commoner species, such as Pied Flycatcher, Redstart, and Willow and Garden Warblers can occur. Some of the more interesting scarce migrants, such as Wryneck, Icterine and Barred Warblers and Red-backed Shrike, may occur when there is no other obvious indication of migration. In recent years seawatching at Southwold has produced regular records of Long-tailed Skua in August–September, and Manx and Sooty Shearwaters, Sabine's Gull and Roseate Tern are annual.

In winter, Hen Harrier and Sparrowhawk are regularly seen especially from Westwood Lodge, and Goshawk is also sometimes present. A handful of Marsh Harrier also usually overwinter and Rough-legged Buzzard, Peregrine and Merlin are not infrequent in some years, while Buzzard is possible at any time of year. Great Grey Shrike is now rare, but an individual may return to establish a winter territory for several years in the manner that made this a good spot for the species in the 1970s. At dusk Barn Owl may be seen around Westwood Lodge, while wintering Short-eared Owl prefer the shore area. The reeds and marshy pools hold wintering Water Rail and Bittern. The mudflats of the Blyth estuary hold the usual common waders, as well as large numbers of Avocet, and there are often Black-tailed Godwit and a few wintering Spotted Redshank. Red-throated Diver and small flocks of Common Scoter are regular offshore, sometimes with a few Velvet Scoter. Twite and Snow Bunting usually winter and should be looked for on the beach or in drier areas around Corporation Marshes. Shore Lark is occasionally seen.

Information

EN, Suffolk Team: Regent House, 110 Northgate Street, Bury St Edmunds, Suffolk IP33 1HP. Tel: 01284 762218. E-mail: suffolk@english-nature.org.uk

RSPB East Anglian Office: Stalham House, Thorpe Road, Norwich, NR1 1UD. Tel: 01603 660066.

SWT: Brooke House, The Green, Ashbocking, Ipswich, Suffolk IP6 9JY. Tel: 01473 890089. E-mail: info@suffolkwildlife.cix.co.uk

18 BENACRE AND COVEHITHE (Suffolk)   OS Landranger 156

Benacre Broad is an interesting wetland on the coast between Lowestoft and Southwold and is part of a NNR, which extends from Kessingland Sluice south to the Broad, and including Covehithe and Easton Broads. Although less extensive than Minsmere or Walberswick the area offers good birding, particularly in autumn and winter.

Habitat

Benacre Broad a natural lake and although once 'fresh', more regular flooding by the sea means that it is now brackish. It is separated from the sea by a narrow shingle beach and water levels fluctuate greatly depending upon sea encroachment and irrigation activities on the surrounding estate. Several bunds have been constructed to protect the reedbeds from seawater, and five artificial lagoons have been created to compensate for the loss of habitat to the sea. To the north and south the Broad is bordered by mature mixed woodland and farmland, and a little further north there are some flooded gravel pits immediately inland of the beach, partially fringed with reeds and sallow bushes (and rapidly disappearing due to coastal erosion). Covehithe Cliffs to the south are being constantly eroded by the sea (which is moving landward faster here than almost anywhere in Britain). Covehithe and Easton Broads are smaller than Benacre and have deteriorated considerably, partially as a result of drainage, and now have little open water.

Access (see map)

Access in the NNR is limited to rights of way and the concessionary path along the private beach.

Benacre Broad Leave the A12 at Wrentham on a minor road east to Covehithe. Beyond the village the road terminates at the sea. Park and walk north along the top of the cliffs. After ¼ mile the path descends to the beach and, after passing a small wood, Benacre Broad lies to the left. Much of the Broad can be seen from the beach and a track along the south side leads to a hide (access unrestricted), which gives good views of the Broad.

Benacre Ness and Kessingland Level Continue north along the beach for c.¾ mile to the gravel pits and Benacre Ness. The latter is a potentially good place from which to seawatch in favourable weather. The flooded pits attract a variety of waterbirds and the bushes here and in the vicinity of Beach Farm are best for passerine migrants. The marshes of Kessingland Level may be worthy of exploration if time permits. Alternative access is from Beach Farm via Benacre village and from Kessingland Beach: in Kessingland village take the B1437 to the coast, park and walk south along the beach.

Covehithe and Easton Broads These lie c.1 and 2 miles south of Covehithe respectively. A footpath leads south from Covehithe village to Covehithe Broad. Easton Broad can be reached along the beach.

Potter's Bridge The B1127 bisects the extensive reedbeds of the Easton Broad valley, with good views from Potter's Bridge.

Birds

A variety of waterbirds breed including Marsh Harrier, seven species of duck (including Gadwall), Water Rail, Reed, Sedge and Grasshopper Warblers, and Bearded Tit. Up to 70 pairs of Little Terns breed on the shingle beach, and also

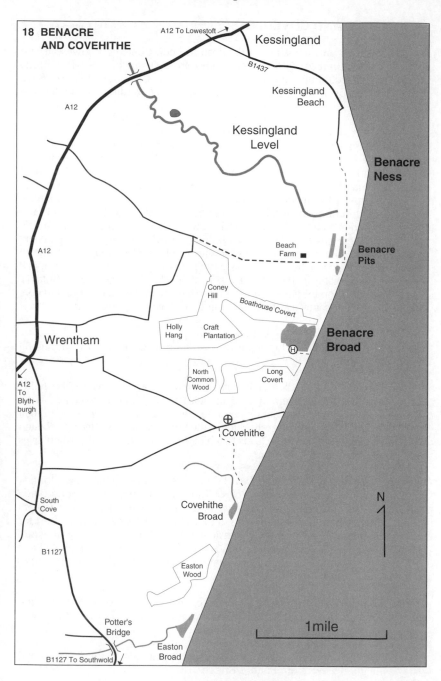

18 BENACRE AND COVEHITHE

A12 To Lowestoft

Kessingland

B1437

A12

Kessingland Beach

Kessingland Level

Benacre Ness

A12

Beach Farm

Benacre Pits

Coney Hill

Boathouse Covert

Holly Hang

Craft Plantation

Benacre Broad

Wrentham

North Common Wood

Long Covert

A12 To Blythburgh

Covehithe

South Cove

Covehithe Broad

N

B1127

Easton Wood

1 mile

Potter's Bridge

B1127 To Southwold

Easton Broad

Common Tern. The woodlands hold most of the typical species including small numbers of Nightingale, as well as Redstart. Woodlark is found on the relict areas of heath, and Wheatear and Hobby sometimes breed. Bitterns formerly bred (and still nest nearby); it is hoped that appropriate management may prompt their return.

Waders are a feature of Benacre Broad in autumn; Avocet is often present and several rarities have been found. Seabirds may be conspicuous offshore at this time and frequently include skuas and auks. A broad variety of migrant passerines may be seen, occasionally including scarce migrants such as Barred Warbler and Red-backed Shrike.

Winter is usually the best season at Benacre. Red-throated Diver is frequent offshore and there may be small numbers of sea ducks, with Scaup, Eider, Common Scoter and Red-breasted Merganser all possible; Long-tailed Duck and Velvet Scoter are less frequent. Goldeneye is usually present on the Broad and Smew and Goosander are regular in small numbers, while Red-necked and Slavonian Grebes may visit. Numbers of dabbling duck are also present, including Wigeon, Teal and Gadwall. Marsh and Hen Harriers regularly hunt the reedbeds, and Buzzard, Goshawk, Sparrowhawk, Peregrine and Merlin are frequent. Several rarer raptors have been seen here, the most likely being Red Kite and Rough-legged Buzzard. Bewick's Swan and White-fronted, Tundra Bean and Egyptian Geese are sometimes found in the area, particularly on Kessingland Level, and Short-eared Owl may also be seen. With luck, Shore Lark and Snow Bunting may be encountered on the beach, and gulls occasionally include Glaucous, Iceland or Mediterranean.

Information

EN, Suffolk Team: Regent House, 110 Northgate Street, Bury St Edmunds, Suffolk IP33 1HP. Tel: 01284 762218. E-mail: suffolk@english-nature.org.uk

19 LOWESTOFT (Suffolk)   OS Landranger 134

Situated near the easternmost point in Britain, the gardens and parks in Lowestoft naturally attract a variety of passage migrants, while the fishing industry inevitably attracts large numbers of gulls in winter. Lowestoft also holds one of the very few colonies of breeding Kittiwakes in southeast England (there is another at Sizewell, see p.162).

Access and Birds

Lowestoft harbour and Ness Congregations of gulls in this area may include Glaucous, Iceland or Mediterranean. The area between the harbour and Lowestoft Ness is generally best. Purple Sandpiper is regular, favouring rocks or man-made structures (the broken concrete defences and seawall between Ness Point and Lowestoft harbour is the best site for Purple Sandpiper in East Anglia). A few Shags and Sanderlings are also usually found in winter.

The only colony of Kittiwake on the coast south of Yorkshire uses not sea cliffs but man-made structures, nesting on ledges on churches, the yacht club and other buildings around the harbour, and especially formerly the South Pier Pavilion. When this was demolished, a purpose-built artificial 'Kittiwake Cliff' was constructed, with the result that the colony increased from c.100 to c.200 pairs; some remain throughout the winter. A few pairs of Black Redstarts also regularly breed, and are best looked for around the warehouses at Ness Point.

Lowestoft North Denes This is a grassy area north of the cricket ground. A camping site in summer, in spring and autumn it attracts gulls, waders, pipits and wagtails. The scrub and woodland on the cliff edge are worth checking for warblers, flycatchers and chats, as are the gardens of Belle Vue Park and Sparrows Nest Theatre. Look for Ring Ouzel on the cricket ground. Kensington Gardens, a small park and bowling green south of Clairmont Pier, are worth checking in autumn when the wind is from the northeast. Scarce migrants have been found here on several occasions.

20 GREAT YARMOUTH AND
BREYDON WATER (Norfolk)

Immediately west of Great Yarmouth lies Breydon Water, a LNR, and further west is the RSPB's Berney Marshes reserve. An excellent variety of wildfowl and waders can be seen during both winter and passage periods. In Great Yarmouth itself, the cemetery regularly attracts rare migrants and the seafront can be productive, especially in winter.

Habitat
Breydon Water is the landlocked estuary of the Rivers Waveney and Yare, and at low tide extensive tidal mudflats are exposed. The Halvergate Marshes, an extensive area of low-lying grazing marshes, lie on either side of the estuary.

Access
Breydon Water Most of the waders on the estuary can be seen in the northeast corner two hours either side of high water as they gather on the last areas of mud to be exposed. A telescope is usually essential. Coming into Great Yarmouth on the A47 dual carriageway, follow signs to the railway station (which involves doubling back on yourself at the second roundabout). Drive past the station frontage into the large Asda supermarket car park by the river, parking in the southwest corner. Walk under Breydon roadbridge to join the Weavers Way footpath along the north shore of Breydon Water. There are two public hides, and although these may be locked, waders can be viewed just as easily from outside.

Great Yarmouth seafront The harbour entrance can be productive for gulls and is accessed by following Marine Parade south into South Beach Road and then to the South Denes Industrial Area (breeding Black Redstart). Mediterranean Gull is, however, best looked for from the central beach area, while the large Little Tern colony can be accessed along the A149 north out of the town, turning right at the traffic lights into Jellicoe Road (signed to the racecourse), following this over the bridge and then turning left into North Drive. From here, it is a short walk to the beach.

Great Yarmouth cemetery The mature trees here consistently attract passerine migrants in both spring and autumn. Access is from the A12: coming into Great Yarmouth from Norwich go straight on at the first two roundabouts and then turn north (left) at the traffic lights into Northgate Street and right at the mini-roundabout into Kitchener Road (which divides the cemetery into its north and south sections). It is possible to park in Kitchener Road or in the pay-and-display car park found by driving to the end of the road and turning right.

RSPB Berney Marshes Accessible at all times from Berney Arms railway station. Otherwise, access is on foot via the Weavers Way footpath (see above) from Great Yarmouth station, a 4-mile walk along the north shore of Breydon Water or by following the Weavers Way from Halvergate (off the B1140 halfway between Reedham and Acle—a 2 mile walk) or from Wickhampton (again, 2 miles each way). The recommended tactic is to take the train from Yarmouth (most frequent on Sundays) and then walk back. Swans, geese and birds of prey are the specialities, and Avocet has recently started to breed.

Burgh Castle and Fishers Marshes For the more energetic, these areas of rough grazing south of Breydon Water hold a similar selection of birds to Berney Marshes. Join the footpath along the south shore of the estuary at Burgh Castle church, and this route also affords the best views of the river channel for diving ducks and grebes.

Birds
Winter wildfowl include Goldeneye, Scaup, Pintail, Wigeon and Dark-bellied Brent Geese on the estuary, with Bewick's and sometimes Whooper Swans, 100–200 White-fronted Geese (Berney/Halvergate Marshes) and occasionally Tundra Bean Geese on the marshes. Hen Harrier, Merlin, Peregrine, Barn and Short-eared Owls, Twite, and Snow and Lapland Buntings are also found in the rough grassland, although the last may be very elusive. Waders include all the usual species, while the gulls should be checked for Glaucous and Mediterranean.

Passage periods bring a wide variety of waders, which may include Avocet, Ruff, Spotted Redshank, Black-tailed Godwit, Whimbrel and occasionally Temminck's Stint, while Broad-billed Sandpiper is nearly annual in May. Other regular migrants include Spoonbill, Little Egret, Garganey, Black and Roseate Terns, and Mediterranean and Little Gulls. Great Yarmouth cemetery regularly holds passerine migrants, and these have included some outstanding rarities.

Breeders include several pairs of Black Redstart around the power station and in the town, Common Tern (on specially constructed rafts) and nationally important numbers of Little Tern: the UK's largest colony of Little Terns breeds on North Denes beach, and from mid-May to late July RSPB wardens are on site.

Information
RSPB Berney Marshes Warden: Mark Smart, Ashtree Farm, Goodchild Marine, Butt Lane, Burgh Castle, Great Yarmouth, Norfolk NR31 9PE. Tel: 01493 700645. E-mail: mark.smart@rspb.org.uk

21 STRUMPSHAW FEN (Norfolk)   OS Landranger 134

The marshes of the Yare Valley, east of Norwich, support some unusual breeding birds, with the RSPB reserves at Strumpshaw Fen and Surlingham (part of their Mid Yare Valley complex of reserves) being among the best areas.

Habitat
Strumpshaw Fen comprises reedbeds, alder and willow carr, damp woodland, open water, and grazing marshes, with similar areas south of the River Yare at Rockland Broad and Surlingham Church Marsh.

Access (see map)
Strumpshaw Fen Leave the A47 just east of Norwich on one of the several exits to Brundall. Follow signs towards Strumpshaw and, 400 yards after passing under the railway bridge on the outskirts of Brundall, turn right (signed Hassingham and Cantley), and immediately right again into Low Road. The reserve car park is on the right after ½ mile. From here cross the railway line on foot to reach the reserve and information centre (open only in summer). There are three circular trails (the Meadow Trail is open only in summer) and four hides, the New Broad Tower hide, in particular, affording excellent panoramic views over the reserve, which is open daily, dawn until dusk.

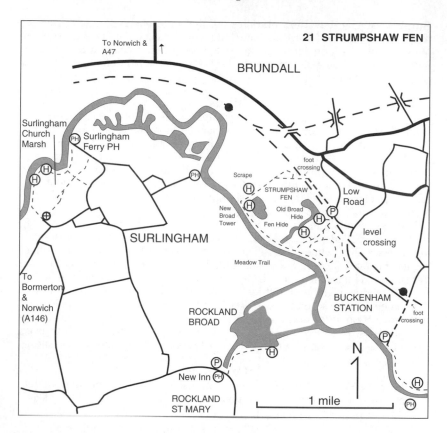

Rockland Broad Most of the RSPB Strumpshaw Fen reserve is north of the River Yare, but an area of carr on the south bank extends as far as Rockland Broad. This is only accessible from Rockland St Mary, which is accessed from the A146 Norwich–Loddon road. A public footpath starts opposite the New Inn in Rockland St Mary and runs to a hide, giving good views over the reedbeds and Rockland Broad.

Surlingham Church Marsh Also south of the River Yare, the RSPB also owns Surlingham Church Marsh, which has a similar range of birds. Park carefully by Surlingham church, from where there is a circular walk around the reserve giving access to the two hides.

Birds

In the areas of carr, Cetti's Warbler is quite common, along with a broad variety of the commoner warblers, including Reed, Sedge and a few pairs of Grasshopper Warblers (Savi's Warbler has bred once at Strumpshaw). Marsh Harrier and Bearded Tit nest regularly but Garganey only breeds sporadically and Bittern is now only an irregular visitor in winter. Other breeders include Pochard, Shoveler, Water Rail, Woodcock, Black-headed Gull (c.70 pairs), Barn and Long-eared Owls and Kingfisher (which is often seen from the Old Broad hide at Strumpshaw). Common birds of the grazing marshes are Lapwing, Redshank and Yellow Wagtail, and a good variety of woodland species include all three woodpeckers, Marsh and Willow Tits, and Redpoll. On passage, Osprey is a surprisingly frequent visitor to

Strumpshaw. The fen attracts roosting Cormorant and occasional visitors are Jack Snipe and Water Pipit, while Hen and Marsh Harriers and Bearded Tit are often present, if elusive.

Information

RSPB Warden: Tim Strudwick, Staithe Cottage, Low Road, Strumpshaw, Norwich, Norfolk NR13 4HS. Tel: 01603 715191. E-mail: strumpshaw @rspb.org.uk

22 BUCKENHAM AND CANTLEY (Norfolk)   OS Landranger 134

The marshes of the Yare Valley, east of Norwich, are important for wildfowl in winter and hold the only regular wintering flock of Taiga Bean Geese in England. Parts of the area are an RSPB reserve (part of the Mid Yare Valley complex of reserves).

Habitat

Buckenham and Cantley are rough grazing marshes adjacent to the River Yare. Recent management has aimed to raise the water table. At Cantley, the settling ponds in the sugar beet factory are attractive to passage waders.

Access (see map)

Leave the A47 just east of Norwich on one of the several exits to Brundall. Follow signs towards Strumpshaw and, 400 yards after passing under the railway bridge on the outskirts of Brundall, bear right (signed to Hassingham and Cantley, and the RSPB's Strumpshaw reserve). There are now two options.

Buckenham Marshes Take the third turning to the right signed to Buckenham and after c.1 mile turn right to park at Buckenham station. Cross the level crossing on foot (it is closed to vehicles) and follow the broad track for ½ mile to the River Yare. Following the riverbank southeast for c.½ mile you reach a hide by the old windmill. This offers panoramic views of the grazing marshes, and visitors are requested not to proceed any further during winter. The Taiga Bean Geese sometimes feed in these fields but a telescope will be necessary to see them at all well (and views are often still poor).

Alternatively, if coming from the RSPB's Strumpshaw reserve, continue along Low Road from the Strumpshaw car park, turn right at the T-junction and cross over the level crossing (toot your horn and wait a few minutes for the gates to be opened). The road continues along the south side of the railway line to Buckenham station, where you should park and then walk to the River Yare.

Cantley Marshes Continue on and, as you approach Cantley, there is a sharp left-hand bend. Take Burnt House Road, which leads straight ahead, and park carefully beside the road at the end. Cross the railway on foot and proceed along the public footpath. Take a telescope and be content to view the geese at a distance, being very careful not to disturb them, even if you have right of way. As an alternative to entering the marshes and the possibility of disturbing the geese, the public footpath over the hill between Burnt House Road and School Lane provides a panoramic view of the area. (Note that School Lane, which leads right from the corner, does not give public access to the railway or marshes.)

Cantley Sugar Beet Factory Park by the roadside at Cantley railway station and cross the railway on foot. Turn left into the British Sugar works. There is a public footpath, marked on the road and pavement in yellow, which gives limited views

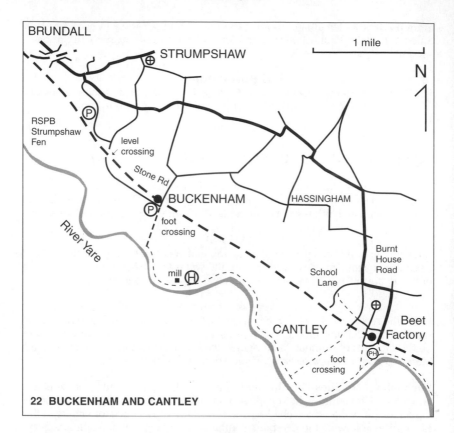

BRUNDALL
STRUMPSHAW
1 mile
N
RSPB
Strumpshaw
Fen
level
crossing
Stone Rd
BUCKENHAM
HASSINGHAM
foot
crossing
River Yare
mill
Burnt
House
Road
School
Lane
CANTLEY
Beet
Factory
foot
crossing

22 BUCKENHAM AND CANTLEY

of the settling ponds. The site is otherwise private (though special access arrangements have been made for rarities). Great care should be taken at this working industrial site, and it is probably only wise to visit at weekends when traffic movements are reduced.

Birds

The flock of Bean Geese, the last to winter regularly in England, is of the form *fabalis* or Taiga Bean Goose (often considered a separate species from Tundra Bean Goose *serrirostris*). These birds breed in central–southern Scandinavia (and the loss of many former wintering flocks in Britain is attributed to a decline in the breeding area and fatalities on migration in Denmark). Up to 500 Bean Geese are present between mid-November and mid-February, but in some seasons may depart by early January. They move around the area, and though Buckenham Marshes have traditionally been favoured, in some recent seasons they have mostly been at Cantley. A smaller flock of White-fronted Geese is also often present. Other birds in winter include up to 10,000 Wigeon, Golden Plover, Water Pipit, Fieldfare, Redwing and vast numbers of corvids—up to 20,000 fly past Buckenham station at dusk. Occasionally Merlin, Hen and Marsh Harriers or Short-eared Owl may visit the area.

Breeders in the area include Marsh Harrier and a few pairs of Cetti's and Grasshopper Warblers.

Information

RSPB Warden: Tim Studwick, Staithe Cottage, Low Road, Strumpshaw, Norwich, Norfolk NR13 4HS. Tel: 01603 715191. E-mail: strumpshaw @rspb.org.uk

23 HICKLING BROAD (Norfolk)

OS Landranger 134
OS Explorer 40

Hickling Broad lies just north of Potter Heigham and only a few miles from the coast. A NNR managed by the Norfolk Wildlife Trust (NWT), a wide variety of species breeds, augmented in spring and autumn by migrant waders, gulls and terns. Winter is often quiet, with the exception of the regular raptor roost and, especially in hard weather, a range of wildfowl.

Habitat

Lying in the upper reaches of the River Thurne, Hickling is the largest of the Norfolk Broads. Originally peat diggings, the broads flooded in the 14th century and now comprise areas of open water surrounded by extensive areas of reed and other fen vegetation, often invaded by scrub and wet carr woodland. Water pollution and neglect resulted in a serious degeneration of the wetland habitats at Hickling (as at many other broads), and the loss of Bittern as a breeder. Past management included the creation of a series of muddy scrapes, which have had a limited attraction for waders and duck, and, more recently, significant efforts have been made to restore the reedbeds, resulting in the return of the Bittern after an absence of 20 years.

Access (see map)

Weavers Way The Weavers Way public footpath skirts the south edge of the broad and accesses a public hide overlooking Rush Hills Scrape (usually the most productive spot on the broad for migrant waders, gulls and terns). Park by Potter Heigham church and walk north along Church Lane for 150 yards; where the road bends sharp left take the footpath to the right for a short distance before turning left to cross a field, continuing over the stile and through the belt of trees to the Weavers Way. Turn right for Rush Hills Scrape. The Weavers Way is also accessible, at the less interesting west end, from Decoy Road, but parking is very limited and vehicles have been vandalised.

Hickling NWT reserve Turn north off the A149 to Hickling Heath and continue to Hickling Green. At the Greyhound Inn turn east into Stubb Road and follow this for 1½ miles, turning right at the NWT sign to the reserve car park. Three trails start here: the Dragonfly Pond Walk passes through woodland and fen to a small pond. The Marsh Walk passes through woodland before accessing three hides overlooking the scrapes (closed April–June), while the Broad Walk passes through reedbeds on a boardwalk before accessing two more hides overlooking the scrapes, and continues to the edge of Hickling Broad, where there is an observation hut. It then returns to the car park, passing Whiteslea Lodge and large areas of reed, which are being managed for Bittern. A recent development is the erection of a 60-foot Tree Tower giving panoramic views over the marshes. The reserve is open all year and the visitor centre is open April–September 10.00–17.00 daily.

Water Trail Mid-May to mid-September, Sunday–Thursday, boat trips from the NWT Visitor Centre explore the reserve via the Hickling Water Trail on the electric-powered *Little Tern*. Booking is essential; for details phone the warden.

Stubb Mill Marsh and Hen Harriers roost in the reeds around Horsey Mere, but are best viewed from the west, with the light behind you (especially important on sunny evenings). Park at the NWT reserve car park and walk back along the access road, turning right at the crossroads and following the road for ½ mile to

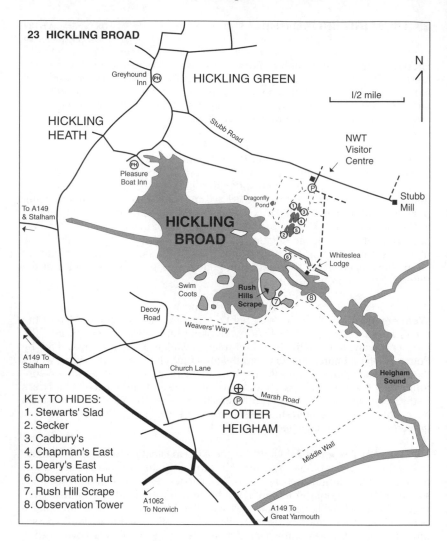

KEY TO HIDES:
1. Stewarts' Slad
2. Secker
3. Cadbury's
4. Chapman's East
5. Deary's East
6. Observation Hut
7. Rush Hill Scrape
8. Observation Tower

Stubb Mill (the lane is often rather wet). Immediately before the mill, a raised bank on the left is the designated viewing area. Marsh Harrier is often present during the day, but roosting Hen Harrier may not appear until c.15.00. Arriving harriers may drop straight into the roost, offering only brief views, or they may quarter the area in search of a last meal; in some cases they are joined by a Merlin, presumably hoping to pick-off small birds flushed by the hunting harrier. This is also an excellent area to see Common Crane on winter evenings.

Birds

Breeding specialities include Bittern, Marsh Harrier and Bearded Tit, and other breeders include Gadwall, Garganey, Ringed Plover, Common and Little Terns, Reed, Sedge and Grasshopper Warblers, and a selection of woodland birds such as Turtle Dove and Redpoll. Sadly, Savi's Warbler has now almost deserted this site (reflecting their virtual extinction as a British breeder), although two singing birds were present in spring 1999; the reeds alongside the Weavers Way are the traditional area for this species, but it is far more often heard than seen.

On passage a wide variety of waders occurs, including regular Black-tailed Godwit, Ruff, Little Stint and, quite regularly, Temminck's Stint. Other migrants may include Spoonbill, Osprey, Black Tern and Little Gull. Marsh Harrier is almost invariably present in the area, and a variety of passerine migrants also recorded.

Winter at Hickling is bleak, but wildfowl can include Gadwall, Goldeneye, Smew, Goosander, Pink-footed Goose and Whooper and Bewick's Swans, as well as Hen and Marsh Harriers, Sparrowhawk, Merlin, Barn and Short-eared Owls and Kingfisher. Occasional Ruffs may join the Golden Plover flocks on the surrounding pastures.

Information

NWT Warden, John Blackburn, Warden's House, Hickling NNR, Stubb Road, Hickling, Norwich NR12 0BN. Tel: 01692 598276. E-mail: johnb@nwt.org.uk

24 WAXHAM AND HORSEY (Norfolk)   OS Landranger 134

This section of the east Norfolk coast can provide excellent birds in winter, with a range of wild swans and geese, and spring and autumn, when it sometimes holds interesting migrants. At all times of year, the resident flock of Common Cranes is a star attraction.

Habitat

At Waxham the coast in bounded by a line of dunes and, immediately inland, lies a narrow band of dense woodland, attractive to migrants. Along the coast towards Horsey the landscape is completely flat, with a mixture of arable fields and pastures, interspersed by reed-lined ditches.

Access

The whole area is accessed from the B1159 between Sea Palling and West Somerton.

Waxham Turn left (east) off the B1159 c.1 mile southeast of Sea Palling, at the sharp right-hand bend. Follow the road past the church and park carefully at the end, around the T-junction. From here walk left, past Shangri-La cottage, to the dunes and beach. It is possible to explore the sycamore woods that run north and south along the coast, immediately inland of the dunes. They are very dense, but with patience and perseverance, interesting birds can sometimes be found. Offshore, especially in late autumn and winter, small numbers of divers, grebes, sea ducks and sometimes Little Gull may be seen.

Brograve Farm to Horsey Corner This stretch of the B1159 is a favourite area for Common Crane and, in winter, sometimes a few wild swans or geese. There are several spots where it is possible to pull off the road to scan the fields (those west of the road being favoured).

Horsey Mere This small broad is a NT reserve. Access is limited to a short track leading to the mere from the Horsey Windmill car park on the B1159. Hen and Marsh Harriers roost in the reeds around the mere, but are best viewed from Stubb Mill, Hickling (see p.179). Interesting wildfowl are sometimes seen on the Mere, with the best views from Horsey Mill in the early morning.

Birds

In the winter herds of Bewick's and Whooper Swans may be found in this area, and Pink-footed Geese are increasingly numerous and regular visitors (over 7,000 in 1997/98). Other geese may include White-fronted and occasionally, Tundra Bean. As well as the fields in the Waxham–Horsey area, it is worth exploring along the B1159 from East Somerton to Sea Palling and Stalham, and minor roads south from there to Hickling. The fields also hold flocks of Golden Plover and, when flooded, may also attract numbers of duck such as Wigeon. Small numbers of raptors, including Barn and Short-eared Owls, Hen and Marsh Harriers and Merlin, winter, but these are well scattered during the day and are best seen when arriving to roost around Stubb Mill, Hickling (see p.179).

Common Crane is resident in the area, but become very elusive in spring and summer and is best seen in autumn and winter, They can often (but not always) be seen from the roadside in fields of winter wheat or recently harvested potatoes, but for such large birds they can vanish into dead ground remarkably easily. Perhaps more reliably, they may be seen in winter in the late afternoon when they roost near Horsey Mere, and are then best viewed from Stubb Mill, Hickling (see p.179). The birds have been breeding in this area since 1982 (the first successful breeding in Britain since c.1600!) and at least 15 were present in winter 2001/2002 (in summer many disperse around Britain, leaving just one pair to attempt to breed).

In spring and autumn the stands of cover at Waxham (and indeed, at any accessible point along the coast), may attract passerine migrants. As well as all the usual migrants, such as Garden and Willow Warblers, Pied Flycatcher and Redstart in autumn, Waxham regularly produces scarce migrants, and has been graced by several Pallas's and Greenish Warblers.

25 WINTERTON (Norfolk) OS Landranger 134

This extensive area of dunes on the coast at Winterton forms a NNR, and regularly attracts migrant passerines in both spring and autumn.

Habitat

A long line of dunes borders the coast, with some damp slacks in the hollows and, on the landward side, some patches of scrub and purpose-built small ponds.

Access

Winterton-on-Sea lies just east of the B1159 and in the village follow signs to the beach car park (fee). From here it is possible to explore the dunes to the north and south, for a distance of c.1 mile in both directions, concentrating on the areas of scrub on the west side of the dune system. Please keep to the paths, and avoid damaging the often delicate dune vegetation.

Birds

In spring and autumn a range of migrant landbirds may be found, with Ring Ouzel, Black Redstart and Firecrest possible in early spring, alongside common species such as Wheatear. Later in the season, in east or southeast winds, scarce migrants such as Bluethroat are sometimes present.

In autumn Winterton is one of the more regular sites on this coast for Wryneck, Red-backed Shrike and Barred Warbler, although all are elusive, and as autumn progresses almost anything could be found. Other birds to look for in late autumn include migrant Woodcock and Long-eared and Short-eared Owls, and Little Gull can occur offshore. Divers and sea duck may be seen in winter and raptors are regularly recorded in winter and spring; the most frequent are Hen Harrier, Sparrowhawk, Rough-legged Buzzard and Merlin.

26 GREAT RYBURGH AND SWANTON NOVERS (Norfolk)

OS Landranger 133

These areas of parkland and ancient woodland between Holt and East Dereham are well-publicised sites for Honey Buzzard which, with luck, can be seen in late spring and summer.

Access

Great Ryburgh Turn off the A1067 2 miles north of Guist southwest onto the minor road to Great Ryburgh. After 1½ miles turn left (south) by the church in Great Ryburgh and follow the road for c.1 mile, bearing left at the junction. The raptor watchpoint is well signed. Park off the road and follow the field border to the viewpoint and scan east towards the tower.

Swanton Novers Turn southwest off the A148 at the roundabout in Holt onto the B1110 towards Guist and East Dereham. After c.7 miles (2 miles south of the staggered intersection with the B1354) turn west at the crossroads on the minor road signed Fulmodeston. After c.½ mile the watchpoint car park lies north of the road.

Birds

Having bred for several years in the vicinity of Swanton Novers Great Wood, the Honey Buzzards have now moved a little further south to the Great Ryburgh area. They are, however, still regularly seen from the Swanton Novers raptor watchpoint, as well as at Great Ryburgh. Honey Buzzard is usually present late May–September, but become especially difficult to see in late August–early September. The optimum time for sightings is 10.00–15.00 on warm sunny days, with scattered cloud and only slight breezes, when they may be seen soaring or in wing-clapping display. They spend a great deal of time perched below the canopy, and a long wait may be necessary for a relatively brief and distant view. Views may sometimes be good, but equally on some days the birds are not seen at all. Other raptors in the area can include Hobby, Sparrowhawk, Common Buzzard and, very occasionally, Goshawk.

27 SHERINGHAM (Norfolk)

OS Landranger 133

In recent years Sheringham has gained a reputation as the premier seawatching station in East Anglia, especially for movements of Long-tailed Skua in September.

Access

Follow signs from the A148 into Sheringham and, at the bottom of the hill near the town centre, turn left (west) at the roundabout onto the A149 coast road. Take the first right over the railway bridge, and then first left (The Boulevard). At the end of the road is a large roundabout and by continuing straight on you reach the coast. Park, go through the archway and down the steps to the lower tier of beach shelters (the best place from which to seawatch). In good sea-watching weather, space is at a premium and latecomers must sit on the upper level (bring a camp chair) or find shelter elsewhere.

Birds

From late August to October strong north to northwest winds, coupled with poor visibility (at least overcast conditions, if not some mist out to sea) are likely to produce interesting movements of seabirds, particularly in early morning. Manx Shearwater, Fulmar, Gannet, Arctic Skua, Kittiwake and a variety of terns are regular, and Sooty Shearwater and Great Skua almost so. If conditions are just right, especially in September, there may be a passage of Long-tailed Skuas, but numbers are very variable and many days can be spent here without a sighting. In addition, they are hard to separate from Arctic Skua so care and practice are required. Nevertheless, Sheringham offers the best chance of seeing this species in south England. Pomarine Skua is also possible, especially as the season advances, and Leach's Petrel may sometimes be seen in small numbers. From late October, there is the chance of a passage of Little Auks, and other notable species from now through the winter include Red-necked and Slavonian Grebes, Red-throated and Great Northern Divers, and a variety of wildfowl and waders.

When seawatching is quiet, the clifftop fields between Weybourne and Sheringham often produce interesting migrants in spring and autumn. Notably, there are autumn concentrations of larks and finches, and Richard's Pipit and Lapland Bunting are recorded quite frequently. The best access is from Weybourne beach car park, walking east along the clifftop path.

28 SALTHOUSE–KELLING (Norfolk)   OS Landranger 132

Lying immediately east of the famous Cley Norfolk Wildlife Trust (NWT) reserve, this area holds a similar range of birds through the year, but in a much more informal setting, without hides, visitor centres etc, though part is owned by the NT and part by the NWT. To the south, the heaths at Salthouse and Kelling are regular haunts of Nightjar.

Habitat

Most of the area north of the A149 coast road comprises rough grazing meadows intersected by numerous ditches, with some pools, while Kelling Water Meadows (also known as Kelling Quags) have been deliberately flooded to attract both breeding and migrant birds. This area is bounded to the north by a high shingle bank which, having been breached by the sea several times in recent years, has been subject to much disturbance in attempts to shore-up the sea defences. South of the coast road the land rises sharply to the Holt–Cromer Ridge, where sandy and gravelly soils support areas of heath at Salthouse and Kelling.

Access (see map)

Salthouse Duck Pond This lies just north of the A149 in Salthouse village, immediately west of the beach road, with ample space to pull off the road. There are often good numbers of gulls around the pond (or loafing in the fields to the north), which occasionally include Mediterranean or Yellow-legged Gulls.

Salthouse Beach A metalled road leads to the beach car park from the A149 on the east side of Salthouse village. Shore Lark and Snow Bunting are regularly

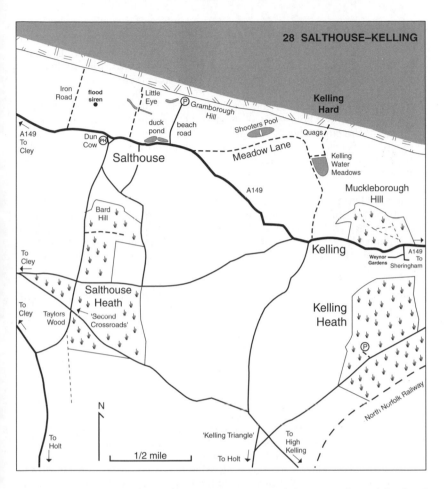

28 SALTHOUSE-KELLING

seen in winter, especially on the wet areas west of the car park, and Lapland Bunting can sometimes be found in the rough pastures. Two small hillocks, Little Eye and Gramborough Hill, lie west and east of the car park, and despite having very limited areas of cover (just a few small bushes) they often hold interesting migrants in spring and autumn. It is possible to walk a circuit west from the car park to Little Eye, then south along a track to the A149, following the coast road east to the duck pond and then the Beach Road north back to the car park.

The Iron Road This track runs north from the A149 to the coast, west of Salthouse village. It can be good for waders in spring and autumn, depending on water levels, but it is not possible to park any closer than the village green (by the Dun Cow pub).

Kelling Quags and Water Meadows This area of grazing marshes lies immediately east of Salthouse Marshes, and includes several pools. In particular, the pool at Kelling Water Meadows often holds interesting ducks and waders. About ½ mile east of Salthouse the A149 bends to the south, heading inland, and at this point a track (Meadow Lane) forks left. Park carefully at the beginning of this track and proceed on foot, checking the Shooters Pool and marshes on the left. After ¾ mile the track turns sharp right towards Kelling, passing alongside the Water Meadows pool. At the bend another track leads east to the beach at Kelling Hard, giving views of several small flooded areas on Kelling Quags. Meadow Lane itself continues to Kelling village, and alternative access is to park on the side road south of the A149 in the village (opposite the gallery) and walk from there.

Muckleburgh Hill This scrub and bracken-covered hill is immediately north of the A149 between Weybourne and Kelling and forms a northern extension of the heaths along the ridge. It holds breeding Nightingale and is attractive to migrants, although the extensive thick cover can be daunting to work. Turn south off the A149 to park in Weynor Gardens and cross the coast road to the hill, where a network of small tracks accesses the whole area.

Salthouse Heath A large area of heath, much of which is covered with bracken, although recent management aims to restore the specialised heather–gorse mosaic characteristic of the north Norfolk heaths. There are breeding Nightjars and Nightingales, and the traditional spot for both is the second crossroads, 1 mile inland of Salthouse village. In some seasons Woodlark also breeds, but can be elusive.

Kelling Heath Another large area of heath; recent management has resulted in rather more heather and gorse than at Salthouse. The heath likewise holds breeding Nightjar and Woodlark, and can be accessed via a maze of tracks from the car park, which lies just east of the road from Weybourne to Holt.

Kelling Triangle Intermittently the haunt of Wood Warbler, the private woods can be viewed from the roadside and still hold a variety of common woodland species.

Birds

On spring passage a wide variety of migrants may occur, including Garganey, Common and Green Sandpipers, Black Tern and Yellow Wagtail, and there are often numbers of Whimbrel in the meadows.

Breeders include Shelduck, Avocet, Redshank, Oystercatcher, Ringed Plover, Yellow Wagtail and Sedge Warbler, and Sandwich, Common and Little Terns regularly patrol the beach, and the former two species may spend time loafing on the pools. Marsh Harrier may visit. Nightingales favour areas of dense blackthorn scrub on Salthouse Heath and Muckleburgh Hill, and Nightjar can be found on the heaths, together with Tree Pipit, Woodlark and, on Kelling Heath, Stonechat.

In autumn a wider variety of migrants may appear, and as well as the species mentioned for spring, waders such as Ruff, Black-tailed Godwit, Curlew Sandpiper and Little Stint may occur. The areas of bramble and other bushes around Little Eye, Gramborough Hill, Kelling Water Meadows, Kelling Quags and Muckleburgh Hill regularly attract interesting passerine migrants, with Barred Warbler being among the more regular scarce migrants. The rough pasture can also produce migrants, including Richard's Pipit and Lapland Bunting, and anything can (and does) turn up.

In winter the pools and flooded meadows hold numbers of Wigeon, Teal, Dark-bellied Brent Geese, Golden Plover and Lapwing, and Barnacle and Tundra Bean Geese are occasional visitors. The small pools behind the shingle ridge hold Redshank, Dunlin and Turnstone, and sometimes Shore Lark can be found around these wet areas (especially in the vicinity of Salthouse), while Snow Bunting is regular, if mobile, along the shingle bank. Red-throated Diver and Red-breasted Merganser are regular offshore. Merlin, Hen Harrier and Short-eared Owl are irregular visitors, but Barn Owl is resident.

29 CLEY (Norfolk)

Cley is probably the best-known mainland birding site in Britain and c.360 species have been recorded in the National Grid 10-km square TG04, including a host of rarities and several firsts for Britain. Cley Marsh reserve covers 435 acres and is owned by the Norfolk Wildlife Trust (NWT), while adjacent Arnold's Marsh is owned by the NT. Birding at Cley is good at any time of year but the greatest diversity of species occurs in spring and autumn.

Habitat

Cley Marsh comprises extensive reedbeds, pools and grazing meadows. A series of scrapes have been excavated which are attractive to wildfowl and waders, and to the east Arnold's Marsh is a naturally flooded area that is attractive to waders and terns. The entire area lies south of a high shingle bank which (usually) protects it from the sea. Rising sea levels threaten the whole area, however, and although several schemes have been proposed to save some or all of the valuable habitat at Cley, notably a new clay bank that would follow the line of the New Cut from Cley Beach Road eastwards, at the time of writing, none has been put into action.

Access (see map)

Cley NWT reserve This lies just east of Cley next the Sea. Access to non-members is by permit only, obtainable daily 1 April–31 October from the NWT visitor centre, which lies south of the A149 c.½ mile east of Cley village, and is open 10.00–17.00 (10.00–16.00, Wednesday–Sunday in November–mid-December). The rest of the year, permits are obtainable from Watcher's Cottage (south of the coast road between the village and the visitor centre), and the reserve is closed on Mondays in November– March. Boardwalks lead from the visitor centre car park and the Watchers Cottage to Avocet, Daukes, Teal and Bishop hides on the south side of the reserve (and east to the East Bank). These hides are usually the best for wildfowl and waders, and the boardwalk out to Daukes Hide passes stands of reeds which can hold Bearded Tit (North hide can be accessed from the beach car park; see below).

Cley coastguards and North Hide Just east of Cley village the Beach Road leads north to the beach car park by the old coastguard lookout. A small cafe is open in summer and on winter weekends, and there are toilets here. Immediately adjacent to the car park, the Eye Pool and Half Moon Pit sometimes hold a few waders, while Eye Field is excellent for Dark-bellied Brent Goose and Golden Plover in winter. The beach car park is also the starting point for those walking to Blakeney Point (see p.190). The shingle bank by the coastguard lookout is the favoured spot for seawatching at Cley, and the bank is favoured by mobile flocks of Snow Bunting in winter. From the car park it is possible to walk east along the base of the shingle bank, and after c.500 yards a track leads south over a stile to the NWT's North hide (permit required, although the North Scrape can be viewed with a telescope from the shingle ridge). The North Scrape is favoured by Cormorant, wildfowl, waders and gulls, but facing directly south, the light is poor for much of the middle of the day. Continuing along the shingle bank, the East Bank is reached after a further 500 yards.

The West Bank This parallels the Beach Road from the beach car park towards the village, and continues, behind the windmill, to Cley Sluice. For its entire length, it affords views west over Blakeney Fresh Marshes, and also east over Cley NWT reserve.

The East Bank This runs between the A149 (where there is a small car park) and the sea, and gives views west over the NWT reserve and east over the Serpentine and Arnold's Marsh. The extensive reedbeds west of the East Bank can be good for Bearded Tit. The wet fields east of the East Bank may hold Water Pipit in winter, while Arnold's Marsh usually has a selection of waders and is especially productive for loafing terns on summer evenings. A walk along the north side, inland of the shingle bank, will give closer views of birds at the back of Arnold's Marsh and Salthouse Broad.

Walsey Hills and Snipes Marsh These lie south of the A149 c.100 yards east of the East Bank car park (and although there is space for a couple of cars to pull off the road at Walsey Hills, it is best to park in the East Bank car park). Walsey Hills is owned by the Norfolk Ornithologists' Association, and an information hut is manned irregularly through the season. The limited areas of cover on the hill and around adjacent Snipes Marsh are attractive to migrants (but are a shadow of their former selves, as much of the hill has been ploughed). Access is by permit, but a permit is not necessary in order to visit the information hut or use the public footpath along the west flank of the hill (this being the best area for migrants). The summit of the hill does give views north over Popes Marsh and Salthouse Broad (favoured by Black Tern in spring).

If time permits, the complete circuit of the East Bank, shingle bank, Beach Road and A149 (no footway, but paralleled for much of the way between the East Bank and Beach Road by the NWT's boardwalk), totalling 3 miles, can be profitable.

Birds

In early spring Wheatear can be seen along the beach, often in the vicinity of North hide, and Long-eared Owl, Firecrest and Ring Ouzel are occasionally found on Walsey Hills. Later in the season a variety of waders occurs, with Temminck's Stint being something of a speciality in May (although not guaranteed, the species is frequently present). Other regular spring migrants include Spoonbill, Garganey, Whimbrel, Black-tailed Godwit, Ruff, Little Gull and Black Tern.

Breeding birds at Cley include Bearded Tit, a reedbed speciality, but numbers fluctuate and it can be hard to see. Late summer and autumn are best, and calm days, when the birds are easier to hear, and may be seen clambering to the top of reed stems, are best. Breeding waders include large numbers of vociferous Avocets, as well as Lapwing and Redshank. Marsh Harrier is frequently present in summer and may breed. Large numbers of Black-tailed Godwits summer, as do a few Ruff. Sandwich, Common and Little Terns visit from the colonies on Blakeney Point, and Roseate and Arctic Terns and Yellow-legged, Mediterranean and Little Gulls are less regular summer visitors. Reed and Sedge Warblers are common in the reeds. Bittern bred until recently (and a single is still present at the time of writing in summer 2002) but was hard to see. The best chance was in June–July when they were feeding young and regularly flew to and from their feeding areas; and the best tactic to see the species (if present) is to choose a spot (such as the East or West Banks) with a panoramic view of the reedbeds and reed-filled dykes, wait and hope.

In autumn, wader passage commences with the arrival of Spotted Redshank and Green Sandpiper in late June, and numbers and variety of species increase to a peak in late August. Typical species include Little Ringed Plover, Little Stint, Curlew Sandpiper, Ruff, Black tailed Godwit, Whimbrel, Greenshank, and Wood and Common Sandpipers. Spotted Crake and Jack Snipe are occasionally seen in autumn, while Water Rail is more frequent at this time. A few Wrynecks and Barred Warblers are found each year, usually in August–September; Walsey Hills is a favoured area, but any cover should be checked.

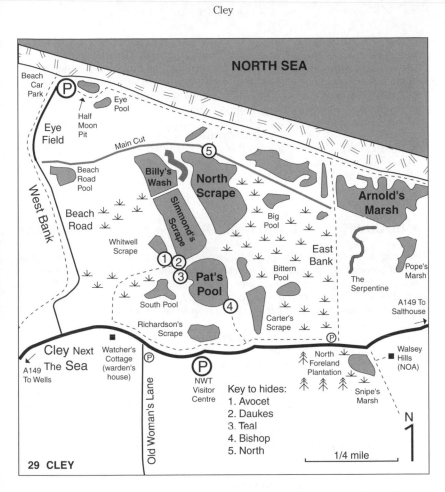

NORTH SEA

Beach Car Park

Eye Pool

Half Moon Pit

Eye Field

Main Cut

Beach Road Pool

West Bank

Billy's Wash

⑤

North Scrape

Arnold's Marsh

Beach Road

Simmond's Scrape

Big Pool

Whitwell Scrape

① ②

East Bank

Pope's Marsh

③ Pat's Pool

Bittern Pool

The Serpentine

South Pool

④

A149 To Salthouse

Richardson's Scrape

Carter's Scrape

Cley Next The Sea

Watcher's Cottage (warden's house)

A149 To Wells

P

North Foreland Plantation

Walsey Hills (NOA)

Snipe's Marsh

NWT Visitor Centre

Key to hides:
1. Avocet
2. Daukes
3. Teal
4. Bishop
5. North

Old Woman's Lane

N

1/4 mile

29 CLEY

Terns are regularly present offshore in summer and autumn, and small numbers of Arctic Skuas are always present in the Cley–Blakeney area at this season, as are Fulmar and Gannet. From late August, north and northwest gales can produce a greater variety of seabirds. Long-tailed Skua is possible earlier in the season, with the chance of Great and Pomarine Skuas increasing in September–October. Manx Shearwater is also regular, but Sooty Shearwater and Leach's Petrel tend to occur only in the best conditions. Storms from late October can produce small 'wrecks' of Little Auks. Little Gull is regular offshore, especially in late autumn, and occasionally Woodcock and Long-eared and Short-eared Owls can be seen flying in off the sea at this time.

In winter Dark-bellied Brent Geese frequent the grassy fields alongside the flocks of feral Greylag and Canada Geese, and Black Brant is sometimes found in the flocks of Brent Geese. In recent years Pink-footed Geese have become much more regular, although they are usually only seen flying over, and occasional parties of Barnacle and White-fronted Geese may also occur; occasionally even a Pale-bellied Brent or Tundra Bean Geese too. Golden Plover and Lapwing also favour the fields, with a few Water Pipits in some of the wetter areas. Barn Owl is resident and seen fairly frequently, but Merlin, Hen Harrier and Short-eared Owl are only occasional. Many dabbling duck winter on the marsh, largely Wigeon, Gadwall, Teal, Pintail, and Shoveler. Goldeneye is frequent on Arnold's

Marsh and Red-throated Diver is always offshore (but can only be seen in calm conditions); Black-throated and Great Northern Divers and Red-necked and Slavonian Grebes are much less common. Snow Bunting inhabits the beach anywhere between Blakeney Point and Weybourne, and are somewhat elusive, while the small and sporadic groups of Lapland Buntings prefer the roughest grazing marshes and are hard to find.

Information
Cley Marsh (NWT) Warden: Bernard Bishop, Watcher's Cottage, Cley, Holt, Norfolk NR25 7RZ. Tel: 01263 740008. E-mail: BernardB@nwt.org.uk
NOA Walsey Hills Warden: Tom Fletcher. Tel: 01263 740875.

30 BLAKENEY POINT AND HARBOUR (Norfolk) OS Landranger 132

The unique 3½-mile shingle spit of Blakeney Point is best known for attracting migrant passerines, sometimes in substantial falls, and until recently for its large colony of terns (some of which have now abandoned the site). The Point is owned by the NT, has been a reserve since 1912 and is now a NNR. It is best visited in spring and autumn for migrants, and in summer for terns.

Habitat
Extensive sand dunes cover much of the point while the spit is largely shingle, which at the Cley end tends to be severely depleted during large winter storms. In places marram grass helps stabilise the dunes and areas of dense *Suaeda* bushes occur on the southern, landward, edge of the spit, particularly at Halfway House, the Hood and the Long Hills. Patches of rank vegetation occur on the point, together with a tiny rectangular patch of stunted trees c.200 yards east of the tea room (the Plantation) and both these and the *Suaeda* bushes are excellent for migrants. To the south, Blakeney Harbour contains extensive well-vegetated saltmarshes.

Access (see map)
Blakeney Point To view the breeding terns in summer the easiest option is to take a tripper boat from Morston quay to the landing stage at Pinchens Creek, and these excursions usually also permit excellent views of Common and Grey Seals. Boats can only operate around high water, however, and allow only limited time on the Point (generally just one hour, and a maximum of three hours); boats operate, according to the tides, daily in April–October and on some weekends in winter (booking advisable July–August).

Alternatively, it is possible to walk to the Point from Cley coastguards. This is a long, tiring walk along the shingle and, if the tide is low, it is easier to walk along the beach where it is firmer underfoot. There is an information centre and tea room at the Point in the old Lifeboat House (open only in summer), and a hide. Visitors should avoid disturbing the tern colony; the main breeding areas are roped-off during summer and dogs are banned April–August, but access is otherwise unrestricted.

In spring and autumn, when searching for migrant passerines, it is best to walk in at least one direction along the muddy and sometimes indistinct track which skirts the landward side of the point (returning along the beach, or taking a boat one way if the tide permits). Areas of cover are scattered along the route (the best being perhaps at Halfway House, the Hood and Long Hills), and at the Point itself the Plantation, lupins and the elder all deserve careful scrutiny. Most

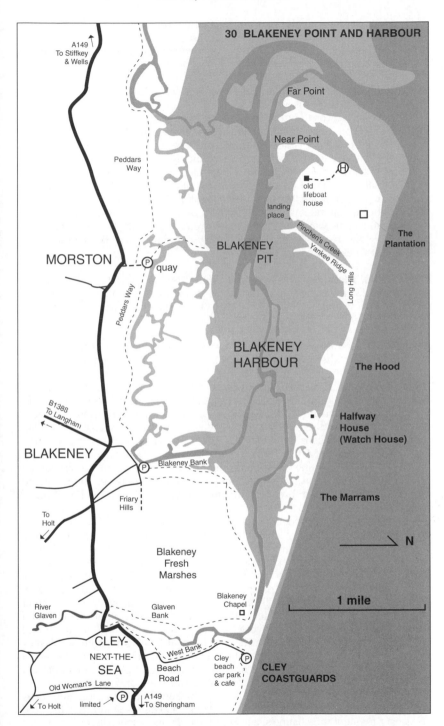

30 BLAKENEY POINT AND HARBOUR

A149
To Stiffkey
& Wells

Far Point

Near Point

Peddars
Way

old
lifeboat
house

landing
place

Pinchen's Creek

Yankee Ridge

The
Plantation

MORSTON

P quay

BLAKENEY
PIT

Peddars Way

Long Hills

BLAKENEY
HARBOUR

The Hood

B1388
To Langham

Halfway
House
(Watch House)

BLAKENEY

P Blakeney Bank

Friary
Hills

To
Holt

The Marrams

N

Blakeney
Fresh
Marshes

Blakeney
Chapel

1 mile

River
Glaven

Glaven
Bank

CLEY-
NEXT-THE-
SEA

West Bank

Cley
beach
car park
& cafe

P

CLEY
COASTGUARDS

Beach
Road

Old Woman's Lane

P

limited

A149
To Sheringham

To Holt

migrants skulk deep in the *Suaeda*, and often only give brief, flight views, although there are exceptions. By far the most successful tactic involves teams of birdwatchers gently chivying birds out of cover; the Point is very hard work for a lone observer.

Blakeney harbour The harbour can be viewed from the track to the Point, but more convenient access is as follows:
1. The look-out at Morston quay car park gives elevated, but distant, views over the harbour. From here a muddy trail leads to the harbour, joining the Peddars Way/Norfolk Coast Path, which in turn skirts the entire landward edge of the harbour. This can be good for Twite and occasionally also Snow Bunting in winter.
2. From the car park on the harbour's edge at Blakeney, the seawall (Blakeney Bank) parallels the main channel, known as Blakeney Pit. There are tidal saltmarshes on the left while the drier rough grassland of Blakeney Fresh Marshes is on the right. At high tide, many waders roost on the saltings. It is possible to follow the bank all the way round the marshes, returning via the Glaven Bank to the main A149 coast road. The bank is extremely popular with walkers during summer, and at weekends year-round.

Friary Hills, Blakeney This area of scattered bushes lies along the seaward edge of Blakeney village, and has good potential for attracting interesting migrants. Follow the road east for 200 yards from Blakeney quay car park.

Birds

At the Point itself there is a colony of terns, but in recent years the numbers breeding have fallen (especially Black-headed Gull, Common Tern and Sandwich Tern, the latter having moved to Scolt Head Island—formerly the colony comprised 1500–3800 pairs of Sandwich Tern, 200–300 pairs of Common Tern and several thousand pairs of Black-headed Gull). Numbers of larger gulls breeding have grown, however, with almost 200 pairs each of Herring and Lesser Black-backed Gulls; this is probably the reason for the decline of the smaller species. In recent seasons, a handful of Roseate Terns have also summered in the area and a few pairs of Arctic Terns and Mediterranean Gulls have bred. Perhaps unaffected by the decline of the main ternery, there is a nationally important population of Little Terns, with up to 215 pairs scattered between the Point and Cley coastguards. Other breeders include Shelduck, Oystercatcher, Ringed Plover and Redshank.

Although migrants do occur in spring, autumn is by far the best time to visit the Point. Falls can occur at any time of day, but are most frequent in the afternoon, and it should be quickly apparent as you walk out whether numbers of birds have arrived or not. In August–September the commonest species are Willow and Garden Warblers, Redstart and Pied Flycatcher, with thrushes, Starling and finches dominant in late autumn. Sadly, perhaps due to the European-wide decline of common birds, substantial falls have become increasingly scarce. Scarcer migrants found annually include Dotterel, Wryneck, Bluethroat, Icterine and Barred Warblers, Red-breasted Flycatcher and Ortolan Bunting (and these and other rarities may occur alone, in the absence of a fall). Offshore, north winds may induce an impressive seabird passage, typically Gannet, Kittiwake and a variety of terns with a few Manx Shearwaters and Arctic and Great Skuas. Pomarine and Long-tailed Skuas, Sabine's Gull and Sooty Shearwater are only occasional.

In winter, Dark-bellied Brent Geese feed in Blakeney harbour alongside many Wigeon and the commoner wintering waders. Goldeneye and Red-breasted Merganser frequent the channels, and sea duck, divers (especially Red-throated) and the rarer grebes are sometimes seen offshore or in Blakeney Pit. The fresh

Golden Oriole

This is a very rare breeding bird, mostly confined to East Anglia. It is also rather uncommon on passage. The East Anglian birds nest in a narrow band of riverbank poplars, but on passage it may turn up in woodland, parkland and gardens. The male's brilliant black-and-yellow plumage is surprisingly effective camouflage amongst spring foliage.

Key sites: Breckland (Lakenheath), Isles of Scilly (migrant).

Common Crane

This magnificent bird is resident in tiny numbers in the Broadland area of Norfolk. Dispersing breeders and young birds may turn up elsewhere, but most records are from East Anglia. It is secretive during the breeding season and vulnerable to disturbance, and therefore it is best looked for in autumn and winter.

Key sites: Hickling Broad, Waxham and Horsey.

Water Pipit

This species is a winter visitor to southern and eastern England. It is most commonly found inland, on marshes, riverbanks and other wetland areas, where it forages for invertebrate food. It is an unobtrusive and shy bird which can be difficult to find. By March, when the species departs for its breeding grounds, many will have acquired their attractive peach-tinted breeding plumage.

Key sites: Hampshire Avon, Christchurch Harbour, Stodmarsh, Minsmere, Chew Valley Lake.

Bittern

This shy, brown heron requires large areas of reedbed – a dwindling habitat in Britain. It is therefore a rare breeding species, with a strong-hold in East Anglia and a few other sites. In winter, numbers are boosted by continental immigrants. Males may be heard 'booming' in spring, but sightings are easier at winter roosts.

Key sites: Minsmere, Walberswick, Cley, Leighton Moss, Rye Harbour (winter), Lee Valley Park (winter – good sightings almost guaranteed!).

marshes also hold Brent Geese, alongside Golden Plover, and raptors, notably Peregrine, may occasionally be seen over the area. Twite can be found in the salt-marshes of the harbour, with Snow Bunting along the beach. Lapland Bunting and Shore Lark are generally in the area but are usually difficult to locate.

Information
Blakeney Point NT Property Manager, Joe Reed, 35 The Cornfield, Langham, Holt, Norfolk NR25 7DQ. Tel: 01263 740480 or 740241 (summer), 01328 830401 (winter). E-mail: abyjrx@smtp.ntrust.org.uk
Ferry Operators, from Blakeney: Graham Bean (01263 740505); Colin Bishop (01263 740753); Roy Moreton (01328 830394). From Morston: John Bean (01263 740038); Jim Temple (01263 740791).

31 STIFFKEY—WARHAM GREENS (Norfolk)   OS Landranger 132

This stretch of coast holds a variety of raptors in the winter, while the area is backed by stands of trees and bushes which are attractive to migrants, especially in autumn. Recent management at Stiffkey has created a new wetland area, Stiffkey Fen, which attracts a range of interesting birds throughout the year.

Habitat
The marshes along this stretch of coast form part of one the biggest expanses of saltmarsh in Europe, and are included within the Holkham NNR. Immediately inland lie areas of mixed farmland, bisected by the Stiffkey River.

Access (see map)
Stiffkey Woods At the west end of Stiffkey village take the minor road (the Greenway) north towards the campsite and park at the end. Immediately to the east lies a narrow belt of trees, Stiffkey Wood, which can be attractive to migrants, while to the west are occasional areas of brambles and rough ground which may also hold a variety of migrants.

Warham Pit Continuing west from Stiffkey Woods, the track eventually reaches an overgrown pit at Warham Greens, attractive to migrants. This can also be accessed by taking the track north off the A149 1 mile west of Stiffkey village (directly opposite the first turning to the south (to Warham) on the A149 west of Stiffkey village); although marked unsuitable for motors, there is a small car park at the end (do not take the track to the north ⅓ mile west of here, also marked unsuitable for motors, because it really is!).

Stiffkey Fen An area of c.30 acres east of Stiffkey has been impounded to create a wet reedbed. Although as yet immature, the area of shallow water that has resulted has attracted many interesting birds. As the reedbed develops the attraction to waders and wildfowl will diminish, although species such as Bittern, Marsh Harrier and Bearded Tit may well appear. The area can be viewed from the sea-wall and the public footpath along the west bank of the River Stiffkey. Park at Morston Quay NT car park and walk west along the coast footpath for just over 1 mile to view.

Birds
In spring, and especially autumn, the area can be productive for passerine migrants, and has attracted a number of rarities, including several Pallas's

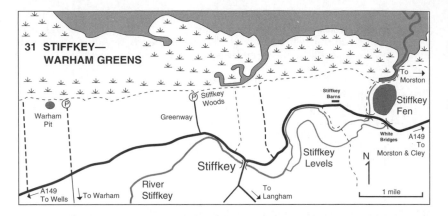

Warblers. Such events are very weather dependent, however, with winds between north and east being best. Migrants at Stiffkey Fen may include Garganey and Mediterranean Gull.

In winter, visitors to the Stiffkey Fen area include Black-tailed Godwit, Ruff and Grey and Golden Plovers, and a variety of the commoner waders are found in the saltmarsh gutters as well as several Little Egrets. A few Hen Harriers roost on the saltings, and Short-eared Owl, Peregrine and Merlin may also occur. It is best to view from the end of the Greenway at Stiffkey or from Warham Pits. Immediately inland, the valley of the Stiffkey River between Stiffkey and Warham has held several Rough-legged Buzzards over the years.

Summer is often quiet, but breeding birds at Stiffkey Fen include Avocet and Shelduck.

32 THE WELLS–HOLKHAM AREA (Norfolk) OS Landranger 132

This stretch of the north Norfolk coast forms part of Holkham NNR. Numbers of migrant passerines, sometimes including rarities, can occur in spring and autumn in appropriate weather conditions. The fields immediately inland of the coast regularly attract a variety of geese in winter, and hold breeding wildfowl and waders, while the sea holds divers, grebes and sea duck in winter.

Habitat

At low tide very extensive sand- and mudflats are exposed along the coast and bordering these is a long series of sand dunes, planted with a narrow belt of pines along a 3-mile stretch from Wells Woods in the east to Holkham Pines in the west (collectively known as Holkham Meals). The northern, exposed side of the pines does not support much vegetation but along the south edge dense areas of scrub and deciduous trees flourish (mainly birches and sallows), especially at the Wells end, where a particularly lush, overgrown hollow is known as the Dell. An area of fields lies between the pines and the A149 coast road, and recent management has raised the water table to create some flooded areas and greatly improve its suitability for both breeding and visiting wildfowl and waders. South of the coast road lie the extensive, walled grounds of Holkham Park, in which grassy parkland is interspersed with stands of mature deciduous woodland and there is a large artificial lake.

194

Access (see map)

Wells harbour The harbour can be viewed from the A149 in Wells town (limited parking on the quay), and from here a minor road signed to the Beach and Pinewoods leads north to a large pay-and-display car park. To the left of this road, the grassy areas attract roosting waders and Dark-bellied Brent Goose. At the car park, the sea wall by the lifeboat station affords views of the outer part of Wells harbour.

Wells Woods From the A149 in Wells town follow the beach road (signed Beach and Pinewoods) to the pay-and-display car park. From here go through the kissing gate and past the north end of Abraham's Bosom (the boating lake, which can occasionally hold a grebe or sea duck in winter). After the next gate, the left-hand path crosses an area of brambles and then follows the south edge of the pines. The Dell (a circular embanked area with birches concentrated along the seaward side) lies on the right after 400 yards, and a long, near-dry pit known as the Drinking Pool is hidden within a dense area of pines 400 yards further. Continuing, the path follows the landward fringe of the woods to Holkham Gap. The path to the right from the kissing gate heads towards the sea, passing the old toilet block.

Lady Ann's Drive and Holkham Gap This private road runs north from the village of Holkham on the A149 coast road, towards Holkham Gap. Parking is available along the drive (toll in summer and at weekends). In winter, numbers of geese are present, often close to the drive.

Holkham Pines A track leads west from Holkham Gap along the south fringe of the woods, and this is good for migrants, especially in late autumn. Walking west, you pass a small pond (Salts Hole) and then reach the George Washington hide which overlooks Meals House Mere, an artificial scrape which attracts a variety of duck. The hide has good views south over Holkham Fresh Marshes for raptors and geese. Continue past Meals House to the Crossroads, where you meet Bone's Drift (access only in summer), and a short track leads from here to the Joe Jordan hide, which has excellent panoramic views over the fresh marshes. Continuing west along the pines you reach the West End and emerge onto Overy Dunes. Migrants can occur at any point along this walk.

Holkham and Overy Fresh Marshes Traditionally a haunt of winter geese, management of this area of rough grazing inland of the pines has created areas of shallow flooding. Large numbers of duck and waders now breed, and the pools attract migrant waders. Access to the marshes is limited. In summer it is possible to walk along Bone's Drift, a track connecting the pines to the A149 which passes a narrow marshy pool which can attract waders and duck. The main areas of flooding at Wroth's Marsh cannot be seen from Bone's Drift, however, and although it is visible from the A149, views are very distant and the road is rather busy (the A149 is a clearway and the nearest parking is in Lady Ann's Drive). The scrape south of Overy Dunes can, however, be viewed from the dunes. In winter, Bone's Drift is closed to prevent disturbance to the geese; view the Fresh Marshes from Lady Ann's Drive, the George Washington and Joe Jordan hides, or from the concessionary path along the line of the old railway at Chalk Drift.

Gun Hill and Overy Dunes This area of dunes holds a few scattered pockets of bushes and although apparently rather bleak, has attracted some five-star vagrants. It can also be good for raptors in the winter. Access is along the seawall (Overy Bank) from the quayside car park at Burnham Overy Staithe, or from the A149 at the Burnham Thorpe turning (though parking is difficult here) or from the west end of Holkham Pines. Bearded Tit is sometimes found in the reeds alongside Overy Bank.

Holkham Park Turn south off the A149 signed "Holkham Hall, Pottery" and park on the right after 400 yards. The road continues to the main gate of the park and a small portal on the left permits access on foot. Immediately beyond, there may be still occasionally wintering Hawfinch in the hornbeams left of the path (they have declined in recent years); the mature woodland holds all three woodpeckers, Nuthatch, Treecreeper and Marsh Tit, and the sharp-eyed observer may spot a roosting Tawny Owl, especially in the evergreen oaks (and the tall cedar tree near the monument), while the lake holds wildfowl, Cormorant (which formerly roosted, but the trees were felled by the estate, presumably to deter them!) and also Black-necked Grebe, which has become increasingly regular. In the south part of the park, the Avenue (leading to the south gate) is a good area for geese and Brambling in winter.

Birds

Geese are the main attraction in winter. Up to 7,000 Dark-bellied Brent Geese frequent the areas of saltmarsh and the fields south of the pines, and the grazing marshes also attract c.350 White-fronted Geese. After a long absence, large numbers of Pink-footed Geese have returned since the early 1980s, with tens of thousands in the area. Early and late winter they favour the fresh marshes, but November–January/February most fly inland in impressive skeins to feed in sugar beet fields. Many roost on the sands at Wells/Warham, but others use Scolt Head Island, and often the best way to see them is at dawn and dusk on their way to and from their roosts. Sometimes small parties of Tundra Bean Geese join the Pink-feet, and there are also resident feral Greylag, Canada and Egyptian Geese on the fields and around Holkham Hall Lake. Other wildfowl include very large numbers of Wigeon (up to 11,000) and Teal, with a scattering of Gadwall and Shoveler. Raptors may include Hen Harrier, Peregrine and Short-eared Owl, and a few Merlins use the area, but are typically elusive; Merlin and Hen Harrier roost at East Hills in Wells harbour.

The usual waders occur in the harbour and on the shore, with many Golden Plover and occasional Ruff in the fields. In Holkham Bay, as well as Red-throated Diver, small numbers of Slavonian and Red-necked Grebes may be found, especially in November. It is best to walk out across the sands to the water's edge just west of the Gap at low water, but beware the rapid advance of the incoming tide. Small numbers of auks, Goldeneye and Red-breasted Merganser, and also variable numbers (large in some winters) of Common and Velvet Scoters and Eider may also be seen, with Snow Bunting, Twite and regularly Shore Lark on the saltmarsh and shore at Holkham Gap. Divers, grebes and sea duck may also occur in the harbour channel, with occasionally a Shag or Red-necked Grebe near the quay. Twite also occur at roadside puddles along Wells beach road, and at Burnham Overy Staithe. In winter Holkham Park supports Hawfinch (especially in February–March), with Goldeneye and Gadwall on the Lake.

Spring migrants in the pines and dunes may include Ring Ouzel and Siskin, and occasionally also Firecrest or Black Redstart. However, autumn is usually more productive. Migrant numbers depend on the weather, however, with NNE winds being best. From early August, a variety of warblers, Pied and Spotted Flycatchers, Redstart, Wheatear and Whinchat occur, with Wryneck, Icterine and Barred Warblers and Red-backed Shrike annual in very small numbers; Greenish Warbler is one of the more regular early-autumn rarities. In mid-September to November the emphasis shifts to thrushes, Goldcrest, finches and buntings, with rather smaller numbers of warblers. Red-breasted Flycatcher and Yellow-browed Warbler are annual (as is Richard's Pipit on the grazing marshes)

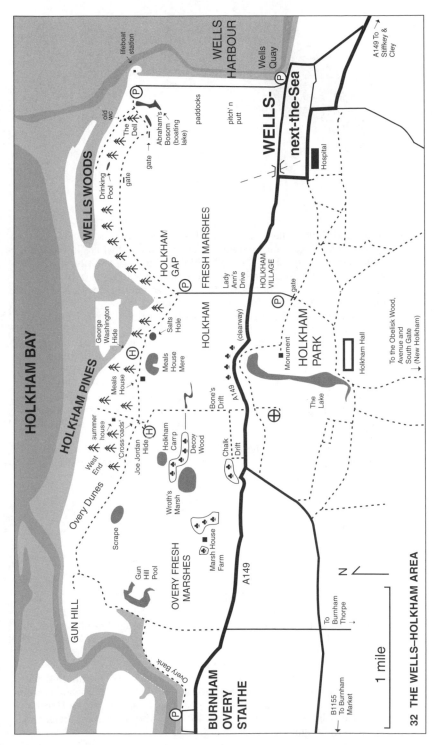

32 THE WELLS–HOLKHAM AREA

Short-eared Owl

and Olive-backed Pipit, Pallas's, Dusky and Radde's Warblers are among the more regular rarities. Passerines migrants may be found anywhere in the pines, although the east end, especially the Dell and Drinking Pool, are perhaps better in early autumn, with the west end being favoured in late autumn. In both spring and autumn, a wide variety of ducks, waders, terns (including Black), and Marsh Harrier may be at the fresh marshes south of the pines.

Breeders include up to 3,000 pairs of Black-headed and a few Herring and Lesser Black-backed Gulls on the marshes at Wells, with Ringed Plover and nationally important numbers of Little Terns on the beach (keep out of the fenced enclosures). Siskin and Crossbill occasionally breed in the pines (and Parrot Crossbill bred near Wells beach car park in 1984 and 1985), with Grasshopper Warbler in the marshy scrub along the south fringes. The grazing marshes hold numbers of Lapwing, Snipe and Redshank. Marsh Harrier and Avocet breed and are usually present in summer, Bittern, Garganey and Bearded Tit have bred, and Spoonbill is an increasingly regular non-breeding visitor.

Information

EN Warden, Ron Harold, Hill Farm Offices, Main Road, Holkham, Wells-next-the-Sea, Norfolk NR23 1AB. Tel: 01328 711183.

33 BURNHAM NORTON (Norfolk)   OS Landranger 132

Forming part of Holkham NNR, this is another area of fresh- and saltmarshes with scattered pools and reedbeds which regularly attracts interesting birds.

Habitat

Three hundred and fifty acres of rough grazing was added to the NNR in 1988 and since then the water table has been raised to encourage breeding and wintering wildfowl and waders.

Access

The easiest access is from the small car park at the north end of Burnham Norton village, following the footpaths north towards the seawall or east towards Overy Mill. Alternative access is on foot along the Norfolk Coast Path from Burnham Deepdale, but this involves a longer walk to reach the interesting areas (and parking space is more limited).

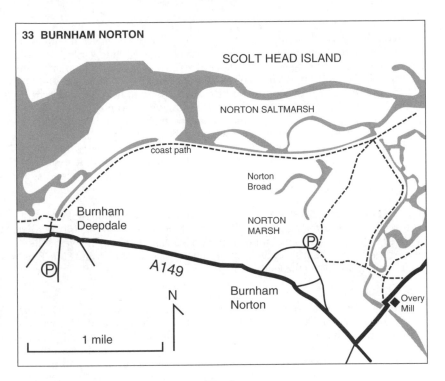

33 BURNHAM NORTON

SCOLT HEAD ISLAND

NORTON SALTMARSH

coast path

Norton Broad

Burnham Deepdale

NORTON MARSH

A149

N

Burnham Norton

Overy Mill

1 mile

Birds

Wintering species include Dark-bellied Brent Goose, Wigeon and a variety of raptors, sometimes including Hen Harrier, Merlin and Short-eared Owl. (Up to 125 Lapland Buntings were formerly present October–March, but the species has now abandoned the site due to grazing pressure on the pastures.) Nearby, Kingfisher can be found on the pond at Burnham Overy Mill.

During passage periods, waders may include Whimbrel, Black-tailed Godwit, Greenshank and Wood Sandpiper, Garganey is regular in spring, and Marsh Harrier and Avocet may be present in summer.

Information

Warden: The Old Chapel, Holkham, Wells-next-the-Sea, Norfolk NR23 1RQ. Tel: 01328 711183.

34 TITCHWELL (Norfolk)   OS Landranger 132

Titchwell is one of the RSPB's premier reserves (indeed, it is now their most visited) and, as a result of effective management, it has become one of the best birding sites on the Norfolk coast. Interesting birds can be found at any time of year, but the greatest diversity is in spring and autumn.

Habitat

The reserve contains brackish and freshwater marshes, sea aster and sea lavender saltmarsh, tidal and freshwater reedbeds, sand dunes, and sandy beach. North of the visitor centre and car park is an area of scrub with some trees.

Access (see map)

Titchwell RSPB reserve Approximately ⅓ mile west of the village of Titchwell on the A149, a track (signed to the RSPB reserve) leads north towards the coast. The car park lies to the right after c.200 yards. The visitor centre, shop and cafe are open weekdays 10.00–17.00 (16.00 November–March), weekends 09.30–17.00 all year, and closed Christmas Day and Boxing Day. From here follow the track north along the embankment to view the marshes, with two public hides to the right of the bank. The footpath eventually reaches the beach, and this is usually a good spot from which to scan for divers, grebes and, especially, sea duck. Additionally, from the visitor centre the Fen Trail leads for c.250 yards through an area of fen and scrub to the Fen hide, which overlooks the reedbed. Access to the reserve is limited to the seawall, the hides and the beach, which are open at all times. No permit is necessary (but there is a car park charge for non-members).

Gypsy Lane Continue east along the A149 through the village of Titchwell and, c.1 mile east of the turning to the RSPB reserve, there is space to pull off the road by a belt of trees. From here a public footpath leads north along the west side of the trees and onto a bank, eventually reaching the beach. Raptors and Little Egret are frequently seen from this path.

Birds

Breeders include Marsh Harrier, Water Rail, Avocet, Reed and Sedge Warblers and Bearded Tit. On the beach there are a few pairs of Ringed Plovers and Oystercatchers. The Fen Trail winds through a scrubby area inhabited by a variety of warblers, sometimes including Grasshopper Warbler, and also attracts passerine migrants. Bittern once bred but is now only an irregular and hard-to-see winter visitor, but recent management has renovated the reedbeds and it is hoped that the species will return to breed; indeed, there are again increasingly regular sightings in summer.

Spring comes late to the north Norfolk coast, but in mid-May and June Titchwell can be an exciting place. As well as the commoner waders, gulls and terns, Spoonbill, Garganey, Little Gull and Black Tern are regular migrants. Indeed, Spoonbills may occur at any time of year, and Little Egrets are now regular year-round and best looked for in the evening when they come into roost. Another resident is the male Black-winged Stilt (affectionately known as Sammy), first seen in August 1993 and still present in 2003.

In autumn, from August to mid-October, a wide variety of passage waders is recorded, including Common and Green Sandpipers. Among scarcer species, Little Stint, Curlew Sandpiper and Black-tailed Godwit are regular. On higher tides, from late summer into winter, large numbers of waders may roost on the saltmarsh, including Oystercatcher, Grey Plover, Knot, Dunlin and Bar-tailed Godwit, and in late summer many of these will still have some summer plumage. Water Rails may be more conspicuous in autumn as its numbers are augmented by migrants, and Spotted Crake is near annual, sometimes making prolonged stays (although much patience may be needed for a sighting). Large numbers of Swallows and martins roost in the reeds, and these may attract a Hobby. Seabird movements can occur offshore after a strong north wind; Gannet and Kittiwake form the bulk with a scattering of Great and Arctic Skuas and the occasional shearwater.

For divers, grebes and sea ducks calm conditions around high tide are best for viewing. In recent winters there has been a large flock of Common Scoter offshore, and there are usually also a few Velvet Scoter too. Red-throated Diver is also regular and Black-throated Diver increasingly so, especially in early winter. There are also usually Slavonian Grebes (which range east to Brancaster) and a handful of Red-necked Grebes. Numbers of Dark-bellied Brent Geese winter in the area, and

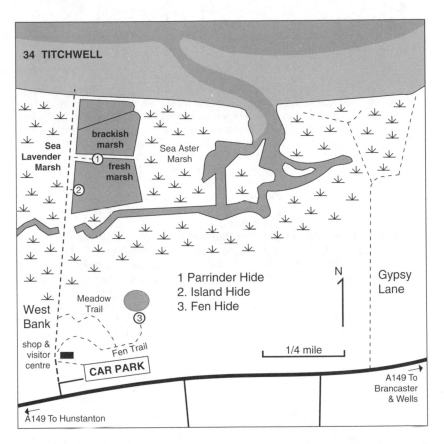

34 TITCHWELL

Sea Lavender Marsh

brackish marsh

(1) fresh marsh

(2)

Sea Aster Marsh

West Bank

Meadow Trail

(3)

Fen Trail

shop & visitor centre

CAR PARK

A149 To Hunstanton

1 Parrinder Hide
2. Island Hide
3. Fen Hide

N

Gypsy Lane

1/4 mile

A149 To Brancaster & Wells

Pink-footed Geese may fly over. The water on the marsh is deeper in winter, and Goldeneye and Red-breasted Merganser are often seen, together with large numbers of dabbling duck, and Cormorant also roosts on the reserve. Waders include large numbers of Golden Plover, and there may also be a handful of wintering Spotted Redshanks and also significant numbers of Ruff. Merlin, Hen Harrier and Short-eared Owl occasionally hunt over the marshes, and small numbers of Hen Harriers roost in the reeds. Snow Buntings are regular on the beach, where they are sometimes joined by Shore Larks. Rock Pipit can be found in the saltmarsh gutters, and there may also be a few wintering Water Pipits (which favour more freshwater habitats). Twite is occasionally also present on the saltmarshes.

Information
RSPB Warden: Titchwell Marsh Reserve, Kings Lynn, Norfolk PE31 8BB. Tel: 01485 210779.

35 HOLME (Norfolk)   OS Landranger 132

Situated on the north coast of Norfolk at the point where an isolated stand of pines marks the entrance to the Wash, Holme is well placed to receive migrants, and the varied habitats make a visit worthwhile at anytime of year. The Norfolk

Wildlife Trust (NWT) owns 600 acres (and leases a further 90 acres at Holme Marsh), while the Norfolk Ornithologists' Association (NOA) operates a private bird observatory from an enclave of seven acres within this area.

Habitat

A small area of saltmarsh lies west of Gore Point but the main habitat is the extensive area of sand dunes. Thickets of sea buckthorn stabilise these in places and are particularly attractive to migrants. Immediately north of the Firs (the NWT warden's house and reserve centre) is a stand of Corsican pines, also attractive to migrants. Just inland of the dunes there is a large brackish pool, Broad Water, and some ponds and scrapes favoured by fresh waders. These are surrounded by reeds, while between the coast and the village is Holme Marsh, an extensive area of rough grassland; management work to raise the water table has made this particularly attractive to winter wildfowl and breeding duck and waders.

Access (see map)

Hunstanton Golf Course and The Paddocks At Holme next the Sea on the A149, take the westernmost road (signed NWT, NOA & Beach) to the sea. The beach car park (fee in summer) is reached after 1 mile and accesses the bushes and scrub on Hunstanton golf course (keep to the seaward edge, away from the greens and fairways; a footpath also skirts the landward edge of the course from the beach car park to Old Hunstanton). To the east and on the seaward side of the houses lies The Paddocks, an excellent area of bushes that are attractive to migrants and can be viewed from the public footpath along its north edge.

Holme NWT and NOA reserves Turn right (east) off the beach road shortly before the beach car park onto a rough private track (toll in summer). After ½ mile a NWT car park lies to the left. From here you can explore the west end of the dunes, following the public footpath east towards the Firs (note that away from the footpath the scrubby areas in the dunes are not open until 10.00, and access is by permit), the Paddocks or walk out on the public footpath towards Gore Point, which can be good for sea duck in winter around high tide. Continuing along the gated track, the NOA and second NWT car parks lie 1 mile further on. The reserves are open daily, 10.00–17.00 (outside these hours the gate is closed). Separate permits, available on site, are required, but it is seldom necessary to enter the NOA area. In the NWT reserve, seven hides overlook Broad Water and the freshwater wader pools, while the pines and scrub on the dunes should be investigated for migrants (please keep to the marked paths and avoid damaging the delicate dune vegetation). During strong onshore winds, seawatching is worthwhile around the period of high tide—watch from the top of the dunes where the footpath cuts through behind the car park at the Firs (the seawatching hide is for NOA members only). Otherwise, the sea is always worth a look for divers, grebes and sea duck.

Birds

Migrant passerines are dependent on suitable weather, north or east winds being best. Wheatear, Whinchat, Redstart, a variety of warblers, and Spotted and Pied Flycatchers are all frequent in spring and autumn, while Black Redstart, Ring Ouzel, Wood Warbler, Firecrest, Red-backed Shrike are also possible, with Wryneck, Bluethroat and Ortolan Bunting much more irregular visitors. Hoopoe and Nightingale are occasional in spring, while in most autumns Barred and Icterine Warblers are noted; Yellow-browed Warbler and Red-breasted Flycatcher are recorded most years, and Long-eared Owl, Woodcock and Lapland Bunting are quite frequent in late autumn. A wide variety of waders

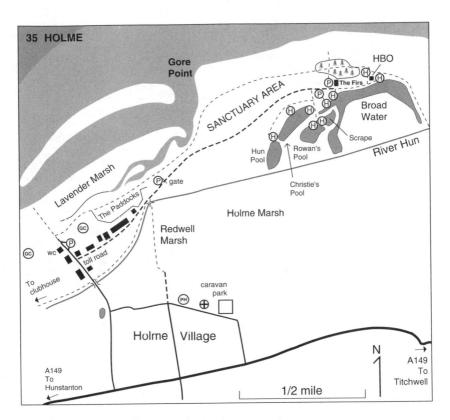

occurs on passage. Offshore, Gannet, Manx Shearwater, and Great and Arctic Skuas are regular from midsummer, together with the occasional Sooty Shearwater or Pomarine Skua.

Breeders include Gadwall, Shoveler, Oystercatcher, Avocet, Ringed Plover, Redshank, Little Tern and Grasshopper Warbler; in 1987, Holme hosted Britain's second record of breeding by Black-winged Stilt. Marsh Harrier and Hobby are frequent visitors in summer.

In winter, Red-throated Diver, Slavonian Grebe, Eider, Long-tailed Duck (off Gore Point at high tide), scoters and Red-breasted Merganser are regular off-shore, and Great Northern and Black-throated Divers and Red-necked Grebe are also regular in small numbers. Up to 700 Dark-bellied Brent Geese and 1,500 Wigeon are regularly present on Holme Marsh, and Pink-footed Geese are increasingly regular visitors. Look too for Hen Harrier, Merlin and Barn Owl, with Kingfisher and Water Rail regular on the pools. Twite and Snow Bunting are often present on the dunes, beach and saltmarsh. Rough-legged Buzzard and Shore Lark are only scarce and irregular visitors, the latter favouring the beach towards Gore Point and Thornham Point.

Information

NWT Warden: Gary Hibberd, The Firs, Broadwater Road, Holme next the Sea, Hunstanton, Norfolk PE36 6LQ. Tel: 01485 525240.

NOA Warden: Jed Andrews, Holme Bird Observatory, Broadwater Road, Holme next the Sea, Hunstanton, Norfolk PE36 6LP. Tel: 01485 525406. E-mail: jedandrews@shrike4.freeserve.co.uk

36 HUNSTANTON AND HEACHAM (Norfolk) OS Landranger 132

The sea off Hunstanton regularly holds numbers of divers, grebes and sea duck in the autumn and winter, and the former season can also be interesting for migrant passerines and sea watching in appropriate weather conditions. Nearby, Heacham is one of the few regular sites in southeast England for Purple Sandpiper.

Habitat

The coast at Hunstanton, a small seaside town, is bordered by low cliffs of chalk, surmounting a layer of carrstone, which extends to form the foundations of the beach and then offshore as a series of reefs. To the south the vast mudflats of the Wash border the coast at Heacham, with a series of old creeks, borrow pits and rough grazing to the landward.

Access

Hunstanton lighthouse The B1161 north of Hunstanton passes close to the coast along the top of Hunstanton cliffs, before joining the A149. There are several shelters along the clifftop, and these are the best spots from which to seawatch. As the B1161 turns east to head inland, a short road leads to the lighthouse and a car park. In season, follow the footpath northwest from here to check for migrant passerines along the edge of the golf course and around Old Hunstanton.

Heacham North Beach Leave Hunstanton south on the A149 and 1½ miles south of the roundabout turn west (opposite the B1454) into Heacham. Follow this road (ignoring side turns) for ¾ mile and then fork right into Station Road to the North Beach. From the car park, explore the beach north towards Hunstanton, looking for Purple Sandpiper on the old groynes. This section of coast can also be accessed from the south end of Hunstanton promenade.

Heacham South Beach Leave the A149 at the southernmost turning to Heacham (signed Heacham Beaches) and, after ¾ mile, turn left, following the road to the car park at South Beach. Walk south from here along the coast. At low water a vast expanse of mud is exposed, with a selection of common waders and large numbers of Common and Black-headed Gulls present. At high water grebes or sea duck may be present. There are a number of chalets with some areas of cover that are attractive to migrants, and immediately inland Heacham harbour (a landlocked creek) can hold interesting ducks. It is possible to follow the coast south to Snettisham Coastal Park (see p.205).

Birds

Sea duck were once a winter speciality at Hunstanton, with numbers of Common Scoter usually present, and often Velvet Scoter too. In recent winters, however, the scoter flock has been off Titchwell (see p.199). Eider may still be present most of the year, but numbers peak in February–March at c.100. Goldeneye and Red-breasted Merganser are usually present, and Scaup may be seen (especially in hard weather). Other wildfowl include Dark-bellied Brent Geese, which favour the shoreline at low tide. Small numbers of divers and grebes are often present; Red-throated Diver and Great Crested Grebe are commonest, but Great Northern and Black-throated Divers and Red-necked and Slavonian Grebes are also possible. Waders may include a handful of Purple Sandpiper, which on a high tide favour the south end of Hunstanton promenade — walk south along the promenade until you reach a concrete ramp entering the sea (the Jet Ski Ramp), also reached by leaving the A149 west on Oasis Way (the B1161), carrying straight on at the roundabout and then turning south into South Beach Road to park after 50 yards. On the south side of this ramp there is a pile of boulders, used by roosting Purple Sandpiper; they are tame, but you should avoid getting too close. At low water they may be found on the mussel beds offshore and the groynes towards Heacham. Other waders include Turnstone and, south along the coast into the Wash, numbers of Curlew, Bar-tailed Godwit, Knot, Dunlin, Redshank and Grey and Ringed Plovers.

In early spring and late autumn Black Redstart may be found (favouring the area of the beach huts bordering the golf course on the north side of Hunstanton, and the chalets at Heacham South Beach). Other interesting passerine migrants, such as Ring Ouzel, may also occur.

Autumn seawatching can be productive at Hunstanton, with gales from a northern quarter being best (NE gales may push numbers of birds into the Wash; some, like the skuas, may escape by moving overland, but many others will return past Hunstanton). Typical species include Fulmar, Gannet and Kittiwake, with Arctic Skua and, later in autumn, Great and sometimes Pomarine Skuas too. Long-tailed Skua and Sabine's Gull are rare, but Little Gull is regular in late autumn and winter (as often in calm conditions as in gales). Manx and Sooty Shearwaters and Leach's Petrel are also possible, together with a variety of grebes, divers, wildfowl and waders. In late autumn and early winter, such conditions may also produce Little Auk among the regular Guillemot and Razorbill.

Breeding birds include small numbers of Fulmars on the cliffs.

37 SNETTISHAM (Norfolk) OS Landranger 132

The Wash is internationally recognised as a major site for wintering wildfowl and waders and the RSPB reserve at Snettisham, on the east side of the Wash c.8 miles north of Kings Lynn, provides access to the wealth and diversity of its birds. The period from late summer into winter is the best time to visit.

Habitat

The RSPB reserve covers 4,500 acres, of which 4,130 acres are intertidal sand and mudflats (extending north towards Heacham South Beach), and 300 acres are saltmarsh. A series of brackish flooded lagoons (created by shingle extraction) and a shingle beach provide further habitats. The south pits have been managed to make them more attractive, and islands have been created which provide roosts for waders and nesting sites for terns.

Access (see map)

Snettisham RSPB reserve Leave the A149 signed to Snettisham Beach and follow the minor road for c.2 miles, where the reserve car park is signed to the left. A well-marked footpath leads from the car park to the beach, through open countryside and scrub on the inland side of the pits. The southernmost pits (with four public hides) are the best and are c.1¼ miles south of the car park. A circular trail accesses all the hides. The reserve is open at all times and a permit is not required. There is currently no visitor centre, but a small reception building within the car park is planned. (Note that the properties at Snettisham beach are private and there is no public access to that area.)

Snettisham Coastal Park Instead of turning into the RSPB car park, follow the Beach Road to its end at the public beach car park. The Coastal Park lies to the north and is an area of sparse stony grassland with areas of scrub and a series of small reed-fringed pools. It can be good for migrants in spring and, to a lesser extent, autumn.

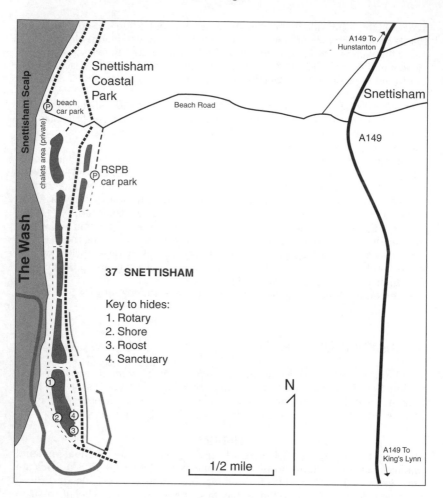

Snettisham Scalp

The Wash

Snettisham Coastal Park

beach car park

chalets area (private)

Beach Road

A149 To Hunstanton

Snettisham

A149

RSPB car park

37 SNETTISHAM

Key to hides:
1. Rotary
2. Shore
3. Roost
4. Sanctuary

1
2 4
3

N

A149 To King's Lynn

1/2 mile

Birds

Waders peak during autumn and winter when up to 120,000 Knot have been counted. At low tide the waders are well scattered over the sand and mudflats, and large numbers are best seen at or just before high tide. Oystercatcher, Knot, Dunlin, Bar-tailed Godwit and Redshank are the commonest species, but Turnstone and Grey Plover are also present. Large numbers roost on the south pits, especially on the fortnightly higher 'spring' tides. Then, from the hides, the spectacle may include 50,000 Knot, 11,000 Dunlin and 6,000 Oystercatcher competing for space, all allowing close views. It is best to visit 2–3 hours each side of high water, and on a 'spring' tide (which coincide with the new and full moons), as these relatively high tides usually flood the mudflats and force the waders onto higher ground, especially the pits at Snettisham, to roost. High water on 'spring' tides usually occurs late evening and early morning, which is fine in spring and autumn but in the winter months 'spring' tides peak during darkness and a late-morning high tide is the best compromise. (Contrariwise, the intervening neap tides leave the mudflats uncovered, and fewer waders move onto the pits to roost—the RSPB produces birdwatchers' tide tables to indicate the best dates each year—available from the Snettisham reserve office, tel: 01485

542689 or the RSPB Titchwell shop). Wildfowl are also numerous, with especially large numbers of Shelduck, and up to 30,000 Pink-footed Geese roost on the mudflats November–February. By day they can frequently be seen feeding on the fields east of the pits and sometimes they are joined by small numbers of Bewick's and Whooper Swans. Large numbers of Dark-bellied Brent Geese are present offshore, while small rafts of Common Scoter and Eider may occasionally be seen on the open water. Many ducks and waders use the pits in winter. Goldeneye and Red-breasted Merganser are invariably present, together with the commoner dabbling and diving ducks. Scaup is also quite regular but Smew and Long-tailed Duck are only occasional. Sometimes Slavonian or Red-necked Grebes or a diver will also visit the pits, or perhaps a Little Auk, and there is a roost of Cormorants. On the beach Snow Bunting is sometimes present.

The variety of waders increases during migration and although there is little habitat here for freshwater species, Black-tailed Godwit, Curlew Sandpiper and Little Stint may sometimes occur on the shore or in the wader roost on the pits. From July wader numbers begin to build up, and at this time large numbers of Knot and Bar-tailed Godwit may be seen with vestiges of their summer plumage. Among other migrants, Arctic Skua is frequent offshore in August–September, and Gannet and Kittiwake may be seen in strong onshore winds, but the area is not noted for good seawatching. Passerine migrants should be searched for in the bushes along the shore. In particular, the area north of the beach car park is graced by the occasional Ring Ouzel.

Midsummer is quiet. Common Tern breeds on the pits together with large numbers of gulls, Oystercatcher, Ringed Plover and Redshank.

Information

RSPB Warden: Jim Scott, 43 Lynn Road, Snettisham, King's Lynn PE31 7RA. Tel: 01485 542689.

38 SANDRINGHAM (Norfolk)   OS Landranger 132

Sandringham Country Park is part of the Sandringham Estate and is open to the public. Areas of mature woodland hold Redstart, Nightingale, Wood Warbler and Crossbill in summer. Golden Pheasant is regularly seen along the minor roads either side of the A149, particularly at dawn; the road to Wolferton is one of the best. The birds here appear to have hybridised historically with Lady Amherst's Pheasant, as they show some characters of the latter species.

39 WAYLAND WOOD (Norfolk)   OS Landranger 144

This stand of ancient woodland lies in southwest Norfolk, between Thetford and East Dereham, and is a prime site for Golden Pheasant. It is an NWT reserve.

Access

Leave Watton south on the A1075 and, after c.1 mile, Wayland Wood is the first stretch of woodland alongside the road. The entrance to the small car park lies to the left of the road, c.100 yards beyond the beginning of the wood. A network of paths allow access to the wood.

Birds

The speciality is Golden Pheasant. This introduced species can be hard to find as it prefers areas of dense cover. Winter or early spring, when males are calling, are the best periods to look and, surprisingly, mid-afternoon is often a good time to see a calling male. Otherwise, early morning and dusk are favoured times for a sighting. Other species include Woodcock, all three woodpeckers and Willow Tit.

40–46 BRECKLAND (Norfolk/Suffolk)   OS Landranger 143 and 144

Breckland is a unique area of sandy heathland and conifer plantations centred around Thetford. Famed for several scarce breeding species, it is best in spring or early summer.

Habitat

Breckland (or The Brecks) lies on an area of light, sandy soil between the Fens to the west (now almost entirely drained) and heavier boulder clays to the east. The Little Ouse River bisects the area, but there is little standing water away from the mysterious ephemeral Breckland meres. Cleared for agriculture in prehistoric times, The Brecks quickly developed heathland on the poorer soils, with continuous farming confined to the richer river valleys. Periodically, however, when demand was high, areas of heath would be ploughed and sown for a season; these were the original "Breck". Thus, traditionally, Breckland was a huge area of heathland, intensively grazed by sheep and rabbits. Following the First World War, however, vast areas were planted with conifers, mainly Corsican or Scots pines, and now only small relics of heath remain. Forestry is now the dominant land-use, and as the plantations have matured, been felled and then replanted, they have provided habitats for a range of interesting species.

Access

There are many interesting areas worthy of exploration, and many species are most easily found by looking for conifer plantations in the right stage of growth (with many of the best areas in the triangle formed by Mundford, Brandon and Thetford. The following sites are particularly notable.

40 LYNFORD ARBORETUM (Norfolk)   OS Landranger 144

The arboretum is favoured by Hawfinch, especially in winter and early spring, and Crossbills is frequently present too, sometimes with Firecrest. (Hawfinch favours the trees at the west end of the arboretum or the large beech trees in the field beyond the lake.) Turn east off the A1065, c.⅓ of a mile north of the Mundford roundabout, on a minor road signed Lynford Hall & Arboretum. After 1 mile (just past the hotel) turn left (north) into the car park. Cross the road to the disabled car park, from where a number of footpaths permit access to the arboretum.

41 WEETING HEATH NNR (Norfolk) OS Landranger 143

Weeting Heath is owned and managed by the Norfolk Wildlife Trust (NWT), and holds several pairs of Stone Curlews, as well as Woodlarks, which are often in the area in front of the west enclosure. Leave Brandon north on the A1065 towards Swaffham and, immediately after the level crossing, turn left on the minor road towards Weeting. After 1¼ miles, turn left (west at the village green in Weeting, next to the phone box and post office, towards Hockwold cum Wilton. After a further mile the reserve car park is on the left (concealed within a belt of pines). The reserve is open April–August, with access restricted to the tracks through the pine belt to the two hides. These overlook a large area of grass heath and are ideal for viewing Stone Curlew, which are easiest to see in early spring; as the season progresses they may only be obvious in early morning and again in late afternoon and evening.

42 MAYDAY FARM (Suffolk) OS Landranger 144

Leave Brandon south on the B1106 and, after 2 miles, turn right (west) into the FC car park at Mayday Farm. From here, walk directly southwest along the Goshawk Nature Trail, which follows the main ride (Shakers Road) for c.¾ mile until a large clearing comes into view to the left (south) of the track and a cross-roads is reached. This is a good spot from which to scan for displaying Goshawk and there is a hide here. There is also Nightjar, Tree Pipit, Woodlark and Crossbill in this area, with Golden Pheasant in the plantations. It is possible to either return directly to the car park or to turn left, and then left and left again, to follow the nature trail on a circuit around the large clearing and rejoin Shakers Road c.½ mile from the car park.

43 THETFORD WARREN (Norfolk) OS Landranger 144

The extensive plantations in this area hold Goshawk, as well as Woodlark and sometimes Crossbill. The car park is at Thetford Warren Lodge, south of the B1107, 1 mile northwest of the A11 Thetford bypass, and c.4 miles southeast of Brandon town centre. From the car park three marked trails permit exploration of Risbeth Wood.

44 EAST WRETHAM HEATH (Norfolk) OS Landranger 144

This reserve of the NWT comprises areas of grassy heath, as well as some wood-land, including hornbeam and ancient Scots pine, and two meres, Langmere and Ringmere. Fed by ground water, these fluctuate mysteriously and sometimes completely dry-up. They may attract wildfowl and occasionally passage waders. Otherwise, the reserve holds Long-eared Owl, Nightjar, wintering Hawfinch (which favours the mature hornbeams around Ringmere) and Crossbill. Leave the A11 at the northeast end of the Thetford bypass on the A1075 towards Watton. After 2¼ miles the reserve car park lies left (west) of the road by the war-den's house (first on the left past the level crossing, 400 yards past the lay-by). There is a signed nature trail, and the reserve is open daily 10.00–17.00.

45 BARNHAM CROSS COMMON (Norfolk) OS Landranger 144

This is the best site for Hawfinch in the Thetford area. Leaving Thetford south-wards on the A134 towards Bury St Edmunds, park in a lay-by on the right about 150 yards after the left-hand turn to The Nunnery. Cross the road and head east straight across the common (short walk). The Hawfinches are on the east side of the common and sit in the big trees by the Anglian Water Pumping Station. They can be seen at any time of day, but are not present in the summer.

46 LAKENHEATH RSPB RESERVE (Suffolk and Norfolk) OS Landranger 143

In a bold step the RSPB has created a completely new 346-acre reedbed on the very edge of the fenland plain, with the aim of attracting up to eight territory-holding male Bitterns. There are, however, no visiting arrangements as yet, although some of the flooded areas can be seen from the footpath along the Little Ouse. The poplar plantations beside the Little Ouse are well known for their breeding Golden Orioles, and now form part of the RSPB reserve. Follow the B112 north from Lakenheath and after c.2½ miles the road crosses the railway adjacent to Lakenheath station. The reserve car park lies left (west) of the road after a short distance. From here, walk north along the road for c.100 yards and then take the footpath west along the south bank of the Little Ouse. The plantations are south of the river after c.1 mile, and there is strictly no access away from the footpath. Early mornings and evenings are the best time for a sighting of Golden Oriole, and the best tactic is to find a point where there is line of sight down a ride or gap in the trees and wait, scanning carefully, for orioles to fly across.

Birds
Breckland birds can be divided into two groups: the traditional heathland specialities and birds of the conifer plantations. Of the first group, Stone Curlew is the most important. It is not, however, confined to relict grassy heaths, for it has adapted to arable fields, where it can breed successfully only with the support of conservation-minded farmers. Stone Curlew can be seen reliably at the NWT Weeting Heath reserve, and visiting birders need look no further for the species. They are in residence mid-March to September. Another heathland speciality, Red-backed Shrike, had its last British stronghold in Breckland, but has now sadly disappeared, and even Wheatear, once relatively common on the sandy heaths, is now rather scarce (and the last Great Bustard was shot in 1838!). Areas of heather and gorse may hold Whinchat and also Nightjar.

The very extensive area of conifer plantations has now matured and is being felled and replanted, and each stage in their growth attracts a particular suite of species. The mature stands hold breeding Goshawk, and there is now a size-able population in Breckland. They are, however, often elusive, and best seen when displaying on clear sunny days in late February–April, usually at 09.30–11.00 and 14.00–15.00. The key to success is to choose the right weather and a locality which offers a panoramic view over a wide area. The plantations also hold large numbers of Sparrowhawk, but Breckland Goshawks, descended from imported falconers' birds, are usually rather large and pale (indicating a north European origin), and are thus relatively easy to distinguish from Sparrowhawk. Mature plantations also attract Crossbill, but the population of this species fluctuates dramatically and while they can be everywhere in some seasons, in other years they may be impossible to find. Listen for the dry *chip, chip* flight calls and in dry weather any water source, such as pools and puddles, is worth checking, as crossbills are thirsty birds. Siskin is a recent colonist, but is uncommon, and the mature plantations hold small numbers of Long-eared Owl, but they are seldom seen. The best chance is to listen for their calls at night in early spring.

Once clear-felled, the large blocks of very young conifers attract Woodlark. These are largely absent in midwinter, but have increased tremendously in recent years (48 territories in 1986 to 420 in 1997!). They prefer recently planted areas of conifers and are easiest to see in late March–late April when in song flight. Nightjars also favour young plantations, as well as heaths, but are late-arriving summer visitors, best looked for at dusk on warm, still, summer evenings. The areas of clear-fell also attract Tree Pipit, and occasionally also Grasshopper Warbler (which also favours the few damper heaths). As the young plantations grow, they form thickets which may hold Golden Pheasant. This introduction from China is hard to find in the dense cover, and is best looked for early and late in the day along forest tracks or the edges of plantations. Hawfinch prefers hornbeams, if available, and although widespread and resident, can be very unobtrusive; it is easiest to find in winter when it forms loose flocks. Some of the other interesting breeding species include Woodcock, Curlew, Lesser Spotted Woodpecker, Nightingale and Redstart, most of which favour deciduous woodland, usually found along watercourses and as disguises along the edges of conifer plantations. Poplar plantations in river valleys support a very small population of Golden Orioles, but numbers fluctuate widely from year to year.

Breckland is generally quiet in winter, although Goshawk and Crossbill may still be found, and there is a chance of a Hen Harrier or Great Grey Shrike on areas of heath or clear-fell, but spring comes early, with both Goshawk and Woodlark best looked for from March.

Information

East Wretham Heath (NWT): Bev Nichols, The Wardens House, East Wretham Heath, Thetford Road, Wretham, Thetford, Norfolk IP24 1RU. Tel: 01953 498339. E-mail: BevN@nwt.org.uk
Weeting Heath (NWT): (April–August). Tel: 01842 827615.

47 OUSE WASHES (Norfolk/Cambridgeshire)　　　OS Landranger 143

The unique wet meadows of the Ouse Washes, in the heart of the East Anglian fens, are renowned as a refuge for wildfowl in winter and for several rare breeding species in summer. Around three-quarters of the total area is now owned and managed by the RSPB, Wildlife Trust for Cambridgeshire and WWT. A visit is profitable at any time of year, but winter is the most spectacular season.

Habitat

The Ouse Washes lie between two straight, almost parallel artificial rivers (or drains), the Old and New Bedford Rivers. The Washes were created in the 17th century as part of the Earl of Bedford's ambitious scheme to drain large parts of the fens, and were designed to flood as necessary in winter to control water levels elsewhere. Although little more than half a mile wide, the Washes extend for over 20 miles between Earith in Cambridgeshire and Denver Sluice near Downham Market in Norfolk. The area is permanent pasture, grazed in summer by cattle and sheep, and regularly flooded in winter; numerous ditches divide the flood plain into 'washes'. Recent management has created a series of permanently flooded lagoons and scrapes. Apart from the high banks along-

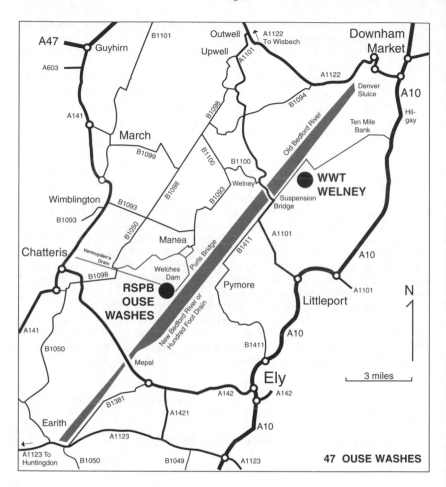

47 OUSE WASHES

side the drains, the area is entirely flat and the few trees grow along the barrier banks.

Access (see maps)

Welney WWT lies on the east bank of the Washes, and is thus best in the morning (and again in the mid-afternoon/evening, when the swans are fed), while the RSPB Ouse Washes reserve faces east and is best in the afternoon. Note that when the Washes are fully flooded, the A1101 is closed where it crosses the Washes and thus a long detour is necessary if travelling between the two reserves.

RSPB Ouse Washes reserve This reserve is jointly owned by the RSPB and the Wildlife Trust for Cambridgeshire. From the A141 at Chatteris take the B1098 signed Upwell and Downham Market. The road turns sharp left after 2 miles and after a few hundred yards crosses Vermuyden's Drain. Immediately after crossing the drain turn right to Manea (signed 4 miles). At the beginning of the village a right turn is signed Purls Bridge, Welches Dam and Nature Reserve. At Purls Bridge the road follows the Old Bedford River to Welches

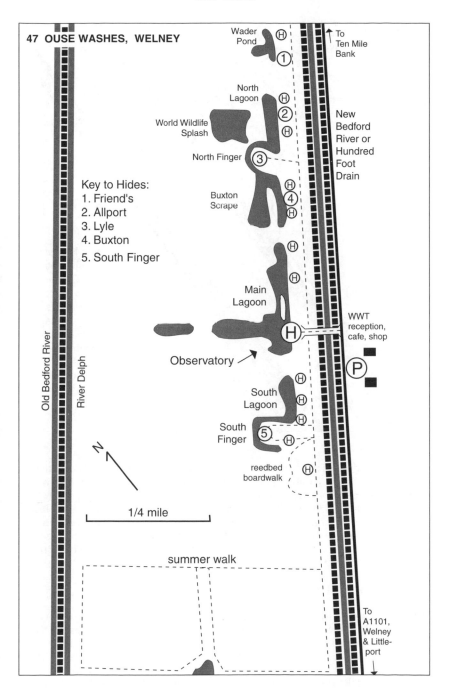

47 OUSE WASHES, WELNEY

Wader Pond

To Ten Mile Bank

North Lagoon

World Wildlife Splash

North Finger

New Bedford River or Hundred Foot Drain

Key to Hides:
1. Friend's
2. Allport
3. Lyle
4. Buxton
5. South Finger

Buxton Scrape

Main Lagoon

WWT reception, cafe, shop

Observatory

South Lagoon

South Finger

reedbed boardwalk

Old Bedford River

River Delph

N

1/4 mile

summer walk

To A1101, Welney & Littleport

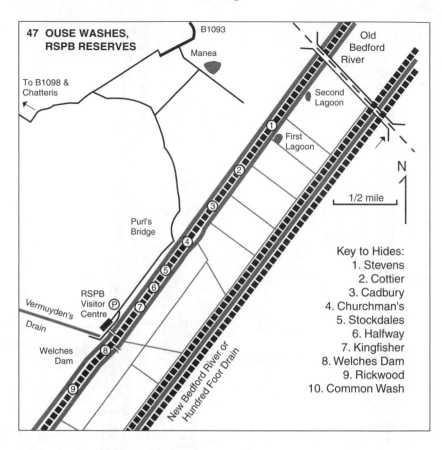

47 OUSE WASHES, RSPB RESERVES

B1093

Manea

To B1098 & Chatteris

Old Bedford River

Second Lagoon

1. Stevens
2. Cottier

First Lagoon

N

1/2 mile

Key to Hides:
1. Stevens
2. Cottier
3. Cadbury
4. Churchman's
5. Stockdales
6. Halfway
7. Kingfisher
8. Welches Dam
9. Rickwood
10. Common Wash

Purl's Bridge

RSPB Visitor Centre

Vermuyden's Drain

Welches Dam

New Bedford River or Hundred Foot Drain

Dam, the headquarters of the reserve, where there is a car park. (Alternatively, turn off the A141 at Wimblington, c.4 miles north of Chatteris, and follow the B1093 to Manea). The Information Centre is open daily (except Christmas Day and Boxing Day) 09.00–17.00, and there is access at all times to the ten hides along 3 miles of the Barrier Bank. They are approached from Welches Dam via the bridge over the river and boardwalk to the Welches Dam hide, and thence via the Haul Road below the Bank. Alternatively, you can park at Purls Bridge and use the floating bridge, a short distance northeast of the point where the road from Manea reaches the river, to access the northern hides, which are often the most productive.

WWT Welney Wildfowl Refuge Leaving the A10 in Littleport, take the A1101 west towards Outwell and Wisbech. After 4 miles the road reaches the New Bedford River and runs alongside it for a further mile. The main road then crosses the river over a suspension bridge to Welney village. Where the road turns northwest over the bridge, continue straight on along a minor road (signed to the Refuge and Ten Mile Bank) alongside the New Bedford River. After c.1½ miles the refuge's car park and reception centre lie to the right of the road; all visitors should report to reception on arrival. (Coming from the north, leave the A10 just south of Hilgay on minor roads to Ten Mile Bank and the refuge; both routes are signed from the A10.) The entrance to the observatory and hides is via a footbridge opposite the car park. The refuge is open daily 10.00–17.00 (with an extension to 18.00 for those already on the reserve) except Christmas Day. The observatory, a spacious hide overlooking a large lagoon, is heated in winter, and a wide variety of wildfowl can be seen at close quarters. In winter, the wild swans and ducks are fed 2–4 times daily in front of the observatory, with the main feed at 15.30. Numbers of Whooper Swans arrive to feed (making this the best place to see this species), but few, if any, Bewick's Swan come to feed, preferring to remain in the fields. The refuge is also open 18.30–20.00, November–late February (not Mondays and Saturdays), when the wild swans are fed by floodlight; booking is essential. There are five other large hides situated along the bank north and south of the observatory, and also several small (2–6 seat) hides, but access to all but the observatory may be impossible at times, due to flooding. From May to August a 2-mile walk across the washes is possible.

Birds

In winter the Ouse Washes hold the largest inland concentration of wildfowl in Britain. The majority are Wigeon, averaging over 35,000 birds, with smaller numbers of Teal, Pintail, Shoveler, Gadwall, Mallard, Pochard, Goldeneye and Ruddy Duck. Over 2,000 Bewick's Swan and up to c.1,300 Whooper Swan also winter (Bewick's reached 6,164 in January 1987). The swans spend most time feeding in harvested fields of potatoes and sugar beet around the washes. A flock of feral Greylag Geese winters at Welney, and may be joined by a handful of Pink-footed or occasionally Tundra Bean or White-fronted Geese. Small numbers of Hen Harrier, Merlin, Peregrine, Sparrowhawk and Short-eared Owl regularly winter but are not guaranteed. Waders include Lapwing, Curlew, Snipe, Golden Plover and Dunlin, with smaller numbers of Ruff and Redshank. Jack Snipe and Water Rail winter but are usually elusive. The flooded washes also provide a roosting site for thousands of gulls, largely Black-headed, as well as Cormorants (which roost on electricity cables), and there are wintering Water and Rock Pipits, Stonechat, Brambling and occasionally Bearded Tit or Twite.

Black-tailed Godwit breeds, having recolonised the area in 1952, although numbers are now rather low (just 12 pairs in 1997). Their spectacular display flights are best observed in spring and early summer. Ruff breeds annually but in variable numbers. Males lek for a brief period in early spring, the majority moving on to leave the females to raise their young. As the season advances, the females become quite inconspicuous. Lapwing, Snipe and Redshank are common breeders, and Avocet has bred since 1997, with eight pairs in 1998. Garganey is among the nine species of breeding duck, but they are unobtrusive in summer and best looked for in spring. Other breeding ducks include Shoveler and Gadwall. Marsh Harrier is frequently present in summer and a pair of Short-eared Owls usually nest. Black Tern has occasionally bred and Little Gull attempted to do so once. Spotted Crake is heard at night and probably breeds, but is unlikely to be seen. Reed Warbler and Yellow Wagtail breed in large numbers. Residents include Great Crested and Little Grebes, Stock and Turtle Doves, Barn and Little Owls, Kingfisher, Corn Bunting and Tree Sparrow.

Spring can be a particularly rewarding time to visit. Several of the breeding species may be easier to see, their numbers being augmented by passage birds (e.g. Garganey, Ruff and Black-tailed Godwit, with up to 2,000 Icelandic Black-tailed Godwit in March–April). Marsh Harrier and Black Tern are regular, as well as a variety of commoner migrants. Waders are more in evidence in autumn, and most of the common species are present from July.

Information
RSPB Site Manager: Cliff Carson, Ouse Washes Reserve, Welches Dam, Manea, March, Cambridgeshire PE15 0NF. Tel: 01354 680212. E-mail: cliff.carson @rspb.org.uk
WWT: Carl Mitchell, Welney WWT, Hundred Foot Bank, Welney, Wisbech, Cambridgeshire PE14 9TN. Tel: 01353 860711. E-mail: welney@wwt.org.uk

48 GRAFHAM WATER (Cambridgeshire)   OS Landranger 153

Two arms of this 1,600-acre reservoir comprise a 370-acre reserve, managed by the Bedfordshire, Cambridgeshire, Northamptonshire & Peterborough Wildlife Trust. Large numbers of grebes and wildfowl winter and passage brings a variety of waders and terns.

Habitat
The reservoir was filled in 1964 and now covers 1570 acres at the highest water levels, with nearly 10 miles of shoreline. There are a number of sheltered creeks and the reservoir is surrounded by small stands of deciduous woodland, an extensive mixed plantation, rough grassland with old hedgerows, and arable fields. Much of the open water is disturbed by sailing and fishing, but the sanctuary at the west end provides an undisturbed area.

Access (see map)
Leave the A1 at the Buckden roundabout onto the B661, which passes the dam and then runs fairly close to the south shore into the village of West Perry. The reservoir can be viewed from two car parks along this road.

Plummers car park Lying to the east of Perry, this is a useful viewpoint.

Mander car park Situated on the west side of Perry, this accesses the Wildlife Trust reserve. A wildlife cabin here acts as an information centre and from the car park nature trails around the west shore of the reservoir lead to five hides.

North-east shore This can be viewed from a minor road that leaves the B661 before the dam and leads to Grafham village. There are two more car parks along this road: Marlow and the very small Hill Farm car park.

Birds
In winter up to 800 Great Crested Grebes are present, and are occasionally joined by one of the rarer grebes or divers. Wintering duck include numbers of Teal, Wigeon, Goldeneye and Pochard. Goosander uses the reservoir as a roost and arrives late afternoon from the direction of the river and gravel pits to the east. Small numbers of Ruddy Duck, Shoveler, Gadwall and Pintail can also be seen, but Long-tailed Duck, Common and Velvet Scoters and Smew are rare visitors. Small numbers of Dunlin and Jack Snipe may winter, with Golden Plover on the surrounding farmland.

On spring passage Turnstone, Green and Common Sandpipers, Greenshank and Dunlin are possible, and in autumn these may be joined by Spotted Redshank, Ruff, Little Stint and Curlew and Wood Sandpipers. Common and Black Terns are regular on both passages, but Arctic Tern is less frequent, occurring mainly in spring. Small numbers of Little Gulls are also seen at these times, and Osprey is fairly regular.

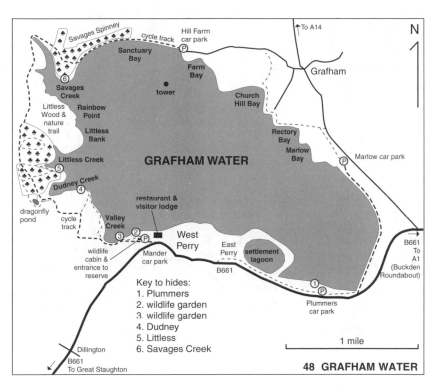

Breeders include Ringed and Little Ringed Plovers, Lapwing, Redshank, Turtle Dove, Yellow Wagtail, Nightingale and Grasshopper, Reed and Sedge Warblers.

Information

Warden: Jo Calvert, c/o The New Lodge, Grafham Water, West Perry, Huntingdon, Cambs PE28 0BX. Tel: 01480 811075 or 812660. E-mail: grafham@cix.co.uk
Bedfordshire, Cambridgeshire, Northamptonshire & Peterborough Wildlife Trust, 3b Langford Arch, London Road, Sawston, Cambridge CB2 4EE. Tel: 01223 712400. E-mail: cambswt@cix.co.uk

49 PAXTON PITS (Cambridgeshire)   OS Landranger 153

Situated immediately north of St Neots and just off the A1, this site has a wide range of breeding species (including Cormorant and Nightingale), as well as a variety of wintering waterfowl and passage gulls, terns and (to a lesser extent) waders.

Habitat

The reserve is centred on a series of flooded, worked-out gravel pits, with areas of both deep and shallow water and several islands. The pits are surrounded by emergent vegetation, reedbeds and mature scrub, within an area of meadows, hedgerows, woodland and the former gardens of the now-demolished Wray House. Nearby, working gravel pits still operate. The area is a LNR, part-owned and managed by Huntingdonshire District Council.

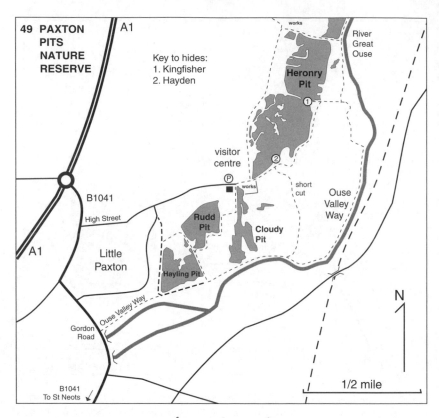

49 PAXTON PITS NATURE RESERVE

A1

Key to hides:
1. Kingfisher
2. Hayden

works

River Great Ouse

Heronry Pit

visitor centre

Ⓟ

works

short cut

Ouse Valley Way

B1041

High Street

A1

Little Paxton

Rudd Pit

Cloudy Pit

Hayling Pit

Ouse Valley Way

Gordon Road

N

B1041 To St Neots

1/2 mile

Access (see map)

Leave the A1, c.2½ miles south of Buckden roundabout, on the B1041 south into Little Paxton. After ⅓ mile turn left (east) onto the High Street and follow this, signed to the reserve, for c.⅔ mile to the car park (on the left) and visitor centre (on the right). The three trails and two other paths, together with the hides, in the reserve are open at all times, and the visitor centre is usually open at weekends and Bank Holidays.

Birds

Approximately 70 species breed annually, including Great Crested and Little Grebes, c.100 pairs of Cormorant, 6–8 pairs of Grey Herons, Sparrowhawk, Ringed and Little Ringed Plovers, Redshank, Common Tern, Turtle Dove, Kingfisher, all three woodpeckers, Yellow Wagtail, up to 20 pairs of Nightingale, Grasshopper, Reed, Sedge and Garden Warblers, Lesser Whitethroat and Corn Bunting. Hobby is a regular non-breeding visitor in summer.

On passage Arctic Tern may be joined by Black Tern and Little Gull, and a variety of waders occurs (although in common with most gravel pit sites, there is only limited habitat for waders), including Dunlin, Ruff, and Common and Green Sandpipers. Other visitors can include Black-necked Grebe, Osprey, Buzzard and Red Kite.

In winter large numbers of Cormorants roost on the pits, with a record-breaking total of 1,200 during cold weather in January 1997. Another notable species that roosts on the reserve is Stock Dove, with over 1,000 sometimes present. Wintering wildfowl include Wigeon, Teal, Gadwall, Goldeneye, Goosander and often Smew, while the rarer grebes, especially Slavonian and Red-necked, may visit, as may Great Northern or Black-throated Divers.

Information

Ranger: Ron Elloway, Visitor Centre, Paxton Pits Nature Reserve, High Street, Little Paxton, St Neots, Cambs. PE19 6ET. Tel: 01480 406795.
Tony How, 63 Gordon Road, Little Paxton, Cambs PE19 4NH. Tel: 01480 474159.
E-mail: tony@howfreeserve.co.uk Internet: www.paxton-pits.org.uk

50 FOWLMERE (Cambridgeshire)   OS Landranger 154

This reserve forms a haven for wildlife within a sea of arable farmland. Though holding no concentrations of wildfowl or waders, it does support an excellent range of common species.

Habitat

Once part of the southernmost extension of the Cambridgeshire Fens, the area was drained long ago and given over to farmland. At Fowlmere, however, upwelling water from a chalk aquifer led to the establishment of a watercress farm in the late-19th century. Once cress growing ceased in the 1970s, the wetter areas were colonised by reeds and willows. The RSPB has raised water levels, created meres and ditches, and removed invading scrub. Now the reserve is centred on a reedbed surrounded by willow and hawthorn scrub and small stands of ash and alder woodland. Adjacent to the reserve are areas of rough grassland, horse paddocks and a poplar plantation, but much of the surrounding land is intensively farmed.

Access

Between Royston and the M11, leave the A10 southeast at Shepreth on the minor road to Fowlmere. After 1 mile turn right (southwest, signed) and the reserve entrance is marked on the south side of the road after ½ mile. The reserve is open at all times, with access along the 2-mile marked trail to four hides.

Birds

Breeders include Little Grebe, Water Rail (numerous but secretive), Turtle Dove, and nine species of warblers (including Grasshopper, Reed, Sedge and Garden Warblers and Lesser Whitethroat). Kingfisher rarely nests on the reserve, but is often seen throughout the year. Corn Bunting still breeds in the surrounding farmland.

In autumn, a few waders (mainly Green Sandpiper) visit the meres, and the Swallow roost can number 400 birds. During winter, a few Snipe are present by the meres, and a small flock of Redpolls and Siskins visit the alders. In the afternoons, hundreds of thrushes, finches and buntings arrive from the surrounding farmland to roost: 500 Fieldfares may roost in the bushes with fewer Redwings and other thrushes, Reed and Corn Buntings may both number 200 in the reeds, and Brambling often joins the Chaffinch roost in the scrub. This concentration of prey attracts raptors, with Sparrowhawk occurring daily, occasional Merlin and Hen Harrier, and Long-eared Owl may be seen at dusk. Bearded Tit and even Bittern are occasional winter visitors.

Information

RSPB Fowlmere: Doug Radford, Manor Farm, High Street, Fowlmere, Royston, Herts SG8 7SH. Tel: 01763 208978.

51 NENE WASHES (Cambridgeshire) OS Landranger 142

Lying just 6 miles east of Peterborough, this area of the Nene Valley attracts significant numbers of wintering wildfowl.

Habitat
The reserve comprises an extensive area of meadows alongside the River Nene that floods during periods of high water levels in winter.

Access
Nene Washes RSPB Reserve Leave the A605 at Whittlesey north on the B1040 (also accessible from the A47 at Thorney). After 1 mile, there are good views over the washes from the road, and the reserve is accessible at all times along the Drove that runs east from the B1040. There are no visitor facilities.

Nene Washes, South Barrier Bank Leave the A60, immediately east of Coates on the minor road north to Eldernell and continue straight ahead to the Barrier Bank. A public footpath runs both east and west from here along the bank, affording good views of the east part of the RSPB reserve, as well as other parts of the Nene Washes.

Birds
Large numbers of wildfowl winter on the reserve, including Bewick's and sometimes Whooper Swans, Wigeon, Teal, Shoveler and Pintail. Such concentrations of prey species attract Hen Harrier, Peregrine, Merlin and Sparrowhawk, and sometimes Short-eared Owl.

Breeders include Shoveler, Gadwall, Garganey, Shelduck, Spotted Crake, Lapwing, Black-tailed Godwit, Snipe and sometimes Ruff, and both Marsh Harrier and Hobby are regular visitors in summer.

Information
RSPB Warden: Charlie Kitchin, 21a East Delph, Whittlesey, Peterborough PE7 1RH. Tel: 01733 205140.

52 WICKEN FEN (Cambridgeshire) OS Landranger 154

Eleven miles northeast of Cambridge, Wicken Fen is among the few remaining examples of the once extensive fens of the Great Level. Its main interest is in winter for waterfowl and a Hen Harrier roost. Wicken Fen is the oldest nature reserve in Britain, and is owned by the NT.

Habitat
The reserve covers 800 acres and consists of four distinct areas: Sedge Fen, St Edmund's Fen, Adventurers' Fen and Baker's Fen. Sedge and St Edmund's Fens have never been drained or cultivated, and sedge and reed are still cut in rotation in the traditional manner, but on St Edmund's Fen natural succession has been permitted to proceed unchecked, and the area has developed into an area of carr with some mature trees and only a few small patches of reeds; similar habitats can also be found in parts of Sedge Fen. Adventurers' and Baker's Fens lie south of Wicken and Monk's Lodes and have undergone periods of drainage and cultivation (though currently wetlands again), but nevertheless hold much of the ornithological interest of Wicken, while the Mere is attractive to wintering

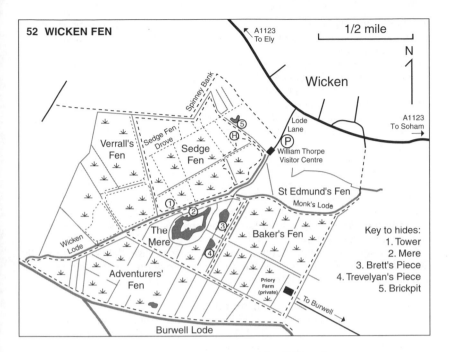

52 WICKEN FEN

wildfowl. Notably, Baker's Fen was purchased in 1993 and a programme to re-establish grazing marsh from arable farmland has resulted in an area that is particularly interesting in winter and passage periods. Recent management throughout Wicken Fen has concentrated on re-growing and restoring reedbeds in the hope of attracting Bitterns to breed again.

Access (see map)

Leave Cambridge north on the A10 and turn right onto the A1123 at Stretham. After 3½ miles, at the beginning of Wicken village, turn right onto a minor road signed Wicken Fen. Park in the large car park on the left a few hundred yards along the track. Continue on foot to the William Thorpe Visitor Centre; permits (entrance free to NT members) and literature are sold here, and a list of recent bird sightings is available. The reserve is open daily 09.00–17.00. There is a choice of three routes. An anticlockwise trail around Sedge Fen takes in the Tower Hide, which affords a view over the entire reserve but is particularly good for watching the Mere on Adventurers' Fen. Various other paths cross the fen. Also on Sedge Fen there is a ¾-mile wooden walkway, permitting access to the less able-bodied, and visitors with families. Finally, there is a clockwise route, c.2 miles in length, around part of Adventurers' Fen. Four hides overlook the various scrapes and the Mere. The flooded areas of Baker's Fen are also viewable at certain points along this route.

Birds

Marsh Harrier, Water Rail and Bearded Tit breed, and Cetti's and Savi's Warblers have done so. Reed, Sedge and Garden Warblers breed in numbers, with a few Lesser Whitethroats, and Grasshopper Warbler nests in the scrubbier sedge areas or reedbeds, especially on Sedge Fen. Areas of carr and woodland hold Woodcock (roding from early March), Turtle Dove and Willow Tit. Sporadically, Spotted Crake has been heard calling at night and Garganey is an irregular summer visitor. Other breeders include Lapwing, Snipe and Redshank. Hobby is a regular non-breeding summer visitor, and Barn Owl is occasionally seen throughout the year.

In winter, the majority of waterfowl gather on or around the Mere and on Baker's Fen; mainly Wigeon and Mallard with smaller numbers of Gadwall, Teal, Shoveler and Pochard, and occasionally Goosander. Canada Goose is usually present on the drier parts of Adventurers' Fen and occasionally a few feral Greylag or White-fronted Geese are seen. Cormorants winter and roost on the island in the Mere. Bittern and Short-eared Owl are present most winters, usually just one or two of each, as well as variable numbers of Bearded Tits. All are best viewed from the Tower Hide or the hides on Adventurers' Fen. The greatest spectacle in winter is the Hen Harrier roost. Numbering up to ten birds, males frequently predominate. They begin to arrive c.1 hour before dusk, usually from the west side of the Tower Hide, which provides an excellent vantage point. Sometimes Merlin or Sparrowhawk is also present. Redpoll and Siskin may winter in the alders, and Golden Plover favours the surrounding farmland and Baker's/Adventurers' Fens.

On passage, reasonable numbers of waders may visit Baker's Fen, mostly Green and Common Sandpipers but sometimes including Black-tailed Godwit and Whimbrel, and Marsh Harrier is regularly recorded.

Information

NT Head Warden: Martin Lester, William Thorpe Visitor Centre, Lode Lane, Wicken, Ely, Cambs CB7 5XP Tel: 01353 720274. E-mail: awnmdl@smtp. ntrust.org.uk Internet: www.wicken.org.uk

CENTRAL ENGLAND

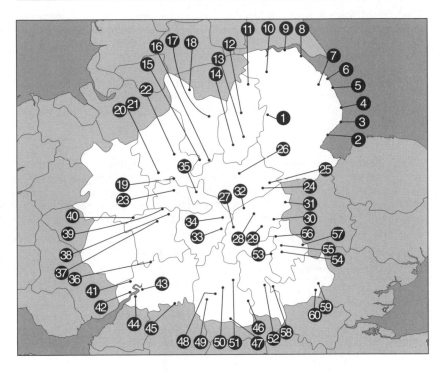

1 LINCOLN: APEX PIT/WHISBY
NATURE PARK (Lincolnshire)

OS Landranger 121

These gravel pits southwest of Lincoln attract a variety of wintering wildfowl, notably a regular flock of Goosander, and also hold an important gull roost.

Habitat

The gravel pits exhibit the typical range of succession, from freshly flooded pits with bare mud to willow carr. The pit complex at Whisby is a Nature Park, jointly managed by local councils and the Lincolnshire Wildlife Trust (LWT), while nearby Apex Pit is a well-established deep-water pit, important for wildfowl and its gull roost.

Access (see map)

Whisby Nature Park Approaching Lincoln from the south on the A46, at the roundabout with the A1434 continue north on the A46 Lincoln bypass and, after c.2 miles, turn west at the sign to Whisby Nature Park and then right into the car park after c.½ mile. There is a visitor centre and several marked trails through the reserve, with four hides overlooking the main pit. The reserve is open during daylight hours. Whisby Pits are best for dabbling duck.

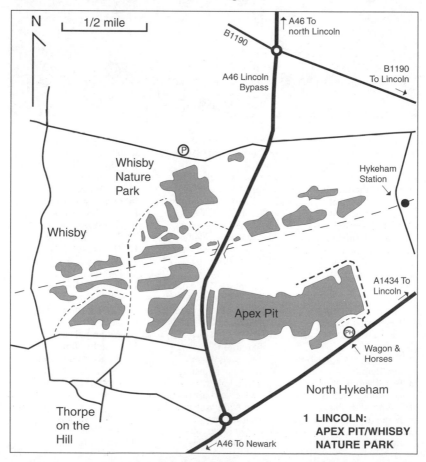

N

1/2 mile

A46 To north Lincoln

B1190

A46 Lincoln Bypass

B1190 To Lincoln

Whisby Nature Park

Hykeham Station

Whisby

A1434 To Lincoln

Apex Pit

Wagon & Horses

North Hykeham

Thorpe on the Hill

A46 To Newark

1 LINCOLN: APEX PIT/WHISBY NATURE PARK

Snow Bunting

This is a charming, and very tough little bird which breeds high in the Cairngorms. Finding them here is very hit-and-miss, but searching is worthwhile as other scarce breeding species like Ptarmigan and Dotterel may also be found in the same habitat. In winter, flocks may be found on beaches at various sites, mainly in the north and east. They are extremely confiding at this time and wonderful close views are possible.

Key sites: Cairngorms (breeding), Sandwich Bay, Walton-on-the-Naze, Salthouse-Kelling, Spurn Point, Ythan Estuary.

Shore Lark

Small parties of the attractive Shore Lark foraging along the strand-line are a rare but welcome sight in Britain. The species visits the east coast of Britain in varying numbers in the winter and very rarely ventures inland, preferring to stick close to the coast or on the beach itself. It can be hard to find with its excellent camouflage, but is often very confiding. There have been a handful of breeding attempts in Scotland.

Key sites: Salthouse-Kelling, Cley beach, John Muir Country Park, Isle of Sheppey.

Stone Curlew

The charismatic Stone Curlew is an extremely scarce and localised British breeding bird, affected by farming changes but also on the edge of its world range. Moreover, its cryptic plumage and crepuscular lifestyle make it difficult to find and easily overlooked. By far the best place to see one is the Brecks of East Anglia, although it does persist here and there in the West Country. It may occasionally appear elsewhere on migration.

Key sites: Weeting Heath.

Wryneck

Britain's oddest woodpecker, the Wryneck is now an extremely uncommon breeder, but more regular as a passage migrant. It makes regular appearances along the south and east coasts in autumn, but can be hard to detect because of its superb camouflage and skulking habits. Long extinct as a breeding species in England, the handful of remaining pairs occupy coniferous woodland in the Scottish Highlands – but finding one is very much a matter of luck rather than judgement.

Key sites: Spurn Point, Blakeney Point, Flamborough Head, Portland, Dungeness, Fair Isle, North Ronaldsay.

Apex Pit Approaching Lincoln from the south on the A46, at the roundabout continue towards the city centre on the A1434 and, after c.¾ mile, turn north in North Hykeham (just beyond the Wagon and Horses pub) onto the sailing club's access track, parking carefully at the sharp right-hand turn. The pit is immediately ahead, and to view the gull roost take the track to the left. Apex Pit is favoured by Cormorant, Goldeneye and Goosander, but the Goosander flock is mobile and best looked for early morning and evening.

Birds

Winter wildfowl include significant numbers of Wigeon, Teal, Gadwall and Pochard, a notable concentration of up to 50 Goosanders, feral Greylag Geese and a handful of Shoveler, Goldeneye and Ruddy Duck. Other waterfowl include Great Crested Grebe and Cormorant. Bittern is occasionally recorded at this season, and Green Sandpiper and Jack Snipe are sometimes found in marshy areas.

Gulls roost on the Apex Pit throughout the year but numbers peak in winter when there may be up to 20,000 Black-headed Gulls, smaller numbers of Common Gulls and up to 500 each of Herring and Great Black-backed Gulls. Careful searching in winter may also produce Glaucous, Iceland or Mediterranean Gulls, while in summer and autumn large numbers of Lesser Black-backed Gull roost, and sometimes one or two Yellow-legged Gulls.

On spring and autumn passage Arctic and Black Terns and Little Gull may pass through, as well as a few waders, typically Common and Green Sandpipers, Redshank and Greenshank. Scarcer spring migrants have included Slavonian and Black-necked Grebes and Garganey.

Breeders include Great Crested and Little Grebes, Ringed and Little Ringed Plovers, Black-headed Gull, Common Tern, Turtle Dove, Kingfisher, all three woodpeckers, Cuckoo, Sand Martin, Reed, Sedge and Garden Warblers, Willow Tit and, notably, several pairs of Nightingales (more than 20 singing males in recent years). Hobby is quite frequent in summer.

Information

LWT: Banovallum House, Manor House Street, Horncastle, Lincolnshire LN9 5HF. Tel: 01507 526667. E-mail: info@lincstrust.co.uk

Whisby Nature Park Warden: Phil Porter, Whisby Nature Park, Moor Lane, Thorpe-on-the-Hill, Lincoln LN6 9BW. Tel: 01522 500676. E-mail: whisby @cix.co.uk

2 THE WASH (Lincolnshire)   OS Landranger 131

The Wash is the largest estuary in Britain, and is formed by the Rivers Witham, Welland, Nene and Great Ouse. It is also the most important for wildfowl and waders, holding internationally important concentrations of Pink-footed and Dark-bellied Brent Geese, Pintail, Oystercatcher, Grey Plover, Knot, Dunlin, Bar-tailed Godwit and Redshank.

Habitat

Vast areas of saltmarsh, tidal sand and mudflats are backed by artificial seawalls that serve to defend areas of reclaimed land, now largely used for arable farming. The excavation of clay to construct these sea banks has formed a series of borrow pits, many overgrown with reeds and sometimes willows. In this flat and featureless region, stands of trees and bushes are otherwise relatively scarce,

Several areas are protected as reserves, notably Frampton Marsh, where both the RSPB and Lincolnshire Wildlife Trust (LWT) possess holdings.

Access (see map)

The pace of birdwatching in this huge area is largely determined by the tides and, ideally, visits should be timed to coincide with high water to view roosting waders, sea duck and, in season, seabirds. In spring and autumn the fortnightly 'spring' tides are ideal, as these usually flood the saltmarshes and force the waders onto drier ground to roost. High water on 'spring' tides usually occurs in late evening and early morning. In contrast, the intervening 'neap tides' leave the mudflats uncovered, and fewer waders move into view of the seawalls, and sea duck also remain distant. In winter 'spring' tides peak during hours of darkness and a late-morning high tide is the best compromise. Access to the seawalls is usually via a maze of minor roads and thus the OS map is especially useful in this area.

Nene Mouth Leave the A17 west on the B1359 towards Long Sutton and, as you enter Sutton Bridge, turn north on the minor road immediately west of the River Nene, following this for 3 miles to the car park by the old lighthouse. Walk north from here along the seawall to the river mouth, which is a good area for sea duck.

Holbeach Marsh Leave the A17 at Holbeach and follow signs through the maze of minor roads north to Holbeach St Matthew. From the phone box in the village take the minor road north for c.1 mile to the car park at the seawall. From here walk east along the seawall to view a vast area of saltmarsh, or north and then west for 2 miles with interesting borrow pits by the bank much of the way. Search for sea duck offshore around high water.

Frampton Marsh RSPB and LWT Reserves Leave the A16 east in Kirton on minor roads to Frampton village and then Roads Farm. The road bends sharply north here and after c.400 yards bear right on the track to the car park. From here, follow the footpath along the south bank of The Haven (River Witham).

Witham Mouth From central Boston follow signs to the docks and thereafter Fishtoft. In the village centre bear right by the pub to Nunn's Bridge. Continue for 2 miles to Cut End on the north bank of the River Witham, parking on the roadside. Walk east for 1 mile to the river mouth where there is a seawatching hide; this is a good site for sea duck.

Hobhole Drain Follow directions as for Witham Mouth, and as you approach Nunn's Bridge the road crosses Hobhole Drain. Immediately beyond the bridge turn sharp right (south) onto the bank of the Drain. Long-eared Owl roosts in the hawthorns on the opposite bank of the drain here.

Birds

Wintering wildfowl include large numbers of Dark-bellied Brent Goose, with a maximum winter count (including the Norfolk sector of the Wash) of 27,742 in 1991–92, and several thousand remain into spring, especially around Frampton Marsh. Also present are Pink-footed Goose (at Holbeach Marsh), Shelduck, Wigeon, Mallard, Pintail (especially at Nene Mouth). Sea duck include Eider and Goldeneye, but other species are much rarer and less predictable. Witham Mouth is favoured by sea duck, and divers and rarer grebes are also occasionally recorded. Other waterfowl include Cormorant. Waders are abundant with

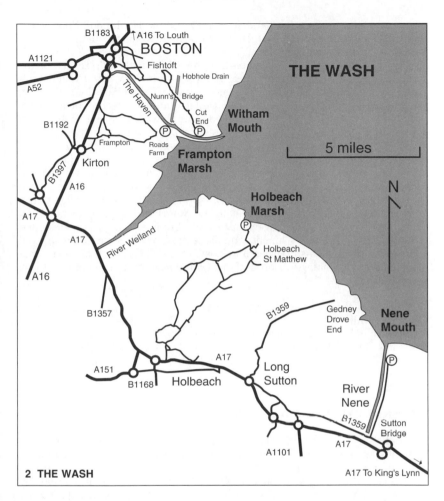

2 THE WASH

huge numbers of Oystercatcher (a minimum of 28,303 in 1991–92), Ringed, Golden and Grey Plovers (10,100), Knot (154,315), Sanderling (378), Dunlin (43,768), Bar-tailed Godwit (9,807), Curlew (at least 3,727), Redshank (2,391) and Turnstone. At low tide most are dispersed over the flats and often offer only very distant views, but at high tide they gather to roost, and on 'spring' tides do so in the fields immediately inland of the seawall. Scarcer waders include Black-tailed Godwit, which may winter at Holbeach Marsh. Large numbers of commoner gulls use the Wash, and Glaucous Gull is occasionally found in winter, with Mediterranean Gull also possible, especially in late summer. Wintering raptors include Hen Harrier, Sparrowhawk, Merlin, Peregrine and Short-eared Owl, with a Long-eared Owl roost at Nunn's Bridge. Wintering passerines include Rock Pipit on the saltmarshes, and in late winter and early spring look for individuals of the Scandinavian race as they begin to assume breeding plumage. Corn and sometimes Snow Buntings occur on the seawalls, as may Twite and Lapland Buntings, which also favour rough ground and stubble fields.

On passage numbers of Ringed and Golden Plovers, Knot, Sanderling and Turnstone are higher than in winter, and there may also be significant totals of Whimbrel, Black-tailed Godwit, Greenshank and Spotted Redshank. In autumn, a few Little Stints and Curlew Sandpipers may join the Dunlin and Knot on the flats and Common, Green and sometimes Wood Sandpipers favour the saltmarsh gutters. As with the other waders, high-tide roosts offer a chance to find the scarcer species, though identifying birds in the tightly packed flocks can be difficult. Interesting waders are more easily found on borrow pits if water levels have fallen in autumn. Terns are regular in summer, especially Common Tern, but also Little and Black Terns and Little Gull in autumn. A feature of autumn is wind-blown seabirds, which may be forced by north gales to shelter in the Wash. They follow the coast in a clockwise direction to leave the Wash at Gibraltar Point. In the appropriate conditions Fulmar, Manx Shearwater, Leach's Petrel, Gannet, Guillemot, Kittiwake and Arctic and Great Skuas (and sometimes Long-tailed and Pomarine Skuas) are possible. The best localities for seabirds are Witham Mouth and Holbeach Marsh. Some species do not leave the Wash via the sea, however, and skuas in particular are prone to move inland, either directly overland or along the rivers (especially the Nene), giving exceptionally good views. The Wash coast is relatively unsheltered but interesting passerines, such as Ring Ouzel, Wheatear, Whinchat and Stonechat, may be found on migration.

Breeders include Marsh Harrier, now relatively numerous, and there are irregular sightings of Montagu's Harrier. Barn Owl is resident and Short-eared Owl sometimes nests.

Information

LWT: Banovallum House, Manor House Street, Horncastle, Lincolnshire LN9 5HF. Tel: 01507 526667. E-mail: info@lincstrust.co.uk

RSPB Lincolnshire Wash Office: John Badley, 61 Horseshoe Lane, Kirton, Boston, Lincs PE20 1LW. Tel: 01205 724678. E-mail: john.badley@rspb.org.uk

3 GIBRALTAR POINT (Lincolnshire)   OS Landranger 122

South of Skegness, Gibraltar Point marks the spot where the Lincolnshire coast turns into the Wash. A Bird Observatory was founded in 1949 to study the resultant concentrations of migrants, and the area also attracts large numbers of wintering birds. It is worth visiting year-round. A NNR, covering 1,500 acres, is managed by the Lincolnshire Wildlife Trust (LWT), and the area has been designated a Ramsar site and SPA.

Habitat

Two major ridges, the East Dunes and the older West Dunes, run roughly north–south parallel to the sea, supporting stands of sea buckthorn and some elder; between these are areas of fresh and saltmarsh. To the south, an extensive sandbar (the Spit) attracts large numbers of roosting waders. Two artificial pools, the Mere and Fenland Lagoon, in the north of the reserve attract migrant ducks and waders. Extensive mudflats and saltmarsh border the Point.

Access (see map)

Leave Skegness seafront south on a minor road signed to Gibraltar Point. Parking is available near the Mere and visitor centre (fee). No permit is required but visitors should keep to roads and marked paths, and not enter marked sanctuary areas. The visitor centre is open daily May–October and at weekends and Bank Holidays during the rest of the year. Basic accommodation is available at the Field Studies Centre (phone for details).

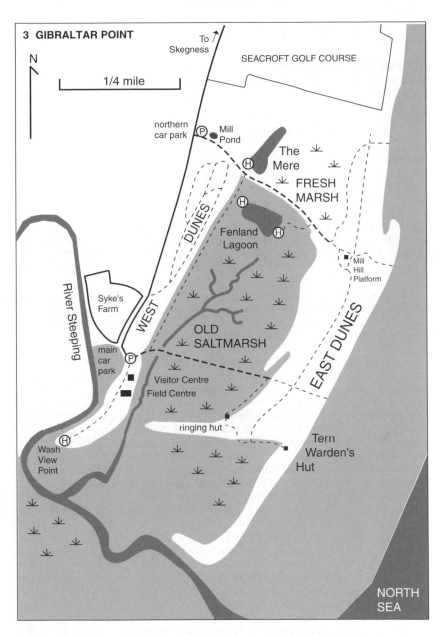

3 GIBRALTAR POINT

N

1/4 mile

To Skegness

SEACROFT GOLF COURSE

northern car park

Mill Pond

The Mere

FRESH MARSH

Fenland Lagoon

Mill Hill Platform

DUNES

WEST

Syke's Farm

River Steeping

EAST DUNES

OLD SALTMARSH

main car park

Visitor Centre
Field Centre

ringing hut

Tern Warden's Hut

Wash View Point

NORTH SEA

The Mere A short walk from the north car park, where there is a public hide.

The Fenland Lagoon There are two hides, at the east and west ends.

The East Dunes Accessed from the north car park or via a well-made path across the freshwater marsh from the main car park. Extensive areas of buckthorn, though difficult to work, provide cover for migrants. The height of the dunes offers an overview in many places (notably at Mill Hill), and at the north

.end of the dunes Shovelers Pool, a small reed-fringed pond surrounded by willows, is especially attractive to migrants.

Mill Hill Observation Platform At the north end of the East Dunes, this provides an all-round view and is ideal for observing movements of diurnal migrants in early morning.

The Wash Viewpoint South of the main car park, this offers panoramic views of the saltmarsh and mud and sand flats of the Wash.

The Spit Wildfowl and waders are best seen as they fly to the Spit to roost at high tide. Largest numbers are in spring and autumn, arriving up to two hours before high tide, and a northwest–northeast wind produces the highest counts. View from the Tern Warden's Hut.

Seawatching This can be a problem in early morning, because of the light, and at low tide. The best place to watch from is the Tern Warden's Hut at the base of the Spit, though in northbound movements a position further north may be better.

Syke's Farm This plantation of mainly deciduous trees lies just west of the access road immediately north of the main car park. Attractive to migrants, access is restricted to LWT members but views from the road are generally sufficient.

Birds

Once spring migration has commenced, east or southeast winds with cloud, rain or poor visibility may produce falls of warblers, flycatchers and chats, sometimes including scarcer species such as Black Redstart, Nightingale, Ring Ouzel, Wood Warbler, Pied Flycatcher and Firecrest. Marsh and, occasionally, Montagu's Harriers pass through, as may Osprey and, from mid-May, Hobby. Visible migration (best viewed from Mill Hill in moderate northwest winds) is a particular feature of Gibraltar Point; as at Spurn, the majority of diurnal migrants (comprising a wide range of species, notably pipits, wagtails, finches and buntings) fly south in spring as well as autumn. Other migrants may include Common, Arctic, Sandwich and Black Terns, Little Gull, and a variety of waders.

Notable breeding birds include Shelduck, Oystercatcher, Ringed Plover and a few pairs of Little Terns. Long-eared Owl breeds nearby and can be seen hunting over the fresh marsh, and Marsh Harrier may summer in the area.

In autumn wildfowl, waders and gulls throng the shore. Large numbers of Common, Arctic and Sandwich Terns offshore may attract all four species of skua, though Arctic Skua is by far the most regular. Black Terns may also pass through and a Mediterranean Gulls put in an appearance, while during onshore northeast winds Manx Shearwater is possible. The Mere and Fenland Lagoon may attract Garganey, Water Rail, Avocet, Little Ringed Plover, Black-tailed Godwit, Little Stint, Curlew and Wood Sandpipers, and Spotted Redshank, in addition to the common waders. From mid-July large flocks of open-shore waders, often still in breeding plumage, roost on the Spit or the beach to the north. Up to 35,000 Knot, 20,000 Oystercatcher, 10,000 Bar-tailed Godwit, 6,000 Dunlin, 4,500 Grey Plover and 2,500 Sanderling have been counted. The largest totals are recorded on 'spring' tides.

In autumn falls of night migrants occur, and these may be substantial with a chance of Wryneck, Icterine and Barred Warblers, and Red-backed Shrike from late August. By October large movements of thrushes, especially Blackbird and Fieldfare, become prominent, as are Goldcrest, tits, finches and buntings. Visible migration is most obvious in south or southwest winds. In late autumn, look for Water Rail, Woodcock, Little Auk (after strong north winds), Long-eared and Short-eared Owls, Richard's Pipit, Yellow-browed Warbler, Firecrest, Great Grey Shrike (which occasionally winters) and Lapland Bunting, and more erratically Rough-legged Buzzard and Waxwing.

Winter brings Red-throated and occasionally Black-throated Divers, auks and sea duck offshore, large numbers of Dark-bellied Brent Geese and sometimes skeins of Pink-footed Geese, a few Whooper or Bewick's Swans, or a Glaucous Gull. There are large numbers of common open-shore waders. Sparrowhawk, Hen Harrier, Peregrine, Merlin and Short-eared Owl are regular and Long-eared and Barn Owls occasional. Rock Pipit, finches (including Redpoll, Twite and Brambling) and Snow and Corn Buntings frequent the saltmarsh, dunes and beach, often in large numbers, but Shore Lark is now an erratic visitor, most likely in late autumn. Occasional wintering Blackcap and Chiffchaff favour the buckthorn and Syke's Farm. Cold weather may bring movements of Lapwing, thrushes and finches. Woodlark is possible in late February–late March, with occasionally up to six present, favouring the close-cropped dune ridges.

Information

Site Manager: Kev Wilson (or Doreen Lilley for bookings for accommodation), Gibraltar Point Field Station, Gibraltar Road, Skegness, Lincolnshire PE24 4SU. Tel: 01754 762677. E-mail: lincstrust@gibpoint.freeserve.co.uk

4 SOUTH LINCOLNSHIRE COAST: CHAPEL ST LEONARDS TO HUTTOFT   OS Landranger 122

This stretch of coast has a restricted range of natural habitats but is rather under-watched and offers the chance to find interesting migrant and wintering birds on the sea, the various borrow pits and in the limited areas of cover along the coast.

Habitat

On this section of coast the foreshore is rather narrow and mostly bounded by artificial seawalls, and the extraction of clay to construct these sea defences has formed a series of borrow pits just inland of the seawall. Comprising deep water fringed by reeds and willow scrub, many of the pits are managed as reserves by the Lincolnshire Wildlife Trust (LWT). Inland are extensive areas of arable farmland, and some sand dunes with stands of sea buckthorn between Huttoft and Chapel St Leonards. An important habitat for migrant passerines is formed by gardens along the coast, especially around Anderby Creek and Chapel St Leonards.

Access (see map)

All points are accessed from the minor road between Sutton on Sea and Chapel St Leonards.

Huttoft Pits Turn east off the A52 at the south end of Sutton on Sea on the minor road signed to Sandilands. After c.⅓ mile the road bends sharply south to parallel the seawall, and after a further c.1 mile there is a pull-in on the inland side of the road, which forms the car park for Huttoft Pits, a LWT reserve. Take the footpath on the opposite side of the road to the hide overlooking the largest pit. (Following the road south for a further 1½ miles there are more borrow pits beside the road, just beyond the turning to the dunes car park at Moggs Eye.)

Huttoft Bank A further c.½ mile south of the Huttoft Pits pull-in, there is a minor crossroads with the west turn signed to Huttoft, while the road to the east leads to the sea. The raised seawall and the car park (fee in summer) offers a vantage for seawatching, best around high tide, and the car can be used as a shelter in poor weather. Gulls roost offshore here.

Anderby Creek Turn east off the coast road 3 miles south of Sandilands to Anderby Creek and park at the end of the road by the dunes. A track runs north, passing some gardens, then a stand of young trees by the open-air sports complex (with a path leading into the trees), and to another patch of trees. The gardens hold migrants but discretion is necessary when peering into them. The small pit among the houses, just inland of the track, attracts occasional sea duck. Another path leads south along the coast from the car park, past the mouth of Anderby Creek, to a patch of scrub with some mature trees. Thirdly, take the track over the dunes to a small shelter which, though affording limited views, can be useful for seawatching.

Wolla Bank and Chapel Six Marshes Continue south on the coast road and tracks lead east to car parks in the dunes at Wolla Bank and Chapel Six Marshes. There are some extensive areas of scrub around these, and a small stand of conifers at Chapel Six Marshes, while the area between the car parks comprises grazed grassland.

Wolla Bank Pit Lies inland of the coast road opposite the turning to Wolla Bank. A LWT reserve, it can be viewed from the road.

Chapel Pit Lies inland of the coast road c.200 yards south of the Chapel Six Marshes turning. A LWT reserve, it can be viewed from the road.

Chapel Point Turn east off the A52 6 miles north of Skegness to Chapel St Leonards and drive through the village for 1½ miles to the northern outskirts at Chapel Point. There is a car park at the coastguards' lookout on the seaward side of the road, with scrub around the car park and on the other side of the road. Chapel Point offers reasonable seawatching from the car park and it is possible to walk south along the seawall past some chalets to the mouth of Willoughby High Drain, and then alongside the drain, turning left into a road, which runs south parallel to the coast. The gardens along the road and the scrub at the channel mouth attract migrants.

Birds

In early spring, passage migrants include Wheatear and sometimes Ring Ouzel, Stonechat, Black Redstart and Firecrest. Later in the season, Yellow Wagtail, a variety of warblers and Whinchat are regular and scarcer species include Redstart, Wood Warbler and Pied Flycatcher. There is little habitat for waders but in both spring and autumn Black-tailed Godwit, Ruff and Whimbrel can be found on areas of short grass, notably at Sandilands golf course.

Breeders include Sparrowhawk, Barn Owl, Grasshopper, Reed and Sedge Warblers, and Water Rail and Bearded Tit may summer.

Autumn passage see arrivals of the 'usual' east coast species such as Redstart, Willow and Garden Warblers and Pied Flycatcher, and sometimes Wryneck, Icterine and Barred Warblers, Red-breasted Flycatcher or Red-backed Shrike. In late autumn Richard's Pipit (on rough grassland south of Anderby Creek and Sandilands golf course), Black Redstart, Yellow-browed and Pallas's Warblers, Firecrest and Great Grey Shrike are some of the scarce migrants to search for,

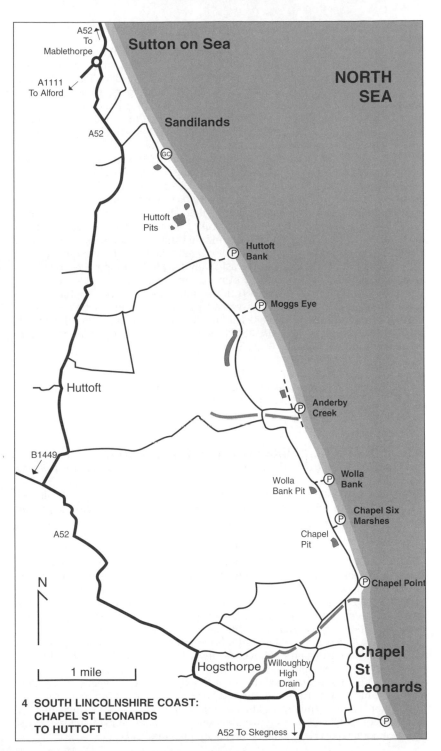

NORTH SEA

Sutton on Sea

A52
To
Mablethorpe

A1111
To Alford

A52

Sandilands

GC

Huttoft
Pits

P Huttoft
Bank

P Moggs Eye

Huttoft

P Anderby
Creek

B1449

Wolla
Bank Pit
P Wolla
Bank

A52

P Chapel Six
Marshes

Chapel
Pit

N

P Chapel Point

1 mile

Hogsthorpe
Willoughby
High
Drain

Chapel
St
Leonards

P

**4 SOUTH LINCOLNSHIRE COAST:
CHAPEL ST LEONARDS
TO HUTTOFT**

A52 To Skegness ↓

and more predictable late-autumn migrants are thrushes, Long- and Short-eared Owls and Woodcock.

Early-autumn gatherings of Common, Sandwich and Little Terns offshore attract Arctic Skuas, and Mediterranean Gulls can also be found with diligence. Low water levels in late summer on the borrow pits (especially Huttoft Pits) attract passage waders, including Common and Green Sandpipers, Greenshank and sometimes Spotted Redshank, Wood and Curlew Sandpipers and Little Stint. Strong onshore winds, especially prolonged north–northeast, may prompt a passage of seabirds, including Gannet, Fulmar, Kittiwake, terns (including Black) and Arctic Skua, and occasionally Manx and Sooty Shearwaters or even Leach's Petrel and Long-tailed Skua. In late autumn sea ducks, Brent Goose, Little Gull, Great and Pomarine Skuas, Guillemot and, sometimes, Little Auk are possible.

Offshore in winter look for Red-throated Diver, Common Scoter and small numbers of Eider. Following strong north winds other sea duck are more likely, including Red-breasted Merganser, Long-tailed Duck, Velvet Scoter and Scaup, as well as Guillemot and a few Razorbills. Winter gull flocks may harbour Glaucous or Iceland Gulls, and flocks of Little Gulls are often present off Huttoft Bank (best searched for in calm weather). Due to the limited foreshore there are few waders but Sanderling and occasionally Purple Sandpiper may occur, as well as Rock Pipit, Twite and Snow Bunting. Inland of the seawalls, the borrow pits may hold occasional sea duck (offering much better views than birds out to sea), Smew, and perhaps also divers or Red-necked and Slavonian Grebes. Further inland still, check the flocks of Lapwing and Golden Plover on the fields for Ruff. The farmland also attracts Peregrine, Merlin, Hen Harrier and Short-eared Owl, and occasionally wild swans or geese.

Information

LWT: Banovallum House, Manor House Street, Horncastle, Lincolnshire LN9 5HF. Tel: 01507 526667. E-mail: info@lincstrust.co.uk

5 NORTH LINCOLNSHIRE COAST: MABLETHORPE TO GRAINTHORPE HAVEN   OS Landranger 113 and 122

This stretch of coastline is well positioned to receive migrants which, despite relatively limited coverage, have included some first-class rarities. It also attracts an excellent range of wintering wildfowl and waders.

Habitat

The dunes and beaches of the Humber gradually narrow as the estuary extends south to Mablethorpe. Tidal sand and mud are backed by saltmarsh and thereafter by a still-evolving dune system. Dunes of variable ages support extensive thickets of sea buckthorn and elder, separated by damp dune slacks which often have freshwater marshes dominated by rushes, sedges and reeds, or areas of willows and sallows. Active management has created some freshwater pools, and dotted along the coast are isolated stands of mature deciduous trees. In the north of the area (from Howden's Pullover northwards) there are also several borrow pits inland of the seawall.

Most of the area is protected. Between Theddlethorpe St Helen and Saltfleet Haven 4½ miles of dunes, foreshore and beach comprise a 1,088-acre NNR, with an additional 95 acres run by the Lincolnshire Wildlife Trust (LWT), while the LWT Donna Nook–Saltfleet Reserve covers another 2,425 acres along 6 miles of coast between Somercotes Haven and Saltfleet, abutting the NNR.

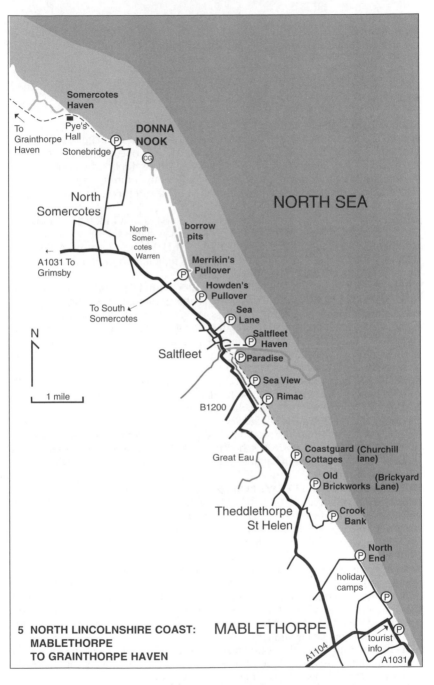

5 NORTH LINCOLNSHIRE COAST: MABLETHORPE TO GRAINTHORPE HAVEN

Access (see map)

These are listed south–north, from Mablethorpe to Donna Nook, and divided between Mablethorpe, Saltfleetby–Theddlethorpe Dunes NNR and Donna Nook–Saltfleet LTNC Reserve.

MABLETHORPE
Mablethorpe seafront The concrete beach shelter by the tourist information is useful for seawatching. There is a car park 200 yards to the south.

Mablethorpe North End Follow the minor road north from Mablethorpe seafront alongside the dunes to the signed car park at North End (or turn off the A1031 halfway between Theddlethorpe and Mablethorpe on a minor road signed North End). From here there is access to the dunes and beach.

SALTFLEETBY–THEDDLETHORPE DUNES NNR
Access is at six points off the A1031, connected by a footpath. Limited parking is available at all six, which are listed south–north. There is open access except to the danger zone—visitors must comply with safety regulations displayed at the entrances.

Crook Bank In Theddlethorpe St Helen, south of the church, turn east off the A1031 at the right-hand bend onto a metalled track and fork right, following Sea Lane for c.1 mile, to Journey's End.

Old Brickworks Follow directions as for Crook Bank, but fork left to Brickyard Lane. Check the copses of trees in Theddlethorpe village.

Coastguard Cottages Leave Theddlethorpe St Helen north on the A1031 and after c.½ mile, at the sharp left-hand bend, turn right into Churchill Road and follow this past Sea Bank Farm to the car park.

Rimac Continue north on the A1031 and, after 1½ miles, the road bends sharp right, and after a further ½ mile sharp left. At this corner take the rough track that leads straight on, over the bridge across the Great Eau, to the car park. A saltmarsh viewpoint lies ahead and though a 1½-mile walk to the sea is necessary in order to seawatch, it can be worthwhile. There are stands of willows and sallows in the freshwater marsh, some interesting freshwater pools, and a belt of willows borders the landward side of the reserve.

Sea View Farm Continue north on the A1031 and, opposite the junction with the B1200, turn east on the metalled track to Sea View Farm. There is a copse of mature trees by the car park, attractive to migrants.

Saltfleet Haven (Paradise) In Saltfleet village the A1031 crosses the Haven and immediately to the south the road bends sharply west while a track leads straight on past Gowts Farm (and crosses the main dyke) to Paradise, where there some mature trees (the copses in Saltfleet village are also worthy of scrutiny).

DONNA NOOK–SALTFLEET LWT RESERVE
Access is at five points, all off the A1031, with limited parking facilities. There is open access to the beach and foreshore but do not enter the danger area, which stretches from Pye's Hall south to Howden's Pullover, when the ranges are in use (usually on weekdays); marker boards are sited at all access points with red flags used to indicate that the shore is in use.

Saltfleet Haven (north bank) In Saltfleet village turn east off the A1031 immediately north of the bridge over Saltfleet Haven on a rough track along the bank of the Haven to a small car park. From here footpaths lead north on either side of the dune ridge and it is possible to walk to the mouth of the Haven (but caution is required as the tidal creeks here are very dangerous), which is a good area for loafing and feeding gulls and terns.

Sea Lane at Saltfleet At the north end of Saltfleet village take Sea Lane for ¼ mile to the car park. The seawall here gives good views over the saltmarsh. It is possible to walk south to Saltfleet Haven or north to Howden's Pullover.

Howden's Pullover Midway between Saltfleet and North Somercotes, Howden's Pullover is signed from the A1031. A rough track leads to the car park on the seawall. Walk south to Saltfleet village or north on the seawall or foreshore, or through the dunes to Donna Nook reserve.

Merrikin's Pullover Just south of North Somercotes turn east off the A1031 on unmetalled roads opposite the turn to South Somercotes.

Donna Nook Follow signs from North Somercotes to Donna Nook, taking the minor road north for 2 miles to the car park at Stonebridge. A public footpath runs northwest along the seawall and it is possible to walk the dunes or along the beach, with patches of cover for migrants, especially the sycamores and elders around the site of the old Pye's Hall, c.1 mile from the car park. Note that on weekdays the bombing ranges are used from c.08.00, and while access to the seawall and dunes is still possible, there is a great deal of disturbance. (The obvious stand of mature trees south of Stonebridge car park is on the RAF base, with no access.) Further on, waders roost at Grainthorpe Haven. The Donna Nook reserve proper can be reached by walking south from Stonebridge for c.1½ miles along the beach before entering the dunes south of the coastguard lookout.

Birds

In winter there are Red-throated Divers and Great Crested Grebes offshore, as well as Common Scoter and Guillemots. Other divers, grebes and sea duck are erratic in their appearances. Brent Goose is regular in some numbers, as are Wigeon, Pintail and Shoveler. Short-eared Owl, Sparrowhawk, Hen Harrier and Merlin are quite frequent and Peregrine reasonably regular. Waders include Jack Snipe and Woodcock in the dunes (and the former also on the foreshore at Rimac) as well as the usual coastal species. Glaucous Gull, especially from January, and Kittiwake may join the commoner gulls. On the saltmarsh and tideline Twite and Snow Bunting are reasonably common (favouring the saltings at Rimac and between Pye's Hall and Donna Nook, and the shingle at the mouth of Saltfleet Haven), but Shore Lark and Lapland Bunting are much less regular, the former having declined greatly but is still possible at Rimac, and the latter favouring areas of damp grassland. Rock Pipit is common on the foreshore and occasionally Water Pipit may be found in 'fresh' habitats (notably on pools near Rimac car park), together with Water Rail. The buckthorn attracts large numbers of Fieldfares, Redwings and Starlings, Stonechats and sometimes a few Blackcaps.

Landbird migrants can be excellent in spring and autumn, with a long list of vagrants recorded in the area. In addition to the usual chats, warblers and flycatchers, scarcer migrants to search for in early spring include Short-eared Owl, Ring Ouzel, Black Redstart, Firecrest and the Scandinavian race of Rock Pipit (on the saltmarshes; Water Pipit favours 'fresh' habitats). In May–June these may be joined by Marsh Harrier, Hobby, Wood Warbler and Pied Flycatcher. Rarer but near-annual late-spring migrants include Bluethroat, Marsh Warbler, Red-backed Shrike, Golden Oriole and Common Rosefinch. Numbers and variety of landbird migrants are usually greater in autumn. In August–September search for Wryneck, Bluethroat, Icterine and Barred Warblers and Red-backed Shrike, all of which are scarce but annual, and may be joined from late September by Ring Ouzel, Black Redstart, 'Siberian' Stonechat, Yellow-browed and Pallas's Warblers, Red-breasted Flycatcher, Great Grey Shrike and Lapland Bunting. Richard's Pipit is something of a specialty, with the dunes north of Rimac car park and the region between Howden's Pullover and Pye's Hall being the best areas. Late autumn can witness arrivals of Long-eared and Short-eared Owls, Woodcock and a few Bearded Tits. A variety of waders occurs on passage and may include Whimbrel, Spotted Redshank (regular in Grainthorpe Haven), Curlew Sandpiper, Little Stint and, sometimes, Wood Sandpiper, with the best range in autumn, but in spring 'trips' of Dotterel are fairly regular, notably on the fields at Donna Nook, and large flocks of Sanderling may pass through.

At sea, onshore winds in autumn may prompt a passage of Gannets, Fulmars and Manx Shearwaters, and sometimes Leach's Petrel and Sooty Shearwater, but in general the area is unproductive for seawatching, being too exposed with no obvious headlands, though the beach shelters at Mablethorpe offer some height and protection. Arctic Skua is regular, attending the flocks of gulls and terns, but Great Skua is quite scarce and Pomarine and Long-tailed Skuas uncommon. In spring and autumn Little Gull and Common, Arctic, Sandwich, Little and Black Terns are often present, with Kittiwake in autumn, and a notable late-summer concentration of terns.

Breeders include Shelduck, occasionally Teal, Water Rail, Oystercatcher, Ringed Plover and, notably, Little Terns in some numbers. Marshy areas have Grasshopper (at Rimac), Reed and Sedge Warblers, and occasionally Short-eared Owl, with Redpolls in the birches and Nightingales may sing from the thickets.

Information

LWT: Banovallum House, Manor House Street, Horncastle, Lincolnshire LN9 5HF. Tel: 01507 526667. E-mail: info@lincstrust.co.uk

EN Saltfleetby–Theddlethorpe: Simon Smith, The Maltings, Wharf Road, Grantham, Lincolnshire NG31 6BH. Tel: 01205 311674. E-mail: simont.smith@ english-nature.org.uk

6 TETNEY MARSHES (Lincolnshire)   OS Landranger 113

This area near the mouth of the Humber estuary holds a selection of migrant and wintering wildfowl and waders, and has an important colony of breeding Little Terns.

Habitat

This RSPB reserve covers 3,111 acres of saltmarsh and dunes between Humberston Fitties and Northcoates Point, with some areas of cover, notably a large hawthorn hedge at Northcoates Point, and two large brackish pools (the MOD Pools) behind the seawall which are especially attractive in spring. Just inland of the seawalls are extensive areas of arable farmland, including a large, relatively recently reclaimed area at Tetney.

Access (see map)

Tetney Marshes RSPB reserve Leave the A1031 at Tetney or North Cotes, taking the minor roads to Tetney Lock, and then the no-through road just north of the bridge over Louth Canal, following this east for c.400 yards to the sharp left-hand bend, where there is limited roadside parking. Follow the footpath for c.1¼ miles along the canal bank to the RSPB warden's caravan. The reserve is open at all times and is wardened in summer. A circular walk of c.3 miles on the embankments encircling the reclaimed fields covers most of the habitats, and at the east end of this circuit, near Northcoates Point, a gate accesses the old seawall and a track which parallels the airfield fence for c.1½ miles to Horseshoe Point. This passes the MOD pools and a track east across the marsh between the two larger pools leads to the shore. The MOD pools attract passage waders in spring but subsequently tend to dry out, although they are temporarily flooded by 'spring' tides in late summer. Breeding Little Terns can be viewed where the track passes through the dunes, and to protect the terns the foreshore between the Haven and MOD pools is out of bounds in summer (as is the Haven track beyond the warden's caravan). Visitors should avoid tern nesting areas and heed warning notices.

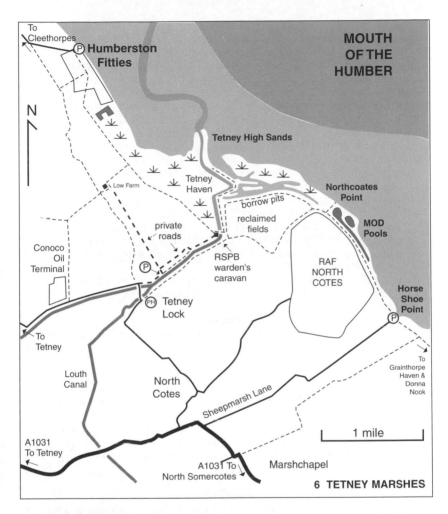

Horse Shoe Point Access is also possible from the A1031 between North Cotes and Marshchapel, taking the signed turn to Horseshoe Point (Sheepmarsh Lane). After 2½ miles there is a small car park by the seawall. This is an excellent spot for open-shore waders. Walking north along the bank, the MOD Pools are reached after c.1 mile and, by continuing, there is access to Northcoates Point and Tetney Marshes RSPB reserve.

Humberston Fitties From the A1031 south of Cleethorpes take the minor road at the roundabout east to Humberston and, after 1 mile, turn south at the next roundabout to Humberston Fitties, where there is a car park by the seawall. Follow the dunes south, through the pines on the sea bank by Fitties holiday camp, to the yacht club, checking the gardens and pines for migrants. It is also possible to follow the seawall for 2 miles from Humberston Fitties to Tetney Marshes RSPB reserve. There are some more areas of bushes and scrub en route which may hold migrants, and the arable fields inland of the bank may have roosting waders and, in spring, occasionally Dotterel.

Birds

The area is excellent for raptors in winter, including Hen Harrier, Sparrowhawk, Merlin and Peregrine. At high tide there are good views of wildfowl from the sea-walls, with numbers of Brent Geese, Wigeon and, sometimes, Common Scoter offshore. A variety of the usual open-shore waders are present, including Grey Plover and Bar-tailed Godwit, and the wader roost can be seen on higher tides from the end of the Haven track, but otherwise only distant views are possible from the seawall. Among flocks of finches and buntings check for Twite and Lapland and Snow Buntings, and Rock Pipit is frequent in the saltmarsh gutters.

At passage times the MOD Pools and adjacent borrow pits (and those nearer the Haven) attract waders, typically including Greenshank and Green Sandpiper, and sometimes also Wood Sandpiper. Other migrant waders favour the salt-marsh and open shore, and may include Golden Plover, Whimbrel, Black-tailed Godwit, Turnstone, Knot, Sanderling, Curlew Sandpiper and Little Stint. Dotterel is annual on passage in the Reclaimed Fields, the fields by the road to Horseshoe Point, or those near Low Farm. Other regular migrants include Marsh Harrier, Common and Sandwich Terns (with a notable late-summer concentration of loafing terns, especially on evening 'spring' tides) and small numbers of passer-ines such as Wheatear and Whinchat.

Breeding birds include Yellow Wagtail, Oystercatcher, Shelduck and up to 100 pairs of Little Terns, which nest on the shore north of the MOD pools.

Information

RSPB Tetney Warden: RSPB North England, 4 Benton Terrace, Sandyford Road, Newcastle-upon-Tyne NE2 1QU. Tel: 0191 2813366.

7 COVENHAM RESERVOIR (Lincolnshire)   OS Landranger 113

Lying c.5 miles north of Louth, this relatively small reservoir lies in a flat and fea-tureless area of arable farmland. Its proximity to the coast has resulted in a reputation for attracting sea duck, grebes and divers in winter, and passage peri-ods can also be interesting.

Habitat

Completed in 1969, open water now covers 200 acres and the banks are steep and concrete-clad, with the outer slopes having grazed turf and some small stands of deciduous trees. The reservoir is used for a variety of watersports, and only the southeast corner is free from disturbance.

Access

Leave Louth north on the A16 and, 1 mile north of Utterby, turn east on a minor road to Covenham and Grainthorpe. Continue straight on at the crossroads and the reservoir is clearly visible on the right. Park in the car park at the northeast corner. Take the steps to the top of the embankment and a footpath circumnavigates the reservoir, with a hide in the quieter southeast corner.

Birds

Wintering wildfowl include Pochard, up to 100 Goldeneye, small numbers of Pintail, Gadwall, Wigeon, Shoveler and Teal, and sometimes Smew, Goosander, Long-tailed Duck, Common and Velvet Scoters or Scaup. Other waterfowl include Little and Great Crested Grebes and reasonably regular single Red-necked or Slavonian Grebes and Great Northern, Black-throated and

Red-throated Divers. Rarer grebes and sea duck may make prolonged visits. Cormorant is regular and may be joined by a few Shags following gales. The reservoir is used by numbers of loafing and bathing gulls, and the roost is of interest; mostly comprising Black-headed and Common Gulls, it also holds small numbers of Herring and Great Black-backed Gulls. Mediterranean, Iceland and Glaucous Gulls are occasional, most regularly in late winter and early spring. Other wintering species include Golden Plover in adjacent arable fields, Sparrowhawk and, sometimes, Green Sandpiper, Merlin, Short-eared Owl, Rock Pipit, Grey Wagtail and Stonechat.

Spring migrants may include Common Sandpiper, Turnstone, Sanderling, transient flocks of Common, Arctic and Black Terns and Little Gull, Wheatear, occasionally Marsh Harrier, Osprey, Black Redstart or Ring Ouzel; scarcer visitors include Temminck's Stint. On autumn passage a greater diversity of waders may be found, despite the rather unattractive concrete banks, and Little Gull and Common and Black Terns. Scarcer visitors include Black-necked Grebe, Marsh Harrier, Osprey, Red-necked and Grey Phalaropes, and coastal gales in late autumn may produce records of Leach's Petrel, skuas or Little Auk

Breeding birds in the area include Barn Owl, Cuckoo and Tree Sparrow.

8 NORTH KILLINGHOLME HAVEN (Lincolnshire)   OS Landranger 113

On the south bank of the River Humber 3 miles north of Immingham, this rather small and compact site is notable for furnishing excellent views of passage waders.

Habitat

Comprising three flooded clay pits, the largest of which has a mosaic of shallow water, reed and sedge beds and islands with varying amounts of exposed mud, there are some mature hedgerows and a patch of hawthorn scrub immediately to the south. The surroundings are a mix of rough grassland and extensive industrial areas. Lincolnshire Wildlife Trust (LWT) manages the pits.

Access (see map)

Leave the A180 Scunthorpe–Grimsby road north on the A160. This road passes South Killingholme and a complex of oil refineries before reaching a roundabout after 3 miles. Turn left here, pass under the railway bridge and, after a further 100 yards, turn left on Rosper Road. After 2 miles, where this road bears to the left, turn right, signed North Killingholme Haven. The two larger pits lie to the right after ¾ mile, either side of the railway crossing, and by remaining in a parked car at the roadside it is often possible to acquire superb views of roosting waders. The road is very busy in working hours and the light is poor in the mornings, making an evening visit best. The smaller pit can be viewed from the Humber seawall, which also affords views over the main wader pit and the estuary.

Birds

On passage Whimbrel, Black-tailed and Bar-tailed Godwits, Ruff, Greenshank, Spotted Redshank, Green, Wood, Common and Curlew Sandpipers and Little Stint are regular, especially in autumn, and there may be a notable build-up of Redshanks, Black-tailed Godwits and Ruffs at the same season. A variety of scarce and rare waders has also been recorded. The largest numbers of waders roost on the pits during the fortnightly 'spring' tides. Shoveler and Wigeon also occur in autumn, and sometimes Garganey. Marsh Harrier is regular in spring, and in May a Long-eared Owl often hunts the adjacent rough grass fields in early evening. During autumn gales, especially from the northeast, seabirds may be forced into the Humber and a variety of auks, gulls, terns and skuas can be seen from the seawall.

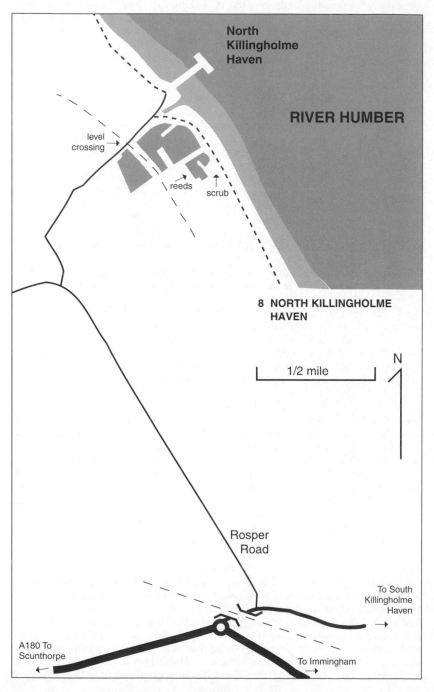

In winter the pits may attract occasional grebes, divers or sea duck, but if water levels remain high wader variety is low. Nevertheless, Redshank and Dunlin are regular, and significant numbers of Snipe are present, along with a few Jack Snipe and Water Rails. Bittern and Bearded Tit are occasional, favouring the reed-filled small west pit. Long-eared Owl roosts in the hawthorn scrub, and Short-eared Owl also winters in the area and may linger into spring.

Breeders include Water Rail and Grasshopper, Reed and Sedge Warblers, with Oystercatcher and Ringed Plover nearby.

Information

LWT, Banovallum House, Manor House Street, Horncastle, Lincolnshire LN9 5HF. Tel: 01507 526667. E-mail: info@lincstrust.co.uk

9 THE INNER HUMBER (Lincolnshire) OS Landranger 112 and 113

The Humber is one of the major rivers in Britain and forms an important landmark for migrating birds. A complex of estuary habitats and borrow pits borders its south shore, offering great potential to the more adventurous birdwatcher.

Habitat

The inner parts of the Humber estuary are formed by rich muddy silts, especially at the confluence of the Rivers Trent and Ouse, with some limited areas of saltmarsh and rough grassland, all bounded by many seawalls.

Access and Birds (see map)

The pace of birdwatching in this vast area is largely determined by the tides, and ideally, a visit should be timed to coincide with high water in order to view roosting waders, sea duck and, in season, seabirds. During spring and autumn the fortnightly 'spring' tides are ideal, as these relatively high tides usually flood the saltmarshes and force waders onto drier ground to roost. High water on 'spring' tides usually occurs late evening and early morning. The intervening 'neap' tides leave the saltmarshes uncovered; fewer waders move within view of the seawalls, and sea duck remain distant. In winter months 'spring' tides peak during darkness and a late-morning high tide is the best compromise.

East Halton Skitter The interest here lies in the areas of rough tidal grassland, which attract wintering Short-eared Owl, Jack Snipe, sometimes Snow and Lapland Buntings, and occasionally Twite. From East Halton take the minor road north to its end at East Halton Skitter. From here walk north along the sea bank, with rough grassland to the east and some borrow pits adjacent to the bank.

Dawson City reserve This reserve at Skitter Ness consists of flooded pits by the sea bank which attract Jack Snipe and a few passage waders. In Goxhill follow signs for North End and continue north on the minor road to Goxhill Haven. Park on the verge and walk southeast along the seawall for 1 mile to view Dawson City reserve. It is possible to continue for 2 miles, with areas of rough grasslands east of the bank, to East Halton Skitter.

New Holland Large numbers of diving and sea duck are attracted to grain and animal feed drifting downstream from spills at the grain terminal. Peak numbers include 2,000 Pochard, 1,000 Tufted Duck, 450 Goldeneye and 250 Scaup, with up to 250 Common Scoter and small numbers of Velvet Scoter, Eider and Long-tailed

Duck in early winter. The period before high water, on calm days, is best; the tide drifts the flocks west towards the Humber Bridge and repeated views are possible as the birds fly back east. Inland, the fields hold large numbers of Golden Plovers and roosting waders. Snow Bunting may be found along the seawall and, just west

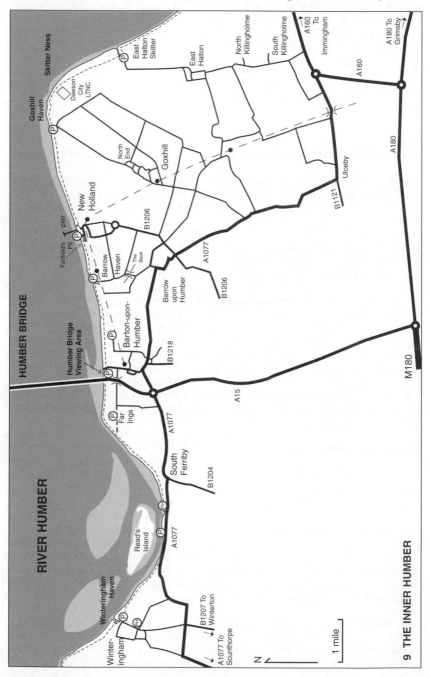

of the pier, Fairfield's Pit, which is a Lincolnshire Wildlife Trust (LWT) reserve, attracts passage waders and breeding Grasshopper Warbler.

Follow the B1206 bypass around New Holland and, once over the level crossing, turn left between the railway and a warehouse, and follow the track around the sharp right-hand bend to park by Fairfield's Pit. To view diving duck walk back to the railway crossing and turn left, then right between the warehouses, to the signed coastal footpath after c.200 yards, and continue around the scrap yard to the seawall.

Barton-upon-Humber A complex of flooded pits stretches almost the entire Humber shore at the foot of the Humber Bridge between Barrow Haven and Chowder Ness, forming a mosaic of open water, reedbeds and scrub. Many are used for fishing or watersports but several are LWT reserves. They attract wildfowl, including up to 50 Scaup and sometimes divers, rarer grebes, Smew and Goosander. Up to three Bitterns winter but are typically elusive. Common Tern and a few Bearded Tits breed, and Garganey and Grasshopper Warbler appear on passage and sometimes nest. Several species of terns occur on passage. Beyond the sea bank, numbers of open-shore waders and seabirds may be seen on the river during autumn storms.

Barrow Haven From the A1077 in Barrow-upon-Humber take the minor road signed to Barrow Haven. After c.⅓ mile the road crosses the Barrow Beck and after a further ¼ mile turns sharp right. Continue straight and park on the right just beyond the level crossing. Take the bridge west across the Haven and turn north through the gate to the seawall. Immediately on the left a stepped path leads to a hide overlooking LWT Barrow Reedbed reserve, and a footpath follows the bank west for 2 miles to Barton Waterside, giving views over the foreshore and a series of pits.

Barton Clay Pits Leave Barton-upon-Humber east on the A1077 and turn north along Falkland Way. After 1 mile the road crosses a railway and after a few hundred yards turns sharply east and passes a series of pits. Park after a further ½ mile in the car park just before the end of the metalled road.

The Humber Bridge Viewing Area Follow signs from the A15 or Barton-upon-Humber town centre to the Viewing Area; from the car park there is access to the Humber bank. Walk west to view the pits west of the bridge, and just west of the Haven Mouth the shelter at the Old Boathouse can be used to watch the river in rough weather for passing seabirds, which are most likely in NE–SE winds on a rising tide.

Far Ings LWT Reserve Follow signs as for the Viewing Area and turn west at the Sloop pub (just north of Barton-upon-Humber railway station) and follow Far Ings road for 1 mile to the visitor centre. Alternatively, turn north off the A1077 ⅓ mile west of the roundabout at its junction with the A15 onto a minor road signed to the Clay Pits and, after 1 mile, turn left at the T-junction into Far Ings Road. The visitor centre is open on summer weekends, and Sunday afternoons in winter, and offers commanding views of the reserve. There are seven hides overlooking the pits, scrapes and foreshore, and the reserve is open in daylight hours. A variety of wildfowl, including Goosander, and sometimes Smew (and Bittern) winter on the pits, which also attract passage waders. Bearded Tit and Water Rail are resident and Grasshopper Warbler sometimes breeds.

South Ferriby Bank Leave South Ferriby west on the A1077 and, after c.½ mile, park just south of the road opposite the Hope and Anchor pub. Cross the main road and the ditch to the right and bear left to the seawall. Follow this east to a hide overlooking the foreshore. The period 2–3 hours before high tide is best.

Read's Island Formerly covering 500 acres, this island has dwindled to 80 acres, but it still attracts roosting waders. Leave South Ferriby west on the A1077 and, after 1 mile, park in either of the two lay-bys to view the mudflats. This is one of the best areas on the estuary for waders, with the period 2–3 hours before high tide best, but on the highest 'spring' tides most waders are forced onto the roost on Read's Island up to 2 hours before high water.

Winteringham Haven Turn off the A1077 on minor roads to Winteringham and turn north by the pub, parking after ½ mile at a right-angled left bend. Either take the footpath to the right along the sea bank to a hide overlooking the estuary or follow the road over the bridge and turn immediately right on a track to the sea-wall, which can then be followed west. Pink-footed Geese were abundant in the past and may be returning (with 1,000+ in winter 1993–94), but are unpredictable and most likely to be seen flying to feed inland. Thousands of Black-headed, Common and Great Black-backed Gulls, along with up to 1500 Herring Gull, roost well offshore, and occasionally Glaucous or Iceland Gulls loaf on the sand bars off Winteringham before going to roost.

Information

LWT: Banovallum House, Manor House Street, Horncastle, Lincolnshire LN9 5HF. Tel: 01507 526667. E-mail: info@lincstrust.co.uk

Far Ings Visitor Centre (LWT), Far Ings Road, Barton-on-Humber DN18 5RG. Tel: 01652 634507. E-mail: farings@lincstrust.co.uk

10 MESSINGHAM SAND QUARRIES (Lincolnshire) OS Landranger 112

This complex of pits lies c.4 miles south of Scunthorpe and harbours a selection of winter wildfowl and passage waders; it has also gained a reputation for attracting scarce migrants and rarities.

Sand Martins

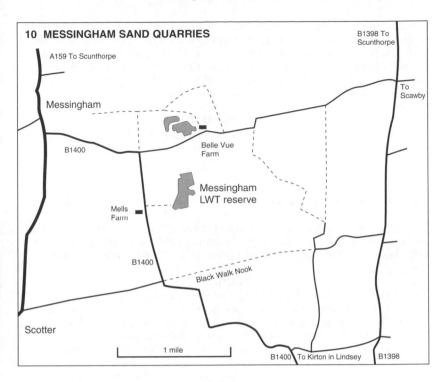

10 MESSINGHAM SAND QUARRIES

B1398 To Scunthorpe

A159 To Scunthorpe

Messingham

To Scawby

B1400

Belle Vue Farm

Messingham LWT reserve

Mells Farm

B1400

Black Walk Nook

Scotter

1 mile

B1400 To Kirton in Lindsey   B1398

Habitat

The extraction of sand and gravel around Messingham has formed a number of flooded pits that demonstrate typical succession from open water to small reedbeds and willow and birch scrub. Part of the area is a reserve of the Lincolnshire Wildlife Trust (LWT), and to the west lies an area of grassland (the site of an old rubbish tip) that is prone to flooding and attracts passage waders.

Access (see map)

Leave Messingham east on the B1400 towards Kirton in Lindsey and, after c.¾ mile, the road turns south at a sharp right-angled bend. Follow the road, and the track to the reserve car park lies to the left after ½ mile. Access is restricted to permit holders only (obtainable from the LWT) and there are three hides. Some of the pits can be viewed from the B1400 adjacent to Mells Farm and from the minor road between the B1400 and Scawby.

Birds

Wintering wildfowl include numbers of Wigeon, Gadwall and Teal, and sometimes Shoveler and Goldeneye, while Goosander and Scaup are occasional, as are wild geese. Sometimes a Bittern, Jack Snipe or Chiffchaff may winter, with Siskin and Redpoll regular in the waterside alders. The area is quite good for raptors, with Peregrine, Merlin, Buzzard and Hen Harrier seen most winters.

On passage the usual waders are regular, parties of Common, Arctic and Black Terns pass through and Little Gull is also possible, especially in spring. Marsh Harrier and Osprey are recorded most years in spring, while in summer there is a build-up of Lesser Black-backed Gull with occasional single Yellow-legged Gulls.

Breeders include Great Crested and Little Grebes, Shelduck, Shoveler, Tufted Duck, Pochard, Ruddy Duck, Lapwing, Oystercatcher, Ringed and Little Ringed

Plovers, Snipe, Redshank, Turtle Dove, Yellow Wagtail, and Reed and Sedge Warblers. There is a notable colony of Black-headed Gulls, and in recent years a male Mediterranean Gull has paired with a Black-headed Gull; the resultant hybrid offspring frequent the colony. Sand Martins breed nearby, and concentrations of Swift and hirundines attract Hobby. The nearby conifer plantations hold Sparrowhawk, Woodcock and Long-eared Owl.

Information

LWT, Banovallum House, Manor House Street, Horncastle, Lincolnshire LN9 5HF. Tel: 01507 526667. E-mail: info@lincstrust.co.uk

11 LOUND (Nottinghamshire)   OS Landranger 120

This extensive complex of gravel pits lies immediately to the west of the River Idle between Retford and Mattersey in northeast Nottinghamshire. It contains a rich variety of habitats and attracts a good variety of wildfowl and waders.

Habitat

The working and disused sand and gravel pits present a typical succession of habitat from bare mud and shallow pools to willow scrub. Some older pits are now used for fishing and watersports, whilst others have been embanked and filled with fly ash from Cottam power station, forming interesting but transient wetland habitats; when filled, they are grassed and turned over to pasture. The western parts of the Idle's floodplain are very sandy and there are areas of relict heathland as well as old hedgerows, pastures and plantations, whilst to the east of the river there are areas of arable fields.

Access (see map)

As is usual with working sand and gravel pits, the favourite localities, both for birds and birdwatchers, are constantly changing.

Leave Retford northwest on the A638 and after 1 mile turn east onto the minor road to Sutton, and then in Sutton turn right signed to Lound.

Belmoor Quarries Proceed along the Lound road and, after 800 yards, take the public footpath southwards. This passes to the east of a trout lake and on to Belmoor Quarries.

Wetlands Wildfowl Centre at the lagoon 800 yards before Lound village the road bends sharp left and a broad track runs straight ahead to the Wetlands Wildfowl Centre. Park after 400 yards to view the ash lagoon to the right and some reclaimed fields. Continue along this track to join Chain Bridge Lane.

Chain Bridge Lane This driveable track joins Lound village centre to the River Idle. Footpaths lead north along the riverbank to Neatholme bridge or south to Tiln and on to Belmoor Quarries (these are not public footpaths, but are frequently used by the general public).

Neatholme Lane This footpath connects Lound village (limited parking) to the River Idle, passing several new pits, especially near the river, which are favoured by wildfowl. At the end of Neatholme Lane the River Idle can be crossed on the footbridge to gain access to an area of carr and rough grassland.

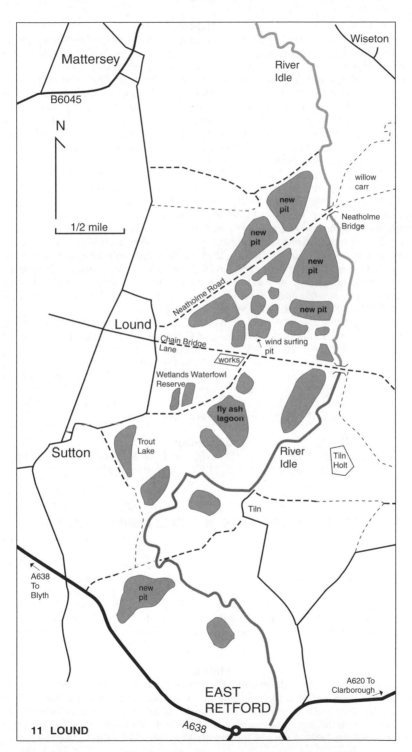

11 LOUND

Birds

Wintering wildfowl include several hundred each of Pochard, Tufted Duck, Gadwall, Teal and Wigeon, and notably there may be about 30 each of Goosander and Goldeneye, with occasional Scaup and Common Scoter, but the highest counts of Pintail and Shoveler are recorded in the early autumn. There are good numbers of Great Crested and Little Grebes and Cormorants are regular visitors throughout the year. There is a notable gull roost, mainly comprising Black-headed but at times holding several hundred each of Common, Herring and Lesser and Great Black-backed Gulls. Mediterranean and Yellow-legged Gulls are fairly regular and Glaucous and Iceland Gulls occasional. Other interesting winterers include Merlin (favouring the arable areas east of the river), Water Rail, Green Sandpiper, Jack Snipe, occasionally Dunlin or Ruff, up to 6,000 Golden Plovers and 4,000 Lapwings on the adjacent fields, Short-eared Owl, Grey Wagtail and Stonechat.

On spring passage Marsh Harrier, Garganey, Arctic and Black Terns, Little Gull, and Kittiwake are regular, and a wide variety of waders is possible. Indeed, at both seasons passage waders are a speciality, and Lound has recorded quite exceptional totals of normally coastal species as well a good numbers of the commoner species (e.g. 100 Dunlin) and a variety in both spring and autumn to rival East Coast sites. Black-necked Grebe is recorded with increasing frequency (in common with many sites in the Midlands). Migrant passerines should not be ignored, and may include Wheatear, Whinchat, Stonechat, Redstart, and occasionally Rock Pipit and Ring Ouzel.

Breeding birds include Sparrowhawk, Greylag Goose, Gadwall, Pochard, Long-eared Owl, Little Ringed and Ringed Plovers, Oystercatcher, Redshank, up to 150 pairs of Black-headed Gulls, about 20 pairs of Common Terns, Turtle Dove, all three woodpeckers, Kingfisher, Sand Martin, Yellow Wagtail, Grasshopper, Reed, Sedge and Garden Warblers, occasionally Shelduck, Curlew, Lesser Black-backed Gull, Nightingale (in plantations near Tiln), and rarely Black-necked Grebe and Garganey, whilst a pair of Little Gulls once attempted to nest. Visiting Hobbies are regularly seen in summer and early autumn.

Information

Lound Bird Club: Paul Hobson (Secretary), 6 St Mary's Crescent, Tickhill, Doncaster, South Yorkshire. Tel: 07940 428326 (after 16.00).

12 THE DUKERIES AT WELBECK AND CLUMBER PARKS
(Nottinghamshire)   OS Landranger 120

Welbeck Park is a well-known site for Honey Buzzards which can be seen from the road with no risk of disturbance, although views are usually distant and much patience may be required. At Clumber Park (National Trust) there is general access and a variety of woodland birds can be seen, including Hawfinches. Honey Buzzards are present most summers, and late May and early June is the best time to visit. For Hawfinches, winter is best, but with perseverance they can also be seen in summer.

Habitat

The area of ancient heathland and woodland that formerly comprised Sherwood Forest has been reduced to small fragments but successive generations of landed gentry have created estates with ornamental lakes set in mixed woodland, parkland, plantations, heathland and farmland. Welbeck Park is privately owned, but the 3,800 acres of Clumber Park are owned by the National Trust.

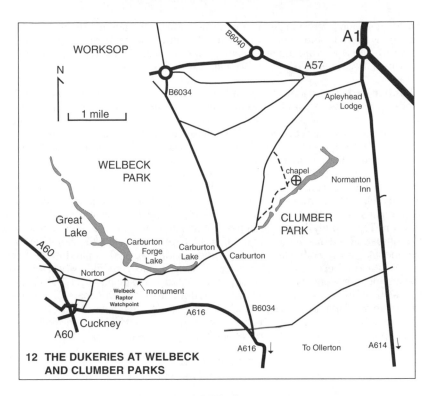

WORKSOP

N

1 mile

B6040

A1

A57

B6034

Apleyhead
Lodge

WELBECK
PARK

chapel

Normanton
Inn

Great
Lake

CLUMBER
PARK

A60

Carburton
Forge
Lake

Carburton
Lake

Carburton

Norton

Welbeck
Raptor
Watchpoint

monument

A616

B6034

Cuckney

A60

A616

To Ollerton

A614

**12 THE DUKERIES AT WELBECK
AND CLUMBER PARKS**

Access and Birds (see map)

Welbeck Raptor Watchpoint From the A616 bear north onto the B6034 towards Worksop, and after 1½ miles turn west at the first crossroads (at a sign saying Carburton). Continue along this minor road for about 1½ miles, passing Carburton Lake, until you reach Carburton Forge Lake (the second section of the Great Lake) and the Bentinck monument on the right, with limited parking (this is a narrow road and common sense should be exercised when parking). Looking north across the lake there is an isolated deciduous wood (Cat Hills plantation) with a large heronry. Honey Buzzards fly over this and/or the lake up to two or three times a day. Alternatively, walk another 300 yards to the gate just to the west of the monument where a tree trunk has been laid on the north side of the road (the 'Welbeck Raptor Watchpoint'). Stay on the road at all times. The whole of the area north of the road is private and well-keepered, with no public rights of way. In any event, the road is the best place to see the birds.

Honey Buzzards have been summering here since at least the early 1960s and they have bred in some years. Although present late May-September, they become especially difficult to see in late August and early September. Normally there are 1-3 individuals present, but up to five have been seen. The optimum time is 10.00-15.00 on warm sunny days, with scattered cloud and only light breezes, when they may be seen soaring or in their wing-clapping display. They spend a great deal of time sitting below the canopy, however, and a long wait may be necessary for a relatively brief and distant view. They may show well, but sometimes are not seen at all.

The area is also good for other species of raptors. Common Buzzards breed and, indeed, are rather more likely to be seen than the Honey Buzzards. Sparrowhawks are frequent and Ospreys are regular in spring and summer and may linger for days or even weeks. Hobbies are also likely in late spring and summer, and Peregrine may visit. The woods around hold all three woodpeckers, Nuthatch, Marsh Tit and Hawfinch, whilst the lake attracts Gadwall and Ruddy Duck.

Clumber Park This is a mosaic of parkland, broad-leaved and coniferous woodlands, scrub, wet meadows, grasslands and heathland. At the crossroads where you turn left for Welbeck Great Lake, turn right instead to Carburton and Clumber Park. Turning right after the first bridge, follow signs to the chapel and park there (fee). The Park is also accessible from the A1 via the A614 at Apleyhead Lodge and Normanton Inn. Immediately behind the chapel is an area of rhododendron, beech, yew, and other conifers. Hawfinches are present in greatest numbers (up to 30) in winter and are quite easy to see, usually in the tops of hornbeams beside the chapel. Early mornings and weekdays with minimum disturbance offer the best chance of finding Hawfinches. The lake may hold wintering Gadwall, Wigeon, Teal, Ruddy Duck, Goldeneye, Water Rail and occasionally Smew or Goosander. Residents in the park include Little and Great Crested Grebes, Woodcock, Tawny and Little Owls, all three woodpeckers, Marsh and the rather scarcer Willow Tits, Nuthatch, Treecreeper, Redpoll and Tree Pipit, whilst winter visitors include Stonechat, Brambling, Siskin, and occasionally Crossbill in the conifers, or Firecrests (which favour the rhododendrons by the chapel). In summer there are Turtle Doves, Nightjars, Yellow Wagtails, Tree Pipits, Woodlarks (try the areas of clear-fell), a few Nightingales and Whinchats, Common Redstarts, Grasshopper and Reed Warblers and Spotted Flycatchers.

Information
NT Clumber Park: Estate Office, Clumber Park, Worksop, Nottinghamshire, S80 3AZ. Tel. 01909 476592.
The Birds of Clumber Park by Austen Dobbs (1976).

13 BLEASBY AND HOVERINGHAM PITS
(Nottinghamshire)   OS Landranger 129

Situated in the Trent valley between Newark and Nottingham, this complex of gravel pits attracts a good variety of migrant and wintering birds; it shot to fame in early 1996 when Europe's first Redhead remained here for several weeks.

Habitat
This part of the Trent valley has been the site of extensive gravel and sand extraction for many years; indeed, many pits have been in-filled and returned to agriculture. Several significant pits remain, however, notably Hoveringham Sailing Lake, which attracts wildfowl but has relatively steep banks, reducing its attractiveness to waders. The very small pit to the west is also used for sailing, and it and the larger lake to the northeast have more gently sloping and better-vegetated banks. To the northeast is Hoveringham Railway Pit, recently (1995) drained and partially in-filled, whilst Gibsmere and the other pits just south of Bleasby also attract a range of wildfowl.

Access (see map)
The area is accessed from the A612 between Newark and Nottingham. By parking at Halleford Ferry it is possible to cover most of the area via footpaths in 3-4 hours. Specific sites are accessed as follows:

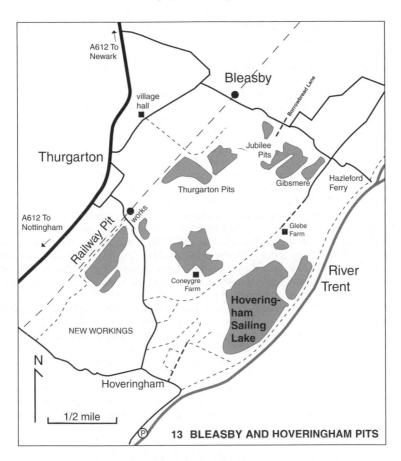

13 BLEASBY AND HOVERINGHAM PITS

Hoveringham Sailing Lake Turn off the A612 about 1 mile northeast of Lowdham onto the minor road to Hoveringham and, after 1¼ miles, turn right at the T-junction in the village. After ¼ mile the road bends sharply to the right and after a further ¼ mile park in the large car park on the left. Walk back to the sharp bend and take the public footpath northeast along the banks of the River Trent for ½ mile to view the Sailing Lake and the smaller pit beyond. This pit holds an interesting winter gull roost, best viewed from the footpath to the sailing club building (SK709 474) which leads to the roost viewing point.

Coneygre Farm Lake Park in Hoveringham village and walk north towards the railway station, taking the public footpath northeastwards on the outskirts of the village to view Coneygre Farm Lake; the footpath continues on to Gibsmere. (It is essential to keep strictly to the footpaths in this area.)

Hoveringham Railway Pit Leave the A612 at Thurgarton on the minor road to Hoveringham and park carefully after ¼ mile near the level crossing. From the crossing take the public footpath southwestwards to view the pit, parallel to the southern side of the railway. As well as wildfowl, this pit also holds a winter gull roost. The small wood just southwest of the pit holds all three woodpeckers, and Marsh and Willow Tits.

253

Hoveringham New Workings Access is from Thurgarton village, via the footpath behind the village hall.

Bleasby Gravel Pits Turn off the A612 at Thurgarton on the minor road to Bleasby. Turn right into the village, follow the road southeastwards past the railway station and, after about 1 mile, park carefully on the roadside at the crossroads. Walk right (southwest) from here to view Gibsmere; it is possible to continue along the footpath to Coneygre Farm Lake. The Jubilee Pits can be viewed from Borrowbread Lane (on foot only – there is no vehicle access).

Birds

Wintering waterfowl include Great Crested and Little Grebes, Cormorant, Tufted Duck, Pochard, Goldeneye, Wigeon, Teal and Gadwall. Small numbers of Goosander and Shoveler occur and occasionally also Pintail, Smew and Scaup. Hoveringham Sailing Lake holds a gull roost, largely Black-headed Gulls with some Common Gulls and small numbers of Herring and Lesser Black-backed Gulls. Mediterranean, Iceland and Glaucous Gulls have also been recorded, and Caspian Gull has been regular in late autumn. The Railway Pit also holds roosting gulls, occasionally including Caspian. Other interesting wintering species include Golden Plovers together with Lapwings in the surrounding fields, and a handful of Grey Wagtails and Stonechats.

Wader passage is unexceptional, with the Railway Pit offering the best habitat. In spring Ringed and Little Ringed Plovers, Dunlin and Green and Common Sandpipers are occasionally joined by Greenshank, Sanderling and Turnstone. In spring, Arctic and Black Terns are also recorded. In the autumn, Black Terns are relatively frequent, and the commoner passage waders may be joined by Grey Plover, Little Stint, or Ruff. Garganey may occur, as may Little Gull.

Breeding birds in the area include Grey Heron, Shelduck, Redshank, Oystercatcher, Turtle Dove, Kingfisher, Cuckoo, Yellow Wagtail and Sedge Warbler, with Common Terns on the Railway Pit. Hobbies are occasional visitors.

14 TRENT VALLEY PITS (Nottinghamshire)   OS Landranger 129

This complex of pits lies in the Trent valley on the eastern outskirts of the City of Nottingham, and comprises Colwick Country Park, the slurry pits at Netherfield, Holme Pierrepont Country Park and the adjacent A52 Pit. The Trent valley is a major 'flyway' for migrants moving across Britain, and thus not surprisingly the area has a reputation for attracting interesting birds throughout the year.

Habitat

This vast conglomeration of gravel working shows every stage of succession, from the freshly-scraped soil of new workings to mature pits with good areas of riparian reeds and willows set amidst meadows and scrub. A notable feature of the complex is that several pits have been heavily landscaped for recreational use.

To the north of the River Trent lies Colwick Country Park, where the gravel workings have been landscaped and planted with a variety of trees and shrubs, interspersed with areas of damp grassland, and bounded to the north by Colwick Woods. Colwick Lake covers 62 acres and is used for trout fishing. The other large pit, West Lake, extends over 24 acres and is used by fishermen and windsurfers year-round and, indeed, being so close to the city, the whole area is heavily used by the general public.

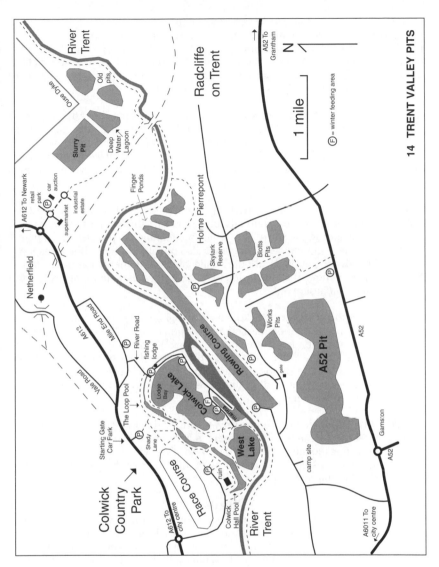

To the east of Colwick lie the disused gravel pits at Netherfield, two of which have been used as a dump for coal slurry, and are separated by a high causeway. The larger tank still has some areas of water and mud which attract waders and roosting gulls and terns, whilst the smaller tank is largely deep water, attractive to wildfowl. The two remaining pits are used by fishermen.

To the south of the River Trent lies Holme Pierrepont Country Park, which is dominated by the National Watersports Centre's 1,000 m rowing course (which has attracted a selection of interesting birds), and the A52 Pit, covering 140 acres and surrounded by pasture. To the east of the A52 Pit lie more recent workings which may attract waders, gulls and terns, whilst to the north is the Nottinghamshire Wildlife Trust's Skylark Reserve, comprising willow carr and a pool with a specially constructed nesting platform for terns. To the east of the rowing course lie areas of grassland and the Finger Ponds.

Access (see map)

Being so close to Nottingham, and largely dedicated to recreation, the whole are is subject to considerable disturbance, especially at weekends, making early morning the best time to visit. Beware also 'car crime', and avoid the quieter, more secluded car parks (especially the Starting Gate car park; the safest car parks are at the fishing lodge and outside Colwick Hall).

Colwick Country Park From Nottingham city centre take the A612 towards Colwick and once past Nottingham Racecourse follow signs for 'water user entrance only', and turn off Mile End Road onto River Road. There are three free car parks and parking is also available within the park for a small fee. Access is also possible using public transport: Netherfield railway station is about 1 mile away, and there are buses from Nottingham city centre. The park is open at all times.

Netherfield Turn south off the A612 to the retail park about 1 mile northeast of Colwick. Continue to the next roundabout and park on the left. From here follow the path southwards to the slurry pits (which are technically private, but in practice there is unrestricted access). Access is also possible using public transport: Netherfield railway station is about 1 mile away and there are buses from Nottingham city centre. The area is due to be developed as a nature reserve, with visitor facilities, including hides.

Holme Pierrepont Country Park Leave Nottingham city centre on the A6011 and turn north on the minor road signed to the National Watersports Centre. There are several car parks. There is open access to the rowing course, Finger Ponds and banks of the River Trent, and whilst the Skylark Reserve is private, it can be viewed from the periphery. Buses run to the Watersports Centre from Nottingham city centre and, of course, the area is severely disturbed during national watersports events.

The A52 Pit This is surrounded by private farmland with restricted access, but the southwest corner can be viewed from the A52, whilst the eastern portion can be seen from the metalled track (which also gives views of the works pits), accessed from the eastbound carriageway of the A52 from the parking area 150 yards east of the 'Happy Eater'.

Birds

Wintering wildfowl include Wigeon, Teal, Gadwall, Shoveler, Pintail, Pochard, Ruddy Duck and Goldeneye. Goosander are only irregular visitors but Smew are annual, as are Red-necked and Slavonian Grebes, the odd diver, and Red-breasted Merganser (the last mainly on passage). Waterfowl favour Colwick and West Lakes, the Deep Water Pit at Netherfield, and the rowing course and A52 Pit, whilst Cormorants roost on the electricity pylons immediately east of Netherfield. In late autumn and winter there are large flocks of Golden Plovers and Lapwings (with up to 4,000 Golden Plovers roosting at Netherfield), often together with a few Ruff, whilst Jack Snipe favour the more waterlogged ground. Occasionally Long-eared Owls may be found roosting in some of the denser areas of scrub (e.g. the railway embankment at Netherfield), and Short-eared Owls sometimes hunt over the rough grassland. Numbers of gulls roost in the area, and Mediterranean Gull is sometimes recorded. The area attracts good numbers of thrushes, pipits and larks, and other interesting wintering species may include Stonechat (favouring the scrub at Netherfield), Blackcap, Chiffchaff, Siskin (up to 100 in the alders at Colwick), Brambling, and up to 60 Tree Sparrows (the last two species often at the feeding area at Colwick).

On spring passage Black-necked Grebe and Garganey are annual, and Black and Arctic Terns and Little Gulls are something of a speciality, particularly after east winds. Wader passage can be good, with Ringed Plover, Ruff, Dunlin, Redshank, Greenshank, Green and Common Sandpipers regular, while Turnstone and Sanderling are also possible, especially in May. The same mix of species occurs in autumn, with a greater chance of Spotted Redshank, Wood Sandpiper, Little Stint and Curlew Sandpiper. Passage waders favour the A52 pit, Holme Pierrepont works pits, and the slurry pits at Netherfield. In both spring and autumn, migrant passerines may include Wheatear and Whinchat.

Breeding birds include Great Crested and Little Grebes, Sparrowhawk, Little Ringed Plover, Common Tern (up to ten pairs on rafts at Colwick, with a late summer post-breeding gathering there), Turtle Dove, Kingfisher, Yellow Wagtail, and Grasshopper, Reed and Sedge Warblers. Hobbies and Yellow-legged Gulls are regular visitors in summer.

Information

Colwick Country Park: Mark Dennis, The Fishing Lodge, Colwick Country Park, River Road, Colwick, Nottingham NG4 2DW. Tel. 0115 987 0785.

Nottinghamshire Wildlife Trust, The Old Ragged School, Brook Street, Nottingham, NG1 1EA. Tel: 0115 958 8242. E-mail: nottswt@cix.co.uk

15 FOREMARK RESERVOIR (Derbyshire)   OS Landranger 128

Lying just 5 miles south of Derby, this reservoir holds significant numbers of wintering Goosanders and, being very deep, seldom freezes, making it an important refuge for diving ducks and gulls during cold weather.

Access (see map)

Turn west off the A514 at Ticknall on the minor road to Milton and, after c.1 mile, turn south through the gates (locked at dusk) to the reservoir. There are two car parks overlooking the north end of the reservoir and a footpath leads south along the east shore to Carver's Rocks NR. Carver's Rocks is also accessible from the A514 c.1¼ miles south of Ticknall (again, the gates are locked at dusk).

Habitat

The reservoir was completed in 1977 and covers 230 acres in an area of undulating farmland at c.110 m above sea level. The banks are largely natural but shelve steeply. The reservoir is used for sailing and trout fishing, but the extreme south end is undisturbed where Carver's Rocks NR, owned by the Derbyshire Wildlife Trust, has a stand of deciduous woodland. An extensive area of conifer plantations lies west of the reservoir at Repton Shrubs.

Birds

Winter waterfowl include significant numbers of Great Crested Grebes and Cormorants, also Pochard, Goldeneye and, notably, up to 200 Goosander. Small numbers of Wigeon, Teal and Shoveler may also occur, and all three divers have been recorded. The gull roost peaks at 10–15,000 birds, largely Black-headed Gull but with numbers of Herring, Lesser and Great Black-backed and Common Gulls. Glaucous and Iceland Gulls are recorded most winters, occasional Kittiwakes are most likely in late winter to early spring, and records of Mediterranean Gull are increasing. The gull roost is best viewed from the shelter of the toilet block in the main dam car park. Other notable species in the area

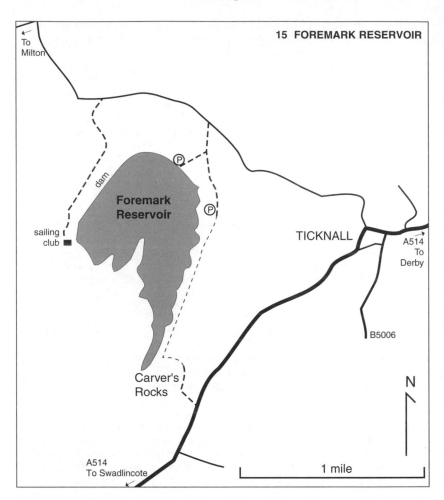

15 FOREMARK RESERVOIR

To Milton

Foremark Reservoir

dam

sailing club

TICKNALL

A514 To Derby

B5006

Carver's Rocks

N

A514 To Swadlincote

1 mile

include Grey Partridge, Little and Barn Owls, and Tree Sparrow, while Carver's Rocks has Siskin and Redpoll.

On spring passage Common and Arctic Terns, Common Sandpiper and Yellow Wagtail are regular, and Osprey is something of a local specialty, with immatures sometimes making prolonged visits. On autumn migration Little Gull, Common Tern and small numbers of waders occur, though water levels have to drop markedly to expose much mud.

Breeding birds include Woodcock, Turtle Dove, Cuckoo, Lesser Spotted Woodpecker, Tree Pipit, Grasshopper Warbler (at the entrance to Carver's Rocks) and Marsh Tit.

16 STAUNTON HAROLD RESERVOIR (Derbyshire)   OS Landranger 128

Only 5 miles south of Derby and slightly east of Foremark Reservoir, this water has shallow shelving banks and is attractive to passage waders and terns, while in winter scarcer grebes or divers are possible.

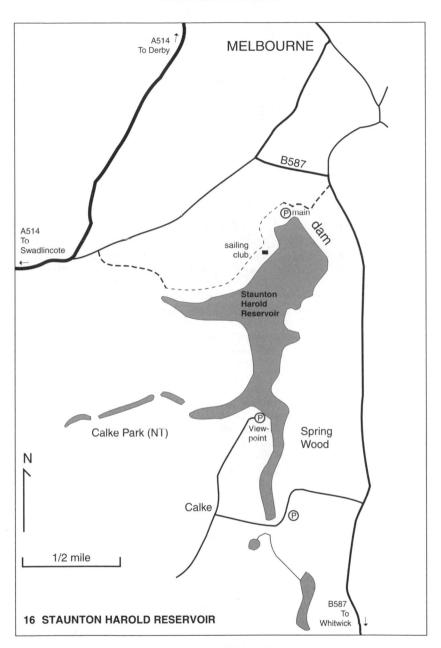

16 **STAUNTON HAROLD RESERVOIR**

Habitat

Completed in 1964, open water covers 216 acres, with gently sloping natural banks. The reservoir is surrounded by farmland and areas of deciduous woodland, including Spring Wood immediately to the southeast, a Derbyshire Wildlife Trust reserve, while Calke Park to the southwest comprises an area of oak-dotted parkland owned by the NT. Sailing and fishing disturb the central and northern parts of the reservoir.

Access (see map)

The reservoir is viewable at three points, all accessed off the B587 south of Melbourne.

Dam End Leave Melbourne south on the B587 and, after c.½ mile, turn west at the signs to the main car park (fee; note the gates are locked at dusk). A footpath runs along the north shore of the reservoir, eventually reaching the A514.

Southern Arm Continue south on the B587 for c.1½ miles and turn west onto a minor road towards Calke. After c.¾ mile the road passes the south tip of the reservoir. This area is favoured by dabbling ducks.

Central Area Continuing along the minor road for c.½ mile, turn north on a minor road to the viewpoint car park.

Birds

Wintering waterfowl include numbers of Great Crested Grebe, Goosander, Goldeneye, Pochard, Wigeon and Teal, as well as Cormorant and, sometimes, small numbers of Ruddy Duck, Shoveler and Pintail. Divers and rarer grebes are recorded relatively frequently. The gull roost is rather small and overshadowed by that at nearby Foremark Reservoir (but is best viewed from just south of the sailing club). Other notable species in winter include Grey Partridge, Little Owl, Water Rail (at the south end), Siskin and Redpoll, while finch flocks in the fields may occasionally include small numbers of Twite.

On spring passage Ringed and Little Ringed Plovers, Dunlin, Ruff, Common Sandpiper, Greenshank, Common, Arctic and Black Terns, White and Yellow Wagtails, and Wheatear are regular, while scarcer migrants have included Black-necked Grebe, Common Scoter, Osprey, Hobby and Little Gull. In autumn greater numbers and a wider variety of waders occur, sometimes including Little Stint and Curlew Sandpiper. Common and Black Terns may pass through, sometimes in large flocks and, again, Black-necked Grebe and Little Gull are among the scarcer visitors. Migrant passerines may include Redstart and Whinchat.

Breeding birds include Turtle Dove, Cuckoo, Kingfisher, a few Grasshopper and Sedge Warblers, and Willow Tit. In some years, Quail may call from adjacent fields.

17 OGSTON RESERVOIR (Derbyshire)   OS Landranger 119

Lying c.6 miles south of Chesterfield, this reservoir has a significant winter gull roost, which regularly attracts 'white-winged gulls', and is also notable for winter wildfowl and sometimes passage waders.

Habitat

Flooded in 1958, open water now covers 206 acres, with natural banks that shelve gently on the north and west shores. The surrounding area is mainly pasture with some small stands of woodland, notably at the Derbyshire Wildlife Trust's reserve of Carr Wood, for which a permit is required. The water is disturbed by sailing and also, in April–October, by trout fishing.

Access (see map)

One mile south of Clay Cross leave the A61 at Stretton west on the B6014 towards Matlock. Follow this road for c.1¼ miles to the car park at the northeast corner of the reservoir (the minor road to Ogston village parallels the east shore,

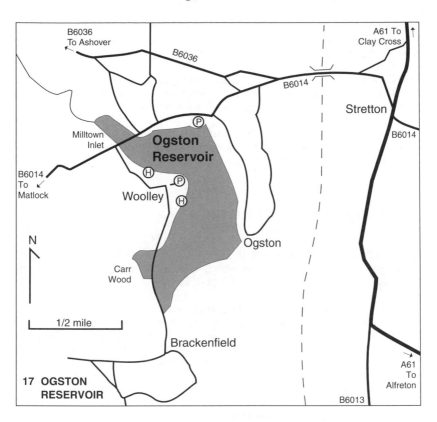

but views are largely obscured). The B6014 then crosses the extreme north tip, separating Milltown Inlet from the main body of water. Immediately beyond this take the minor road south towards Woolley and Brackenfield, which offers good views of much of the reservoir, with a car park at Woolley. The Ogston Bird Club has three hides and members receive a key for these (see Information). Otherwise, there is no access to the water's edge.

Birds

Wintering wildfowl may include several hundred each of Pochard, Wigeon and Teal, as well as small numbers of Goosander and sometimes Goldeneye. Shoveler, Pintail, Gadwall and Scaup are more erratic in appearance, but Little and Great Crested Grebes are usually present, and often also Cormorant. Rarer grebes and divers may occur, and divers may make prolonged visits. The main attraction in winter is the gull roost, best viewed from the road along the west perimeter and Woolley car park. Commonest is Black-headed Gull, of which counts may top 8,000, while Herring and Lesser Black-backed Gulls may both peak at over 1,000 and Great Black-backed at over 600, but Common Gull is scarce, with just a few tens of birds. Iceland, Glaucous and Mediterranean Gulls may all occur in very small numbers, as does Yellow-legged Gull, and Ring-billed Gull has also been recorded. Great patience is usually required, however, to pick out these rarities, and a telescope is essential.

On spring passage Arctic Tern may pass through, sometimes with Black Tern or Little Gull, and scarcer migrants have included Common Scoter and Osprey, but wader passage is generally poor. If water levels fall in autumn, Ringed and Little Ringed Plovers, Common Sandpiper, Greenshank and Dunlin are all regular, with a smattering of scarcer species possible, such as Ruff, Oystercatcher, Whimbrel and Spotted Redshank. Other migrants may include Garganey, occasionally Osprey and, in late autumn, Rock Pipit.

Breeders include Little and Great Crested Grebes, Grey Heron (15–20 pairs near Carr Wood), Tufted Duck, Common Tern (on specially constructed rafts), Grasshopper and Sedge Warblers, and sometimes Little Ringed Plover, while Sparrowhawk, Little Owl, Kingfisher and Grey Wagtail breed in the vicinity.

Information
Ogston Bird Club: Membership details from Mrs Ann Hunt, 2 Sycamore Avenue, Glapwell, Chesterfield, Derbyshire S44 5LH.

18 THE UPPER DERWENT VALLEY
(Derbyshire) OS Landranger 110

Lying c.12 miles west of Sheffield, this section of the Peak District is notable for its thriving population of Goshawk which, with luck, can be viewed from the roads and public footpaths with no risk of disturbance.

Habitat
Nestled in the High Peak region, the three reservoirs of Howden, Derwent and Ladybower were constructed at the turn of the century. As is typical of reservoirs in upland areas, they are deep with steeply shelving banks and are relatively birdless. The surrounding valleys have been extensively planted with conifers, while the higher slopes, rising to 2,077 feet, are a mosaic of rough grassland and moorland, with some relict oak woodlands.

Access (see map)
The A57 Sheffield–Glossop road passes across the valley and the south part of Ladybower Reservoir. Immediately to the west, a minor road (signed Derwentdale) runs north along the west edge of all three reservoirs, passing several small car parks from which footpaths lead to the moors. This road terminates near the north end of Howden Reservoir at Kings Tree, where there is a small car park. For wintering raptors, follow the footpath to Slippery Stones and into the Derwent Valley to view the surrounding crags. On Sundays and, in April–October, on Saturdays and Bank Holidays, the road is closed at Fairholmes, where there is a car park and information centre. From here there is a shuttle service to the two northern reservoirs, saving the walk to Windy Ridge Corner (probably the best spot for Goshawk); bicycles can also be hired.

The entire area is very popular with a range of outdoors enthusiasts and to minimise disturbance (and ensure parking space) an early-morning arrival is recommended. Note too that bad weather is possible year-round and you should be adequately prepared if you wander far from the roads, with appropriate clothing, footwear, a compass and the relevant OS map.

Birds
The prime attraction is Goshawk, a species which despite much persecution has been increasing in numbers in Britain during the last three decades. Most originate, however, from escaped or released falconers' birds, and are very large and pale (being from high latitudes) making them easier to separate from Sparrowhawk. The best chance of a sighting is in February–early April in fine weather with light winds, when they display over the plantations and ridges. Sparrowhawk also indulges in

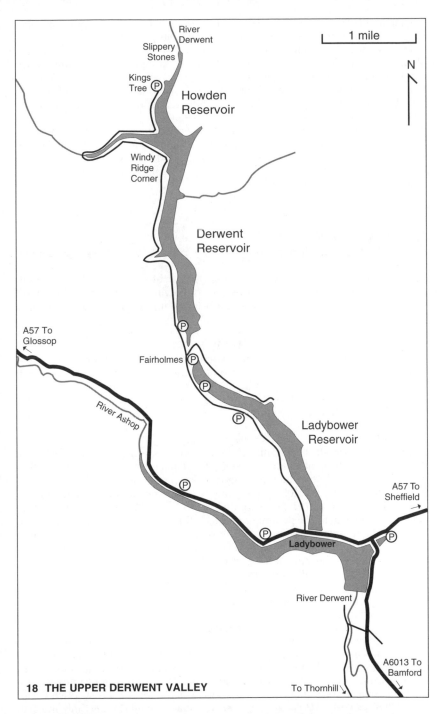

1 mile

N

River
Derwent

Slippery
Stones

Kings
Tree (P)

Howden
Reservoir

Windy
Ridge
Corner

Derwent
Reservoir

A57 To
Glossop

(P)

Fairholmes (P)

(P)

River Ashop

(P)

Ladybower
Reservoir

(P)

A57 To
Sheffield

(P)

Ladybower (P)

River Derwent

A6013 To
Bamford

To Thornhill

18 THE UPPER DERWENT VALLEY

similar displays. Goshawk can be seen at other times of the year but much more
luck is required. Other residents include Red Grouse on the heather moors, Grey

Wagtail and Dipper on the streams (and occasionally around the reservoirs, with Dipper favouring the River Derwent below Ladybower) and Raven.

The area is also worth investigating in winter. Raptors may include Peregrine, Merlin, Hen Harrier and, occasionally, Buzzard. Rough-legged Buzzard sometimes occurs but is very erratic. The woodland may hold Siskin (notably in larches and alders near water), Redpolls and, following invasions, numbers of Crossbills may also be present, also favouring the larches. The reservoirs hold little of interest in winter apart from a few Goosander.

Breeders include Red-breasted Merganser and Common Sandpiper around the reservoirs, Ring Ouzel and Tree Pipit on the slopes, a few Redstart and Wood Warbler in relict stands of deciduous woodland, and Curlew and Golden Plover on the higher moors. If it has been a 'good' crossbill year, some may stay to breed but they are very early nesters.

19 CHASEWATER
(Staffordshire and West Midlands)   OS Landranger 128 and 139

Set amid landscaped colliery spoil heaps and scattered urban development on the West Midlands border, Chasewater is heavily disturbed by a variety of water sports but still attracts interesting birds and holds a large and interesting gull roost.

Habitat
Chasewater is a canal-feeder, and open water covers nearly 250 acres with largely natural banks. Much of the surrounding area has been reclaimed and landscaped, but some areas of marsh and scrub remain, notably below the dam around Anglesey Basin, around Plant Swag, in Willow Vale, around Jeffrey's Swag and along Big Crane Brook.

Access (see map)
Just west of Brownhills turn north off the eastbound carriageway of the A5 into Pool Road. Pass the grandstands to the right and, after c.¼ mile, turn left into the complex of car parks by the amusement park. This is usually the best place to observe the gull roost, which can be watched from the car, though a telescope is essential. In summer a charge is made to park, so it is better to continue to the end of the dam where it is possible to park on the verge. A well-defined footpath encircles the reservoir, though the south shore and section east of Target Point are usually best for waders, and the heath and scrub below the dam are attractive to passerines. The small pool north of the old railway causeway, known as Jeffrey's Swag, is generally less disturbed. This is accessible from Norton East, where there is limited roadside parking. It is generally best to avoid weekends and holidays, and early mornings are preferable.

Birds
Chasewater holds only small numbers of wintering duck, notably up to 100 Goldeneye, often with small numbers of Ruddy Duck and Goosander, and a handful of Wigeon, Gadwall and Shoveler. Rarer grebes and divers are also recorded quite regularly, notably Black-throated Diver. But the casual visitor can expect to see little except the sizeable winter gull roost, which is relatively easy to work. Up to 12,000 Black-headed Gulls, 2,000 Lesser Black-backed and Herring Gulls and 100 Great Black-backed Gulls roost from c.15.00 (though they may not settle if disturbance is heavy, and may even abandon the roost altogether). Glaucous and

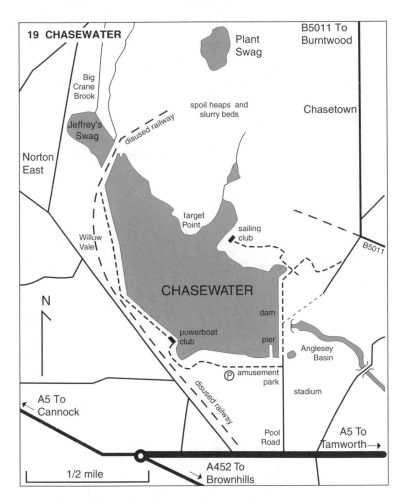

Iceland Gulls are often present, this being one of the more regular sites in central England for the latter; the period Christmas–March is best. Mediterranean Gull and Kittiwake may also occur but are harder to find. The small pools and water's edge may attract a few Jack Snipe and Water Rails. A flock of Twite was regular in winter on the surrounding waste ground, but recent landscaping has led it to largely abandon the area.

On passage small numbers of waders may occur, though the water level is kept as high as possible to facilitate powerboats. Flocks of terns and Little Gull may also make brief appearances and a variety of migrant passerines occurs in the surrounding scrub.

20 BELVIDE RESERVOIR (Staffordshire)   OS Landranger 127

Approximately 7 miles northwest of Wolverhampton and just south of the A5, this relatively small reservoir is important for breeding, moulting and wintering wildfowl and for passage waders.

265

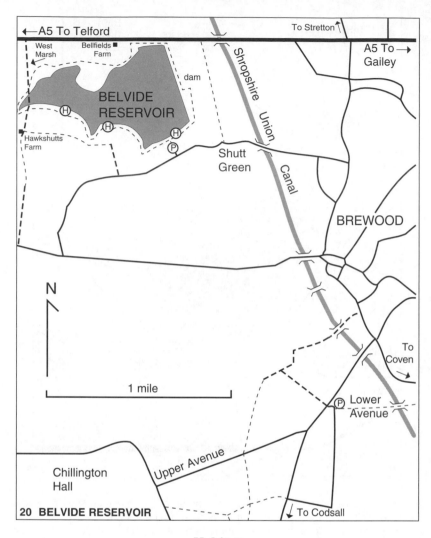

20 BELVIDE RESERVOIR

Habitat
Built as a canal-feeder, the reservoir covers 182 acres and has largely natural banks. It is situated in mixed farmland, with a small wood on the southeast shore; otherwise the immediate surroundings are largely wet grassland.

Access (see map)
Leave the M6 at junction 12 and take the A5 west, across the roundabout at the junction with the A449 at Gailey, and then take the third turning south (towards Brewood) after c.2 miles. After ¾ mile turn right, over the canal and though the hamlet of Shutt Green, parking at the car park on the right adjacent to the wood. Access is strictly by permit only, issued by the West Midland Bird Club (see Information). There are three hides available to permit holders (keys are issued with the permit). Otherwise, a small section of the west shore can be viewed from the footpath south of the A5 (but note that there is no parking along this private road).

Birds

Wintering wildfowl include numbers of Shoveler (occasionally as many as 500), Teal, Wigeon, Ruddy Duck, Pochard, Goldeneye, a few Goosander and, especially in late winter, Gadwall and Shelduck. The gull roost holds up to 20,000 Black-headed, 1,000 Lesser Black-backed and 500 Herring Gulls, and Glaucous, Iceland and Mediterranean Gulls are occasional.

On passage some of the more regular waders are Ringed and Little Ringed Plovers, Ruff, Whimbrel, Little Stint, Dunlin, Sanderling, Green and Common Sandpipers, and Greenshank. Common, Arctic and Black Terns and Little Gull pass through in small numbers. Other migrants include Black-necked Grebe (especially in spring) and Garganey (especially in late summer), and a variety of passerines.

Breeders include Little and Great Crested Grebes, Shoveler, Tufted and Ruddy Ducks, Redshank, Snipe, and Reed and Sedge Warblers, with Curlew in nearby farmland; Shelduck, Gadwall, Teal, Garganey and Pochard have occasionally nested.

Information

Belvide permits: Miss M. Surman, 6 Lloyd Square, 12 Niall Close, Edgbaston, Birmingham B15 3LX.

21 CHILLINGTON LOWER AVENUE (Staffordshire)   OS Landranger 127

About 2 miles south of Belvide Reservoir, this is a good site for Hawfinch.

Habitat

Planted to frame the approach to Chillington Hall, the Avenue supports stands of beech and, especially at the west end, hornbeam.

Access (see map on p.266)

Leave the A5 c.2 miles west of the roundabout with the A449 at Gailey on minor roads to Brewood. Follow signs towards Coven and, after ½ mile, turn right at the crossroads towards Codsall, into Codsall Road. After ½ mile turn left to park carefully on the verge, exploring the Lower Avenue on foot. As Hawfinch is rather shy, early-morning visits are preferable, and it is best to avoid weekends.

Birds

Though Hawfinch may, with luck, be found year-round, the optimum period is late winter to early spring. Great Spotted Woodpecker, Nuthatch and Treecreeper also occur.

22 BLITHFIELD RESERVOIR (Staffordshire)   OS Landranger 128

Blithfield is the largest reservoir in the West Midlands and is important for wildfowl and passage waders. It provides interesting birdwatching year-round, especially in autumn and winter.

Habitat

Blithfield covers 790 acres, has largely natural banks (extending for 9 miles) and is surrounded by agricultural land. The east shore has been extensively planted with conifers and there is some deciduous woodland. Areas of marsh fringe the inflows at the north end, with willow scrub and, especially on the upper reaches of the River Blithe, alders. If the water level drops in autumn extensive mudflats are exposed.

Access (see map)

The B5013 Rugeley–Uttoxeter road crosses the reservoir via a causeway (limited parking at either end), affording views of much of the open water, including that used by the gull roost. Access is otherwise by permit only (fee), issued on behalf of the South Staffordshire Waterworks Company by the West Midland Bird Club (see Information). There are eight hides and visitors can walk the entire shoreline, though the north half is less disturbed and generally has the best variety of birds.

Birds

In winter Red-necked Grebe and divers (especially Great Northern) are occasional. Large numbers of duck occur: up to 1,600 Wigeon and 600 Teal have

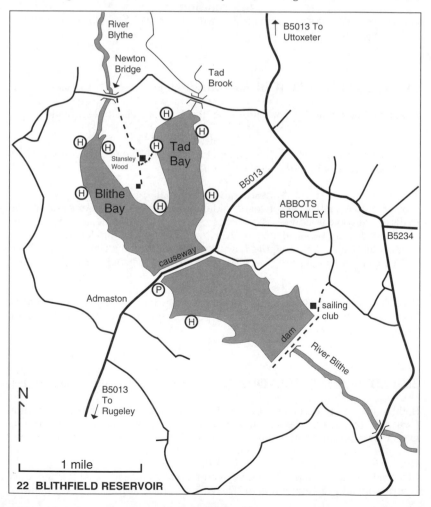

22 BLITHFIELD RESERVOIR

been noted, as well as a few Gadwall, Shoveler and, sometimes, Pintail. There may be up to 80 Goosander and 80 Goldeneye, and a maximum of 630 Ruddy Duck has been recorded, with up to 400 regular in midwinter. Smew and sea duck sometimes appear, especially during hard weather (though Common Scoter and Scaup may visit at any time of year). Several hundred Canada Geese are resident and up to 30 Bewick's Swans are fairly frequent in winter, while Cormorant, though regular, is generally present only in early morning. The large gull roost often has 1–2 Glaucous and/or Iceland Gulls, and there have been several records of Mediterranean Gull. The best time is Christmas–March, especially for Iceland Gull, and a telescope is essential. Siskin and Redpoll are regular visitors in surrounding trees, notably the alders by the River Blithe.

Passage periods can be very good. Osprey, Hobby and Peregrine have appeared in most recent autumns and sometimes stay long periods. Wader numbers are generally low in spring, but in autumn large numbers may be present, mostly Ringed Plover and Dunlin. In addition, Little Stint and Curlew Sandpiper occur regularly, especially in September. Ruff, Whimbrel, Black-tailed Godwit, Jack Snipe, Spotted Redshank and Green Sandpiper are also regular, with a chance of Sanderling and Turnstone. Common, Arctic and Black Terns and Little Gull are quite frequently present. Pintail and Garganey often occur in autumn, with Rock Pipit regular late in the season. Breeding birds are unexceptional but include Great Crested Grebe, Sparrowhawk, Kingfisher and Lesser Spotted Woodpecker.

Information
Blithfield permits: Miss M. Surman, 6 Lloyd Square, Niall Close, Edgbaston, Birmingham B15 3LX.

23 SANDWELL VALLEY (West Midlands)   OS Landranger 139

Sandwiched between Birmingham and West Bromwich, the area is an oasis of green amid the vast urban sprawl of the Midlands, and attracts a remarkably rich variety of birds year-round.

Habitat
The River Tame meanders through the north part of the valley, and a balancing lake (Forge Mill Pool) has been constructed next to the river, with the east end forming part of an RSPB reserve. Adjacent to the M5, Swan Pool is much more disturbed but can produce surprises. Otherwise the valley has four golf courses, active farmland and areas of rough grass, together with several small stands of mixed woodland.

Access (see map)
From junction 1 on the M5 take the road towards Birmingham city centre and, beyond West Bromwich Albion football ground, turn left into Park Lane. To access Swan Pool and the country park, park on the left after 1½ miles. For the RSPB reserve continue along Forge Lane and at the T-junction turn right into Newton Road, continue over the railway bridge and take the second right into Hampstead Road. After ⅔ mile turn right into Tanhouse Avenue, with the reserve entrance on the left. From the car park, walk over the railway bridge to the reserve entrance. Alternatively, the balancing lake can be viewed from the pull-in on Forge Lane. Avoid weekends and Bank Holidays, as disturbance is especially heavy at these times.

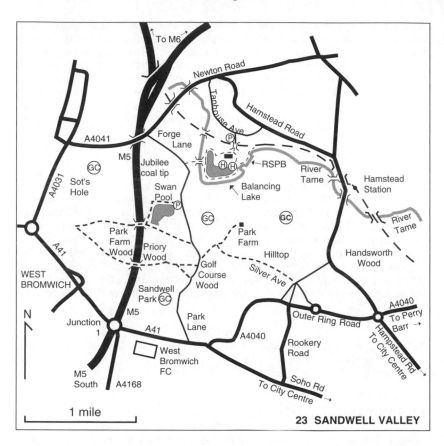

23 SANDWELL VALLEY

Birds

Breeders include Yellow Wagtail, Sedge and Reed Warblers, Lesser Whitethroat and, sometimes, Whinchat and Grasshopper Warbler. Residents include Sparrowhawk, Stock Dove, Green and Great Spotted Woodpeckers, Willow Tit and Tree Sparrow.

In spring and autumn regular visitors include Redshank, Common Sandpiper, Little Ringed Plover and, sometimes, Oystercatcher, as well as Common, Arctic and occasionally Black Terns. Spotted Crake has appeared on several occasions in autumn. A variety of passerines is regular on passage, including White Wagtail (spring), Tree Pipit, Whinchat and Wheatear, and occasionally Redstart and Pied Flycatcher.

In winter Snipe is numerous and there may also be Jack Snipe and Water Rail, while flocks of Corn Bunting can be found in areas of rough grassland. Look too for Stonechat, Grey Wagtail, Siskin and Redpoll. Regular wildfowl include reasonable numbers of Pochard and Teal, and often a few Goldeneye, Wigeon and Ruddy Duck.

Information

Senior Ranger, Sandwell Valley Country Park, Salters Lane, West Bromwich, West Midlands B71 4BG. Tel: 0121 553 0220/553 2147.

RSPB Sandwell Valley: Colin Horne, 20 Tanhouse Avenue. Great Barr, Birmingham B43 5AG. Tel: 0121 357 7395.

24 EYEBROOK RESERVOIR (Leicestershire and Rutland) OS Landranger 141

Approximately 3 miles north of Corby, this reservoir holds a variety of winter wildfowl and passage waders, and in hard weather often attracts interesting birds. It is managed as a reserve.

Habitat

The reservoir was completed in 1940 and open water covers 400 acres with natural, gently shelving banks. There is an area of marsh near the inlet at the north end and the east shore has been extensively planted with conifers. The reservoir is used for trout fishing but is otherwise undisturbed.

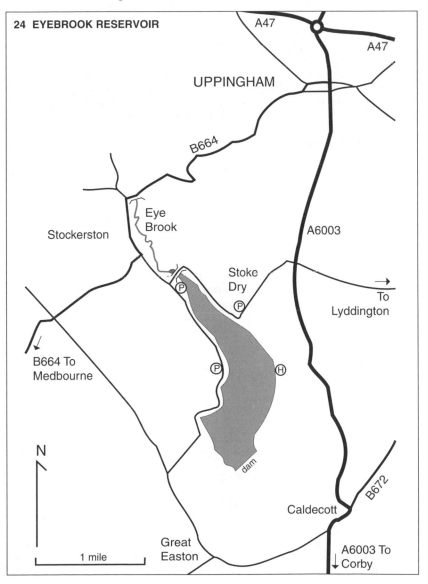

Access (see map)

From the A6003 between Corby and Uppingham take the minor road west to Stoke Dry and continue through the village to the reservoir. The road runs around the north end and then parallels the west shore with limited roadside parking at three points. The bridge over Eye Brook at the north tip and the west shore are best for passage waders. Access off the road is only granted to members of the Leicestershire and Rutland Ornithological Society and there is a hide for their use. Casual visitors can obtain good views from the road.

Birds

Wintering wildfowl include Bewick's Swan, with a maximum of up to 80 occasionally present in midwinter, together with feral Greylag Geese. Wigeon is numerous, peaking at c.1,000, and up to 100 Ruddy Ducks may occur, together with small numbers of Goldeneye, Goosander, Smew, Shoveler, Pintail and, sometimes, Red-crested Pochard. Hard weather can bring sea duck, especially Scaup, as well as Slavonian and Red-necked Grebes, and divers, particularly Great Northern. Peregrine is sometimes seen, and wintering waders include up to 2,000 Golden Plover, 150 Dunlin and the occasional Green Sandpiper or Jack Snipe. The large gull roost is comparatively easy to work, though a telescope is essential. It is best watched from the north half of the west shore. A handful of Mediterranean Gulls are regular, notably in late autumn and early spring, but can be hard to find. In winter Glaucous and Iceland Gulls may be found, but neither is regular.

Common Scoter, White Wagtail and Water Pipit sometimes occur in early spring and Hobby is quite regular in spring and early summer (the north end of the reservoir is best). Black-necked Grebe is increasingly frequent on passage from late March and other spring migrants may include Garganey, small numbers of waders depending on the water level, Common, Arctic and Black Terns, Kittiwake and Little Gull.

Osprey is recorded almost annually in autumn and this season, when water levels have dropped, is also best for waders. Little Stint and Curlew Sandpiper are annual, and other species may include Ruff, Black-tailed Godwit, Spotted Redshank and Greenshank. Yellow-legged Gull may occur from late summer.

Breeders include Great Crested Grebe, Ruddy Duck, Gadwall and occasionally Shelduck or Teal, and look for Little Owl on the Stockerston Road.

25 RUTLAND WATER (Leicestershire and Rutland)   OS Landranger 141

Rutland Water is the largest reservoir in Britain. Since its construction in 1975 it has become one of the most important wildfowl sanctuaries in Britain (it is an SPA and a Ramsar site), and is well worth visiting, especially during winter and passage periods. Nine miles of shoreline (comprising one-third of the total) along the west arms form two reserves of the Leicestershire and Rutland Wildlife Trust (LRWT), covering 450 acres, and the Anglian Water Birdwatching Centre at Egleton is home to the annual British Birdwatching Fair.

Habitat

As well as 3,100 acres of open water, at the west end of the reservoir there are purpose-built islands, shingle banks and three lagoons, with areas of scrub woodland at Gibbet Gorse and Gorse Close, and stands of mature deciduous woodland at Lax Hill. Other interesting habitats include ancient meadows and reedbeds.

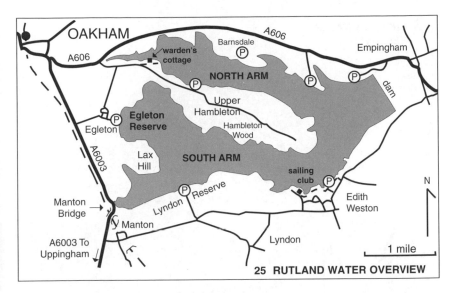

25 RUTLAND WATER OVERVIEW

Access (see maps)

Rutland Water lies 1 mile southeast of Oakham and is easily accessed from the A1 via the A606 west of Stamford, and from the A47 along the A6003 north of Uppingham.

Egleton Reserve and Anglian Water Birdwatching Centre From the A6003 1 mile south of Oakham take the minor road to Egleton. The entrance to the reserve is at the southernmost point of the village and is well signed. It is open 09.00–17.00. A permit is required by non-members of the LRWT, and is available from the Anglian Water Birdwatching Centre. There are 10 hides and a woodland trail through Lax Hill and Gorse Close. Visitors must keep to the paths.

Lyndon Reserve Leave the A6003 eastwards, c.2½ miles south of Oakham, to Manton and take the first turning on the left after the village to the Interpretative Centre. Access from the A1 is via the A606, following signs to Edith Weston and Manton. There are five hides and a nature trail through Gibbet Gorse. The reserve is open 10.00–16.00 daily (except Mondays) May–October, and on Saturdays and Sundays November– April. A permit is required by non-members of the LRTNC, and is available from the centre. Visitors must keep to the paths. The Manton Bridge area is one of the better areas for waders and can be viewed from the Shallow-water hide.

South arm The elevated cycle track east of the Lyndon Reserve Centre offers good views over the south arm, with signed car parks at Edith Weston.

Dam area Often holding congregations of ducks in winter, especially diving ducks, and also good for divers, this may be the last area to freeze in cold weather. A signed car park near the north end is accessible from the A606.

North shore Two signed access points to the shore off the A606 afford views of the reservoir for ducks, gulls, and terns.

North arm Best viewed from the Hambleton Peninsula, at the end of the minor

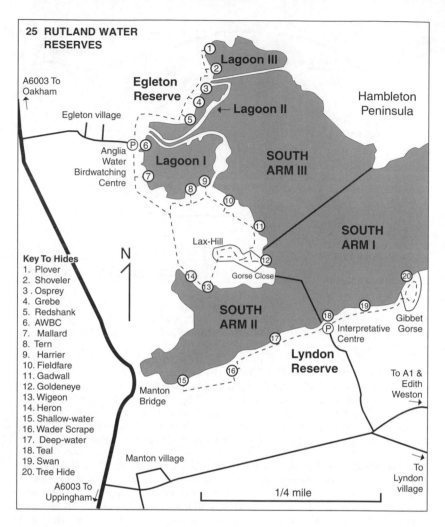

25 RUTLAND WATER RESERVES

A6003 To Oakham

Egleton village

Egleton Reserve

Lagoon III

← Lagoon II

Hambleton Peninsula

Anglia Water Birdwatching Centre

Lagoon I

SOUTH ARM III

SOUTH ARM I

N

Lax-Hill

Gorse Close

SOUTH ARM II

Gibbet Gorse

Interpretative Centre

Lyndon Reserve

To A1 & Edith Weston

Manton Bridge

Manton village

A6003 To Uppingham

To Lyndon village

1/4 mile

Key To Hides
1. Plover
2. Shoveler
3. Osprey
4. Grebe
5. Redshank
6. AWBC
7. Mallard
8. Tern
9. Harrier
10. Fieldfare
11. Gadwall
12. Goldeneye
13. Wigeon
14. Heron
15. Shallow-water
16. Wader Scrape
17. Deep-water
18. Teal
19. Swan
20. Tree Hide

road by the warden's cottage or from the car park just northwest of Upper Hambleton.

Birds

All three divers are near-annual in winter, with Great Northern the most likely. Red-necked and Slavonian Grebes are also almost regular in winter, while Great Crested Grebe has peaked at the astonishing total of over 1,000, with up to 800 regularly present. Other waterfowl include several hundred Cormorants. Wildfowl include feral Greylag and Snow Geese, up to 4,500 Wigeon, 1,500 Gadwall, 2,500 Tufted Duck, 2,000 Pochard, 400 Ruddy Duck and 400 Goldeneye, and peak autumn counts of 750 Shoveler and 1,800 Gadwall are outstanding. Species occurring in smaller numbers include Pintail, Goosander (usually c.50 but up to 120) and, notably, Red-crested Pochard (up to seven have occurred, mainly in autumn and winter) and Smew (including up to seven males each winter). Small numbers of Scaup are regular and other sea duck appear in ones and twos.

Osprey

Water Rail and Jack Snipe winter in marshy areas, and grassy areas, especially the slopes of the dam, often attract a large flock of Golden Plovers. Other waders include up to 20 Ruff and 120 Dunlin as well as Black-tailed Godwit and Green Sandpiper. Numbers of gulls use the reservoir to roost. Largely Black-headed and Common Gulls, the roost also attracts Herring Gull and up to 400 Great Black-backed Gulls. Yellow-legged and Mediterranean Gulls are regular, and records of Glaucous and Iceland Gulls are increasing. The roost is rather scattered but is best watched from Gadwall or Goldeneye hides on Egleton Reserve. Short-eared Owl occurs in declining numbers; in good years up to ten hunted over rough ground, but in the 1990s numbers were much lower. Occasionally Long-eared Owl is found roosting in the scrub, particularly at Lax Hill and Gibbet Gorse, though they are difficult to find. Peregrine is a regular visitor and occasionally Bearded Tit and Cetti's Warbler are recorded. Other notable species at this season include Tree Sparrow (especially at the feeders by the Birdwatching Centre), Siskin and Redpoll in the alders (behind lagoons II and III and at Lyndon Reserve) and Brambling (try Barnsdale Wood).

Black-necked Grebe is quite frequently seen, especially in spring, late summer and autumn (usually on Lagoon III or the north arm), while Garganey and Common Scoter are also regular on passage, up to 14 Garganey being present in autumn. On passage, Osprey is regular, and in 1996 young Osprey chicks were reintroduced into England at Rutland Water as part of a translocation programme. The project has been a success and Ospreys have now bred successfully at Rutland water (2002). Waders may include all of the usual species such as Ringed and Little Ringed Plovers, Greenshank, Redshank, Common Sandpiper and Dunlin, as well as Grey Plover, Turnstone, Black-tailed Godwit, Whimbrel and Spotted Redshank. Wood Sandpiper, Little Stint and Curlew Sandpiper are annual, usually in autumn, and Pectoral Sandpiper nearly so. The lagoons, Manton Bay and north arm are best for waders. Little Gull, Kittiwake, and Common, Arctic and Black Terns are regular migrants, favouring the main water. Migrant passerines include Wheatear and Whinchat, occasionally Redstart, with Rock Pipit regular in late autumn (especially on the dam).

Great Crested and Little Grebes, Cormorant (45+ pairs), Grey Heron, Greylag and Egyptian Geese, Shelduck, Ruddy Duck, Gadwall, Shoveler and, sometimes, Garganey breed, as do Oystercatcher, Lapwing, Little Ringed Plover, Redshank and 20–50 pairs of Common Terns on specially constructed rafts. Astonishingly, an Avocet laid eggs in 1996, the first recorded breeding attempt at a freshwater site anywhere in the world. The woods hold Sparrowhawk, Long-eared Owl, all three woodpeckers and Nuthatch, with Nightingale at Barnsdale and Hambleton Woods and, in 1996, also the Egleton Reserve. Grasshopper, Reed and Sedge Warblers breed in waterside vegetation, with Turtle Dove, Garden Warbler and Tree Sparrow in scrub. Hobby often hunts over the area from spring to early autumn, being most regular in the evening.

Information
Anglian Water Bird Watching Centre, Egleton Nature Reserve, Egleton, Oakham, Rutland LE15 8BT.
LRWT Warden: Tim Appleton, Fishponds Cottage, Stamford Road, Oakham, Leicestershire LE15 8JA. Tel: 01572 770651. E-mail: awbc@rutlandwater.org.uk
An annual report is produced on the birds of Rutland Water.

26 SWITHLAND RESERVOIR (Leicestershire and Rutland) OS Landranger 129

This relatively small reservoir holds a variety of wintering wildfowl and a notable gull roost that regularly includes Mediterranean Gull.

Habitat
A little over 1 mile from north to south and less than ½ mile wide, the reservoir is bisected by a viaduct carrying the Great Central Railway and is crossed at the south end by the minor road between Rothley and Swithland, the bridge having caused a shallow, reed-fringed lagoon to form at the inflow. Though water levels fluctuate con-

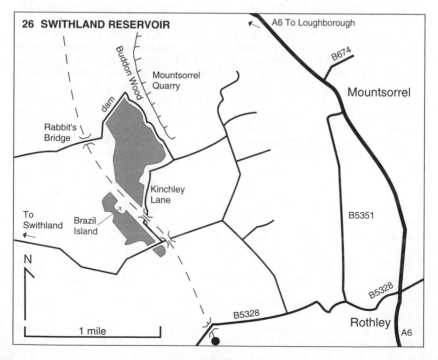

siderably, exposing areas of shoreline, this is mostly stony and attracts few waders. The water is, however, relatively undisturbed. To the north, Buddon Wood has been reduced to a narrow strip of birches by the expansion of Mountsorrel Quarry.

Access (see map)

Access to the reservoir is by permit only, which are strictly limited, but most areas can be seen from the road.

North and west shores Leave the A6 west at Rothley on the B5328 and, after 1 mile, turn north on the minor road to Swithland. After 1 mile the road passes under a railway bridge and immediately beyond this turn north into Kinchley Lane, which runs beside the south part of the reservoir before passing under the railway and continuing along the east and north shores. This is a very narrow lane and caution should be exercised, especially when parking. The gull roost is best watched on overcast evenings from Kinchley Lane (on sunny days this faces the setting sun; access to better viewpoints is limited to permit holders).

South shore Alternatively continue along the minor road towards Swithland village and, ¼ mile past the railway bridge, park at the east end of the bridge at the south tip of the reservoir.

Birds

Wintering wildfowl include small numbers of Wigeon, Teal, Gadwall, Shoveler, Pochard and Goldeneye, with a notable concentration of up to 250 Ruddy Ducks. Goosander and Pintail are occasionally recorded but divers, rarer grebes, Smew and sea duck are all scarce and irregular. Up to 50 Cormorants gather in the late afternoon to roost. Other interesting wintering species include up to three Peregrines (around Mountsorrel Quarry), Water Rail, Green Sandpiper, Grey Wagtail, Siskin and Redpoll. Among the prime attractions of Swithland in winter is the gull roost, which may hold up to 15,000 birds (though numbers have fallen following the closure of Mountsorrel tip). Mediterranean Gull is regular November–March, with up to three recorded together, although they are usually hard to locate. Occasionally Glaucous or Iceland Gulls occur but these have been especially hit by the closure of the tip. In March–April occasional Kittiwakes may appear, and in late summer and autumn Yellow-legged Gull is regular in small numbers.

Migrants in spring may include Arctic and Black Terns, Little Gull, small numbers of waders and occasionally Garganey, Osprey or Wood Warbler (the last favouring Buddon Wood). On autumn passage Black-necked Grebe is near-annual in late summer, a variety of waders occurs, most regularly Ringed and Little Ringed Plovers, Common Sandpiper, Greenshank and Dunlin, and sometimes Garganey and Black or Arctic Terns.

Breeders include Little and Great Crested Grebes, Ruddy Duck, Sparrowhawk, Common Tern (on specially constructed rafts), Kingfisher, Lesser Spotted Woodpecker, Reed and Sedge Warblers, and Marsh and Willow Tits, while Pochard, Gadwall and Shoveler have bred and Cormorant summers. Hobby is a fairly frequent visitor.

27 DAVENTRY RESERVOIR (Northamptonshire)   OS Landranger 152

This small reservoir on the outskirts of Daventry attracts a variety of winter wildfowl and passage waders.

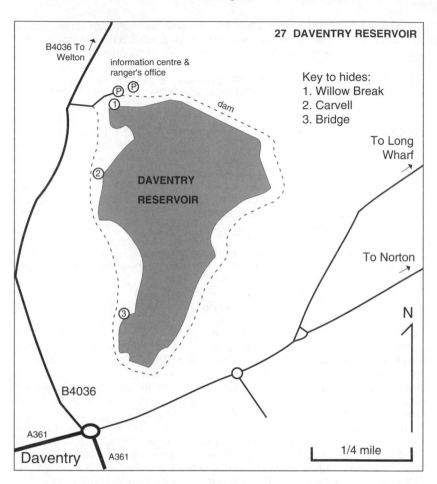

27 DAVENTRY RESERVOIR

B4036 To Welton

information centre & ranger's office

dam

Key to hides:
1. Willow Break
2. Carvell
3. Bridge

To Long Wharf

DAVENTRY RESERVOIR

To Norton

N

B4036

A361

Daventry A361

1/4 mile

Habitat

Built in the 19th century as a canal feeder, Daventry Reservoir covers 130 acres with gently shelving natural banks, and is encircled by a narrow ring of mature deciduous woodland, broken only at the dam. The reservoir and surrounding area are operated as a country park by Daventry District Council and facilities include an information centre, adventure playground and a cafe along the track to the dam, while coarse fishing is permitted mid-June to mid-March.

Access (see map)

Leave Daventry northeast on the B4036 towards Welton and Watford, and Daventry Reservoir Country Park is signed to the right after c.¾ mile. The reserve is encircled by a 2-mile footpath, which accesses three hides. The small Willow Break hide, nearest the car park, overlooks a woodland feeding station, and has free access, but Bridge hide is only accessible with a combination to the locks, obtainable from the ranger's office at the car park.

Birds

Wintering wildfowl include small numbers of Pochard and Wigeon, and a few Shoveler; divers, rarer grebes, Shag and a variety of sea duck have also been recorded. Golden Plover and Snipe occur around the water's edge. There is a small gull roost, mainly comprising Black-headed Gulls but Yellow-legged and Mediterranean Gulls are annual (and both are possible in summer and autumn). The roost is best watched from near the site of the old Carvell hide.

On spring passage Arctic and Black Terns and Little Gull may occur, especially after east winds, and Osprey and Common Scoter sometimes pass through. Of note in late summer and autumn is the occasional occurrence of Black-necked Grebe, and on autumn passage a variety of waders is possible, including Ringed and Little Ringed Plovers, Dunlin, Greenshank, Common and Green Sandpipers and Ruff, with Little Stint, Curlew Sandpiper and Spotted Redshank reasonably regular. At both seasons interesting passerines may occur, such as Redstart, Whinchat, Wheatear, Ring Ouzel (spring) and Rock Pipit (late autumn).

Breeders include Great Crested Grebe, Common Tern (on specially constructed rafts), Green and Great Spotted Woodpeckers and, sometimes, Grasshopper Warbler, while Shoveler has bred.

Information
Daventry Country Park: Dewi Morris, Reservoir Cottage, Northern Way, Daventry, Northants NN11 5JB. Tel: 01327 877193. E-mail: dmorris1@daventrydc.gov.uk

28 PITSFORD RESERVOIR (Northamptonshire)   OS Landranger 141 and 152

Just 6 miles north of Northampton, Pitsford Reservoir holds a variety of duck in winter and waders on passage, and is worth a visit during these periods. Indeed, with a species list of over 224, it is the premier site in Northamptonshire. Part of the north shore is a reserve of the Beds, Cambs, Northants & Peterborough Wildlife Trust (BCNPWT), and the area northwest of the dam is part of Brixworth Country Park.

Habitat
The reservoir was filled in 1955 and covers 800 acres with natural, gently shelving banks. The perimeter of the north half has been extensively planted with conifers, and there is also a mature oak copse; otherwise the surrounding land is farmed.

Access (see map)
The reservoir lies just to east of the A508 and slightly west of the A43. Access is via the following points.
1. The causeway on the minor road to Holcot from the A508 at Brixworth. There are car parks at the west end and at the Fishing Lodge at the east end of the causeway.
2. Either end of the submerged road north of the causeway.
3. Pitsford: leave the village on the road signed 'Reservoir Car Park'.
4. The anglers' car park, outside the reservoir perimeter fence and just north of the sailing club, is a good place to observe the gull roost (although the reservoir is usually disturbed by boats until near dusk at weekends).
5. The dam end, where there are car parks and toilets at either end of the dam, and also an information centre, cafe etc. at Brixworth Country Park at the northwest end.

The reservoir is intensively used for sailing, trout fishing and walking, and there is public access to the entire shoreline south of the causeway (except the sailing club grounds). Wigeon prefers more open areas of the south section, and the dam area can be good unless there are boats present. Otherwise, Scaldwell

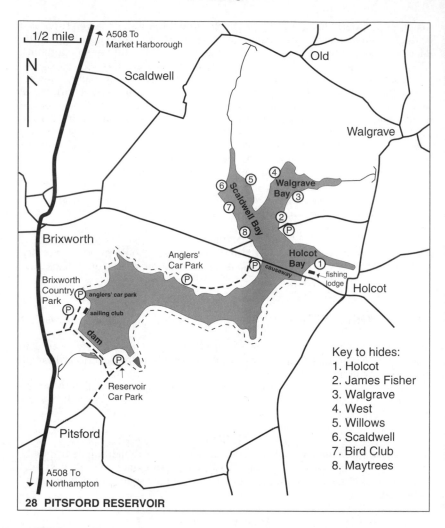

28 PITSFORD RESERVOIR

Key to hides:
1. Holcot
2. James Fisher
3. Walgrave
4. West
5. Willows
6. Scaldwell
7. Bird Club
8. Maytrees

and Walgrave Bays north of the causeway are best for waders, and the north half is also better for most ducks. Access to this half of the reservoir is by permit only. Annual and day permits (fee) are issued by Anglian Water and are available from the Fishing Lodge by the causeway (open mid-March to mid-November, 08.00–dusk; opening times variable in winter) or from the BCNPWT. There are eight hides on the reserve north of the causeway, but the small hide near the dam is for the use of 'authorised' gull watchers only.

Birds

In late autumn and early winter there are often 100–200 Dunlin present if water levels are low. Winter wildfowl include up to 1,200 Tufted Duck, 1,000 Wigeon and 750 Teal, as well as smaller numbers of Pintail, Gadwall, Shoveler, Pochard, Goldeneye, Ruddy Duck and up to 60 Goosander. Red-crested Pochard, Smew, Red-breasted Merganser, Scaup and Common Scoter are annual, as are rarer grebes and divers (especially Great Northern). Numbers of Cormorants are present year-round. There is a large gull roost, sometimes holding 20,000 birds, largely Black-headed and Common Gulls, with smaller numbers of Lesser and Great Black-backed and Herring Gulls. One or two Mediterranean, Glaucous and Iceland Gulls are recorded fairly regularly most winters. Wintering passerine flocks may include Corn Bunting and Tree Sparrow.

On passage there can be a good variety of the usual waders, with Golden and Ringed Plovers, Greenshank and Ruff among the commonest, and Little Stint, Curlew Sandpiper and Spotted Redshank are annual. Tern passage is also good: Common, Arctic and Black are regular, as is Little Gull, while Arctic Skua appears surprisingly frequently. Osprey is annual, especially in August, and Black-necked Grebe and Marsh Harrier are also reasonably regular in autumn.

Breeders include Great Crested Grebe, Shoveler, Gadwall, Tufted Duck and, occasionally, Ruddy Duck. Eight species of warbler nest in the surrounding area, including Grasshopper, and Hobby is quite frequent.

Information
BCNPWT Warden: Cliff Christie, Lings House, Billing Lings, Northampton NN3 4BE. Tel: 01604 405285. E-mail: northwt@cix.co.uk
Pitsford Water Lodge: Dave Francis, Brixworth Road, Holcot, Northamptonshire NN6 9SJ. Tel: 01604 780148. E-mail: pitsford@cix.compulink.co.uk

29 EARLS BARTON GRAVEL PITS (Northamptonshire)   OS Landranger 152

Lying in the Nene valley just south of Wellingborough, this complex of gravel pits attracts a wide range of waders and wildfowl throughout the year.

Habitat
Within this section of the Nene Valley there is a series of gravel pits stretching over 3½ miles between Wollaston and Earls Barton. Both working and restored pits exhibit a typical succession of habitats. In the centre of the complex and surrounded by older pits lies Summer Leys LNR, managed by Northamptonshire County Council. It comprises a large landscaped pit with gently shelving banks, specially created islands and a scrape, surrounded by extensive plantations of deciduous trees. The reserve is bounded to the north by a disused railway and grazing meadows alongside the River Nene.

Access (see map)
Summer Leys LNR Leave the A45 5 miles east of Northampton on the B573 to Great Doddington. After ¼ mile (just west of Great Doddington), turn right (south) on Hardwater Road towards Wollaston and follow this road over the River Nene by Hardwater Mill. The reserve car park is on the left after a further ⅔ mile. A 2-mile trail circles the reserve, with three hides near the car park. The reserve is open at all times.

Two pits lie east of Summer Leys and can be viewed from the gates along the single-track road that runs north to the river, c.⅓ mile west of the reserve car park.

Pits further west and newer ones to the east can also be explored by walking along the disused railway track in either direction.

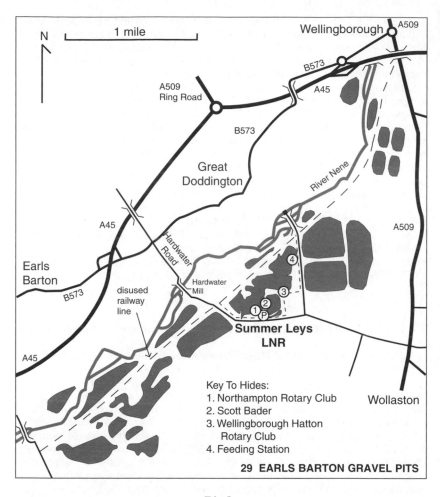

N

1 mile

Wellingborough A509

A509
Ring Road

B573

B573

A45

Great
Doddington

River Nene

A45

Hardwater
Road

A509

Earls
Barton

B573

disused
railway
line

Hardwater
Mill

④

③

②

① P

**Summer Leys
LNR**

Wollaston

A45

Key To Hides:
1. Northampton Rotary Club
2. Scott Bader
3. Wellingborough Hatton
   Rotary Club
4. Feeding Station

29 EARLS BARTON GRAVEL PITS

Birds

Wintering wildfowl include up to 500 Wigeon as well good numbers of Pochard, small numbers of Teal, Pintail and Shoveler, and up to 40 Goldeneye. Parties of Bewick's Swan occasionally visit, and a few Smew winter (e.g. 15 in 1998/99). Other notable wintering species include Water Rail, Golden Plover, Dunlin and Green Sandpiper. Small numbers of gulls are present, regularly including a few Common and Lesser Black-backed Gulls, and occasionally Mediterranean Gull. The feeding station attracts parties of Tree Sparrow throughout the day.

On spring passage Garganey, a variety of waders including Turnstone, Ruff, Dunlin, Sanderling, Bar-tailed Godwit, Whimbrel, Green Sandpiper and Greenshank, Little Gull, and Arctic and Black Terns occur, while migrant passerines may include White Wagtail, Whinchat and Wheatear. In autumn a similar variety of waders may occur, with the addition of Black-tailed Godwit and, from late August, sometimes Little Stint and Curlew and Wood Sandpipers. Scarcer migrants have included Black-necked Grebe, Little Egret, Marsh Harrier and Red-crested Pochard. In late autumn there is a build-up of Golden Plovers in the area, sometimes topping 1,000 birds.

Breeding birds on the reserve and surrounding pits include Great Crested and

Little Grebes, Grey Heron, Greylag and Canada Geese, Gadwall, Sparrowhawk, Oystercatcher, Ringed and Little Ringed Plovers, Lapwing, Redshank, Black-headed Gull, Common Tern, Cuckoo, Sand Martin, Yellow Wagtail, Reed and Sedge Warblers, Tree Sparrow and, sometimes, Shoveler. Cormorant is present in summer and Hobby, Garganey and Kingfisher are regular.

Information
Chris Haynes, Countryside and Tourism, Northamptonshire Council, PO Box 163, County Hall, Northampton NN1 1AX. Tel: 01604 237 227. E-mail: country-side@northamptonshire.gov.uk

30 DITCHFORD GRAVEL PITS (Northamptonshire) OS Landranger 152 and 153

Sandwiched between Wellingborough, Higham Ferrers and Rushden, this complex of gravel pits in the Nene Valley has a broad variety of habitats and attracts a wide range of species, as well as having an exciting list of rarities to its credit.

Habitat
The gravel pits, varying in age, demonstrate the succession from bare sand and gravel with shallow pools to stands of mature willows. One of the most attractive to birds is also the largest, and lies immediately west of Higham Ferrers.

Access (see map)
Old Pits From the A6 in Higham Ferrers turn west at the Queen's Head pub into Wharf Road, parking in the small car park at the foot of the hill. Cross the A45 dual carriageway via the footbridge, and there is then largely free access to the pits.

New Pits To view the newer pits leave the A45 north on Ditchford Lane, which is the minor road that connects with the B571. After crossing the river at the traffic lights there is a dirt road immediately on the left. Pedestrian access is possible along this dirt road in working hours, and access by car in the evenings and at weekends. The second pit on the left is favoured by waders, and the newest pits are further on.

Birds
Wintering wildfowl include over 100 each of Wigeon, Teal, Gadwall, Tufted Duck and Pochard, with smaller numbers of Shoveler and a few Goldeneye. Scaup, Common Scoter and Red-crested Pochard are occasional. The largest lake immediately west of Higham Ferrers usually has the best variety of wildfowl. Cormorant is regular and there are large pre-roost gatherings of gulls in late afternoon, including many Common, Herring and Lesser and Great Black-backed Gulls, but most gulls appear to roost elsewhere. Glaucous, Iceland and Mediterranean Gulls are occasional. Other winter visitors include Water Rail, Stonechat and up to three Water Pipits, which favour the wet grassland along the River Nene, with Green Sandpiper and Grey Wagtail also possible by the river.
  Passage waders favour the west pits, with Dunlin, Ringed and Little Ringed Plovers, Green and Common Sandpipers, Ruff and Greenshank all regular, and Black-tailed and Bar-tailed Godwits, Little Stint and Curlew and Wood Sandpipers possible, especially in autumn. A variety of scarce and rare species has also occurred. Common, Arctic and Black Terns are fairly regular on passage, and Shelduck and Garganey also occur.

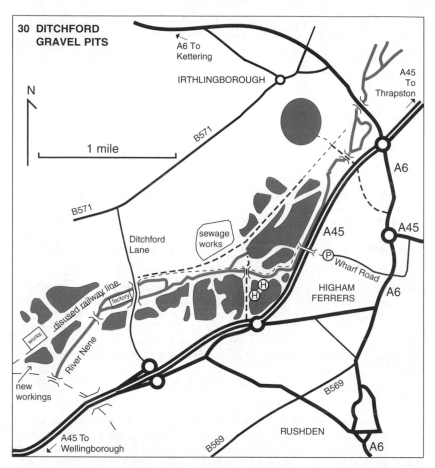

30 DITCHFORD GRAVEL PITS

N

1 mile

A6 To Kettering

IRTHLINGBOROUGH

A45 To Thrapston

A6

B571

A45

A45

B571

sewage works

Ditchford Lane

Wharf Road

HIGHAM FERRERS

A6

disused railway line

factory

works

River Nene

new workings

A45 To Wellingborough

B569

B569

RUSHDEN

A6

Breeders include Little and Great Crested Grebes, up to ten pairs of Grey Herons, Greylag and Canada Geese, a few Pochard, Shoveler, Shelduck, Gadwall, Tufted and Ruddy Ducks, Ringed and Little Ringed Plovers, Lapwing and Redshank. Common Tern formerly bred and is usually present in summer, while Wigeon, Garganey, Teal and Oystercatcher may also oversummer. Reed and Sedge Warblers are common and Cetti's Warbler has occurred and may recolonise. Sparrowhawk, Kingfisher and Willow Tit nest in the area and Hobby is frequent in summer.

31 THRAPSTON GRAVEL PITS (Northamptonshire)   OS Landranger 141

This complex of gravel pits occupies c.3½ miles of the Nene Valley immediately north of Thrapston. A wide range of habitats is present, and the area has an important concentration of wintering Goosander.

Habitat

As is usual with gravel workings, the pits are of various ages and the more recently excavated pits lie at either end of the complex. Thrapston Lake is the largest

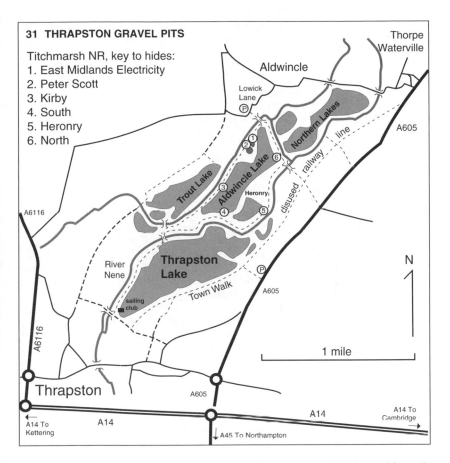

31 THRAPSTON GRAVEL PITS

Titchmarsh NR, key to hides:
1. East Midlands Electricity
2. Peter Scott
3. Kirby
4. South
5. Heronry
6. North

Thorpe Waterville

Aldwincle

Lowick Lane

Northern Lakes

A605

Trout Lake

Aldwincle Lake

Heronry

disused railway line

A6116

River Nene

Thrapston Lake

Town Walk

A605

sailing club

A6116

N

1 mile

Thrapston

A605

A14

A14 To Kettering

A14 To Cambridge

A45 To Northampton

and deepest, with several small wooded islands at its east end: it is used for sailing and fishing. The older central area of the complex forms the Titchmarsh Reserve of the Beds, Cambs, Northants & Peterborough Wildlife Trust (BCNPWT), which includes an overgrown duck decoy now occupied by a heronry, while the largest pit on the reserve is surrounded by rough grassland, with stands of reeds at the west end and several islands that may attract nesting Common Tern, ducks and waders.

Access (see map)

Thrapston Lake Leave the A14 north on the A605 and, after c.¼ mile, continue north over the roundabout. After a further c.¾ mile park in the lay-by on the left and follow the footpath beside the field to the disused railway line ('Town Walk') to view Thrapston Lake. This path continues back into Thrapston, passing through mature trees and scrub that attract migrants and hold several species of warbler, sometimes Nightingale and, in winter, occasionally Hawfinch.

Titchmarsh NWT Reserve Centred around Aldwincle Lake, the reserve also includes Heronry Lake and the heronry itself (no access). Turn west off the A605, 2 miles northeast of Thrapston, at the Fox Inn, to Thorpe Waterville. Take the minor road (past the pit) to Aldwincle and turn first left into Lowick Lane, with the entrance to the reserve on the left after 400 yards (take the bridge over

Harpers Brook), and a small car park opposite. The Nene Way Long-Distance Footpath runs along the west edge of the reserve, giving access to the East Midlands Electricity and Peter Scott hides (overlooking the wader scrapes), and Kirby hide (overlooking the main lake). Another footpath from the bridge follows Brancey Brook along the north side of the reserve, and the River Nene south along the east perimeter, giving access to the North and South hides (overlooking the main lake) and Heronry hide. Alternatively, at the Thrapston end, from 'Town Walk' turn northeast along the disused railway and, after c.1 mile, a footpath west crosses the river to access the reserve. Entrance is possible at all times.

Birds
Wintering wildfowl include large numbers of Wigeon (peaking at over 1,000), several hundred each of Pochard and Tufted Duck, and smaller numbers of Gadwall, Teal and Shoveler. Goosander is something of a specialty, with over 100 regular in February, and similar numbers of Goldeneye also occur. Red-necked and Slavonian Grebes sometimes visit. Cormorant, Water Rail and Kingfisher are fairly frequent, and Hawfinch is sometimes found.

On passage a variety of waders occurs, including Dunlin, Ruff, Greenshank, Common Sandpiper, Turnstone and Bar-tailed and Black-tailed Godwits. Common, Arctic and Black Terns and Little Gull may occur; all favour Thrapston Lake. Other visitors are Shelduck, Garganey (occasional), and White Wagtail may occur in spring.

Breeders include Little and Great Crested Grebes, Greylag and Canada Geese, and c.40 pairs of Grey Herons. Several waders breed, notably Oystercatcher and Ringed and Little Ringed Plovers, as well as Common Tern, at Titchmarsh Reserve, and Redshank, Snipe and a few Curlews nest nearby. Other breeders are Nightingale, Reed, Sedge and Grasshopper Warblers, and Tree Sparrow. Hobby is a frequent visitor.

Information
BCNPWT, Lings House, Billing Lings, Northampton NN3 4BE. Tel: 01604 405285. E-mail: northwt@cix.co.uk

32 STANFORD RESERVOIR
OS Landranger 140
(Northamptonshire/Leicestershire)

Between Rugby and Husbands Bosworth, this small reservoir on the Leicestershire border attracts good numbers of winter wildfowl and is also interesting on passage. Indeed, for its size, a relatively large number of scarce migrants and rarities has been recorded.

Habitat
A drinking-water reservoir set in arable farmland, open water covers 180 acres with a narrow belt of trees along the northwest shore, more extensive areas of woodland just to the north and south, and hawthorn and willow scrub at Blower's Lodge Bay in the southeast corner of the reservoir, which is a reserve of the Beds, Cambs, Northants & Peterborough Wildlife Trust (BCNPWT). There are also some limited stands of reeds.

Access (see map)
The northeast tip of the reservoir, at the inlet stream, can be viewed from the minor road between South Kilworth and the A50 at Welford, with a convenient car park. Otherwise access is restricted to permit holders (obtainable from Severn

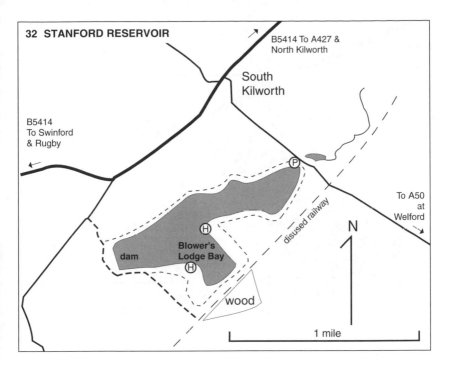

Trent Water Authority or BCNPWT). Leave South Kilworth on the B5414 and the reservoir entrance is on the left after 1 mile. A footpath encircles the reservoir, and there are two hides either side of the mouth of Blower's Lodge Bay.

Birds

Wintering wildfowl include numbers of Wigeon (up to 1,850) and Coot, as well as Teal, Shoveler, Pochard, Tufted Duck and Ruddy Duck (often over 100), up to 90 Gadwall, and a few Pintail, Goosander and Goldeneye. Wild swans, rarer grebes (especially Black-necked) and divers are occasional. The large gull roost can hold as many as 2,000 Lesser Black-backed, and Mediterranean, Glaucous and Ring-billed Gulls have been recorded (the west hide offers the best vantage for gull watching). Check the dense hawthorn scrub at Blower's Lodge Bay for the occasional wintering Long-eared Owl.

On passage a variety of waders may occur, including Little Ringed and Ringed Plovers, Dunlin, Ruff, Greenshank and Green and Common Sandpipers, with Little Stint, Curlew and Wood Sandpipers, Spotted Redshank, and Black-tailed and Bar-tailed Godwits possible, especially in autumn. Common, Arctic and Black Terns are relatively frequent.

Breeding birds include Great Crested and Little Grebes, Common Tern (on purpose-built rafts), Grasshopper, Sedge and Reed Warblers, and Hobby may visit.

Information

Severn Trent Water Authority, Avon House, Demountford Way, Cannon Park, Coventry CV4 7EJ.
Warden: Phil Richardson, Blower's Lodge Bay Reserve, 10 Bedford Cottages, Great Brington, Northampton NN7 4JE. Tel: 01604 770632.
BCNPWT, Lings House, Billing Lings, Northampton NN3 4BE. Tel: 01604 405285.
E-mail northwt@cix.co.uk

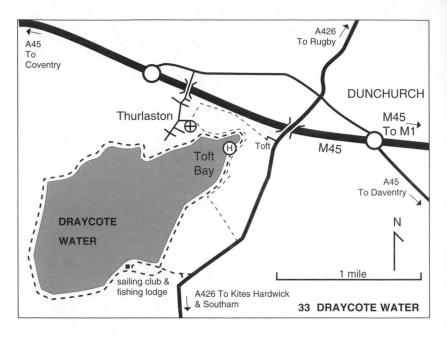

Map labels:
A45 To Coventry
A426 To Rugby
DUNCHURCH
Thurlaston
M45 To M1
Toft
Toft Bay
M45
DRAYCOTE WATER
A45 To Daventry
N
1 mile
sailing club & fishing lodge
A426 To Kites Hardwick & Southam
33 DRAYCOTE WATER

33 DRAYCOTE WATER (Warwickshire)   OS Landranger 140 and 151

Draycote Water lies just southwest of Rugby. Though heavily disturbed by sailing and fishing it attracts a variety of duck in winter, often including a few sea duck, as well as divers and grebes.

Habitat

The reservoir covers c.700 acres and the shoreline is partly natural and partly concrete embankments. There is a small marsh at the northeast end, overlooked by a hide.

Access (see map)

The entrance is off the A426 2 miles south of Dunchurch. A permit is required for vehicular access, available from the Severn Trent Water authority or their agent (but at the time of writing, June 2002, new permits are not being issued). It is possible to drive clockwise around the entire perimeter, viewing from the car. It is possible to walk the shore without a permit. Otherwise, a small section of the northeast end is visible from a public footpath which leaves the A426 c.½ mile northeast of the entrance, skirts the shore and continues to Thurlaston (where it is accessed via Church Lane).

Birds

In winter divers are regular, especially Great Northern, and often make long stays. A few hundred Wigeon occur, together with small numbers of Gadwall and Shoveler. Diving duck are more numerous and there are usually c.50 Goldeneye and smaller numbers of Goosander and Ruddy Duck. Common and Velvet Scoters, Red-breasted Merganser, Scaup and Eider have all been recorded and several of these may be present simultaneously, together with Smew. There is a huge gull roost, mainly Common and Black-headed, but Glaucous is fairly frequent, sometimes together with Iceland. There are several winter records of Mediterranean and Little Gulls, but Kittiwake is more frequent at this season, especially after severe coastal gales. Surrounding pasture sometimes attracts a Short-eared Owl.

Wader passage is poor, Common Sandpiper and Dunlin being the most frequent species. Black, Common and Arctic Terns and sometimes Little Gull also occur on passage.

Information

Permits: Severn Trent Water Authority, Avon House, Demountford Way, Cannon Park, Coventry CV4 7EJ. Tel: 01203 416510. (Agent: Kites Hardwick Filling Station, on the A426 500 yards south of reservoir entrance.)

34 BRANDON MARSH (Warwickshire)   OS Landranger 140

Situated just southeast of Coventry, this 210-acre wetland attracts an excellent variety of breeding, wintering and passage birds. It is managed by Warwickshire Wildlife Trust.

Habitat

Centred around old colliery subsidence pools in the Avon Valley and many gravel pits, the area also has marsh, reedbeds, grassland, willow scrub and small stands of woodland.

Access (see map)

Leave Coventry south on the A45 and, just beyond the roundabout at the junction with the A46, turn north off the eastbound carriageway into Brandon Lane (if approaching from the W, continue past Brandon Lane towards Coventry and perform a U-turn at the roundabout). Proceed along Brandon Lane and turn right after 1 mile to the nature centre car park. There are five hides and a nature trail. The reserve is open 09.00–17.00 on weekdays and 10.00–16.30 at weekends (there is a charge for non-members of the Trust).

Birds

Wintering wildfowl usually include up to 400 Teal and smaller numbers of Wigeon, Gadwall, Shoveler, Goldeneye, Pochard and Tufted Duck. Wintering waders include Snipe, with Jack Snipe in late autumn and early spring, and occasional Woodcock, Dunlin, Common or Green Sandpipers. Raptors include Sparrowhawk, and sometimes Long-eared and Short-eared Owls. Frequently, a few Bearded Tits are present October–November and may remain until March, while Corn Buntings roost in the marsh.

On passage Black-necked Grebe, Garganey and Marsh Harrier are occasional in spring, and waders may include Ringed and Little Ringed Plovers, Curlew, Ruff, Greenshank, Common and Green Sandpipers, Dunlin and occasionally Sanderling (in May). Small numbers of Common and Arctic Terns may pass through and Spotted Crake has occurred several times in autumn.

Breeders include Little and Great Crested Grebes, Tufted and Ruddy Ducks, Snipe, Redshank, and occasionally Garganey, Gadwall or Shelduck. Kingfisher is frequent, several pairs of Water Rails breed and up to 50 pairs of Reed Warblers, together with a few Grasshopper and Cetti's Warblers. The woodland holds all three woodpeckers and Turtle Dove, and Hobby is a fairly regular visitor in summer.

Information

Warwickshire Wildlife Trust, Brandon Marsh Nature Centre, Brandon Lane, Coventry CV3 3GW. Tel: 01247 6302912. E-mail: admin@warkswt.cix.co.uk

35 TAME VALLEY (Warwickshire)   OS Landranger 139

The Tame Valley between Tamworth and east Birmingham has a complex of gravel workings that have become one of the premier birdwatching localities in the Midlands.

Habitat

Sand and gravel extraction have produced a chain of pits which have been landscaped and put to a variety of uses, including water sports and, at Lea Marston and Coton, water purification. These are surrounded by farmland, rough grassland and scrub. In the south of the area, at Ladywalk, gravel pits are used to recirculate power station cooling water.

Access

Ladywalk Reserve Jointly run by the power company and West Midland Bird Club (WMBC), access is through Hams Hall power station and by permit only, available to members of the WMBC. Leave the M42 at junction 9 and take the A446 south for ½ mile, turning left towards Lea Marston. At the sharp left bend, continue straight on over the railway, to the power station entrance. Several hides overlook the marsh. The warm water in the pits seldom freezes and thus is particularly attractive in cold weather.

Coton Pools Leave the M42 at junction 9 and take the A4097 east towards Kingsbury. After 1½ miles turn right at the first roundabout onto a minor road and park carefully on the verge after ½ mile. Coton Pools lie on the left (east) side of the road, and the north pool can be seen from the road but to view the south pool follow the public footpath from the railway bridge.

Lea Marston Balancing Lakes Follow directions as for Coton Pools, but view to the right, on the west side of the road. There is a hide.

Kingsbury Water Park Leave the M42 at junction 9 and take the A4097 east towards Kingsbury. After 1½ miles turn left at the roundabout (signed to the Water Park) and follow the minor road for ½ mile to the entrance. Follow signs to Far Leys car park. It is usually best, however, to continue over the M42 and turn right immediately after into a small lane, then turn left at the sign to Broomey Croft. Follow this road, forking right to leave the caravan park to the left, through the barriers to the car park. A path leads from here north to the two hides. Throughout the park there is a network of marked trails, and Broomey Croft car park is most convenient for the best areas. (Closed on Christmas Day.)

Dosthill Gravel Pits Follow directions to Broomey Croft car park (under Kingsbury Water Park). Walk north along the canal towpath and the pits are on both sides of the canal after c.1 mile. View from the canal side, the bridge or the public footpath to the A4091. In recent years this has been the best area in winter within the Tame Valley, attracting Red-necked and Black-necked Grebes and Smew.

Birds

Wintering wildfowl include large numbers of Pochard and Tufted Duck (notably at Lea Marston), as well as Goldeneye, Wigeon, Shoveler, Gadwall, and a few Ruddy Duck, Goosander and Pintail. Occasional divers, rare grebes or sea duck occur, and a Ferruginous Duck was fairly regular at Coton for several years. Water Rail may be seen, especially in cold weather, and in recent years 2–3 Bitterns have overwintered at Ladywalk. Up to 500 Golden Plovers may be found in fields around Drayton Bassett (just west of the A4091). Rock and Water Pipits may occur in late autumn, and the latter may also overwinter. A handful of Redshank, Green Sandpiper and, sometimes, Ruff may occur at the same season and, quite extraordinarily, even single Spotted Redshank and Wood Sandpiper have wintered. The concentration of birds attracts raptors, and Sparrowhawk, Merlin and Short-eared Owl are possible.

A variety of waders occurs in spring, including Dunlin, Ruff, Whimbrel, Green and Common Sandpipers, Turnstone and Sanderling, and Temminck's Stint is almost annual. Parties of Common, Arctic or Black Terns may pass through, augmenting the breeding Common Terns. Osprey and Marsh Harrier make brief visits most years. A slightly reduced variety of waders occurs on autumn passage, with a build-up of Little Ringed Plover and Green Sandpiper in July–August.

Breeders include Great Crested and Little Grebes, 5–6 pairs of Shelducks, Gadwall, Shoveler, Tufted and Ruddy Ducks, Water Rail, Oystercatcher, Little Ringed and a handful of Ringed Plovers, Redshank, Snipe, c.20 pairs of Common Terns (on Canal Pool at Kingsbury), Turtle Dove, Little Owl and Kingfisher. Garganey has occasionally bred. Breeding passerines include Whinchat, Black Redstart (on Hams Hall Power Station), nine species of warbler including a few Grasshopper, Spotted Flycatcher, Willow Tit, Redpoll and Corn Bunting.

Information
Kingsbury Water Park Manager, Bodymoor Heath Lane, Sutton Coldfield, West Midlands B76 0DY. Tel: 01827 872660. E-mail: parks@warwickshire.gov.uk

36 BREDON'S HARDWICK AND THE
AVON VALLEY (Worcestershire/Gloucestershire)   OS Landranger 150

This area of gravel pits and water meadows in the Avon Valley on the border with Gloucestershire has gained a reputation for attracting interesting birds, with passage waders and winter wildfowl the main attractions.

Habitat
Like all gravel pits, the habitat is dynamic, though the pits are currently under sympathetic management. The fields beside the River Avon are prone to flood in winter, and some (notably Twyning Great Meadow) are still managed traditionally and are of great botanical interest.

Access (see map)
Bredon's Hardwick New Pit Leave Tewkesbury northeast on the B4080 and, after 1 mile, park carefully on the verge just before Bredon's Hardwick, viewing the 'New Pit' from the five-barred gates at the roadside. The pit is well vegetated and careful scrutiny over a period of time may be necessary to find all of the birds present.

Avon Valley, Worcestershire bank In Bredon's Hardwick a concealed public footpath runs between the houses directly to the river, overlooking three very wet meadows that are good for waders, especially Golden Plover in December–April. The Fishing Pit to the south attracts grebes and ducks and small numbers of waders. More water meadows can be viewed from Fleet Lane and the fisherman's footpath on the south bank of the river.

Twyning Great Meadow Continue on the B4080 into Bredon, then follow signs to the church and riverbank to view the meadow over the river.

Avon Valley, Gloucestershire bank Leave the M50 at junction 1 and, from the roundabout south of the motorway, take the minor road to Twyning and thereafter Twyning Green. Park at the riverbank by the Fleet Inn and follow the footpath south along the west bank of the river (which continues for 2 miles, meeting the A38 just north of Tewkesbury).

Birds
In winter wildfowl on the pits or flooded meadows may include up to 2,500 Wigeon, 400 Teal and 80 Pintail, as well as Shoveler, Goldeneye, Goosander and

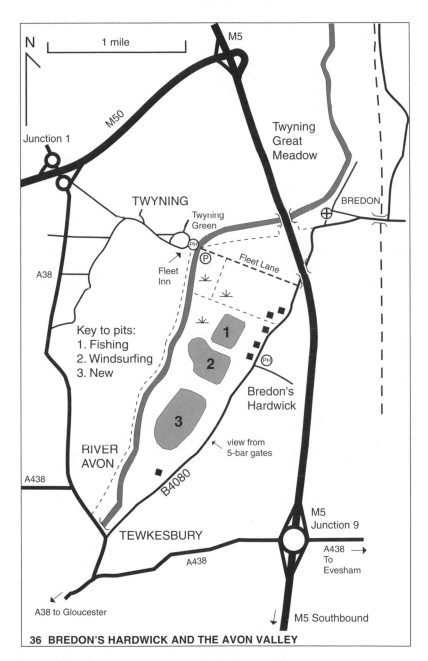

36 BREDON'S HARDWICK AND THE AVON VALLEY

occasionally Smew or Scaup on the pits or river. Parties of White-fronted Geese or Bewick's Swans may pass through, the latter in some numbers if the meadows are flooded. Cormorant is always present, Peregrine is regular and Merlin may visit. The fields attract large numbers of Lapwings and Golden Plovers and, if flooded, sometimes also Dunlin and Redshank, while wintering passerines may include Stonechat and large flocks of Fieldfare and Redwing.

On passage a variety of waders has occurred, with Ruff and Whimbrel among the more frequent. Other migrants include Shelduck, Garganey, Common Tern and a variety of passerines, notably Yellow Wagtail, including birds of the continental form, Blue-headed Wagtail.

Breeders in the area include Gadwall, Sparrowhawk, Hobby, Oystercatcher, Little Ringed Plover, Redshank, Curlew, Snipe, Little Owl, Kingfisher, Yellow Wagtail and Corn Bunting.

37 UPTON WARREN (Worcestershire)   OS Landranger 150

Also known as the Christopher Cadbury Wetland Reserve, this compact site (split into two halves) can produce a variety of birds, especially wildfowl and waders. The area is a reserve of the Worcestershire Wildlife Trust (WWT), covering c.65 acres.

Habitat
The extraction of underground salt deposits has resulted in a number of subsidence pools, the Moors Pool to the north and the three Flashes (themselves saline) to the south. Between these is a relatively unproductive gravel pit. The pools are surrounded by rough grassland, with scrub bordering the Henbrook and alders the River Salwarpe.

Access (see map)
The area lies east of the A38, 2 miles southwest of Bromsgrove, and can also be reached by leaving the M5 at junction 5, proceeding north along the A38 for 2 miles. Access is restricted to members of the WWT or other affiliates of the RSNC, and is otherwise by advance permit from the WWT (SAE please). There is a total of seven hides and the reserve is closed Christmas Day.

Moors Pool Turn east off the A38 by the AA box ¼ mile north of the Swan Inn, following a farm track for 200 yards and then parking on the left. There are three hides, one adjacent to the car park overlooking the North Moors Pool, the other two either side of Moors Pool. Alternatively, park at the Swan Inn and cross the A38, proceeding on foot through the gate opposite and following the path beside the River Salwarpe to the hides. Moors Pool is best for wildfowl, with Jack Snipe and Water Rail favouring the North Moors Pool, and warblers and passerine migrants the adjacent vegetation.

The Flashes Park in the sailing centre car park adjacent to the A38 just south of the Swan Inn (the turning is opposite Webb's Garden Centre) and follow the path beyond the sailing centre, around the south shore of the gravel pit and over the Henbrook to the hides. The Flashes are best for passage waders (an early-morning visit after overnight rain is recommended), and are usually quiet in winter, though often hold numbers of Teal and an occasional Green Sandpiper at this season.

Birds
Winter brings small numbers of dabbling duck, including Wigeon and Gadwall, up to 120 Shoveler, and also Ruddy Duck and occasional Scaup, sea duck or sawbills. There are usually several Water Rails, Jack Snipe and Green Sandpipers, and often Siskins and Redpolls in the riverside alders.

It is during passage periods that Upton Warren, especially the Flashes, comes into its own. Regulars include a roost of up to 110 Curlews, and July–August gatherings of up to 25 Green Sandpipers and 2,000 Lapwings. In addition, almost any

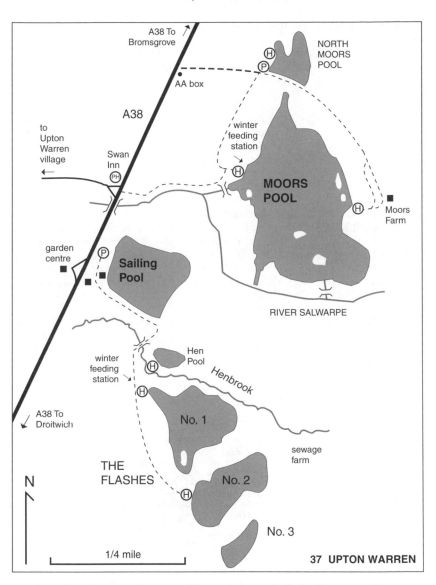

37 UPTON WARREN

species of wader may turn up. Other migrants include Garganey, Common, Arctic and Black Terns, and a variety of passerines, notably Whinchat.

Breeders include Ruddy Duck, Sparrowhawk, Water Rail, Little Ringed Plover, Redshank, Curlew, Common Tern, Kingfisher, Yellow Wagtail and several warblers, including Sedge, Reed and Grasshopper. A feature of summer and early autumn is the regular evening forays of Hobbies among the Swallows and martins.

Information

Worcestershire Wildlife Trust, Lower Smite Farm, Smite Hill, Hindlip, Worcestershire WR3 8SZ. Tel: 01905 754919.

A.F. Jacobs, 3 The Beeches, Upton Warren, Bromsgrove, Worcestershire B61 7EL. Tel: 01527 861 370. E-mail: worcswt@cix.co.uk

38 BITTELL RESERVOIRS (Worcestershire)   OS Landranger 139

Just south of Birmingham, these reservoirs were built as canal-feeders and have a long ornithological history. A variety of wildfowl is usually present in winter, and small numbers of waders move through on passage.

Habitat

Upper Bittell is the larger water, covering 100 acres, with small areas of marsh and shallow water at the northeast end, but is generally much disturbed by watersports. Lower Bittell covers 57 acres and is bisected by a causeway (the north portion being known as Mill Shrub). Much less disturbed, it is surrounded by woodland and extensive areas of rough grassland. Both reservoirs have natural banks. Between the two, stands of swampy woodland follow the course of a small stream.

Access (see map)

Lower Bittell The B4120 between Barnt Green and Alvechurch (accessed via the A441 from junction 2 of the M42) follows the south shore of the reservoir, giving limited views, though parking is difficult. From here turn north on Bittell Farm Road towards Hopwood; parking is easier and there are views of the open water over the hedge. Proceed to the sharp right-hand bend (limited parking) and then pass over the causeway between Lower Bittell and Mill Shrub, with good views from the road.

Upper Bittell From the right-angled bend at Lower Bittell causeway follow the lane north beside the stream for ½ mile to view Mill Shrub pool. At the two small ponds turn right over the stile by the old pump house on a public footpath along the top of Upper Bittell dam. Alternatively, proceed along the track

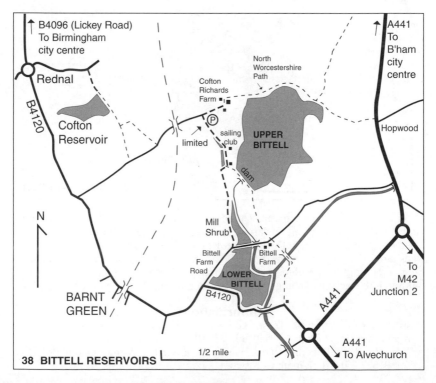

past the two ponds and, after ⅓ mile, turn right to Cofton Richards Farm (limited parking at the corner). Follow the North Worcestershire Path over the fields until it parallels a short section of the north shore of the reservoir, giving limited views in a few places.

Birds

Winter is perhaps the most interesting season, with regular Teal, Wigeon, Pochard, Ruddy Duck, Goldeneye and a few Shoveler and Goosander, while other sawbills, sea duck and rarer grebes are occasional. Jack Snipe and Water Rail may be found in the wetter areas, with Grey Wagtail, Redpoll and Siskin along the stream. There is a small gull roost, but it almost exclusively comprises Black-headed Gulls.

On passage small numbers of waders are recorded, including Ringed and Little Ringed Plovers, Ruff, Dunlin, Greenshank, Common Sandpiper and occasionally Turnstone, Little Stint or Curlew Sandpiper, as well as Black, Common and Arctic Terns. Waders tend to make rather short visits (perhaps because of the sterility of the mud due to fertiliser runoff). Hobby is fairly regular in late summer, and Rock Pipit may occur in late autumn.

Residents include Sparrowhawk, Kingfisher, all three woodpeckers and Willow Tit.

39 LICKEY HILLS (Worcestershire)   OS Landranger 139

This area of woodland on the outskirts of Birmingham is heavily used for recreation but still supports a notable range of breeding birds, including Tree Pipit, Pied Flycatcher, Redstart and Wood Warbler.

Habitat

Rising to 956 feet, the hills are cloaked by large areas of planted conifers, mixed with some extensive stands of beech and oak, more open birch woodland with bilberry, gorse and heather on some of the steeper slopes, and some open grassy areas.

Access (see map)

Leave Birmingham south on the A38 and, at the roundabout by Longbridge car plant, continue straight ahead on Lickey Road (the B4096). At the next roundabout in Rednal turn right on Old Birmingham Road, parking on the left by the visitor centre. From here a network of footpaths radiates into the woods. Alternatively, continue to the top of the road and, at the crossroads, turn left into Twatling Road, turning immediately left again on the track to a small car park (or continue along the road and park on the left-hand verge). An alternative point of access is off the B4120 between Barnt Green and Rednal, where there is very limited roadside parking. There is free public access to the whole area.

Birds

Residents include Sparrowhawk, all three woodpeckers, Nuthatch and Marsh Tit. Breeding summer visitors include tiny numbers of Pied Flycatcher (three pairs in 1995), Wood Warbler (especially on the slopes of Cofton Hill) and Redstart. Additionally Tree Pipit can be found on the summit of Rose Hill, and several pairs of Firecrests bred in 1975.

During invasion years, areas of conifers often attract Crossbills, and in winter Siskin, Redpoll and Brambling can usually be found, the latter favouring the stands of beech along Twatling Road.

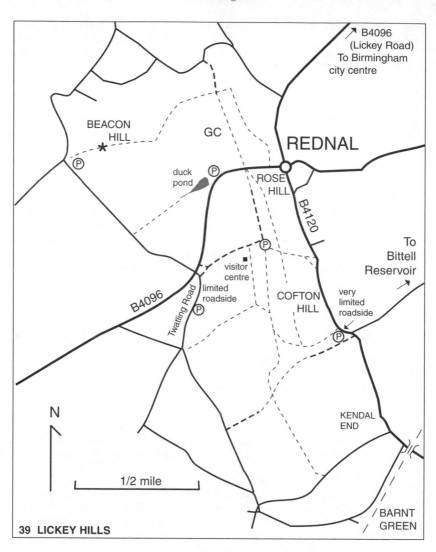

39 LICKEY HILLS

B4096
(Lickey Road)
To Birmingham
city centre

BEACON
HILL

GC

REDNAL

duck
pond

ROSE
HILL

B4120

To
Bittell
Reservoir

visitor
centre

limited
roadside

COFTON
HILL

very
limited
roadside

B4096

Twatling Road

KENDAL
END

N

1/2 mile

BARNT
GREEN

Information

Visitor Centre, Lickey Hills Country Park, Warren Lane, Rednal, Birmingham B45 8ER. Tel: 0121 447 7106. E-mail: visitorcentre@lickeyhills.fsnet.co.uk

40 THE WYRE FOREST (Worcestershire)   OS Landranger 138

West of Bewdley, this area of ancient woodland is not only scenic but also holds an excellent selection of woodland birds. Portions of the forest are protected as an NNR and as reserves of the Worcestershire Wildlife Trust (WWT) and West Midlands Bird Club.

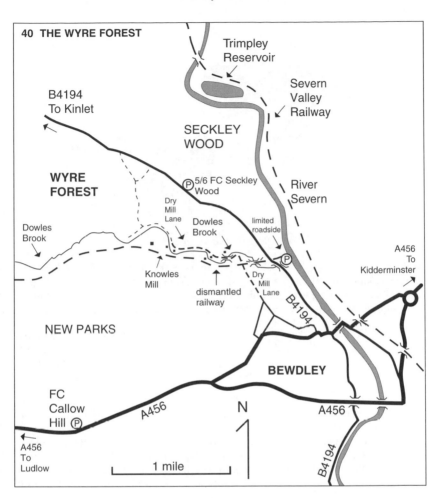

Habitat

The forest covers over 6,000 acres and contains some of the best stands of ancient woodland in Britain, predominantly oak, but just over half of the forest is conifer plantations, managed by the FC. Dowles Brook runs through one of richest and most diverse areas of the forest, including meadows and abandoned orchards.

Access (see map)

Dowles Brook Leave Bewdley northwest on the B4194 Kinlet road. After c.1 mile the road crosses Dowles Brook; limited roadside parking is available on the bridge and on the left between the bridge and the disused railway line. A few yards further, there is a small entrance on the left-hand side (just beyond the railway embankment). From here take the footpath west beside the embankment for a short distance before crossing Dowles Brook and reaching Dry Mill Lane. This follows Dowles Brook (again crossing the stream) and, after 1 mile, is Knowles Mill on the opposite bank. Take the footbridge to the Mill and follow the footpath through Knowles Coppice (WWT reserve) to the old railway line, which can be followed back to the road. This circular walk should deliver most or all of the specialities.

Buzzard and Magpies

Seckley Wood Continue on the B4194 towards Kinlet and, c.2½ miles from Bewdley, park at the FC picnic site on the right. There are three marked trails and, after initially following the red trail, leave it on the path past Seckley Beech to a track that offers panoramic views over the River Severn and Trimpley Reservoir.

New Parks Leave Bewdley west on the A456 Ludlow road and, after 2½ miles, park on the right at the FC Callow Hill car park and visitor centre. From here follow the red or green marked trails through the principal area of coniferous forest. The red trail is 3½ miles long and is connected by footpaths to Dowles Brook.

Birds

Residents include Mandarin (along Dowles Brook, and sometimes feral Wood Duck), Buzzard, Goshawk, Sparrowhawk, Woodcock, Kingfisher, all three woodpeckers, Grey Wagtail, Dipper, Marsh and Willow Tits, Nuthatch, Raven, Siskin and Hawfinch. In summer these are joined by Cuckoo, Turtle Dove, Tree Pipit (especially along the old railway line), Redstart, Wood and Garden Warblers and Pied Flycatcher (notably at Knowles Coppice and around Knowles Mill). Search also for Nightjar and Firecrest.

In autumn and winter there may be sizeable finch flocks, including Brambling, Siskin, Redpoll and, sometimes, Crossbill.

Information

Michael Taylor, Lodge Hill Farm, Bewdley, Worcestershire DY12 2LY. Tel: 01299 400686.

41 SYMONDS YAT (Gloucestershire) OS Landranger 162

Since 1982 a pair of Peregrines has nested at Symonds Yat Rock, in the Wye Valley between Chepstow and Monmouth, with viewing facilities laid on by the RSPB. The Peregrines are resident, but most active June-August when feeding young.

Habitat

The lower Wye valley in bounded by steep limestone cliffs, some of which rise to 300 feet, with stands of coniferous, deciduous and mixed forest in the valley.

Access

Leave the A4136 at Coleford northwards on the B4432, parking in the large car park on arrival at Symonds Yat. Alternative access is south off the A40 at Goodrich, via the B4229, crossing the Wye via a narrow minor road. From the car park a short trail leads over a footbridge to the viewpoint. The eyrie is located on the cliffs south of the river, a little upstream of the viewpoint. From the car park, a variety of trails leads into deciduous woodland to the south.

Birds

Breeding raptors in the area include Buzzard, Sparrowhawk and Kestrel, in addition to Peregrine. The adjoining woodlands hold a range of typical forest species, including Wood Warbler, whilst Dipper and Grey Wagtail can be found on the River Wye.

Information

Ivan Proctor, The Puffins, Parkend, Lydney, Gloucestershire GL15 4JA. Tel: 01594 562852.

42 FOREST OF DEAN (Gloucestershire)   OS Landranger 162

The Forest of Dean cloaks a large area between the confluence of the rivers Wye and Severn and holds an excellent variety of woodland birds, including some sought-after specialities such as Nightjar, Pied Flycatcher and Hawfinch. May and June are the best months to visit.

Habitat

The Forest of Dean is a relict of the ancient wildwood that once covered Britain but, sadly, large areas have been felled and replaced with conifers and Pendunculate Oak. The RSPB's Nagshead reserve protects one of the largest and best stands of deciduous woodland, consisting largely of mature plantations of Pendunculate Oak, with some Beech and stands of conifers, whilst a fast-flowing stream runs from the Cannop Ponds through the oak woodland.

Access

The following sites are recommended:

RSPB Nagshead Leave the B4234 westwards at Parkend on the minor road towards Coleford and, on the outskirts of Parkend, turn north at the RSPB sign onto a track, following this for ½ mile to the reserve car park. Access is unrestricted, and there are several waymarked trails, whilst an Information Centre is manned at the car park during weekends, April-August. Around 50 pairs of Pied Flycatchers nest on the reserve, and Wood Warbler and Redstart are also common, whilst the plantations and clearings on the northern and western fringes of the reserve hold Tree Pipit, Whinchat and Redpoll.

Speech House Hotel This lies to the south of the B4226 between Cinderford and Coleford, with a car park opposite (Redstarts and Pied Flycatchers breed around this car park). The arboretum and blocks of conifers to the south and east hold Willow Tit, Siskin and Common Crossbill.

Woodgreen's Lake Hobbies may hunt over this large, rush-fringed pool, which attracts Common and Jack Snipe in the winter; the lake is a reserve of the Gloucestershire Wildlife Trust. The block of forest to the north, between the B4226 and A4136, hold Hawfinches, with Nightjars in the clearings.

Cannop Ponds These are signed off the B4234 north of Parkend. Look for Dippers on the stream, and explore the oak woodland to the southeast. The surrounding trees hold Siskins and Redpolls in winter.

Birds

Resident woodland species in the forest as a whole include Buzzard, Sparrowhawk, Woodcock, all three woodpeckers, Dipper, Marsh and Willow Tits (the latter favouring dense stands of young conifers, reflecting their normal choice of habitat on the Continent), Nuthatch, Treecreeper, Raven, Common Crossbill and a few pairs of Siskins. Hawfinch is a speciality, and the key to finding the species in winter is to track down stands of Hornbeams, under which they can be seen quietly feeding.

Summer visitors include Nightjar (in the clearings formed by clear-felling and replanting conifers), Tree Pipit, Grey Wagtail, Redstart, a few pairs of Stonechats and Whinchats, Grasshopper Warbler (in areas of young conifers), Wood and Garden Warblers, over 100 pairs of Pied Flycatchers, and a few pairs of Firecrests. Hobbies breed in the area and may visit.

In winter variable numbers of Bramblings arrive, and large numbers of Siskins and Redpolls augment the local breeders.

Information

RSPB Nagshead, Warden: Ivan Proctor, The Puffins, Parkend, Lydney, Gloucestershire GL15 4JA. Tel: 01594 562852. E-mail: ivan.proctor@rspb.org.uk
Gloucestershire Wildlife Trust, Dulverton Building, Robinswood Hill Country Park, Reservoir Road, Gloucester GL4 6SX. Tel: 01452 383333. E-mail: info@gloucesterwildlifetrust.co.uk

43 FRAMPTON (Gloucestershire)   OS Landranger 162

Flooded gravel pits on the outskirts of this picturesque village hold small numbers of wildfowl, whilst views of the Severn estuary are possible from Frampton Breakwater; some good flashes attract passage waders.

Habitat

At Frampton the southern, larger pit is deep with steep banks and often disturbed by sailing, whilst the smaller northern pits are shallower, more heavily vegetated and less disturbed. Frampton Breakwater overlooks the vast Severn Estuary.

Access (see map)

Leave the M5 at junction 13 west onto the A419, and after ⅓ mile turn south at the roundabout onto the A38. After a further ½ mile turn west on the B4071 to Frampton on Severn. After 1½ miles turn left into the village.

Frampton Pools Continue on to the village green in Frampton and park either in the small car park by the post office at the northern end of the green, or on the roadside at the far end of the green. A public footpath runs from the southern end of the green along a track to the yacht club, from which the larger pit can be scanned. Carry on diagonally left across the field to the gate. View the northern pit straight ahead through the trees, and this track can be followed to a scrubby area that is good for warblers and Nightingale. Returning to the gate, follow this footpath back towards the village green but, before reaching the houses, take another footpath which leads north past the western edge of the pits.

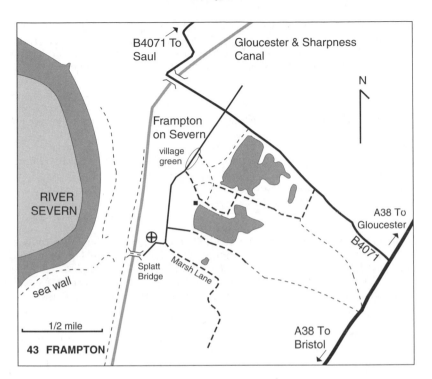

Frampton Breakwater Continue straight through the village to Splatt Bridge, which spans the Gloucester and Sharpness Canal. Park and cross the bridge, scanning the canal for grebes or ducks; the small reedbed by the bridge is worth a look for migrant warblers (and the small pool along Marsh Lane holds Reed and Sedge Warblers). From here there are two options:
1. Walk south along the canal towpath for 200 yards, where a gate on the right marks the start of a path to the seawall. Continue south along the seawall, reaching Frampton Breakwater after 1 mile. There are two flashes by the seawall.
2. Go through the gate adjacent to the bridge and follow the seawall round to the north; there is a flash after about ½ mile (note there is no public right of way, and access is at the discretion of the landowner).

Birds
Wintering wildfowl on the pits include Pochard, Teal, Shoveler, Gadwall, a handful of Goldeneye, and sometimes the odd Smew; there are also regularly numbers of Cormorants. Water Rails winter but are typically elusive, Siskins and Redpolls may be found in the waterside alders, and Chiffchaffs may also winter, whilst the rarer grebes, divers, or Bitterns are occasionally recorded.

On the estuary, wildfowl and waders, as described under Slimbridge, may be seen in somewhat less artificial (and consequently less comfortable) conditions. The pools may hold Jack Snipe, and raptors such as Peregrine, Merlin or Short-eared Owl may occur.

On passage Garganey are sometimes found, and small numbers of Common, Arctic and Black Terns and Little Gulls. Wader passage on the pits is not notable, and typically the longer-legged shanks and sandpipers are attracted.

Breeding birds include Ruddy Duck (it was from Slimbridge that British Ruddy Ducks originated), a resident flock of Mandarins (which may peak at over 50 in the autumn), and there are resident flocks of feral Greylag and Canada Geese, often joined by other geese of captive origin. Water Rails sometimes breed, but Turtle Doves and Kingfishers are regular. Breeding passerines include Reed Warbler and several pairs of Nightingales. Hobbies may visit at any time in summer.

44 SLIMBRIDGE (Gloucestershire)   OS Landranger 162

Slimbridge is the headquarters of the Wildfowl and Wetlands Trust, formed in 1946 by the late Sir Peter Scott. The area was chosen because of the largest flock of wintering White-fronted Geese in Britain, and these remain the major attraction, together with a flock of Bewick's Swans. A visit is best in winter, when some 30,000 wild birds visit the reserve.

Habitat
Reclaimed meadows form an area of 1,000 acres known as the New Grounds, while 200 acres of grassy saltmarsh outside the seawall are known as the Dumbles. Beyond this, large areas of mud are exposed alongside the River Severn at low water. Some shallow pools and scrapes have been created inside the seawall, attracting waders, and these are visible from the Trust's hides.

Access
Leave the M5 at junction 14 and drive north along the A38, turning left after 8 miles onto a minor road signed Slimbridge. The reserve is 2 miles from this turning. Coming from the north, the turning is 4 miles from junction 13 on the M5. The WWT's Slimbridge headquarters now boasts a smart new Visitor Centre, with every facility imaginable. There are exhibitions, a cinema, an art gallery and a restaurant, as well as nature trails and a tropical house for hummingbirds. Visitors can view the wild geese from three towers and sixteen hides, accessible through the Trust's collection. This is open daily, 09.30-17.00 (to 16.00 November-March), except Christmas Day. There is a charge for non-WWT members. As well as the wild geese, the collection of captive waterfowl has grown into the world's largest and best.

Birds
Some White-fronts arrive in early October, but numbers remain low until late November, when they begin to build up rapidly, peaking in the New Year. In recent years, numbers have averaged around 1,500, but can rise to over 5,000 in cold weather. Most will have departed by early March. One or two Lesser White-fronted Geese used to be found most winters, but are less regular now. Individuals of several other species of geese can usually be found with the White-fronts. They require a good telescope and a great deal of patience to find. Several hundred Bewick's Swans winter; they feed on the fields and roost on the estuary, but also visit Swan Lake where they can be seen at very close range. Nine species of duck are regularly present, including large numbers of Wigeon as well as Pintail, Gadwall, and Shoveler, and many come into the collection to feed. A Peregrine is almost always present in winter, and a Kingfisher may be seen from a special hide in the grounds. Waders include several thousand Lapwings and Golden Plovers in the fields, as well as the common open-shore species.

Waders are more varied on passage, and can include Whimbrel, especially in spring, and Black-tailed Godwit in autumn.

Information

The Wildfowl and Wetlands Trust, Slimbridge, Gloucestershire GL2 7BT. Tel: 01453 890333. E-mail: slimbridge@wwt.org.uk Website: www.wwt.org.uk

45 COTSWOLD WATER PARK

(Gloucestershire and Wiltshire) OS Landranger 163

Straddling the county border four miles south of Cirencester, this complex of over 70 gravel pits attracts a good variety of birds throughout the year, although wildfowl and passage waders are the main draw.

Habitat

The extraction of gravel since 1920 has left a series of flooded pits situated amidst typical lowland farmland.

Access (see map)

Turn off the A419 3½ miles SE of Cirencester at the Spine Road Junction onto the B4696 signed to the Water Park. After ¼ mile the road crosses the old Thames-Severn Canal and there is a car park and the Gateway Visitor Centre. A map is displayed here and at other car parks, and as footpaths and rights of way change as new pits are developed, these should be consulted for the most up-to-date information. In such a big area it is hard to single out specific sites, but the Cleveland Lakes pits 74 and 68c (viewable from the 'Twitchers Gate') are often very productive for wildfowl, while the silt beds (pits 68c and 68d, accessed from the Waterhay car park) have been the best site in the county for waders for many years. Pit 44 is good for Smew, pit 46/48 for Nightingales, pits 57 and 41 for Hobbies, and 57 also for wintering wildfowl. The Shorncote reedbed is being managed to attract Bitterns, and this area is also good for waders, especially pits 79, 87, 84, 85a and 85b, and these are accessed from the parking area by pits 31/32.

Birds

On passage a good variety of waders occur, the more regular species including Turnstone, Oystercatcher, Whimbrel, Ruff, Greenshank, Common and Green Sandpipers, and Dunlin. Other migrants include Shelduck and a few Garganey, whilst Common Terns are fairly regular migrants; odd Black and Arctic Terns may also occur.

Breeding birds include Great Crested and Little Grebes, Grey Heron, Sparrowhawk, Ringed and Little Ringed Plovers, Curlew, Redshank, a few pairs of Common Terns, Cuckoo, Kingfisher, Sand Martin, Reed and Sedge Warblers, Lesser Whitethroat, and small numbers of Nightingales. Hobbies are regular in summer, attracted in part by the large flocks of feeding swifts, swallows and martins. Notable, too, are several pairs of feral Red-crested Pochards, and Dippers on some of the streams in the area.

Winter wildfowl within the complex include large numbers of Wigeon, Teal, Pochard and Tufted Duck, with a scattering of Ruddy Duck, Shoveler, Gadwall and Goldeneye, and a few Goosander. Divers, the rarer grebes, and small numbers of Smew may also occur, especially in hard weather. Other wintering species include Cormorant, Water Rail, large flocks of Lapwings and Golden Plovers, Common Snipe, a few Jack Snipe, and Siskin, whilst a gull roost at pit 16 near South Cerney attracts large numbers of Black-headed Gulls and several hundred Common and Lesser Black-backed Gulls; other large gulls are scarce.

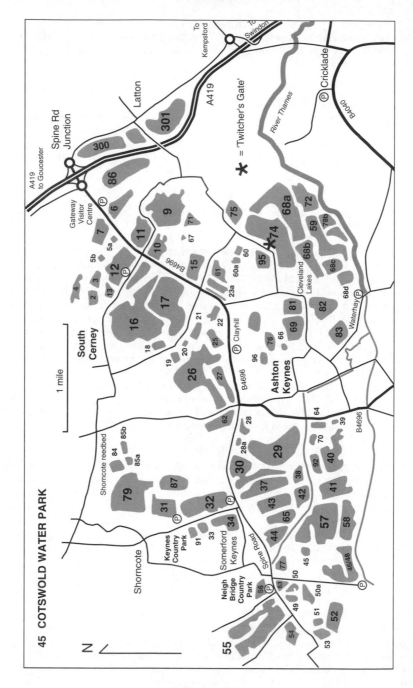

Information
Cotswold Water Park Society, Keynes Country Park, Shorncote, Cirencester,
Gloucestershire GL7 6DF. Tel: 01285 862777.

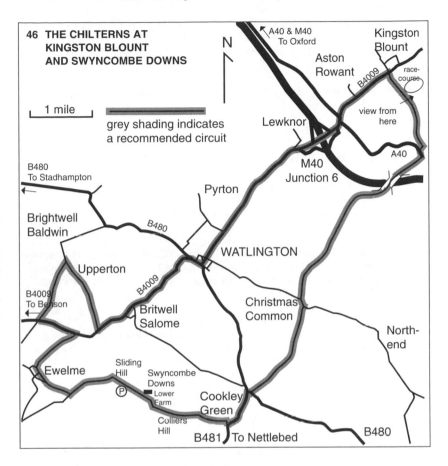

46 THE CHILTERNS AT KINGSTON BLOUNT AND SWYNCOMBE DOWNS (Oxfordshire)   OS Landranger 165 and 175

Following the highly successful reintroduction programme, 142 pairs of Red Kites are breeding in the Chilterns (2002) and these are among the more reliable sites to find the species.

Habitat

The Chiltern escarpment, with numerous wooded stands, is ideal habitat for raptors.

Access (see map)

Kingston Blount Leave the M40 at junction 6 northeast on the B4009. Turn south upon entering Kingston Blount, signed to the 'racecourse'. Passing the racecourse after ½ mile, continue to the base of the Chilterns escarpment to view.

Swyncombe Downs Leave Watlington southwest on the B4009 and, after c.2 miles, take the minor road south to Ewelme and follow minor roads towards Cookley Green. After c.2 miles park carefully by the roadside near Sliding Hill and Mower Farm to view the escarpment.

A circuit of minor roads between Kingston Blount and Swyncombe Downs should, in all but the worst weather, produce sightings of Red Kites and, notably, they are seen regularly from the M40 (but beware the perils of too much 'rubbernecking').

Birds
Red Kite is regular in spring and summer, and Sparrowhawk, Buzzard and Hobby are also possible.

47 THE WESSEX DOWNS AT CHURN (Oxfordshire)   OS Landranger 174

The Wessex ('Berkshire') Downs comprise an area of open, chalkland habitats in south Oxfordshire that can be interesting at any season, though a certain amount of luck is required and blank days are possible.

Habitat
Prior to the Second World War almost the entire area was unimproved grassland grazed by sheep and rabbits but large parts are now cultivated, with some areas of permanent grassland associated with racing stables and remnant stands of woodland.

Access (see map)
Exploration of public rights of way is recommended, notably the Fair Mile and Ridgway, with three main access points off the A417 between Harwell and Streatley:
1. At the west edge of Blewbury leave the A417 south on Bohan's Road. Follow this concrete road through two left bends and park carefully on the grass verge near Churn pig farm.

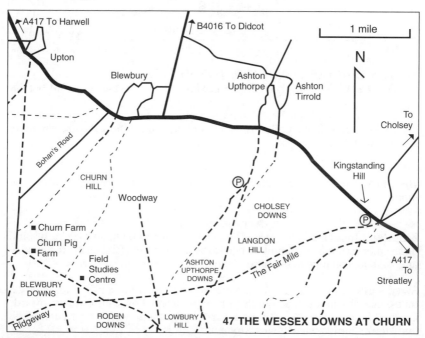

2. On the A417, east of Blewbury, park at the end of the Fair Mile on Kingstanding Hill. The Fair Mile footpath can be followed west for several miles.
3. Turn south off the A417 4 miles northwest of Streatley (opposite the turn to Aston Upthorpe) and follow the track to park after ⅔ mile. From here walk south for c.1 mile to the Fair Mile.

Birds
Breeding birds include Sparrowhawk, Buzzard, Hobby, Red-legged and the scarcer Grey Partridge, Lapwing, Curlew, Little Owl, Meadow Pipit and Corn Bunting. In summer variable numbers of Quails use the area and the occasional pair of Stone Curlews may persist.

On passage the escarpment forms a 'leading line' for migrating birds, attracting Wheatear, Ring Ouzel and Whinchat at both seasons, with good numbers of thrushes in autumn and, in May, sometimes a Montagu's or Marsh Harrier.

In winter there are large flocks of Lapwing and Golden Plover, but raptors probably hold the greatest interest, with Hen Harrier and Short-eared Owl regular (the former roosts near the disused railway line), and Merlin and Long-eared Owl occasional. Interesting passerines, such as Stonechat, are also possible and the mixed flocks of finches and buntings sometimes contain Tree Sparrows.

48 FARMOOR RESERVOIRS (Oxfordshire)   OS Landranger 164

Completed in 1976 and lying just 5 miles west of the centre of Oxford, these two reservoirs adjacent to the River Thames are attractive to birds in winter and passage periods.

Habitat
A causeway separates the reservoirs and open water covers 378 acres, but both have concrete banks, reducing their attractiveness to waders. To the west, 10 acres bounded by a meander of the Thames comprise Pinkhill Meadow NR, an area of shallow pools and willow scrub. Adjacent to the Thames are flood meadows, shrubs and trees.

Access (see map)
Leave Oxford west on the B4044 and, upon entering Farmoor village, turn south on the B4017. The reservoirs' entrance and car park are on the right after c.½ mile. Access is by permit only, available from the gatehouse or by post from Thames Water. The gates are open from dawn to 30 minutes after dusk. Access is restricted to the embankment, and while a circuit of both reservoirs is worthwhile, the central causeway should be adequate for a short visit. Farmoor II is often disturbed by windsurfing and sailing, and though Farmoor I is generally disturbed only by fishermen, watersports are increasing here too (early mornings are perhaps best). Away from the reservoirs, there is access to public footpaths and the Thames towpath, which afford limited views of the reservoirs. Access to Pinkhill Meadow NR is restricted to the hide and confined to keyholders (details from the warden's office at the gatehouse).

Birds
Winter wildfowl include up to 60 Goldeneye and 1,000 Wigeon, with smaller numbers of Goosander, Pintail, Gadwall and Shoveler, and at times oddities such as divers or sea duck. Indeed, Great Northern Diver and rarer grebes are reasonably

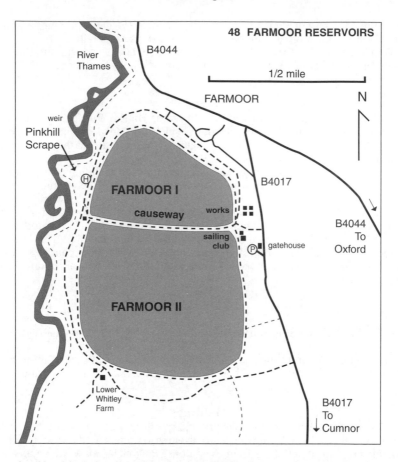

regular. Notably, in hard weather the reservoirs may be the last of the local waters to freeze, thus attracting large numbers of wildfowl. Numbers of Cormorants use the reservoirs, roosting at Farmoor II, and Kingfisher is often present. The gull roost holds up to 5,000 Black-headed, 2,500 Lesser Black-backed, 2,000 Herring and small numbers of Common and Great Black-backed Gulls. Iceland, Glaucous and Mediterranean Gulls are occasionally present. The best place to watch the gull roost is the west end of the causeway (with the sun behind you).

On passage Black, Common and, sometimes, Arctic Terns and Little Gull occur (the latter two especially in spring). The most regular waders are Dunlin, Redshank, Common Sandpiper, and Ringed and Little Ringed Plovers, but a variety of other species is possible, including Ruff, Greenshank, Curlew Sandpiper, Little Stint and Sanderling. Migrant passerines may include Yellow Wagtail, Wheatear, Whinchat and, especially in late autumn, Rock Pipit. Large numbers of Swallows, martins and Swifts occur, especially in late summer, when up to four Hobbies may be present, and Osprey is annual, mainly in spring.

Breeding birds include Common Tern, which use specially constructed rafts, Kingfisher and House Martin.

Information
Thames Water, Amenity and Recreation Officer, Nugent House, Vastern Road, Reading RG1 8DB.

49 STANTON HARCOURT GRAVEL PITS (Oxfordshire) OS Landranger 164

Lying in the Windrush Valley just 6 miles west of Oxford city centre, this complex of over 30 sand and gravel pits includes Dix Pit, one of the top birding sites in the county.

Access (see map)

Many pits have restricted access and are heavily disturbed by watersports (though almost all can be viewed from a right of way, but note that these are sometimes re-routed). Four sites are best both for ease of access and ornithological interest.

Dix Pit The most important in the complex for wintering wildfowl. From Stanton Harcourt follow signs to the municipal tip. Pass through the entrance gate and follow the approach road (Draw Road) around the pit to the public dump. Park well off the road, to the left, just before the weighbridge, and view the pit. The other end of the lake can be viewed from the approach road near the gate. (Be sure to note the gate closing times—you may be locked in! If in doubt park outside the gate and walk.)

Linch Hill Pits Three pits managed by the ARC for fishing and water sports. The entrance is on the B4449 c.1¼ miles south of Stanton Harcourt. Entrance is free.

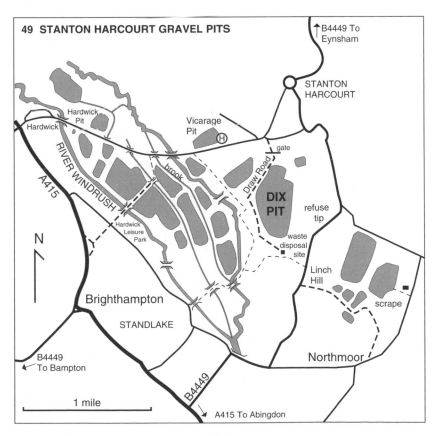

Northmoor Scrape A shallow pit, favoured by waders, Garganey and Hobby. View from the footpath running past the college to the pit, accessed via the gated minor road north of Northmoor village.

Vicarage Pit A reserve managed by The Wildlife Trust for Berkshire, Buckinghamshire and Oxfordshire. View from the minor road between Stanton Harcourt and Hardwick (limited roadside parking) or from the hide in the southeast corner. This pit's ornithological interest has apparently declined in recent years.

Birds

Winter wildfowl include Goldeneye, Goosander, Ruddy Duck, Wigeon, Gadwall, Pintail (up to 70), Shoveler and Shelduck, and occasionally Red-crested Pochard (of unknown but presumably captive origin). The resident Canada Geese may be joined by feral/escaped Bar-headed, Snow, Greylag and Barnacle Geese. Cormorant is regular, and Black-necked and Slavonian Grebes reasonably frequent in winter. Large numbers of gulls use the adjacent tip and many spend time loafing on Dix Pit; there is also a large gull roost with similar species to Farmoor Reservoirs, with which there is considerable interchange (see p.270). In particular, Glaucous, Iceland and Mediterranean Gulls are occasionally recorded, and Yellow-legged Gull is regular in August and January. The surrounding fields and the dry pits hold large flocks of Lapwings, which are joined by a few Golden Plovers, and Common and Green Sandpipers occasionally overwinter. Raptors sometimes include Short-eared Owl or Merlin.

On passage a variety of waders is recorded, often including Greenshank and Ruff. Common, Arctic and Black Terns and Garganey also pass through, and Osprey is possible. Migrant passerines may include Wheatear, Whinchat and wagtails.

Breeders include Great Crested and Little Grebes, Grey Heron, Redshank, Black-headed Gull, Common Tern, Turtle Dove, Little and Barn Owls, Kingfisher, Sand Martin, Nightingale and Corn Bunting, and in summer Hobby often visits.

Information

Berkshire, Buckinghamshire and Oxfordshire Wildlife Trust, The Lodge, 1 Armstrong Road, Littlemore, Oxford OX4 4XT. Tel: 01865 775476. E-mail: bbowt@cix.co.uk

50 PORT MEADOW, OXFORD (Oxfordshire)   OS Landranger 164

Within walking distance of Oxford city centre, this area holds a variety of winter wildfowl and waders, and a few interesting migrants on spring passage.

Habitat

Common land owned by the City Council, the area is largely unimproved grazing meadows between the River Thames and Oxford Canal, and is prone to flood in winter.

Access (see map)

Access to Port Meadow is unrestricted but the area is best worked early in the day before birds are pushed off by disturbance.

1. Leave Oxford city centre north on Walton Street and, after c.½ mile, turn left into Walton Well Road and continue to the car park at the end. From here a surfaced track leads north to the end of Aristotle Lane. This is the best access point, especially when the area is flooded.

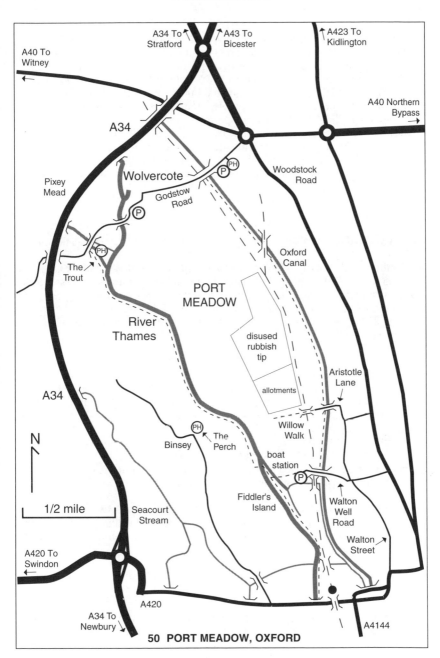

50 PORT MEADOW, OXFORD

2. Leave Oxford city centre north on Woodstock Road, turning west at the Wolvercote roundabout into Godstow Road. Park after c.1 mile on the left by the River Thames.

Continue on Godstow Road to the Trout pub and take the towpath south along the west bank of the Thames, which affords good views in times of flood, and is often best for waders.

Birds

Wintering wildfowl include up to 1,000 Wigeon as well as numbers of Teal, and smaller parties of Gadwall, Shoveler and Pintail. In cold weather Goldeneye and Goosander sometimes occur on the river. Small flocks of White-fronted Geese often winter, and there may be up to 4,000 Golden Plover, 2,000 Lapwing, 70 (1,000) Snipe, 40 Dunlin, ten Ruff and small numbers of Redshank. Many gulls use the area as a pre-roost. Other notable wintering species may include Water Rail, Grey Wagtail, Redpoll and Tree Sparrow.

On spring passage a few waders may occur, as well as Shelduck and occasionally Garganey. By autumn however, the meadow has largely dried out and is much less attractive, but Wheatear and Whinchat may pass through at either season.

Breeders in the area include Sparrowhawk, Cuckoo, Sedge Warbler and Tree Sparrow, and Hobby may visit.

51 OTMOOR (Oxfordshire)   OS Landranger 164

Just 7 miles northeast of Oxford, this area comprises the floodplain of the River Ray and in the 19th century held breeding Black Terns and Bitterns. Today, despite drainage, much is 'unimproved' and it still attracts wintering wildfowl and an interesting variety of breeding birds. Part of the area is an RSPB reserve covering 250 acres, and it is hoped that by regenerating extensive areas of reed Bitterns will return to the area.

Habitat

The area comprises a low-lying plain, once highly prone to flooding, drained by the River Ray. Most has now been converted to agriculture but Fowls Pill still has water year-round and can cover a large area in winter. There are large areas of unimproved grassland with some scrub, and some mature woodland at Noke Wood and the Spinney.

Access (see map)

There is, as yet, no organised access to the RSPB reserve but the entire area can be successfully explored using existing footpaths.

Fowls Pill From Beckley drive (or walk) north along the narrow road and park by the gate and right turn to the rifle range. Continue walking north towards Fowls Pill in the centre of the moor, but do not proceed beyond the gate onto the moor if red flags are flying.

Noke Wood Park in Beckley and follow the footpath past the church and then northwest through the wood.

Oddington Park at Oddington village green and walk east along Oddington Lane. On crossing the River Ray at the bridge either continue straight or turn south to follow the river.

Charlton-on-Otmoor Park in Charlton-on-Otmoor and, from the Crown pub, take Otmoor Lane southeast.

Birds

In winter the Fowls Pill area (and numerous ditches and dykes on Otmoor) attracts Teal, Wigeon, and occasionally small numbers of Gadwall, Pintail and

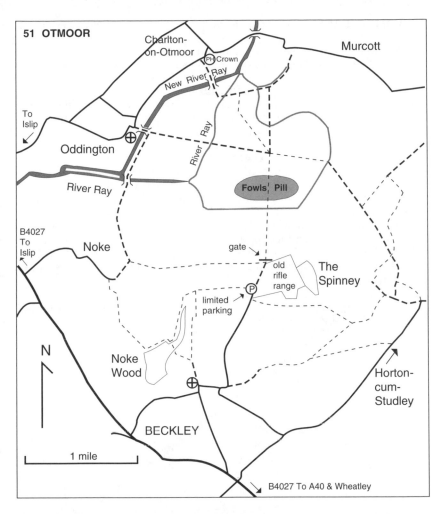

Shoveler. Waders include Snipe, Golden Plover and, sometimes, Jack Snipe or Woodcock, and look too for Water Rail. Sparrowhawk and Short-eared Owl are fairly frequent, and sometimes Hen Harrier or Merlin may be present. Look for Little Owl in the willows by the River Ray, and wintering passerines may include flocks of thrushes, finches, buntings and, sometimes, Stonechat.

On passage a variety of waders has been recorded. Look for Garganey and harriers in spring, while at both seasons Wheatear, Whinchat, Redstart and other passerine migrants may occur.

Breeders include Hobby, Curlew (most vocal at dawn and dusk), Snipe, Turtle Dove, Cuckoo, Kingfisher, all three woodpeckers, Yellow Wagtail, Sedge and Garden Warblers, Lesser Whitethroat, Willow Tit, Corn Bunting and, sometimes, Quail. There is a substantial population of Grasshopper Warblers and Nightingale also breeds.

Information

RSPB Site Manager, Neil Lambert, c/o Lower Farm, Noke, Oxford OX3 9TX. Tel: 01865 848385.

52 WILLEN LAKES (Buckinghamshire)   OS Landranger 152

Situated on the western outskirts of Milton Keynes, this site attracts a range of winter wildfowl, including Goosander, and a variety of passage waders.

Habitat
There are two lakes, separated by a road, the North Lake containing a large island that has a specially designed wader scrape on it. The surrounding area is open parkland with some shrubby areas.

Access (see map)
Leave the M1 southwest at junction 14 on the A509 towards Milton Keynes, turning north after c.1½ miles at the third roundabout onto V10 Brickhill Street and then taking the second turning on the right to the small car park by Willen Lake.

Alternatively, continue north along Brickhill Street and turn right onto H4 Dansteed Way. Turn right again into Millington Gate, go over the roundabout and turn right into Willen Gate, proceeding to the small car park by the North Lake. Footpaths encircle both lakes, but the wader scrape is best viewed from the hide near the weir between the lakes, and the North Lake is generally most productive.

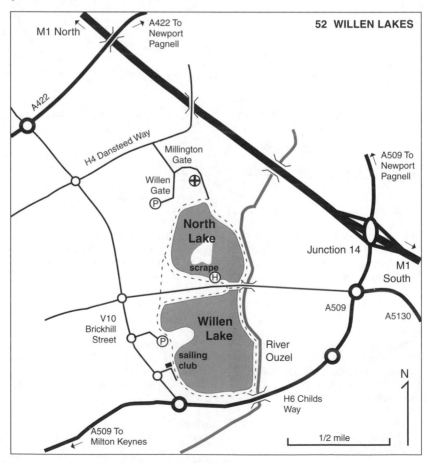

Birds
Wintering wildfowl include Wigeon, Teal, Shoveler, Pintail, Pochard and up to 30 Goldeneye, while small numbers of Goosander are regular. Other waterfowl include Cormorant, divers, rarer grebes, sea duck, and Whooper and Bewick's Swans are occasional visitors. There is a notable gull roost, and among the commoner species one or two Mediterranean Gulls are regular, and Iceland and Glaucous Gulls have been recorded. In late winter and early spring Kittiwake may also appear in the roost. Other notable winterers include Snipe, and occasionally Jack Snipe or Short-eared Owl.

In spring, flocks of Common, Arctic and Black Terns and Little Gulls may pass through. On both spring and autumn passage a variety of waders has been recorded, including the more usual Oystercatcher, Ruff, Dunlin, Green and Common Sandpipers and Ruff, while Grey Plover, Turnstone, Curlew, Whimbrel, Black-tailed Godwit, Knot, Sanderling, Curlew Sandpiper and Little Stint are also regular, especially in autumn and, unusually, some of these have been recorded in small flocks, while the scarce Temminck's Stint is almost annual. Among passerines, Rock and Water Pipits, Yellow and White Wagtails, Wheatear and Whinchat are regular. Scarce passage migrants include Osprey, Common Scoter, Garganey, Mandarin, Ring Ouzel, Redstart and Black Redstart.

Breeding birds include Little and Great Crested Grebes, Sparrowhawk, Ringed and Little Ringed Plovers, Redshank and Sedge Warbler, and a Hobby occasionally visits, especially on late spring and summer evenings. Gadwall has bred, and Black-winged Stilt attempted to breed in 1993.

53 LITTLE BRICKHILL (Bedfordshire/Buckinghamshire) OS Landranger 165

The speciality of this site is the introduced Lady Amherst's Pheasant, with winter and early spring the best times to visit.

Habitat
Mixed woodland with stands of oak, chestnut and larch.

Access (see map)
Leave the A5 dual carriageway at Little Brickhill roundabout east on the minor road to Woburn, forking right after c.½ mile to park after a further ½ mile in the small lay-by on the left-hand side by the Bedfordshire/ Buckinghamshire county

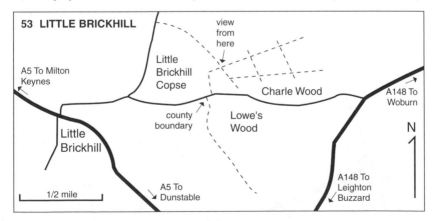

boundary sign (or on the roadside just to the west). Follow the public footpath north into Charle Wood uphill for c.400 yards, bearing right to an obvious meeting place of two broad rides. The best tactic is to wait quietly here for the pheasants to emerge on these rides (or in the ride which runs parallel a little to the south); a mounted telescope is useful. The rhododendron scrub by the road itself is also worth checking.

Birds
Lady Amherst's Pheasant is most easily seen early and late in the day. In addition, these woods hold Woodcock, Grasshopper Warbler and occasionally Redstart and Wood Warbler.

54 BROGBOROUGH LAKE (Bedfordshire)   OS Landranger 153

This relatively small lake between Milton Keynes and Bedford holds a large winter gull roost, notable for being one of the few regular localities for 'white-winged' gulls in the Home Counties.

Habitat
This deep, largely steep-sided flooded clay pit, is screened by a line of poplars to the north, while elsewhere there are extensive areas of scrub with a small

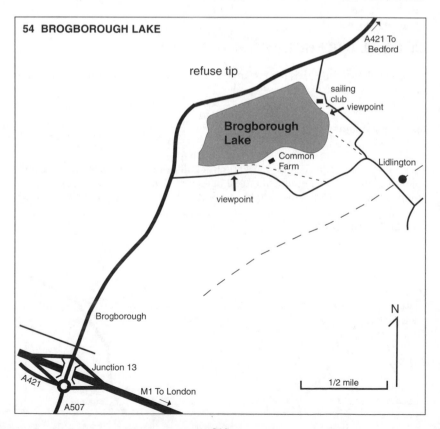

54 BROGBOROUGH LAKE

A421 To Bedford

refuse tip

sailing club
viewpoint

Brogborough Lake

Common Farm

Lidlington

viewpoint

Brogborough

Junction 13

A421

M1 To London

A507

N

1/2 mile

stands of reeds in the south corner. The lake is disturbed by windsurfing and fishing.

Access (see map)

Leave the M1 north at junction 13 on the A421 towards Bedford. After c.1½ miles turn right on the minor road to Lidlington. There is access to the lake shore along a public footpath at one point along the south shore, and the gull roost is best viewed at the southwest end of the lake from this minor road, where there is a convenient gap in the hedge. The east end of the lake can be seen from the short footpath just south of the sailing clubhouse.

Birds

The principal attraction in winter is the large gull roost, which holds significant numbers of Black-headed, Common, Herring and Lesser Blackbacked Gulls, together with Great Black-backed Gull. Among rarer species, Mediterranean and Yellow-legged Gulls are regular in very small numbers in autumn and winter, with a few Iceland and Glaucous Gulls in the latter period, and Kittiwake is possible in late winter and early spring. Wintering wildfowl include numbers of Pochard and up to 30 Goldeneye. Other waterfowl include Great Crested Grebe and up to 30 Cormorants (which roost on the island). The rarer grebes (especially Red-necked), sawbills and sea duck are occasional. Other notable winter visitors include Water Rails, and a few Corn Buntings roost in the reeds.

On spring passage, Common Scoter, Arctic and Black Terns and Little Gull may pause briefly, and migrant passerines can include Yellow Wagtail and Grasshopper and Sedge Warblers. Terns also pass through in autumn, but the banks are too steep to attract many waders.

Breeders include Shelduck, Ruddy Duck, Common Tern, Turtle Dove, Cuckoo, Kingfisher and Reed Warbler, and Hobby is a fairly frequent visitor.

55 PRIORY COUNTRY PARK (Bedfordshire)   OS Landranger 153

Close to Bedford town centre, this site attracts a range of wintering wildfowl and a variety of passage migrants.

Habitat

Comprising 90 acres and bordered to the south and east by the River Great Ouse, the Country Park contains a large (62-acre) disused gravel pit fringed by reeds and willows, while immediately to the northeast of the main lake are Finger Lakes, a pair of small overgrown pits. Elsewhere there are plantations of deciduous trees and areas of grassland, which at Fenlake and near the sewage works to the east may flood in winter.

Access (see map)

Being so close to an urban area and used for a variety of outdoor activities, the Country Park is prone to disturbance, especially at weekends. Early mornings are generally best.

Main Entrance Leave Bedford town centre east on the A428 (towards the A1 and Huntingdon) and, after 1 mile, turn south on the A418. After ½ mile, at the playing fields, turn east into Barkers Lane. The entrance to the Country Park car park is on the right after ½ mile. There is a visitor centre near the car park, and from here footpaths circuit the lakes and access two hides.

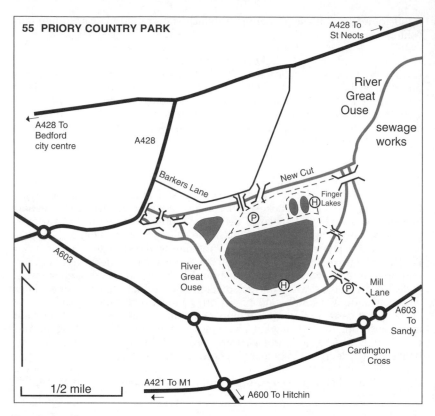

Southern Entrance Leave Bedford town centre east on the A6003 (towards Sandy) and, after 2 miles, turn north at the double roundabout into Mill Lane and continue to the car park. From here, footpaths lead to the lakes.

Birds

Wintering wildfowl include Wigeon, Teal, Gadwall, Shoveler, Pochard, small numbers of Goldeneye and occasionally Shelduck, Pintail, sawbills or Ruddy Duck. Other notable wintering species include Cormorant, Water Rail and Snipe.

On passage a variety of waders may pass through, but due to the lack of habitat, many simply fly over, with Little Ringed Plover, Greenshank and Common and Green Sandpipers among the more regular, with the best variety recorded in spring. Also, particularly in spring, Osprey occasionally occurs and parties of Common, Arctic and Black Terns and Little Gull may pass through. Other migrants include Grey, White and Yellow Wagtails, Whinchat, Wheatear, and occasional Shelduck, Jack Snipe, Kittiwake and Water Pipit in early spring.

Breeders include Great Crested and Little Grebes, Kingfisher, Cuckoo, Lesser Spotted Woodpecker, Nightingale (around Finger Lakes), Reed, Sedge and Garden Warblers, and Spotted Flycatcher. Hobbies may also visit, especially on summer evenings.

Information

Errol Newman, Warden's Office, Visitor Centre, Priory Country Park, Barkers Lane, Bedford MK41 9SH. Tel: 01234 211182.

56 HARROLD ODELL COUNTRY PARK (Bedfordshire) OS Landranger 153

Around 7 miles northwest of Bedford, this series of gravel pits and associated habitats holds an interesting variety of species and is worth visiting year-round.

Habitat

Centred around a series of abandoned gravel pits beside the River Great Ouse, the 144-acre park also includes riverside meadows and riparian willows and alders. At the east end of the main lake there is an interesting area of reeds and willow carr, while part of a specially created island is regularly cleared of vegetation to attract passage waders.

Access (see map)

Just north of Bedford leave the A6 west on minor roads to Oakley, and continue via Pavenham and Carlton towards Odell. Just south of Harrold the road crosses the River Great Ouse, and the entrance to the country park is on the right after 100 yards. There is an information centre at the car park and the main lake is circumnavigated by a footpath, with a hide on the south shore, and side paths to the river and reedbeds.

Birds

Wintering wildfowl include up to 300 Wigeon, Teal, Shoveler, Gadwall, Pochard, Goldeneye, small numbers of Goosander and occasionally Smew, as well as feral

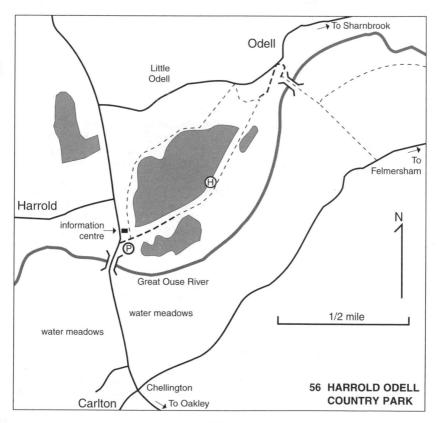

56 HARROLD ODELL COUNTRY PARK

Canada and Greylag Geese, while parties of Bewick's Swans may pass through in November. Other notable winter visitors include Water Rail, Snipe, Grey Wagtail, Siskin and Redpoll in the riverside trees, and sometimes Stonechat. Bittern and Bearded Tit are occasionally recorded.

On passage small numbers of common waders are regular, including Little Ringed Plover, Dunlin and Common Sandpiper and, especially in May, occasionally Turnstone and Sanderling, with Curlew, Whimbrel, Greenshank, Green Sandpiper and Ruff more likely in autumn. Common, Arctic and Black Terns are also possible, especially in late April and May. Black-necked Grebes may pass through in late summer and autumn. Migrant passerines can include White Wagtail and Wheatear.

Breeders include Little and Great Crested Grebe, Sparrowhawk, Ringed Plover, Redshank, Common Tern (on purpose-built rafts), Grey and Yellow Wagtails, Reed and Sedge Warblers, and Willow Tit. Hobby is a regular visitor, especially on late summer evenings.

Information
Bill Thwaites, Harrold Odell Country Park, Carlton Road, Harrold, Bedford MK44 7DS. Tel. 01234 720016.

57 THE LODGE (Bedfordshire)   OS Landranger 153

The Lodge is the headquarters of the RSPB and is surrounded by an area of partially wooded heathland with a good range of common birds.

Habitat
The Lodge is located on relict heathland, once part of Sandy Warren. Some is still heath, but much has developed into secondary woodland or is plantation. Two ponds have been established, and The Lodge itself is surrounded by formal gardens.

Access
Leave Sandy on the B1042 towards Cambridge and turn right into the car park after 1½ miles. From here a series of well-marked trails permit exploration of the area, and there is a hide. The reserve is open from dawn until dusk, and the shop is open 09.00–17.00 on weekdays and 10.00–17.00 on weekends.

Birds
Resident species include Sparrowhawk, Woodcock, Tawny Owl, all three woodpeckers and Nuthatch. In summer these are joined by Cuckoo, Turtle Dove, Tree Pipit, Garden Warbler, Lesser Whitethroat and Spotted Flycatcher. In winter Brambling, Siskin and Redpoll may occur, and Crossbill and Hawfinch are occasional visitors.

Information
RSPB, The Lodge, Sandy, Bedfordshire SG19 2DL. Tel: 01767 680551.

58 TRING RESERVOIRS (Hertfordshire)   OS Landranger 165

Lying northwest of Tring, this complex of four reservoirs has a long ornithological history and, with a fine range of habitats, attracts interesting birds throughout the year.

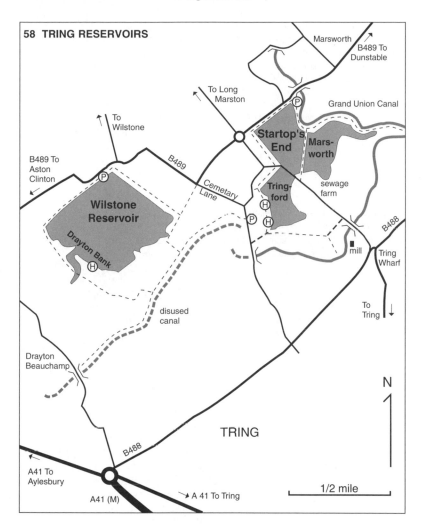

58 TRING RESERVOIRS

Marsworth

B489 To Dunstable

To Long Marston

Grand Union Canal

To Wilstone

Startop's End

Mars-worth

B489 To Aston Clinton

B489

Cemetary Lane

Tring-ford

sewage farm

Wilstone Reservoir

Drayton Bank

mill

B488

Tring Wharf

disused canal

To Tring

Drayton Beauchamp

N

TRING

B488

A41 To Aylesbury

A41 (M)

A 41 To Tring

1/2 mile

Habitat

The reservoirs were built in the 19th century as canal feeders. Wilstone is the largest and has concrete banks to the north and natural banks to the south, with substantial stands of woodland along the water's edge and a marsh and damp meadow at the extreme south tip. To the east, the rather smaller Tringford has natural banks bordered by meadows and, in the south sector, woodland. Stantop's End and Marsworth also have largely natural banks, with a substantial reedbed at Marsworth, while to the east of these is a sewage farm which can be interesting at times. The reservoirs are managed by Friends of Tring Reservoirs.

Access (see map)

Wilstone Reservoir Leave the A41 north at Aston Clinton on the B489 towards Dunstable, parking on the right after c.2½ miles in the small car park by the reservoir embankment (note, the area has a bad reputation for car crime). Take the path onto the bank, walking right to reach Drayton Bank and the hide (the footpath continues and it is possible to circuit the reservoir via the disused canal). Alternatively, continue along the B489 and after a further ½ mile continue straight at the sharp left-hand bend into Cemetery Lane, parking in the large car park on the left after ¼ mile. From here cross the road and follow the footpath across the field to a stile and then turn right to the reservoir bank.

Startop's End and Marsworth Reservoirs Continue on the B489 and park on the right in the pay-and-display car park just before the Grand Union Canal. From here footpaths run along the north and west shores, and east shore of Startop's End, with a lane connecting them (making it possible to undertake a circular walk); the track along the east shore also affords views over Marsworth Reservoir.

Tringford Reservoir A footpath runs along the west and south shores and accesses two hides, accessible either from the large car park on Cemetery Lane or from the lane which separates Tringford and Startop's End (take the footpath through the wood to the hides).

Birds
Wintering wildfowl include small numbers of Wigeon, Shoveler, Gadwall, Teal, Pochard, Goldeneye and Ruddy Duck, and occasionally Goosander, Smew and sea duck. There is a large gull roost, which mainly comprises Black-headed Gulls with a scattering of Lesser Blackbacked Gulls. 'White-winged' gulls are rare, but Mediterranean Gull is sometimes recorded, and Kittiwake is possible, especially in late winter and early spring. Other notable wintering species include Corn Bunting, which roosts in the reeds, Siskin, Redpoll, Chiffchaff, Blackcap, Common and Jack Snipes (especially at the sewage farm), and occasionally Bearded Tit or Bittern, which if present are best looked for at dawn and dusk flying between the reedbeds at Marsworth and Wilstone.

On spring passage small numbers of waders pass through, including Curlew, Common and Green Sandpipers, Redshank and Dunlin, and other migrants may include Shelduck, Common Scoter, flocks of Common, Arctic and Black Terns and Little Gull, White and Yellow Wagtails, Whinchat, Wheatear, and occasionally Garganey and Osprey. In autumn a greater variety of waders is possible, with Greenshank, Ruff, Curlew Sandpiper and Little Stint more likely than in spring, and Black-necked Grebe is occasionally recorded.

Breeders include Great Crested and Little Grebes, Grey Heron, Ruddy Duck, Gadwall, Pochard, Sparrowhawk, Water Rail, Little Owl, Kingfisher, Reed and Sedge Warblers, and Willow Tit. Hobby is a regular visitor on spring and summer evenings. The reservoirs are famous as the site of England's first breeding Black-necked Grebes (1919) and Britain's first breeding Little Ringed Plovers (1938).

Information
Friends of Tring Reservoirs, Rob Young, Falcon House, 28 Tring Road, Long Marston, Hertfordshire HP23 4QL.
British Waterways, Watery Lane, Marsworth, Tring, Hertfordshire HP23 4LZ. Tel: 01442 825938. Internet: www.tringreservoirs.btinternet.co.uk

59 RYE HOUSE MARSH (Hertfordshire) OS Landranger 166

Lying east of Hoddesdon, the Rye Meads area contains a variety of wetland habitats and is notable for regular wintering Bitterns and breeding Common Terns. A small portion forms the RSPB's Rye House Marsh reserve and other areas are managed by the Hertfordshire and Middlesex Wildlife Trust (HMWT).

Habitat

A complex of wet meadows, carr woodland and reedbeds has been supplemented with specially constructed scrapes, while a large part of the area is occupied by sewage treatment ponds.

Access

Rye House Marsh RSPB and HMWT reserves From the A414 northeast of Hoddesdon turn south on Toll Road towards Rye Park and Hoddesdon. Shortly before Rye House railway station turn north into the RSPB car park (there is also a car park on the south side of the road here). Alternatively, turn east off the A10 in Hoddesdon and follow signs for Rye Park into Rye Road. Pass Rye House railway station, cross the River Lea and park on the left. The reserve and visitor centre are open daily 10.00–17.00 (except Christmas and Boxing Days). There is free access to the Ashby hide from the car park, but access to the rest of the RSPB reserve (four additional hides) and the HMWT reserve (one hide) attracts a charge to non-members of these organisations.

South Lagoons Access to the pools south of Toll Road is possible through the Rye Meads Ringing Group (details in their annual report, available at the RSPB visitor centre). A ringing hut is manned most weekends, from where permission may be sought to explore these lagoons.

Birds

In winter small numbers of Water Rails are present—best looked for from the hides, as is Bittern. Both are very secretive, but with patience may show well. Water Pipit, Green Sandpiper and Common and Jack Snipes also winter, and may be found by careful scrutiny of the water's edge. Other winterers include Cormorant (on the North Lagoons), Pochard, Shoveler, Teal and Grey Wagtail, with Siskin and Redpoll in alders. Stonechat and Beaded Tit are irregular visitors.

On passage small numbers of Little Ringed Plover, Greenshank, Common and Green Sandpipers, Yellow Wagtail, Whinchat and Wheatear may pass through, with occasional Garganey and Pintail in late summer.

Breeders include Gadwall, Common Tern (which use specially constructed rafts) Turtle Dove, Kingfisher, and nine species of warbler including Grasshopper, Sedge and Reed Warblers. Hobby is regular and Cetti's Warbler has bred.

Information

RSPB Rye House Marsh, Rye Meads Sewage Treatment Works, Stanstead Abbotts, Hertfordshire SG12 8JY. Tel: 01279 793720.

HMWT, Grebe House, St Michael's Street, St Albans, Herts. AL3 4SN. Tel: 01727 858901. E-mail: info@hmwt.org.uk

60 LEE VALLEY PARK (Hertfordshire)

The River Lee Country Park is one of 5 sites that make up Lee Valley Park. These flooded gravel pits close to London form an important refuge for many species, especially wildfowl, and are part of an important series of wetlands which includes Rye House Marsh to the north (Site 59). However, the park's main claim to fame is its Bittern Watchpoint. In the last few years, this site has become the most reliable place in Britain to see this elusive species, and not just fleeting flight views either. Here, you can see Bitterns on the ground.

Habitat
The park is a complex of open water, wooded islands, reedbeds and marshy areas.

Access
From Waltham Abbey, close to junction 26 of the M25, take the B194 north for 1½ miles. Turn left into Stubbins Hall Lane and Fishers Green car park is on the left. The Bittern Watchpoint is close to the entrance and is open daily, free of charge. Other hides are free at weekends, but require permits at other times (purchased from Lee Valley Park Information Centre).

Birds
Bittern is the star attraction, but a good variety of other wetland species can also be seen here.

Information
Lee Valley Park Information Centre, Abbey Gardens, Waltham Abbey, Essex EN9 1XQ. Tel: 01992 702200. E-mail: info@leevalleypark.org.uk

WALES

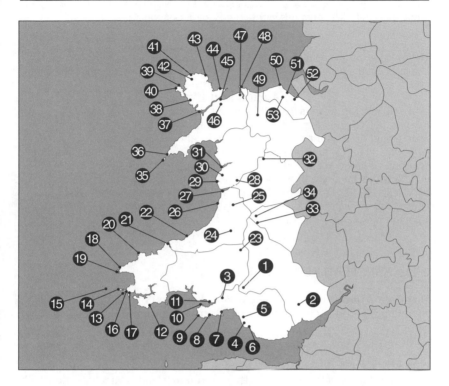

1 FFOREST FAWR (Breconshire)   OS Landranger 160

This largely afforested upland area is excellent for Nightjar, which is best looked for in June–July. The area lies within the Brecon Beacons NP.

Habitat

The area lies on the south flank of the Brecon Beacons and comprises very large blocks of conifer plantations, interspersed with clear-fell and newly replanted zones.

Access and Birds

Leave Neath northwest on the A465 and, after c.10 miles, turn north at Glyn-neath onto the A4109 and after 4 miles fork right onto the A4221, turning right (north) after 1 mile on a minor road into Coelbren. After 300 yards turn right at the T-junction and follow this road for ⅔ mile through the village. At the end turn right at another T-junction and then fork left, following a minor road east for c.4 miles, initially along the north fringe of the forest and then north through the forest, to park at SN 907139. From here follow the footpath for 1½ miles northwest towards Pant Mawr. Nightjar can be seen in this area around the clearings and on the adjacent moorland.

2 LLANDEGFEDD RESERVOIR (Gwent)   OS Landranger 171

This large reservoir is immediately east of Pontypool and attracts numbers of wintering wildfowl, including Bewick's Swan, with the possibility of divers, rarer grebes or sea ducks.

Habitat

Built in 1964, the drinking-water reservoir covers c.400 acres. It is fed by Sor Brook, a tributary of the River Usk. The surrounding land is largely farmed, with some woodland on the ridges, which fringe the reservoir to the east and west.

Access (see map)

Leave Pontypool north on the A4042. There is a hide.

Birds

Wintering wildfowl include large numbers of Wigeon, Teal and Pochard, as well as Goldeneye and Ruddy Duck, and Bewick's Swan and Goosander regularly use the reservoir as a roost, the swans feeding by day on Olway Meadows and the Goosanders probably coming from the River Usk. Divers and rarer grebes are occasional visitors, as are sea duck (notably Long-tailed Duck). Numbers of Common, Herring and Black-headed Gulls roost, and Siskin and Redpoll occur in the waterside trees. Residents include Great Crested Grebe, Sparrowhawk and Buzzard, while Cormorant and Grey Heron are regular visitors, and Merlin, Peregrine and Goshawk have been recorded.

On passage a variety of waders pass through, with Ringed and Little Ringed Plovers, Oystercatcher and Common and Green Sandpipers being among the more likely. Other migrants have included Osprey and Hobby. Breeding summer visitors include Yellow Wagtail.

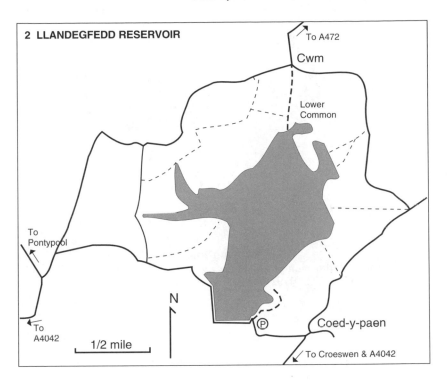

2 LLANDEGFEDD RESERVOIR

To A472

Cwm

Lower
Common

To
Pontypool

To
A4042

N

1/2 mile

Coed-y-paen

To Croeswen & A4042

3 CWM CLYDACH (Gower)   OS Landranger 159

Lying just 7 miles north of the centre of Swansea, this woodland reserve holds a typical range of Welsh species, and is best visited in May–June.

Habitat
Oak woodland with some stands of birch and beech, and ash and alder on damper ground along the Afon Clydach. Slopes above the woodland have areas of heather and bracken.

Access
Leave the M4 north at junction 45 on the A4067 and, after c.1⅔ miles, turn left (west) at the crossroads in the centre of Clydach on a minor road. The reserve car park is adjacent to the New Inn pub in Craig-cefn-Parc after 2 miles. The reserve is open at all times, with access along the signed path by the river. (By following the road for another c.3 miles past the upper car park, higher ground can be accessed, with a picnic site overlooking Lliw Reservoirs.)

Birds
Breeders include Sparrowhawk, Buzzard, Tawny Owl, all three woodpeckers, Redstart, Wood and Garden Warblers, Pied and Spotted Flycatchers, Nuthatch, Treecreeper and Raven, with Tree Pipit, Whinchat and Wheatear at the woodland edges and on open ground above it, and Dipper and Grey Wagtail along streams. Winter is typically quiet, but visitors may include Woodcock, Kingfisher, Siskin and Redpoll.

Dipper

Information

RSPB Warden: Martin Humphreys, 2 Tyn y Berllan, Craig Cefn Par, Clydach, Swansea SA6 5TL. Tel: 01792 842927.

4 KENFIG (Glamorgan)   OS Landranger 170

Kenfig, north of Porthcawl, has a variety of habitats attracting a range of wildfowl, raptors and waders in winter and on passage. The area is a NNR and a Special Area of Conservation (under the EU Habitats Directive).

Habitat

Kenfig Pool is a natural 70-acre dune-slack lake, surrounded by areas of reeds and sallows and set within c.1,200 acres of dunes (both mobile and fixed), with areas of wet dune-slack between them. The reserve is flanked on the seaward side by Kenfig Sands. At Sker Point there is a small area of rocky shore and the tiny Sker Pool attracts waders, especially after bad weather.

Access (see map)

Leave the M4 at junction 37 (Pyle) south on to the A4229 towards Porthcawl. After ½ mile turn north (right) on the B4283, under the motorway and through Cornelly past the Greenacre pub. After c.1 mile turn west (left, signed to the reserve) at the crossroads, on a minor road over the motorway, past the Angel pub, and straight on for ½ mile to the car park. The reserve centre is open Monday–Friday 14.00–16.30, weekends and Bank Holidays at least 10.00–16.30. The reserve is managed by Bridgend County Borough Council and there are no restrictions on access, except to the reedbeds on the west shore during the breeding season (March–July). Otherwise it is possible to walk around the pool and there are two hides (always open), one at the southwest corner of the pool and the other on the north shore, approached via a 100-yard boardwalk through the reedbed from the north inlet (reached via a track that starts at the bus shelter on the road near the Prince of Wales Inn, and convenient for those arriving by bus from Porthcawl/Bridgend). Sker Point is reached by walking though the dunes from the car park.

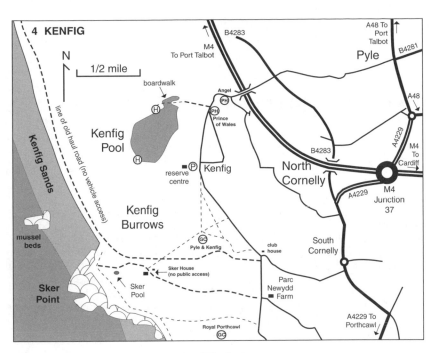

Birds

Winter wildfowl include Teal and Pochard, usually smaller numbers of Wigeon, Shoveler, Gadwall (up to 80) and Goldeneye, and occasionally Smew, Scaup and Long-tailed Duck. Numbers, especially those of diving ducks, increase when near-by Eglwys Nunydd Reservoir is disturbed by water sports (most likely at weekends). Divers, rarer grebes and Whooper and Bewick's Swans are irregular. Around the pool there are often Water Rail, Jack Snipe, a few Chiffchaffs and, much less frequently, Cetti's Warbler. Merlin and Peregrine may hunt over the area, and occasionally Hen Harrier and Short-eared Owl are recorded. In the fields at Sker Farm there are usually several hundred Golden Plovers. On the beach and rocks at Sker Point are Grey Plover, Sanderling, Purple Sandpiper and Turnstone.

Breeders include Great Crested Grebe, Oystercatcher, Ringed Plover, Snipe and Redshank, with Stonechat and Grasshopper Warbler in rough vegetation in the dunes, and Reed and Sedge Warblers around the pool. Teal occasionally breeds, and Shoveler, Garganey and Ruddy Duck have also nested.

Purple Heron has occurred several times in spring and Bittern in late autumn, especially after east winds or cold weather. Passage also occasionally brings Garganey and Scaup to the pool. Waders occur on both Kenfig and Sker Pools and the beach; the range of habitats means that a good variety is often present. Notable are relatively large numbers of Whimbrel in both spring and autumn. Common, Sandwich and Black Terns are regular migrants, but Arctic and Little Terns and Little Gull are less frequent. Small numbers of passerine migrants occur, and Aquatic Warbler has been recorded several times in August–September. Seawatching from Sker Point can be worthwhile, although there is no shelter. In May–August on a rising tide in early morning, Manx Shearwater, Fulmar, Gannet and Common Scoter can be seen, the latter two mainly in late summer, when there are also occasionally Great or Arctic Skuas. A west wind is likely to push birds inshore and produce the best views. In September, gales can produce occasional Storm or even Leach's Petrels.

Information
Warden: David Carrington, Kenfig Reserve Centre, Ton Kenfig, Pyle, Bridgend CF33 4PT. Tel: 01656 743386. E-mail: carridg@bridgend.gov.uk

5 EGLWYS NUNYDD RESERVOIR
(Glamorgan)   OS Landranger 170

This concrete-banked water covers 200 acres and attracts a range of waterfowl in winter.

Access
Leave the M4 at junction 38 and, from the roundabout, take the lane past the British Oxygen Company works to the reservoir. Parking is, strictly speaking, not permitted inside the gates (your car may be locked in) but most birders do so and rely on anglers or sailors to unlock the gate in the event that it is closed (*bona fide* birdwatchers have not been challenged); otherwise enter on foot through the same gate.

Birds
In winter the commoner ducks are frequently joined by divers, grebes, Goosander and sea duck. There are few waders on passage, but Common and Arctic Terns and Little Gull are quite frequently seen.

Information
Steve Moon, Glamorgan Bird Club. Tel: 01656 643170 or contact Kenfig Reserve Centre (see above).

6 OGMORE ESTUARY (Glamorgan)   OS Landranger 170

This relatively small estuary, tucked away to the east of Porthcawl, holds large numbers of wintering waders and gulls, which regularly include scarcer species such as Mediterranean, Iceland and Ring-billed Gulls.

Habitat
To the south of the river mouth the coast is flanked by low rocky cliffs at Ogmore-by-Sea, but to the north it is guarded by the extensive dune system of Merthyr Mawr Burrows (which, with Kenfig Dunes, is a Special Area of Conservation under the EU Habitats Directive). Upstream, there are stands of woodland towards Merthyr Mawr.

Access (see map)
Leave the A48 c.3 miles southeast of Bridgend west on the B4524 to Ewenny (or take the B4265 south to Ewenny c.½ mile east of Bridgend) and then follow the B4524 southwest to Ogmore-by-Sea.

Portobello Island Two miles beyond Ewenny (and c.1 mile before reaching the coast) pull off the road onto the grassy area on the right (by the bye-laws sign, near Portobello House). From here walk northeast along the river to view Portobello Island, a good area for roosting gulls and waders, and also for wintering Water Pipit.

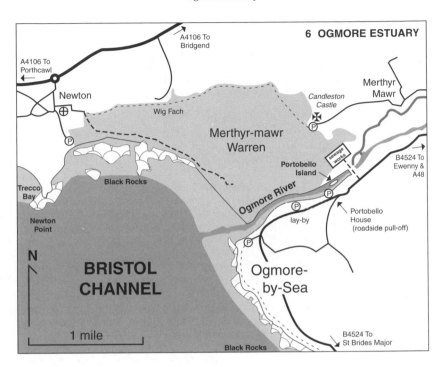

Ogmore River Continue towards Ogmore-by-Sea on the B4524 and park in the pull-in on the right after c.½ mile. This offers views of the river channel, with Goldeneye and other ducks possible in winter.

Ogmore-by-Sea Continue towards the sea and park in the car park just north of the village. This offers good views of the river mouth and the area of saltmarsh on the north shore. It is also possible to follow the coastal footpath south from here, with resident Rock Pipit, Wheatear on passage, a chance of Peregrine and Chough (which sometimes forage on the short turf at the north end of the car park) and, in winter, occasional Snow Bunting.

Newton, Porthcawl Alternative access to the estuary is from the north, along the coast from the car park in Beach Road, Newton.

Birds
The estuary supports huge numbers of gulls and careful checking regularly produces Mediterranean Gull, with Ring-billed Gull also possible; the gulls roost at Portobello Island. Wintering waders include Turnstone, Ringed Plover, Sanderling, Dunlin and Redshank, with especially large numbers of Oystercatcher. Wildfowl often include Goldeneye on the river channel, and sometimes Scaup, Red-breasted Merganser or Smew.

On passage a variety of waders occurs, including Whimbrel, Black-tailed Godwit, Greenshank, Green Sandpiper and, in spring, Little Ringed Plover and occasionally also Wood Sandpiper. Wheatear also occurs.

Breeding birds in the area include Shelduck, Redshank, Rock Pipit, Stonechat and (in 1998) Wheatear.

7 BLACKPILL (Gower)

Blackpill lies immediately west of Swansea. The beach is similar to hundreds of others but, since Britain's first Ring-billed Gull was found here in 1973, the species has occurred regularly, together with small numbers of Mediterranean Gull. February–April is probably the best period to visit.

Habitat

Blackpill is the last part of the shore of Swansea Bay to be covered at high tide. Clyne Stream runs out across the beach and provides birds with bathing facilities, while roosting gulls use the sand bar, sea and beach.

Access

Leave Swansea on the A4067. The road runs beside the beach and the best place to watch from is the boating pool, between the Clyne and the B4436 turning. The period around high tide is usually the most productive on neap tides; an earlier arrival is desirable on 'spring' tides.

Birds

The high-tide gull roost, often of several thousand birds, consists mainly of Black-headed and Common Gulls, but each year four or five Ring-billed Gulls are recorded, most frequently in February–April, and often stay for long periods. Mediterranean Gull is commoner and may be found at any time, though early spring to July is best. Iceland and Glaucous Gulls are sometimes recorded in winter, and Kittiwake also occurs. The usual waders are present at Blackpill, which is used as a roost, including Grey Plover and Sanderlings. On the sea there are occasionally divers or sea duck (Eider, Common and Velvet Scoters, Red-breasted Merganser and Goldeneye are possible), and a Peregrine is often present.

Little Tern occurs in spring and late summer, and Little Gull is regular in March–June. Small numbers of Curlew Sandpiper are frequent in autumn; other possibilities include Little Stint and Black-tailed Godwit, and there is a notable concentration of up to 500 Sanderlings. Offshore in late summer and autumn there are sometimes a few skuas and small numbers of terns, which may include Black Tern.

8 OXWICH (Gower)

Oxwich Bay, on the south shore of the Gower Peninsula, is a NNR. An excellent range of habitats attracts an appropriate diversity of birds, and a visit is worthwhile at any time, especially in spring and summer.

Habitat

Two miles of sandy beach are backed by dunes and bordered to the north and south by limestone cliffs. Nicholaston Pill flows across the beach attracting roosting gulls and waders. Behind the dunes are freshwater marshes with areas of open water, c.100 acres of reedbeds, and alder and willow carr. The small saltmarsh is rather dry and consequently unattractive to birds. To the north and south, Nicholaston and Oxwich Woods are both largely deciduous.

Access (see map)

Oxwich village is on a minor road south off the A4118; good views of the marsh are possible from this road. The reserve is managed by the Countryside Council

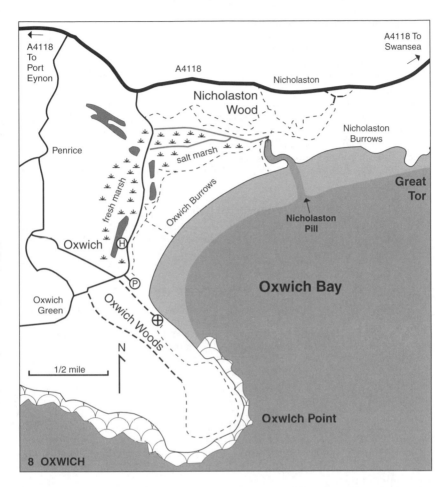

for Wales and there is open access to the dunes and beach, and marked paths in Nicholaston and Oxwich Woods (the lower path in the former has good views of the marsh). The freshwater marsh and carr are closed to casual visitors, though there is a hide and marsh tower affording good views over two sections of the area. A suggested route is to park at the car park, walk along the beach, over Nicholaston Pill, through Nicholaston Wood to the road, and back along it through the marsh to the car park. The latter is a good vantage point from which to scan the Bay, especially the sheltered area in the lee of the headland. Oxwich Point also has views of the Bay and can be reached by following the footpath southeast from the village past the church and through Oxwich Wood.

Birds

In winter there are sometimes Great Northern Diver or Common Scoter offshore, and on the marsh occasionally Gadwall or Shoveler. Green Sandpiper may winter, and there is occasionally a Bittern, especially in early spring. Turnstone and Purple Sandpiper frequent the rocks and Sanderling the beach. Mediterranean, Glaucous and Iceland Gulls are occasionally found in the gull roost. Kingfisher and Grey Wagtail are regular. The woodland and carr sometimes have Siskin and Redpoll, and often Woodcock, Blackcap, Chiffchaff and Firecrest.

Garganey and Marsh Harrier are occasional spring visitors, and Purple Heron has been recorded several times, while more regular migrants include Common and Sandwich Terns. Offshore, Fulmar, Manx Shearwater, Gannet, Shag and Common Scoter may appear in spring and summer. Osprey has been recorded in autumn, and Hobby may appear on late-summer evenings, hunting roosting hirundines.

Breeding birds on the marsh include Little Grebe, Shelduck, Teal, Pochard and Water Rail. Several hundred pairs of Reed Warblers are joined by Sedge and Grasshopper Warblers. Bearded Tit bred in the 1970s and 1980s, but is now merely an irregular winter visitor. Cetti's Warbler is the most recent colonist, though more difficult to see. The woods have Buzzard, a heronry (Penrice Woods), Sparrowhawk, all three woodpeckers, Nuthatch, Treecreeper and Marsh and Willow Tits.

Information

Countryside Council for Wales, RVB House, Llys Felin Newydd, Phoenix Way, Swansea Enterprise Park, Llansamlet, Swansea SA7 9FG. Tel: 01792 763500.

9 GOWER COAST NNR AND WORMS HEAD

(Gower) OS Landranger 159

Between Worms Head and Port Eynon Point c.7 miles of coast are managed by the Countryside Council for Wales (CCW), Glamorgan Wildlife Trust and NT. Approximately 100 acres of cliff around the Worm form the NNR proper. The entire area provides fine clifftop walking, but the real attractions are Worms Head in late April–July for breeding seabirds, and Port Eynon Point for summer and autumn seawatching.

Habitat

Worms Head is a mile-long grass-topped promontory at the southwest tip of the Gower Peninsula that is separated from the mainland at high tide. The adjacent coast has areas of scrub along the cliffs, terminating at Port Eynon Point, Gower's southernmost point.

Access (see map)

Worms Head Park in the large car park in Rhossili and walk c.1 mile along the clifftop path to the disused coastguard's lookout (now a summer information kiosk) overlooking the Head. The rocky causeway is only passable for 2½ hours either side of low water. Check the times of the tides before you cross or risk being stranded for seven hours. Tide tables are posted at the coastguard houses in Rhossili, and there is sometimes a CCW warden at the lookout in summer who can advise. The best route across the causeway is on the north side. The seabirds are on the north of the Head, visible from certain points on Middle Head (many nesting ledges are only visible from a boat). Visitors must keep to the footpath.

A footpath runs east along the coast from the Worm to Port Eynon Point, and is accessible in several places from the B4247.

Port Eynon is at the terminus of the A4118. Park just south of the village and follow the footpath south for ½ mile past the youth hostel to the Point.

Birds

At Worms Head there are several hundred pairs of breeding Razorbills, Guillemots and Kittiwakes and a few Fulmars, Shags and Herring and Great Black-backed

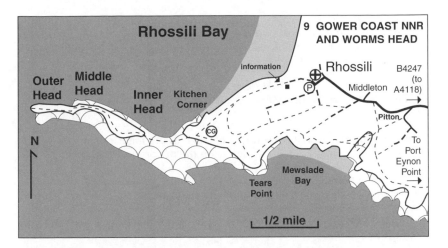

Gulls. Small numbers of Puffins may be present in summer, though they are often elusive. Non-breeding Cormorant, Gannet and Manx Shearwater can often be seen offshore in spring and summer, shearwaters most commonly in early morning. Erratically, at any time except midsummer, large flocks of Common Scoter, sometimes with a few Velvets, are off the Worm. With luck, Peregrine and Chough may be seen, and other breeding birds include Rock Pipit, Stonechat, Wheatear, Jackdaw and Raven on the clifftop.

A few Arctic and sometimes Great Skuas, as well as Gannet, shearwaters, auks, and terns occur on passage. Particularly at Port Eynon, southwest gales may bring very small numbers of Storm Petrel (June–August), Sooty Shearwater (late July–early August) and Pomarine Skua (most likely in September). Passerine migrants such as Wheatear, warblers and, sometimes (in late autumn and winter), Black Redstart occur along the clifftop.

In winter there are Red-throated Divers offshore and occasionally Great Northern, as well as Eider and Red-breasted Merganser. The rocks at the Worm usually attract a flock of Purple Sandpipers and Turnstones (some of which may oversummer).

Information

Countryside Council for Wales, RVB House, Llys Felin Newydd, Phoenix Way, Swansea Enterprise Park, Llansamlet, Swansea SA7 9FG. Tel: 01792 763500.

10 BURRY INLET, SOUTH SHORE
(Gower)   OS Landranger 159

The south shore of the Inlet is largely owned by the NT, while Whiteford Burrows NNR covers a large area of the dunes and foreshore. The Inlet's populations of Oystercatcher, Knot and Pintail are internationally important. Ideally a visit should be in winter, timed to coincide with the fortnightly 'spring' tides, which usually occur in early morning and evening.

Habitat
The River Loughor forms a broad estuary, the Burry Inlet, into which flow four smaller rivers. Two-thirds of the Inlet is tidal flats and the remainder saltmarsh

(one of the largest in Britain), concentrated on the south shore. Whiteford Burrows, a large dune system covering over 500 acres and extending for 2 miles north–south, guards the south entrance to the Inlet and has been planted in places with Corsican pines.

Access (see map)

Penclawdd to Crofty The B4295 gives views of the shore from Penclawdd to Crofty.

Salthouse Point This old causeway projects into the inner estuary. Leave the B4295 at the crossroads in Pen-caer-fenny on the minor road north to the Point.

Llanrhidian Marsh Accessible from the minor road between Crofty and Llanrhidian which parallels the B4295. Old earth platforms at Wernffrwd and near Crofty make useful vantages, especially at high tide. The area is good for ducks, with Greenshank and Green Sandpiper on autumn passage; both species often winter.

Weobley Castle The heavily grazed saltings below Weobley Castle are used by roosting waders on high 'spring' tides. Large numbers of Golden Plovers winter and the area also attracts raptors. Good views can be obtained from the castle.

Whiteford NNR Continue on unclassified roads south of Landimore to Llanmadoc and Cwm Ivy. Follow the signed footpath past the pine plantations to the marsh. The track winds through the dunes for c.2 miles to Whiteford Point, giving views of Groose and Landimore Marsh from the stile before plunging back into the conifers. Just after the path re-emerges from the plantations, a hide overlooks the Inlet at Berges Island, a good spot for Brent Goose. Black-necked and Slavonian Grebes may be seen from the hide on a rising or falling tide. Further on, Whiteford Point is used by roosting waders on lower tides, and the sea has grebes and divers. Cormorants roost on the abandoned lighthouse, and Eider and Brent Geese frequent the rocks and mud at its base. A suggested route would be to visit the hide on a rising tide, walk to the Point on the falling tide and finally back to Cwm Ivy along Whiteford Sands, a total of 5 miles.

Birds

In winter, Great Crested and Slavonian Grebes are regular in small numbers, but Black-necked Grebe is no longer guaranteed. Red-throated Diver may also be seen, and sometimes Great Northern. Wildfowl include up to 1,000 Brent Geese, 200 Shelduck, large numbers of Wigeon, Pintail and Teal, and a few hundred Shoveler. Up to 200 Eider frequent the mussel beds around Whiteford Point, along with small numbers of resident Red-breasted Merganser. Common Scoter can be seen west of the Point, and irregularly very small numbers of Scaup, Long-tailed Duck, Velvet Scoter and Goldeneye also occur here or in the river channel. Waders include Sanderling and maxima of 17,000 Oystercatchers, 1,500 Curlews, 3,000 Knots, 2,800 Dunlins, 600 Redshanks and 300 Bar-tailed Godwits. Several hundred Turnstones frequent the mussel beds off the Point, together with a few Purple Sandpipers. Small numbers of Greenshank and Spotted Redshank winter, mainly at Whiteford but also at Llanrhidian Marsh, together with a few Green Sandpipers and Black-tailed Godwits. Buzzard and Sparrowhawk are resident and regularly joined in winter by Merlin, Peregrine, Hen Harrier and Short-eared Owl.

In spring there can be large numbers of Whimbrel. Other migrants include terns, especially Common and Sandwich, but sometimes also Black.

In summer Eider is still present, as are numbers of non-breeding terns. Around

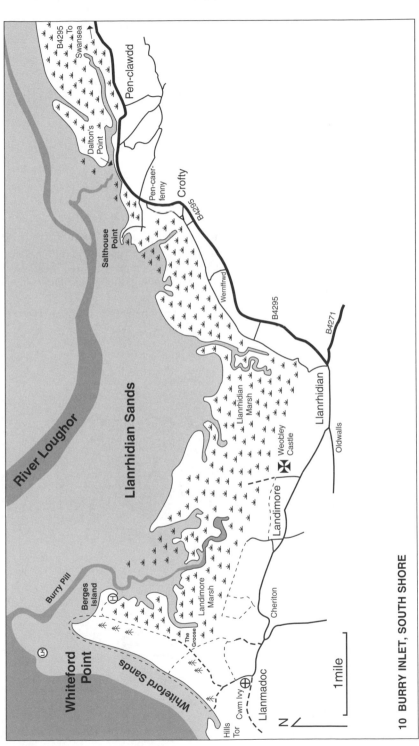

10 BURRY INLET, SOUTH SHORE

Cwm Ivy you may find Raven or Grasshopper Warbler, but Whiteford is generally quiet at this season.

Information

Countryside Council for Wales, RVB House, Llys Felin Newydd, Phoenix Way, Swansea Enterprise Park, Llansamlet, Swansea SA7 9FG. Tel: 01792 763500.

11 PENCLACWYDD (Carmarthenshire)   OS Landranger 159

Overlooking the north shore of the Burry Inlet and lying just south of Llanelli, this relatively new WWT refuge of 220 acres has already gained a reputation for attracting unusual birds, as well as regular wintering wildfowl, waders and raptors. Little Egret is frequently present.

Habitat

Opened in 1991, the Centre's habitats include areas of saltmarsh and mudflats bordering the north shore of the Burry Inlet, together with wet meadows, reedbeds specially constructed lagoons, and a scrape in the upper saltmarsh.

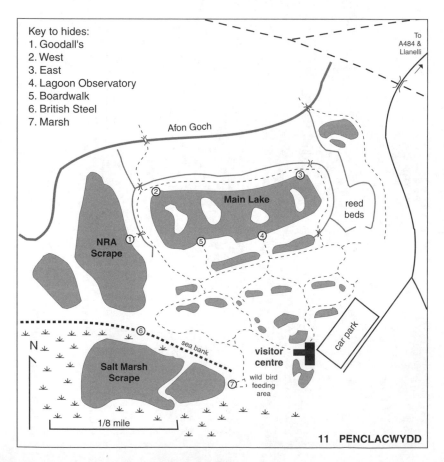

Key to hides:
1. Goodall's
2. West
3. East
4. Lagoon Observatory
5. Boardwalk
6. British Steel
7. Marsh

To A484 & Llanelli

Afon Goch

Main Lake

reed beds

NRA Scrape

Salt Marsh Scrape

sea bank

car park

visitor centre

wild bird feeding area

N

1/8 mile

11 PENCLACWYDD

Access (see map)

The reserve is off the A484 Llanelli–Swansea road, via the minor road off the roundabout (2 miles east of Llanelli) to Penclacwydd (signed with a duck). Open daily 09.30–18.00 April–September, 09.30–17.00 October–March (closed Christmas Eve and Christmas Day; the visitor centre closes 30 minutes earlier). Facilities include a visitor centre, restaurant, six hides and the heated Lagoon Observatory. There is also a collection of captive waterfowl.

Birds

Wintering wildfowl include Red-breasted Merganser, Goldeneye, Teal, Wigeon, Pintail, Brent Goose and family parties of Whooper Swans, and occasionally Bewick's Swan and Scaup. Waders include numbers of Oystercatcher, Curlew and Redshank, and Black-tailed Godwit is present year-round. A handful of Greenshank and Spotted Redshank may winter and Golden and Grey Plovers, Knot and Bar-tailed Godwit sometimes occur in small numbers. Water Rail and Jack Snipe also winter but are typically secretive. Raptors may include Hen Harrier, Merlin and Short-eared Owl, as well as the resident species.

On passage a wider variety of waders may be present, including Whimbrel, Ruff and Green and Common Sandpipers and, in autumn, also Wood and Curlew Sandpipers and Little Stint. Common, Arctic and Sandwich Terns may visit, and Garganey is possible. Spoonbill, Mediterranean Gull, Marsh Harrier and Osprey are occasional visitors.

Residents in the area include Little Grebe, Greylag Goose (feral), Shelduck, Gadwall, Shoveler, Pochard, Buzzard, Sparrowhawk, Peregrine, Water Rail, Redshank, Barn Owl, Kingfisher and Raven. Little Egret has been almost constantly present on the reserve or nearby estuary in recent years. Breeding summer visitors include Grasshopper, Sedge and Reed Warblers, and Common and Lesser Whitethroats.

Information

Dr Geoff Proffitt, WWT, Penclacwydd, Llwynhendy, Llanelli, Carmarthenshire SA14 9SH. Tel: 01554 741087.

12 CASTLEMARTIN PENINSULA (Pembrokeshire)   OS Landranger 158

Largely a live-firing range used for tank training, the Peninsula has a wild and unspoilt coast with some good seabird colonies, as well as breeding Chough, while Bosherston Ponds hold a variety of wintering wildfowl. Bosherston Ponds and Stackpole Warren are NNRs.

Habitat

The coast is bounded almost exclusively by cliffs, only infrequently broken by small coves and bays. The area immediately inland is covered by short turf, with scrub in more sheltered places. Bosherston Ponds are artificial and were formed in the 18th and 19th centuries by the construction of dams across what had been a sea-drowned marshy valley, cut off from the sea by sand dunes. The ridges between the ponds are cloaked in deciduous woodland.

Access (see map)

Stackpole Head From Pembroke, follow signs south for the unclassified road to Stackpole, and then to the car park at Stackpole Quay. It is a 1 mile walk south to the Head. Breeding seabirds include a small number of Puffins, as well as

Guillemot, Razorbill and a handful of Kittiwakes (the latter declined from c.140 pairs in 1985 to just five in 1997).

Bosherston Ponds Take the B4319 south from Pembroke and turn south to Bosherston, parking in the car park near the church, following footpaths to the ponds.

St Govan's Head Take the B4319 south from Pembroke and turn south to Bosherston, bearing right in the village to the car park at St Govan's Chapel (note the cliff-nesting House Martins here). From the car park walk c.½ mile south and east to the head. Seawatching here may produce Manx Shearwater (especially in early mornings and evenings) and Gannet.

Elegug Stacks Turn south off the B4319 immediately west of Merrion Barracks onto a minor road, parking at the coast after c.1¾ miles. The road passes through a live firing range, with access for much of the year only at weekends, on Bank Holidays and in the evenings. The area is closed when the gate is shut and red flags are flying. The four stacks lie just offshore and are an excellent place to see breeding seabirds at very close range, including c.6,000 Guillemots, 650 Razorbills, 200 pairs of Kittiwakes, 100 pairs of Herring Gulls, smaller numbers of Fulmars and Lesser Black-backed Gulls, and a few Shags and Great Black-backed Gulls.

Range East The Pembroke Coast Path runs east from Elegug Stacks to the car park at St Govan's Chapel, but is closed during firing (as above).

Birds
Breeding seabirds include Fulmar, Shag, Guillemot, Razorbill, a handful of Puffins, Kittiwake, Herring Gull and a few Great and Lesser Black-backed Gulls. Manx Shearwater and Gannet can be seen offshore throughout the summer.

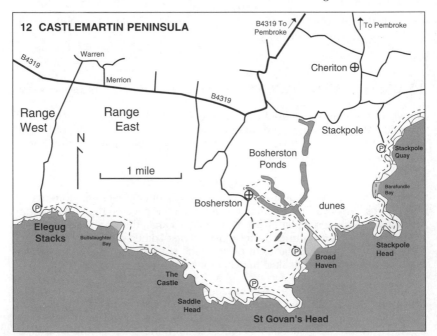

Peregrine, Raven and Chough are resident on the cliffs. Look also for Rock Pipit and Stonechat.

Wintering waterfowl on Bosherston Lakes include small numbers of Gadwall, Pochard, Scaup, Goldeneye and Goosander, while the reeds hold Water Rail and often a wintering Bittern. Kingfisher is resident around the ponds. Offshore, there may be a few Red-throated Divers and sometimes Great Northern. Fulmars return to the colonies by January.

Information
Pembrokeshire Coast NP, County Offices, St Thomas's Green, Haverfordwest, Dyfed SA61 1QZ.

13 SKOKHOLM ISLAND (Pembrokeshire)   OS Landranger 157

In 1933 Ronald Lockley established Britain's first bird observatory on Skokholm, building the country's first Heligoland traps. Ringing ceased in 1976 and the island is now managed as a reserve by the Wildlife Trust, West Wales. The island is now best known for breeding seabirds and migrants, and the best time to visit is May–September.

Habitat
One mile long, the island covers 242 acres, with cliffs rising to 160 feet. The exposed west and southwest sides have a short sward, extensively excavated by rabbits, Puffins and Manx Shearwaters. The more sheltered east side is dominated by bracken, with some rocky outcrops. The island's summit has a network of dry stone walls and dykes which, together with the rocky scree and cliffs, shelter nesting Storm Petrels. There are two ponds, the more southerly is surrounded by a marsh. The only buildings are the lighthouse and old farm buildings.

Access
Accommodation is available on a weekly basis, Saturday–Saturday, April–October, and also for short breaks (weekends or mid-week) on a scattering of dates throughout the season. Up to 15 people can be accommodated observatory style (full board); contact The Wildlife Trust, West Wales, Islands Booking Officer for details. The *Dale Princess* leaves Martin's Haven at 13.00 each Saturday. Day trips (guided walk only) are also organised from Martin's Haven on Mondays June–late August, for details contact the Wildlife Trust, West Wales. Always check sailing times in rough weather. Cars can be left at Martin's Haven car park.

Birds
Breeding birds include c.46,000 pairs of Manx Shearwaters and c.5,000–7,000 pairs of Storm Petrels. Both tubenoses are strictly nocturnal on land but are very vocal and can be heard at night, and be seen at twilight or on moonlight nights. Other seabirds include 147 pairs of Fulmars, Razorbills (1,011 individuals), Guillemos (774 individuals), c.2,500 pairs of Puffins, and 387 pairs of Herring, 3,270 pairs of Lesser Black-backed and 46 pairs of Great Black-backed Gulls (all counts refer to 1998). Peregrine, Buzzard, Oystercatcher, Rock Pipit, Chough and Raven also breed. Although present, albeit intermittently, from late March, Puffin is best seen from early June, when feeding young. The breeding auks depart by mid-August (and Puffin slightly earlier, by the end of the first week of August).

Passage periods bring the usual thrushes, chats, warblers and flycatchers. Spice is provided by the regular autumn occurrence of Wryneck, Black Redstart,

Bluethroat, Icterine, Melodious and Barred Warblers, Red-breasted Flycatcher and Lapland Bunting, and there have been numerous other rarities.

Information
Wildlife Trust of South and West Wales, Welsh Wildlife Centre, Cilgerran, Cardigan SA43 2TB. Tel: 01239 621212. E-mail: wildlife@wtww.co.uk

14 SKOMER ISLAND (Pembrokeshire)   OS Landranger 157

One mile offshore, Skomer has a large and easily accessible seabird colony. It is best visited in late April to mid-July, though migrants may be seen in autumn. The island is a NNR, managed by the Wildlife Trust, West Wales.

Habitat
Skomer covers 720 acres. The central plateau of grassland, bracken and heath has masses of bluebells and red campion in spring, when the cliff slopes are a blaze of thrift and sea campion. The sward is dissected by a maze of rabbit, Puffin and shearwater burrows.

Access
Skomer is open daily (except Mondays but including Bank Holidays) 1 April (or Good Friday, if earlier) to 31 October, 10.00–18.00, except for four days in early June. The *Dale Princess*, operated by the Dale Sailing Company, sails from Martin's Haven where there is a car park (fee). Boats leave at 10.00, 11.00 and 12.00 (with additional departures depending on demand), allowing c.5 hours on the island. Access is restricted to the 4-mile nature trail and a landing fee is payable to the island's warden. The boat may also make circumnavigations of the island in early afternoon, without landing. During rough weather, especially north winds, the boat may be delayed or even cancelled, so always check on sailing times. The Lockley Lodge Information Centre at Martin's Haven can advise on sailings; it is usually manned from Easter to late September/October.

The Pembrokeshire Coast NP organises a guided walk on Wednesdays during the height of the season, and on Tuesday and Friday evenings a 'Seabird Spectacular' (aboard the *Dale Princess* out of Martin's Haven) to see rafting Manx Shearwaters (and permitting good views of Skomer cliffs and the colonies). Both can be booked through the NP Information Centre in Haverfordwest.

Basic chalet accommodation is available on Skomer and it is also possible to stay on the island on a weekly basis as a volunteer; in return for help in running the reserve, volunteers receive free accommodation and boat crossings. Contact the Trust for details.

Birds
Breeding seabirds include Fulmar (638 pairs), Manx Shearwater (c.102,000 pairs— apparently 50% of the world population!), Storm Petrel (55 pairs), Puffin (maximum of 9,235 individuals), Guillemot (10,890 individuals), Razorbill, Kittiwake (2,092 pairs), Lesser Black-backed (c.12,000 pairs), Herring (299 pairs) and Great Black-backed Gulls (53 pairs), Cormorant (16 pairs) and Shag (three pairs; all figures refer to 1998). Other breeders are Teal, Shoveler, Buzzard, Peregrine, Curlew, Oystercatcher, Little and Short-eared Owls, Rock Pipit, Wheatear, Raven and Chough. The shearwaters are largely nocturnal, only return- ing to land after dark, but the Trust has a mini-camera in a burrow, relaying

pictures to a TV monitor in the Information Room, affording visitors views of the underground activities. Nevertheless, an overnight stay is essential to experience the spectacle of thousands of shearwaters returning to their burrows. By late August and early September the adults have departed, but the full-grown young are then leaving their burrows at night to exercise their flight muscles before making a final departure. Otherwise, Manx Shearwaters may come inshore in rough weather and can sometimes be seen from a boat, especially on the Seabird Spectaculars. Although present, albeit intermittently, from late March, Puffin is best seen from early June, when feeding young. The breeding auks have departed by mid-August (and Puffin slightly earlier, by the end of the first week of August).

Skomer attracts numbers of passerine migrants but its size and extensive cover make them harder to find than on Skokholm. Wintering birds include Short-eared Owl, Hen Harrier and Merlin (and in 1981–1990 a flock of c.100 Barnacle Geese; feral birds from Sweden, they spent the early winter in the West Midlands).

Information
Juan Brown, Skomer Island, Marloes, Pembrokeshire SA63 2BJ. Tel: 07971 114302. E-mail: skomer@wtww.co.uk
Pembrokeshire Coast NP, Information Centre, 40 High Street, Haverfordwest, Pembrokeshire. Tel: 01437 760136. (Main Office: County Offices, St Thomas's Green, Haverfordwest, Pembrokeshire SA61 1QZ. Tel: 01437 764636.)
Wildlife Trust of South and West Wales, Welsh Wildlife Centre, Cilgerran, Cardigan SA43 2TB. Tel: 01239 621212. E-mail: wildlife@wtww.co.uk
Lockley Lodge Information Centre, tel: 01646 636234.
Dale Sailing Company, tel: 01646 631636.

15 GRASSHOLM (Pembrokeshire)   OS Landranger 157

Lying 10 miles offshore, Grassholm covers 22 acres. The 32,000 pairs of Gannet form the third-largest colony in the world (records go back to 1860, when there were just 20 pairs). Other seabirds include Shag, Razorbill, Guillemot, Kittiwake, and Herring and Great Black backed Gulls. The island is (frustratingly) also very good for small birds on passage, and is an NNR.

Access
The Dale Sailing Company organises trips circumnavigating the island from April, and these may record Manx Shearwater as well as the breeding seabirds (especially in the evening). The crossing takes 1–1½ hours. Landing is not permitted.

Information
Lockley Lodge Information Centre, tel: 01646 636234.
Dale Sailing Company, tel: 01646 631636.

16 MARLOES PENINSULA (Pembrokeshire)   OS Landranger 157

This area holds some interesting breeding birds, notably Peregrine and Chough, and offers the chance of seeing seabirds without venturing offshore to the breeding islands.

Access and Birds (see map on p.309)

Wooltack Point Large numbers of Manx Shearwater assemble offshore each evening in the breeding season and, depending on the weather, may be seen from the mainland. Seabirds are best seen from c.2 hours before until two hours after high tide from Wooltack Point (follow the footpath a few hundred yards northwest from Martin's Haven); at other times they tend to congregate in Broad Sound and St Brides Bay, and views are more distant.

Marloes Peninsula From the coastal footpath, on either the north or south sides of the Peninsula east of Marloes, Peregrine, Buzzard, Raven and Chough can be seen, and Stonechat and Grasshopper Warbler breed in the rough ground. Passerine migrants occur and have included rarities.

Marloes Mere Leave Marloes west on the minor road past Marloes Court and park after c.1 mile at the junction. Follow the track west past the youth hostel and the Mere, where there is a public hide (continuing, this track connects with the coast path opposite Gateholm). The Mere is a reserve of the Wildlife Trust, West Wales, and largely comprises areas of rushes and cotton grasses. Numbers of wildfowl winter, including Wigeon, Teal and up to 50 Shoveler.

Dale Aerodrome Worth checking in autumn, when post-breeding gatherings of up to 40 Chough have been recorded in September–October (and Buff-breasted Sandpiper has been seen several times in September). From Marloes a narrow track runs south to Little Marloes Farm and a footpath follows the runways south and east to Dale.

Westdale Bay A good spot for Chough. Follow the track west from Dale Castle for ½ mile to the Bay.

St Ann's Head Another chance for Chough. Take the minor road south from Dale to the lighthouse.

Information

Wildlife Trust of South and West Wales, Welsh Wildlife Centre, Cilgerran, Cardigan SA43 2TB. Tel: 01239 621212. E-mail: wildlife@wtww.co.uk
Pembrokeshire Coast NP, Information Centre, 40 High Street, Haverfordwest, Pembrokeshire. Tel: 01437 760136. (Main Office: County Offices, St Thomas's Green, Haverfordwest, Pembrokeshire SA61 1QZ. Tel: 01437 764636.)

17 GANN ESTUARY (Pembrokeshire)   OS Landranger 157

This small estuary can be interesting in winter and passage periods.

Habitat

Close to the mouth of the Milford Haven estuary and facing into the sheltered waters of Dale Roads, a shingle ridge separates the sand and shingle beach from a small area of saltmarsh, where gravel extraction has left several pools varying from fresh to brackish in nature.

Access (see map)

The lower reaches can be seen from the B4327 north of Dale, with a small car park at the west end of the estuary affording good views of the flats. From here,

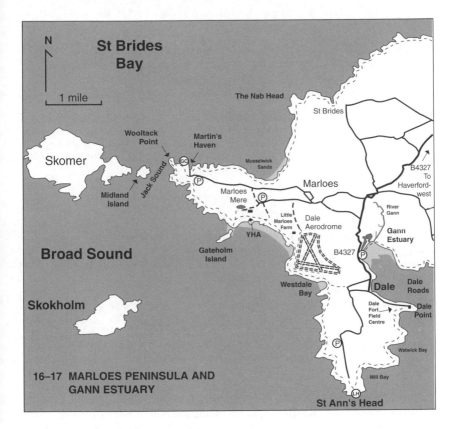

N

St Brides Bay

1 mile

The Nab Head

St Brides

Wooltack Point

Martin's Haven

Skomer

Jack Sound

Musselwick Sands

B4327 To Haverford- west

Marloes

Midland Island

Marloes Mere

River Gann

Little Marloes Farm

Dale Aerodrome

Gann Estuary

YHA

Broad Sound

Gateholm Island

B4327

Westdale Bay

Dale

Dale Roads

Skokholm

Dale Fort Field Centre

Dale Point

Watwick Bay

16–17 MARLOES PENINSULA AND GANN ESTUARY

Mill Bay

St Ann's Head

it is possible to walk north below the shingle ridge that separates the estuary from the lagoon and then across the tidal ford over the River Gann. The area is best in the period around high water and is heavily disturbed in summer, when early-morning visits are likely to be most productive.

Birds
Winter brings a few Red-throated Divers and occasional Great Northern and Black-throated Divers and Slavonian Grebe to Dale Roads, especially in rough weather, with Little Grebe on the lagoon. Goldeneye and Red-breasted Merganser are regular on the sea. Wintering waders include Grey and Ringed Plovers and Turnstone, and regularly also Greenshank, which favour the upper part of the estuary and the high-banked channel of the river. Little Egret and Spoonbill are possible in autumn and winter.

Information
Pembrokeshire Coast NP, Information Centre, 40 High Street, Haverfordwest, Pembrokeshire. Tel: 01437 760136. (Main Office: County Offices, St Thomas's Green, Haverfordwest, Pembrokeshire SA61 1QZ. Tel: 01437 764636.)

18 ST DAVID'S PENINSULA (Pembrokeshire)   OS Landranger 157

This area of relict maritime heaths with a mosaic of heathland, willow scrub and patches of open water, set amid mixed farmland, is notable for the range of raptors that is present, especially in winter, including good numbers of Hen Harrier, and for resident Chough on the coast.

Access (see map)

Dowrog Common Comprising a mixture of heather, gorse and some open pools, this is a reserve of the Wildlife Trust, West Wales, and is crossed by a minor road which leads north off the A487 2 miles east of St David's (towards Gwrhyd Mawr), with a small car park near the northwest end.

Tretio Common Crossed by a minor road north off the A487 at Carnhedryn Uchaf, 3¼ miles east of St David's.

Vachelich Moor (St David's Airfield Common) This lies north of the now disused St David's Airfield. Turn south off the A487 on the minor road to Caerfarchell, c.3 miles east of St David's, viewing the common to the west after ½ mile. The area may also attract harriers.

Trefeiddan Pool Viewable from the minor road west of St David's towards St Justinian lifeboat station.

Pen Dal-aderyn and Point St John From the car park at St Justinian follow the coastal footpath south towards Dal-aderyn or north towards Point St John for a chance of Chough.

Lleithyr Farm Pool Leave the A487 just outside St David's north on the B4583, follow the road round the right-angle left bend, and after a further 1¼ miles, turn right (east) on the narrow minor road to Lleithyr. After ⅓ mile, where the road bends sharply right, follow the footpath along the track past the farm to view the pool on the left after ¼ mile.

St David's Head From St David's, follow the B4583 to the car park at Whitesands Bay. From here follow the coastal footpath north towards St David's Head, looking for Chough en route.

Porth Clais and Nine Wells These two short, narrow valleys on the south side of the Peninsula can be excellent on occasion for passerine migrants, especially in autumn. They have attracted rarities and given more intensive watching could rival better-known sites in southwest Britain. Porth Clais is accessible along a minor road southwest from St David's, with public footpaths running down both sides of the valley. Nine Wells lies on the A487, 2¼ miles east of St David's, and footpaths similarly run south to the sea.

Birds

Residents include Peregrine, Buzzard and Sparrowhawk, and breeding species on the heaths and rough ground include Stonechat and Grasshopper and Sedge Warblers, with Water Rail in some of the wetter areas. Passage brings occasional Garganey to the pools.

In winter a greater variety of raptors may be seen. Merlin and Short-eared Owl join the resident species, while Hen Harrier are at low density and possible anywhere in the day, but up to 14 have been recorded roosting on Dowrog

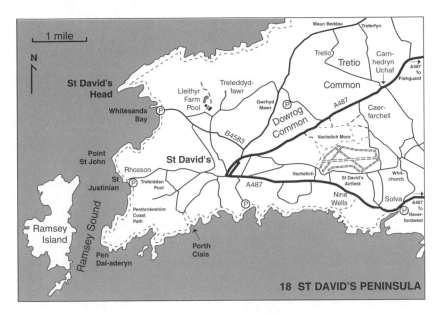

18 ST DAVID'S PENINSULA

Common. It is best to watch from the road and keep a sharp eye in all directions, as the harriers arrive low and fast and quickly drop to the ground (though they may fly again and move to a different roost site, making accurate counts more difficult). Small numbers of Wigeon and Teal occur on the various pools.

Information
Wildlife Trust of South and West Wales, Welsh Wildlife Centre, Cilgerran, Cardigan SA43 2TB. Tel: 01239 621212. E-mail: wildlife@wtww.co.uk
Pembrokeshire Coast NP, Information Centre, 40 High Street, Haverfordwest, Pembrokeshire. Tel: 01437 760136. (Main Office: County Offices, St Thomas's Green, Haverfordwest, Pembrokeshire SA61 1QZ. Tel: 01437 764636.)

19 RAMSEY ISLAND (Pembrokeshire)   OS Landranger 157

The second-largest of the Pembrokeshire islands (after Skomer), Ramsey is now an RSPB reserve and NNR, and worth visiting in spring and summer for its breeding seabirds and Chough.

Habitat
The island covers 650 acres and was, until very recently, farmed (current management includes some agricultural practices). The lower, east side of the island largely comprises fields with several ponds, while the south portion is mostly heather and bracken. There are two hills, Cann Llundain in the south, rising to 450 feet, and the slightly lower Carn Ysgubor in the north. The coast, especially in the west, is bounded by high cliffs, with spectacular sea caves and inlets, and Ramsey has a series of satellite islets.

Access
The island is accessible daily (except Fridays), 1 April–31 October, weather permitting. Boats leave the lifeboat station in St Justinians, near St David's, at 09.45 and 13.00 and also, in July–August, at 10.30 (but there is a limit of 80 visitors per day in the latter period). Boats also circumnavigate the island daily, weather permitting, in order to view the seabird colonies on the west cliffs. Advance bookings can be made by ringing 01437 721686 or 0800 163621.

Birds
Breeding seabirds include Guillemot, Razorbill, Kittiwake and c.1,000 pairs of Manx Shearwaters, although the latter come ashore only at night; there are no Puffins on Ramsey. Early-evening gatherings of Manx Shearwaters can sometimes be seen from nearby shores. Other breeding birds include Peregrine, Buzzard, Lapwing, Wheatear, Raven and Chough.

Like all of the Pembrokeshire islands, Ramsey attracts migrants during passage periods and has hit the headlines with records of transatlantic vagrants (Yellow-rumped Warbler in 1994 and Indigo Bunting in 1996).

Information
RSPB Ramsey Island: Ian Bullock, Tegfan, Caerbwdi, St David's, Pembrokeshire SA62 6QP. Mobile tel. 07836 535733.

20 STRUMBLE HEAD (Pembrokeshire)   OS Landranger 157

This is the top seawatching station in Wales and one of the best in Britain. Some seabirds can be seen throughout spring and summer (mostly from the nearby breeding colonies on the Pembrokeshire islands), but late August–early October is the best time to visit for the scarcer species. An added bonus is resident Chough in this area.

Habitat
The Head lies at the west end of the Pencaer Peninsula and rises to a maximum of c.100 feet, comprising grass and heather-clad slopes with rocky outcrops.

Access
Strumble Head Well signed along minor roads from the A40 at Fishguard harbour, there is a car park directly opposite the lighthouse rock and, while it is possible to seawatch from the car here, the best place is the disused War Department building below the road on the right, just before the car park, which has been renovated as an observation centre by the Pembrokeshire Coast NP Authority. Dawn onwards is best. The coastal footpath east from the Head towards Carreg Gybi is good for Chough.

Fishguard harbour This can be good for divers, grebes and sea duck, and Ring-billed, Mediterranean, Little and Iceland Gulls are sometimes recorded.

Dinas Head Leave Fishguard east on the A487 and, after c.3 miles, turn north at Dinas Cross on the minor road to Bryn-henllan. Continue north through the village to the car park at the base of the Head. The coastal footpath circumnavigates the Head with a chance of Chough, while Razorbills and Guillemots nest on Dinas Island.

Birds

Manx Shearwater is regularly seen offshore March–October, especially in early mornings and evenings. Cormorant, Shag and Gannet are also present almost year-round, and other regulars in spring and summer include Fulmar, Razorbill, Guillemot, Kittiwake and other gulls.

The best autumn seawatching conditions are a southwest gale veering west or northwest. Shearwaters, including Sooty and occasionally Mediterranean or Great, may occur, together with Leach's Petrel in late autumn. Storm Petrel is rare, while Cory's and Little Shearwaters and Sabine's Gull have been recorded. Great and Arctic Skuas are regular, Pomarine less so and Long-tailed is rare (but annual). Red-throated Diver, Common Scoter, Little Gull, Kittiwake, auks and terns (including Black Tern) are other regulars. Passerine migrants too, should not be ignored.

Breeding birds include Fulmar, Herring Gull, Chough, Raven, Stonechat and Grasshopper Warbler, and Peregrine is often present.

21 WELSH WILDLIFE CENTRE (Pembrokeshire)   OS Landranger 145

Lying near the mouth of the Afon Teifi immediately south of Cardigan, this site holds a variety of the commoner wildfowl and waders, and, notably, breeding Cetti's Warbler. The area is a reserve of the Wildlife Trust, West Wales.

Habitat

The Centre's 250 acres of varied habitats include the upper estuary, fresh and salt-water reedbeds, grazing marshes and pools, and the wooded gorge of the river.

Access (see map)

Welsh Wildlife Centre Leave the A487 Cardigan bypass at the west roundabout south on the A478 and, after c.2 miles, turn east (left) at Pen-y-bryn on the minor road to Cilgerran, signed to the Centre. After c.1 mile (before the village) turn north on a minor road to the Centre car park (a further 1½ miles distant; free to Trust members but £5 to non-members). The reserve is open all year, 10.00–17.00. There is a visitor centre with a shop, information area and restaurant (open Easter–early November), seven hides and four trails.

Lower Teifi Estuary The lower reaches of the estuary north of Cardigan can be seen from the B4546 on the west shore, and from the B4548 on the east shore, the latter road running along the shoreline towards the mouth.

Birds

Wintering wildfowl include Shelduck, Wigeon, Shoveler, Gadwall and Teal, with Goldeneye, Red-breasted Merganser and Goosander on the river, and wintering waders include Oystercatcher, Ringed Plover, Dunlin, Bar-tailed Godwit, Curlew and Redshank. Jack Snipe and Water Rail are often present (the latter in some numbers), but are typically elusive. Raptors in the area include Sparrowhawk, Buzzard and sometimes Peregrine, and interesting passerines include Redpoll, Siskin and occasionally Brambling.

On passage a greater variety of waders occurs, including Ruff, Common and Green Sandpipers, Spotted Redshank and Greenshank, and scarcer migrants have included Little Egret, Garganey, Osprey, Marsh Harrier and Bearded Tit.

Breeding birds include Water Rail, Cetti's, Grasshopper and Reed Warblers, and Barn Owl, Kingfisher, Grey Wagtail and Dipper.

Information

Chris Lawrence, Manager, Welsh Wildlife Centre, Cilgerran, Cardigan SA43 2TB.
Tel: 01239 621212. E-mail: chris@wtww.co.uk

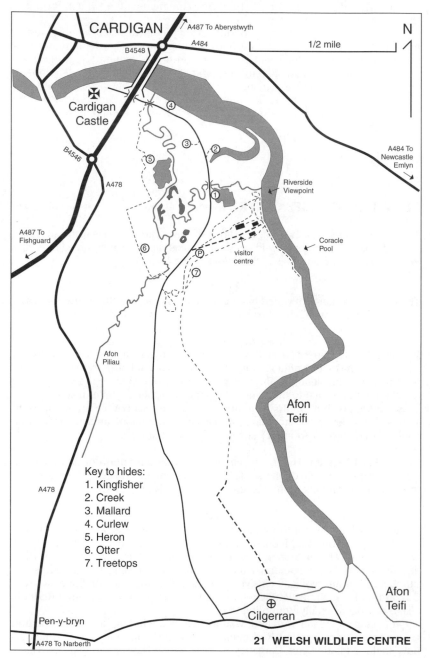

Key to hides:
1. Kingfisher
2. Creek
3. Mallard
4. Curlew
5. Heron
6. Otter
7. Treetops

21 WELSH WILDLIFE CENTRE

22 THE LOCHTYN PENINSULA
(Ceredigion)   OS Landranger 145

This small peninsula on the coast c.6 miles southwest of New Quay is a well-known site for Chough, and also holds a few breeding seabirds.

Access
Leave the A487 north at Brynhoffnan on the B4334 to Llangranog. From the seafront follow the coast path north for c.1 mile to the Peninsula (parking can be tricky in summer).

Birds
Chough is resident in the area and may be especially numerous in late summer. Small numbers of Guillemots, Razorbills and Kittiwakes also breed. Although the breeding cliffs are difficult to view (being more visible from a boat), the birds can be seen on the sea and flying to and fro. Look for Peregrine along the cliffs. In winter, small numbers of Red-throated Diver are present offshore and Common Scoter may be seen throughout the year.

23 DINAS AND GWENFFRWD AND AREA
(Carmarthenshire)   OS Landranger 146 or 147

The RSPB reserves of Dinas and Gwenffrwd, c.10 miles north of Llandovery in the upper Tywi catchment, total almost 7,000 acres. Their range of habitats and birds is typical of this part of Wales. May–June is the best time to visit; summer visitors have arrived and are singing, and there is a chance of Red Kite if the weather is good. Nearby Crychan Forest holds Goshawk, best looked for in fine weather in March–April.

Habitat
Dinas RSPB reserve covers just 129 acres and comprises a steeply wooded knoll at the confluence of the Doethie and Tywi, rising to over 1,000 feet, with hanging oak woods and small areas of alder carr and marshland. Gwenffrwd is far larger and reaches 1,343 feet at Cefn Gwenffrwd, with areas of moorland, hanging oak woods and farmland, as well as woodland in the valleys.

Access (see map)
Dinas RSPB reserve Leave Llandovery north on unclassified roads to Rhandirmwyn and continue towards Llyn Brianne dam. The Dinas Information Centre is at Nant-y-ffin, after a further 4 miles, and is open 10.00–17.00 Easter–late August. The nature trail and reserve are open at all times.

Gwenffrwd RSPB reserve For access to Gwenffrwd (daily, Easter–August) report at Dinas Information Centre. The number of visitors to Gwenffrwd is restricted by limited parking, and access is permitted only to RSPB members.

Nant Melyn reserve At Rhandirmwyn turn west and cross the Tywi via Rhandirmwyn bridge. Turn right at the T-junction for Cwrt-a-Cadno and continue for 2⅔ miles past Towy Bridge Inn to the bridge over the Nant Melyn. Here a footpath leads uphill to the north through an area of deciduous woodland. Nant Melyn is a reserve of the Wildlife Trust of South and West Wales.

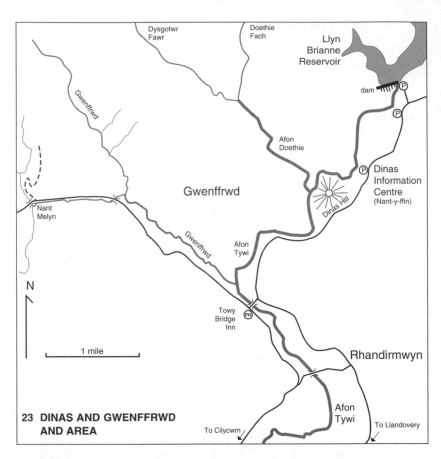

23 DINAS AND GWENFFRWD AND AREA

The Irfon Valley A good area for Dipper. Leave the A483 northwest at Llanwrtyd Wells on a minor road towards Abergwesyn. This parallels the river, with several parking places from which to scan for Dipper, Grey Wagtail and Common Sandpiper.

Crychan Forest (Dyfed; OS Landranger 160) A very extensive area of conifer plantations that holds Goshawk, best looked for March–April. Five miles northeast of Llandovery, turn east off the A483 on a minor road opposite the Talgarth pub in Cynghordy. Almost immediately, fork left and follow the road for c.2½ miles to a picnic site. From here take the main track to a large clearing, which offers a good view over the forest. Alternative access points are Sugar Loaf picnic site, east off the A483, 2¾ miles north of Cynghordy, and Banc Cefngarreg, reached by forking right (not left) after turning in Cynghordy and following the narrow road southeast for c.1 mile.

Birds

A specialty of mid-Wales is Red Kite, which can sometimes be seen in the area. The best chance is in the first half of the year and good weather is essential; there are few birds and a good deal of luck is required. Resident Buzzard and Sparrowhawk are much commoner, and Merlin and Peregrine can sometimes be seen, as can Raven. A few Red Grouse persist on higher ground, but rampant

Pied Flycatcher

over-grazing has greatly reduced their numbers and they are hard to find. In summer they are joined by Wheatear, with Tree Pipit and Whinchat in areas of scattered trees. Along streams and rivers Goosander, Common Sandpiper, Grey Wagtail, Sand Martin and Dipper breed, and Kingfisher may also visit. Summer visitors to woodlands include Redstart, Wood Warbler and Pied Flycatcher, which join resident Woodcock, Green, Great and Lesser Spotted Woodpeckers, Marsh and Willow Tits, Nuthatch, Treecreeper, Siskin and Redpoll.

Information

RSPB Dinas and Gwenffrwd, Warden: Tony Pickup, Troedrhiwgelynen, Rhandirmwyn, Llandovery, Carmarthenshire SA20 OPN.

24 CORS CARON (TREGARON BOG)

(Ceredigion)   OS Landranger 146

Tregaron, c.15 miles southeast of Aberystwyth, is a good area for Red Kite, especially in winter. Cors Caron NNR, to the north of the village, covers 2,016 acres of Tregaron Bog.

Habitat

Cors Caron contains areas of raised bog covered with heather, grass, moss and patches of birch and willow carr. Peat cutting to the east of the Afon Teifi has created some small flashes, and a scrape has been created in front of the observation tower. The surrounding area is a mixture of deciduous woodland and pasture rising to more rugged hills.

Access (see map)

Cors Caron NNR Owned by the Countryside Council for Wales, access to the NNR is restricted but the nature trail along the disused railway line leading after c.1 mile to an observation tower is always open. In winter wildfowl and raptors, notably Red Kite, can be seen from here. The trail starts at the B4343, c.2½ miles north of Tregaron, just beyond Maes-llyn Farm; roadside parking is limited. A permit is required to enter the rest of the reserve but the interesting species can be

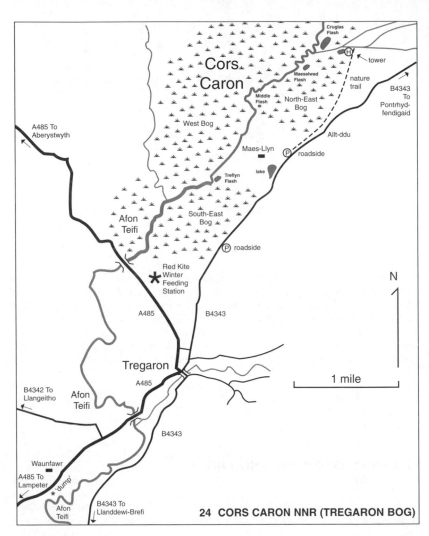

24 CORS CARON NNR (TREGARON BOG)

seen from the road or nature trail. Approximately 1 mile northwest of Tregaron village on the A485 there is a Red Kite feeding station, operational in winter.

Tregaron dump A private dump, just east of the A485 c.1½ miles south of the village (near the track to Waunfawr), where rendered fat is put out, attracts kites, especially in late afternoon, December–February. The species can be seen from the B4343 and A485, parking carefully off the road.

Tregaron to Llanwrtyd Wells The minor road east from Tregaron to Llanwrtyd Wells crosses hill country, with oak woods and plantations. Red Kite is possible as well as the usual woodland species in summer.

Tregaron to Devil's Bridge (OS Landranger 135 or 147) Continuing north from Tregaron to Devil's Bridge, the triangle formed by the B4343 between Pont-rhyd-y-groes and Devil's Bridge and the minor road that leaves the B4343 at

Pont-rhyd-y-groes to the northwest and bends back after 2 miles northeast to Devil's Bridge, is a good area to look for Red Kite, especially in early spring.

Birds
Red Kite, Sparrowhawk, Buzzard, Peregrine and Raven are resident in the area. Kites can be seen over the bog, soaring over the hills east of the B4343 or indeed just about anywhere. Barn Owl, Water Rail and Dipper occur all year. A good spot for the latter is Tregaron Bridge.

Winter brings wildfowl: up to 50 Whooper Swans occur November– March, and irregularly there are small numbers of Bewick's Swans. Wigeon, Teal and Mallard form the bulk of the wintering duck, with smaller numbers of Gadwall. The resident raptors are joined by Hen Harrier, Short-eared Owl and, sometimes, Merlin. Other visitors include Stonechat and Redpoll.

Summer visitors to the bog include Sedge Warbler, with Grasshopper Warbler and Redpoll in scrubbier areas. Teal, Curlew, Snipe and Redshank breed, and there is a Black-headed Gull colony. Marsh Harrier is also a summer visitor. Small numbers of Tree Pipit, Redstart, Whinchat, Wood Warbler and Pied Flycatcher breed in the remnant oak woods and scrubby hillsides, especially on the east side of the B4343, joining the resident Nuthatch, Treecreeper and Willow Tit. On passage small numbers of waders may be seen on the scrape.

Information
Countryside Council for Wales, Tregaron Warden: Paul Culyer, Neuaddlas, Tregaron, Ceredigion SY25 6LG. Tel: 01974 298480. E-mail: p.culyer@ccw.gov.uk

25 VALE OF RHEIDOL AND DEVIL'S BRIDGE
(Ceredigion)   OS Landranger 135

This attractive valley holds a good variety of woodland and riverside birds.

Habitat
The lower reaches of the River Rheidol comprise a narrow floodplain with the river meandering past oxbow lakes and gravel islands; there are also several gravel pits. Upstream it is dammed to form the Gwm Rheidol Reservoir and beyond this the valley is cloaked with extensive stands of sessile oak woods, while at Devil's Bridge there is a spectacular waterfall. At Devil's Bridge the Coed Rheidol NNR is managed by the Countryside Council for Wales, while Coed Simdde Lwyd Reserve is owned by the Wildlife Trust, West Wales.

Access
Vale of Rheidol Approximately 5 miles east of Aberystwyth on the A44 take the minor road south at Capel Bangor to Dolypandy. Continue, paralleling the Afon Rheidol, for 3½ miles to the Powergen Information Centre at the dam, from where a nature trail circuits the reservoir.

Coed Simdde Lwyd In the lower reaches of the valley, this reserve is accessible along a very narrow road past the Powergen Information Centre, with extremely limited parking at SN 703787, from where a footpath runs upslope.

Devil's Bridge Reached by narrow-gauge steam train from Aberystwyth (Easter to mid-September) and via the A4120. At the bridge there is a 400-foot cascade. From the car park above the falls a path descends through mixed woodland.

Birds

Around the reservoir Goosander (has bred), Red-breasted Merganser, Common Sandpiper, Kingfisher, Sand Martin, Dipper and Grey Wagtail frequent the river, and Tree Pipit, Redstart, Wood Warbler and Pied Flycatcher the woods. At Devil's Bridge the usual species occur in summer and Sparrowhawk, Buzzard, Raven and occasionally Red Kite may be seen overhead.

Information

Wildlife Trust of South and West Wales, Welsh Wildlife Centre, Cilgerran, Cardigan SA43 2TB. Tel: 01239 621212. E-mail: wildlife@wtww.co.uk

26 ABERYSTWYTH AREA (Ceredigion) OS Landranger 135

The nodal point for the RSPB Ynys-hir Reserve and the Vale of Rheidol, there are some spots worth checking around the town of Aberystwyth, especially in winter.

Access and Birds

Aberystwyth harbour Ring-billed Gull has been recorded several times, usually in January–early April. The best time to check the harbour is on a falling tide when the gulls congregate on the newly exposed mud. In late winter and early spring up to 24 Mediterranean Gulls have also been noted, together with Little Gulls. Glaucous and Iceland Gulls are also sometimes seen in winter, and there are often Purple Sandpipers by the promenade. Wintering Black Redstart is almost annual around the harbour buildings or in the remains of Aberystwyth Castle.

Aberystwyth to Borth Chough occurs on the cliffs between Aberystwyth and Borth, usually closer to Borth; a footpath follows the coast, accessible at Aberystwyth, Clarach Bay and Borth. The small outflow at Clarach Bay attracts gulls, occasionally including Mediterranean. Take the minor road to the sea off the B4572 at Clarach (north off the A487, 1 mile east of Aberystwyth).

27 DYFI ESTUARY (Ceredigion and Meirionnyd) OS Landranger 135

The Dyfi (or Dovey) is the largest estuary emptying into Cardigan Bay. A small flock of wintering Greenland White-fronted Geese is of special interest, and at all times of year the area's range of habitats should guarantee an interesting day. The estuary, Ynys-las Dunes and Cors Fochno (Borth Bog) are a NNR. Ynys-hir, an RSPB reserve covering c.1,000 acres, lies on the south shore of the estuary with an additional large area in the adjacent Llyfnant Valley.

Habitat

Approximately 5 miles long by 1½ miles at its widest, three-quarters of the estuary comprise sand flats and the remainder saltmarsh, concentrated on the south shore and near the seaward end. The mouth of the estuary is guarded to the south by the extensive dune system of Ynys-las, and to the southeast lies Cors Fochno (Borth Bog) which, at c.1,400 acres, is the largest unmodified raised mire in Britain. Further inland, the south shore is fringed by extensive water meadows, and south of the A487 lie open hillsides and conifer plantations, as well as deciduous woodland. Oak woods border the north shore of the estuary.

Access (see map)

Ynys-las Dunes Leave the A487 on the B4353 and turn north at Ynys-las on the minor road to the Dunes. There is a car park, information centre (open daily 10.00–17.00, April–October, and weekends, 10.00–16.00, November–March) and nature trail. From here you can view the river mouth and look out to sea (early morning and high tide are best for seawatching). Several shingle ridges attract concentrations of gulls and waders at high tide, especially during passage periods. Gulls also roost on the sea anywhere between Ynys-las and the cliffs at Borth, and can be viewed from the B4353 between Ynys-las and Borth.

Afon Leri The sand flats behind the Dunes attract waders and a good place to watch from is the mouth of the Afon Leri. A short track north off the B4353 follows the west bank of the river, affording views of the flats, and a footpath on the east bank accesses the saltings. The tidal channels of the Afon Leri and Afon Cletwr are worth checking in late summer for passage waders.

Cors Fochno A permit from the Countryside Council for Wales is required to enter Cors Fochno (available from Ynys-las Information Centre). The bog and Aberleri water meadows can also be viewed from the Afon Leri embankment where a public footpath follows the west bank from the B4353, via a railway bridge, south to Borth. After 1⅓ miles it connects with another public footpath west to the B4353, with a public hide overlooking the Aberleri Marshes. Although of great interest in other respects, the bog is nowadays of only limited interest for birds (Black Grouse having disappeared and the Greenland Whitefronts largely favouring other habitats).

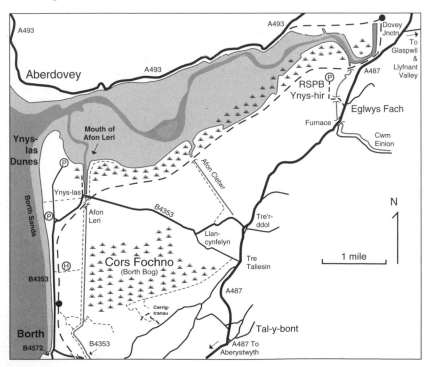

Ynys-hir RSPB reserve Off the A487 c.6½ miles west of Machynlleth, the entrance is signed in Eglwysfach. Report to reception on arrival. The reserve is open daily 09.00–21.00 (or sunset if earlier). There are nature trails and seven hides giving views of the estuary, wader scrape and woods (the best place on the Dyfi to watch waders is the Saltings hide at Ynys-hir on a rising tide).

Llyfnant Valley The minor road off the A487 through the Llyfnant Valley to Glaspwill makes an excellent walk for woodland species, with Dipper on the small river.

Einion stream This also has Dipper and Grey Wagtail, with Red-breasted Merganser and Common Sandpiper on the higher reaches. A minor road from Furnace follows the stream (well above it in places) and there is a good tea shop at the end.

Birds

Winter brings a flock of c.100 Greenland White-fronted Geese, which feeds on the saltmarsh or on Cors Fochno and adjoining arable land, and roost on the estuary sands. Present early October–early April, the birds are best seen from the RSPB reserve on a high rising tide. Whooper Swans may visit and Bewick's Swan sometimes appears in February–March. Other wildfowl include significant numbers of Shelduck, Wigeon, Mallard and Teal, and small numbers of Pintail and Goldeneye, while Red-breasted Merganser is always present in the channel. The occasional Merlin, Peregrine, Red Kite and Hen Harrier occur in winter and the commoner waders are joined by small numbers of Sanderlings on the beach and Black-tailed Godwits on the estuary. Offshore in winter there are often up to 100 Red-throated Divers off the estuary mouth, and large numbers of Great Crested Grebes, occasionally with a Great Northern Diver or a few Scaup, Long-tailed Duck or Velvet Scoter. Parties of Eider and large numbers of Common Scoter are present almost year-round, as are Cormorant, Shag and Gannet.

Spring passage brings a slightly wider variety of waders, and concentrations of up to 1,000 Curlew on the estuary. Up to seven Mediterranean Gulls have been seen in early spring at the Borth gull roost, where there have also been records of Ring-billed, Iceland, Glaucous and Little Gulls.

Breeding species on the saltmarshes include Oystercatcher and Snipe, and Dyfi Marshes is now the most important breeding site for Lapwing and Redshank in Wales. A few pairs of Ringed Plovers nest at Ynys-las, and Shelduck, Red-breasted Merganser, Teal, Sparrowhawk, Buzzard, Water Rail, Barn Owl, all three woodpeckers, Tree Pipit, Stonechat, Whinchat, Redstart, Grasshopper, Sedge and Wood Warblers, many Pied Flycatchers, Willow Tit and Raven all breed on the RSPB reserve at Ynys-hir. Goosander breeds in the area and is often seen in spring, and Kingfisher is frequently seen on the RSPB reserve at Domen Las at the mouth of the Einion stream. Red Kite is only irregularly seen in the area, mostly in spring and summer. Black Grouse formerly occurred on Cors Fochno, but has long since deserted the area.

Midsummer is rather quiet, but autumn brings passage waders, including Black-tailed Godwit, Green Sandpiper, Greenshank and Spotted Redshank; as in spring, there is a concentration of Curlews on the estuary. Large numbers of terns gather off the river mouth in late summer, mostly Sandwich, with smaller numbers of Common, Arctic and Little and occasionally Black or Roseate, while in late summer huge numbers of Manx Shearwaters can be seen in the bay from Ynys-las, particularly in early morning and late evening. In autumn, north gales may push some interesting birds inshore, included Storm and Leach's Petrels and Sooty Shearwater, and parties of Guillemots are regular in October and April.

Information

RSPB Ynys-hir Warden: Dick Squires, Cae'r Berllan, Eglwys-fach, Machynlleth, Powys SY20 8TA. Tel: 01654 781265. E-mail: dick.squires@ rspb.org.uk
Countryside Council for Wales, Warden: Mike Bailey, Plas Gogerddan, Aberystwyth, Ceredigion SY23 3EE. Tel: 01970 821100.
Ynys-las Information Centre, tel: 01970 871640.

28 DYFI FOREST (Meirionnyd)   OS Landranger 124 and 135

This area, bounded by the Afon Dyfi (River Dovey) to the southeast and the A470 and A487 to the north and west, is worth exploring for moorland and woodland birds in spring and early summer.

Habitat

The hills rise to 2,213 feet, with areas of moorland fragmented by conifer plantations.

Access

Access is via the roads and footpaths, especially from the A487 and a minor road which parallel the River Dulas on the west and east sides of its well-wooded valley.

Birds

Red Grouse, Wheatear and the occasional Golden Plover and Ring Ouzel breed on the moors, while the plantations have Redpoll, Siskin and, sometimes, Crossbill. Black Grouse can, with much luck, be found around the young plantations; early morning is best (try the area west of the A487, especially north of Pantperthog; this area is also good for Crossbill). Deciduous woods hold Redstart, Wood Warbler and Pied Flycatcher, with Common Sandpiper and Dipper on the river and streams. Buzzard may be seen anywhere.

29 BROAD WATER (Meirionnyd)   OS Landranger 135

This small estuary holds a selection of wildfowl and waders, and also a colony of Little Tern. It holds some interest throughout the year.

Habitat and Access

The estuary of the Afon Dysynni is accessed via the minor road north of the A493 in Tywyn, paralleling the railway, to reach the estuary near its mouth. A public footpath follows the south shore of the Dysynni (in places), east from the mouth to Bryncrug.

Birds

The estuary has small numbers of wintering wildfowl and can be good for waders at low tide. Large numbers of gulls roost here. At the river mouth there is a small Little Tern colony, wardened during the breeding season, and this area is generally good for gulls and terns plus sea duck.

30 CRAIG-YR-ADERYN (Meirionnyd) OS Landranger 124

Inland along the Dysynni Valley a precipitous crag towers almost 700 feet above the farmland of the valley floor. This is Craig-yr-Aderyn (Bird Rock), which holds a unique colony of breeding Cormorants, as well as Chough.

Access
Leave the A493 at Bryncrug (2½ miles northeast of Tywyn) on a minor road along the valley. The rock is on the right after 3 miles and is a reserve of the North Wales Naturalists' Trust.

Birds
Up to 40 pairs of Cormorants breed (of the British race *carbo*), as well as Chough and Jackdaw, and Raven, Peregrine and Buzzard occur in the area. Outside the breeding season Cormorants roost on the rock, and may be seen in late afternoon and evening.

31 MAWDDACH ESTUARY (Meirionnyd) OS Landranger 124

This extremely scenic estuary holds a variety of commoner wintering wildfowl and waders, while the surrounding woodlands hold all the usual Welsh species. A visit at any time is likely to be productive, though May–June is best for woodland birds.

Habitat
The Afon Mawddach rises within Snowdonia NP and reaches the sea at Barmouth, after passing through c.7 miles of sand and mud flats. The mouth of the estuary is guarded by a narrow spit, which extends north from Fairbourne on the south shore, and in its shelter lies a relatively small saltmarsh. Arthog Bog, now an RSPB reserve, is a relict of once-extensive areas of peat on the south shore. The upper reaches of the estuary are bounded by extensive stands of deciduous woodland and conifer plantations, including the RSPB reserve of Coed Garth Gell, which largely comprises birch and sessile oak.

Access (see map)
RSPB Penmaenpool The RSPB operates an information centre in the old signal box at Penmaenpool on the A493. Open daily, 11.00–17.00, late May–early September (weekends only April–May), information on the latest sightings is available and there are good views from the higher floor of the box over the upper reaches of the estuary.

Penmaenpool–Morfa Mawddach Walk From Penmaenpool signal box it is possible to walk west for c.5½ miles to Morfa Mawddach station (from where you can cross to Barmouth via a 1-mile-long footbridge). This walk gives excellent views over the entire lower estuary. Walking east along the old railway from Penmaenpool signal box gives views over the upper estuary, including some stands of reeds and willow scrub.

Arthog Bog RSPB reserve Accessible at all times via the Penmaenpool–Morfa Mawddach Walk from Morfa Mawddach station. The bog has a selection of breeding passerines, including Grasshopper Warbler and Common Whitethroat.

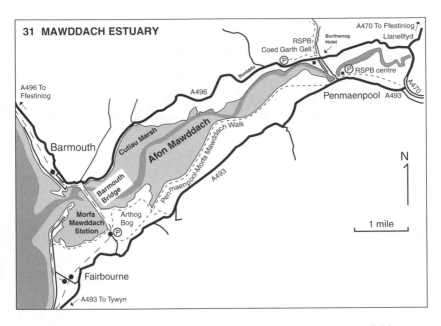

31 MAWDDACH ESTUARY

Fairbourne Bar The minor road that follows the railway north from Fairbourne gives views of the mouth of the estuary, which is a good area for terns.

Barmouth/Cutiau Marsh On the north shore of the estuary, this area of salt-marsh can be viewed from lay-bys on the A496 c.2 miles east of Barmouth.

Coed Garth Gell RSPB reserve Accessible at all times along the footpath from the lay-by on the A496 opposite the Borthwnog Hotel.

Birds

Small numbers of waders winter, including Oystercatcher, Golden and Ringed Plovers, Turnstone, Curlew, Bar-tailed Godwit, Redshank and Dunlin. Occasionally Greenshank may winter. Wildfowl include Wigeon, Teal, Goldeneye and Red-breasted Merganser, while interesting passerines include Dipper and, sometimes, Siskin and Redpoll.

On passage a variety of waders occurs including Whimbrel and all of the wintering species, although being in the far west, birds such as Little Stint and Curlew Sandpiper are infrequent. In late summer there are congregations of Common and Sandwich Terns off the estuary mouth, and sometimes Arctic and Little Terns. Osprey has been recorded on passage.

Breeders include Shelduck, Red-breasted Merganser, Oystercatcher, Snipe, Redshank, Grasshopper, Sedge and Reed Warblers, with Common Sandpiper, Grey Wagtail and Dipper by the river and its tributaries. The surrounding hills and woodlands have resident Sparrowhawk, Buzzard, all three woodpeckers, Nuthatch, Treecreeper and Raven, joined in summer by Tree Pipit, Whinchat, Redstart, Wood and Garden Warblers, and Pied and Spotted Flycatchers.

Information

RSPB Mawddach Valley: Reg Thorpe, Abergwynant Lodge, Penmaenpool, Dolgellau LL40 1YF. Tel: 01341 422071. E-mail: mawddach@ rspb.org.uk

Oystercatcher

32 LAKE VYRNWY (Montgomeryshire)   OS Landranger 125

The largest remaining area of heather moorland in Wales is in the Berwyn Mountains, and the RSPB has a reserve at Lake Vyrnwy, c.15 miles east of Dolgellau. Mostly managed by agreement with Severn Trent Water, Forest Enterprise and the Lake Vyrnwy Hotel, the total area of the reserve is c.26,000 acres. The best time to visit is May–June for summer visitors to the woodlands, but the reserve as a whole is worth visiting at any season.

Habitat

Lake Vyrnwy is the largest man-made lake in Wales, nearly 5 miles long and covering 1,100 acres. It was formed when the Afon Vyrnwy was dammed in 1891. Fringed by scrub woodland and meadows, heather and grass moorland rise to nearly 2,000 feet, with a network of streams and large areas of conifer plantations, and c.200 acres of deciduous woodland.

Access (see map)

Lake Vyrnwy Take the B4393 from Llanfyllin (northwest of Welshpool) to Llanwddyn, from where the road circumnavigates the lake. The reserve is open at all times, with access along public roads and footpaths. The RSPB information centre is on the minor road 100 yards south of the west end of the dam. It is open 10.30–16.30 daily April–Christmas (or dusk if earlier), weekends only Christmas–March. There may be a video link to interesting nests (e.g. Peregrine). The Coed y Capel hide is by the car park and the Lakeside hide on the northeast shore of the reservoir. There are three nature trails: the Grwn-oer Trail is 1½ miles long, the Rhiwargor Island Trail 2 miles (taking in the Centenary hide), and the Graig Garth-Bwlch Trail 3 miles long (taking in the Garrison Wood hide).

Minor roads north and west of Lake Vyrnwy The two minor roads that lead north and west from the head of the reservoir are very good for moorland species. The south road leaves the B4393 at Pont Eunant and climbs to c.1,600 feet before dropping into the upper watershed of the River Dyfi and Dinas Mawddwy. The other heads north over the watershed and descends past the conifer-clad hills of Penllyn Forest through Cwm Hirnank to Bala.

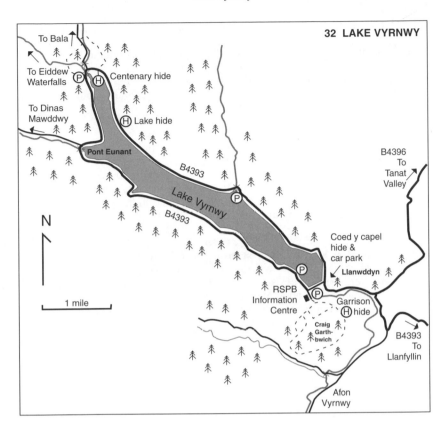

Birds

The moorland has a fine range of breeding species including Buzzard, Hen Harrier, Merlin, Red Grouse, Curlew, Short-eared Owl, Wheatear, Whinchat, Stonechat and Raven. Peregrine and Red Kite also visit the area (and Peregrine sometimes nests on the dam, with a closed-circuit TV relay to the RSPB visitor centre). Ring Ouzel is scarce but can sometimes be found near Eiddew Waterfalls. Areas of deciduous woodland hold Woodcock (may be seen roding over Grwn-oer trail), Tawny Owl, Green and Great Spotted Woodpeckers, Willow Tit, Nuthatch and Treecreeper, and these are joined in summer by Redstart, Garden and Wood Warblers, and Spotted and Pied Flycatchers. In the conifers there are Goshawk, Sparrowhawk, Grasshopper Warbler (young plantations), Crossbill, Redpoll and Siskin. The woodland fringes attract Tree Pipit and, sometimes, Black Grouse. Along the streams and around the reservoir Great Crested and Little Grebes, Grey Heron, Teal, Red-breasted Merganser, Goosander, Common Sandpiper, Kingfisher, Grey Wagtail and Dipper occur.

Waders occasionally appear on passage, especially at the north end of the reservoir, and Osprey may pass through. In winter, wildfowl include Whooper Swan, Wigeon, Teal, Pochard, Goldeneye and Goosander, and there is a roost of Black-headed Gulls, while Great Northern Diver may also turn up.

Information

RSPB Centre Manager: Jo Morris, Bryn Awel, Llanwddyn, Oswestry, Salop SY10 0LZ. Tel: 01691 870278. E-mail: lake.vyrnwy@rspb.org.uk

33 CARNGAFALLT (Breconshire and Radnorshire)   OS Landranger 147

Lying in the Wye and Elan Valleys near Rhayader, these woodlands hold a typical range of breeding birds, including Redstart, Wood Warbler and Pied Flycatcher, and are best visited in May–June. Nearby, at Gigrin Farm, a Red Kite feeding station offers superb views of this, the most graceful of raptors, through the winter.

Habitat

The woodlands in the upper Wye Valley are some of the best in Wales for birds, and the adjacent hill farms and moorland areas have the usual range of upland birds. Gigrin Farm lies in the Wye Valley between 700 and 1,200 feet and is entirely grazed. The RSPB has three woodland reserves in the area (Dyffryn, Cwm and Cwm yr Esgob), and an upland reserve at Carngafallt on the plateau southwest of the confluence of the Elan and the Wye.

Access

Gigrin Farm Red Kite feeding station Leave Rhayader south on the A470 towards Builth Wells and after c.⅓ mile turn left (east) to Gigrin Farm (signed). There is an entry fee. The birds are fed daily, mid-October to mid-April, at 14.00 (15.00 BST), when a scattering of meat and bones is put out in a field next to the farm. Several hides permit excellent views, but the kites are tame and will swoop low over the track even with people present. Numbers vary, but usually at least ten come to feed, sometimes as many as 30 (70 in January 1999), together with Buzzard, Raven and other corvids.

Dyffryn Wood Leave Rhayader south on the A470 and after 1 mile park in the lay-by as woodland appears on the left (east) side of the road. Access to the reserve is possible at all times. The A470 follows the River Wye and it is worth stopping where possible to scan the river for waterbirds.

Carngafallt Common This area of c.650 acres is dominated by heather and is accessible from a minor road, between Llanwrthwl (off the A470 3 miles south of Rhayader) and Elan village, which runs along the south margin of the plateau.

Birds

Breeders in the woodlands include Woodcock, Lesser Spotted Woodpecker, Redstart, Wood and Garden Warblers, Pied Flycatcher and Willow Tit. Hawfinch and Tree Sparrow are also possible, and areas of conifers hold Siskin and Redpoll. At woodland fringes look for Tree Pipit, Whinchat and Wheatear and, overhead, Red Kite, Sparrowhawk, Buzzard, Peregrine and Raven. Rivers and streams hold Goosander, Common Sandpiper, Kingfisher, Grey Wagtail and Dipper.

In winter the uplands are largely devoid of birds and the woodlands are usually very quiet, but at this season the feeding station at Gigrin Farm provides a guaranteed Red Kite spectacle.

Information

Gigrin Farm, South Street, Rhayader, Powys LD6 5BL. Tel: 01597 810243.
RSPB Carngafalt, Warden: The Cwm, Llanwrthwl, Llandrindod Wells, Powys LD1 6NU. Tel: 01597 811169.

34 ELAN VALLEY (Radnorshire) OS Landranger 147

This area, much favoured by tourists, provides a typical cross-section of the birds of Welsh uplands and waterways, including Peregrine and Red Kite. Late April–June is the best time to visit.

Habitat

The area comprises a mosaic of habitats—moorland, blanket bog, woodland, rivers and reservoirs—covering c.70 square miles in the catchment of the rivers Elan and Claerwen. Set aside to protect the watershed, most of the area is leased by the Elan Valley Trust, with largely open access. Craig Goch, Penygarreg, Garreg-ddu and Caban-Coch Reservoirs lie in the valley of the River Elan and were constructed in the late-19th century to supply drinking water to Birmingham, while Claerwen Reservoir in the valley of the same name was opened in 1952 (the system now also supplies parts of south and mid-Wales). Penygarreg, Garreg-ddu and Caban-Coch Reservoirs are bordered by stands of sessile oak woodland, and there are also large blocks of conifers. Claerwen and Craig Goch Reservoirs lie at higher altitudes, and upland areas are largely sheep-walk, dominated by purple moor-grass, with rather restricted areas of heather.

Access

Leave Rhayader west on the B4518. The reservoirs are well signed and much of the four waters in the Elan Valley can be seen from surrounding minor roads. A visitor centre with ample parking lies near Caban-Coch dam and is open daily 10.00–18.00 mid-March to late October. Offering a shop, cafe and exhibitions, there is also an information desk with full details of the 80 miles of leafleted walks and nature trails, and a Countryside Ranger service. The Elan Valley Trail runs for 6 miles from the visitor centre to Craig Goch dam beside the reservoirs, and Cnwch Wood Nature Trail climbs through excellent sessile oak woodland. There are also car parks at Penygarreg and Craig Goch dams, and at the dam of the massive Claerwen Reservoir. Upland species are best sought in the watershed between the Elan and Claerwen Valleys (open access). A less strenuous option is to follow the road north and west from Pont ar Elan at the head of Craig Goch reservoir to Cwmystwyth, scanning en route for raptors.

Birds

Breeders include Great Crested Grebe, Teal, Goosander and Common Sandpiper around the reservoirs and Grey Wagtail and a few Dippers along streams and rivers. Red Grouse (in heather-dominated areas), Snipe, Golden Plover and a very few Stonechats are present in the uplands all year, while Dunlin, Tree Pipit, Whinchat and Wheatear are summer visitors; the latter is common and may be seen from the roads, but Golden Plover and Dunlin are found only on the highest moors. Buzzard, Peregrine and Red Kite are resident and usually easy to see, but Merlin is rare and Short-eared Owl usually present only in good vole years. (Woodcock, Curlew, Lapwing and Ring Ouzel have been lost as breeders.) Sessile oak woodland holds breeding Redstart, Wood Warbler and Pied Flycatcher, with small numbers of Lesser Spotted Woodpecker and Hawfinch. The conifers hold Goshawk and Siskin and, in invasion years, Crossbill; Parrot Crossbill bred in 1990.

In winter, wildfowl on the lakes may include Pochard, Goldeneye and Goosander, and the surrounding moorland occasionally produces a Hen Harrier or Merlin.

Information

Hyder PLC & Elan Valley Trust, Pete Jennings, Rangers Office, Elan Valley Visitor Centre, Rhayader, Powys LD6 5HP. Tel: 01597 810880. E-mail:pete@elanvalley.org.uk

35 BARDSEY ISLAND (Caernarfon)   OS Landranger 123

Bardsey lies 2 miles off the Lleyn Peninsula and the Bird Observatory was established in 1953. Several scarcer migrants are nearly annual, and Bardsey has a very long list of rarities to its credit. The best times to visit are late April–early June and August–early November, and ideally a visit should be timed to coincide with the first ten days after a new moon to have the best chance of witnessing a lighthouse 'attraction'.

Habitat

Bardsey covers 444 acres and is dominated by the 548-foot-high Mynydd Enlli (the 'Mountain'), the upper areas of which are covered by bracken and rocky outcrops. The steep east slopes are riddled with Manx Shearwater and rabbit burrows. The Observatory garden, the four withy beds and a small pine plantation provide cover for migrants. The south of the island has a lighthouse, which in certain weather conditions following a new moon can attract hundreds or even thousands of nocturnal migrants. Nights with thick cloud cover or a 'smoke haze' obscuring the horizon are best, but such conditions formerly resulted in many fatalities. A 'false' light was built nearby in 1978 and has greatly reduced the death toll. Large numbers of birds are now trapped and ringed and an 'attraction' is certainly a unique experience.

Access

The island boat leaves Porth Meudwy, 1 mile southwest of Aberdaron at 08.30 on Saturday or the first suitable day thereafter; delays are possible in either direction during bad weather. Day trips can be organised from Porth Meudwy. The Observatory is open late March–early November and bookings are taken on a weekly basis Saturday–Saturday. Up to 12 people can be accommodated on a self-catering basis in the large stone-built farmhouse in single, double or triple rooms, and two midsummer courses are operated on a full-board basis. There are two seawatching hides and another in a small bay. In addition, Bardsey Island Trust has several holiday cottages for hire on the island.

Birds

Spring migration commences in late March with the usual assortment of chats, warblers and flycatchers as well as diurnal migrants, but late spring is best for rarities, with Hoopoe and Woodchat Shrike among the more regular.

Ten species of seabird breed, notably c.3,000 pairs of Manx Shearwaters, as well as small numbers of Fulmar, Shag, Razorbill, Guillemot, Herring, Lesser Black-backed and Great Black-backed Gulls, and Kittiwake. Peregrine, Oystercatcher, Little Owl, Rock Pipit, Stonechat, Wheatear, Raven, and c.7 pairs of Choughs add interest. Small numbers of non-breeding Storm Petrels may come ashore at night.

Return passage begins in late July with a trickle of warblers and these are joined by chats, Goldcrest and flycatchers as the autumn progresses—light east or southeast winds are best. October is the premier month for migration, with the possibility of large falls of night migrants such as Redwing and Blackbird, movements of Skylark, Starling and finches, and Icterine, Melodious and Yellow-browed Warblers, Firecrest and Red-breasted Flycatcher are all nearly annual. Bardsey also has potential for seawatching. There may be large numbers of Manx Shearwaters, Kittiwakes, Guillemots and Razorbills, as well as Gannets, terns and Arctic Skuas, plus a few Sooty Shearwaters and Great Skuas, while Leach's Petrel, Pomarine Skua, Sabine's Gull and Little Auk are all scarce but regular; the largest and most varied movements occur in September–early October following strong west or northwest winds.

Information

Bird Observatory Warden: Steven Stansfield, Bird Observatory, Cristen, Bardsey Island, off Aberdaron, Pwllheli, Caernarvonshire LL53 8DE. Tel: 07855 264151. E-mail: steve@bbfo.freeserve.co.uk

Bookings Secretary (SAE please): Alicia Normand, 46 Maudlin Drive, Teign-mouth, Devon TQ14 8SB. Tel: 01626 773908. E-mail: bob&lis@solfach.freeserve.co.uk

Bardsey Island Trust: Simon Glyn, Stable Hen, Tywyddyn Du, Cricceith, Caernarvonshire LL52 0LY. Tel: 01758 730326.

36 LLEYN PENINSULA (Caernarfon)   OS Landranger 123

This can be as good as Bardsey for migrants, and rarities have also been recorded, while resident Chough is an added bonus.

Habitat and Access

Porth Meudwy This sheltered valley is attractive to migrants. Leave Aberdaron west on the minor road to Uwchmynydd and turn left after ½ mile. Park in the lay-by after a further ½ mile and follow the track east through the steep-sided valley to the beach, checking for migrants in the dense bracken, gorse and honeysuckle en route. It is possible to take the steps to the clifftop path which runs south to Pen y Cil, and in summer small numbers of seabirds, as well as Peregrine and Chough, can be seen.

Braich y Pwll This is the headland opposite Bardsey. Leave Aberdaron west on the minor road to Uwchmynydd and follow the road to the coastguard buildings. There is plenty of parking along this road and the headland is crossed by several footpaths. It is good for seabirds and Chough in summer, with potential for seawatching and migrants.

Birds

In summer, Fulmar, Gannet, Shag, Cormorant, Herring and Great Black-backed Gulls, Kittiwake, Razorbill and Guillemot may be seen around the cliffs or offshore, with Manx Shearwater possible, especially in the evenings. Peregrine, Little Owl, Rock Pipit, Stonechat, Wheatear, Raven and Chough also haunt the cliffs, with Garden and Sedge Warblers and Common and Lesser Whitethroats at Porth Meudwy.

In spring and autumn migrants may turn up in any area of cover, and the commoner species may be joined by Turtle Dove, Redstart and Black Redstart, Whinchat and Ring Ouzel, while several rarities have been recorded. Offshore at Braich y Pwll, especially in autumn, Sooty Shearwater, Leach's Petrel and a variety of terns may occur, especially in strong west or northwest winds.

37 NEWBOROUGH WARREN (Isle of Anglesey)   OS Landranger 114

The Warren and adjacent coast harbour an excellent variety of wildfowl, waders and raptors. The treeless southeast section of the Warren and much of its coastal perimeter is a NNR, managed by the Countryside Council for Wales (CCW). The best time to visit is during winter and passage periods, but summer is also interesting.

Habitat

The Warren is an area of sand dunes covering over 3,000 acres, two-thirds of which (Newborough Forest) have been planted with Corsican pine. Southwest of the dunes is Ynys Llanddwyn, a rocky promontory connected to the mainland by a narrow strip of sand which is covered on the highest tides. North of the Warren is the Cefni estuary, largely comprising the extensive Malltraeth Sands, but with some salt-marsh along its south shore. At the head of the estuary, and separated from it by an embankment known as the Cob, is Malltraeth Pool. This is an excellent spot for passage waders, as are the adjacent fields when flooded (although recently water levels have varied erratically, and when high there are few waders). In the dunes is a small pool, Llyn Rhos-ddu, while Llyn Coron, a larger lake, lies north of the Warren. Finally, on the south flank of the Warren, lies the Braint estuary.

Access (see map)

Within the NNR, permits are required for areas away from designated routes and public rights of way.

Malltraeth Pool This can be viewed from the A4080 and the Cob (be careful not to disturb birds if using the Cob). The River Cefni upstream of the bridge can also be good for wildfowl.

Cefni Estuary Walk south from the Cob along the seaward side of the forest to view the saltmarsh. In winter a few Hen Harriers roost in this area, as well as Ravens; other raptors are also frequent.

Ynys Llanddwyn An excellent spot in winter. Divers are often present offshore, together with Slavonian and Great Crested Grebes and Common Scoter. Purple Sandpiper and Turnstone occur on the rocky shore. Drive southwest from Newborough on a minor road past the cemetery and then follow the track through the forest to the FC car park (information centre open in summer). Walking west along the shore, the island is reached after 1 mile. Alternatively, walk for 2½ miles from Newborough directly to the island through the forest.

Llyn Rhos-ddu A public hide overlooks this small lake. In winter Ruddy Duck, Shoveler, Gadwall and Water Rail can be seen, and raptors hunt the surrounding dunes. Access is via the short track to the small car park from the A4080 at Pen-lon.

Llyn Parc Mawr This pool has a hide, accessible along forest tracks from the A4080 c.1 mile northwest of Newborough. The pool attracts waterfowl, and woodland passerines come to drink, sometimes including Crossbill.

Llyn Coron Footpaths run along the west, southeast and north shores of the lake, accessible from car parks along the A4080 via a short walk across dry heathland. Llyn Coron supports wintering wildfowl, sometimes including wild swans, as well as breeding Great Crested Grebe, Stonechat, Grasshopper and Sedge Warblers, and summering Ruddy Duck.

Birds

In winter, Cormorant, Shag, all three divers (particularly Great Northern and Red-throated), and Great Crested and Slavonian Grebes are joined offshore by numbers of Common Scoter, and occasionally Eider or Long-tailed Duck. There are up to 250 Pintail and many Wigeon (up to 1600 on Llyn Coron), plus Goldeneye and a few Shoveler, Gadwall and Ruddy Duck. Flocks of Canada and feral Greylag Geese roam the area, and occasional Pink-footed and White-fronted

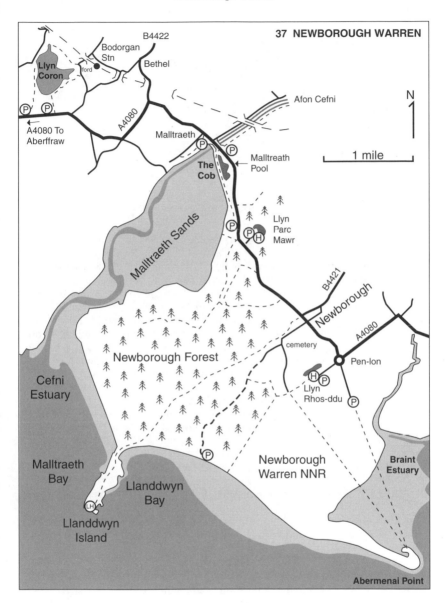

37 NEWBOROUGH WARREN

Geese join them. Both Whooper and Bewick's Swans may winter. Peregrine, Merlin, Buzzard, Hen Harrier, and Barn and Short-eared Owls can be seen, and waders include Knot and Grey Plover, and sometimes Spotted Redshank and Greenshank, with Turnstone and Purple Sandpiper on Ynys Llanddwyn. Small flocks of Snow Buntings may occur along the shore.

Passage can be good, with a wide variety of waders. Little Stint, Sanderling, Curlew Sandpiper, Black-tailed Godwit and Spotted Redshank may all occur.

Breeders include Great Crested and, sometimes, Little Grebes, Shelduck, Teal, Red-breasted Merganser, Oystercatcher and Ringed Plover, while Herring, Lesser Black-backed and Black-headed Gulls, Tree Pipit and Whinchat nest in the dunes,

Bewick's Swans

together with Stonechat and, occasionally, Short-eared Owl. Sparrowhawk, Coal Tit, Siskin, Redpoll and, sometimes, Crossbill breed in the plantations, together with the elusive Golden Pheasant. At Ynys Llanddwyn there are breeding Cormorants and a few Shags, Rock Pipits and Stonechats, and Turnstone summers. Often there are terns offshore, mostly Common, Arctic and Sandwich, but occasionally also Little or Roseate. Other breeders in the area include Barn and Little Owls, Grasshopper, Reed and Sedge Warblers, and Common and Lesser Whitethroats. Newborough was famous in the past for its breeding Montagu's Harriers and Merlins, but sadly these have long since gone.

Information
Countryside Council for Wales, Newborough Warren, Warden: W. Sandison, CCW North West Area, Bryn Menai, Holyhead Road, Bangor, Caernarvonshire LL57 2JA. Tel: 01248 716422.

38 VALLEY WETLANDS (Isle of Anglesey)   OS Landranger 114

Lying just north of the RAF Valley airbase, Llyn Penrhyn is just one of the many lakes on Anglesey, and supports a typical range of species. It is an RSPB reserve.

Habitat
The lake is surrounded by reedbeds, areas of sedges and willow carr. To the south lies an area of heathland with some rocky outcrops.

Access
Leave the A5 c.2 miles west of Bryngwran on minor roads south to Llanfihangel yn Nhowyn and on to Dowyn. There is limited roadside parking on the right-hand side, just past the RAF camp and just before the railway bridge, and from here public footpaths skirt the south and west flanks of the lake. There is no other access.

Birds
Wintering wildfowl may include Bewick's Swan and Goldeneye, as well as resident breeding wildfowl. The area attracts raptors, including Sparrowhawk, Hen Harrier, Peregrine, Merlin and Short-eared Owl.

Breeders include Little and Great Crested Grebes, feral Canada and Greylag Geese, Gadwall, Teal, Shoveler, Pochard, Ruddy Duck, Oystercatcher, Lapwing and Redshank.

Information
RSPB Valley Wetlands Warden: Maes y Ffynnon, Penrhasgarnedd, Bangor, Gwynned. tel: 01248 363800.

39 HOLYHEAD HARBOUR (Isle of Anglesey)   OS Landranger 114

The harbour is worth visiting in winter for divers, grebes and sea ducks.

Habitat
A sheltered harbour surrounded by piers and a long breakwater.

Access (see map on p.334)
In Holyhead, park near the end of the A5 near the sailing club or near Soldiers Point. There is access on foot along the breakwater, though many of the birds can be seen from its base at Soldiers Point.

Birds
In winter divers are usually present in the harbour, especially Black-throated and less often Great Northern. Red-necked Grebe is also sometimes seen, late winter being the best period. One or two Black Guillemots are regular, and sea ducks may include Common Scoter and Red-breasted Merganser.

In autumn Gannet, Manx Shearwater and a variety of terns may be seen off-shore, but in good seawatching conditions, Penrhyn Mawr at South Stack RSPB reserve or Point Lynas are better.

40 SOUTH STACK (Isle of Anglesey)   OS Landranger 114

Situated 3 miles west of Holyhead, on Holy Island at the west extremity of Anglesey, South Stack cliffs and their hinterland of maritime heath are an RSPB reserve. The best time to see the seabirds is May–June.

Habitat
The reserve includes both North and South Stacks, and these rise to nearly 400 feet. South Stack is connected to the mainland by a footbridge and a flight of steps that gives access to its lighthouse. Landward of the cliffs, areas of heather and gorse heath rise to 853 feet at Holyhead Mountain, and there is a separate area of heathland to the south, at Penrhos Feilw Common.

Access (see map)
South Stack Cliffs From the A5 in Holyhead follow signs from just before the ferries via Llaingoch and Twr to South Stack. There is a large car park and access is possible at all times along the public paths. The information centre at Ellin's Tower (a short walk from the main car park) overlooks the main auk colony, and provides a video link to the ledges; there are also good views from the steps to the lighthouse and from the lighthouse itself (which re-opened in 1997). The Tower is open daily Easter–early September, 11.00–17.00, and during this period a warden is present. Visitors should keep to the roads and paths.

Penrhos Feilw Common (The Range) Follow minor roads south from South Stack or leave the A5 at Dyffryn on the B4545 to Trearddur and then take the minor coast road through Penrhosfeilw, parking at Gors-goch. There is open access to Penrhos Feilw Common along tracks from the road south of South Stack. Penrhyn Mawr is a good spot to seawatch from; boulders and shattered rocks provide some cover.

Birds
Nine species of seabird breed, including Fulmar, Kittiwake, Herring, Great Black-backed and Lesser Black-backed Gulls, a few pairs of Shags, up to 3,000 Guillemots, and smaller numbers of Razorbills and Puffins. Other breeders include Peregrine, Kestrel, Stock Dove, Little Owl, Rock Pipit, Raven and 4–5 pairs of Choughs, which can be seen around the cliffs and RSPB car park, and in winter in fields along the approach road. The heath has breeding Stonechat and Common Whitethroat, with Lapwing and Redshank on Penrhos Feilw Common.

Gannet and Manx Shearwater can sometimes be seen offshore in summer and autumn, the shearwaters being commonest in July–August when up to 1,000 a day occur; they are especially numerous in early morning and evening. Common and Arctic Terns are also present offshore and, in spring, Great Northern and Red-throated Divers, Common Scoter and Arctic Skua are regular, and Pomarine Skuas probably annual. No special conditions are required for seawatching at this season, and interesting birds may be seen at any time of day. In autumn, by contrast, an early-morning watch in strong northwest winds is recommended: Sooty

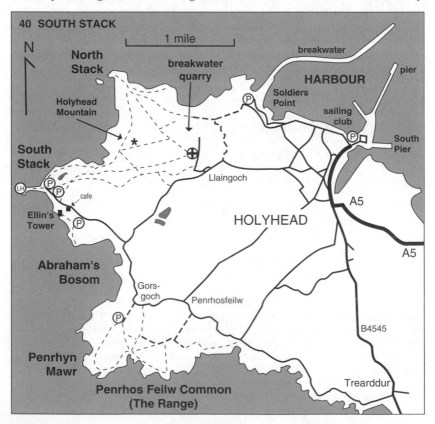

40 SOUTH STACK

Shearwater, Storm and Leach's Petrels, and Pomarine and Long-tailed Skuas are possibilities, while Great and Arctic Skuas and large numbers of Kittiwakes and auks are regular.

On passage the heaths attract harriers, Short-eared Owl, Whimbrel and other waders (sometimes including Dotterel), Wheatear, Ring Ouzel and warblers, and there can be large movements of diurnal migrants in late autumn. In winter Red-throated Diver, Common Scoter and Red-breasted Merganser occur offshore, while Hen Harrier and Merlin hunt the heaths. Choughs may have formed large nomadic flocks, making them difficult to locate at times, though they are often in the grassy fields bordering the approach road to the reserve, and they may roost at Holyhead Breakwater Quarry Country Park (see map).

Information
RSPB South Stack, Warden: Alastair Moralee, Plas Nico, South Stack, Holyhead, Anglesey LL65 1YH. Tel: 01407 764973.

41 CEMLYN LAGOON (Isle of Anglesey) OS Landranger 114

On the north coast of Anglesey, this small lagoon holds important colonies of breeding terns, in some years including Roseate Tern. During passage and winter periods, a variety of wildfowl and waders occurs.

Habitat
A shingle storm beach has sealed off the entrance to Cemlyn Bay and formed a saline lagoon. The area is owned by the NT and managed as a reserve by the North Wales Wildlife Trust.

Access
Leave Holyhead on the A5 and take the A5025 north towards Amlwch. After c.11 miles, turn northwest in Tregele on an unclassified road signed to Cemlyn. There are car parks at both the east (Traeth Cemlyn) and west (near Bryn Aber) ends of the shingle ridge. The lagoon can be viewed from the shingle ridge, but it is best to avoid 'skylining' as this will inevitably alarm the birds. During the breeding season access to some areas is restricted, and a summer warden is present.

Birds
Breeders include variable numbers of Sandwich, Common, Arctic and Roseate Terns. Sandwich Tern has peaked at over 1,000 pairs but conversely Roseate Tern has all but disappeared from Anglesey and can no longer be expected at this site (the formerly important Anglesey population has, apparently, moved across the Irish Sea to nest at Rockabill in Co. Dublin). Other breeding species include Shelduck, Red-breasted Merganser, Oystercatcher, Ringed Plover, Redshank and Black-headed Gull. Others in the area include Yellow Wagtail, Wheatear, Sedge Warbler and Common Whitethroat.

On passage Little Tern may join the locally breeding species and waders can be interesting, with Grey Plover, Sanderling, Common, Curlew and Purple Sandpipers, Whimbrel and Turnstone all possible. Manx Shearwater may occur at sea, as can Leach's Petrel and a variety of skuas during onshore winds.

In winter numbers of wildfowl use the lagoon, including up to 400 Wigeon, as well as Teal, Shoveler, Pochard and Goldeneye, and Bewick's and Whooper Swans are regular visitors. Hen Harrier, Peregrine and Barn Owl can be found hunting in the general area. Offshore, look for Red-throated and Great Northern Divers, Great Crested Grebe, Eider, Common Scoter, Razorbill and Guillemot.

Information

North Wales Wildlife Trust, Chris Wynne, 376 High Street, Bangor, Caernarvonshire LL57 1YE. Tel: 01248 351541. E-mail: nwwt@ cix.co.uk

42 LLYN ALAW (Isle of Anglesey)   OS Landranger 114

This is the largest area of fresh water in Anglesey and holds spectacular concentrations of wintering wildfowl (the largest of any inland water in Wales).

Habitat

The lake covers 777 acres and is surrounded by reedbeds and areas of fen vegetation, as well as some mixed woodland.

Access (see map)

The lake is approached via minor roads from Llanerchymedd on the B5111. There are three car parks, with a visitor centre at the southwest end of the lake and a hide overlooking the northeast sector. The area is managed as a reserve by Welsh Water and there is open access, except to the sanctuary area at the northeast end.

Birds

Wintering wildfowl include Mute, Whooper and, sometimes, Bewick's Swans, Pink-footed and occasionally White-fronted Geese, Ruddy Duck, Wigeon, Gadwall, Teal, Shoveler and Pochard. Sea duck may occur, including Long-tailed Duck. Snipe, Curlew and Golden Plover may be found around the lake

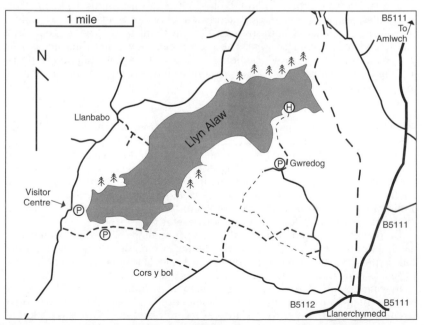

and in surrounding pastures, with Peregrine, Merlin, Hen Harrier, Sparrowhawk and Barn and Short-eared Owls all hunting the area.

On passage small numbers of commoner waders occur, as well as some scarcer species such as Spotted Redshank, Wood Sandpiper and, in some autumns, Little Stint and Curlew Sandpiper. There may also be terns and sometimes Little Gull.

Breeders include Great Crested Grebe, Grey Heron, feral Greylag and Canada Geese, Gadwall, Oystercatcher, Common Tern, Whinchat, Grasshopper and Sedge Warblers, and Common and Lesser Whitethroats.

Information
Welsh Water, Head Ranger: Jim Clark, Visitor Centre, Llyn Alaw Reservoir, Llantrisant, Holyhead, Anglesey LL65 4TW. Tel: 01407 730762. E-mail: llynalaw @amserve.net

43 POINT LYNAS (Isle of Anglesey)   OS Landranger 114

Situated at the northwest tip of Anglesey, this is an excellent seawatching station.

Habitat
A narrow promontory projecting north for c.½ mile, with a lighthouse at the tip.

Access
From the A5025 southeast of Amlwch follow minor roads via Llaneilian to the Point, parking just before the gate on the lighthouse road. The period immediately after dawn is best for seabirds.

Birds
Manx Shearwater may be seen offshore throughout summer and autumn, and other regular species include Fulmar, Gannet and Kittiwake, with large numbers of terns in early autumn, sometimes including a few Black, and Razorbill and Guillemot in late autumn, with occasional Puffin, Black Guillemot or Little Auk All four species of skua are possible in autumn, though Pomarine and Long-tailed are scarce, and Leach's Petrel and Sooty Shearwater may occur during N–NW autumn gales. Numbers of visible passerine migrants also pass through.

In winter small numbers of divers and grebes may be present offshore, and sea duck can include Red-breasted Merganser, Eider, Scaup and Goldeneye.

Resident species around the head include Rock Pipit, Stonechat and Raven.

44 FEDW FAWR (Isle of Anglesey)   OS Landranger 114

A handful of pairs at Anglesey's eastern tip are the only breeding Black Guillemots south of St Bees Head.

Access
Leave Beaumaris north on the B5109 to Llangoed and follow a minor road north for 1 mile to Mariandyrys. Follow this to the bottom of a hill, cross a bridge and turn right to park (at SH 605810). Walk uphill towards Penmon, passing a farm entrance after c.50 yards and take a track north (left) after 200 yards down the extremely narrow road to Fedw Fawr (it is possible to drive this

lane but there are few passing places and only a very limited parking/turning area at the end).

Birds

Black Guillemot is usually present in the boulder scree at the foot of the cliffs below the car park (normally c.6 pairs in the area) or is viewable from the coastal footpath. There are also a few Razorbills and Guillemots, and other breeding birds in the area include Shag, Peregrine, Rock Pipit, Stonechat, Raven and Chough, while the Common Gulls breeding in nearby quarries are the only ones in Wales.

45 ABER (Caernarfon)   OS Landranger 115

The Lavan Sands, northeast of Bangor, hold internationally important numbers of Oystercatcher and Curlew, and specialities are the wintering Black-necked and Slavonian Grebes and concentrations of moulting Great Crested Grebes and Red-breasted Mergansers. Traeth Lafan LNR covers over 6,000 acres of the sands, which are a Special Area of Conservation (EU Habitats Directive).

Habitat

The mouth of the Afon Ogwen, together with Bangor Flats, forms the muddy west extremity of Lavan Sands, which can be up to 3 miles wide at low water and extend east to Llanfairfechan.

Access (see map)

Divers, grebes and sea ducks are best looked for around high water, and waders are best seen 1–2 hours either side of high tide. A footpath follows the shore from Aber Ogwen to Llanfairfechan, with access at the following points.

Porth Penrhyn Accessible from the A5122 in Bangor, with views over Bangor Flats.

Aber Ogwen Leave the main A55 North Wales Expressway north on the A5122 towards Bangor, turning right after 1 mile to Tal-y-bont, and then taking a minor road left after a further ½ mile to the coast beyond Aber Ogwen Farm. At the end of this lane there is a car park and just before this a track leads through the gate to a hide overlooking the estuary and a small pool. This is a good spot for wintering Water Rail, Black-tailed Godwit, Spotted Redshank, Greenshank and Kingfisher, and is generally productive for ducks and waders.

Morfa Aber Leave the A55 dual carriageway at Abergwyngregyn, where a minor road passes under the railway to the shore, and there is a car park and hide. It is possible to walk northeast from here to the mouth of the Afon Aber, another good area for waders and ducks.

Llanfairfechan Sewage Farm (Morfa Madryn) This is accessed from the eastbound carriageway of the A55 c.1 mile SW of Llanfairfechan, at a small sign for 'training centre', following the lane to view the filter beds on the right. These regularly attract wintering Chiffchaffs and Firecrests. Continue on foot over the railway to the shore, where there is a hide. Waders roost on the small promontory and there may be Twite on the saltmarsh.

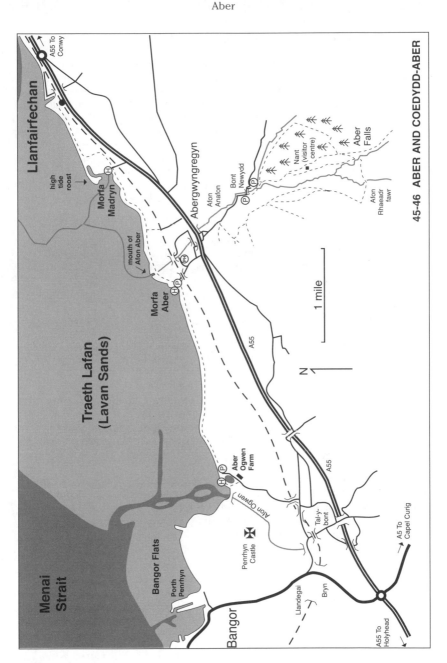

45-46 ABER AND COEDYDD-ABER

Llanfairfechan Offshore from Llanfairfechan promenade there are regularly small numbers of divers, Black-necked and Slavonian Grebes, and sea duck.

Birds

In winter there are numbers of Great Crested Grebe and Red-throated Diver off-shore, as well as a few Great Northern Divers. Black-throated Diver is uncommon, tending to occur only on passage. Small numbers of Slavonian and Black-necked

Grebes are regular, together with Red-breasted Merganser, Goldeneye and Common Scoter, and a few Long-tailed Ducks and Velvet Scoter. Other wildfowl include large numbers of Wigeon, Teal and Shelduck, and a few Pintail and Shoveler. Commoner waders include internationally important numbers of Oystercatcher and Curlew, and these are joined by a few Greenshanks and Turnstones, and occasional Spotted Redshank and Black-tailed Godwit. Water Rail, Kingfisher, Chiffchaff and Firecrest occur in small numbers around marshy areas and pools, and there is occasionally a Water Pipit at the sewage farm. A flock of up to 30 Twite often winters on the shore, and Snow Bunting is sometimes present.

Passage brings a greater variety of waders and there is a concentration of Great Crested Grebes and Red-breasted Mergansers on the sea in early autumn; over 500 of the former and 400 of the latter have been recorded. Common and Sandwich Terns are also present on passage. Breeders include Shelduck, while Peregrine is resident in the area.

Information
Traeth Lafan LNR, Director, Planning and Economic Development Department, Council Offices, Caernarfon, Caernarvonshire LL55 1SH. Tel: 01286 679381.

46 COEDYDD ABER (Caernarfon)   OS Landranger 115

This scenic valley, partly a NNR, holds a typical selection of birds in the woods and on the rivers and streams, and is best in spring and early summer.

Habitat
From Aber, the river valley climbs to Aber Falls and the Carneddau uplands, passing through extensive areas of mixed deciduous woodland in the lower part of the valley and dry acid oak woodland on the higher slopes, giving way to scrub at higher levels, within grazed grassland. There are also extensive conifer plantations.

Access (see map)
Leave the A55 North Wales Expressway at Abergwyngregyn, then take the minor road south to Bont Newydd, parking after 1 mile in either the Countryside Council for Wales or adjacent FC car parks. From these a nature trail follows the valley for c.1 mile to Aber Falls, with an information centre en route. It is possible to return via an alternative route, climbing fairly steeply at first through open country and then descending through conifer plantations; a permit is required away from the marked trails but should be unnecessary.

Birds
On the rivers and streams are Red-breasted Merganser, Dipper, Grey Wagtail and, sometimes, Kingfisher, while the woods have resident Green and Great Spotted Woodpeckers, Willow Tit, Nuthatch and Treecreeper, with Siskin and, in invasion years, Crossbill in the conifers. Summer visitors include Redstart, Garden and Wood Warblers, and Pied Flycatcher, with Tree Pipit, Ring Ouzel, Whinchat and Wheatear on the moors; the scree slopes around Aber Falls are particularly good for Ring Ouzel. Look for Buzzard, Sparrowhawk, Peregrine and Raven overhead.

Information
Countryside Council for Wales Warden: Duncan Brown, Bryn Menai, Ffordd Caergybi, Bangor, Caernarvonshire LL57 2JA. Tel: 01286 650547.

47 CONWY (Caernarfon)

This new RSPB reserve lies on the east shore of the Conwy estuary and was purpose-built in 1993 from spoil. As well as holding a variety of waders and wildfowl, it has already gained a reputation for attracting rare waders.

Habitat

The reserve is sandwiched between the main A55 dual carriageway to the north and the tidal reaches of the River Conwy to the south and west, and was constructed with the huge quantities of spoil produced by the construction of the Conwy road tunnel. Two large reed-fringed lagoons have been created, with numerous small islands, and the reserve also has several ponds, areas of salt-marsh beside the river and grassland.

Access (see map)

Conwy RSPB reserve Leave the A55 North Wales Expressway at the junction with the A456 for Conwy (the first junction west of the Llandudno exit, and immediately east of the Conwy tunnel) and turn south off the roundabout to the reserve (signed). The reserve is open daily 10.00–17.00 (or dusk if earlier) and there is a visitor centre with a shop, toilets and window giving panoramic views of the reserve, trails circumnavigating the reserve, and four hides.

Caer-Hun Lying in the Conwy Valley south of Conwy, this is a good site for Hawfinch in late winter and early spring. Leave Conwy south on the B5106 and, c.1 mile south of Ty'n-y-groes, park near the churchyard. Hawfinch favours the adjacent tall trees. Nearby, the River Conwy has held a regular wintering Iceland Gull.

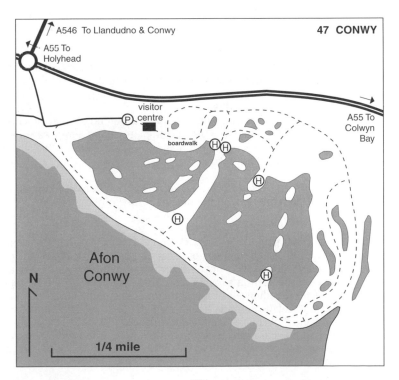

Birds

Wintering wildfowl include Shelduck, Wigeon, Teal, Gadwall, Shoveler, Pochard, Goldeneye and Red-breasted Merganser, as well as Little and Great Crested Grebes. Numbers of commoner waders are present, including Snipe and Lapwing, and other high tide estuarine species such as Oystercatcher, Curlew, Redshank and Dunlin roost on the lagoons, perhaps joined by a Spotted Redshank or Greenshank. Water Rails skulk in the reedbeds, Kingfisher and Grey Wagtail may visit, and the gull flocks may hold occasional Mediterranean. Sparrowhawk, Buzzard, Peregrine and Raven breed in the area and are seen all year.

On passage a wider variety of waders is present, with Knot, Sanderling, Black-tailed and Bar-tailed Godwits, Whimbrel and Common and Green Sandpipers all possible, while scarcer species have included Wood Sandpiper and Little Stint. Terns, including Common and Sandwich, may bathe in the lagoons, and passerines can include White and Yellow Wagtails, Sand Martin and Wheatear, as well as Twite from the adjoining hills. Osprey and Marsh Harrier have been recorded.

Breeders include Little Grebe, Shelduck, Oystercatcher, Lapwing, Ringed and Little Ringed Plovers, Redshank, Common Sandpiper, Reed and Sedge Warblers, and Common and Lesser Whitethroats.

Information

RSPB Warden: Ian Higginson, Conwy RSPB Reserve, Llandudno Junction, Conwy LL33 9XZ. Tel: 01492 584091.

48 GREAT ORME HEAD (Caernarfon) OS Landranger 115

Lying immediately north of Llandudno, this massive headland forms the east boundary of Conwy Bay and is noted for its numbers of breeding seabirds.

Habitat

The head covers c.2 square miles and rises to 675 feet. Largely composed of limestone, there are areas of deeply fissured limestone pavement.

Access (see map)

From Llandudno, Marine Drive encircles the head (though parts may be closed for repair at times). A minor road also bisects the plateau and a tramway climbs to the top. From the tramway's summit, a nature trail leads west to the seabird cliffs. The whole area is a Country Park.

Rhos-on-Sea Small numbers of Purple Sandpipers, together with Turnstones, roost along the promenade here and at nearby Rhos Point.

Birds

Breeders include c.100 pairs of Fulmars, Cormorant, Shag, over 1,200 pairs of Kittiwakes, Herring Gull, small numbers of Great and Lesser Black-backed Gulls, c.700 pairs of Guillemots and 100 pairs of Razorbills. Puffin formerly nested, and occasional birds are still seen in summer, and also notable are the cliff-nesting House Martins. Other breeding species include Peregrine, Little Owl, Rock Pipit, Wheatear, Stonechat and Raven, and Chough, though not breeding here, also visit.

On passage a variety of species may occur, including Black Redstart in early spring and late autumn, and Dotterel, which has been recorded several times on the limestone pavement. Seawatching can be productive, with Leach's Petrel possible in September–October following northwest gales, together with Manx and,

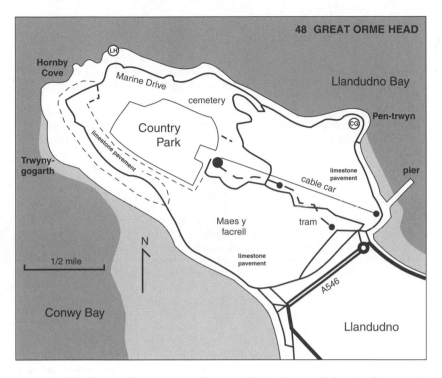

occasionally, Sooty Shearwaters, Gannet, Kittiwake, and Arctic, Great and Pomarine Skuas.

In winter few birds are found, but there are usually small numbers of Red-throated and Great Northern Divers and Common Scoter offshore, Turnstones and Purple Sandpipers on the Head, and Chough is most likely at this season.

49 MYNYDD HIRAETHOG (Denbighshire) OS Landranger 116

Situated in the extensive upland block between Ruthin and Betws-y-Coed, this mosaic of moorland, conifer forest and open water offers a good range of upland species. April–June is the optimum time to visit.

Habitat
Extensive areas of rolling moorland rise to 1,760 feet and are interspersed by huge blocks of conifer plantations, with Clocaenog Forest to the southeast being one of the largest areas of forestation in the principality. Mynydd Hiraethog has several areas of open water, both natural (Llyn Aled and Llyn Bran) and man-made (Aled Isaf, Alwen and Brenig Reservoirs).

Access
Access to the area is from the A453 southwest from Denbigh.

Foel Lwyd A minor road heads north from the A453 near Pont y Clogwyn (SH 929567) past Llyn Aled and Aled Isaf Reservoir to the high point at Foel Lwyd (1,325 feet). Upland species are possible along this route.

Mynydd Hiraethog forests Leave the A453 south on the B4501, which passes through extensive stands of conifers. There are several parking places and exploration may be worthwhile anywhere, though sites with a panoramic view are best for scanning for raptors such as Goshawk. There is a nature trail at Pont-y-Brenig at the northwest tip of Llyn Brenig Reservoir, an archeological trail at the northeast tip of Llyn Brenig, and visitor centres on the south shores of both Llyn Brenig and Alwen Reservoir.

Gors Maen Llwyd This is a reserve of the North Wales Wildlife Trust, accessed from the B4501 immediately north of Llyn Brenig, with a hide near the lake shore. Merlin, Hen Harrier, Red and Black Grouse, Wheatear and Whinchat occur in the area.

Birds
The moorland's specialities include breeding Golden Plover and a handful of Dunlin (listen for the mournful cry of Golden Plover in the early morning and trilling purr of Dunlin; the latter often follows the former), as well as Lapwing, Snipe and Curlew. Red Grouse favour heather moors but Black Grouse prefer the interface of moorland and woodland; it is scarce and generally hard to find (look and listen for lekking males in early morning in spring and October). Raven may be seen anywhere, but Wheatear and Redstart favour stone walls, Ring Ouzel areas of crags and scree slopes, and Whinchat and Tree Pipit the moorland fringes. Breeding raptors may include Short-eared Owl, Hen Harrier, Merlin and Peregrine, but all are at low density; Buzzard is more likely to be seen. There are also several colonies of Black-headed Gulls on the moors. Streams and rivers have Common Sandpiper, Dipper and Grey Wagtail, the former also nesting on reservoir shores. Breeders on the lakes and reservoirs include Great Crested Grebe, and Cormorant and Grey Heron may visit. The conifer plantations hold Goshawk and Sparrowhawk, Long-eared Owl, Siskin and, in invasion years, Crossbill. Hawfinch can sometimes be seen in the Alwen Valley below Pentre-llyn-cymmer.

In winter the reservoirs hold small numbers of Wigeon, Teal, Pochard, Goldeneye and Goosander, as well as itinerant family parties of Whooper Swans. Occasional raptors can still be seen, and Snow Bunting may visit the barer upland areas.

Information
North Wales Wildlife Trust, 376 High Street, Bangor, Caernarvonshire LL57 1YE. Tel: 01248 351541. E-mail: nwwt@cix.co.uk

50 POINT OF AIR (Flintshire) OS Landranger 116

This site, at the mouth of the Dee Estuary, is excellent for concentrations of wintering waders and wildfowl, has notable late-summer concentrations of terns, and can be good for seawatching in autumn.

Habitat
Extensive sandy flats and a small area of dunes guard the northwest mouth of the Dee Estuary, while the Point is a shingle spit surmounted by a lighthouse. In its shelter, large areas of saltmarsh have developed.

Access
Leave Prestatyn east on the A548 and, after c.2½ miles (just beyond the end of a section of dual carriageway) turn northwest at the roundabout on Station Road to Talacre, proceed to the shore and park. An RSPB reserve with open access,

Hawfinch

This big, bright but very shy finch is found in much of England and Wales. It requires mature deciduous trees, either within woodland or scattered among more open countryside. It is especially fond of hornbeams. Hawfinches can be difficult to detect, especially in the breeding season, and the best chance of seeing them is during the winter. Certain favoured sites attract good numbers which feed and roost together.

Key sites: Bedgebury, Breckland, Wolves Wood, New Forest.

Little Ringed Plover

These summer visitors only began to nest in Britain in 1938, and have benefited greatly from the recent creation of a new habitat here – flooded gravel workings. They breed beside freshwater lakes with areas of unvegetated shoreline or islands, and will desert a site if it becomes overgrown. They favour similar habitats on passage, rarely occurring on the coast. These active, energetic little birds are often seen scurrying about hunting invertebrate prey close to the water's edge.

Key sites: Grafham Water, Paxton Pits, Messingham Sand Quarries, Rutland Water.

Grasshopper Warbler

A dull-plumaged bird with a distinctly mouse-like ability to creep about invisibly in deep cover, the Grasshopper Warbler (often nicknamed 'Gropper') is fairly widespread in scrubby and marshy habitats. It is usually detected by its thin, reeling song, often delivered at dusk. It is commonest in northern and western areas, but has declined quite sharply over the last fifty years.

Key sites: Penclacwydd WWT, Walberswick, the Wirral Coast, Barons Haugh.

Black Grouse

A rare and declining species of the uplands of northern England, Wales and Scotland, the Black Grouse is rarely easy to find. Lengthy explorations of suitable habitat on foot are often the best bet, but views are usually brief. Early risers might choose to visit one of the known regular lekking sites, where the birds gather to perform their spectacular displays early on spring mornings.

Key sites: Braco Moor, Langdon Common, Mynydd Hiraethog, Loch Ruthven.

the Point is not wardened. A public hide overlooking the high-tide wader roost is reached from the seawall that leads from the end of the road south towards the colliery. Otherwise it is possible to walk west along the beach to the lighthouse, the best position for seawatching (early morning and a high tide are best) or east to the point, but do not disturb the high-tide wader roost. Note that the whole area is badly disturbed in summer.

Up to 60 pairs of Little Terns breed at Gronant, west of the Point of Air. Take the road to the caravan site north of the A548 at Gronant (1½ miles west of the Talacre turning). There is an RSPB summer warden.

Birds

In late summer and autumn there are gatherings of terns at the point, often including several thousand Common Terns, several hundred Little and Sandwich Terns, and small numbers of Arctics. Careful searching may reveal Roseate Tern too, and Black Terns also pass through in autumn. These congregations attract Arctic Skua, which are almost constantly present. In strong northwest gales, seawatching can be productive (though, on balance, the Wirral shore may be better, see p.393). Leach's Petrel is possible after 2–3 days of gales, as are Manx Shearwater, Fulmar, Great, Pomarine and Long-tailed Skuas, and Sabine's Gull. In both spring and autumn, small numbers of passerine migrants, such as White and Yellow Wagtails, Wheatear and Ring Ouzel, may be present in the dunes.

In winter large numbers of wildfowl occur, including Shelduck, Wigeon, Teal, Pintail and Shoveler, with a few Common Scoter, Goldeneye and Red-breasted Mergansers on the sea, together with Red-throated Diver, Guillemot and Razorbill. Scarcer wildfowl may include Brent Goose. Huge numbers of waders (up to 20,000) roost at the Point in winter; mostly Oystercatcher, Knot, Dunlin and Redshank, others include Grey Plover, Black-tailed and Bar-tailed Godwits, Sanderling and Turnstone. The congregations of potential prey species attract a variety of raptors, including Peregrine, Merlin, Hen Harrier and Short-eared Owl. A few Twite and Snow Bunting may occur, together with Water Pipit and, very occasionally, Shore Lark.

Information

RSPB Warden: Gareth Stamp, Burton Point Farm, Station Road, Burton, South Wirral, Cheshire CH64 5SB. Tel: 0151 336 7681. email: colin.wells@rspb.org.uk

51 FLINT AND OAKENHOLT MARSHES
(Flintshire)   OS Landranger 117

This area of the Welsh shore of the inner Dee Estuary is freely accessible and holds much the same selection of waders and raptors as Pont of Air to the north and Connah's Quay to the south.

Access

Leave the A548 at Flint and park by the ruined castle. From here it is possible to walk both north and south along the shore.

Birds

In winter large numbers of Oystercatcher, Knot, Dunlin and Redshank are present, together with Grey and Golden Plovers, Bar-tailed and Black-tailed Godwits, and Turnstone. Wildfowl may include numbers of Teal and Wigeon, and Pintail is also possible. Raptors are attracted by the concentrations of birds, notably

Peregrine, Merlin and, sometimes, Hen Harrier. A specialty of the area is Twite, and good numbers may be present along the tideline or in the saltmarshes.

52 CONNAH'S QUAY (Flintshire) OS Landranger 117

This reserve, on the Welsh bank of the Dee, offers the chance to see large numbers of waders on passage and in winter.

Habitat
Three hundred acres of saltmarsh, mudflats and grassland scrub, meadow and open water around Connah's Quay power station are a reserve, owned by Powergen and managed by the Deeside Naturalists' Society (DNS). A scrape and raised bank (for roosting waders) have been constructed, and large numbers occur in the 2 hours before high water, when the tide is 29½ feet high or more.

Access
Take the A548 northwest from Connah's Quay towards Flint; the power station entrance is on the right. There is a field studies centre, four hides overlooking the estuary and a nature trail. An advance permit is necessary and will be checked at the gate. Apply to the DNS or power station manager. Casual visitors may visit on a Public Open Day; these are held once a month on a Saturday or Sunday, generally when tides are suitable.

Birds
In winter, wildfowl, raptors and waders may be seen, including Pintail, Goldeneye, up to 1,000 Black-tailed Godwits and a few Spotted Redshanks, as well as the common estuarine species. Peregrine and Merlin may visit, and Twite is an irregular visitor to the saltmarsh.

On passage there is a greater selection of waders, including up to 100 Spotted Redshanks in autumn.

Information
Warden: R. A. Roberts, 38 Kelsterton Road, Connah's Quay, Flintshire CH5 4BJ.

53 HALKYN (Flintshire) OS Landranger 117

This is a traditional locality for Lady Amherst's Pheasant, and though some birdwatchers consider them to be too domesticated, to others they are as 'wild' as the population introduced into Bedfordshire. It is also a good site for Hawfinch.

Access
Halkyn lies just off the A55 dual carriageway directly southwest of Flint, and is accessed via the B5123. The churchyard, on a slight hill east of this road, is the site for Lady Amherst's Pheasant and Hawfinch. Do not wander into nearby back gardens.

Birds
Lady Amherst's Pheasant can be seen at any time of day but early morning when there is least disturbance is best, and January–March is the optimum period. Similarly, Hawfinch is best looked for when the churchyard is undisturbed.

NORTHERN ENGLAND

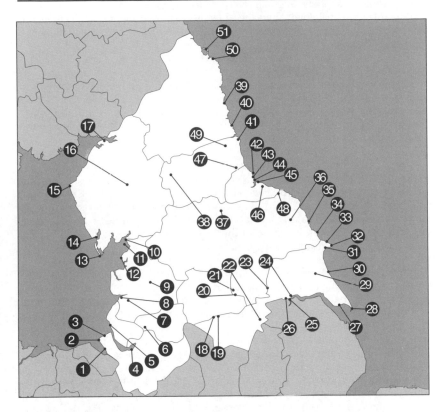

1 The Inner Dee Estuary
2 Hilbre and Red Rocks
3 The Wirral Coast
4 Frodsham Lagoons and the Weaver Bend
5 Seaforth and Crosby Marina
6 Pennington Flash Country Park
7 Martin Mere
8 South Ribble Marshes
9 Pendle Hill
10 Leighton Moss
11 Morecambe Bay
12 Heysham
13 South Walney
14 Hodbarrow
15 St Bees Head
16 Haweswater
17 Bowness-on-Solway and Campfield Marsh
18 Pugneys Country Park

19 Wintersett Reservoir and Anglers Country Park
20 Fairburn Ings
21 New Swillington Ings
22 Potteric Carr
23 Derwent Valley
24 Whitton Sand and Faxfleet Ponds
25 Blacktoft Sands
26 Swinefleet Pea Fields
27 Cherry Cobb Sands and Stone Creek
28 Spurn Point
29 Tophill Low
30 Hornsea Mere
31 Bridlington Harbour and South Beach
32 Flamborough Head
33 Bempton Cliffs
34 Filey
35 Scarborough and Scalby Mills

36 Wykeham Forest
37 Arkengarthdale and Stonesdale Moor
38 Upper Teesdale
39 Druridge Bay Area
40 Seaton Sluice to St Mary's Island
41 Whitburn
42 Hartlepool
43 Seaton Carew, North Gare and Seaton Snook
44 North Teesside
45 South Gare
46 Coatham Marsh and Locke Park
47 Hurworth Burn Reservoir
48 Scaling Dam Reservoir
49 Washington WWT and Barmston Pond
50 The Farne Islands
51 Lindisfarne

1 THE INNER DEE ESTUARY (Cheshire)

The Dee estuary supports internationally important populations of ten species of wader and three of wildfowl. Along the Cheshire shore of the inner estuary there are several excellent sites, holding year-round interest (though quiet in midsummer).

Habitat

The east shore of the estuary (east of the canalised Dee) has extensive areas of inaccessible mudflats backed by large saltmarshes; the upper, drier parts of the marsh are grazed by sheep except where protected (as at the RSPB's Gayton Sands reserve, which covers a large area mudflats and saltmarsh on the north-east shore of the estuary). The hinterland is a mixture of farmland and some heavy industry.

Access (see map)

Heswall Beach (OS Landranger 118) Leave the A580 in Heswall west at the traffic lights on minor roads into Lower Heswall and head downhill to Banks Road, parking in the car park at its west end overlooking the estuary. From here walk north for 200–500 yards along the shore to view. This may now be the best area for waders on the Cheshire shore of the Dee, with a rising tide from 2½ hours prior to high water onwards being best.

Gayton Sands RSPB reserve Leave the A540 on the B5136 or B5134 west to Neston. After passing under the railway in the town, take the B5135 to Parkgate and follow the road sharply right along the edge of the saltmarsh. At the right-angle right turn (where the B5135 turns away from the coast), continue straight on to the Old Baths car park. There are good views from here and, for the more active, a public footpath runs northwest along the shore. The area is best in the period 1–2 hours either side of high water. Parkgate is especially good for wintering wildfowl, notably up to 10,000 Pintail (i.e. the entire Dee population). On high 'spring' tides, roosting waders include up to 200–300 Black-tailed Godwits, and on the very highest tides (33 feet plus) Water Rail and Jack Snipe are forced to leave the marshes, only to be preyed upon by Grey Herons. It is also a good area for raptors (though the Hen Harrier roost has sadly declined). Other attractions are flocks of finches and buntings, and a few Water Pipits.

The Wirral Way This long-distance footpath runs parallel to the coast northwest of Neston along the line of a dismantled railway; a footpath leads inland from Old Baths car park to connect with the Wirral Way. The track-side scrub and adjacent arable attracts a variety of warblers in summer, and finches and buntings in winter.

Neston Reedbed This small reedbed near the sewage works holds Reed and Sedge Warblers in summer, and small numbers of Grasshopper Warblers can be found in the scrubbier margins. In Neston, turn south off the B5135 where it meets the coast to a car park, and from here follow the footpath south along the edge of the saltmarsh to the reedbed.

Burton Marshes At Burton an area of saltmarsh is managed as a refuge by the Dee Wildfowlers Club. Leave the A540 on minor roads into Burton and follow the minor road through the village towards Neston. As you leave the village turn left into Station Road, crossing the railway after c.½ mile and continuing for a few hundred yards to view the saltmarshes at Denhall Lane. Waders may be present on the pools here, and the area is good for wildfowl.

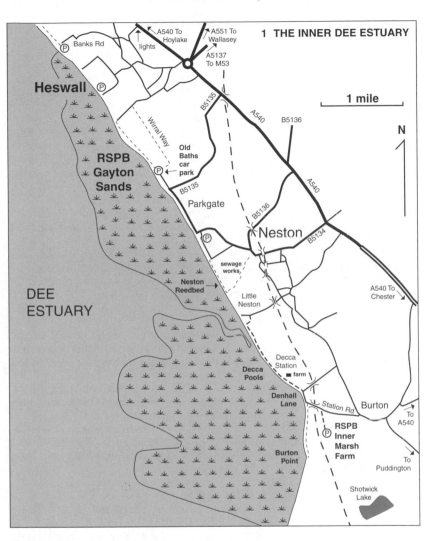

1 THE INNER DEE ESTUARY

Decca Pools From Denhall Lane, Burton, it is possible to follow the public footpath north to Little Neston. Just beyond Denhall House Farm (and below Decca station) a series of saltmarsh pools is particularly attractive to waders. View from the embankment.

Inner Marsh Farm RSPB reserve Lying in an area of former saltmarsh at Shotwick Fields, and separated from the estuary by the Wallasey–Wrexham railway, a series of artificial pools and scrapes now attracts an excellent variety of wildfowl and waders. Leave Burton on Station Road (as for Burton Marshes) and after ½ mile, just *before* the road crosses the railway, turn left along a narrow track signed Burton Point Farm. At the end is the small RSPB car park. Access to the reserve is limited to RSPB members. (Notably, to the south of the area and over the Welsh border, Shotwick Lake is now the only site in the principality for Corn Bunting.)

Birds
Wintering wildfowl include large numbers of Pintail, as well as Shelduck, Teal and Wigeon. Diving duck such as Red-breasted Merganser and Goldeneye occur in the river channel, and may be distantly visible across the saltmarshes. Once famous for its geese, protection has resulted in the return of small numbers of White-fronted and Pink-footed Geese (notably at Burton Marshes), and small numbers of Bewick's Swans may also be seen (they roost at Inner Marsh Farm). The Dee holds large numbers of waders; dispersed at low water, the estuarine species such as Oystercatcher, Bar-tailed Godwit, Curlew, Redshank, Knot and Dunlin are best seen roosting on the upper saltmarshes at high tide, especially at Burton. Scarcer species include variable numbers of Black-tailed Godwits and occasional wintering Greenshank and Spotted Redshank (e.g. on Decca Pools). These concentrations attract raptors; Merlin, Sparrowhawk, declining numbers of Hen Harrier and Short-eared Owl. Peregrine and Raven are year-round visitors. The saltmarsh gutters hold wintering Rock Pipits, and there are much smaller numbers of Water Pipits (which favour 'fresher' habitats, such as flooded fields or pools on the upper saltmarshes). The grazed marshes and adjacent fields hold large flocks of Golden Plovers and Lapwings. Large numbers of finches and buntings feed along the strand line, and the commoner species are joined by Tree Sparrow, a few Twites, variable numbers of Bramblings, Corn Buntings and sometimes Lapland Buntings. The saltmarsh cover harbours Water Rails and Jack Snipes, but these are seldom seen unless forced out by the very highest tides.

Passage also brings large numbers of waders, with a greater variety than in winter. Whimbrel is more frequent in spring, but autumn is generally better; Ruff, Common, Green and Curlew Sandpipers, Little Stint, Greenshank and Spotted Redshank may all occur. Black Tern is frequent, especially in the upper estuary. Passerines may include White and Yellow Wagtails, Wheatear and Ring Ouzel, and other notable migrants include Spoonbill and Little Egret (both increasingly frequent), Garganey, Marsh Harrier, Osprey, Hobby and Spotted Crake.

Breeders include Shelduck, Oystercatcher, Redshank, a large colony of Black-headed Gulls at Inner Marsh Farm, sometimes a few Stonechats, and Grasshopper, Reed and Sedge Warblers, while Common Tern may visit from colonies on the Welsh shore of the estuary.

Information
RSPB Gayton Sands Warden: Colin Wells, Burton Point Farm, Station Road, Burton, South Wirral, Cheshire CH64 5SB. Tel: 0151 336 7681.

Wirral Country Park Centre: Martyn Jamieson, Head Ranger, Station Road, Thurstaston, Wirral CH61 0HN. Tel: 0151 648 4371/648 3884. E-mail: wirral countrypark@wirral.gov.uk

2 HILBRE AND RED ROCKS (Cheshire)   OS Landranger 108

Lying at the mouth of the Dee estuary, Hilbre is well known as a site for roosting waders (immortalised by legions of bird photographers) and as an excellent seawatching station, with Leach's Petrel a speciality. The adjacent Red Rocks peninsula on the mainland is also attractive to waders and can offer exciting autumn seawatching, and both areas attract small numbers of migrant passerines.

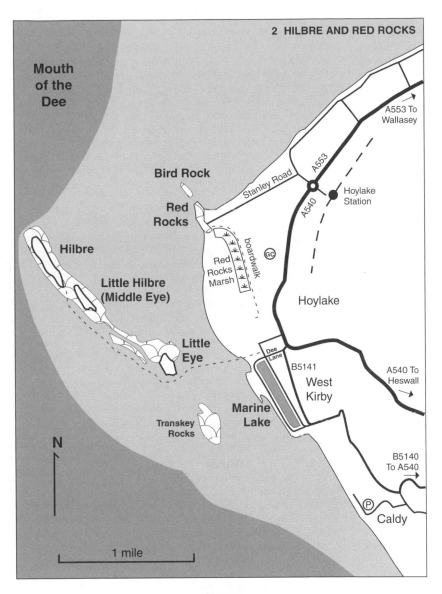

2 HILBRE AND RED ROCKS

Mouth
of the
Dee

Bird Rock

Red
Rocks

Hilbre

Little Hilbre
(Middle Eye)

Little
Eye

Transkey
Rocks

N

A553 To
Wallasey

A553

A540

Stanley Road

Hoylake
Station

GC

boardwalk

Red
Rocks
Marsh

Hoylake

Dee
Lane

B5141

West
Kirby

A540 To
Heswall

Marine
Lake

B5140
To A540

P

Caldy

1 mile

Habitat

Lying c.1½ miles off Hoylake are three sandstone islands: Little Eye covers only
½ acre, Little Hilbre is larger and Hilbre, the largest island, is 11 acres in extent
with cliffs rising to 55 feet on the west shore. The islands are sparsely vegetated
and separated from the mainland for three hours either side of high water. Hilbre
is a Wirral Council reserve. At Hoylake, sand from the mouth of the River Dee has
formed two low dune ridges which sandwich a dune-slack marsh with stands of
reeds and alder and willow scrub. Inland is the Royal Liverpool Golf Course and,
at the north end of the dunes, areas of sandstone are exposed at Red Rocks,
forming a short promontory, with the furthest rocks (Bird Rock) cut off at high
tide. Red Rocks Marsh is a reserve of the Cheshire Wildlife Trust.

Access (see map)

Hilbre Reached on foot from West Kirby. Start from the slipway on the promenade opposite Dee Lane (just north of the Marine Lake, see below for access), walk directly northwest to the south end of Little Eye (the most southerly island), and then, keeping Little Eye on your right, to Little Hilbre and over the rocks past the small tidal pool to the gate at the south end of Hilbre. This takes c.1 hour and you should start, *at the latest*, three hours before high tide (do not attempt the crossing in foggy conditions). The paddocks and bungalows are private. Hilbre Bird Observatory operates a ringing station and seawatching hide. No accommodation is available. The period around high tide is most productive for seawatching, and the hide can be used by arrangement with the observatory or Wirral Council Ranger, otherwise the north end of Hilbre, above the Lifeboat House, is a good spot to watch from, providing conditions are not too bad.

Red Rocks From West Kirby, walk north along the foreshore, past Red Rocks Marsh to Red Rocks Point. Alternatively, from the A540, turn northwest towards the coast at the roundabout by Hoylake Station and after 200 yards first left into Stanley Road and park. The Point lies at the far end of the road. The scrub around the dune slacks attracts migrant passerines (especially the small poplar plantation at the north end), as do the trees and gardens along Stanley Road. Access to Red Rocks Marsh is restricted to the foreshore or the boardwalk on the inland side of the marsh. Bird Rock off Red Rocks Point is an island at high tide, and when undisturbed holds roosting waders. The Point is also a worthwhile seawatching station, offering a similar range of species to Hilbre, but from a more accessible spot.

West Kirby Marine Lake This may hold one or two sea ducks, grebes or divers, especially in the early morning. Leave the A540 at West Kirby railway station and follow signs for the Marine Lake west to the beach.

Caldy Beach Road Access off the B5140 south from West Kirby. In some seasons numbers of Scaup can be seen, with high water being best.

Birds

The wader roost on Little Eye and/or Little Hilbre has declined in recent years but remains one of the attractions of the area. Wintering waders include large numbers of Oystercatcher, Curlew, Black-tailed Godwit, Dunlin and Knot, smaller numbers of Grey and Ringed Plovers, Bar-tailed Godwit, Sanderling and Turnstone, and up to 50 Purple Sandpipers. A similar range of species may roost at Bird Rock, Red Rocks, and at low water these waders (except Purple Sandpiper) are scattered over the estuary. In winter there are also small numbers of divers off the estuary mouth, mostly Red-throated, with Great Northern scarce and Black-throated only occasional. Small numbers of Scaup, Red-breasted Merganser and Goldeneye frequent the river channel and mouth, together with a few Common Scoter, Guillemot and Razorbill. Other wildfowl include Shelduck, Wigeon, and often a few Dark-bellied Brent Geese around Hilbre. Gulls regularly include Mediterranean, Little or Glaucous, but Iceland Gull is quite rare. Snow Bunting is sometimes found in the dunes, with Stonechat in the scrubby areas. The concentrations of waders attract Peregrine, and other raptors may include Sparrowhawk and Merlin.

In spring and autumn small falls of migrants occur, such as White and Yellow Wagtails, Whinchat and Wheatear. The best conditions are light to moderate SE–SW winds, coupled with poor visibility and perhaps rain or drizzle. However, by two hours after dawn, most have left Hilbre, though some falls occur later in the day. The scrub at Red Rocks tends to hold birds for longer; being on the west coast, however, scarce migrants are just that, rare! Visible passerine migration can also be interesting and usually occurs in the first four hours after dawn.

Autumn is best for seawatching. From September to early November, following 2–3 days of northwest gales, Leach's Petrel is virtually guaranteed, along with small numbers of Manx Shearwaters, and occasionally Sooty Shearwater and Sabine's Gull. A deep low centred on the Faeroes and moving slowly east will produce the necessary gales. Fulmar, Gannet, Kittiwake and Arctic Skua are regular offshore in autumn, but Great and Pomarine Skuas are scarce and Long-tailed is rare. The occasional shearwater or skua occurs in early spring, and Little Gull may be seen from June. Late-summer congregations of terns occur off the mouth, occasionally including Roseate, and up to 1,000 Little Terns appear in mid-August off Red Rocks and Hilbre.

Breeders include Shelduck at Hilbre, with Grasshopper, Reed and Sedge Warblers at Red Rocks.

Information

Permits for Hilbre (only necessary for groups of more than six) are available free from the Wirral Country Park Centre, Station Road, Thurstaston, Wirral CH61 0HN. Tel: 0151 648 4371/648 3884; open 10.00–17.00 daily. E-mail: wirralcountrypark@wirral.gov.uk Visits to the observatory are by arrangement with J.C. Gittins, 17 Deva Road, West Kirby, Wirral L48 4DB (SAE please). Tel: 0151 625 5428.

Cheshire Wildlife Trust, Grebe House, Reaseheath, Nantwich, Cheshire CW5 6DA. Tel: 01270 610180. E-mail: cheshirewt@cix.co.uk

3 THE WIRRAL COAST (Cheshire)   OS Landranger 108

In autumn, northwest gales push large numbers of seabirds inshore, notably Leach's Petrel, and the Wirral is one of the best sites in the country for this species, with a variety of other seabirds also on offer. In spring and autumn there is also the possibility of passerine migrants.

Habitat

The north coast of the Wirral Peninsula is guarded by a system of fixed dunes, backed by market gardens and built-up areas. There are occasional patches of cover for migrants, but numbers of birds are usually small. The main interest centres on autumn seawatching.

Access

Dove Point, Meols Offers seawatching from the shelter of a car and the potential of the closest views of seabirds, but only at high tide (when the sands of East Hoyle Bank are completely covered). On lower tides and in calmer weather, numbers of gulls and terns, sometimes including Mediterranean Gull, roost on the sands here. Access is from A553 at Hoylake, driving to the northeast tip of the promenade.

Leasowe Lighthouse A good place to seawatch from, though it may no longer be possible to take a car onto the seawall. Leave Wallasey west on the A551 and, at the sharp left-hand bend a few hundred yards beyond the hospital, take the rough track straight ahead along the seawall; the lighthouse is clearly visible ½ mile ahead.

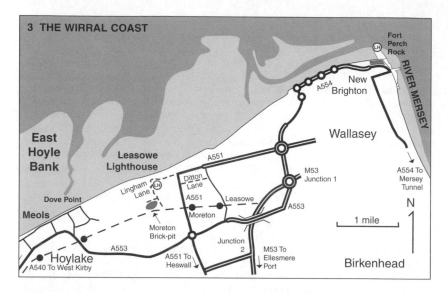

Leasowe Common Lying immediately behind the seawall, this is a good area for migrants in spring and autumn, has breeding Grasshopper Warbler, and may hold Black Redstart, Stonechat, Twite and Snow Bunting in winter. From Leasowe lighthouse follow Lingham Lane to the south, checking the hedges for migrants, past Lingham Farm and reaching Moreton Brick-pit after ½ mile. This attracts bathing and loafing gulls, regularly including Glaucous and Mediterranean.

Ditton Lane This runs between the A551, ⅓ mile north of Moreton station, and Wallasey. The willow and alder scrub here may hold good numbers of migrants.

New Brighton Good for seawatching, with the period around high tide preferable (but not essential as at Meols); Leach's Petrel may be seen trying to exit from the mouth of the Mersey (and are sometimes observed upriver as far as Seacombe Ferry). The A554 follows the coast for 1 mile to the marine lake and lighthouse, and the shelters near the Fort Perch Rock are ideally placed for seawatching, as is a parked car along the seafront.

Birds
Autumn seawatching is the prime attraction, and following 2–3 days of northwest gales Leach's Petrel is virtually guaranteed, sometimes in large numbers, as well as small numbers of Manx Shearwater, and occasionally Sooty Shearwater and Sabine's Gull. A deep low centred on the Faeroes and moving slowly east will produce the necessary gales. Fulmar, Gannet, Kittiwake and Arctic Skua are regular offshore in autumn, but Great and Pomarine Skuas are scarce and Long-tailed rare. The occasional shearwater or skua occurs in spring. In spring and autumn small numbers of passerine migrants may be present, such as White and Yellow Wagtails, Wheatear and Ring Ouzel, and several rarities have occurred.

In autumn and winter small numbers of waders occur along the coast, with Turnstone and sometimes Purple Sandpiper around the fort at New Brighton. Throughout the year, gulls should be carefully checked. Mediterranean and Little are frequent, with small numbers of Glaucous, and an Iceland Gull appeared in midwinter every year from 1957 to 1985.

4 FRODSHAM LAGOONS AND THE WEAVER BEND (Cheshire)

OS Landranger 117

This area, sandwiched between the M56 and the Manchester Ship Canal, attracts a variety of waders and wildfowl in winter and on passage, and is especially favoured by Curlew Sandpiper and Little Stint in autumn.

Habitat

Dredgings from the Manchester Ship Canal are pumped into embanked lagoons at Frodsham. When full, these slowly dry out, resulting in a succession of habitats from bare mud to pasture. Together with the surrounding farmland they form a complex of freshwater and brackish habitats. Beyond the ship canal, Frodsham Score is an area of grazed saltmarsh and to the north, where the River Weaver flows into the Manchester Ship Canal, the resultant estuarine habitats add further variety.

Access (see map)

The Weaver Bend Leave the M56 at junction 12 and take the A56 south into Frodsham. Just before a set of traffic lights turn right into Ship Street and follow the road to the right and then turn left to a bridge over the motorway. Cross this and follow the public footpath to the gate (some birdwatchers drive to the gate, but the road is private beyond the motorway). Continue along the footpath to the Weaver Bend. The patch of mud around the small island by the ICI Tank is especially favoured by waders.

Frodsham Lagoons In Frodsham continue along the A56, past the main shopping area and then turn right into Ship Street. Cross the motorway bridge onto the public footpath that follows the private track. The track soon forks, to the right is Tank No. 5 and the Weaver Bend, while the left track passes along the south edge of No. 5 Tank and skirts No. 6 Tank.

Birds

Wintering wildfowl include variable numbers of Shelduck, Wigeon, Teal and Mallard, which often favour Frodsham Score or the Weaver Bend, with smaller

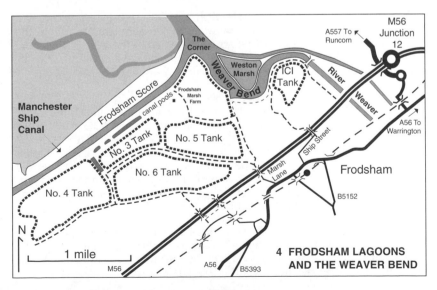

numbers of Pintail. Pochard, Goldeneye and sometimes Scaup favour the River Weaver. Wild swans and geese are only erratic visitors, as are Great Crested Grebe, Cormorant, Smew and Ruddy Duck, but these may also be found on the river, especially in cold weather. Waders on the pastures and on Frodsham Score include large numbers of Lapwing and Golden Plover, as well as Snipe, Redshank, Dunlin and sometimes Ruff. The estuary attracts more of these species, and sometimes a wintering Little Stint; on big tides waders roost on the wetter lagoons. The concentrations of prey attract Sparrowhawk, Peregrine, Merlin and Short-eared Owl. Other notable winterers include Water Rail and sometimes Twite.

Garganey may occur on spring passage, as can a variety of waders, including Ringed Plover, Common Sandpiper, Greenshank, Sanderling and Ruff, and Little Gull, Common, Arctic and Black Terns. Passerine migrants include White and Yellow Wagtails, Rock and Water Pipits, Wheatear and Whinchat. Autumn passage is more protracted and more varied; in addition to the above, Turnstone, Black-tailed Godwit, Spotted Redshank, Knot, Curlew and Green Sandpipers, and Little Stint are possible, and in some years Little Stint and Curlew Sandpiper may be relatively numerous, while a variety of rare waders has appeared over the years. Large numbers of the commoner species, such as Ringed Plover and Dunlin, may be forced off the Mersey to roost on the lagoons during 'spring' tides. Other notable migrants may include Spoonbill, Little Egret, Hobby and Spotted Crake.

Breeders in the area include Oystercatcher, Ringed and Little Ringed Plovers and Grasshopper, Reed and Sedge Warblers.

5 SEAFORTH AND CROSBY MARINA (Lancashire)   OS Landranger 108

Lying within Liverpool Freeport, Seaforth NR has an enviable reputation as a centre for the close study of gulls, the venue for the largest spring concentrations of Little Gulls in Britain, and a first landfall for ship-hopping American passerines, while adjacent Crosby Marina attracts occasional sea duck sheltering from harsh weather, and small numbers of waders.

Habitat
Seaforth consists of single fresh- and saltwater lagoons, bordered by rubble and sand bunds and wet grasslands. The reserve is owned by the Mersey Docks and Harbours Company and managed by the Lancashire Wildlife Trust. Crosby Marina lies immediately to the north and is heavily disturbed by watersports.

Access (see map)
Seaforth NR Exit the M57/M58 at their northern/western terminus (junction 7) and take the A5036 southwestwards. At the junction with the A565 exit the dual carriageway following signs for the Freeport (dock gates 99–103). Park at the Freeport entrance on Crosby Road and walk the ½ mile to the reserve, which is open 09.00–17.00 (£1 donation expected). Three hides overlook the pools and the bund used by roosting and loafing birds. For waders the period 2–3 hours before high tide is best, but gulls are less governed by the tides, with late morning and afternoon being the best periods.

Crosby Marina Access immediately north of the Freeport entrance, parking at the marina. Though heavily disturbed, some parts of the shoreline are quieter and the surrounding short turf attracts a few passage waders. Seawatching is best along the estuary sea defences near the coastguard lookout.

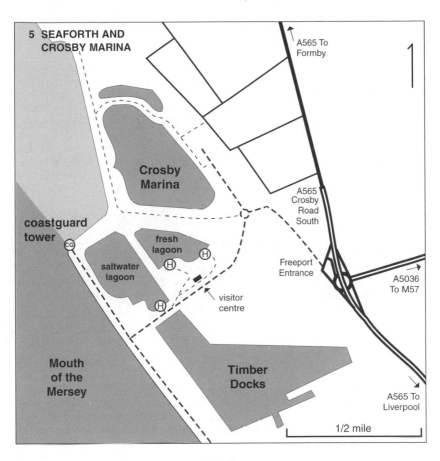

Birds

Gulls are the major focus at Seaforth. All of the commoner species are regularly recorded in large numbers, but scarce visitors are the greatest fascination. Small numbers of Kittiwakes are present year-round. Little Gull is present offshore most of the year, but is seldom seen in winter unless westerly storms force numbers inshore. Spring is the peak period for the species, and in late March–April large numbers may be present at Seaforth, with the peak count of 683 recorded in April 1989. Small numbers may summer and flocks are also recorded in autumn, especially following onshore winds. Mediterranean Gull is similarly recorded in very small numbers throughout the year, most regularly in September–early April (especially mid–late March). Yellow-legged Gull (formerly treated as a race of Herring Gull) is most frequent in mid-June to July (immatures) and mid-October to November (adults). Glaucous and Iceland Gulls, on the other hand, are most regular in winter–early spring. Ring-billed Gull is also annual, with spring (immatures) and early winter (adults) being the most likely periods.

Wintering wildfowl include Shelduck, Teal, Pochard, Scaup, Goldeneye and Red-breasted Merganser, and other notable waterbirds include numbers of Cormorant, Snipe and a few Jack Snipe. Good numbers of waders roost on the pools at Seaforth, largely Oystercatcher and Redshank, with smaller numbers of Ringed Plover, Turnstone, Bar-tailed Godwit, Dunlin and Knot. Occasionally Snow Bunting is found around the marina.

On passage large numbers of Common Terns are recorded, peaking at over 1,000 in August, and Sandwich Tern is also regular in small numbers, but Arctic, Little and Black Terns are scarce. Waders may include Whimbrel, Black-tailed Godwit and Common Sandpiper, with Curlew Sandpiper, Sanderling and Little Stint most likely in autumn. Migrant passerines include numbers of White Wagtails in spring, with Yellow Wagtail and Wheatear at both seasons. Two vagrant American sparrows have been recorded, Song Sparrow and White-crowned Sparrow, and although these almost certainly arrived aboard ships, they are officially deemed 'wild' unless known to have been fed en route! A stunning male Blackpoll Warbler was a one-day highlight of a recent spring. Autumn gales may prompt an excellent passage of seabirds, notably Leach's Petrel, which is regular after northwest gales. Manx and Sooty Shearwaters and all four species of skua are also possible (though Long-tailed is, of course, scarce), and Storm Petrel is occasionally seen after late-summer gales.

Breeders include Ringed Plover and a handful of Common Terns.

Information

Steve White, Seaforth Nature Reserve, Port of Liverpool, Liverpool L21 1JD. Tel: 0151 920 3769. E-mail: 1wildlife@cix.co.uk

Lancashire Wildlife Trust, Cuerden Park Wildlife Centre, Shady Lane, Bamber Bridge, Lancashire PR6 6AU. Tel: 01772 324129. E-mail: lancswt@cix.co.uk

6 PENNINGTON FLASH COUNTRY PARK

(Greater Manchester)   OS Landranger 109

This large country park on the outskirts of Leigh shot to fame in 1994 when Britain's first Black-faced Bunting spent several weeks there. On a more prosaic level, it regularly attracts a variety of wildfowl and waders, often including a few Smew, and Long-eared Owl also sometimes winters. The site is owned and managed by Wigan Council.

Habitat

Subsidence due to coal mining has resulted in a large area of open water. The northwest quadrant was filled with colliery waste (Ramsdale's Ruck, now grassland and birch scrub but currently under development), while the south part was filled with domestic refuse. The remainder forms a shallow lake totalling over 170 acres, with another 20 acres of smaller pools and scrapes in the northeast reserve area and some stands of reeds. The surrounding land comprises expanses of rough grassland, meadows and scrub, while areas of derelict land and landfill have been landscaped and planted with a variety of trees and shrubs, and developed as a golf course.

Access (see map)

Leave the A580 (signed for the Country Park) north onto the Leigh by-pass. After c.1 mile turn southwest (left) onto the A572 and the entrance to the Country Park is on the right after c.400 yards. There is a car park at the main entrance or you can follow the track around the east perimeter of the Flash to park at the information centre. A network of well-made paths and tracks permits exploration of the entire area, especially the reserve area on the northeast margin of the flash, while tracks along the south and west shores are productive in autumn and winter. There are seven hides. The Country Park is popular in summer, and much of the area away from the sanctuary area is disturbed by watersports and anglers, especially at weekends.

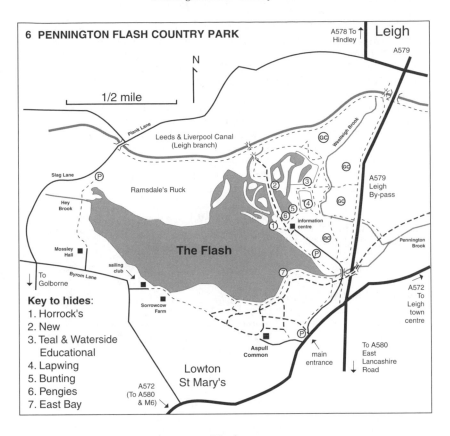

6 PENNINGTON FLASH COUNTRY PARK

A578 To Hindley

Leigh

A579

N

1/2 mile

Plank Lane

Leeds & Liverpool Canal
(Leigh branch)

Westleigh Brook

GC

GC

GC

A579
Leigh
By-pass

Slag Lane

P

Ramsdale's Ruck

Hey
Brook

2

3

GC

4

5

6

1

information
centre

GC

Pennington
Brook

Mossley
Hall

The Flash

P

sailing
club

7

To
Golborne

Byrom Lane

A572
To
Leigh
town
centre

Key to hides:
1. Horrock's
2. New
3. Teal & Waterside
   Educational
4. Lapwing
5. Bunting
6. Pengies
7. East Bay

Sorrowcow
Farm

Aspull
Common

Lowton
St Mary's

A572
(To A580
& M6)

main
entrance

To A580
East
Lancashire
Road

Birds

Wintering wildfowl include several hundred each of Mallard, Teal, Pochard and Tufted Duck, with smaller numbers of Shoveler, Wigeon, Goldeneye and often a few Ruddy Ducks. Shelduck, Gadwall, Scaup, Red-breasted Merganser, sea ducks and Whooper and Bewick's Swans are scarce, but occasional Smew and Goosander may take up winter residence. Other notable waterfowl include large numbers of Cormorants, and Water Rail, but the rarer grebes and divers and Bittern are only occasional. Up to 100 Snipes may be present, and large numbers of Golden Plover and Lapwing winter in the agricultural areas to the south and may visit at times. Occasionally Water Pipit, Redshank and Dunlin also use the area. A handful of Long-eared Owls winter between mid-November and mid-March, and are best looked for when roosting in dense thickets, from New hide. A large gull roost forms in winter; mostly Black-headed Gull, there are also good numbers of Lesser Black-backed and Herring Gulls, occasionally, Mediterranean, Iceland and Glaucous Gulls, while Yellow-legged and Ring-billed Gulls have been recorded. Great Spotted Woodpecker does not breed in the Country Park and is only a visitor, as are Tree Sparrow and Siskin, while Brambling is regular at the feeding station in most winters.

On spring migration small numbers of waders may appear, including Oystercatcher, Ringed and Little Ringed Plovers, Curlew, Black-tailed Godwit, Dunlin and Common Sandpiper, with Sanderling and Turnstone possible in May. Common, Arctic and Black Terns may also pass through. Black-necked Grebe has been regular in spring since 1992. Other migrants include White Wagtail and sometimes Water Pipit and Wheatear (try Ramsdale's Ruck), and Common Scoter, Garganey, Marsh Harrier, Osprey and Yellow Wagtail are scarce at this season. Autumn passage is more protracted, but with many of the same species possible, though Greenshank, Spotted Redshank, Green Sandpiper, Little Stint and Ruff are more likely. Migrant passerines, such as Redstart, Spotted Flycatcher and Tree Pipit, are also possible.

Residents include Great Crested and Little Grebes, Tufted Duck, Kingfisher, Willow Tit (2–3 pairs breed and the species is regular at the feeding station in winter), and Redpoll, while Grey Heron is almost always present. Other breeders (mostly present in small numbers) include Shelduck, Gadwall, Shoveler, Pochard, Ruddy Duck, Oystercatcher, Ringed and Little Ringed Plovers, Redshank, Common Tern (on rafts in the main flash), Grasshopper, Reed, Sedge and Garden Warblers, and Lesser Whitethroat.

Information

Peter Alker, Ranger, Pennington Flash Country Park, St Helens Road, Leigh WN7 3PA. Tel: 01942 605253.

7 MARTIN MERE (Lancashire)   OS Landranger 108

Martin Mere is a WWT Refuge and intensive management has produced an excellent wetland area that attracts large numbers of ducks, Pink-footed Geese and swans in winter, as well as a variety of waders on passage.

Habitat

In the centre of the south Lancashire mosses, Martin Mere was once a large lake. But, like the rest of the mosses, the Mere was drained to leave an area of winter flood water. This relict of past glories was purchased by the WWT in 1972, the area of flood increased and many permanent pools and scrapes established, surrounded by damp pastures.

Access (see map)

The refuge is on a minor road between the B5246 at Holmeswood (S of Mere Brow on the A565) and the A59 at Burscough Bridge, and is signposted from Burscough Bridge and Mere Brow. Open daily from 09.30 until 16.30 (November–February; closed Christmas Day) or 17.30 (rest of the year), there is an entrance fee for non-members of the WWT. There is an education centre, exhibition hall and a collection of captive wildfowl and flamingos, as well as nine hides overlooking the Mere.

Birds

In early winter the Lancashire Pink-foot population converges on Martin Mere and can peak at 34,000 prior to dispersal. Many leave Lancashire (for Norfolk) but some feed on Altcar Moss and others move to Marshside (see p.402), and large numbers continue to spend the day at Martin Mere, being augmented by others coming to roost. The Pink-feet are often joined by family parties of other geese, and sometimes by lone Snow or Canada Geese of one of the small subspecies, both of which are likely to be genuine vagrants from North America. There are also several hundred feral Greylag Geese and smaller numbers of feral Barnacle Geese in the area. A flock of up to c.2,000 Whooper Swans has built up, together with up to 100 Bewick's Swans, some of which arrive from the Ribble in the evening. Ducks are numerous. Wigeon has topped 25,000 and Teal can peak at

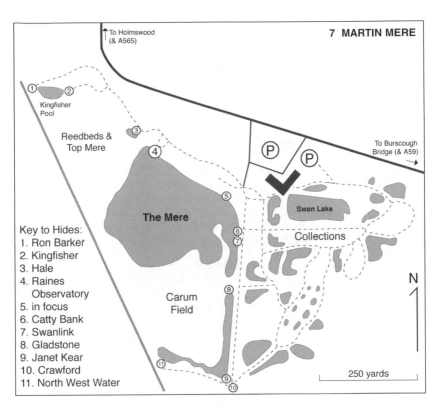

To Holmswood (& A565)

Kingfisher Pool

Reedbeds & Top Mere

To Burscough Bridge (& A59)

The Mere

Swan Lake

Collections

Key to Hides:
1. Ron Barker
2. Kingfisher
3. Hale
4. Raines Observatory
5. in focus
6. Catty Bank
7. Swanlink
8. Gladstone
9. Janet Kear
10. Crawford
11. North West Water

Carum Field

N

250 yards

10,000, while up to 3,000 Pintail can be present in early winter. There are also up to 2,000 of Shelducks, and smaller numbers of Gadwalls, Shovelers and Pochards and often also a few Ruddy Ducks, Goldeneyes, and sometimes Scaup and Goosanders. Hen Harrier and Merlin are regular and the area is especially good for Peregrine. Corn Bunting and Tree Sparrow may be seen in winter around the refuge, and Long-eared Owls are regular in late summer.

Many of the same species can be seen in the surrounding mosses (now merely fields, though still liable to occasional flooding), by touring lanes in the area, especially those across Altcar, Plex and Halsall Mosses. The area to work is the rectangle between the A5147 in the east and A565 in the west, and the A570 in the north and B5195 in the south.

On passage a variety of waders occurs, with Ringed and Little Ringed Plovers, Curlew, Dunlin, Common Sandpiper, Spotted Redshank and Greenshank being likely, and Black-tailed Godwit a speciality, with large numbers sometimes present. Golden Plover and Lapwing congregate in autumn and winter and may be joined by over 100 Ruff. Garganey and Common, Arctic and Black Terns may also be recorded on passage, with numbers of Yellow Wagtails and, in spring, White Wagtail. Also in spring, the persistent searcher may sometimes find trips of Dotterel in the surrounding mosses, especially on Altcar Moss, and Martin Mere is the most regular site in the north-west for Temminck's Stint and Green-winged Teal.

Breeders include Shelduck, Gadwall, Shoveler, Pochard and large numbers of Mallards. Small numbers of other species, as well as 'pricked' or otherwise injured geese and swans, may also summer. Other breeders are Lapwing, Snipe, Redshank, Barn Owl and Sedge Warbler, and Oystercatcher, Little Ringed Plover and Ruff have bred, while numbers of Black-tailed Godwits may summer, together with one or two Marsh Harriers.

Information
Patrick Wisniewski, WWT Martin Mere, Fish Lane, Burscough, Ormskirk, Lancashire L40 0TA. Tel: 01704 895181. E-mail: christine@ martinmere.co.uk

8 SOUTH RIBBLE MARSHES (Lancashire)   OS Landranger 102 and 108

Lying between Southport and Blackpool, the Ribble Estuary is one of the most important in Britain, supporting internationally important populations of Pintail and nine species of wader, particularly Knot, Sanderling and Bar-tailed Godwit. This provides excellent birdwatching, especially in autumn and winter. Large parts of the south shore form a NNR, created in 1979 to prevent the drainage and reclamation of the saltmarshes, while Marshside Marsh is an RSPB reserve.

Habitat
The outer estuary is sandy, attracting tourists to Southport, Lytham St Anne's, and Blackpool. The inner estuary is also mostly sandy, but fortunately attracts fewer people. The Ribble has one of the largest areas of tidal flats and saltmarsh in the country, the latter mainly on the south shore. The saltmarshes are grazed in summer by cattle and inland of the sea walls lie reclaimed pastures, which may flood in winter.

Access (see map)
Southport Marine Lake Lying at the base of Southport pier, this is rather disturbed and only Cormorant, Goldeneye and Red-breasted Merganser are regular. In winter gales divers, Shag and sea ducks sometimes seek shelter here, while Snow Bunting may be found on the nearby beach. In autumn northwest gales can push seabirds onshore, and at high tide a few Leach's Petrel and Manx Shearwater may be seen from the pier, but it is not as good as Squires Gate on the north shore of the Ribble.

Southport Marine Drive This follows the coast northeast from Southport Marine Lake to the Banks roundabout on the A565, with car parks by the Marine Lake and near the sand depot; stopping on the road is otherwise prohibited, though there are several pull-offs. The golf course at Marshside attracts small numbers of migrants during passage, and ½ mile north of the sand depot, the fields inland of the road are excellent. Large flocks of Pink-feet spend the day feeding here, usually roosting on Southport Sands. Bewick's Swan, as well as small numbers of Whoopers, also frequent the fields and roost at Martin Mere. The area attracts raptors, including a roost of c.5 Hen Harriers. When the fields are wet they may hold Golden Plover and Black-tailed Godwit, and sometimes Little Stint. On the seaward side of the road, Crossens Marsh is not attractive to feeding waders, but has a huge roost on the highest tides in spring and autumn (30 feet or more). Twite is occasional on the saltings, and Lapland Bunting is sometimes present.

In the NNR, Crossens, Banks, and Hesketh Out Marshes are visible from a public footpath along the seawall. Access is from Crossens Pumping Station, just off the A565, and at Hundred End (on a minor road north from the A565). There are no restrictions on access to Crossens and Banks Marshes, except for the study-sanctuary zone. Access to this and Hesketh Out Marsh is only by permit. While a

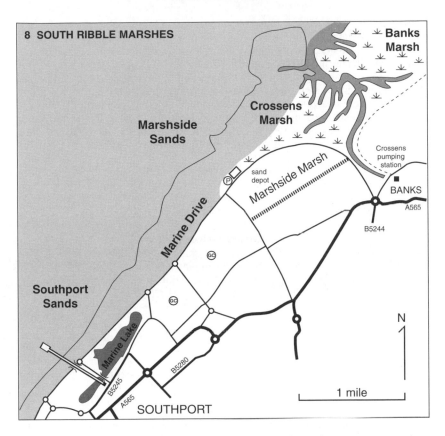

8 SOUTH RIBBLE MARSHES

Banks Marsh

Marshside Sands

Crossens Marsh

Crossens pumping station

sand depot

Marshside Marsh

BANKS

A565

B5244

Marine Drive

Southport Sands

Marine Lake

B5245

B5280

A565

SOUTHPORT

N

1 mile

pleasant walk, you are unlikely to see more than from the more convenient Marine Drive.

Birds

Wintering species include Pink-footed Goose, which favours Marshside and may peak at 10,000 birds, and is often joined by singles or family parties of other species, notably a Greater Snow Goose that has been returning to the area for several years and is generally considered to be wild. There are also up to 200 Bewick's and a few Whooper Swans. Other wildfowl include large numbers of Pintail, as well as Shelduck and a few Gadwall and Shoveler. The grazing marshes hold large numbers of Golden Plover and Redshank, as well as a few Ruff. At high tide small numbers of sea duck may appear offshore, including Eider, Scaup, Goldeneye and Red-breasted Merganser. Waders on the shoreline are dominated by Knot, up to 70,000, as well as hordes of other common species. Up to 1,000 Black-tailed Godwits may be present, and occasional Little Stint, Spotted Redshank and Greenshank winter. The wader roost can be watched from Marine Drive, by parking at the sand depot. Hen Harrier, Peregrine, Merlin and Short-eared Owl can all be seen. Wintering passerines include Rock Pipit, Stonechat and often Twite, with a few Lapland Buntings on the saltmarshes (these are very elusive and only likely to be detected in flight, giving their distinctive *tricky-tick* call), while the rather erratic Snow Bunting prefers sandier areas. On the highest tides, Water Rail and Jack Snipe may be forced from the saltmarshes to seek shelter on drier ground.

In spring a trickle of passerines follow the west coast, notable species including White Wagtail bound for Iceland, Wheatear (the larger and brighter 'Greenland' Wheatear passing in May), and Ring Ouzel. Other possible migrants include Marsh Harrier and Garganey. Spring movements of waders are rapid, but autumn passage is more leisurely, with large influxes from late July, and huge flocks of moulting waders on the estuary. Wintering species are joined by Curlew Sandpiper, Little Stint and up to 4,000 Black-tailed Godwits. In autumn, northwest gales can push seabirds inshore, occasionally including Leach's Petrel and Manx Shearwater, but the area is not particularly productive for seawatching, with sites such as Heysham to the north and Seaforth to the south being better (see p.411 and p.396).

Breeding birds include several thousand pairs of Black-headed Gulls, a few hundred pairs of Herring and Lesser Black-backed Gulls and Common Terns on the marshes, as well as a few Arctic Terns, large numbers of waders, particularly Redshank, Shelduck, Shoveler and Corn Bunting.

Information
EN Warden: Kevin Wilson, Pier House, Wallgate, Wigan, Lancs WN3 4AL. Tel: 01942 820342. E-mail: north.west@english-nature.co.uk

RSPB Marshside: Tony Baker, Beechwood, Cat Tail Lane, Scarisbrick, Southport, Lancs PR8 5LW. Tel: 01704 233003. E-mail: tony.baker@rspb.org.uk

9 PENDLE HILL (Lancashire)   OS Landranger 103

Lying on the southeast flanks of the Ribble Valley, this is a traditional stopover for migrant Dotterel in spring, and is best visited in mid-April to mid-May.

Habitat
The lower slopes of the hill are occupied by pastures bounded by dry-stone walls or hedges. These grade into rocky, bracken-covered slopes on the upper hill, with sparse grass and heather at the summit. Predictably, numerous streams run-off the hill, providing variety.

Access
Leave the M65 at junction 13 north on the A682 at Barrowford and, after ¾ mile, turn northwest on minor roads to Barley. Continue through the village on the minor road towards Downham, and, after a further ¾ mile, a public footpath follows a track west to Pendle Side and Pendle House and then a steep, stepped path ascends to the summit (it is possible to pull off the road here, but it may be better to park in Barley and walk the road). There are also many footpaths around the lower slopes. Dotterel often occurs on the summit plateau around the beacon at the north end of the hill, on short heather or recently burnt areas. The area is popular with walkers, especially at weekends.

Birds
Trips of Dotterel may be present from mid-April, but the largest numbers are likely to be seen in the first two weeks of May, prior to departure for the Scottish breeding grounds (recent counts have been as high as 32, but trips are usually rather smaller). Note that, although regular, the species is *not* guaranteed. Other migrants should include the larger and brighter Greenland race of Wheatear, Whinchat and Ring Ouzel, along with Golden Plover and Curlew. Visiting raptors may include Peregrine, Merlin and Short-eared Owl (but are thin on the ground here).

Breeders include small numbers of Red Grouse, Golden Plover and Twite around the summit, with Ring Ouzel in the gullies, Wheatear on the rocky slopes and around dry-stone walls, Redstart in areas of scattered bushes and trees, and Snipe, Redshank and Yellow Wagtail in wetter pastures. Look for Grey Wagtail and Dipper along streams.

10 LEIGHTON MOSS (Lancashire)   OS Landranger 97

Lying close to the northeast corner of Morecambe Bay, this is one of the RSPB's premier reserves, and holds one of the few remaining populations of Bitterns in Britain (three booming males in 1997), as well as Marsh Harrier and Bearded Tit. In winter a broad variety of wildfowl is present. A visit is worthwhile at any time, other than when the moss is completely frozen in cold weather, but to see Bittern May–June or winter, when hard frosts may force them to feed in the open, are probably best.

Habitat
Once an arm of the sea, Leighton Moss was embanked, drained and ploughed, but then allowed to re-flood in 1917. It is now a freshwater marsh, extensively overgrown with reeds, willow and alder carr, with large areas of open water and specially constructed scrapes and islands.

Access (see map)
Access is from the M6 spur, junction 35a north of Carnforth, onto the A6 and then via minor roads through Yealand Redmayne and on towards Silverdale. The car park and visitor centre are well signed at Myers Farm, near Silverdale Station. A public causeway runs across the reserve, with a public hide that is always open. Access to the rest of the reserve and its four additional hides is by permit only, available from reception. The reserve is open daily (except Christmas Day) 09.00–21.00 (or dusk if earlier), and the visitor centre daily 10.00–17.00.

The north end of the RSPB's Morecambe Bay Reserve is adjacent to Leighton Moss; the Eric Morecambe and Allen Pools are especially convenient (see p.408)

Birds
Winter brings large numbers of ducks, including Teal, Wigeon, Pintail, Shoveler, Pochard, and a few Gadwall, Goldeneye and Goosander. Feral Greylag Goose is resident, and other (probably wild) birds may arrive to roost, while small parties of Whooper or Bewick's Swans occasionally visit. Bittern is present, though difficult to see, as is Water Rail, but both may become bolder if the pools freeze over. Water Pipit is occasional around the muddy edges, with Siskin and Redpoll in the carr, and Hen Harrier may visit, joining resident Sparrowhawk, Buzzard and Barn Owl. Hawfinch is resident in Silverdale, and with patience and luck can be seen around Woodwell. Other woodland birds include Woodcock, all three woodpeckers, Nuthatch and Marsh Tit.

Breeding species include Bittern, Marsh Harrier (first bred 1987, four nests in 1997), Teal, Shoveler, Gadwall, Pochard, Oystercatcher, Black-headed Gull and occasionally Garganey, while Spotted Crake has bred twice. The reedbeds hold Bearded Tit and Reed Warbler, with Sedge and Grasshopper Warblers in scrubbier areas. Cetti's Warbler was recorded in 1996 and may colonise.

A fortunate visitor may find a Jack Snipe in early spring or late autumn, feeding quietly along the edge of the reeds, or perhaps a Garganey. Osprey and Spoonbill are also reasonably regular on passage. Little Gull and Black Tern are more

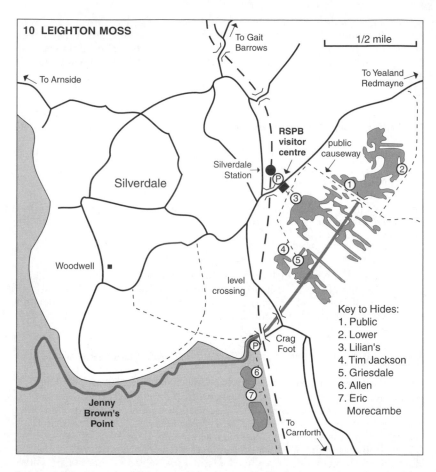

10 LEIGHTON MOSS

To Gait Barrows

1/2 mile

To Arnside

To Yealand Redmayne

RSPB visitor centre

public causeway

Silverdale Station

Silverdale

Woodwell

level crossing

Crag Foot

Jenny Brown's Point

To Carnforth

Key to Hides:
1. Public
2. Lower
3. Lilian's
4. Tim Jackson
5. Griesdale
6. Allen
7. Eric Morecambe

frequent in spring, but Common Tern is equally likely in autumn, also the best period for passage waders, which can include Common and Green Sandpipers, Greenshank and Spotted Redshank. The autumn roost of Starlings attracts hunting Sparrowhawk, and sometimes a Merlin, Peregrine or even a Hobby.

Information

RSPB Warden: Robin Horner, Myers Farm, Silverdale, Carnforth, Lancashire LA5 0SW. Tel: 01524 701601.

11 MORECAMBE BAY (Lancashire and Cumbria) OS Landranger 96, 97 and 102

Morecambe Bay is the largest and, for birds, the most important intertidal area in Britain, attracting up to 200,000 waders in winter. It is of international importance for Shelduck, Wigeon, Pintail, and nine species of wader, particularly Knot. The best time to visit the bay is in winter and during passage periods. The RSPB manages a large reserve between Silverdale and Hest Bank.

Habitat

Morecambe Bay covers c.120 square miles of tidal mud and sand, and is a complex of five estuaries, those of the rivers Wyre, Lune, Keer, Kent and Leven. There are large mussel beds and the flats are fringed by heavily grazed saltmarsh, especially in the upper reaches of the rivers.

Access (see map)

It is important to note the state of the tide, as the sea can be up to 7 miles distant at low water. Fortnightly 'spring' tides are generally best and predictions for Liverpool are more or less correct. Access is at the following points.

WYRE ESTUARY AREA (OS Landranger 102)
Attractions include seawatching at Rossall Point, Fleetwood, and concentrations of Black-tailed Godwits on passage.
Rossall Point, Fleetwood Lying at the west end of the promenade near the coastguard station, the point attracts a few Purple Sandpipers as well as Turnstone, which may number 1000 by spring. There are often Common Scoter and Red-breasted Merganser offshore, sometimes Red-throated Diver, and occasionally Twite and Snow Bunting on the foreshore. For several years a female Kentish Plover wintered at the Point, and was best looked for near the old Rossall coastguard station at high tide. In September–October northwest gales push seabirds inshore, notably Leach's Petrel (see Heysham, p.411, for details).
Knott End-on-Sea Leave the A588 on the B5377/B5270 to Knott End-on-Sea from where you can walk east along the shore for 2½ miles to Fluke Hall.

LUNE ESTUARY AREA (OS Landranger 102)
As well as the usual wildfowl and waders, this area is excellent for Pink-footed Goose, which feeds on farmland at Cockerham Moss and roosts on Pilling Sands.
Pilling The wader roost is best seen from Lane Ends car park, on the seawall just off the A588 north of the village. It is also worth visiting Fluke Hall on a rising tide, by turning-off to Pilling from the A588 and following signs in the village to the car park on the shore.
Cockerham–Pilling–Eagland Hill The low fields in the Cockerham–Pilling–Eagland Hill area are good for Pink-footed Goose and Whooper Swan, especially in mid-February to mid-March. Numbers vary between 500 and 11,000, and the flocks often include family parties of other geese. It is necessary to drive the maze of lanes to find the geese.
Cockersand Point Half a mile north of Cockerham on the A588, a lane leads west to Bank End Farm, from where a path follows the coast northwest for c.2 miles to Cockersand Point. Alternatively, leave the A588 at Thurnham on the minor road to Cockersand Abbey, just a short distance from the Point. There is a wader roost on lower tides, sea duck offshore, and late-summer congregations of terns.
Conder Green Turn west off the A588 in Conder Green at the Stork Inn and park by the disused railway embankment in the shore car park.
Glasson Dock Take the B5290 off the A588 at Conder Green to Glasson Dock. Waders are visible from the road over the disused railway embankment and the area is productive during passage periods.
Middleton Salt Marsh Follow signs from Heysham south on minor roads to Middleton, turning right at the first junction in the village, signed Middleton Sands. Park at Potts Corner from where there are good views of the sands and a footpath runs southeast through the marsh. There is a large wader roost (this site and Pilling Lane Ends are the best places to guarantee large numbers of a variety of waders at high tide), and late-summer concentrations of terns. Sunderland Point is worth checking for migrant passerines in the right conditions.

KEER ESTUARY AREA (OS Landranger 97)

Morecambe Promenade Good for waders at low water, on neap tides waders roost around the jetty, while on higher tides numbers of smaller species roost on the new groynes along the seafront north to Teal Bay. For sea duck watch from the Stone Jetty (just behind the Midland Hotel); Red-breasted Merganser, Goldeneye, Scaup and Eider are regular, and Long-tailed Duck and Common Scoter also occur, along with Great Crested Grebe and Red-throated Diver; sea duck etc are best seen on calm days 2–3 hours *before* high water. Gulls can include Mediterranean. A similar range of seabirds as at Heysham harbour may occur following gales, though the area is not as good if winds are WNW or from further north (rather than from the west or WSW).

Hest Bank RSPB reserve At the south tip of Morecambe Bay and once the best place to see large numbers of waders, but saltmarsh erosion has taken its toll and now only small numbers of Curlew and Oystercatcher roost, with most of the smaller waders now using the groynes on Morecambe seafront. Wildfowl and raptors are now the area's principal attractions. Cross the railway at the level crossing at Hest Bank signal box on the A5105 (plenty of parking space) and walk north for good views.

Carnforth Saltmarsh Reached by taking the footpath along the north bank of the River Keer near Cote Stones Farm. Leave the A6 into Carnforth and take the minor road past the station towards Silverdale. After c.1 mile turn left at the junction and at a sharp right-hand bend take the road straight ahead to Cote Stones, forking left after 100 yards to the riverbank. The old slag heaps offer good vantage points. The *Juncus*-dominated inner saltmarsh is good for Jack Snipe, there is a wader roost, and the slag banks may attract Twite and Snow Bunting, especially in cold weather.

RSPB Eric Morecambe and Allen Pools Two lagoons have been constructed on the saltings of the RSPB reserve, overlooked by hides on the seawall. This is a prime spot to watch waders and a good area for Greylag Goose. Several hundred pairs of Black-headed Gulls breed (and Mediterranean Gull bred in 1997), and migrants have included Garganey, Mediterranean and Little Gulls, and Black Tern, with Marsh Harrier wandering from nearby Leighton Moss (see p.405). Leave the Carnforth–Silverdale road at Crag Foot (just south of Leighton Moss), passing under the railway bridge to the car park. Hides are open 09.00–21.00 (or dusk when earlier).

KENT ESTUARY AREA (OS Landranger 96 and 97)

Notable are flocks of Greylag Geese that frequent the upper estuary, especially the mosses at Foulshaw and Brogden, and Meathop Marsh, between the Kent Viaduct and Holme Island, which are sometimes joined by small numbers of White-fronted, Pink-footed or Barnacle Geese. Diving duck favour the deeper channel around Kent Viaduct, and the limestone whaleback of Humphrey Head provides shelter in west and northwest storms, and in such conditions seabirds may occasionally be seen from Kents Bank railway station.

Upper Kent Estuary, east shore The south side of the upper Kent estuary can be viewed either from the east end of Arnside promenade, looking over the railway wall, or from Sandside promenade, 1½ miles north of Arnside. Waders roost but not on the highest tides. This area is good during passage and there is a large gull roost, which is the most northwesterly site for multiple records of Mediterranean Gull, especially in July–August, and sometimes attracts scarcer species such as Glaucous Gull.

Upper Kent Estuary, west shore Leave the A590 south at the Derby Arms, Witherslack, on the minor road to Ulpha. After 2 miles take the footpath towards Sampool Bridge and view Brogden and Foulshaw Mosses from the sluice at Crag Wood.

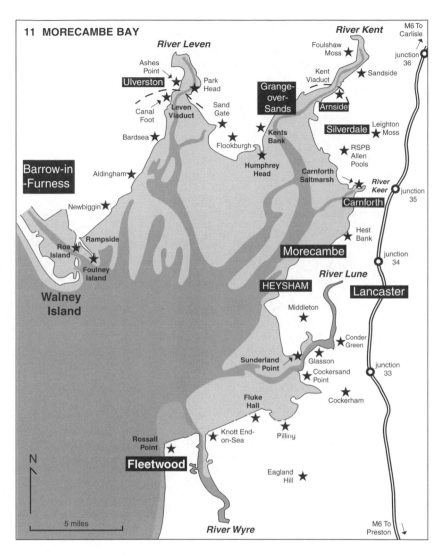

Lower Kent Estuary The lower Kent estuary can be viewed from the footpath to New Barns and Blackstone Point from the west end of Arnside promenade. There is a wader roost, except on higher tides.

Kents Bank Railway Station A good vantage point, with large numbers of Pintail and Shelduck, and the possibility of sea duck, grebes and divers in rough weather.

Humphrey Head Follow signs from Flookburgh, off the B5277. The Head is a reserve of the Cumbria Wildlife Trust and is a good site to observe visible migration, while a number of scarce migrants have occurred in recent years.

LEVEN ESTUARY AREA (OS Landranger 96 and 97)
The extensive saltmarshes at Flookburgh are good for waders, raptors, gulls, and sometimes grey geese. The Leven Estuary has the usual mixture of wildfowl and waders, occasionally including Whooper Swan and grey geese.

Flookburgh Marshes One of the most important areas for roosting waders, which favour West Plain, but may also use East Plain (note that the wader roost at Out Marsh has declined in importance during recent years). West Plain can be viewed by walking west from West Plain Farm (south on a minor road from Flookburgh to Cark airfield) on the Cumbrian Coastal Path to Cowpren Point. High 'spring' tides are best.

Sand Gate Marsh At Flookburgh, off the B5277, proceed west along the main street of the village to a vantage point on the shore beyond Sand Gate Farm to view Sand Gate Marsh. The area has a wader roost on higher tides and is productive for wildfowl, especially on a rising tide, with a large gull roost.

Leven Estuary, east shore The east side of the Leven can be reached from the B5278 1½ miles north of Flookburgh, along the minor road to Old Park and the Park Head car park on the shore. Walking north from here along the road, the viaduct just south of Low Firth offers good views over the estuary.

Leven Estuary, west shore The Leven estuary is best viewed from the west shore. From the A590 in Ulverston take the minor road east, past the entrance to the Glaxo chemical works, to the Bay Horse Inn at Canal Foot to view. More extensive areas can be accessed by taking a minor road from the A590 at Newland (just north of Ulverston) to Plumpton Hall. Walk north along the shore from here, under the railway and on towards Ashes Point. There is a wader roost and it is a productive area during passage.

Bardsea to Roa Island The A5087 parallels the coast from Bardsea to near Roa Island. Waders roost at Bardsea (a track runs northeast off the main road to Wadhead Scar, just north of the turn-off to the village; distant views can also be had of Chapel Island, which holds roosting wildfowl and waders), Aldingham (take the minor road into the village to view the shore) and Newbiggin (visible from the main road). Sea duck occur off Bardsea, including Red-breasted Merganser, Goldeneye and Scaup, as well as Red-throated Diver.

Foulney Island From the A5087 at Rampside take the minor road to Roa Island and, about halfway along the causeway to the island, park and follow the track southeast over the granite-block causeway to Foulney Island, which is a Cumbria Wildlife Trust reserve. The island is a good watchpoint for wildfowl (numbers of Eiders and sometimes other sea ducks) and waders, and, in bad weather, also seabirds, while passerine migrants also occur. In winter Twite and occasionally Snow Bunting may be found along the shore, with raptors over the rough ground. In summer, numbers of Common, Arctic, Sandwich and Little Terns and Black-headed Gull breed at the Slitch Ridge at the south tip.

Walney Island See p.413.

Birds

In winter small numbers of Red-throated Divers appear offshore. Raptors include Peregrine, Merlin, Short-eared Owl and occasionally Hen Harrier. Pink-footed Goose is regular, feeding inland and roosting in the Bay. As many as 1,000–4,000 use sandbanks in the Lune, and are joined by a handful of White-fronted Geese. The Pilling/Cockerham area is also favoured. Greylag Geese concentrate on the RSPB reserve at Carnforth, roosting on the Keer estuary or at Leighton Moss in early winter, and the Lune estuary in the latter part. Other wildfowl include Pintail and a few Shoveler. Sea duck occur in small numbers: Scaup, Goldeneye and Red-breasted Merganser being sometimes joined by Common Scoter, Eider or Long-tailed Duck. The commonest wader is Knot, which can total 50,000. Oystercatcher, Curlew, Bar-tailed Godwit, Redshank and Dunlin are also numerous, with small numbers of Turnstone and a few Ringed Plover and Sanderling. Purple Sandpiper is regular at Heysham and Fleetwood. The saltmarshes attract Rock Pipit, but Snow Bunting and Twite are uncommon.

Passage periods produce more waders but fewer wildfowl. Most waders are commoner in autumn, from July, than in spring. Exceptions are Knot (up to 70,000), Ringed Plover and Sanderling. Autumn passage also produces a greater variety, which may include Little Ringed Plover, Curlew Sandpiper, Little Stint, Spotted Redshank or Black-tailed Godwit. Other passage visitors include terns, and in autumn the right conditions can produce seabirds at Heysham harbour or Fleetwood.

Small numbers of waders oversummer, when breeders include Shelduck, Red-breasted Merganser and Shoveler. Common and a few Arctic Terns breed on the saltmarshes, together with Oystercatcher, Redshank, Wheatear (Carnforth slag tips) and occasionally Dunlin, but the commonest birds are Meadow Pipit and Skylark.

Information

RSPB Morcambe Bay: information, including tide details, is available at the Leighton Moss visitor centre or by writing to the warden, c/o Leighton Moss reserve (see p.405).

12 HEYSHAM (Lancashire) OS Landranger 96, 97 and 102

Heysham harbour is probably the only mainland site in Britain guaranteed to produce Leach's Petrel following southwest to west gales (west to northwest elsewhere).

Habitat

The two nuclear power stations are surrounded by stands of cover, and the northeast sector of the compound has been made into a reserve with a mosaic of habitats, including wetland. Offshore, the warm-water outflows can be particularly attractive to gulls and terns.

Access (see map)

Heysham harbour Straightforward from the A683. On entering Heysham turn right at the Moneyclose Inn traffic lights, and after c.¼ mile turn left at the T-junction (by the helipad). Almost immediately turn right and then follow the road, which eventually narrows to a 'private' road, to the tip of the breakwater. This is the best seawatching station. Waders roost on the helipad.

Heysham Bird Observatory and NR Enter Heysham on the A683 and turn left at the Moneyclose Inn traffic lights signed to Ocean Edge caravan site and power station public observation tower. After c.300 yards, turn right to the NR car park. Any bushes around the power station can hold birds, especially those by the observation tower, along Moneyclose Lane, and bordering the caravan site and golf course. The reserve is open at all times, with vehicle access to the car park possible at least 09.30–18.00 (can be longer in summer and shorter in winter).

Red Nab Follow directions as for the Observatory but ignore the turning to the NR car park and instead park carefully at Ocean Edge caravan site car park. Proceed to the shore on foot, turning right and following the seawall to the outfalls and hide. Waders roost on Red Nab (although not on the highest tides). The outfalls are best 2–3 hours before high water, especially during onshore winds, but may be birdless around high tide.

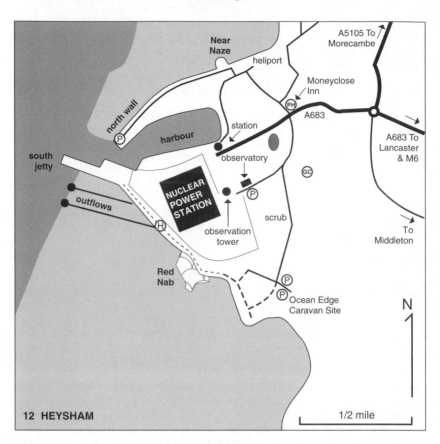

12 HEYSHAM

1/2 mile

Birds

On spring passage in mid-April to mid-May numbers of seabirds, particularly Arctic Tern, can be seen moving north; early mornings are best, preferably with a rising tide and an east wind. Red-throated Diver, Gannet, Kittiwake and skuas are also seen in variable numbers in this period. April–August gales can produce Fulmar and more terns.

In September–October SW–WNW gales (especially after strong west winds) should produce Leach's Petrel (on the second day of the storm and thereafter), as well as Arctic and some Great Skuas. Shearwaters are rare, as is Gannet (Leach's Petrel is often commoner than Gannet in autumn). The north harbour wall is the best place to watch from, although petrels should be visible, albeit more distantly, from the outfall hide. The warm-water outflows attract gulls and terns, including Mediterranean and Little Gulls, and Black and Arctic Terns.

The power station lights act like a huge lighthouse. Sizeable falls of passerines occur in spring and autumn, and have included scarce migrants; indeed, Heysham boasts a very impressive list for a west coast site, including remarkable numbers of Yellow-browed Warbler. The best conditions are either southeast winds around the west flank of an anticyclone, or southeast winds ahead of a warm front with the edge of the cloud cover coinciding with dawn.

In winter small numbers of Purple Sandpipers are occasionally found (though the large and once-regular flocks have now abandoned the area), and a variety of other common waders occurs; in recent winters a spectacular high-tide roost of Knot has appeared on the helipad at a viewing range of c.50 m. Up to 17,000 have occurred in November– February. Winter gales may produce Little Gull and Kittiwake, and oddities such as Great and Pomarine Skuas or Little Auk may be caught up in such movements.

Information
Heysham Nature Reserve: Pete Marsh, 17 Albion Street, Lancaster LA1 1DY. Tel: 01524 66775. E-mail: pbmarsh@btopenworld.com

13 SOUTH WALNEY (Cumbria)   OS Landranger 96

South Walney is the south part of Walney Island, which forms the west flank of Morecambe Bay and thus naturally shares its huge population of waders. This position also concentrates migrants and has led to the establishment of a Bird Observatory. A few semi-rarities and rarities are recorded annually. The best times for migrants are April–early June and August–early November, but for wildfowl and waders winter is better. South Walney is a reserve of the Cumbria Wildlife Trust.

Habitat
There is a variety of habitats: low dunes and sandy beaches are interspersed with areas of gravel, bracken, marsh, and brackish and fresh water, with one substantial patch of elder. The limited cover is concentrated around the five Heligoland traps and coastguard cottages. Saltmarsh and mudflats fringe the east side of South Walney, and the Spit protects the sheltered tidal basin of Lighthouse Bay and is used by large numbers of roosting waders.

Access (see map)
Cross the roadbridge from Barrow-in-Furness to Walney Island, turn left at the traffic lights, and after 400 yards fork right by the King Alfred Hotel into Ocean Road. Turn left after c.½ mile into Carr Lane (signed for the caravan site) and continue for c.1¼ miles to Biggar village and on past the rubbish tip. Just before the South End caravan site fork right, signed to the nature reserve, onto a rough track which cuts across the island past South End Farm to the reserve (stopping not permitted). South Walney Nature Reserve is open all year, 10.00–17.00 (or 16.00 September–April). There is a permanent warden. Entrance is by permit, and is restricted to the hides and two nature trails. A hide overlooks the gull colony and three others face the Irish Sea and Morecambe Bay, excellent for seawatching in wet and windy weather. A cottage accommodating up to eight people is available all year on a self-catering basis. Bookings are taken by the week, although October–Easter daily rates may be available, and it may be possible to accept individuals at a reduced rate. A six-berth caravan is also available.

Birds
Large movements of diurnal migrants occur during passage periods, and in spring a few Marsh Harriers are usually recorded. Calm, overcast or hazy weather is most likely to produce a fall of night migrants. Among the commoner species, Black Redstart, Red-breasted Flycatcher, Yellow-browed and Melodious Warblers, and Firecrest are annual. Seawatching during or after strong west winds in August–September can produce Fulmar, Gannet, Manx and sometimes Sooty Shearwaters, and Leach's Petrel, while Great and Cory's Shearwaters are virtually annual. Another possibility is Pomarine Skua, though you are more likely to see Great and Arctic Skuas, and large numbers of Kittiwake, Common, Arctic and

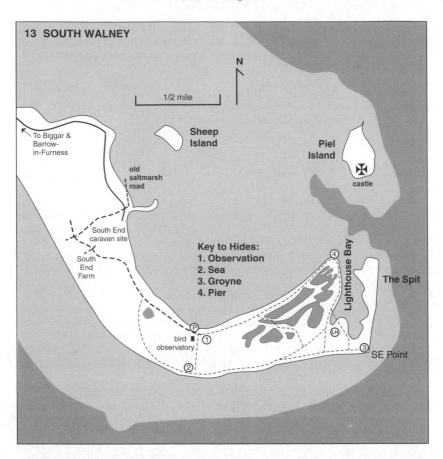

13 SOUTH WALNEY

N

1/2 mile

Sheep Island

Piel Island

To Biggar & Barrow-in-Furness

old saltmarsh road

castle

South End caravan site

South End Farm

Key to Hides:
1. Observation
2. Sea
3. Groyne
4. Pier

Lighthouse Bay

The Spit

P

bird observatory

LH

SE Point

Sandwich Terns, Guillemot, Razorbill and Common Scoter. Migrant waders usually include some of the scarcer species such as Curlew Sandpiper or Little Stint, especially in autumn.

Winterers include Red-throated Diver on the sea, with up to 5,000 Common Eiders and 2,000 Common Scoters, as well as a handful of Velvet Scoters, Red-breasted Merganser, Scaup and Goldeneyes. There are also large numbers of Wigeon, Teal and Shelduck, as well as Whooper Swan, Greylag and Brent Geese, Pintail and Shoveler, and occasional visitors include Black-throated and Great Northern Divers, Red-necked Grebe and Long-tailed Duck. Merlin and Peregrine are daily visitors, and there are sometimes Short-eared Owl or Hen Harrier too. All of Walney Island attracts raptors, so keep a sharp look-out from the car. Little Auk is almost annual following northwest gales, and there have been spectacular hard-weather movements of wildfowl and passerines. Waders include up to 12,000 Oystercatchers, 12,000 Knots and 3,000 Dunlins, and significant numbers of other common species. The pier hide affords good views of the Spit, which is used by roosting waders.

Breeding birds include 1,200 pairs of Eiders, c.200 pairs of Sandwich and a few of Common, Arctic and Little Terns, 20,000 pairs of Herring Gull, 30,000 pairs of Lesser Black-backed Gull, and c.60 pairs of Great Black-back. There are small numbers of Shelduck, Oystercatcher and Ringed Plover. Peregrine breeds in the area and is often seen.

Information

Warden: Mick Venters, South Walney Nature Reserve, 1 Coastguard Cottages, Walney Island, Barrow-in-Furness, Cumbria LA14 3YQ. Tel: 01229 471066. E-mail: cumbriawt@cix.co.uk

14 HODBARROW (Cumbria)   OS Landranger 96

Lying north of the Duddon Estuary and Barrow-in-Furness, this RSPB reserve holds a ternery and numbers of wildfowl and waders, especially on passage.

Habitat

Formerly an industrial site, part of the area has been developed as a holiday complex, but the major portion is now a reserve, with a complex of lagoons and smaller pools, marshy areas, overgrown lime tips, slag banks and scrub.

Access (see map)

Leave the A5093 by Millom Station, taking Devonshire Road into the centre of Millom. Turn right into Mainsgate Road (signed to the reserve), and after c.½ mile left at the T-junction and the car park is just beyond the entrance to the rubbish tip. From here follow the track around the lagoon to the hide (it is possible to drive, but the track has many pot-holes and is very bumpy). The hide overlooks the ternery on the island, which is also used by roosting waders and wildfowl. In autumn and winter, visits timed to coincide with high tide are likely to be most productive, when waders arrive to roost. Alternative access is on foot from Haverigg via the entrance to the caravan site.

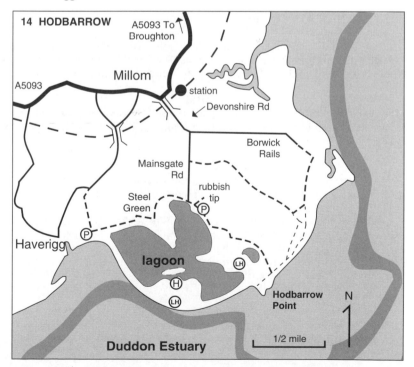

415

Birds

Breeders include numbers of Sandwich Terns, usually accompanied by a handful of pairs of Common, Arctic and Little Terns; the ternery lies on a specially created island in the south of the lagoon, which also has breeding Oystercatcher and Ringed Plover. Other breeding species include Great Crested and Little Grebes, Shelduck, Red-breasted Merganser, Sparrowhawk, Stock Dove, Barn Owl, Lesser Whitethroat and Grasshopper Warbler, with Peregrine in the area.

In late summer there is a build-up of moulting Red-breasted Mergansers, and numbers may peak at 350. Other possible migrants include Garganey, a variety of waders including Black-tailed Godwit, Ruff and, in some years, Little Stint and Curlew Sandpiper, as well as Black Tern and Little Gull. Areas of scrub and other cover can harbour passerine migrants, occasionally including scarcer species such as Black Redstart, Ring Ouzel and Pied Flycatcher. As at other west coast sites, White Wagtail is a feature of spring migration.

Winter brings small numbers of divers and grebes, and wildfowl may include Whooper Swan, Wigeon, Teal, Pochard, Scaup, Goldeneye and Long-tailed Duck, with divers and sea duck especially likely following winter storms. Waders include Golden Plover, Black-tailed and Bar-tailed Godwits, Sanderling, Turnstone and notably a few Spotted Redshanks and Greenshanks. Such concentrations attract raptors, and gull flocks should be perused for the occasional Glaucous, Iceland or Mediterranean.

Information

RSPB Site Manager: Norman Holton, North Plain Farm, Bowness-on-Solway, Wigton, Cumbria CA7 5AG. E-mail: norman.holton@rspb.org.uk

15 ST BEES HEAD (Cumbria)   OS Landranger 89

To the west of the Lakeland fells, St Bees Head holds a colony of seabirds, including England's only breeding Black Guillemots. The Head is an RSPB reserve, and is best visited April–mid-July for breeding birds and in autumn for seawatching.

Habitat

Red sandstone cliffs rise to 300 feet and are topped by areas of gorse and bramble (especially at Fleswick Bay) and grassland, with large fields ringed by dry-stone walls in the hinterland.

Access (see map)

Leave Whitehaven south on the B5345. At the staggered crossroads in St Bees take the road straight ahead and turn right after 400 yards at the T-junction. The car park is a further ½ mile. From there take the cliff path north for c.2½ miles to the lighthouse at North Head (the path continues to Whitehaven). There are safe observation points overlooking the seabird colonies en route, with the best views from Fleswick Bay north to the lighthouse. Alternative access is to leave Whitehaven south on the B5345, turning west after c.2 miles on minor roads to Sandwith. Park near the post office and walk 2 miles west, past Tarnflat Hall, along the private road to North Head. The reserve is open at all times.

Birds

The 5,000 pairs of breeding seabirds include large numbers of Guillemots, but many fewer Razorbills and only a few Black Guillemots and Puffins; Black Guillemot should be looked for around the base of the cliffs at Fleswick Bay. There

Long-eared Owl

Though widespread, this is probably our most elusive owl. The easiest way to see one is to visit one of the communal winter roosts, which form in thick scrub cover at a variety of sites. They may also be seen arriving from the sea at autumn migration watchpoints. Breeding sites have a mixture of dense woodland and open countryside. In spring, listen for the low, pumping 'hoo-hoo-hoo-hoo' of the male.

Key sites: Lower Derwent Valley, Pennington Flash, North Teeside, The Wash, Gibraltar Point.

Pomarine Skua

For seawatchers, a passage of 'Poms' is about as good as it gets. These large, powerful skuas do not breed in Britain but adverse weather conditions during their spring and autumn migration may bring them close to the east and west coasts of Britain. Good numbers are often logged from watchpoints in Kent, Sussex, Hampshire and Dorset during May, but the biggest numbers are off North Uist. In autumn, the east coast is more reliable.

Key sites: Beachy Head, Dungeness, Portland, Flamborough Head, Bowness-on-Solway, Outer Hebrides.

Great Grey Shrike

The largest shrike to visit Britain, this species is an uncommon passage migrant and winter visitor which is almost always seen alone. Certain sites seem to be frequented by wintering individuals year after year, and are usually in fairly open country. Moorland and heathland are particularly favoured, and there is a bias to the east side of Britain. These birds are adept hunters, preying on small birds and mammals.

Key sites: Hartlepool, Ashdown Forest, Thursley Common, Walberswick.

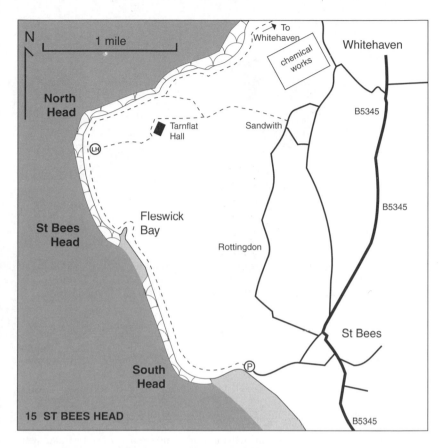

15 ST BEES HEAD

are also Fulmar and Kittiwake, c.600 pairs of Herring Gull, a single pair of Great Black-backed Gull, and, in recent years, a few Cormorants. Other breeding species include Raven, Peregrine, Little Owl, Rock Pipit, Stonechat and Corn Bunting.

The Head can be good for seawatching, especially in strong southwest winds. Red-throated Diver and Manx and Sooty Shearwaters are possible, especially in late summer and autumn, as are Storm and Leach's Petrels, together with Gannet, Great and Arctic Skuas, and Sandwich, Common and Arctic Terns. Small numbers of passerine migrants may occur along the cliffs and in the well-vegetated gully at Fleswick Bay.

Information

RSPB Site Manager: Norman Holton, North Plain Farm, Bowness-on-Solway, Wigton, Cumbria CA7 5AG. E-mail: norman.holton@rspb.org.uk

16 HAWESWATER (Cumbria)   OS Landranger 90

This area of Lakeland fells and valleys around the scenically attractive Haweswater reservoir in the valley of Mardale is famous as the home of England's only breeding Golden Eagles, and also holds a range of other upland birds. A large part of the area is an RSPB reserve.

Ring Ouzel

Habitat

The fells are bisected by rocky streams and crowned by rocky crags, while in the valley near the dam, Naddle Forest comprises steep woods of oak and mixed conifers. Haweswater itself is artificial, and is 4 miles long by ½ mile wide.

Access

From junction 39 on the M6, take the A6 north and in Shap follow signs for the minor road to Haweswater and Bampton Grange. Bear left in Bampton Grange, past the church and over the bridge, for Burnbanks and Mardale. The route passes the dam and then a narrow road follows the southeast flank of Haweswater (with views of the lake and the adjoining fells en route), with a small car park at the road terminus at the south end of the reservoir. Access to the reserve is possible at all times, and the eagle observation post is open 09.00–18.00, April–August, when a warden is present. Naddle Forest is best accessed via the public footpath from the road above the dam. The area is very popular with tourists, thus weekends and especially Bank Holidays are busy.

Birds

The Golden Eagles occupy Riggindale Valley near the head of the reservoir and have bred here since 1969, though they have been unsuccessful in most recent years (four out of five); perhaps the presence of walkers on High Street, just above the nest site, causes too much disturbance. Late summer and autumn, when any young have fledged, is perhaps the best time to observe them. Peregrine, Raven and Ring Ouzel also breed among the high crags and rocky screes, with Wheatear around the boulders on the valley floors. Above the road, mixed oak, ash and birch woodland holds good populations of Sparrowhawk, Buzzard, Woodcock, Pied Flycatcher, Garden and Wood Warblers, Tree Pipit and Redstart. The reservoir edge and feeder streams are good for Dipper, Grey Wagtail, Common Sandpiper and Goosander, with Teal and Greylag Goose around the reservoir. The adjoining pine and larch woods hold Sparrowhawk, Siskin and, in some years, Crossbill is also seen. On the island at the south end of the reservoir is one of the few inland breeding colonies of Herring and Lesser Black-backed Gulls and there are also ground-nesting Cormorants (of the British race *carbo*).

In winter there is a large gull roost (up to 12,000 birds, mainly Common and Black-headed Gulls), and Teal, Wigeon and Goldeneye are regular with occasional sawbills and divers.

Information
RSPB Warden: Bill Kenmir, 7 Naddlegate, Burn Banks, Penrith, Cumbria CA10 2RL.

17 BOWNESS-ON-SOLWAY AND
CAMPFIELD MARSH (Cumbria)   OS Landranger 85

The Solway is one of Britain's largest estuaries and is of international importance for both wildfowl and waders. The north, Scottish, shore is perhaps the most famed ornithologically, but the Cumbrian shore is notable too, both for wildfowl and for the regular spring passage of Pomarine Skua moving east along the Firth between mid-April to mid-May.

Habitat
The south shore of the estuary is bordered by extensive areas of saltmarsh east and west of Bowness-on-Solway. Here, where the saltmarsh narrows (and terminates) at the narrowest point of the Firth, there was formerly a railway bridge, of which the remnants of its embankment, Herdhill Scar, now form a useful 'seawatching' station.

Access (see map)
Bowness-on-Solway Leave Carlisle west on the B5307 and, after c.13 miles, turn north near Kirkbride on the minor road to Bowness-on-Solway. In Bowness turn left at the T-junction where the road meets the coast and park after c.¼ mile at the RSPB car park to view the estuary.

Herdhill Scar From the RSPB car park walk west along the road for c.½ mile to the point where the dismantled railway crosses the road. From here it is a scramble through gorse and over sandstone blocks for 600 yards to the tip of Herdhill Scar (it can be hazardous when wet or otherwise slippery; the Scar is not part of the RSPB reserve). This is the best spot to observe spring skua passage. Pomarine Skua is possible during the second half of April and the first two weeks of May. The best weather conditions are west winds, coupled with cloud and showers. The skuas fly east over the estuary and presumably continue overland to the North Sea.

Campfield Marsh RSPB reserve This holds the largest wader roost on the Solway. Follow directions to Bowness-on-Solway as above, turning left in Bowness along the coast road. Park in the lay-bys at West Herdhill or Maryland Farm to view north over the marsh and estuary, including the wader roosts and wader scrape at Maryland Farm. There is no access to the saltmarsh, and while escorted tours of the farmland and raised mire are possible by arrangement with the warden, for normal birdwatching purposes these are unnecessary.

Birds
Wintering wildfowl include Whooper Swan, up to 10,000 Barnacle Geese and 15,000 Pink-footed Geese, as well as Greylag and large numbers of Wigeon and Pintail; Barnacle Goose favours the saltmarsh while Pink-feet are usually encountered on agricultural land. On the sea occasional Red-necked Grebe, Guillemot and Scaup are seen (high water being best). Waders include Lapwing and Golden Plover on the grazing marshes and Grey Plover, Dunlin, Knot, Bar-tailed Godwit, Turnstone and Sanderling on the shore. Large numbers of the commoner gulls roost on the estuary. The huge numbers of birds attract raptors, including Hen Harrier, Peregrine, Merlin and Short-eared Owl. Look for Twite

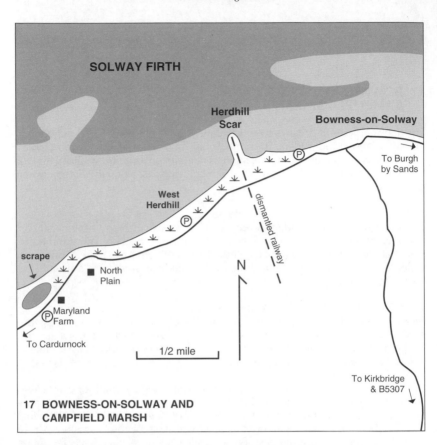

17 BOWNESS-ON-SOLWAY AND CAMPFIELD MARSH

and Snow Bunting along the tideline and Rock Pipit in the saltmarsh gutters, which may also hold Jack Snipe.

On spring passage Pomarine, Great and Arctic Skuas may be observed moving east over the estuary, and in autumn Arctic and Great Skuas and Kittiwake may seek shelter in the Firth, especially in stormy conditions. A variety of waders may appear, including Whimbrel, Greenshank, Green and Common Sandpipers, Little Ringed Plover and, most frequently in autumn, Wood Sandpiper, Spotted Redshank, Curlew Sandpiper and Little Stint. There is a notable build-up of Black-tailed Godwit at Bowness in August–September. Other notable migrants have included Garganey, Little Gull and Black Tern, and oddities such as Little Egret and Spoonbill have occurred.

Residents include Teal, Shoveler, Oystercatcher, Redshank, Curlew, Snipe, Barn Owl, Grey Wagtail and Stonechat. Ruff may oversummer and areas of scrub hold breeding Grasshopper Warbler and Lesser Whitethroat.

Information
RSPB Site Manager: Norman Holton, North Plain Farm, Bowness-on-Solway, Wigton, Cumbria CA7 5AG. E-mail: norman.holton@rspb.org.uk

18 PUGNEYS COUNTRY PARK (West Yorkshire) OS Landranger 110 and 111

Lying on the southern marches of Wakefield, this area attracts a range of water-birds throughout the year. It is owned by Wakefield Council.

Habitat
The Country Park is an area of restored and landscaped gravel pits containing three lakes surrounded by farmland with, to the southwest, a small wood. The larg-er of the lakes covers 75 acres and is used for boating, but nevertheless attracts wildfowl in winter. To the south a smaller pool is managed as a reserve, with well-vegetated banks, including a reedbed. To the north lies another, smaller pool.

Access (see map)
Leave the M1 north at junction 39 on the A636 towards Wakefield. After ¾ mile turn right at the roundabout (signed for the Country Park) on the B6378 and turn into the car park after 100 yards. From here footpaths encircle the larger lake. To reach the reserve, turn right from the car park and follow the path around the west end of the lake, branching right through the wood to a hide overlooking the south lake. The small north pool (Cawoods) can be viewed by walking left from the car park. The main lake is heavily disturbed in summer, especially at week-ends, making early-morning visits preferable.

Birds
Wintering wildfowl include up to 100 Wigeon and Pochard, as well as small num-bers of Goldeneye, Gadwall, Teal and Shoveler. Other notable winter visitors include Water Rail, and large numbers of Golden Plovers use the surrounding fields. Occasional visitors in winter include divers, rarer grebes, Bittern, Whooper

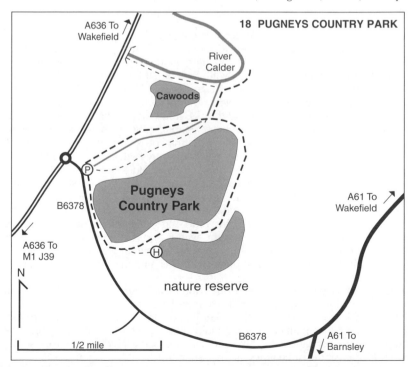

and Bewick's Swans, Pintail, Goosander and Smew. There is a respectable gull roost, which sometimes holds Glaucous, Iceland or Mediterranean Gulls.

On migration a variety of commoner waders occurs, as well as Common, Arctic and Black Terns and Lesser Black-backed Gull, and Shelduck is sometimes noted in spring. Reed and Sedge Warblers are breeding summer visitors to the south lake, and Little Ringed Plover and Common Tern have nested. Residents include Great Crested and Little Grebes, Ruddy Duck and Sparrowhawk.

19 WINTERSETT RESERVOIR AND ANGLERS COUNTRY PARK (West Yorkshire) OS Landranger 110 and 111

Lying southeast of Wakefield this area contains a broad variety of habitats and attracts an equally wide range of birds, especially waterbirds. It is worth visiting throughout the year, but especially in spring and autumn.

Habitat
The largest water in the complex, Wintersett Reservoir (the 'Top Reservoir') is bounded by farmland with some stands of deciduous woodland and large areas of willow scrub, as well as stretches of marshy and rocky shore; it is used for watersports. To the west lies Cold Hiendley Reservoir (the 'Low Lake'), which has mature deciduous woodland at the west end and much riparian vegetation, and borders Haw Park, an area of conifer woodland that is now a LNR owned by Wakefield Council. Anglers Country Park Lake is a former opencast coal mine and following restoration is surrounded by areas of open meadow and recently planted trees, interspersed with rough ground. The 'Pol' is a small scrape on the southwest flank of the Lake.

Access (see map)
Wintersett Reservoir Leave Wakefield south on the A61 and turn left on the B6378 towards Walton and then, after c.¼ mile, right on the B6132 towards Royston. After 2 miles turn left on a minor road to Ryhill. Pass under the railway bridge and then alongside Haw Park, turning left at the sign for Cold Hiendley and Ryhill. After 1 mile turn left again, at the sign to Anglers Country Park. This road passes the southeast flank of Wintersett Reservoir and then, ⅔ mile from the turning, the road cuts across the northeast arm of the reservoir, separating the main water from Botany Bay. Park by the causeway to view. The water may be disturbed by sailing or windsurfing, and the wildfowl often fly to Anglers Country Park Lake. Alternatively, the area can be accessed off the A638 southeast of Wakefield, following signs to Crofton and turning left in the village towards Ryhill, bearing left in Wintersett, just past the Anglers Retreat pub, to the reservoir.

The north shore of the reservoir can be viewed by leaving the Anglers Country Park car park (see below), crossing the road and walking to West Riding Sailing Club. Bear right for 50 yards to view the water, and it is possible to follow this path along the north and west shores, eventually reaching a bridge from which Cold Hiendley Reservoir can also be seen (this is a good spot for Water Rail).

Anglers Country Park Continue from Wintersett Reservoir for ½ mile and turn left at the sign for the Country Park. The car park lies to the right after ½ mile. The Country Park is also signed off the A638 Wakefield–Doncaster road at Crofton. From the car park a path encircles the lake, passing a hide overlooking the 'Pol' scrape on the west flank of the lake and also accessing a hide on the west shore, which is open at the same times as the park centre.

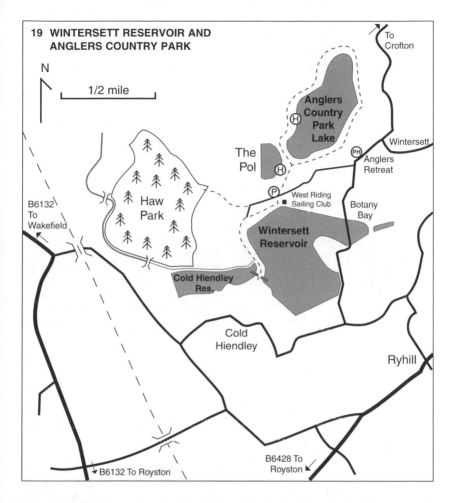

Haw Park Walk west from Anglers Country Park along the road, taking the track to the right through a gate to the park, where there is a network of paths.

Birds

Winter wildfowl in the complex include a few Bewick's and Whooper Swans and occasional White-fronted and feral Greylag Geese, and sometimes also a few Pink-footed Geese. Ducks include numbers of Wigeon, Pochard and Tufted Duck, with smaller numbers of Gadwall, Teal, Pintail, Shoveler, Goldeneye and Goosander (up to 20 roost on Anglers Country Park Lake). Water Rail, Jack Snipe and Stonechat winter. Occasional visitors include divers and rarer grebes, Merlin, Short-eared Owl, Bittern and Smew. A substantial gull roost, on either Wintersett Reservoir or Anglers Country Park Lake, may hold occasional Glaucous, Iceland or Mediterranean Gulls.

On passage in both spring and autumn Black-necked Grebe may turn up, as well as Cormorant, Shelduck, Hobby, Little Gull, Common, Arctic and Black Terns and, especially in spring, Garganey, Marsh Harrier and Osprey are possible. A variety of waders occurs on passage, sometimes including scarcer inland species such as Oystercatcher, Whimbrel or godwits. In late summer, parties of Crossbill sometimes appear in Haw Park.

Residents include Great Crested and Little Grebes, Ruddy Duck, Sparrowhawk, all three woodpeckers (though Lesser Spotted is scarce), Kingfisher, Little and Long-eared Owls and Willow Tit. Tree Pipit, Redstart, Whinchat, Grasshopper, Sedge and Reed Warblers and Lesser Whitethroat are breeding summer visitors.

20 FAIRBURN INGS (West/North Yorkshire) OS Landranger 105

These shallow lakes were formed by mining subsidence and the variety of habitats created has proved very attractive to birds within an otherwise industrial area. Fairburn lies alongside the A1, 4 miles north of the A1/M62 interchange. It is best during migration seasons or in winter. The reserve is managed by the RSPB on behalf of Leeds City Council.

Habitat
Once an area of extensive flood meadows, subsidence has produced a mosaic low spoil heaps and permanent lakes (over one-third of the reserve is open water). The pools at the east end of the reserve have little fringing vegetation and subsidence has continued to reduce the reedbeds, though floating islands have been constructed to help compensate for the loss. Abandoned spoil heaps have been colonised by a variety of plants and planted with trees. At the west end of the reserve, low-lying pasture is still subject to flooding and subsidence, and the resulting shallow flashes are attractive to wildfowl and waders.

Access (see map)
Access to the reserve is from the A1. Approaching from the south, turn west c.4 miles north of the junction with the M62 into Fairburn village and continue to Caudle Hill. From the north, turn off the A1 signed 'Fairburn ¼'. The road crosses the motorway to the village, where you turn right immediately after the Wagon and Horses pub, at the sign for 'Castleford', into Gauk Street and then right at the T-junction into Caudle Hill.

Cut Lane From Caudle Hill turn left into Cut Road car park after c.⅓ mile. From there walk the Cut, a lane bordered by large hawthorns. This gives views of Village Bay and then accesses two public hides on the causeway among the spoil heaps on the south flanks of Village Bay and Main Bay. The hides are open at all times.

Main Bay Continuing west along Caudle Hill, a lay-by on the left after c.1 mile gives views over Main Bay.

Visitor Centre Continuing west along the road for a further ½ mile (and bearing left at the fork in the road), the visitor centre and car park is on the left. This is open weekdays 11.00–16.00 and Saturdays and Sundays 10.00–17.00; maps and guides are available here, as well as up-to-date information on species present on the reserve. From here a boardwalk leads to Pickup hide which overlooks the Pickup Pool, a shallow scrape.

Newfield Plantation Rather than bearing left, fork right along the road towards Ledston and Kippax and take the footpath along the south flank of Newfield Plantation, which is a good area for woodland species.

Phalarope Pool Continue west for 1 mile from the visitor centre along the road

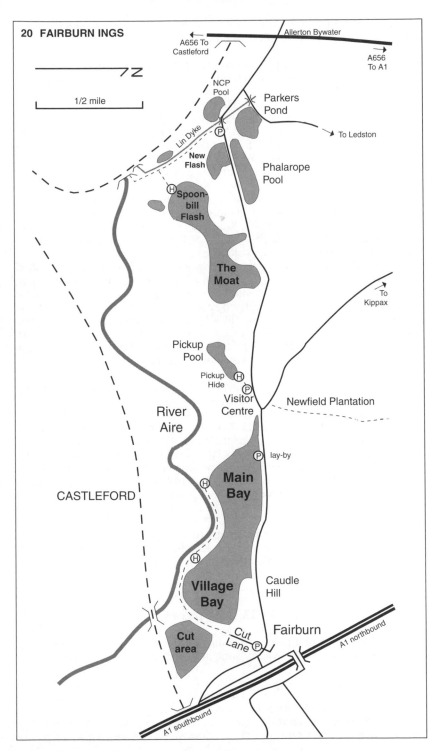

towards Castleford, and Phalarope Pool, a series of shallow, reed-fringed pools at Ledston Ings, lies to the north of the road.

Lin Dyke After a further ½ mile, a car park lies to the south of the road and a trail leads along Lin Dyke through the west end of the reserve to a hide over-looking Spoonbill Flash.

Birds

Many wildfowl winter including a regular herd of Whooper Swan, with as many as 100 sometimes present. These tend to feed in fields during the day, arriving to roost in the evening. Bewick's Swan may also occur. Wintering waterfowl include large numbers of Coot, Wigeon and Teal, as well as Gadwall, Pintail, Shoveler, Pochard and Goldeneye, and occasionally Scaup, Goosander and Smew, while Ring-necked Duck is one of the regular rarities. Occasional Bittern may winter, and divers or rarer grebes are sometimes recorded. A large gull roost frequently attracts Glaucous or Iceland Gulls, sometimes Mediterranean Gull and, in early spring or late autumn, Kittiwake. Redpoll feeds on the alders and birches and is sometimes joined by a few Siskins. Up to 7,000 Golden Plovers roost in the area, and Merlin may visit.

Small numbers of waders occur on passage, sometimes including Spotted Redshank and Green and Wood Sandpipers. Tern passage can be notable, particularly in spring following east winds. The main species are Common, Arctic and Black Terns (this being one of the best sites in Yorkshire for the latter). A few Little Gulls are regular at these times. In July–August Common Scoter is fairly frequent. In autumn large numbers of hirundines can be seen, many of them roosting on the reserve, and Hobby, Marsh Harrier and Osprey are occasionally recorded. Water Rail is resident and Spotted Crake has occurred several times in autumn.

Summer is comparatively quiet. Several species of wildfowl breed including Gadwall, Shoveler, Pochard and Ruddy Duck, and occasionally Garganey and Shelduck. Lapwing, Snipe and Redshank favour the shallow flashes at the west end of the reserve, Kingfisher breeds, and Little Ringed Plover and Reed Warbler almost reach the northerly limits of their breeding ranges here. A colony of Black-headed Gull nests on Priest-holme and in 1978 a pair of Little Gulls attempted to breed among them. Common Tern also breeds. The scrub and deciduous woodland attract a variety of common warblers (occasionally including Grasshopper Warbler) and Whinchat, and Sparrowhawk, Little Owl and Corn Bunting are resident.

Information

RSPB Information Warden, Chris Drake, Fairburn Ings Visitor Centre, Newton Lane, Fairburn, Castleford, West Yorkshire WF10 2BH. Tel: 01977 603796.

21 NEW SWILLINGTON INGS (West Yorkshire)   OS Landranger 104

Lying southeast of Leeds, this area of mining subsidence in the Aire Valley is very attractive to wintering wildfowl, roosting gulls and, in spring and autumn, passage waders.

Habitat

Over the years mining subsidence in the area bounded to the south by the River Aire has produced a number of shallow flashes, and though most are now filled in, Astley Lake was restored as a reserve in 1987. Shallow with gently shelving banks, it con-

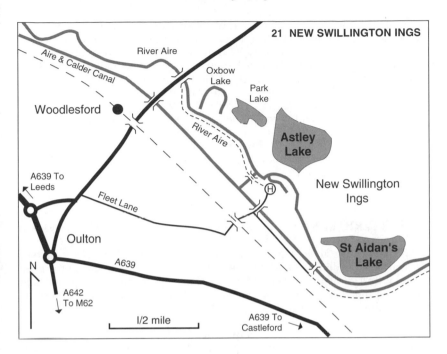

tains 14 small islands. Immediately to the west lie two areas of water; Park Lake and Oxbow Lake. To the east, within a loop of the river, St Aidan's Lake is a larger and more extensive sheet of water.

Access (see map)

From the A642 in Oulton turn east (just south of the Kwik-Save supermarket and opposite the Old Masons Arms pub) into Fleet Lane. Follow this for c.1 mile, under a railway bridge and over the Aire and Calder Canal, to the car park adjacent to Bayford oil terminal. An elevated hide looks north from here over the river and Astley Lake; managed by the New Swillington Ings Bird Group, the hide is open to the public at weekends and on Bank Holidays, with access at other times by arrangement. From the car park walk west along the south bank of the river to Fleet Plantation (a stand of birch and alder) or east to view Fleet Lane Pond and then to Lemonroyd Lock, just beyond which is a viewpoint for St Aidan's Lake. Alternatively, turn southeast off Fleet Lane just before the bridge over the canal and drive for ½ mile to a footbridge, which gives views of St Aidan's Lake.

British Coal plans to drain St Aidan's Lake and develop the area to the north of the river for recreation, including re-opening public footpaths through the area. This may cause much disturbance.

Birds

Winter wildfowl include significant numbers of Wigeon, Gadwall, Teal, Pochard, Goldeneye and Ruddy Duck, and smaller numbers of Goosander and Pintail, while scarcer visitors include Whooper and Bewick's Swans, Greylag Goose, Smew and Peregrine. Merlin is fairly regular in the area at this season, with Golden Plover in the fields, Siskin in Fleet Plantation and Water Rail is usually present, if secretive. Large numbers of gulls roost on St Aidan's Lake, and Kittiwake and Glaucous and Iceland Gulls are sometimes present in the roost.

On passage Black-necked Grebe is occasional in spring (several pairs bred here in the 1940s), as is Common Scoter, and Water Pipit can be found in the early season. Other possible migrants include Little Gull, Sandwich, Arctic and Black Terns, and less regularly Garganey, Osprey or Hobby. A variety of waders is recorded on passage, sometimes including Grey Plover, Sanderling, Little Stint, Wood or Curlew Sandpipers, godwits and Turnstone.

Residents include Little and Great Crested Grebes, Cormorant, Canada Goose, Shelduck, Sparrowhawk, Kingfisher and Green Woodpecker, while Common Tern and a few Sedge and Reed Warblers are breeding summer visitors.

Information
New Swillington Ings Bird Group Secretary, Peter Griffin, 4 Fleet Lane, Oulton, West Yorkshire LS26 8HX.

22 POTTERIC CARR (South Yorkshire) OS Landranger 111

Lying just 2 miles southeast of Doncaster city centre, this wetland is a reserve of the Yorkshire Wildlife Trust. Its greatest claim to fame must surely be the presence in 1984 of a pair of Little Bitterns, which raised three young (the first confirmed breeding record in Britain). More usually, a wide variety of birds is present throughout the year, making a visit worthwhile at any time.

Habitat
An area of relict fenland, the carr was partially drained before succumbing again to subsidence and reverting to wetland. It is now a complex of subsidence and artificial pools, drainage dykes and areas of wetland, with extensive areas of *Phragmites* (notably at Low Ellers and Decoy Marshes), together with willow carr, birch woodland, maturer stands of oak in Black Carr Wood, and grassland. Railway embankments, both used and disused, crisscross the area.

Access (see map)
Leave the M18 at junction 3 north on the A6182 towards Doncaster. After 1 mile, at the first roundabout, take the third exit, signed 'no through road', and turn right after 50 yards into the reserve car park. Access is by permit only, available on a daily or annual basis; apply to 36 Selhurst Crescent, Bessacarr, Doncaster (tel: 01302 530778). The reserve is open from dawn until dusk, and the Field Centre is open for hot and cold refreshments on Sundays 10.00–15.00. There are three marked trails and eight hides, with those nearest the field centre overlooking a passerine-feeding station and a small pool frequented by Water Rail and Kingfisher.

Birds
Breeders include Great Crested and Little Grebes, Gadwall, Shoveler, Teal, Ruddy Duck, Sparrowhawk, Water Rail, Little Ringed Plover, Woodcock, Snipe, Redshank, Black-headed Gull (c.250 pairs), Turtle Dove, Cuckoo, Little and Long-eared Owls, Kingfisher, Green and Great Spotted Woodpeckers, Tree Pipit, Grasshopper, Reed and Sedge Warblers, Tree Sparrow, Redpoll and Corn Bunting.

On spring migration Shelduck is regular, and east winds may bring parties of Common, Arctic and Black Terns. A variety of waders passes through in spring and autumn, depending on water levels, including Ringed and Little Ringed Plovers, Redshank, Greenshank, Common and Green Sandpipers and occasionally Black-tailed Godwit and Wood Sandpiper. Other occasional migrants include Black-necked Grebe, Garganey, Honey Buzzard, Marsh and Hen Harriers, Osprey, Hobby, Kittiwake, Little Gull and Black Tern.

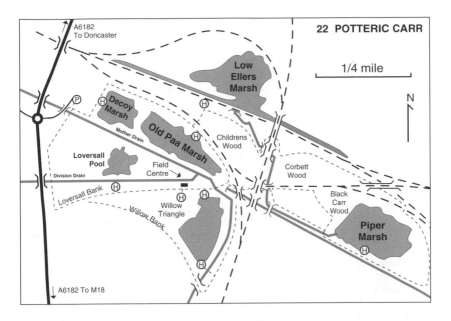

22 POTTERIC CARR

1/4 mile

N

A6182
To Doncaster

Low
Ellers
Marsh

P

Decoy
Marsh

Mother Drain

Old Paa Marsh

Childrens
Wood

Loversall
Pool

Division Drain

Field
Centre

Corbett
Wood

Loversall Bank

Willow Bank

Willow
Triangle

Black
Carr
Wood

Piper
Marsh

A6182 To M18

Wintering wildfowl include Wigeon, Gadwall, Teal, Pintail, Shoveler and Pochard, with Goldeneye, Smew and Goosander sometimes present. Look for Jack Snipe with the resident Water Rail around the pools, and wintering passerines may include Grey Wagtail, Stonechat and Siskin. Bittern is occasionally found in winter, and other irregular visitors include Cormorant, Whooper and Bewick's Swans, Pink-footed and Greylag Geese, Merlin, Short-eared Owl and Bearded Tit.

23 DERWENT VALLEY (East/North Yorkshire)   OS Landranger 105

This area is prone to seasonal flooding and can hold significant numbers of wildfowl in winter, while at Wheldrake Ings, owned by the Yorkshire Wildlife Trust (YWT), careful management of the habitat provides year-round interest, with exceptional numbers of breeding ducks and waders, and a variety of passerines. The area forms the Lower Derwent Valley NNR.

Habitat
The YWT Wheldrake Ings Reserve lies in the floodplain of the River Derwent, and comprises seasonally flooded meadows with stands of willow along riverbanks and an area of permanent open water. Around the car park lie mature hedges, scrub and rough ground, which are attractive to passerines. To the south, towards Aughton and Bubwith Ings, water levels in the meadows are more closely controlled and the river valley floods much more rarely.

Access (see map)
Access in the NNR is restricted to the nine hides and marked footpaths.

Wheldrake Ings Leave the A64 York ring-road on the A19 towards Selby. After 1 mile turn left at Crockey Hill to Wheldrake village and continue for 3½ miles through the village towards Thorganby. The road bends sharp right and, after ½ mile, turn left between two old stone gateposts onto an unsigned sealed track, with a car park after ¼ mile. From here cross the bailey bridge over the River Derwent and turn right, over the stile, to follow the riverbank footpath south. There are five hides. After ¼ mile a hide overlooks the main ings (often flooded in winter) and after a further ½ mile, by the wind pump, a track forks left to a second hide overlooking the main flash. Between 1 April and 30 June access is restricted to YWT members, but there is public access outside this period.

North Duffield Carrs Leave North Duffield east on the A163 towards Bubwith and turn north into the well-hidden car park after ¾ mile. From here walk 150 yards to the hide, which overlooks a large, well-vegetated pool on the west bank of the river and the meadows beyond.

Bubwith and Aughton Ings Continuing east towards Bubwith on the A163 the road crosses a narrow bridge over the River Derwent, with parking on both the east and west sides of the bridge. In winter it may be worth walking north along the east bank of the river to view Bubwith Ings and Aughton Ings, some 2 miles from the bridge.

Skipwith Common This has breeding Sparrowhawk, Woodcock, Turtle Dove, Long-eared Owl, Nightjar, Tree Pipit, Redstart, Lesser Whitethroat and a few Grasshopper Warblers, as well as Black-headed Gull and Snipe around the pools. Access is from Skipwith village, bearing right (southeast) just south of the Hare and Hounds pub on the road through the village to access a track on the opposite side of the triangular village green. Follow the track for c.1 mile to the crossroads (the best area for Nightjar), and turn right (west) to reach the car park after a further ½ mile. The area is a reserve of the YWT.

Birds

The numbers and variety of wintering wildfowl depend upon the extent of the flood waters. In good seasons, both Bewick's and Whooper Swans occur, as well as up to 5,000 Wigeon and several thousand Teal and Pochard, with smaller numbers of Gadwall, Pintail, Shoveler, Goldeneye and Goosander. Occasionally, rarer grebes or divers may appear in winter, as can parties of Bean, Pink-footed or White-fronted Geese, and Cormorant. Sparrowhawk is resident and in winter may be joined by Short-eared Owl, Peregrine, Merlin, Hen Harrier and, sometimes, Goshawk. Large flocks of Golden Plover and Lapwing winter, together with small numbers of Dunlin, Ruff, Curlew and Redshank.

On passage, depending on water levels, a variety of waders may occur, including Whimbrel, Common and Green Sandpipers, Dunlin, and sometimes Ruff or Black-tailed Godwit may stay late into spring and even display. Black-necked Grebe appears most springs, as do parties of Common Tern and sometimes Arctic and Black Terns and Little Gull. Hobby occurs in late summer, and there is a chance of Marsh Harrier or Osprey in both spring and autumn.

Breeders include Little and Black-necked Grebes (usually c.5 pairs of the latter, but 13 pairs in 1994), Cormorant (at Wheldrake Ings), Greylag Goose, Shelduck, Shoveler, Garganey (30+ pairs in 1998), Wigeon, Gadwall, Teal, Pintail (20 pairs in 1998), Pochard, Ruddy Duck, Marsh Harrier, several pairs of Goshawk, Water Rail, Lapwing (360 pairs in 1998), Snipe, Curlew, Redshank, Ruff (25 lekking males in 1998), and sometimes a few pairs of Black-tailed Godwit. Black-headed Gull, Turtle Dove, Barn and Little Owls, Kingfisher, Yellow Wagtail, Grasshopper, Sedge and Reed Warblers, and Corn Bunting also nest, as occasionally does Great Crested Grebe. Outstanding are the populations of Spotted Crakes (30+ calling birds in 1998), Corncrake (eight calling birds in 1998) and Quail (c.10 in 1998). These three species are, of course, much more likely to be heard than seen (and the best time to hear Spotted Crake is at night).

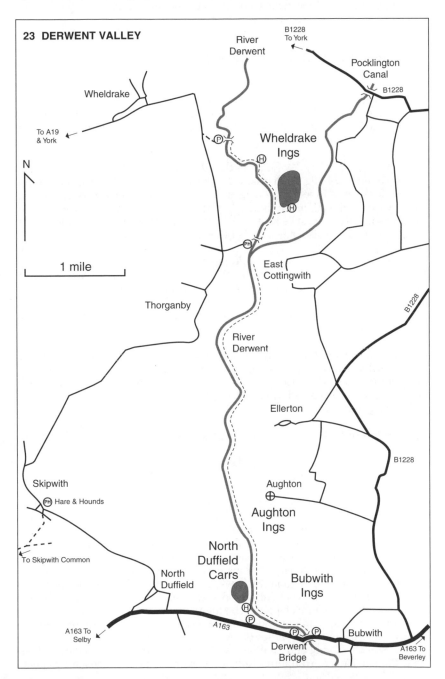

23 DERWENT VALLEY

Information

Yorkshire Wildlife Trust, 10 Toft Green, York YO1 1JT. Tel: 01904 659570. E-mail: yorkshirewt@cix.co.uk

EN, Tim Dixon, Genesis 1, Science Park, University Road, Heslington, York YO10 5DQ. Tel: 01904 435500. E-mail: york@english-nature.org.uk

24 WHITTON SAND AND FAXFLEET PONDS
(East Yorkshire)   OS Landranger 106

Lying at the head of the Humber estuary, just below the confluence of the Ouse and the Trent (and almost opposite the RSPB's Blacktoft Sands Reserve), this area attracts very large numbers of wildfowl and waders, and forms part of the Humber Wildfowl Refuge.

Habitat
Whitton Sand is a large sandbank, c.2 miles long, that is only covered on the highest tides (over 16 feet). In consequence it is an important roost site, being the only exposed bank in the upper Humber on low and medium tides. On the Humber shore to the west lie Faxfleet Ponds, two lagoons fringed by sallows and reeds, and there are also large stands of reeds along the shore.

Access
From the M62 junction 38 take the B1230 southwest towards Newport and Gilberdyke. Continue through Newport and turn south on the minor road to Faxfleet, which is reached in just over 3 miles. At the southernmost point of the village, where the road bends sharp right, carry straight on to a small car park by the Humber bank.

Whitton Sand From the car park walk northeast for ¾ mile along the Humber Bank, past Faxfleet foreshore, to view the Sand from Bowes Landing. Check the foreshore for waders en route and, for roosting waders on a high tide, the hour before high water is best at Bowes Landing; on lower tides flocks will be scattered and viewing more difficult.

Faxfleet Ponds Walk west from the car park for ½ mile along the Humber Bank.

Birds
Waders in winter should include Golden and Grey Plovers, Bar-tailed Godwit, Dunlin, and sometimes Knot, Sanderling and Turnstone. Wintering wildfowl include up to 2,000 Pink-footed Geese, which fly to feed south of the Humber in Lincolnshire and sometimes roost overnight on Whitton Sand. Up to 200 feral Greylag Geese are resident, and a few Brent Geese visit. Wigeon, Teal and Pintail (September–October) occur in large flocks, and small numbers of Shoveler, Pochard, Scaup, Goldeneye and Goosander can also be expected. Occasionally, parties of Whooper or Bewick's Swans may be present. In winter, raptors may include Peregrine, Merlin, Sparrowhawk and sometimes Hen Harrier or Short-eared Owl. Large numbers of gulls are present, with up to 50,000 Common Gull roosting on the Sand. Rock Pipit may be found along the tideline, a few Bearded Tit can be seen around the ponds or in the reeds along the foreshore, together with Water Rail, and small parties of Twite pass through in early spring.

On passage in spring and autumn a variety of waders may be found, such as Little Ringed Plover, Whimbrel, Ruff, Greenshank, Spotted Redshank, Green

Sandpiper and Black-tailed Godwit, with Little Stint and Wood and Curlew Sandpipers present some years. Common Scoter is sometimes seen flying west over the estuary in the evening (July–August). Passage periods may also bring Marsh Harrier and Osprey, and small numbers of Common, Arctic, Sandwich and Black Terns and Little Gull, and larger numbers of Lesser Black-backed Gull, while Black-headed Gull may peak at 50,000 in autumn. The ponds hold a large hirundine roost, and a variety of common passerine migrants may occur.

Breeders on the ponds include Little and Great Crested Grebes and Sedge and Reed Warblers, with Turtle Dove in the area. Barn and Little Owls are resident.

25 BLACKTOFT SANDS (East Yorkshire)   OS Landranger 112

Blacktoft Sands is an RSPB reserve lying at the confluence of the Rivers Ouse and Trent on the south side of the Humber estuary. Several uncommon species breed and the artificial lagoons attract a variety of waders.

Habitat
The east part of the reserve consists of an area of mudflats and saltmarsh at the confluence of the Trent and the Ouse, while the majority of the area, bounded to the south and west by a flood bank, is a tidal reedbed (the second largest in Britain), within which six brackish lagoons have been excavated. Other habitats include areas of flooded grassland and willow scrub.

Access (see map)
Leave Goole on the A161 to Swinefleet and Crowle (signed RSPB). Fork left in Swinefleet on a minor road to Reedness. Continue for c.5 miles, through Reedness, Whitgift and Ousefleet. Approximately ½ mile east of Ousefleet, turn left into the signed reserve car park, immediately before the road bends sharply right. The Ian Prestt Reception hide is situated within the car park, with a shop (open 09.00–17.30 or dusk if earlier), and views over the reserve. The reserve is

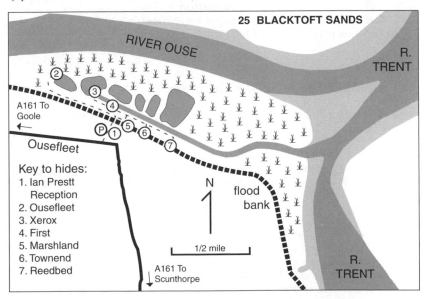

25 BLACKTOFT SANDS

RIVER OUSE

R. TRENT

A161 To Goole

Ousefleet

N

flood bank

1/2 mile

A161 To Scunthorpe

R. TRENT

Key to hides:
1. Ian Prestt Reception
2. Ousefleet
3. Xerox
4. First
5. Marshland
6. Townend
7. Reedbed

open daily 09.00–21.00 (until sunset September–April), with six hides giving good views of the lagoons and reedbed. High 'spring' tides push the greatest number and variety of waders from the Humber estuary onto the lagoons.

Birds

Large numbers of commoner duck winter on the Humber estuary and visit the reserve, including Wigeon, Teal and Pochard, and a few Goosander, Red-breasted Merganser and Goldeneye may also be present. Flocks of Pink-footed Geese and wild swans, especially Whooper, sometimes fly over. Wintering waders include up to 2,500 Golden Plover, and Jack Snipe is sometimes present. Merlin, Peregrine, Short-eared Owl and Hen Harrier are regular, with up to five of the latter roosting in the reeds. Occasionally Bittern may winter, and Sparrowhawk, Little Grebe, Water Rail, Kingfisher, Bearded Tit and Reed Bunting are resident, with large numbers of Bearded Tit sometimes present in winter.

During migration seasons a wide variety of waders pass through and are best viewed from the hides. Many are often only visible at high tides when their feeding areas on the Humber estuary are covered. Characteristic species include Little Stint, Curlew Sandpiper, Ruff, Black-tailed Godwit, Greenshank and Spotted Redshank, and several rare waders have been found in recent years. The best periods for waders are May and July–August with greater numbers during the latter. In spring, Temminck's Stint, Black Tern and Little Gull are occasional, and other irregular visitors include Osprey, Montagu's Harrier, Hobby, Little Egret and Spoonbill.

In summer, Redshank, Lapwing and Snipe nest on the lagoons alongside Pochard, Teal, Shoveler, Gadwall, Shelduck and feral Canada and Greylag Geese, and Ruddy Duck has also bred. A few pairs of Little Ringed Plovers breed on the lagoons. Avocet breeds on artificial islands (16 pairs in 1996). One or two pairs of Short-eared Owls and Grasshopper Warblers nest in grassy areas. Large numbers of Reed Warblers breed in the reedbeds, together with Sedge Warbler and a few pairs of Marsh Harriers. Blacktoft is an important breeding site for Bearded Tit (usually c.40 pairs but up to 100 pairs in some years). They are most visible September–early November.

Information

RSPB Warden, Pete Short, Blacktoft Sands Reserve, Hillcrest, Whitgift, Nr. Goole, East Yorkshire DN14 8HL. Tel: 01405 704665. E-mail:simon.wellock@rspb.org.uk

26 SWINEFLEET PEA FIELDS (East Yorkshire) OS Landranger 112

Lying close to Blacktoft Sands RSPB Reserve, this area is a traditional spring stopover for Dotterel.

Access

Leave Swinefleet southeast on the A161 towards Crowle and expanses of flat fields appear on either side of the road. Continue to a sign on the right for 'Peat Works" and scan the fields for the next 2 miles.

Birds

Dotterel may be present any time mid-April to late May, with numbers depending on the season and weather (and how many people look). They frequent fields of peas and young wheat, and can be very hard to see if they are in the furrows or sitting among the crops. A telescope and patience are essential requirements for the search.

27 CHERRY COBB SANDS AND STONE CREEK
(East Yorkshire)   OS Landranger 113

This area along the north bank of the Humber harbours one of the largest wader roosts on the estuary and, over the years, has also attracted a number of major rarities.

Habitat
Cherry Cobb Sands comprise the largest expanse of raised saltmarsh on the north shore of the Humber, bordered by flat, featureless farmland.

Access
Leave Hull east on the A1033 and, after passing through Thorngumbald and adjacent Camerton, turn sharp right on a minor road signed 'Paull'. After 200 yards turn left to Cherry Cobb Sands and Stone Creek. Continue on this minor road for 2½ miles, passing the hamlet of Thorney Crofts and follow the road left, now almost parallel to the Humber Bank, for c.3 miles until you reach Stone Creek. (Alternatively, leave the A1033 just west of Keyingham on the minor road to Cherry Cobb Sands.)

Cherry Cobb Sands Park by the Humber bank and follow it on foot northwest to view Cherry Cobb Sands for waders (a rising tide is best).

Stone Creek/Sunk Island From the parking area walk left along the track to the bridge over the creek and then cut right, back to the Humber Bank. Follow this for c.1 mile to the small wood, checking for migrants en route.
   To check the fields to the east, drive left along the track from the parking area for a few yards to the bridge over Stone Creek and follow the made-up road left for c.400 yards to park where the road leaves the creek, scanning the surrounding fields. Continuing, the road runs through farmland, which may hold plovers and raptors, to Sunk Island Farm and it is then possible to cut north back to the main A1033 at either Ottringham or Patrington.

Birds
Wintering wildfowl include Brent Goose, Wigeon, Teal and Pintail. Good numbers of waders are present, especially Grey Plover, Curlew, Knot, Dunlin, Redshank and Bar-tailed Godwit. Occasionally small numbers of Bewick's Swans may be found. On higher tides roosting waders, notably Curlew, Golden Plover and Lapwing, use the fields east of Stone Creek. Wintering raptors in the area may include Peregrine, Merlin, Sparrowhawk and, sometimes, Hen Harrier.
   On passage the typical estuarine waders are usually present, including Whimbrel, Ruff, Greenshank and sometimes Black-tailed Godwit, Little Stint or Curlew Sandpiper. In late autumn the area has harboured a couple of extreme rarities, including a Green Heron from North America (together with a Great White Egret!) in dykes at Stone Creek in November 1982. Clearly, anything is possible!

28 SPURN POINT (East Yorkshire)   OS Landranger 113

Lying 32 miles southeast of Hull (on a road to nowhere), Spurn was site of the first Bird Observatory to be established on mainland Britain, in 1946, and is an excellent place to observe migrants and arguably the premier site in mainland Britain for rarities. Spurn NR is owned by the Yorkshire Wildlife Trust.

Habitat

Spurn is a narrow sand and shingle spit, c.3½ miles long, extending into the mouth of the Humber. The base of the peninsula is farmed, and includes Beacon Ponds and Easington Lagoons, but the spit really begins at the observatory, and is only c.30 yards wide at the Narrow Neck. Indeed, it has been breached by the sea several times in recent years, although the road is always maintained to give access to the tip. Sea buckthorn forms extensive and largely impenetrable thickets, with occasional elder bushes and areas of marram grass. To the seaward there is a narrow beach, while on the Humber shore are the extensive mudflats of Spurn Bight.

Access (see map)

Spurn Head Leave Hull on the A1033 through Keyingham and on to Patrington, and then take the B1445 to Easington, continuing on a minor road to Kilnsea. The road bends sharp left and then, at the junction (with the caravan site to the left), turn sharp right and continue for 1 mile to the entrance of the reserve. The Canal Scrape and hide lie to the right just before the gate. The Observatory is based at Warren Cottage at the base of the peninsula and offers simple self-catering accommodation for up to 17 people. There is a resident warden, and a seawatching hide behind Warren Cottage for the use of observatory residents.

Access to the peninsula is unrestricted, apart from the Bird Observatory garden, the various RNLI, pilots' and coastguards' buildings, and the Point Camp area. There is a charge for cars using the road along the peninsula, usually collected near the Observatory. An Information Centre is situated outside the Bird Observatory, and there is a car park there and at the tip of the peninsula.

Visible migration is best watched from the Narrow Neck, ¾ mile south of the gate. Movements usually peak in the first few hours of daylight and west winds are most productive. This can also be a good place to seawatch from. Otherwise migrants can occur anywhere but the buckthorn is difficult to work. It is better to concentrate on:

* The trees and hedges around Kilnsea, especially at the churchyard and near the Crown and Anchor pub.
* Beacon Lane, which is bordered by hedges.
* The Canal Zone, an area of farmland with hedges and ditches.
* The Big Hedge, a mature belt of hawthorns which runs east–west across the base of the peninsula, c.100 yards north of the entrance gate.
* The trees and bushes around Warren Cottage.
* Chalk Bank, which is especially good for larks, pipits, wheatears and Snow Bunting.
* Near Chalk Bank, a hide on the Humber Shore overlooks a raised sand and shingle beach, used by roosting waders.
* The Point Camp area, especially the sycamores and elders around the old parade ground, and the stands of sea buckthorn by the lighthouse.

Easington Lagoons Just outside Easington, heading towards Spurn, there is a sharp right-hand bend. At the bend carry straight on along the track to park at the clifftop. Walk south from here to the lagoons and hides. The lagoons are good for waders if water levels are low, especially at high tide. In winter they attract the occasional duck or grebe and there are often many Snow Buntings, occasionally Lapland Buntings and raptors.

Beacon Ponds Lying north of Kilnsea, access is by walking north from Beacon Lane or by continuing south from Easington Lagoons. Birds are similar to Easington Lagoons.

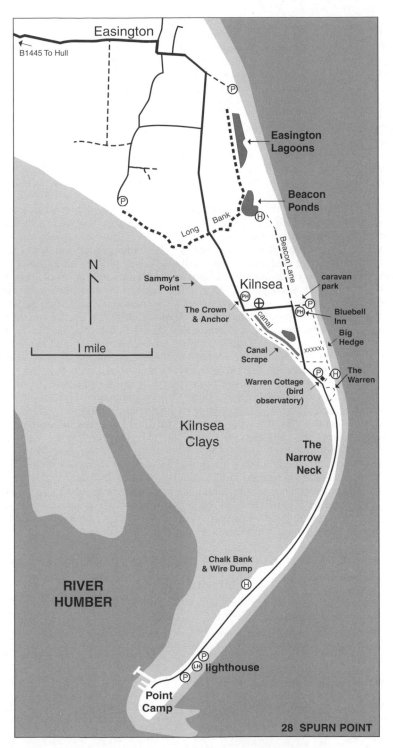

Easington

B1445 To Hull

Easington
Lagoons

Beacon
Ponds

N

Sammy's
Point

Kilnsea

caravan
park

The Crown
& Anchor

Bluebell
Inn

Big
Hedge

I mile

Canal
Scrape

The
Warren

Warren Cottage
(bird
observatory)

Kilnsea
Clays

The
Narrow
Neck

RIVER
HUMBER

Chalk Bank
& Wire Dump

lighthouse

Point
Camp

28 SPURN POINT

Birds

Visible migration commences in March with Lapwing, Starling, Rook, Jackdaw and Chaffinch on the move. A peculiarity of Spurn is that birds appear to be moving the 'wrong' way in spring, that is south or south-southeast. In March–April Rock Pipits of the Scandinavian race may occur on the saltmarsh and lagoons. East winds in late March–April will bring Black Redstart, and later on flycatchers, chats and warblers; Wryneck, Bluethroat, Icterine and Marsh Warblers, Red-backed Shrike and Common Rosefinch occur most years. Easterlies also bring movements of Black, Common and Arctic Terns in the first few hours of daylight.

Late summer sees passages of waders and terns offshore, especially in strong west or southwest winds, as well as large movements of Swift. From late August to early November, NW–NE winds may prompt a passage of seabirds. Regular are Sooty Shearwater, skuas (sometimes including Pomarine and occasionally Long-tailed), and, from October, Little Auk, while Little Gull can peak at 100 on a very good day. Large numbers of waders frequent the estuary, with a good variety on Beacon Ponds and Easington Lagoons. Spotted Redshank is regular, with Little Stint and Curlew Sandpiper in some years.

Autumn passerine migration commences in late July with movements of Sand Martin, Swallow, and Pied and Yellow Wagtails. August produces a trickle of warblers, mainly Willow, but towards the end of the month and into September the pace increases with Redstart, Whinchat, Wheatear and Pied Flycatcher joining a wide variety of warblers. East winds are most likely to produce interesting birds and there is a chance of Wryneck, Red-backed Shrike, Bluethroat, Icterine or perhaps even a Greenish Warbler. Spurn is *the* locality on the British mainland for Barred Warbler. In October diurnal migrants (pipits, Linnet, Greenfinch and sometimes Twite) increasingly dominate the scene, but there can be large falls of Robins, thrushes or Goldcrests. Flocks of Meadow Pipits may occasionally be joined by a Richard's, and in late October Spurn has consistently produced records of Pallas's Warbler, as well as Yellow-browed Warbler and Red-breasted Flycatcher. Long-eared Owl is regular and may be flushed from the buckthorn; Short-eared Owl tends to pass straight through. There can be large arrivals of thrushes in bad weather, especially Blackbird.

Winter is comparatively quiet. Large numbers of Red-throated Divers can occur offshore and wildfowl on the Humber include Brent Goose, often around the Narrow Neck. Hen Harrier, Merlin and Short-eared Owl may, with luck, be seen and in early winter there are often large numbers of thrushes feeding on the buckthorn berries. Snow Bunting is regular, numbers varying from a few dozen to a several hundred. Hard-weather movements can occur: fleeing birds can be seen moving south in early morning, especially if it is clear, and some may pause to feed.

Breeding birds include a few pairs of Little Tern around Easington.

Information

Warden: Spurn Bird Observatory, Kilnsea, Patrington, Hull, Yorkshire HU12 0UG.

29 TOPHILL LOW (East Yorkshire)   OS Landranger 107

This complex of reservoirs lies north of Hull, between Beverley and Great Driffield. Sympathetic management in recent years has produced a range of habitats and the site now holds year-round interest (although noted for winter wildfowl and passage waders) and a reputation for attracting the rare and unusual.

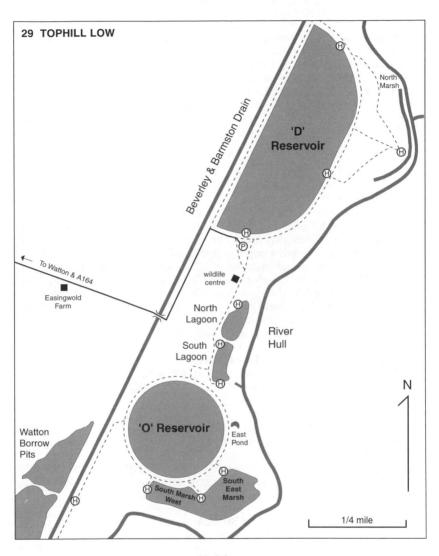

29 TOPHILL LOW

Habitat

Lying in the valley of the River Hull and just 9 miles from the east coast, the varied habitats include two large reservoirs, as well as lagoons, marshes, scrub and some small stands of woodland. The reserve is owned by Yorkshire Water and managed in collaboration with Tophill Low Wildlife Group.

Access (see map)

Turn east off the A164 at the south end of Watton (c.6 miles north of Beverley) onto a large looping lay-by and then immediately east again on a narrow minor road. After 2 miles, where the road turns sharply north (back towards Hutton Cranswick), continue straight and then fork right to the pumping station entrance after 2 miles. The reserve is open daily except Mondays and Tuesdays, and day permits are available from the car park. A well-marked system of paths accesses 13 hides (but not the residential and operational areas).

Birds

Winter wildfowl usually include large numbers of Mallard, Teal, Wigeon and Tufted Duck, as well as Gadwall, Pintail, Shoveler, Pochard, Goldeneye and Ruddy Duck (numbers of some of these peak in autumn). Parties of Whooper and Bewick's Swans may be present, and other waterfowl include Cormorant (numbers peak in autumn) and occasionally rarer grebes or divers, Smew, Goosander and sea duck, notably Long-tailed Duck, Common Scoter and Scaup. The reserve has an impressive list of rare diving ducks to its credit. Large numbers of Lapwing and Golden Plover winter in the area, with Corn Bunting in the surrounding fields, and a handful of Long-eared Owls roost on the reserve. Short-eared Owl is an occasional winter visitor. There is a very large gull roost, mainly Black-headed and Common Gulls. Jack Snipe join resident Water Rail in dense cover at the water's edge, while Bearded Tit sometimes appears in late autumn, and notable winter passerines include Rock Pipit, Siskin, Redpoll and, sometimes, Brambling.

On passage Garganey and Osprey are occasionally seen, and Spotted Crake has been recorded several times. A variety of waders occurs, including Dunlin, Ruff, Greenshank, Spotted Redshank, Green and Common Sandpipers and Ringed Plover, with less frequent species including both godwits, Whimbrel, Little Stint and Wood and Curlew Sandpipers. Common, Arctic and Black Terns are regular, and Sandwich Tern and Little Gull are sometimes recorded. Small numbers of passerine migrants occur, such as Tree Pipit, Yellow and White Wagtails, Wheatear and Whinchat.

Residents included Little and Great Crested Grebes, up to 500 Greylag Geese, Shelduck, Sparrowhawk, Water Rail, Little Ringed Plover, Little and Tawny Owls, Kingfisher, and Grasshopper, Sedge and Reed Warblers.

Information

Tophill Low Nature Reserve Warden, Peter Izzard, Watton Carrs, Hutton Cranswick, Driffield, East Yorkshire YO25 9RH. Tel: 01377 270690.

30 HORNSEA MERE (East Yorkshire)   OS Landranger 107

This large natural lake lies very close to the sea and is highly attractive to wildfowl and migrants, and holds a notable concentration of Little Gulls in early autumn. It is worth a visit at any season.

Habitat

Lying just under 1 mile from the sea, the Mere is c.1½ miles long and ½ mile wide, with the 300 acres of open water being used for sailing and fishing (the east end is most disturbed). Bordering the town of Hornsea at the seaward end, the surrounding vegetation includes grassy fields, with large reedbeds at the west end, stands of deciduous woodland on the north and west sides, and reeds and scrub along the south shore.

Access (see map)

Access is only possible at two points (the B1244 parallels the north shore but there are no viewpoints along this road).

Kirkholme Point From the B1242 in Hornsea town centre follow signs to 'The Mere and Car Park' via the track to Kirkholme Point. An information centre is situated in The Bungalow left of the entrance to the boating complex and is open at weekends, May–August. Parking is available in business hours, and there is a cafe. The Point is a good spot to look for gulls and terns over the Mere.

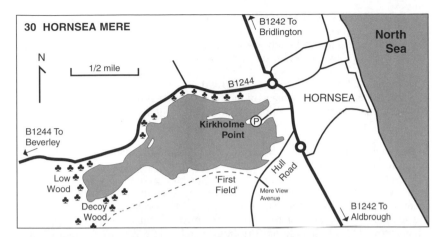

South Shore Travelling south out of Hornsea on the B1242 towards Aldbrough, turn right into Hull Road (opposite the garage). Park after c.800 yards in Mere View Avenue and take the public footpath opposite along the south shore of the Mere. The first ½ mile gives the best views (and is known as 'First Field'), after this reeds and trees obscure the water, although the footpath continues to the west end at Wassand.

There is no other access to the reserve.

Birds

In winter there are large numbers of Wigeon, Pochard and Tufted Duck, notable concentrations of 100–200 Gadwall and Shoveler, and occasionally as many as 400 Goldeneye. A few Goosander and Ruddy Duck are also regular, and occasional sea duck, notably Long-tailed Duck, may occur. The resident feral Greylag and Canada Geese and Mute Swans are sometimes joined by small numbers of Bewick's or Whooper Swans or feral Barnacle Geese. Around the Mere's fringe a few Jack Snipe and Water Rail find cover, and occasionally a Hen Harrier is seen. Bittern and Bearded Tit are rather irregular.

In early spring a few Rock Pipits of the Scandinavian race occur. Subsequent passage brings Garganey and possibly Marsh Harrier, Osprey and terns, including Black and Arctic.

Breeders include Great Crested Grebe, Pochard, Shoveler and Gadwall. In the waterside vegetation are Reed and Sedge Warblers with Corn Bunting in the fields. Sparrowhawk, Great Spotted Woodpecker and Treecreeper nest in areas of trees. There are late-summer concentrations of Cormorant, gulls and terns, most notably Little Gull, which is generally present early May–October and can peak at over 100. In midsummer, good numbers of Manx Shearwater may be seen offshore at Hornsea.

Red-necked, Black-necked and Slavonian Grebes may occur in ones and twos in autumn and winter, but are irregular, as is Red-throated Diver. In autumn both Ferruginous Duck and Red-crested Pochard have appeared several times and a careful check through the ducks is worthwhile. Little Gull continues to occur, often with migrant terns and, as in spring, Black Tern is regular. If water levels fall exposing some mud a variety of waders may occur. There is a large roost of hirundines in the reedbeds, and these are hunted by Sparrowhawk and occasionally Hobby. There may be migrants in the surrounding woods, fields and hedges, and sometimes these include scarcer species such as Wryneck or Red-backed Shrike.

Information

RSPB Warden: 11 Carlton Avenue, Hornsea, East Yorkshire HU18 1JG.

31 BRIDLINGTON HARBOUR (East Yorkshire)   OS Landranger 101

Bridlington harbour and beach are worth a look, especially in winter for gulls, waders and, in rough weather, seabirds sheltering in the harbour.

Habitat
The harbour is sheltered by piers and to the south is South Beach, part of a series of strands that extends from Bridlington to Spurn Head.

Access
In Bridlington follow signs for South Beach, with parking available near the harbour and, especially in winter, in nearby side streets.

Mid-May to mid-September there are regular sailings of the *MV Yorkshire Belle* from North Pier in Bridlington harbour to view the seabird colonies at Flamborough and Bempton. The boat carries 200 passengers and full facilities are available on board for the 2½ hour cruise (details from the skipper, P. Richardson, 28 Roundhay Road, Bridlington, tel: 01262 673582). Longer cruises for birdwatchers are sometimes arranged, as are 'pelagics' in August–October to search for skuas and shearwaters, details from the RSPB visitor centre at Bempton or their North England Regional Office (tel: 0191 2324148). See also p.443 for details of cruises from North Landing on Flamborough Head.

Birds
In winter, divers, grebes, Cormorant, Shag, sea ducks and auks may seek shelter in the harbour, especially during rough weather, when they may give excellent views. At low tide the exposed mud attracts numbers of commoner waders, with Turnstone, Purple Sandpiper and Rock Pipit on the harbour walls and rocks on the seaward side of the South Pier. When fishing boats are unloading their catches the large assemblage of gulls regularly includes Kittiwake and sometimes Glaucous, Iceland or Mediterranean. Otherwise, the gulls may be found loafing on South Beach (especially on falling or low tides), together with a variety of waders, notably Grey Plover, Sanderling and Turnstone.

32 FLAMBOROUGH HEAD (East Yorkshire)   OS Landranger 101

Flamborough Head provides the best seawatching on the east coast and is rivalled as a seawatching site in Britain only by west Cornwall. Landbird migrants also occur in significant numbers and have included many rarities.

Habitat
The chalk cliffs of Flamborough Head rise to 250 feet and the peninsula projects over 6 miles into the North Sea. Largely comprising farmland, the network of hedges and some small plantations provide cover for migrants. Variety is provided by a couple of golf courses and a large pond near the Head. Danes Dyke, an ancient fortification, runs north-south at the base of the headland and holds much more extensive stands of cover, as does South Landing. Along the clifftop there are also areas of scrub and stunted hedges that attract migrants, notably at Selwicks Bay.

Access (see map)
Access to the area is via the B1255 from Bridlington. Flamborough Head is private farmland, with access only along roads and public footpaths. In particular,

the gardens around the Head are private and residents' privacy should be respected at all times.

THE OUTER HEAD

1. Fog Signal Station Park in the public car park and walk the metalled road to the foghorn. This is the traditional seawatching site, in the shelter of the walls of the building or on the grassy ledges below. Take great care on the potentially treacherous cliff edges. Seabirds can be seen at all times, but the best numbers and variety are likely when there is a strong northwest to east wind coupled with poor visibility. The Cliff End Cafe, on the right just before the car park, is a regular meeting point for birdwatchers.

2. Gorse Field An area of rough grazing with a dense stand of gorse lies immediately east of the car park. Although there is no public access, it is worth scanning the hedges and the field from the car park or from opposite the toilets.

3. South Cliff Path This runs from the fog station towards Old Fall. There is little cover but in autumn the stubble fields and areas of rank grass may hold larks, pipits and buntings, notably Lapland Bunting and occasionally Richard's Pipit.

4. Old Fall Hedge Perhaps the best area for large numbers of migrants. Park in the car park by the new lighthouse and walk back along the road to the entrance to the footpath (signed 'New Fall'). Old Fall Plantation lies immediately to the east and is also very attractive, but is private and any temptation to enter must be resisted; with patience most of the birds in the wood can be seen from the public footpath (a mounted telescope is useful).

5. Roadside Pool This is easily viewed from the road and the surrounding sallows may hold migrants (it is a potentially good area for Bluethroat). Park in the car park by the new light and walk back to the area.

6. Selwicks Bay A scenic bay just north of the car park, the bramble at the head of the Bay offers a first landfall for tired migrants (keep to the well-marked path in this sometimes precipitous area). The areas of low scrub along the north cliff path to North Landing may also be worth a look.

7. Golf Course A good area for larks, pipits, wagtails and Wheatear, especially in early morning. The course is private but can be seen from the north cliff path or the road.

8. Breil Nook One of the best areas on the Head for breeding seabirds, with spectacular numbers present in April–July. Access is from Selwicks Bay or North Landing along the clifftop footpath.

NORTH LANDING AND THORNWICK BAY

1. North Landing From Flamborough follow signs to North Landing. Park in the car park and follow any of the many footpaths along the clifftop or around the hedges. Between Easter and late August there are regular boat trips, weather permitting, from North Landing to view the seabird colonies on the north side of the Head (details from Richard Emmerson, Westcarr, Woodcock Road, Flamborough, tel: 01262 850575; see also p.442 for details of cruises from Bridlington).

2. Thornwick Bay Approaching North Landing on the road from Flamborough, turn left just before the Viking Hotel on the track to Thornwick Bay (car park and cafe). En route you pass a small area of reeds on the left which may hold migrants.

SOUTH LANDING AREA

1. South Landing One of the best areas on the Head for migrants, but the extensive areas of cover can make it hard (and time-consuming) to work thoroughly. Follow signs from Flamborough village along South Sea Road to the pay-and-display car park. Public footpaths surround the wood and it is also worth checking the boulder beach; particularly productive areas are the ravine running south to the sea and the bridge at the east end of the wood. Follow the footpath east along the clifftop to Book and Grosbeak Gullies, with more areas of cover attractive to migrants.

2. Beacon Hill The highest point on the Head and well positioned for observing visible migration and also any raptors in the area. On entering Flamborough on the B1255 from Bridlington turn first right and drive south through Hartendale housing estate. There is limited parking near Beacon Farm and from here follow the footpath south to the hill.

DANES DYKE SOUTH
Another large area of cover which, like South Landing, may be hard to work but can hold numbers of migrants. Signed from the B1255, park in the car park at the south end, with free access to all of the woodland south of the B1255; the ravine nearest the sea is perhaps the most productive area. A footpath leads west across Sewerby golf course, which may hold larks, pipits, wagtails, Wheatear etc. especially in early morning.

Birds
There is always Gannet offshore at Flamborough and Fulmar is common all year, with larger numbers in spring and early autumn. Occasional 'blue' Fulmar, dark birds from northerly populations, are seen. Manx Shearwater is also quite common March–November and, of the rarer shearwaters, Sooty is regular July–October and can total several hundred on good days, and small numbers of Mediterranean occur in late summer. Great (August–October) and Cory's (scattered records April–October) are both much rarer. Little Shearwater, the rarest of all, has been seen on a handful of occasions in June–October. Arctic is the commonest skua; peak passage is in the last ten days of August and the first half of September. Great Skua can also appear in large numbers, up to 100 in a good day, especially in September and sometimes October. Though Pomarine Skua occurs in spring, autumn is better. It usually occurs in small numbers, only a handful even on a good day. Singles are present by late August and are increasingly frequent in September. Occasionally, it appears in large numbers and in these 'invasions' most are seen October–early November. Long-tailed Skua is very uncommon and tends to be associated with the main Arctic Skua passage in the last few days of August and September. Sabine's Gull is also uncommon, with a mean c.15 a year, but sometimes as many as 100 Little Gulls can be seen in a day, especially in late autumn. Other species that appear on spring and autumn seawatches are divers (mainly Red-throated), ducks, waders, gulls and terns, especially Common, Arctic and Sandwich, but also including Black. In late autumn Little Auk may occur, occasionally in large numbers. For the breeding seabirds, which are present offshore in large numbers for much of the year, see Bempton Cliffs (p.445).

During passage periods there are occasionally large falls of migrants on the Head, with good numbers of thrushes, warblers, flycatchers and finches. These follow the same pattern as at other east-coast sites. Wryneck, Redstart, Black Redstart, Ring Ouzel, Whinchat, Wheatear and Pied Flycatcher occur regularly, together with a variety of warblers. Icterine and Yellow-browed Warblers, Firecrest, Red-breasted Flycatcher and Ortolan Bunting are annual in very small numbers, and Flamborough is *the* locality on the east coast for Yellow-browed Warbler. Late spring and late autumn are generally best for scarce migrants and rarities.

In winter, fishing boats going to and from Bridlington pass close to the Head, and their attendant gulls should be checked for Glaucous and Iceland. All three divers are regular in winter, though Great Northern is scarce. A regular group of Black-throated Divers winters in Bridlington Bay and can sometimes be seen from the Head. Shag, auks, Scaup, scoters and especially Eider are frequent offshore in

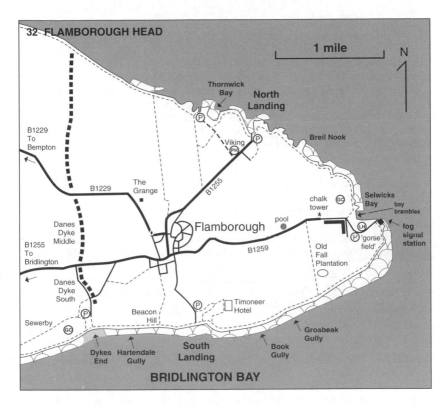

small numbers. The occasional Arctic or Great Skua may appear, and much less often a Pomarine. There may be large movements of seabirds in severe weather at this season. Peregrine can appear anywhere in the area. Other notable winter visitors include a few Snow Bunting and Rock Pipit of the Scandinavian race, which can be recognised in early April as they begin to assume summer plumage.

Residents include Feral Pigeon (many appearing to be wild-type Rock Doves), and Corn Bunting.

33 BEMPTON CLIFFS (East Yorkshire)   OS Landranger 101

Lying on the north flank of the great chalk outcrop of Flamborough Head, Bempton Cliffs support one of the largest seabird colonies in Britain, and are best visited May–mid-July.

Habitat
Bempton Cliffs rise to 400 feet and extend for 4 miles to Flamborough Head, and are topped by mixed farmland.

Access
Leave Bridlington north on the minor road to Buckton and turn east on the B1229 to Bempton, from where you take Cliff Lane (by the White Horse Inn) to the reserve car park and visitor centre (open March to November). Alternatively, coming from the north, leave the A165 just south of Reighton (opposite The

Dotterel Inn) on the B1229 to Bempton. Access to the cliffs is unrestricted but can be very dangerous, especially when wet. A footpath runs along the clifftop for the length of the reserve with several safe observation points. Bempton is wardened April–August. See p.443 and p.442 for details of cruises to view the seabird cliffs from North Landing at Flamborough and from Bridlington.

Migrants can be found at Bempton in season, and the most productive area has traditionally been the area of scrub and boggy ground near the seaward end of Hoddy Cows Lane, which runs north from near the pond in Buckton (½ mile west of Bempton village). This area can also be accessed by walking west on the clifftop path from the reserve car park.

Birds
In summer there are as many as 80,000 pairs of Kittiwake between Bempton and Flamborough, as well as thousands of Guillemot, Razorbill and Puffin, several hundred Herring Gull and Fulmar, and a few Shag. Over 1,000 pairs of Gannet at Bempton until recently constituted the only mainland colony in Britain. Rock Dove also breeds on the cliffs, as do Jackdaw and Tree Sparrow, and Peregrine is sometimes seen around the colonies. Corn Bunting nests in the clifftop fields.

Information
RSPB Bempton Cliffs Visitor Centre, Cliff Lane, Bempton, Bridlington, East Yorkshire YO15 1JF. Tel: 01262 851179.

34 FILEY (North Yorkshire) OS Landranger 101

Filey has gained a reputation in recent years as a premier site for both seawatching and scarce and rare passerines (indeed, it now rivals the more traditional sites to the south, Flamborough and Spurn). It is worth a visit in spring and autumn, and also has a good range of seabirds, notably often including Little Auk in late autumn. Nearby, the small Filey Dams reserve lies just inland of the coast behind Filey town, and is owned by Scarborough Council and managed by the Yorkshire Wildlife Trust.

Habitat
A typical seaside town, the beach at Filey is sandy, and north of the town lies Carr Naze, a cliff promontory that terminates in Filey Brigg, a long, narrow finger of low rocks that is almost covered by the sea at high tide. The Brigg is backed to the north and south by eroded cliffs of boulder clay that are penetrated by two well-wooded gullies, Arndale and Church Ravines. Above the cliffs are a large car park and caravan site, bordered by trees and shrubs, and to the northwest arable land. Protected to the north by Carr Naze and the Brigg, Filey Bay may shelter seabirds in rough weather. Filey Dams reserve comprises a marshy area and artificial scrapes surrounded by farmland.

Access (see map)
Filey Brigg From the A1039 in Filey follow signs to Filey Country Park and park in the metalled area in the far right-hand corner. From the car park footpaths lead over Carr Naze to the seawatching hide at the base of the Brigg; operated by the Filey Brigg Ornithological Group, this may be locked but visiting birdwatchers are welcome when it is manned, and regular or holiday visitors can hire a key for a small charge. It is possible to scramble onto the Brigg from near the seawatching hide, but it is a treacherous descent. Access to the beach is oth-

erwise via steps on the south side, part way along the promontory. The scrub around the Country Park car park often holds interesting migrants.

Cleveland Way From the Country Park car park it is possible to follow this footpath northwest along the clifftop, checking the fields and hedgerows for migrants and wintering buntings.

Arndale Ravine The small copse is excellent for migrant passerines. Access is from the Country Park Stores in the car park, via a gate signed 'Filey Sailing Club'.

Church Ravine The large trees here also hold migrants. From the Country Park car park follow the footpath around the seaward side of the caravan site to the bottom of the ravine. Walking up the ravine, under the footbridge, and bearing right brings you back to the Country Park entrance. Alternatively, leave the Country Park car park and turn left into Ravine Road towards Coble Landing, parking along the road.

Glen Gardens Another migrant trap. Access is from the south end of the seafront via the steps near the White Lodge Hotel, or from the town centre roundabout, heading east along Station Avenue and turning second right into West Avenue, with the entrance to Glen Gardens on the left opposite the small car park. The gardens along the entire seafront may hold migrants.

Filey Dams reserve This lies on the west side of Filey. Leave the A1039 at the south entrance to the Wharfdale Estate (small letterbox on corner) and bear left and then right into the estate, and park after 650 yards at the end of the road. A hide adjacent to the car park overlooks the Main Pool, while the East Pool hide lies 200 yards away by a signed path. There is no other access.

Birds

Well placed for seawatching, Filey has an impressive reputation and, unlike Flamborough Head, where one is forced to watch from the top of high cliffs, the low vantage offers a better chance of seeing petrels in favourable conditions. In autumn Manx and Sooty Shearwaters are regular, with occasional Mediterranean Shearwater; as at all North Sea seawatching stations, the two large shearwaters, Great and Cory's, are rare. Strong northwest winds may bring small numbers of Leach's Petrels and all four skuas are regularly recorded, though Long-tailed is scarce. Large numbers of terns use the Brigg at high tide and can include Black, together with Little Gull in late September/early October. Seawatching may also produce divers, grebes, sea ducks, waders (sometimes including Grey Phalarope) and auks, including Little Auk Both Grey Phalarope and especially Little Auk are most likely in late autumn following strong northerlies and occasionally take shelter in the bay.

As well as seabirds, Filey attracts many passerine migrants in season. Wryneck, Richard's Pipit, Icterine, Barred and Yellow-browed Warblers, Red-backed Shrike and Red-breasted Flycatcher are annual in autumn. Easterlies in spring also produce records of shrikes, together with Bluethroat. During passage periods, Filey Dams attracts passerine migrants, together with 'fresh' waders and Garganey.

Winter brings all three divers (best seen in the bay around high tide), Red-necked and sometimes Slavonian Grebes, Common and Velvet Scoters, Eider, Goldeneye, Long-tailed Duck and Red-breasted Merganser to Filey Bay. Gulls, including Glaucous and occasionally Iceland, follow the fishing boats to Coble Landing, and the Brigg supports a large flock of Purple Sandpipers, as well

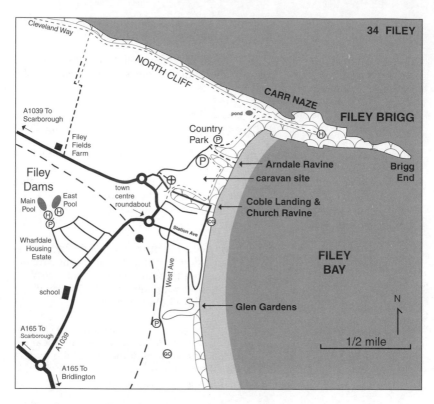

as often large numbers of Dunlins around the grassy Country Park car park. Small numbers of Snow and Lapland Buntings are regular around the car park and coastal fields, with Rock Pipit along the shoreline.

Breeders include Fulmar, Cormorant, Herring Gull, Kittiwake, Razorbill, Guillemot, Puffin, Rock Dove and Rock Pipit.

Information

Filey Brigg Ornithological Group, Lez Gillard (Recorder), 12 Sycamore Avenue, Filey, North Yorkshire YO14 9NU. Tel: 01723 516383. E-mail: lez.gillard@talk21.com

35 SCARBOROUGH AND SCALBY MILLS
(North Yorkshire)   OS Landranger 101

Scarborough, a popular holiday resort, is also strategically situated on an east-facing coast, with the castle promontory forming a natural migrant trap. In autumn and winter a number of interesting gulls and other seabirds can also be found.

Habitat

The coast is largely built-up but Scarborough Peasholme Park and the area around the Mere provide stands of cover attractive to migrants, as do the well-wooded slopes of Castle Hill. Immediately south of Castle Hill lies the harbour, which provides shelter to seabirds, especially in rough weather. To both north and south, sandy beaches are interspersed by areas of rocky coastline, and north of Scarborough at Scalby Mills, Scalby Beck meanders across the beach, providing a bathing and loafing area for gulls.

Access (see map)

Scalby Mills Leave Scarborough north on the A165 towards Whitby. After c.2 miles, at the Ivanhoe Inn, turn right into Scalby Mills Road, continuing for ½ mile to the seafront car park. View the beach and stream from here, with good numbers of gulls and, in season, terns, especially around low water; evenings are particularly good. Look for waders on the beach and Common Sandpiper, Kingfisher, Grey Wagtail and Dipper on Scalby Beck, where it passes through a steep ravine before spilling onto the strand. In March–April, Rock Pipit of the Scandinavian race is regularly seen on the beach by the stream. The slopes of the beck have areas of cover that should be checked for migrants by crossing the bridge over the beck and following the stepped path up. A good walk in winter is south from here along the sea front; if you have left your car at Scalby Mills, there arc regular buses back from Scarborough.

Peasholme Park This lies near North Bay adjacent to the A165. From the roundabout take Northstead Manor Drive and park in the car park adjacent to the nearby swimming pool (200 yards on the right), walking across the road to the park. As well as attracting passerine migrants, the lake may hold sea duck in rough weather.

Castle Hill Access is best from the north end of Marine Drive, parking near the small cafe and gift shop, and taking the path to the castle walls, bearing right to pass under an obvious archway. The south-facing slopes have the most productive areas of cover. Over 2,000 pairs of Kittiwakes as well as a few Fulmars and Herring Gulls nest on Castle Hill cliffs, and can be watched from Marine Drive as they cruise overhead.

Marine Drive The main promenade in Scarborough, this can be a good seawatching vantage, with the advantage of being able to use a car for shelter. The Drive is, however, closed in really rough weather.

Scarborough harbour Easily accessed from South Bay sea front, pedestrian access is possible to the three breakwaters (the outer, east pier from near the fun fair at the entrance to Marine Drive). In winter the east pier is linked to the central pier (Vincent Pier) by a footbridge, which commands a good view of the entire harbour. Gulls may be found in the harbour or loafing on nearby buildings, especially those along the west pier. In rough weather, look for divers, grebes, Shag, sea ducks and auks in the harbour. Rock Pipit and Turnstone can also be found, with large numbers of Purple Sandpipers on the seaward flanks of the outer pier.

The Mere Leave Scarborough south on the A64 and, after c.1 mile, turn left on the B1427 (signed A165 Filey and Bridlington) into Queen Margaret's Road. Cross the railway bridge and the entrance to the Mere lies on the right after 300 yards. The lake is encircled by a driveable track. Though busy in summer, Reed Warbler and sometimes Kingfisher may be present, and stands of cover around the lake are attractive to migrants.

Cornelian Bay Leave Scarborough south on the A165 coast road and, after c.2 miles, turn left into either of the entrances to Cornelian Drive, taking the rough track from here east towards the sea, parking just beyond the large farm building

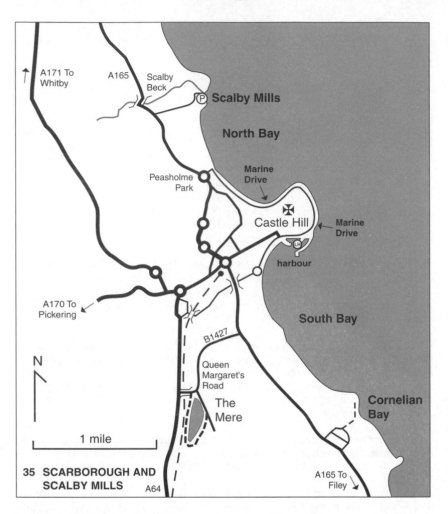

35 SCARBOROUGH AND SCALBY MILLS

on the right. The Cleveland Way runs along the clifftop and you can view the sea from here or take the path to the left, down the cliffs. The slopes have plenty of cover to attract migrants, the beach and rocky sills hold good numbers of waders, especially Purple Sandpiper, and the bay may have sea duck.

Birds

In winter look for divers offshore; the majority are Red-throated but Black-throated or Great Northern are sometimes seen. Grebes may include Red-necked and Slavonian, and other waterbirds include Cormorant, Shag, Common Scoter, Red-breasted Merganser, Goldeneye, Guillemot and Razorbill. In rough weather all may be seen in the harbour and, especially in late autumn, there may be Little Auk too. In such conditions look also for Grey Phalarope, which favours Scalby Mills. Gulls are a feature of the area, with regular records of Glaucous, Iceland, Mediterranean and Little. Commoner waders occur, with particularly impressive numbers of Purple Sandpipers. Residents include Kingfisher, Grey Wagtail and Dipper, and the local Rock Pipits may be joined by birds of the Scandinavian race, although these cannot be identified until they assume breeding plumage in early spring.

On passage an excellent variety of passerine migrants may occur, including a notable list of rarities. Seawatching can also be interesting, with numbers of shearwaters and skuas given winds from the north.

36 WYKEHAM FOREST (North Yorkshire) OS Landranger 101

Lying a little over 6 miles west of Scarborough, this area has become well known in recent years as a venue for watching Honey Buzzard. A visit late May–July in suitable weather offers the best hope of a sighting. The area forms part of the North Yorkshire Moors NP.

Habitat
The area has been extensively planted with exotic conifers, bordered to the northwest by Trouts Dale, with areas of pasture and stands of deciduous woodland, and to the north by the River Derwent.

Access
High Wood Brow Viewpoint Turn north off the A170, 6 miles west of Scarborough, at Downe Arms Hotel in Wykeham, and drive north on a minor road through the forest for c.4 miles to High Wood Brow crossroads. Turn left here and park in the signed car park on the right after ½ mile (if full, there is another small parking area on the left after a further 200 yards). From the car park walk north, past the barrier, for 300 yards to the observation platform, which has panoramic views over the forest and Trouts Dale. Honey Buzzard is present late May–late August but is difficult to see after midsummer. The optimum time is 09.00–13.00, on warm sunny days with scattered cloud and only light breezes, when they may be seen soaring or in wing-clapping display. They spend much time sitting below the canopy, and a long wait may be necessary, but views are often exceptionally good. Visiting birdwatchers are asked to keep to the viewpoint, and indeed, the chances of seeing Honey Buzzard away from there are slim. The viewpoint is managed by the FC.

River Derwent Continuing north from the crossroads at High Wood Brow on a steep narrow road and, after descending for c.1 mile, turn right at the T-junction towards Hackness. After c.½ mile stop just beyond Hilla Green at the bridge over the River Derwent. A footpath follows the right bank of the river, with a chance of Kingfisher, Grey Wagtail and Dipper.

Birds
Several pairs of Honey Buzzard are thought to be in the region, and other raptors include Sparrowhawk and occasionally Hobby, Merlin and Goshawk (the latter especially in late summer). Residents include Green and Great Spotted Woodpeckers, Siskin, Redpoll and Crossbill.

Summer visitors include several pairs of Nightjar, which favour the areas of clearfell before the trees have grown too high (any clearings along the road north of North Moor are worth checking at dusk), as well as Tree Pipit, Redstart and Whinchat.

In winter the forest is quiet, but raptors may be seen, including Goshawk in early spring and, in more open areas, Peregrine, Merlin or Hen Harrier. Crossbill may be more obvious, especially in years with high populations.

Information
FC, Pickering Office, Head Ranger, tel: 01751 472771.

37 ARKENGARTHDALE AND
STONESDALE MOOR (North Yorkshire)   OS Landranger 91 and 92

This section of the Yorkshire Dales holds a typical selection of upland birds and is one of the better areas for Black Grouse. There is little to see, however, outside spring and early summer.

Habitat
Juncus moor interrupted by gullies and streams on Stonesdale Moor, with hill pasture in Arkengarthdale.

Access
Arkengarthdale (OS Landranger 92) Leave the A6108 c.5 miles west of Richmond on the B6270 towards Kirkby Stephen. After c.5 miles, turn north in Reeth on a minor road towards Langthwaite and into Arkengarthdale. After 3 miles turn right (north) on the minor road towards Scargill and the A66. The best area for Black Grouse is the moorland west of the road around Shaw Farm (NZ 004053). The area can also be accessed by turning south off the A66 south of Barnard Castle on a minor road and following this for c.7 miles to Shaw Farm.

Stonesdale Moor (OS Landranger 91) Leave the A685 in Kirkby Stephen south on the B6259 towards Hawes and, after 1 mile, turn east on the B6270 towards Gunnerside and Richmond. After c.9 miles, just west of Keld, turn north on the minor road signed 'West Stonesdale and Tan Hill' to Stonesdale Moor. (Alternatively, approach the area from the A6108 near Richmond, via the B6270 past Arkengarthdale and on for c.13 miles to Keld.) After c.2 miles there is a grassy lay-by on the left near a small bridge, with another lay-by on the left after a further c.1 mile; both spots may produce Black Grouse. Continuing north to Tan Hill, a right turn at the T-junction takes you to Arkengarthdale.

Birds
Black Grouse are declining in Britain, for unknown reasons, and the remaining groups are best looked for when lekking in early mornings in April–May. To avoid disturbance, if at all possible it is best to use the car as a hide, using a window-mounted telescope. The birds often favour wet, rushy fields. Other species to look for include Red Grouse on the heather moor between Tan Hill and Arkengarthdale, Peregrine, Golden Plover, Oystercatcher, Curlew, Snipe, Redshank, Dunlin, Short-eared Owl and Wheatear, with Common Sandpiper, Dipper and Grey Wagtail on the streams and rivers, and Ring Ouzel elusive around rocky outcrops. In the Swale Valley along the B6270 look for Goosander along the river.

38 UPPER TEESDALE (Durham)   OS Landranger 92

Perhaps most famous botanically (and for the failure in the 1960s to prevent Cow Green Reservoir from damaging one of the great natural wonders of Britain), Upper Teesdale does possess ornithological attractions, notably Black Grouse (best in looked for in March–April), a variety of other moorland birds and high concentrations of breeding waders (best June–early July).

Habitat
Upper Teesdale comprises a mosaic of habitats, with moorland and hill pastures on higher ground and unspoilt hay meadows and areas of deciduous woodland

in the valleys. There are many small tarns and of course the large Cow Green Reservoir, which straddles the border of Cumbria and Co. Durham, in the Tees Valley above Cauldron Snout. Part of the area is a NNR.

Access

Langdon Common Holding one of the largest Black Grouse leks in Britain, the area is best visited in the first couple of hours after dawn, although some birds may be present throughout the day. Leave Middleton-in-Teesdale northwest on the B6277 and, after 7½ miles, the road crosses Langdon Beck. After a further ½ mile take the minor road north (signed Weardale and St John's Chapel) and in ¼ of a mile, the road passes over a cattle grid, with room to pull off the road soon afterwards. Continuing, after another ½ mile the road crosses Langdon Beck, with a parking area shortly afterwards. Black Grouse lek in the valley to the right of the road leading down to the beck between the cattle grid and the bridge, and although it is just possible to park, the road is narrow and it is far better to park by the bridge and walk back. Stay on the road at all times; the birds may be quite distant but a mounted telescope will give good views. If the birds are absent, check the area north and west of the B6277 between Langdon Beck and the turn-off and the minor road north to the cattle grid. Look also for Common Sandpiper and Dipper on the beck, and Red Grouse on the slopes of Three Pikes (west of the minor road).

Widdybank Fell and Cauldron Snout An excellent area for breeding moorland birds. Leave Middleton on Tees northwest on the B6277 and, after c.7 miles turn left at Langdon Beck onto the minor road towards Cow Green Reservoir. After c.½ mile turn south on a rough farm track signed Widdybank Farm and Cauldron Snout Fall. After 1 mile there is a small car park on the right (just before the farm). From here, follow the Pennine Way west along the north bank of the Tees towards Cauldron Snout (c.2 miles). The river runs through a deep valley past Cronkley Scar and Falcon Clints, with Peregrine, Merlin, Red Grouse, Ring Ouzel, Raven and Twite all possible, as well as the usual river birds. By following the track north from Cauldron Snout to Cow Green Reservoir car park, and then the road back towards Langdon Beck, a circular route of c.7 miles around Widdybank Fell (which rises to 1,715 feet), good numbers of breeding moorland waders may be seen.

High Force The highest waterfall in England. Leave Middleton on Tees northwest on the B6277 and, after c.4½ miles, park on the right by the hotel. Cross the road and take the track for 600 yards to the falls. The surrounding mixed woodland holds Woodcock, Wood Warbler, Pied Flycatcher and, in invasion years, Crossbill, with Common Sandpiper, Grey Wagtail and Dipper on the river.

Eggleston Common Comprising excellent heather moorland, this is a good area for raptors in winter. Leave Eggleston village north on the B6278 towards Stanhope. After 2½ miles the Common lies to the east of the road.

Barnard Castle Woods These hold the typical deciduous woodland species, with Goosander, Dipper and Grey Wagtail on the river. Park at Barnard Castle and take the footpath from the village green (west of the castle) along the north bank of the River Tees for c.2½ miles.

Birds

In this region Black Grouse favour areas of hill pasture, grazed by sheep, to lek. British (and especially English) populations have declined in recent years, making this a threatened species. Other breeders include a variety of waders, with

Oystercatcher, Golden Plover, Lapwing, Snipe, Curlew, Redshank and a few Dunlin and Ringed Plover. Indeed, Upper Teesdale west of Forest-in-Teesdale holds one of the densest concentrations of breeding waders in Britain. In addition, Common Sandpiper joins resident Goosander, Grey Wagtail and Dipper on the River Tees (and Red-breasted Merganser and Goldeneye may also summer). Wheatear and Ring Ouzel are relatively common summer visitors, the latter favouring areas of crags and rocky slopes. Red Grouse frequent areas of heather, and small numbers of raptors breed, including Merlin, Peregrine, Sparrowhawk and Buzzard. Stands of woodland hold a variety of typical residents, including Woodcock, Great Spotted Woodpecker, Marsh Tit and Nuthatch, which are joined in summer by Tree Pipit, Redstart, Garden and Wood Warblers, and Pied Flycatcher. Occasionally Crossbill and Siskin may be found in the conifer plantations.

Winter is bleak but Black Grouse is easiest to see in late winter and early spring, Red Grouse remain on the heather and the occasional Hen Harrier, Buzzard, Peregrine, Merlin or Short-eared Owl may be seen hunting, occasionally joined by a Rough-legged Buzzard (the prime area for raptors being around the Eggleston–Stanhope road), with Raven also possible, especially in the west.

Information
EN, Stocksfield Hall, Stocksfield, Northumberland NE4 7TN. Tel: 01661 845500. E-mail: northumbria@english-nature.org.uk

39 DRURIDGE BAY AREA (Northumberland) OS Landranger 81

This 5-mile stretch of the Northumberland coast forms a single conservation area and contains several excellent birdwatching sites, holding interest throughout the year. Seabirds, wildfowl, waders and migrant landbirds provide an exceptionally rich 'mixed bag' of interesting species.

Habitat
Druridge Bay extends for c.6 miles along the Northumberland coast and is fringed for most of its length by sand dunes and a narrow sandy beach, with the mouth of Chevington Burn (Chibburn Mouth) attracting loafing and bathing gulls and terns, and areas of low rocks at both the northern and southern extremities. Formerly a mixture of farmland and collieries, open-cast mining in the 1970s devastated much of the hinterland, but with its demise these areas of industrial dereliction have been 'landscaped' and returned to a variety of uses, including conservation (mining having recently ceased south of Druridge Bay Country Park, the area of the former Chevington Burn is now being developed as another wetland). Notably, immediately inland of the coast lie a series of relatively small areas of open water. Cresswell Pond and the Warkworthlane Ponds in the south of the area are 'natural' (being a product of subsidence), but the rest are artificial. Much of the former farmland cover was stripped during mining operations, but has now been replaced by shelter belts and plantations of conifers and mixed woodland trees, as well as native scrub species planted by various conservation bodies.

Access (see map)
Coquet Island RSPB Reserve. Lying 1 mile off the coast at Amble-by-the-Sea, this small island holds important colonies of seabirds, notably Puffin, Black-headed Gull and Sandwich Tern. A few Roseate Terns breed, but these are most likely to be seen at Hauxley NR. No landing is permitted, but boat trips around

the island may be advertised from Amble Marina in the summer months (tel: D. Gray 01665 711975 or G. Easton 01665 710384). Otherwise, the breeding species can be seen all along this coast as they commute to and fro, with the coastguard lookout at Hauxley providing one of the closest vantage points.

Hauxley NR Centred upon an artificial freshwater pool, the reserve also has areas of planted reedbeds and scrub. The area is at its best from spring to early autumn, and is probably the most reliable site on the east coast to find Roseate Tern, which sometimes visit to loaf or bathe (the Tern hide being the best view-point), while waders use the pool as a roost site. Leave the A1068 east on the minor road to High Hauxley, c.1 mile south of Amble. As the road passes through the village it turns sharply right and then, after c.300 yards, at the right-angle left bend, turn south at the sign to the reserve car park. For non-members of the Northumberland Wildlife Trust (NWT), permits can be obtained at the nature centre (valid also for Druridge Pools and Cresswell). Four hides overlook the main pool, and the surrounding fields are also worth checking. To the south, the dunes and foreshore form part of Druridge Bay CP, while to the north the dunes near the coastguard lookout are a LNR. The entire stretch of coast can be interesting, with the dunes east of the Tern hide best for autumn seawatching, while the area of the lookout affords views in summer of seabirds going to and from Coquet Island. (Note that the wood at Low Hauxley has no public access.)

Hadston Carrs Turn east off the A1068 c.1 mile south of the turning for Hauxley (and about halfway to the turn for Druridge Bay CP) on the minor road to Hadston Carrs, turning south at the seafront. This gives easy access by car for seawatching.

Druridge Bay Country Park (Hadston Country Park) Leave the A1068 around Broomhill at the signed turning to the Country Park. There are several lay-bys overlooking Ladyburn Lake, with the main car park, visitor centre (including a blackboard detailing the latest sightings) and toilets at the seaward end of the lake. In winter, the car park at the watersports slipway also gives good views. A footpath circles the lake, and from the main car park access through the dunes to the beach is also possible (with the option of walking north to Hauxley or south to the Chibburn Mouth). The area is at its best in winter, and is somewhat prone to disturbance in summer, as all but the west end of Ladyburn Lake is used for watersports April–September.

Druridge Pools NR Managed by the NWT, this area is best from late autumn to late spring for wildfowl and waders. The main pool is a product of reclamation following the cessation of open-cast mining, but the NWT created the two south scrapes; these pools are separated by fields that are prone to flooding. Leave the A1068 at Widdrington east on the minor road to Druridge and, after c.1 ½ miles, turn north (at the sharp right-hand bend) signed NWT and NT. After paying the car park fee (non-members), drive north parallel to the coast. Within a few hundred yards, park on the right to access Budge hide, which overlooks the wader scrapes and wet fields, and after ½ mile another car park accesses the walkway to the Oddie hide overlooking the main, deep-water, pool, and an unnamed hide south of the track views a small pool and the wet fields to the south. Though unlocked, non-members should obtain a permit from the Hauxley Information Centre or the visitor centre at Druridge Bay CP. Access is possible on foot north along the dunes to Chibburn Mouth.

Cresswell Pond A product of subsidence, this shallow brackish lagoon is fringed by saltmarsh and reeds, separated from the sea by a narrow sandbar and surrounded by pasture. Managed by the NWT, it is of interest year-round, but is best in spring and autumn. Leave the A1068 east at Ellington roundabout and turn left in the village on the minor road to Cresswell. Continue north, parallel with the coast, towards Widdrington, to view the pond from the lay-by at Blakemoor Farm entrance or, after a further ¼ mile, from the small car park (opposite the track to Warkworthlane Ponds); from the latter it is also possible to walk east through the dunes to seawatch. The British Alcan hide overlooks the south part of the pond and is accessed from the track to Blakemoor Farm (non-members of the NWT should obtain a permit from the information centre at Hauxley).

Warkworthlane Ponds These five small subsidence pools lie c.1 mile southwest of Cresswell Pond (and nowhere near the village of Warkworth). The surrounding fields are good for Whooper Swan (sometimes as many as 100, and occasionally also Bewick's Swan), but the ponds are most interesting in spring and autumn for passage waders. Access is from the A1068, ¼ mile north of Ellington roundabout, turning off northwest towards Warkworth Lane Cottage and then parking carefully by the caravan site reception area. Follow the footpath past the touring caravans and Pond A, and then bear left around the residential caravans to join the main bridleway between Ellington and Highthorn. Bear left along this for ¼ mile to view Pond B (the largest) or straight at the junction onto the footpath through the trees to view Ponds C and D. The small Pond East can be viewed from a lay-by on the A1068 ¾ mile north of Ellington roundabout. Alternatively, from the car park at Cresswell Pond, follow the footpath around the north edge of the pond for ¾ mile to Ponds C and D, and then continue on the main bridleway to Ponds A and B.

Snab Point Accessed along the minor road south from Cresswell, the car park here is a convenient point from which to seawatch.

Birds

Wintering waders on the foreshore include Ringed and Grey Plovers, Turnstone, Curlew, Bar-tailed Godwit, Redshank, Sanderling, Dunlin, Knot and Purple Sandpiper, with good numbers of Lapwing and Golden Plover around the fields; the latter are sometimes joined by a handful of Ruffs (especially at Druridge Pools). Eider and Common Scoter are present offshore year-round, and are joined in autumn and winter by Red-breasted Merganser, Goldeneye, a few Long-tailed Duck and Velvet Scoter, and sometimes Scaup. The sea also has small numbers of Red-throated Diver and Slavonian Grebe, and occasionally other divers or rarer grebes. The freshwater pools are favoured by Shelduck, Teal, Wigeon, Gadwall, Shoveler, Pochard, and sometimes small numbers of Pintail. A handful of Smew is often present, commuting between the various freshwater pools, and Ruddy Duck is a recent colonist. The pools may also attract sea duck, especially during periods of bad winter weather. Flocks of Whooper Swan are regular, but wide ranging (although they favour the area around Warkworthlane Ponds), and there is occasionally also a few Bewick's Swans. Occasional parties of Greylag Geese may be found in the coastal fields, but Pink-footed, Barnacle and Pale-bellied Brent Geese are irregular. The dunes and coastal fields may also hold flocks of Twite and Snow Bunting (often favouring the fields where cattle are fed), and less frequently the elusive Lapland Bunting or even Shore Lark. Such concentrations of birds attract Peregrine, Merlin, Short-eared Owl and sometimes Hen Harrier. In winter Mediterranean, Iceland and Glaucous Gulls are occasionally recorded together with the commoner gulls.

On spring passage both Black Tern and Little Gull are possible, as are Marsh Harrier, Osprey, Hobby and Garganey. In autumn, and to a lesser extent in

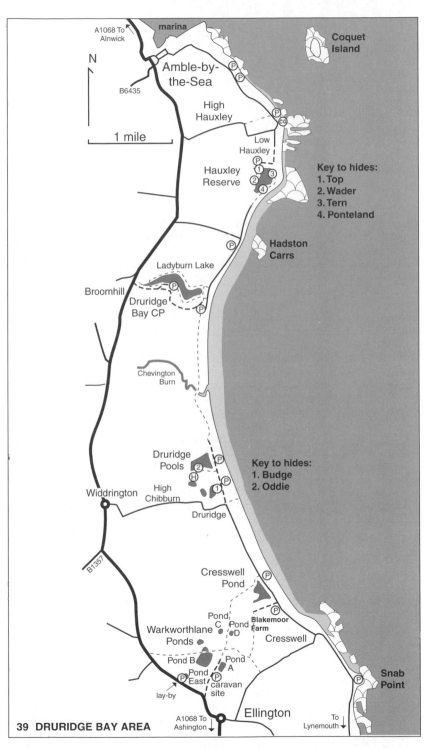

Key to hides:
1. Top
2. Wader
3. Tern
4. Ponteland

Key to hides:
1. Budge
2. Oddie

39 DRURIDGE BAY AREA

spring, a variety of waders may occur, both on the foreshore and around the various pools. Little Ringed Plover, Ruff, Whimbrel, Greenshank and Common Sandpiper are likely at either season (as is the rarer Wood Sandpiper or Black-tailed Godwit), but autumn is more likely to produce Spotted Redshank, Green and Curlew Sandpipers and Little Stint. Cormorant, Gannet and Fulmar are almost constantly present offshore. Autumn seawatching can be productive, with divers, Red-necked Grebe, Manx and sometimes Sooty Shearwaters, Arctic and sometimes Great, Pomarine and even Long-tailed Skuas, Kittiwake and auks all possible in the right conditions (usually strong winds with a northerly component). In late autumn and winter, storms may promote movements of Little Auk along the coast, and sometimes produce a Grey Phalarope. In both spring and autumn a superb array of passerine migrants has been recorded, with many scarce and rare species. Migrants may be found in any cover on the coast, with no area particularly favoured (and apparent concentrations of rarities being due to numbers of birdwatchers rather than birds). Scarcer species such as Ring Ouzel and Black Redstart are regular, as are the typical east coast autumn specialities: Wryneck, Icterine and Barred Warblers and Red-backed Shrike, and anything is possible.

Breeders include Little Grebe, Shelduck, Ruddy Duck, Sparrowhawk, Ringed Plover, Common Sandpiper, Barn and Little Owls, Sand Martin (in some years), Rock Pipit, Yellow Wagtail, Whinchat, Stonechat (in the dunes), Wheatear, Grasshopper, Sedge and Garden Warblers, Spotted Flycatcher, Tree Sparrow and a few Corn Buntings, and sometimes Pochard, Gadwall and Shoveler. Breeding birds on Coquet include up to 13,000 pairs of Puffins, c.4,000 pairs of Black-headed Gulls and c.2,000 pairs of Sandwich Terns, as well as several hundred pairs of Eiders, Fulmars and Common and Arctic Terns, and, most notably, c.30 pairs of Roseate Terns. Of course, all these can be seen along the entire stretch of coast throughout the spring and summer (gulls and terns bathing and loafing on the pool at Hauxley), together with resident Herring and Great Black-backed Gulls and, in spring and summer, Lesser Black-backed Gull.

Information

Northumberland Wildlife Trust (NWT), The Garden House, St Nicholas Park, Jubilee Road, Gosforth, Newcastle-upon-Tyne NE3 1AA. Tel: 0191 284 6884. E-mail: mail@northwt.org.uk

NWT, Druridge Bay Reserves: Jim Martin, Hauxley NR, Low Hauxley, Amble, Morpeth, Northumberland. Tel: 01665 711578.

40 SEATON SLUICE—ST MARY'S ISLAND
(Northumberland)   OS Landranger 88

This section of coast has three principal attractions, wintering waders, spring and autumn passerine migrants, and seawatching, with both Seaton Sluice and St Mary's Island being well-established watchpoints.

Habitat

Much of this coast is bounded by areas of rocky sills that, together with the adjacent sandy and muddy beaches, hold numbers of waders. To the north, Rocky Island at Seaton Sluice is a traditional seawatching venue, while to the south, St Mary's Island (marked by an old lighthouse) is also a good seawatching station, though inaccessible at high tide. It also has some areas of cover, which may hold migrants, as may the rough ground along the low clifftops of the mainland and the fields immediately inland of the coast, but Whitley Bay Cemetery, with stands of trees and shrubs, is perhaps the best area for migrants.

Access (see map)

Seaton Sluice At the north end of Seaton turn east off the A193 immediately south of the bridge over the Seaton Burn and park just south of the harbour by the Kings Arms pub. Cross the wooden footbridge opposite onto Rocky Island,

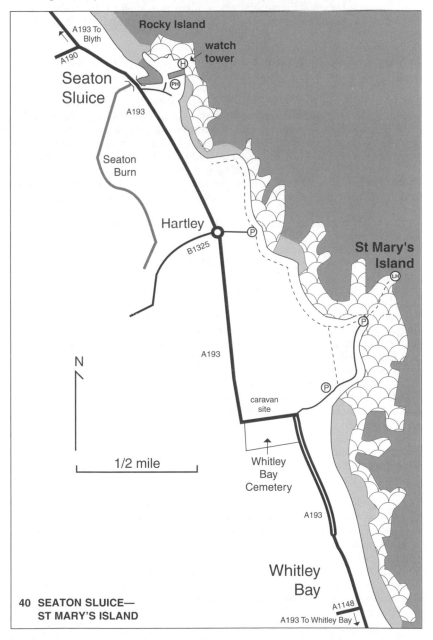

**40 SEATON SLUICE—
ST MARY'S ISLAND**

walk straight to the sea and then around the island to the white wooden tower. This is the Northumberland and Tyneside Bird Club's seawatching hide and is kept locked, with access only to members, but it is possible to seawatch from the shelter of the wall here. Alternatively, find a sheltered position on the mainland near the Kings Arms.

Hartley Turn east off the A193 at the roundabout in Hartley, taking the minor road to the radio masts by the sea, where there is a small car park. From here, footpaths run north along the coast to Seaton Sluice and south to St Mary's Island, giving views of the coastal fields and beaches.

St Mary's Island (Bait Island) Leaving Whitley Bay north on the A193 turn sharply east immediately as the dual carriageway ends onto a road leading to the point overlooking the island. There are large car parks at the point and midway along this road (the field adjacent to the latter is maintained as a sanctuary for feeding and roosting waders 1 October–31 March). The island is only accessible on foot, and is cut off from the mainland around high water; it is best to depart as the tide falls and return to the mainland as the tide rises (details of access and tide times are available from North Tyneside Library or Tourist Office). There is a seawatching hide on the island, operated by North Tyneside Council, and keys and information on opening times etc. are available from the information centre on the island (where there is also a cafe).

Whitley Bay Cemetery Leaving Whitley Bay north on the A193, park at the cemetery entrance on the left just before the dual carriageway ends.

Birds

Autumn is perhaps the peak season. Fulmar and Gannet are almost constantly present offshore, and auks and terns from colonies on the Farnes are regular in summer and autumn, whatever the weather, attracting marauding Arctic Skuas, and from midsummer Manx Shearwater is often present offshore. From late August strong to gale-force winds from the north may prompt movements of seabirds. Sooty and Balearic Shearwaters may join the Manx, and Sabine's Gull and Long-tailed Skua are possible. As autumn progresses, Pomarine and Great Skuas become more likely, and geese and ducks appear, while late-autumn and winter gales may produce Little Auk

Passerine migrants can be interesting, and the typical scarce migrants of the east coast, Icterine, Barred and Yellow-browed Warblers and Red-backed Shrike, are recorded most years, and the area has produced a good list of rarities.

Spring passage is quieter, but seabirds include numbers of terns, and passerines may include Ring Ouzel and Black Redstart, with Bluethroat and Red-backed Shrike possible in May–early June.

In winter good numbers of waders are present along the coast, especially Golden Plover, Lapwing and Oystercatcher, with smaller numbers of Knot, Redshank, Turnstone, Sanderling, Curlew, Grey and Ringed Plovers and Purple Sandpiper. The clifftop fields hold wintering thrushes, finches and buntings (sometimes including Snow or Lapland Buntings), with Stonechat around bushier areas, which attract raptors such as Peregrine, Merlin and Short-eared Owl. Large numbers of Black-headed Gulls roost on the sea, and both Glaucous and Iceland Gulls are sometimes recorded. Eider are resident, and wintering sea duck may also include Common Scoter, Red-breasted Merganser and Goldeneye, and Red-throated Diver is also regular.

41 WHITBURN (Durham)

Due largely to the activities of a group of keen local birders, this section of coast has gained an enviable reputation in recent years for the number and variety of migrants that occur, including many rarities, and for the sometimes outstanding seawatching. In addition, the cliffs hold numbers of breeding seabirds.

Habitat
The mouth of the River Tyne is flanked to the south by dunes at South Shields, and further south the coast is bounded by limestone cliffs (topped with areas of short turf known as The Leas), which reach 90 feet near Whitburn. At the foot of the cliffs sandy beaches and extensive rock shelves ('Steels') are exposed at low tide. As usual, any area of cover, from parks, cemeteries and gardens to the scrappiest bush, can and do attract migrant passerines.

Access (see map)
South Shields Congregations of gulls around the mouth of the Tyne, especially birds following fishing boats back into harbour in late afternoon, can be viewed by turning north off the A183 at the roundabout by the Sea Hotel onto the B1344 (signed Riverside). There are several pay-and-display car parks overlooking the sea. In the evening gulls roost on the sea south of the pier and can be viewed from near the Gypsies Green Stadium.

South Shields Leas An area of close-cropped turf that attracts buntings and sometimes also waders. It lies immediately east of the A183 between South Shields and Marsden.

Marsden Quarry This abandoned limestone quarry has limited areas of cover and is a LNR with free access. It is good for migrants such as Ring Ouzel and Black Redstart in spring but is better during autumn falls and has attracted several rarities. Turn west off the A183 in Marsden on the A1300 and, after c.175 yards, turn south at the roundabout into Quarry Lane. The entrance to the quarry lies on the right after 500 yards, and there is limited parking. The well-vegetated grounds of adjacent Marsden Hall are private, but some of the area can be viewed from the quarry.

Marsden Bay and Rock Marsden Rock is a 90-foot-high stack lying just offshore and holding a large colony of Cormorants. Numbers of other seabirds also breed on the two smaller stacks of Jack Rock and Pompey's Pillar, and on the magnesian limestone cliffs of the mainland south to Lizard Point (together these comprise the most important seabird colonies between the Farnes and Bempton Cliffs). The rock and cliffs can be viewed from the Marsden Bay car park, which lies east of the A183, c.550 yards south of the junction with the A1300, and from the footpath which follows the clifftop south from there.

Lizard Point Together with Whitburn Observatory and Souter Point, this is the best seawatching station, and has the advantage of easy access. Park off the A183 just north of the Souter Lighthouse (it is possible to seawatch from the car here in bad weather).

Whitburn Observatory The large seawatching hide here provides shelter in rough weather. Normally locked, keys can be obtained from the Durham Bird Club. Access is by walking south for c.⅔ mile from Lizard Point or by walking c.½ mile east to the coast from Whitburn Lodge Hotel and then south along the cliffs to the Observatory (passing a small pool that sometimes holds waders and areas of rough ground that may attract Snow and Lapland Buntings).

Souter Point Perhaps the best position for seawatching, but lacks a hide. Access is from Whitburn Lodge Hotel as for the Observatory, but continue south past the seawatching hide for a further 500 yards; there is no access along the clifftop path when red flags are flying.

Whitburn cemetery This small cemetery may hold migrants. It lies west of the A183 in Whitburn, c.350 yards north of the Jolly Sailors pub.

Whitburn churchyard Another site to search for migrants. Turn west off the A183 at the Jolly Sailors pub in Whitburn onto the B1299. Turn first left into Church Lane and the churchyard lies on the right after 100 yards.

White Steel and Cornthwaite Park, Whitburn Rock shelves (the 'Steels') flank the cliffs for over 1 mile at Whitburn, and attract numbers of waders. Park to the east of the A183, just behind the garage on the southern outskirts of Whitburn, to scan the Steels with a telescope. Cornthwaite Park lies west of the road and can be attractive to migrants, with the best areas of cover at the Nern end.

Mere Knolls cemetery This holds large numbers of mature trees attractive to migrants. On the northern outskirts of Sunderland turn west off the A183 at the traffic lights into the B1291 (Dykelands Road). The cemetery lies north of the road after 300 yards and it is possible to park on the roadside.

Birds

Spring migration brings a scatter of commoner species such as Wheatear, Whinchat and Redstart as well as scarcer species such as Ring Ouzel and Black Redstart, while Bluethroat and Marsh and Icterine Warblers are annual in May. Seawatching in spring is relatively quiet, but small numbers of Manx Shearwaters, skuas and terns are seen.

In summer the cliffs around Marsden Rock hold up to 300 pairs of Fulmar, 200 pairs of Cormorant, 5,000 pairs of Kittiwake and 150 pairs of Herring Gull. A few Razorbills now breed, but Shag has yet to do so. Ringed Plover and Rock Pipit also nest. Offshore, Puffin, Guillemot and Razorbill and Common, Arctic and Sandwich Terns are regular. Notable breeding landbirds include Sparrowhawk, Little Owl (around Marsden Quarry), Tree Sparrow and Corn Bunting.

Inevitably, autumn holds the greatest promise for the migrant hunter. All of the regular east coast species are recorded, especially during the classic conditions of southeast or east winds coupled with overcast skies or precipitation. Wryneck, Icterine and Barred Warblers, Red-backed Shrike and Red-breasted Flycatcher are annual, and look too for Long-eared and Short-eared Owls and Woodcock. In addition, the area is notable for rare *Phylloscopus* warblers, with regular Yellow-browed Warbler and several records of Pallas's Warbler. Richard's Pipit is another near-annual species in late autumn. Wader passage is limited by the available habitat, but a wide variety may be recorded over the season on the beaches and 'Steels'. In autumn seawatching comes into its own. Manx Shearwater is present all summer, as are terns, with a few Roseate and Black Terns passing each year. Gannet and Fulmar are present offshore year-round. The largest numbers and variety of seabirds are recorded during strong winds from the north, and in gales resultant movements may be spectacular. From August Sooty Shearwater may occur, with up to 100 per day in the right conditions. A few Balearic Shearwaters are also seen annually, but large shearwaters

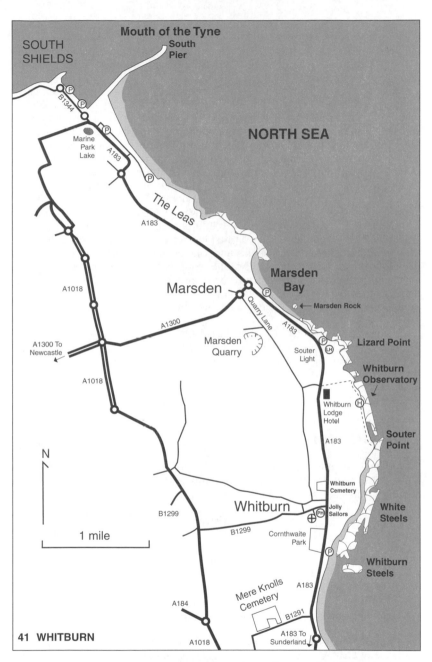

41 WHITBURN

are rare. Leach's Petrel is sometimes seen from shore late in the season, but Storm Petrel is rare (although they are present offshore, as demonstrated by the capture of many birds using tape lures at night). Perhaps the most exciting seabirds are the skuas, and all four species are possible, with Arctic and Long-tailed more likely in early autumn and Pomarine and Great in the latter part of the season (until November or even December). Large numbers of Kittiwakes are regular, as is Little Gull, with Sabine's Gull putting in an occasional appearance. Auks are regular, with Little Auk occurring in significant numbers in late autumn and early winter during strong northerly winds. Other species seen during seawatches include numbers of ducks, and a feature of October is a short passage of Barnacle and Pink-footed Geese.

Offshore in winter small numbers of Red-throated Diver are regular, and Great Northern and Black-throated Divers and Red-necked Grebe are occasionally found. Fulmar is present year-round (except sometimes for a short period mid-winter), as is Cormorant (roosting on Marsden Rock) and there is often also Shag. Sea duck are uncommon, however, with just a handful of Eiders and Common Scoters being regular. Wintering waders include large numbers of Lapwing and Golden Plover (the latter favouring the fields around the Observatory and Whitburn Lodge, as well as the 'Steels')', and the 'Steels' and beaches attract Oystercatcher, Turnstone, Ringed Plover, Sanderling, Dunlin, Redshank, Curlew and small numbers of Grey Plover, Bar-tailed Godwit and Knot. Purple Sandpiper is something of a speciality, with up to 100 between South Shields Pier, Lizard Point, the 'Steels' and the rocks near the Observatory. Large numbers of gulls are present and Mediterranean, Iceland and Glaucous Gulls are often found. Gulls often follow fishing boats back to North Shields Fish Quay and it is always worth checking carefully for rarities such as Ivory and Ross's Gulls. Other notable wintering species include Merlin, Short-eared Owl, Rock Pipit and occasionally Snow Bunting, while Shore Lark, Twite and Lapland Bunting are rare.

Information
Kevin Spindloe, Durham Bird Club, 31 Comrie Road, Hartlepool, Tyne & Wear TS25 3AJ. Tel: 01429 867550.

Whitburn Bird Observatory, Tony Armstrong, 39 Western Hill, Durham City DH1 4RJ. Tel: 0191 386 1519. E-mail: ope@globalnet.co.uk

42 HARTLEPOOL (Cleveland)   OS Landranger 93

Hartlepool's geographical location on a promontory almost surrounded by the sea makes it a first landfall for many migrants, and also places it in pole position to witness movements of seabirds along the east coast.

Habitat
As with any migrant trap, arriving birds frequent any cover that is available, which in Hartlepool means gardens and the taller trees of the various cemeteries and parks. The decline of the fishing industry has reduced the town's attractiveness to gulls, but the Fish Quay Dock remains a magnet for these scavengers.

Access (see map)
The following largely follows Britton & Day (1995).

Hartlepool Headland The most productive area for migrants, this lies 1½ miles northeast of Hartlepool town centre, largely separated from it by the docks and marina complex. Leave the town centre north on the A179 and follow this left at the roundabout (the right turning is to the docks). Turn right after 50 yards, at the Middleton Road traffic lights, into Lancaster Road. Bear right at the mini-roundabout and continue along Northgate to the headland, following signs to the Maritime Museum and Fish Quay. Turn left (just before the bus depot) into Middlegate and park in the car park on the right after 100 yards. Searching for

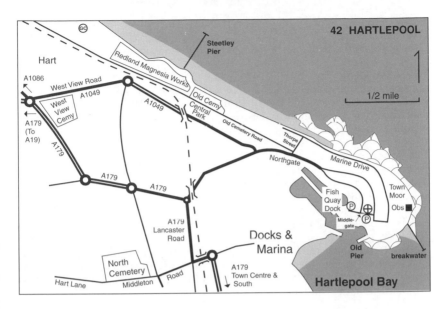

migrants here involves checking any patch of cover; the side streets from the sea-front southwest of the observatory being especially productive. Care and consideration are needed when looking into private gardens; a good relationship has been established between local birders and residents that should not be compromised by visitors. In particular, follow any advice or instructions from local birdwatchers. Other recognised hotspots include.

St Mary's churchyard Opposite the car park, access is possible if the wooden gate is open.

Fish shop trees Bordering the east side of the small park, next to the car park, near Verill's fish-and-chip shop.

The Croft The sloping park opposite the chip shop.

Olive Street trees Head along Middlegate, then turn left into Durham Street, right into Friar Terrace and left into Olive Street.

Doctor's garden At the junction of Durham Street and Friar Terrace.

Bowling green Across Marine Crescent from Olive Street, and the shrubs around the perimeter extend to the adjacent tennis courts. One of the classic spots.

Town Moor An extensive grassy area north of the bowling green, between the road and sea. Good for wheatears, pipits etc.

Memorial garden On the seafront, beside Cliff Terrace, just southwest of the Observatory.

Hartlepool Headland Observatory The seawatching tower hide lies near the lighthouse, just north of the breakwater at the tip of the Headland. Access is on foot from the bowling green (walking towards the sea and then turning right) or by parking in Moor Terrace. Keys are available to members of the Teesmouth Bird Club, and visitors are welcome if there is space.

Fish Docks Quay Approaching the Headland, turn right off Northgate into Abbey Street (just before the bus depot) and park in the quayside car park by the Golden Anchor pub. Gulls occur on the adjacent roofs as well as on the water.

North cemetery From Hartlepool town centre, rather than turning right for the Headland, continue straight at the traffic lights onto Middleton Road and the cemetery is on the right after ¼ mile, with good stands of mature trees.

West View cemetery From Hartlepool town centre, bear left (not right, as for the Headland) at Lancaster Road mini-roundabout, and follow the A179 over two more roundabouts. At the third, turn right on the A1049 West View Road and the cemetery is almost immediately on the right. Again, it has good numbers of mature trees.

Old cemetery and Central Park From Hartlepool town centre, bear right (as for the Headland) at Lancaster Road mini-roundabout, but then turn left after ¾ mile into Thorpe Street (signed to Redland Magnesia) and immediately left into Old Cemetery Road. The cemetery lies on the right after ½ mile, and though sparsely vegetated, is near the sea and thus first landfall for some birds. Central Park is to the left, and has been extensively planted with trees.

Marine Drive Leave the town as for Old Cemetery, but continue along Thorpe Street towards the sea. Marine Drive follows the coast for ½ mile, and is good for sea ducks; it is possible to walk around the entire Headland from the end of Marine Drive to the Old Pier.

Birds

Migrant landbirds can be exciting in both spring and autumn, although the latter season is invariably best. In spring, scarcer species include Ring Ouzel and Black Redstart early in the season with Bluethroat, Icterine Warbler and Red-necked Shrike possible in May–June. In autumn, east winds combined with poor weather may produce falls, and as well as the classic east coast migrants such as Redstart and Pied Flycatcher, scarcer species may appear, with Wryneck, Barred, Yellow-browed and Pallas's Warblers, Firecrest, Red-breasted Flycatcher and Great Grey Shrike joining the list of spring species.

Seawatching interest increases in midsummer, when numbers of Manx Shearwater, Razorbill and Puffin are possible, but it is mid–late August that the season really gets underway. The best conditions are strong winds with a northerly component. Sooty and occasionally Mediterranean Shearwaters may join the regular Manx Shearwaters, and Arctic Skua is normally present offshore. These may be joined by a few Long-tailed Skuas in late August–September, with Great and Pomarine Skuas becoming more likely as the season progresses. Other seabirds include large numbers of Fulmars, Gannets, auks, Kittiwakes, and sometimes Little or even Sabine's Gulls, and numbers of terns, often including Arctic and sometimes also Roseate or Black. As autumn progresses ducks feature more heavily, including Goldeneye and a variety of sea ducks. Seawatching in late autumn–winter can also produce Little Auk, sometimes in large numbers in the right conditions (i.e. northerly gales).

In winter the small numbers of Great Crested Grebe and Red-throated Diver on the sea are joined occasionally by Great Northern Diver or Red-necked Grebe. Up to 100 Purple Sandpipers winter on the rocks (especially near the breakwater), and Sanderling joins the commoner waders on Steetley Beach. Variable numbers of Eider and Common Scoter are found off the Headland, sometimes joined by a Velvet Scoter or Long-tailed Duck, with Red-breasted Merganser in Hartlepool Bay. Other seabirds include Cormorant and a few Guillemots. Large numbers of gulls occur in the area, with Mediterranean, Iceland and Glaucous regularly recorded.

Breeders include small numbers of Kittiwakes on the docks and old piers.

Information

Chris Sharp, Teesmouth Bird Club, 20 Auckland Way, Hartlepool, Cleveland TS26 0AN. Tel: 01429 865163.

43 SEATON CAREW, NORTH GARE AND SEATON SNOOK (Cleveland)

OS Landranger 93

This area lies on the north side of the Tees estuary and is particularly interesting in late summer for the concentrations of terns and attendant skuas, and in autumn–early winter for migrant passerines.

Habitat

Seaton Snook is a promontory of sand, mud and rock within the Tees estuary, used by roosting waders, while the river mouth is protected by an artificial break-

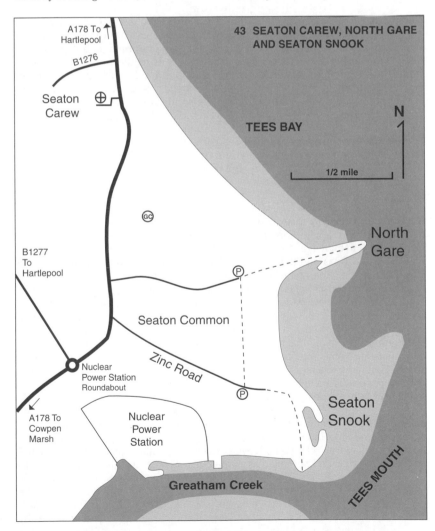

water, the North Gare. To the north lie extensive areas of beach and dunes, backed by a golf course and the grazed land of Seaton Common. Stands of cover, attractive to migrants, lie between North Gare and the golf course, and in the cemetery at the seaside village of Seaton Carew.

Access (see map)

The area is accessed from the A178 north of Middlesborough (and can be combined with a visit to Seal Sands and the wader pools of North Teesside, see p.469).

Seaton Snook Turn sharply southeast off the A178 c.300 yards north of the nuclear power station roundabout on the Zinc Road. After ¾ mile park at the end of the road. Walk onto the sands and bear right, reaching the Snook after 650 yards. Waders may be roosting here, but can be anywhere along the beach. In late summer, the large tern roost attracts skuas. You can walk west along the seawall, past the nuclear power station, for 1 mile to view Greatham Creek.

North Gare The most convenient route to North Gare is along the minor road that leaves the A178 1 mile south of Seaton Carew (and 300 yards north of the Zinc Road). Follow the road for ½ mile to the large car park, and then walk ¼ mile onto the breakwater, checking areas of cover to the north for migrants. North Gare is good for sea duck, Purple Sandpiper and Snow Bunting in winter, and for seabirds in autumn. There is little shelter here for seawatching, and Hartlepool to the north or South Gare to the south are better in the right conditions. It is possible to walk south from the Gare along the beach to Seaton Snook.

Seaton Carew cemetery Entering Seaton Carew from the south on the A178, turn west just past Seaton Hotel into Church Street, with the cemetery at the end of the road after just 50 yards. The churchyard holds passerine migrants, including annual Yellow-browed Warbler.

Birds

In winter Red-throated Diver and Great Crested Grebe may be seen on the sea, together with a few Common Scoter, Eider, Red-breasted Merganser and Goldeneye, and there is a scattering of Guillemots and Cormorants. Other sea duck, Black-throated Diver and the rarer grebes may sometimes also be found. Raptors may include Peregrine, Merlin and Short-eared Owl, hunting over the rough ground of Seaton Common or harassing the waders on the beach. The beach and estuary hold the commoner waders, notably Golden Plover on Seaton Common, Sanderling on the beaches and Purple Sandpiper at North Gare. Gulls are abundant and often include Kittiwake and sometimes Glaucous, Iceland and especially Mediterranean. Very mobile flocks of Snow Bunting haunt the beaches and dunes, and there are sometimes Lapland Bunting and Twite in the rough pastures of Seaton Common, together with Stonechat. Shore Lark is rare.

Passage periods are the most exciting. Gannet, Fulmar and Manx Shearwater are regular offshore in late summer and autumn (especially if the wind has a northerly component), together with Kittiwake and sometimes Sooty Shearwater and, in late autumn, Little Auk Gatherings of up to 2,500 terns occur off the estuary mouth, mostly Sandwich and Common but sometimes also Black, Arctic and, in July–August, Roseate Tern and also Little Gull. These congregations attract up to 100 Arctic Skuas and, in some years, a Long-tailed Skua may linger too. Great and Pomarine Skuas can be seen offshore, but usually only after periods of northerly winds. Up to 100 Little Terns may be found on the beach in spring. Among landbird migrants, the usual chats, warblers and flycatchers are sometimes joined in spring by Marsh Harrier, Ring Ouzel, Black Redstart or Red-backed Shrike, and in autumn also by

Woodcock, Wryneck, Barred, Icterine and Yellow-browed Warblers, Red-breasted Flycatcher and Great Grey Shrike. Breeders include Ringed Plover.

44 NORTH TEESSIDE (Cleveland) OS Landranger 93

This area holds a series of pools and tidal creeks around the Tees estuary that, although surrounded by a grim industrial landscape, regularly hold interesting birds and have attracted an astonishing number of rare waders. Seal Sands is a NNR.

Habitat

The Tees estuary has been extensively reclaimed for industry, leaving just 250 acres of intertidal mud at Seal Sands. Despite this, the remaining Seal Sands retain their attraction for wildfowl and waders, holding internationally important populations of Shelduck, Knot and Sanderling. The mudflats are bounded to the north by Greatham Creek, a steep-sided channel, and west of the A178 this is bordered by areas of relict saltmarsh. Separated from the mudflats by slag reclamation banks are a number of areas of marsh, rough grazing and several pools.

Access (see map)

Haverton Hole Three deep freshwater subsidence pools and a shallower scrape that is more attractive to waders. The area is interesting in summer for breeding Ruddy Duck, Water Rail, Little Ringed Plover, Whinchat and Reed and Sedge Warblers, migrant Marsh Harrier, Garganey, waders, Black Tern and occasionally Black-necked Grebe, and in winter for irregular Scaup and sometimes a roosting Long-eared Owl. Access is from the A1046 at Haverton Hill, turning north at the traffic lights onto the B1275 (Hope Street) and continuing straight to Cowpen Bewley Road. As the village ends, turn right on the last rough track and park at the end of the allotments. Continuing on foot, the raised track gives views of the Main Pool and Rough Pools. The newer scrape (designated for conservation) can be seen by continuing along Cowpen Bewley Road for c.300 yards to the next rather rough track on the right, driving this for 300 yards to view. Prone to disturbance, the area is best visited early in the day.

Saltholme Pools These two freshwater subsidence pools lie beside the A178 1 mile north of Port Clarence (just beyond the start of a short section of dual carriageway), with the Back Saltholme Pool lying 300 yards to the west being more open. The roadside pools can be especially good for waders in dry autumns. It is essential to park right off the road here.

Dorman's Pool A shallow, slightly saline flash, this is probably the best wader pool on North Teesside, especially in wetter autumns when water levels do not fall far. Turn east off the A178, c.75 yards south of Saltholme Pools, on the private ICI road, cross the level crossing and turn left along a track past the south end of Dorman's Pool (it is worth stopping and scanning). Fork left and left again to the parking area for more views. From here it is possible to walk along the east side of the pool to the hide; this is kept locked, but a key is available to members of Teesmouth Bird Club. Technically, a permit from ICI (issued by the Teesmouth Bird Club, SAE please) is required to enter the area of Dorman's Pool and Reclamation Pond, but birdwatchers are rarely challenged; nevertheless, regular visitors should obtain one.

Reclamation Pond An embanked lagoon which sometimes attracts interesting waders and is often used by roosting and loafing gulls and terns, and attracts ducks, notably, Shoveler, in winter. Access is as Dorman's Pool, either viewing from the parking area (final fork right instead of left) or by following the track along the south shore.

Hargreaves Quarries This area of rough ground with many small flashes and areas of reed and willow scrub lies south of the main access road for Dorman's Pool and Reclamation Pond. It is attractive to passerines, wintering Short-eared Owl, and sometimes Long-eared Owl too.

Fire Station Pool A smallish area of water adjacent to Seal Sands roundabout, it attracts waders.

Long Drag Pools The Long Drag marks the west perimeter of the reclaimed area of Seal Sands. Turn east off the A178 at the Seal Sands roundabout towards Seal Sands Industrial Estate and park at the private sign after c.½ mile. From here walk north along the Long Drag to view the pools, scrub and reeds. Access is also possible from Seal Sands hide (see below).

Cowpen Marsh Lying west of the A178 and south of Greatham Creek, this has fresh- and saltmarsh, and though once a reserve is now used for salt extraction. The area can be viewed from the main A178 (pulling completely off this busy road) but it is probably best to turn west off the road, ½ mile north of Seal Sands roundabout, onto a very short track, viewing Holme Fleet from the gate. The Gatenby public hide overlooks the north of the marsh. Access is from the A178 1 mile north of Seal Sands roundabout, parking west of the road at Cowpen Marsh car park (by the small stands of trees). From here walk north along the A178, turning left after 300 yards, just before the Greatham Creek bridge, over the stile to the hide. At high water many of the waders that feed on Seal Sands roost on the saltmarsh near the hide.

Seal Sands These hold large numbers of waders, best seen on a rising tide; at high water they are absent, but numbers of diving ducks can then be seen on Greatham Creek from Seal Sands hide. Access is from Cowpen Marsh car park, walking north along the A178 to Greatham Creek as for the Gatenby hide, but taking the track east along the south bank of the creek for ½ mile to Seal Sands public hide. From here it is possible to walk south along the Long Drag, but the road along the south perimeter of Seal Sands is private.

Tidal Pool South of Greatham Creek and visible as you walk to Seal Sands hide.

Greenabella Marsh An area of rough grassland north of Greatham Creek that may attract raptors, and viewable from the track to Seal Sands hide or the A178.

Birds

On the estuary and marshes wintering wildfowl include large numbers of Shelduck, Wigeon and Teal as well as Gadwall, Pintail and Shoveler. Greylag Goose is resident, and occasional wild White-fronted Geese may join them; Brent Goose and Whooper and Bewick's Swans are also sometimes recorded. Diving duck congregate off the mouth of Greatham Creek by Seal Sands hide and, although erratic, may include hundreds of Goldeneye and Pochard, and often Scaup; in rough weather Eider, Common Scoter, Red-breasted Merganser and sometimes Velvet Scoter, Goosander and Long-tailed Duck may join the commoner species. Large numbers of waders feed on Seal Sands, mostly Knot,

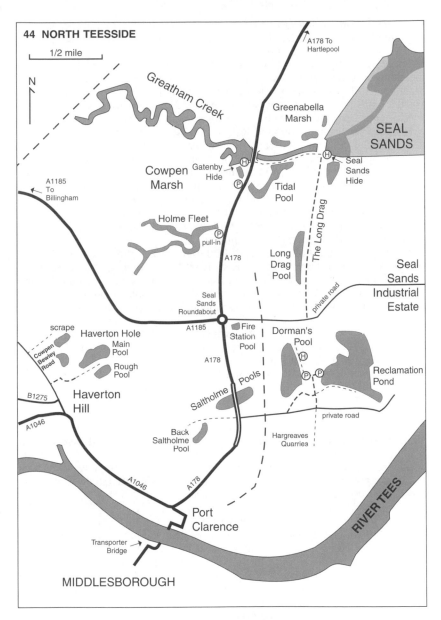

44 NORTH TEESSIDE

1/2 mile

N

Greatham Creek

A178 To
Hartlepool

Greenabella
Marsh

SEAL
SANDS

Cowpen
Marsh

Gatenby
Hide

Seal
Sands
Hide

Tidal
Pool

A1185
To
Billingham

Holme Fleet

pull-in

A178

Long
Drag
Pool

The Long Drag

Seal
Sands
Industrial
Estate

private road

Seal
Sands
Roundabout

A1185

Fire
Station
Pool

Dorman's
Pool

Reclamation
Pond

scrape

Haverton Hole

Main
Pool

Cowpen
Bewley
Road

Rough
Pool

A178

Saltholme Pools

private road

B1275

Haverton
Hill

A1046

Back
Saltholme
Pool

Hargreaves
Quarries

A1046

A178

RIVER TEES

Port
Clarence

Transporter
Bridge

MIDDLESBOROUGH

Dunlin and Redshank, but also Oystercatcher, Ringed and Grey Plovers, Curlew and Bar-tailed Godwit, and a few Sanderling. Golden Plover favours rough pastures and may be joined by a Ruff, Black-tailed Godwit or Spotted Redshank, and even Avocet may winter on the estuary. Such numbers of birds attract raptors, with Sparrowhawk, Peregrine and Merlin regular, Short-eared Owl favouring rough pastures, Hen Harrier scarce but increasing, and sometimes Long-eared Owl may roost in areas of dense thorn bushes, notably at Haverton Hole and Hargreaves Quarries. Around marshy pools there may be Water Rail and Jack Snipe, and gulls are abundant, with Mediterranean, Iceland and Glaucous irregularly recorded. Interesting passerines can include Rock Pipit, Stonechat and often Twite along the Long Drag. Lapland Bunting winters in very small numbers in rough pastures, but is very elusive.

On spring passage Marsh Harrier is regular, as are Garganey and Little Gull, but the main interest, as in autumn, is the waders. Regular species include Whimbrel, Ruff, Greenshank and Common Sandpiper, and almost anything is possible, with Temminck's Stint virtually annual. Autumn passage is more varied, with waders again taking centre stage. Black-tailed Godwit, Green and Wood Sandpipers, Greenshank, Spotted Redshank, Little Stint and Curlew Sandpiper are all regular, and Pectoral Sandpiper is nearly annual. Regular rarities have included Wilson's Phalarope and White-rumped Sandpiper. Large numbers of terns, principally Sandwich and Common but occasionally including one or two Roseate and Arctic, loaf on Seal Sands and attract a few Arctic Skuas. Interesting gulls and terns may also be found on Reclamation Pond. As in spring, Marsh Harrier and Garganey are regular, but Black Tern is surprisingly scarce, though there have been several records of White-winged Black Tern. Wild Barnacle Geese may pass through in late autumn.

Breeders include numbers of duck in the marshes, Little and Great Crested Grebes, Water Rail, Oystercatcher, Redshank, Snipe, Ringed Plover, some of Britain's most northerly Little Ringed Plovers, sometimes a few Common or even Little Terns, as well as Cuckoo, Yellow Wagtail, Whinchat, Stonechat, Reed and Sedge Warblers, and occasionally Grasshopper Warbler.

Information

Chris Sharp, Teesmouth Bird Club, 20 Auckland Way, Hartlepool, Cleveland TS26 0AN. Tel: 01429 865163.

Mike Leakey, English Nature, c/o British Energy, Tees Road, Hartlepool TS25 2BZ. Tel: 01429 853325. E-mail: northumbria@english-nature.org.uk

45 SOUTH GARE (Cleveland)   OS Landranger 93

Lying south of the mouth of the River Tees, this artificial breakwater and its immediate environs is attractive to passerine migrants, especially in spring, and also attracts concentrations of terns and skuas.

Habitat

A relict of the dunes and saltmarshes that once protected the mouth of the Tees, the area comprises a mosaic of dunes, mudflats, and fresh- and saltwater pools, while the Gare itself was built in the 19th century from iron-ore slag. On the southwest flanks of the Gare lie Bran Sands, which hold good numbers of the commoner estuarine waders.

Access (see map)

Just west of Redcar, leave the A1085 (opposite the junction with the A1042) north on a minor road towards Coatham. After ¼ mile turn left at the roundabout and follow this road, sharp right and left over the old railway at Fishermen's crossing, and onto the Gare access road. This is a narrow private road and despite the 'no entry' signs, is open to birdwatchers (with the exception of one Sunday each year in September when it is closed to traffic for legal reasons). The road extends for 3 miles, almost to the tip of the breakwater, and when stopping it is best to pull right off the road to avoid obstructing traffic.

Coming from Redcar, to the east of the access road lies a golf course, and

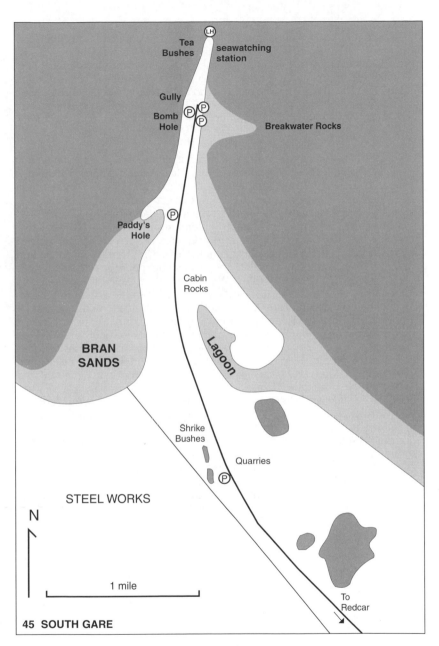

45 SOUTH GARE

scattered along the road are bushes, which sometimes hold migrants. Next is a large freshwater pool (with other, smaller, pools further from the road) worth checking for migrant waders. West of the road are the Shrike Bushes, an area of reeds and scrub, which very often attracts migrants; just opposite the Quarries is a similar but rougher area. Further north, to the east of the road the Lagoon is an area of mud and sand that is periodically flooded, backed by saltmarsh, rough grassland and dunes; at its south end is a stand of *Suaeda*, traditional migrant habitat but difficult to work. Immediately north of the Lagoon the expanse of slag known as Cabin Rocks can be good for migrants. The Gare end is normally the most productive area for passerine migrants, notably the Tea Bushes, Gully, Bomb Hole and Paddy's Hole, although the limited cover means that birds may filter inland fairly rapidly. At the very end of the road it is possible to seawatch from the car around high water (the sea is too distant at low tide), otherwise seek shelter at a point almost at the tip of the Gare. Off the very tip, the Breakwater Rocks hold loafing ducks, waders and gulls.

Birds

The Gare is at its best during spring and autumn, and a large variety of migrants can occur, including Black Redstart and Ring Ouzel in early spring, with Marsh Harrier, Garganey and Black Tern later in the season and Wryneck, Bluethroat, Red-backed Shrike and Common Rosefinch scarce migrants worth looking for in May–early June. The variety of birds is greater in autumn, with Icterine and Barred Warbler possible in August–September, in addition to Wryneck, Bluethroat and Red-backed Shrike, and a chance of Richard's Pipit, Yellow-browed Warbler, Red-breasted Flycatcher, Great Grey Shrike and Lapland Bunting later in the autumn, as well as the regular commoner east coast migrants such as Woodcock, Redstart, Willow Warbler, Goldcrest, Pied Flycatcher, and oddities such as Long-eared and Short-eared Owls. Passage waders in autumn may include Greenshank, Little Stint and Curlew Sandpiper (on the estuary or the pools), as well as Green and Common Sandpipers.

The Gare can be productive for seawatching, but is somewhat overshadowed by Hartlepool to the north; except in the severest gales, most birds cross Tees Bay well out to sea. Nevertheless, a variety of shearwaters and skuas is possible, and in late-autumn or winter gales species such as Grey Phalarope and Little Auk may seek the shelter of the Gare.

Breeders include Little Grebe, Water Rail, Ringed Plover, Snipe, Little Tern and Sedge Warbler, while Common Tern breeds nearby and small numbers of Eider and Sandwich Tern summer. By August the large numbers of terns at the estuary mouth include small numbers of Arctic and sometimes one or two Roseates. Notably, these concentrations attract numbers of Arctic Skuas, and in some years a Long-tailed Skua (including adults with full tails) may linger.

In winter Red-throated Diver is regular on the sea, as are Cormorant, Eider, Red-breasted Merganser and Guillemot, and these are often joined by Shag, Common and Velvet Scoters and Long-tailed Duck, and occasionally a Great Northern Diver or Red-necked Grebe. The various fresh pools attract dabbling ducks, mostly Wigeon and Teal. Large numbers of gulls often include Mediterranean and occasionally a Glaucous or Iceland. Waders include the usual species on Bran Sands, including Sanderling and Grey Plover, with Purple Sandpiper on the rocks and breakwaters, together with Rock Pipit. Such large concentrations of birds regularly attract Peregrine, with Merlin and Short-eared Owl over rougher ground. Large flocks of Snow Buntings are found on the beach, especially around the mouth of the Lagoon.

46 COATHAM MARSH AND LOCKE PARK

(Cleveland)   OS Landranger 93

Lying immediately west of Redcar, these two adjacent sites attract a variety of wild-fowl and waders, as well as passerine migrants in spring and autumn. Coatham Marsh is a reserve of the Tees Valley Wildlife Trust (TVWT).

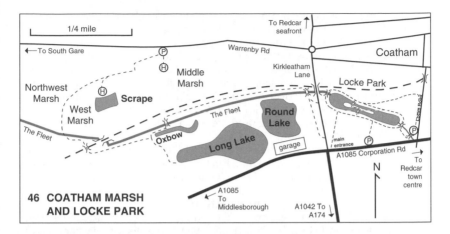

1/4 mile

To South Gare →

To Redcar seafront

Warrenby Rd

Kirkleatham Lane

Coatham

Locke Park

Middle Marsh

Northwest Marsh

West Marsh

Scrape

The Fleet

The Fleet

Oxbow

Long Lake

Round Lake

garage

main entrance

A1085 Corporation Rd

To Redcar town centre

N

46 COATHAM MARSH AND LOCKE PARK

A1085 To Middlesborough

A1042 To A174

Habitat

Coatham Marsh is bisected by the Saltburn–Darlington railway and the Fleet, an old saltmarsh channel. South of the railway a rubbish tip has been landscaped to form low hillocks and two artificial lakes (Long Lake and Round Lake), while north of the railway the relict saltmarsh is still prone to flooding, and a scrape has been excavated at the west end. Locke Park is a small town park centred on a small lake and planted with a variety of trees and shrubs. Backing the Saltburn–Middlesborough railway, areas of cover along the line and the gardens to the north are also attractive to migrants.

Access (see map)

Coatham Marsh On the west outskirts of Redcar turn north off the A1085 at the traffic lights, opposite the junction with the A1042, into Kirkleatham Lane. After ¼ mile turn west at the roundabout (towards South Gare) into Warrenby Road, and park on the right after c.¼ mile (just after the road rises over a disused railway) in the reserve car park. There is free access to the reserve, and a large hide overlooks the old saltmarsh at Middle Marsh (kept locked, keys available from the warden on payment of a deposit), while a more basic, unlocked hide provides views of the scrape. The footpath from here continues to the Oxbow, Long Lake and Round Lake, and then to Kirkleatham Lane.

Locke Park, Redcar Just east of Coatham Marsh, access is from Locke Road on the east perimeter and from Corporation Road (the A1085) along the south side (ignore the main entrance with the large Locke Park sign and park in the unfenced car park 100 yards to the east). Best in spring and autumn, there is usually little of note in midsummer and winter.

Birds

Early-spring migrants may include Black Redstart, Ring Ouzel and Firecrest, as well as wandering Hawfinch at Locke Park, while later in the season falls of Scandinavia-bound birds such as Chiffchaff and Pied Flycatcher may also include a Bluethroat or Red-backed Shrike. A visit to both Locke Park and Coatham Marsh can be rewarding during such falls. Passage waders can include Green, Common and Wood Sandpipers (the latter favours the Oxbow), Greenshank, Ruff and Little Ringed Plover, with Garganey, Osprey and Black Tern annual at Coatham Marsh.

In autumn the usual east coast migrants are regular and Yellow-browed Warbler is something of a speciality of Locke Park in October. In addition to the waders listed above, Coatham Marsh may attract Black-tailed Godwit, Whimbrel, Spotted Redshank, Curlew Sandpiper and Little Stint.

Wintering wildfowl include Teal, Wigeon, Pochard, small numbers of Shovelers and sometimes Goldeneye, Scaup, Pintail or Gadwall; sea ducks, divers and the rarer grebes are occasional. Large numbers of Oystercatcher winter on Coatham Marsh, and a Jack Snipe may be found among the Snipe, and similarly Ruff or Golden Plover occasionally join the large flocks of wintering Lapwing. Other species to watch for include Sparrowhawk, Merlin, Water Rail, Short-eared Owl and Kingfisher, and Peregrine, Stonechat, and Snow and Lapland Buntings are possible.

Residents at Coatham Marsh include Little Grebe and Snipe, and Shelduck, Sedge Warbler and occasional Little Ringed Plover, Grasshopper and Reed Warblers are breeding summer visitors. Common Tern may visit at this season.

Information
Tees Valley Wildlife Trust, Bellamy Pavilion,Kirkleatham Old Hall, Kirkleatham, Redcar, Cleveland TS10 5NW. Tel: 01642 759900. E-mail: teesvalleywt@cix.co.uk

47 HURWORTH BURN RESERVOIR (Durham)   OS Landranger 93

Lying a little north of the Teesside conurbation, this small reservoir is notable for winter wildfowl and a good wader passage, especially in autumn.

Habitat
Covering just 32 acres, the south, dam end of the reservoir is deepest, while the north half and the two cut-offs are shallower and areas of mud can be exposed when water levels are low. The surroundings are largely farmland.

Access (see map)
Leave the A19 west on the B1280 towards Wingate and, after c.½ mile, turn left (southwest) on a minor road towards Trimdon, following the road right and then right again to the reservoir. There is space to park on the roadside by the access road, 100 yards past the outflow stream. A public footpath follows the access

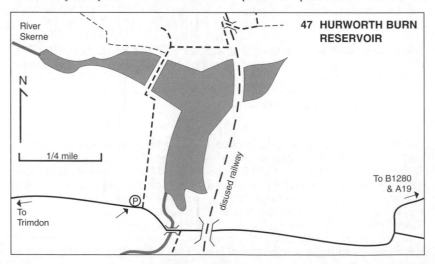

River Skerne

47 HURWORTH BURN RESERVOIR

N

1/4 mile

disused railway

To B1280 & A19

P

To Trimdon

track along the west flank of the reservoir, giving views of most of the water, and then bisects the northwest arm before splitting, the right fork running along the north shore and meeting a disused railway line often used by hikers.

Birds

Wintering wildfowl include Teal, Wigeon and Pochard, with small numbers of Goldeneye, often a few Goosander and sometimes Scaup or Pintail. Other notable waterbirds include Cormorant, Curlew, Snipe, Redshank and Water Rail. Occasionally Peregrine or Merlin is seen, as well as the regular resident Sparrowhawks. There is a small gull roost, largely Common and Black-headed Gulls, but occasionally including a white-winged gull.

Wader passage can be exciting, especially in autumn, but depends at both seasons upon water levels. Possibilities include Ringed Plover, Whimbrel, Black-tailed Godwit, Ruff, Greenshank, Spotted Redshank, Green, Wood and Common Sandpipers, with Curlew Sandpiper and Little Stint in autumn. Shoveler, Common Tern and Grey Wagtail may also appear, and other possible migrants are Black-necked Grebe, Garganey, Black Tern and Little Gull, although the large autumn flocks of the last species are no longer a feature.

Breeders include Little and Great Crested Grebes, Shelduck, Oystercatcher, Little Ringed Plover, and sometimes Common Sandpiper and Redshank. Other summer visitors include Turtle Dove and Lesser Whitethroat, and Little Owl, Lesser Spotted Woodpecker and Tree Sparrow are scarce residents.

48 SCALING DAM RESERVOIR
(Cleveland and North Yorkshire)   OS Landranger 94

Lying on the edge of the North Yorkshire Moors, this upland reservoir is surprisingly productive for wintering wildfowl and passage waders, and the surrounding moorland has resident Red Grouse and is good for raptors, especially in winter.

Habitat

The reservoir was constructed in the 1950s and covers c.125 acres, with large areas of mud exposed as water levels drop. The water is used for sailing Easter–October, but c.20 acres in the southwest corner have been set aside as a sanctuary, and there are areas of waterside willows here. The reservoir lies at an altitude of 625 feet and is bordered to the south by heather moorland and a block of conifers.

Access (see map)

The reservoir lies immediately south of the A171, 12 miles west of Whitby. At the west end the yacht club car park gives access to a public hide overlooking the sanctuary area, while raptors are best watched for from upper parts of this car park. Walking west along the A178 for 50 yards gives access to Bog House Lane. This in turn accesses several footpaths across the moors, and in summer (22 March–30 September) access is also permitted to a path along the entire south side of the water. There is also a public car park at the east end of the reservoir.

Birds

Wintering wildfowl include feral Greylag Goose, Wigeon, Teal and small numbers of Pochard, Goldeneye and Goosander (the latter usually spend the day to the south on the River Esk); a few Whooper Swans, Bean Geese, Scaup, Shoveler,

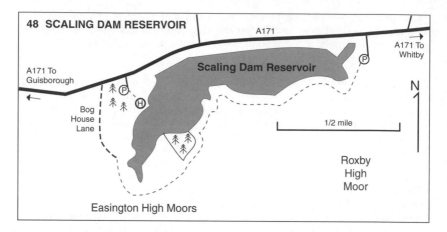

48 SCALING DAM RESERVOIR

A171

A171 To Whitby

A171 To Guisborough

Scaling Dam Reservoir

Bog House Lane

1/2 mile

N

Roxby High Moor

Easington High Moors

Gadwall and Pintail are also quite regular (as are feral Pink-footed Geese with the Greylag; wild Pink-feet and White-fronts are scarce). Divers, Red-necked Grebe, sea duck, Smew and Red-breasted Merganser are occasional. Other notable water-birds include Little Grebe and Cormorant, and the gull roost may hold Glaucous or Mediterranean Gulls as well as large numbers of Black-headed, and there can be many Lapwing and Golden Plover in the reservoir's hinterland. Interesting passerines may include Water Pipit, Stonechat, Willow Tit (along Bog House Lane), Brambling and Snow Bunting. A major focus in winter is the concentration on raptors on the moorland, especially Hen Harrier, but also Merlin, Peregrine, Sparrowhawk and Barn and Short-eared Owls. Afternoons and evenings are best. Long-eared Owl is sometimes found in the conifers.

Breeders include Great Crested and Little Grebes, Teal, Woodcock, Whinchat, Lesser Whitethroat and occasionally Ringed and Little Ringed Plovers, and Black-headed Gull, and Red-necked and Black-necked Grebes may summer. Red Grouse is resident on the adjacent moors, and may be joined in summer by Merlin and Short-eared Owl, as well as Curlew, Snipe and Redshank.

On passage, Marsh Harrier may occur in spring, together with Black-necked Grebe, Little Gull, Black and Arctic Terns and a handful of waders. If water levels fall a much greater variety of waders is possible in autumn, with Ruff, Black-tailed Godwit, Green, Common and Curlew Sandpipers, Greenshank, Spotted Redshank and Little Stint all regular. Marsh Harrier is again possible, as is Osprey.

49 WASHINGTON WWT AND BARMSTON POND
(Durham)   OS Landranger 88

Lying between the urban sprawls of Sunderland and Washington, this small area holds a variety of wetland and woodland birds, with waders on passage, and the waterfowl collection provides additional year-round interest.

Habitat
Washington is owned by the WWT and c.20 per cent of the 100-acre grounds are occupied by a collection of over 100 species of swans, geese and ducks, the remainder comprising a mosaic of brackish and freshwater pools, and small stands of reeds and woodland on the north bank of the River Wear (still tidal at

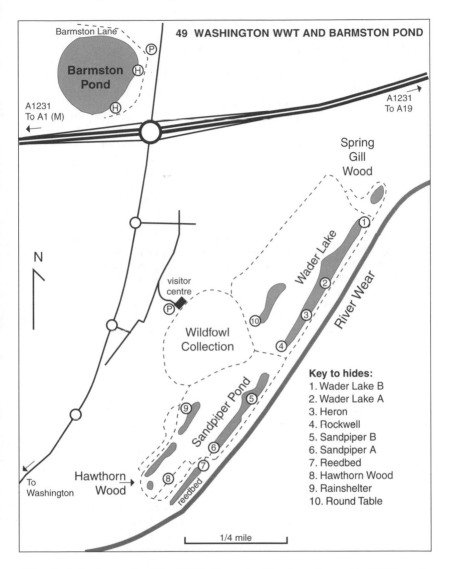

49 WASHINGTON WWT AND BARMSTON POND

Barmston Lane

Barmston Pond

A1231
To A1 (M)

A1231
To A19

Spring Gill Wood

Wader Lake

River Wear

visitor centre

Wildfowl Collection

Sandpiper Pond

N

Key to hides:
1. Wader Lake B
2. Wader Lake A
3. Heron
4. Rockwell
5. Sandpiper B
6. Sandpiper A
7. Reedbed
8. Hawthorn Wood
9. Rainshelter
10. Round Table

Hawthorn Wood

reedbed

To Washington

1/4 mile

this point). To the north of the A1231, Barmston Pond was formed in 1970 by subsidence and is owned by Sunderland City Council and managed as a reserve. A freshwater pool, there are shallow scrapes at both ends and the pond is managed to provide ideal feeding conditions for passage waders in autumn.

Access (see map)

Washington WWT From the south, turn east off the A1 (M) at junction 64 just south of Gateshead on the A195. Continue on the A195 past its junction with the A182 and then, after 1 mile, turn right at the second roundabout on a minor road and follow signs to the WWT. Alternatively, leave the A19 just west of Sunderland on the A1231 towards Washington. After 1 mile turn left at the roundabout on a minor road, and then left again after c.300 yards at the next roundabout, following signs to the WWT car park. The grounds are open daily (except Christmas

Day) 09.30–17.00 April–October and 09.30–16.00 in winter, the Peter Scott Visitor Centre and Glaxo-Wellcome Wetlands Discovery Centre closing ½ hour earlier. There are ten hides overlooking the pools, notably the slightly brackish Wader Lake, which is attractive to dabbling ducks, waders, gulls and terns, and also has a heronry, and The Reservoir (from Rainshelter hide) which attracts diving ducks and Wigeon, while the Hawthorn Wood Feeding Station is operative mid-September–Easter. The River Wear may hold grebes and Goldeneye, and can be viewed from the track along Wader Lake.

Barmston Pond Turn north off the A1231 at the roundabout signed for the Nissan works. Park after a short distance on the left, at the start of Barmston Lane (near the gate of the Nissan European Technology Centre). From here a track follows the east shore of the pond, and there are two hides, while a third hide lies along Barmston Lane and overlooks the reservoir used to control water levels in the pond.

Birds

Wintering wildfowl at Washington include many Pochard and Teal and a few Wigeon, Shoveler, as well as up to 60 Goldeneye, often with a handful of Goosander. Other notable waterfowl include Great Crested and Little Grebes and Cormorant. Scarcer visitors include Whooper Swan and Smew, and the rarer grebes, divers and Bittern have been recorded here or on the adjacent river. Long-eared Owl breeds nearby and may sometimes be found roosting in areas of dense cover. Waders include up to 200 Redshank, a few Snipe and occasionally Jack Snipe, and small numbers of Water Rail occur throughout. Wintering Siskin and Redpoll may be found anywhere in the grounds. and the feeding station attracts woodland birds such as Great Spotted Woodpecker, Willow Tit and Bullfinch, with Brambling possible in late winter, and these in turn attract hunting Sparrowhawk. Barmston Pond has a similar range of waterfowl and there is some interchange with Washington. The surrounding fields may hold Merlin, Short-eared Owl and Golden Plover, and there is a possibility of a hunting Long-eared Owl at dusk.

On passage a variety of waders may occur at Washington and Barmston Pond (the latter being particularly productive in autumn), including Common Sandpiper, Greenshank, Dunlin, Ruff and Black-tailed Godwit, with Green and Wood Sandpipers and Temminck's Stint among the scarcer species. In spring Osprey, Marsh Harrier, Buzzard, Hobby and Garganey may pass through, and in autumn there are concentrations of Grey Heron and Common Tern on Wader Lake and Barmston Pond, with other terns, Little Gull and Garganey scarce visitors. Waders at this season may include Spotted Redshank, Little Stint and Curlew Sandpiper, in addition to those species listed for spring.

Breeders include a small number of Grey Heron (viewed at eye level from Heron hide or via a video link), Sparrowhawk, feral Shelduck and Gadwall, Lapwing, Little Ringed Plover, Oystercatcher, Redshank, a handful of pairs of Common Terns (on Wader Pool), Stock Dove, and Reed, Sedge and Garden Warblers.

Information

WWT, Andrew Donnison (Grounds Manager), District 15, Washington, Tyne & Wear NE38 8LE. Tel: 0191 416 5454. E-mail: wetlands@euphony.net

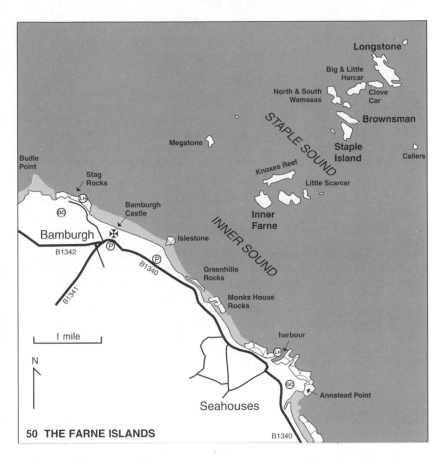

Longstone

Big & Little
Harcar

North & South
Wamseas

Clove
Car

Brownsman

Megstone

Staple
Island

Callers

Budle
Point

Knoxes Reef

Little Scarcer

Stag
Rocks

LH

GC

Bamburgh
Castle

Inner
Farne

Bamburgh

Islestone

B1342

P

INNER SOUND

P

B1340

Greenhills
Rocks

B1341

Monks House
Rocks

I mile

N

harbour

LH

GC

Annstead Point

Seahouses

50 THE FARNE ISLANDS

B1340

STAPLE SOUND

50 THE FARNE ISLANDS (Northumberland)   OS Landranger 75

Lying off the Northumberland coast between Bamburgh and Seahouses, the
Farne Islands hold superb, easily accessible seabird colonies, and the short boat
trip is guaranteed to add to the excitement. The best time to visit is May–early July.
The islands belong to the NT and are a NNR.

Habitat

These small islands, comprising ten larger outcrops and numerous smaller rocks,
totalling 28 in all, lie 1½ miles or more offshore. Most are rocky stacks, but Inner
Farne and Staple Island are flatter, providing habitat for nesting terns.

Access (see map)

Weather permitting, boats run daily from Seahouses harbour, from April to late
September. Tickets are available from the boat kiosks at the quay, but it is best
to book in advance, especially during busy holiday periods. Seahouses Tourist
Office can advise; one of the boatmen most regularly used by birders is Billy
Shiels (or the *Glad Tidings* boats). Sailings commence at 10.00, and several itin-
eraries are available, either landing on Inner Farne and/or Staple Island, or
non-landing (check on booking). Half-day trips allow only one hour ashore,

however, and as there is so much to see, a full-day trip may be preferable. An entrance fee is payable on landing and leaflets are available for the nature trails on the islands.

Birds

Over 65,000 pairs of 14 species of seabirds breed. Puffin is the most numerous, with c.34,000 pairs, followed by Guillemot (16,000 pairs), Kittiwake (6,000 pairs), Arctic Tern (3,000 pairs), Sandwich Tern (2,700 pairs) and Shag (c.2,000 pairs). There are several hundred pairs of Cormorant, Fulmar, Lesser Black-backed, Herring and Black-headed Gulls, Razorbill and Common Tern, but just a handful of Roseate Terns (3–4 pairs). The terns breed on Inner Farne, Staple Island and Brownsman. Of special note was a lone female Lesser Crested Tern, known as 'Elsie', which summered annually between 1984 and 1997 on Inner Farne. Usually paired with a Sandwich Tern, hybrid young were raised on three occasions. Other breeding birds include 1,100 pairs of Eider, as well as Mallard, Ringed Plover, Oystercatcher, Rock Pipit, Pied Wagtail, Swallow and sometimes Shelduck.

Passage brings divers, shearwaters, waders and skuas to this coast, as detailed under Lindisfarne–Seahouses, and passerine migrants to the islands, although for obvious reasons, these are usually seen only by the islands' wardens.

Information

NT Warden: John Walton, 8 St Aidan's, Seahouses, Northumberland NE68 7SR. Tel: 01665 720651.

Seahouses Tourist Office. Tel: 01665 720884.

Billy Shiel, Southfield Avenue, Seahouses, Northumberland. Tel: 01665 720308.

51 LINDISFARNE (Northumberland)   OS Landranger 75

Lindisfarne, on the Northumberland coast, is an excellent area for birdwatching during winter and passage periods, especially for divers, grebes, wildfowl and waders. The area supports internationally important populations of Pale-bellied Brent Goose, Knot, Dunlin and Bar-tailed Godwit. On passage a wide variety of passerines has been recorded. Lindisfarne NNR covers 8,101 acres and includes Budle Bay. The adjacent coast between Bamburgh and Seahouses has essentially the same population of divers, grebes and sea duck as Lindisfarne, and also attracts passage migrants.

Habitat

The intertidal flats are sheltered from the sea by the dune systems of Goswick Sands, Holy Island and Ross Links. Budle Bay is another sheltered tidal basin, while the 4-mile stretch of coast from Bamburgh to Seahouses has several rocky sections.

Access

Within the NNR, permits are not required for access to the shore or causeway, but remember that farmland is private.

Holy Island (see maps) The island is c.3 miles long by 1½ miles wide at the widest point. From the Snook, areas of sand dunes extend along the north shore, via a rather narrow strip at the Links, to Emmanuel Head. South of the Links lies farmland, and the village, priory and castle. The road to the island is well signed

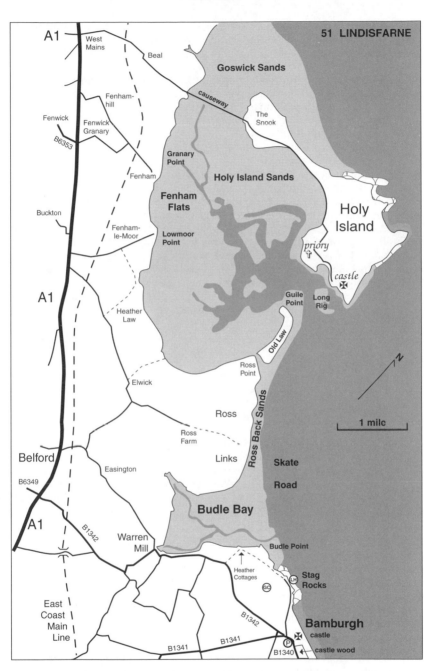

51 LINDISFARNE

off the A1 at West Mains Inn. It is impossible to use the causeway for at least two hours either side of high water, and the strength of the wind and the height of the tide must also be taken into account. Tide tables are displayed on the causeway and in the village. The causeway itself is a well-made tarmac road. The following areas are worthwhile.

1. In the dunes of the Snook there is a scattering of bushes and clumps of willows and hawthorns, notably in the garden of Snook House and the bushes and pools to the west, which may harbour migrants, while the dunes attract pipits. It is possible to park along the access track.

2. Off Sandon Bay and North Shore look for Red-breasted Merganser and Shag, and Sanderling on the beach. It is possible to park along the road (tides permitting) and walk through the dunes to the North Shore. The Links and dunes area also attract migrants, and may harbour Long-eared or Short-eared Owls or Woodcock in late autumn.

3. The fields at Chare Ends attract larks, finches and buntings, sometimes including Twite or Lapland Bunting.

4. The Heugh (an igneous dyke by the coastguard tower south of the priory, complete with benches), affords views over Fenham Flats and south towards Ross Back Sands, and notably of Long Rig and Black Law for roosting waders and gulls. The adjacent harbour also attracts gulls and is worth checking for divers and grebes, especially on a rising tide, while the freshwater pools in the nearby fields attract passage waders (over the wall behind the car park kiosk).

5. Any area of cover around the village is worth checking in spring and autumn for migrants, but especially the gardens east of the road between Chare Ends and the Lindisfarne Hotel, the trees opposite the North View Restaurant, the trees around the main car park and St Mary's churchyard, and the gardens on the eastern periphery of the village. Migrants tend to leave the island during the day, thus in suitable weather an early-morning visit is best.

6. The walled garden just north of the castle attracts migrants (once including Red-flanked Bluetail!), and the close-cropped turf by the lime kiln larks, wheatears and buntings.

7. The stunted hedges along the Straight and Crooked Lonnens, and the garden of the house north of the Crooked Lonnen, also attract migrants, with waders, finches, buntings and sometimes wildfowl in adjacent fields. Access is past the 'visitor farm', 300 yards north of the main car park.

8. The Lough attracts 'fresh' waders and duck, and holds breeding Little Grebe, Shoveler and 200–300 pairs of Black-headed Gull. The Paul Greenwood Memorial hide overlooks the east end.

9. You can seawatch from the high dunes at Snipe Point on the north coast or the cliffs at Coves Bay or Nessend, from the shelter of the white stone beacon at Emmanuel Head (the best point) or Castle Point, but these are probably no better than Bamburgh or Seahouses.

Holy Island is simply too large an area to cover in its entirety in a single day, and thus a long weekend or even a one-week visit could be contemplated. A half-day visit, preferably in the morning, provides sufficient time to cover a variety of habitats, with a circular walk from the main car park, along either the Straight or Crooked Lonnen to the coast, to Emmanuel Head, and then completing the square along the other lonnen. Another circular walk would be to check the gardens around the village, then the Heugh and Castle, returning along the Crooked Lonnen.

Holy Island Causeway (see maps) From the A1 at West Mains, take the minor road to Beal. Continue to the shore and causeway (from the base of which a public footpath runs along the shore). The causeway to Holy Island, with lay-bys either side of the white refuge tower, is the best viewpoint to see large numbers of waders, which favour Holy Island Sands and Fenham Flats. Sea duck may sometimes be seen on the channel by the refuge, with Whooper Swan on the flats, especially in autumn, while this is also an excellent vantage point to observe the hordes of wintering wildfowl, notably Wigeon and Pale-bellied Brent Goose.

Fenham Flats (see map) There is open access to the foreshore here, although it may be disturbed by wildfowling 1 September–20 February. This is a good area for Pale-bellied Brent Goose and Wigeon, and is best an hour or so either side of high water. Access is from the A1 at three points, although parking is limited at all of these. Note that it is unwise to venture onto the mudflats.
1. The minor road to Fenwick Granary and Fenham (opposite the B6353 turning to Fenwick), continuing to the shore.
2. The minor road to Fenham-le-Moor and on to Lowmoor Point, where a small hide is usable at your own risk. Good for waders and wildfowl on the rising tide.
3. A signed wildfowlers footpath runs north from the hamlet of Elwick for c.1 mile to the shore. From here two circular routes are possible: north to Lowmoor Point, returning via Fenham-le-Moor and the footpath to Heather Law, or rather longer, east to Guile Point, returning via Ross Back Sands and Ross Farm.

Ross Back Sands (see map) A good area to view divers, grebes, sea duck and other wildfowl on Skate Road, with Sanderling and Grey Plover on the beaches, Snow Bunting around the dunes, a variety of raptors, and Hooded Crow around the coastal pastures. Terns breed around Guile Point. A footpath runs east from Ross Farm (park on the verge) along a tarmac road and then over Ross Links to Ross Back Sands, with access north towards Guile Point along the shore (note that Old Law and Guile Point are separated from Ross Point at high tide).

Budle Bay (see map) Very good for wildfowl and waders, especially if Fenham Flats are disturbed by shooting.
1. The B1342 between Warren Mill and Budle offers views over the southeast shore of the bay, and parking is possible along the verge. There is also roadside parking at Warren Mill.
2. The minor road west from Warren Mill towards Easington, with the 'Belford' lay-by on the north side of the road, gives distant panoramic views of the bay and fields between Easington and Ross, which may be used by Greylag Goose when not in the bay.
3. From Budle a footpath runs to Heather Cottages and the golf course, past Budle Point, which is a good spot to view the bay and sea. The path then skirts the golf course to Bamburgh lighthouse.

Bamburgh to Seahouses (see map) This section of the coast is bounded by large areas of rocks and extensive sandy beaches, notable for divers, grebes and sea ducks. On the landward side, areas of cover attract passerine migrants.
1. The B1340 parallels the coast from Bamburgh to Seahouses, with open access to the foreshore.
2. From the centre of Bamburgh you can drive along a narrow, concealed minor road (the Wynding) to the lighthouse. Beyond the houses, it is possible to park by the foreshore on the cliff at Stag Rocks (marked as 'Harkess Rocks' on the OS map), using the wall of the lighthouse as shelter to view the sea; this is the best spot for divers, grebes and sea duck.
3. Bamburgh Castle Wood and the numerous stands of bushes in the dunes to the south should be checked for passage migrants. There are car parks opposite the castle and in the dunes to the south.
4. Seahouses harbour attracts small numbers of gulls, including Glaucous and occasionally Iceland, and holds large numbers of Eiders in winter.
5. The public park/bowling green opposite the north pier in Seahouses should

Red-breasted Mergansers

be checked for passerine migrants in season (see The Farne Islands, p.481).
6. It may be worth seawatching from near the old lookout at Annstead Point (known as Snook or North Sunderland Point on the OS map), accessible by following the footpath south along the cliffs from the harbour.

Birds

In winter Red-throated Diver and Slavonian Grebe are quite common offshore; Black-throated is the second commonest diver but is distinctly scarce, as is Great Northern. Red-necked Grebe is regular but uncommon, and the sea also has Cormorant, Shag, and many Eider and Common Scoter, with smaller numbers of Long-tailed Duck and Red-breasted Merganser, a few Goldeneye and Velvet Scoter, and more erratically Scaup. Up to 4,000 Greylag Geese occur, mainly in the fields between Budle Bay and Ross, or on the flats of Budle Bay, and are sometimes joined by small numbers of Pink-footed or a few White-fronted and Bean Geese. The flats hold the largest flock of wintering Pale-bellied Brent Goose in Britain. They belong to the declining Svalbard and Franz Josef Land populations, which number only c.5,000 birds. These winter in Denmark and at Lindisfarne, which holds half of the population, numbers peaking at c.2,500 in December. Dark-bellied Brent Goose may also be present, and numbers of Barnacle Geese pass through in autumn and spring. A small flock of 20–30 (formerly up to 440; many have now transferred to Cresswell or the Ashington area) Whooper Swan uses the fields and flats and is sometimes joined by a few Bewick's. Wigeon has peaked at 40,000 and typically 15,000 are present, while Shelduck and Teal are also common, with a few Pintail and Pochard. Peregrine, Merlin and Short-eared Owl are regular, and there is sometimes a Hen Harrier. Of waders, Dunlin is by far the commonest and Knot is also abundant, together with the usual estuarine species, but Sanderling and Purple Sandpiper occur in relatively small numbers (the latter favours Nessend on Holy Island and Stag Rocks at Bamburgh). There is occasionally a wintering Spotted Redshank or Greenshank. Occasionally Glaucous Gull puts in an appearance and Iceland is even more rarely seen. Snow Bunting can be quite common, especially on Ross Links. Shore Lark, Twite and Lapland Bunting are only occasional. Grey Wagtail and sometimes Dipper can be found at Warren Burn outlet.

Seawatching can be good during passage periods. Gannets and Manx and sometimes Sooty Shearwaters are noted offshore in autumn, together with six species of tern, though Little is scarce and Roseate quite rare. Arctic Skua is almost constantly present in autumn, and sometimes Great too, but Pomarine and Long-tailed are unusual. Waders frequent the flats, but it is worth checking any area of fresh water as well. Black-tailed Godwit, Greenshank, Spotted Redshank and Wood Sandpiper occur at both seasons, but Little Stint and Curlew Sandpiper almost exclusively in autumn. Large falls of migrants are occasional in autumn, including huge arrivals of thrushes, and sometimes Woodcock, Jack Snipe and Long-eared Owl in late autumn. Wryneck, Shore Lark, Black Redstart, Bluethroat, Red-backed Shrike, and Ortolan and Lapland Buntings may occur at either season, but all are scarce and a visitor would be lucky to see any of these. The equally elusive Barred and Yellow-browed Warblers, Red-breasted Flycatcher and Great Grey Shrike almost exclusively occur in autumn, as does Waxwing, albeit sporadically.

Breeders include small numbers of Fulmar (on Lindisfarne Castle and at Coves Bay), Eider, Shelduck, Ringed Plover and Oystercatcher, as well as Common, Arctic and Little Terns. Seabirds from the Farnes can be seen moving along the coast, as well as Gannet and Manx Shearwater from further afield.

Information

EN (Site Manager):, Phil Davey, Beal Station, Berwick-on-Tweed TD15 2PB. Tel: 01289 381470.

SCOTLAND

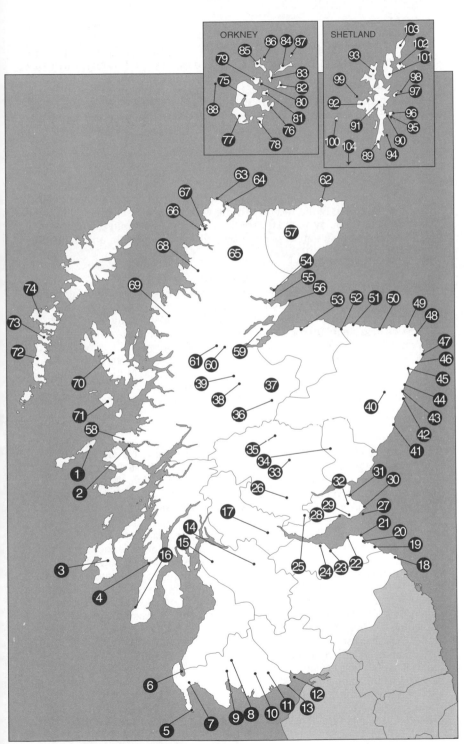

1 COLL (Argyll)

Coll is an island within the south sector of the Inner Hebrides. Lying at the west end of the island and covering over 3,000 acres, the RSPB reserve was established specifically to benefit Corncrake, which has declined disastrously in Britain in the 20th century. Coll now has c.40 pairs of Corncrakes and the population in the reserve has risen from six pairs in 1991 to 28 in 1996. The island also holds numbers of breeding waders and raptors, and is at its best in spring and early summer, although winter can be good for divers and wildfowl.

Habitat

Coll is largely cloaked in heather but the RSPB reserve comprises two extensive dune systems together with machair (stabilised lime-rich dunes of shell sand covered by herb-rich sward) and productive hay meadows, as well as heather stands in the centre of the reserve. To the west, the reserve is bounded on the north coast by Feall Bay and to the south by Crossapol Bay, with extensive sandy beaches. The two bays are separated by the west dune system and flanked by rocky headlands.

Access

Coll is served several times a week by a car ferry operated by Caledonian MacBrayne from Oban to Arinagour (the ferry goes on to call at Tiree). The crossing can be excellent for seabirds, especially in spring and autumn.

On Coll take the B8070 southwest from Arinagour, and this road provides good opportunities to see moorland birds, including Red-throated Diver on the smaller lochans. The RSPB reserve is accessed by turning south (left) at Arileod, and then continuing for c.½ mile (forking right at the turning to the castle) to park just beyond the next cattle grid. This track continues to Crossapol Bay, and there is an information bothy at Totronald. The reserve is open all year, but vehicles must not be taken onto the machair and there is no access to the hay meadows.

Birds

With up to 30 calling Corncrakes, this is potentially a good area to find this elusive species. Present April–September, they generally cease calling in late July. But, although easy to hear (they call most frequently at night, 22.00–05.00; listen from the road between Uig and Roundhouse), sightings are hard to come by. Early in the season is best, when the vegetation is still short, but a great deal of persistence is usually required.

The machair has a high density of breeding waders, with Lapwing, Snipe, Dunlin and Redshank, and other species in this habitat include Shelduck and Wheatear. Other breeders on the reserve include Rock Dove, Raven and Twite, with Red-throated Diver, Greylag Goose, Teal and Arctic Skua in moorland areas. Hen Harrier, Peregrine, Merlin and Short-eared Owl may visit, and along the coast Fulmar, Shag, Eider and Common, Arctic and Little Terns nest. Gannet is often present offshore, and Manx Shearwater, Puffin, Razorbill and Guillemot breed on the Treshnish Isles to the southeast and are often present off Coll (look for shearwaters especially in the evening).

Winterers include numbers of Barnacle and Greenland White-fronted Geese, as well as 500–700 Greylag. Interestingly, the RSPB has a flock of c.40 feral Snow Goose that breed on Mull. Offshore, there are good numbers of divers (especially Great Northern, which may linger well into spring) and small numbers of sea duck, mainly Long-tailed Duck (sometimes c.100) but also a few Common Scoter and Scaup; Feall Bay is favoured by sea duck as well as divers.

Information
RSPB Warden, Charlie Self, Totronald, Coll, Argyllshire PA78 6TB. Tel: 01879 230301.
Caledonian MacBrayne Ltd, The Ferry Terminal, Gourock PA19 1QP. Tel: 01475
650100.

2 ORONSAY (Argyll)

Access and Birds
Lying just south of the Isle of Colonsay, Corncrakes cling on in Oronsay, with
three pairs in 1995. The RSPB has leased the entire 1,470-acre island in the hope
of increasing the population to around 10 pairs. There are no visiting arrangements.

3 ISLAY (Argyll)   OS Landranger 60

Adjacent to Jura and c.12 miles off the southwest coast of Scotland, Islay's major
draw is its wintering geese. Up to 70% of Greenland's breeding Barnacle Geese
and 25% of its White-fronted Geese winter here. A visitor to Islay is thus guaranteed not only a wide diversity of species, but also a superb spectacle. The RSPB
has a very extensive reserve at Loch Gruinart, covering over 4,000 acres.

Habitat
The southernmost of the Inner Hebrides, Islay is a large island (c.150,000 acres).
The varied habitats include deciduous plantations around houses and farms,
conifer plantations, extensive areas of scrub, moorland, cliff (including the spectacular Mull of Oa), dunes, machair, freshwater and sea lochs, rivers, streams,
marshes and arable land. The extensive areas of peat bog are important to the
Greenland White-fronts. Islay lacks high hills, but the Paps on neighbouring Jura
dominate the north horizon.

Access (see map)
Caledonian MacBrayne operates car and passenger ferries daily from
Kennacraig, 7 miles southwest of Tarbert on the Kintyre peninsula, to Port Ellen
and Port Askaig on Islay, and the two-hour voyage is good for divers and other
seabirds. There are daily services. Alternatively, British Airways Express operate
flights from Glasgow. The Islay Field Centre (located in the same building as the
youth hostel in Port Charlotte, and open March–October) acts as an information
centre for birdwatchers and other naturalists. For full details of accommodation
contact the tourist board. Wintering geese and raptors are widespread, and
exploration with the OS map is strongly recommended, but the following spots
are worth highlighting.

Gruinart Flats The south end of Loch Gruinart is an important area for geese,
especially Barnacle Goose, and is part of the RSPB reserve. The B8017 crosses the
flats and affords good views of the south of the reserve, while the minor road north
along the Ardnave Peninsula gives views of the west. Park at Aoradh Farm on the
B8017, where the RSPB visitor centre is open daily 10.00–17.00. A short way to the
north along the Ardnave road a path leads to a hide on a raised bank between two
flooded fields, which are good for wildfowl in winter and waders in summer (walk
from the visitor centre or park in the small car park opposite the hide). Lapwing,

Redshank, Snipe, Mallard, Teal and Shoveler breed in the fields, Garganey occurs in spring (and has bred, as has Gadwall) and Black-tailed Godwit also turns up on passage. In winter, the fields attract many Wigeon, Teal and Greenland White-fronts. Numbers of Barnacles roost on the Loch's saltings, and the tidal flats are also used by a variety of waders, best viewed from the road along the east shore. The whole area attracts raptors such as Hen Harrier (up to 12 roost in the area), Buzzard, Golden Eagle and Peregrine.

Ardnave Loch Good in winter for a variety of ducks. View from the end of the minor road along the Ardnave Peninsula. Leaving your car by the Loch, a short walk into the dunes should produce feeding Chough, as well as Snow Bunting and Twite in winter, especially where cattle are being fed.

Loch Gruinart, east shore Waders and wildfowl feeding in Loch Gruinart can be more easily seen from the east side where the minor road, which runs north from the B8017, follows the shore, than from the west side.

Sanaigmore Breeding seabirds can be seen here: drive to the end of the B8018 and walk west. Also, look for Great Northern Diver and Black Guillemot in the bay.

Loch Gorm Holds 10–12 pairs of Common Scoters, and the area supports wintering Greenland White-front and Whooper Swan. The Loch is circumnavigated at a distance by minor roads.

Saligo Bay Good for raptors, including Golden Eagle and Peregrine, over the massif to the north, and for passing seabirds. Park at Saligo Bridge.

The Rhinns The dunes at Machir Bay on the northwest coast often have feeding Chough and, together with the Ardnave Dunes, are one of the best places on the island to find the species. Peregrine can be often be seen around the cliffs at the south end of Machir Bay, and the cliffs also hold small numbers of breeding seabirds. The forestry plantations on the Rhinns have very small numbers of Black Grouse and are frequented by Short-eared Owl and Hen Harrier. Greenland White-fronts feed in the fields around the peninsula.

Frenchman's Rocks This, the most westerly point on the island, is the best seawatching station on Islay. Access is from the A847 at Portnahaven, taking the track west off the minor road, which runs north to Claddach, and then walking to Rubha na Faing. The first hour of daylight is best (the westerly aspect can result in terrible light in the evening).

Port Charlotte Often has Black Guillemot in winter, with regular Great Northern Diver just offshore and less frequent Purple Sandpiper.

Bruichladdich On the west shore of Loch Indaal, this is a spot for Greenland White-front, and the mudflats adjacent to the A847 at Traigh an Luig to the north are good for waders. There are several lay-bys constructed specifically for birdwatchers. Bruichladdich pier is a good year-round spot for Common Scoter, and also favoured by Black-throated Diver and Purple Sandpiper.

Loch Indaal holds all three divers, up to 50 Slavonian Grebes, Eider, Redbreasted Merganser, 1,000+ wintering Scaup, 50+ Common Scoters (present all year) and a variety of waders. Greenland White-fronted and Barnacle Geese are very regular in the fields behind Bruichladdich (and also behind Port Charlotte).

Islay

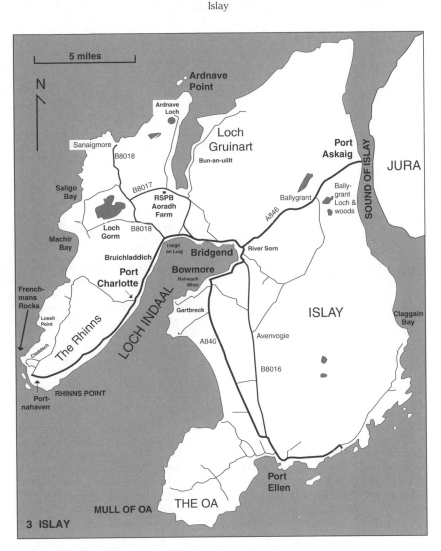

3 ISLAY

Bridgend There are waders on the flats at Bridgend (best an hour either side of high water), Pintail and Shoveler favour the river channel, and Barnacle Geese roost in Bridgend Bay; view from the A847 and A846 north and south of Bridgend, while a hide overlooks the bay, accessed from a small car park off the A847 at the end of the cattle mart fence, ½ mile north of Bridgend (this is the best place to watch thousands of Barnacle Geese arriving to roost). The bridge over the River Sorn is a good spot to look for Dipper.

Bowmore Situated on Loch Indaal, this attracts waders, sea duck, Wigeon and Whooper Swan, with divers and grebes offshore (see Bruichladdich). The Loch can also be viewed from the B847 between Bowmore and Bridgend, with the lay-by ½ mile north of Bowmore by the hydro-board generating station, being a particularly good vantage point. The rubbish tip southwest of Bowmore may hold white-winged gulls, and is a particularly good spot for Raven (up to 60 have occurred in autumn), while the coast to the southwest, from Ronnachmore to Gartbreck, is good for waders.

493

B8016 Crosses an extensive area of mosses good for Greenland White-fronted and Barnacle Geese, especially the north end, while Hen Harrier is regular in summer.

Port Ellen There may be divers, grebes and sea duck around the harbour mouth.

The Oa The south cliffs are good for Golden Eagle, Peregrine, Raven and Chough, with breeding seabirds in summer and occasional Snow Bunting along the clifftops in winter. They can be reached along a minor road southwest from Port Ellen.

Claggain Bay At the end of the road leading east from Port Ellen, the Bay is good for Great Northern and Red-throated Divers, with moulting Red-breasted Mergansers in late summer. Nearby woods are good for Siskin and Redpoll, and Twite are always present on the shore in winter.

Port Askaig Holds Black Guillemot, often year-round, and there are usually Arctic Skuas in the Sound (from their small breeding colonies on Jura).

Ballygrant Loch and Woods Accessible by turning south on a minor road in Ballygrant and parking by the entrance to the woods. The Loch has breeding Little Grebe, Tufted Duck and Mute Swan, the occasional Coot in winter, and is visited by Red-throated Diver. A track leads through the woods to Port Askaig, passing Loch Allan en route, where there is a small heronry. Woodland birds include Redstart, Blackcap, Wood Warbler, Spotted Flycatcher, Siskin and Redpoll.

Birds

In winter, Great Northern Diver is quite common offshore, and there are a few Red-throated and Black-throated Divers and some Slavonian Grebes. Wildfowl include Whooper Swan (especially on Loch Gorm, but most have moved further south by midwinter) and up to 35,000 Barnacle Geese. The latter usually peak in October–November, immediately following their arrival in Britain; numbers then fall slightly as they disperse. They favour the pasture around the head of the two sea lochs, and are joined by up to 13,000 Greenland White-fronts. These tend to be more scattered, occurring in smaller, but tamer, flocks on the best grass (a recent development, as they were formerly secretive, favouring rough, unimproved grassland); a good place to see them is the RSPB's Loch Gruinart Reserve, where special management is attracting substantial numbers. A small flock of Greylag frequents the Bridgend area. There may be one or two wild Snow Geese, as well as vagrant Canada Geese of one of the small subspecies, and occasional Pink-footed and Brent Geese. Up to 1,200 Scaup frequent the harbour at Bowmore and sometimes move to Bruichladdich or Port Charlotte. They are joined by Slavonian Grebe, Goldeneye, Eider, Red-breasted Merganser and a few Common Scoters. There are large numbers of Wigeon and Teal, and dabbling duck concentrate on the shores of inner Loch Indaal, which also attracts small numbers of waders. Purple Sandpiper and Turnstone occur on rockier sections of coastline. Glaucous and Iceland Gulls appear in winter and, like Black Guillemot, can be found in the harbours, while Brambling and Snow Bunting may occur in reasonable numbers, depending on the year.

Red-throated Diver is resident and frequents small lochs as well as the sea and sea lochs. Breeding seabirds include Fulmar, Cormorant, Shag, Kittiwake, Common, Arctic and Little Terns, Razorbill, Guillemot and Black Guillemot.

These are joined on the cliffs by Rock Dove, and non-breeding Arctic Skuas may be present offshore. Shelduck, Teal, Wigeon, Eider and Red-breasted Merganser are widespread, but Shoveler and Common Scoter are distinctly uncommon, with only a handful of pairs, and a Whooper Swan occasionally summers. Breeding waders include Oystercatcher, Ringed and Golden Plovers, Curlew, Snipe, Redshank, Common Sandpiper and a few Dunlin. A few pairs of Golden Eagle are resident, as well as Buzzard, Hen Harrier, Peregrine, Merlin, and Barn and Short-eared Owls, and these may be joined in winter by wandering White-tailed Eagles from the re-introduction programme on Rhum. Small numbers of Red Grouse breed on the moors, and a very few Black Grouse persist in birch scrub and tussocky grass at the edge of plantations. Conifers also hold Siskin and Redpoll. In summer, Tree Pipit, Whinchat and Wood Warbler are present, and a few pairs of Corncrake return (three calling birds at the RSPB's Loch Gruinart reserve in 1999 and a minimum of seven pairs on the island). Rock Pipit, Twite and Stonechat are all widespread residents. There are up to 50 pairs of Chough (a decline from almost 100 pairs in 1986, presumably due to changes in farming practices) and Raven is widespread.

On passage Manx Shearwater and Arctic Skua are regular off Frenchman's Rocks, and Sooty Shearwater and Great Skua are reasonably frequent. Onshore gales may also produce sightings of Storm and Leach's Petrels. A variety of waders also passes through, with species such as Greenshank and Black-tailed Godwit joining the regular wintering and breeding species.

Information

RSPB Warden: Yvonne Brown, Bushmills Cottages, Gruinart, Bridgend, Isle of Islay PA44 7PS. Tel: 01496 850505. E-mail: yvonne.brown@rspb.org.uk

Islay Field Centre, Port Charlotte, Isle of Islay PA48 7TX. Tel: 01496 850288.

Tourist Information Centre, Morrison Court, Bowmore, Isle of Islay. Tel: 01496 810254.

Caledonian MacBrayne Ltd, The Ferry Terminal, Gourock PA19 1QP. Tel: 01475 650100.

British Airways Express. Tel: 01345 222111.

4 WEST LOCH TARBERT (Argyll)   OS Landranger 62

Access and Birds

West Loch Tarbert, a long, sheltered sea loch, has all three divers in winter, as well as Slavonian Grebe, Glaucous and sometimes Iceland Gulls. These can be seen around the harbour and from the ferry en route for Islay.

5 MULL OF GALLOWAY (Dumfries & Galloway)   OS Landranger 82

Lying at the tip of the Rinns Peninsula, this is the southernmost point in Scotland, and the cliffs hold large numbers of breeding seabirds, as well as affording good views south over the Solway Firth and Irish Sea to the Isle of Man. The best time to visit is April–July.

Habitat

The granite cliffs rise to a maximum of c.260 feet.

Access

Take the A716 south from Stranraer to Drummore, then the B7041 south to Damnaglaur and finally a minor road south to the lighthouse at the point. The reserve is open at all times. There are several shore walks along the cliffs, and good views of the colonies can be obtained near the lighthouse. Guided walks are organised May–August. An information point is usually open April to September, 10.30–17.00 Tuesdays–Saturdays (phone to confirm times).

Birds

Breeders on the cliffs include Fulmar, Cormorant, Shag, Kittiwake, Guillemot, Razorbill and small numbers of Black Guillemots. A few Puffins summer, but no longer breed. Over 2,000 pairs of Gannets breed on Scare Rocks, a small rocky outcrop 7 miles to the east (also an RSPB reserve) and Gannet is often visible at sea; Manx Shearwaters are also frequently seen offshore, especially in September. Stonechat, Twite and Corn Bunting are resident on the head. In spring and autumn, migrant passerines may also occur on the headland.

Information

RSPB Warden: Paul Collin, Gairland, Old Edinburgh Road, Minnigaff, Newton Stewart, Wigtownshire DG8 6PL. Tel: 01671 402861.

6 LOCH RYAN AND STRANRAER
(Dumfries & Galloway)   OS Landranger 76 and 82

Loch Ryan is a large, sheltered sea loch with small numbers of divers, grebes (notably Black-necked Grebe) and sea duck. The best time to visit is winter. Nearby, Portpatrick often holds Black Guillemot and Corsewall Point is a good seawatching station, best in autumn.

Habitat

The Loch has a rather narrow shoreline, with only two significant areas of mud, around the Wig and on the south shore.

Access

Loch Ryan The A77 follows the east and south shores as far as Stranraer, while the A718 hugs the west shore north to the Wig. Most of the diving duck and Wigeon occur on the south shore, but Eider are scattered over several areas. Most birds can be seen by stopping at regular intervals and scanning the shore and Loch.

Portpatrick (OS Landranger 82) Portpatrick, southwest of Stranraer on the A77, is a good spot for Black Guillemot. The area around the harbour is best—the birds nest in the harbour walls. Check the gulls here as well.

Corsewall Point Leave Stranraer north on the A718 to Kirkcolm and follow signs for Corsewall/Barhills, bearing right on a single-track road on reaching the lighthouse. It is possible to seawatch from a car, but views are better from the rocks.

Birds

Winter brings small numbers of Slavonian and Black-necked Grebes and all three divers to Loch Ryan, although Red-throated is the most numerous. Red-necked Grebe is occasional. Sea duck include several hundred Eider, with smaller numbers of Common Scoter, Scaup, Goldeneye and Red-breasted Merganser, and sometimes Long-tailed Duck. There have been several King Eiders over the years (Cairnryan on the east shore has been favoured by this species). Wigeon can peak at around 2,000. A handful of Black Guillemot winter, together with small numbers of waders. Glaucous Gull is an occasional visitor, and parties of Twite may be found, especially on the Wig. Black Guillemot and white-winged gulls can also be sought at Portpatrick.

A constant stream of Gannets pass Corsewall Point in summer and autumn, as well as Cormorant, Shag and auks. Mid-August–late October brings Manx Shearwater, Leach's and Storm Petrels, Kittiwake, skuas and occasionally Sabine's Gull, especially in strong westerly winds.

7 WEST FREUGH AIRFIELD
(Dumfries & Galloway)   OS Landranger 82

Access and Birds
Up to 30 Hen Harriers roost here in late October, numbers falling to c.12 in winter. Sparrowhawk, Peregrine, Merlin and Short-eared Owl can also be seen. Leave Stranraer south on the A77 and turn southeast onto the A716 and then take the B7077 towards Glenluce. Finally, after 4 miles, turn southwest onto the B7084. The harriers can be seen on the north side of the road, 1 mile south of the junction with the A757. You should not attempt photography in this sensitive MOD area. About 500 Greenland White-fronts occur around West Freugh, but are difficult to pinpoint. Try the fields north of the A757, east of Lochans. There are also up to 3,000 Greylag, as well as several feral Snow Geese, based on Loch Inch, Castle Kennedy.

8 GLEN TROOL (Dumfries & Galloway)   OS Landranger 77

Part of Galloway Forest Park, this attractive valley is worthy of exploration.

Habitat
Conifer plantations with areas of relict oak and birch woodland around Loch Trool.

Access
Leave Newton Stewart northwest on the A714 Girvan road and turn east after c.9 miles on a minor road at Bargrennan, bearing right at Glen Trool village to the Glen. There are three way-marked trails, and a 4½-mile trail circles Loch Trool (leaflet from the FC).

Birds
Hen Harrier, Peregrine and occasionally Golden Eagle and Black Grouse can be seen in winter from the road, while in summer the deciduous woods around Loch Trool at Buchan, Glenhead and Caldons hold Tree Pipit, Redstart, Wood Warbler, and Pied Flycatcher, with Crossbill and Siskin in the conifers.

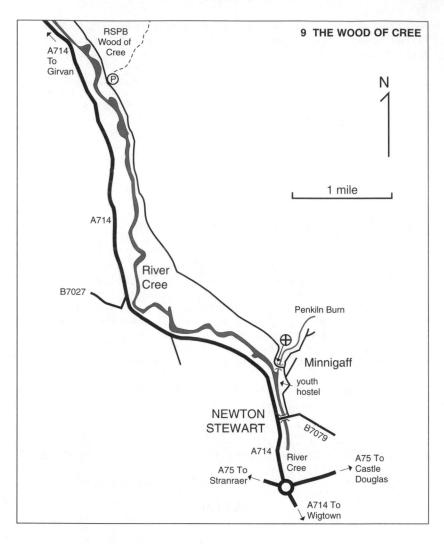

9 THE WOOD OF CREE (Dumfries & Galloway)   OS Landranger 77

This large deciduous woodland on the east slopes of the Cree Valley, part of the largest remaining stand of ancient woodland in south Scotland, is an RSPB reserve and holds a variety of typical woodland birds.

Habitat
The wood largely comprises oak, birch and hazel, while alongside the river is an area of meadows.

Access
The reserve lies 4 miles northwest of Newton Stewart. Just north of the town centre turn east off the A714 on the B7079. The road crosses the River Cree and, immediately beyond, turn left (north) on the minor road to Minnigaff. Follow this

past the youth hostel and then bear left to cross Penkiln Burn, bearing left again beyond the church. Follow the minor road, which runs parallel to, and east of, the A714 and River Cree, for c.4 miles to the reserve car park, from which signed trails lead into the woods.

Birds
Residents include Buzzard, Sparrowhawk, Woodcock and Great Spotted Woodpecker, with Willow Tit in the riverside scrub and Barn Owl in surrounding open areas. In May–June look also for Tree Pipit, Redstart, Garden and Wood Warblers, and Pied and Spotted Flycatchers, with Goosander, Common Sandpiper, Dipper, and Grey Wagtail on streams and river, Teal, Oystercatcher, Snipe and Water Rail in riverside meadows, Grasshopper Warbler in scrub and Curlew and Whinchat at the woodland/moorland interface.

Information
RSPB Warden: Paul Collin, Gairland, Old Edinburgh Road, Minnigaff, Newton Stewart, Wigtownshire DG8 6PL. Tel: 01671 402861.

10 LOCH KEN (Dumfries & Galloway)   OS Landranger 77, 83 and 84

To the northwest of Castle Douglas, Loch Ken is a long, shallow loch that attracts Greenland White-fronted and Greylag Geese. To the west, the NTS has a large wildfowl refuge near Threave Castle. For wintering wildfowl, October–March is the peak period, and for breeding birds May–June.

Habitat
The River Dee was dammed during a hydro-electric scheme in 1935 to form Loch Ken, a shallow lake surrounded by areas of meadows and freshwater marsh, the latter especially at the head of the loch (technically, only the north sector is known as Loch Ken, the stretch below the viaduct being the River Dee). If water levels fall in summer, expanses of mud are exposed, especially along the southwest shore. The surrounding area comprises farmland, open hillsides and woodland.

Access (see maps)
Carlingwark Loch A 105-acre pool visible from the B736 (old A75) immediately south of Castle Douglas; it has diving ducks, notably Goldeneye and Goosander.

Castle Douglas to Bridge of Dee Greylag and a few Pink-footed Geese are regular, but although Bean Geese were formerly seen around Threave and south of Castle Douglas (anywhere between Gelston and Netherhall), they are now rare, erratic and unpredictable. Pink-feet can usually be seen in the pastures west of the B736, 1–2 miles south of Castle Douglas. The geese are highly mobile and you must be prepared to search the area.

Threave Wildfowl Refuge The Threave Estate lies southwest of Castle Douglas and is open all year (no charge). Access is at Kelton Mains Farm, off the A75 1 mile west of Castle Douglas. There is a map at the car park showing the network of trails and the location of the four hides; the Blackpark Marsh hide gives views over farmland for geese, the Lamb Island hide overlooks the river and fields, and the Stepping Stones and Castle hides on the riverbank overlook more farmland and, again, the river. Greylag and Pink-footed Geese (and occasionally a few

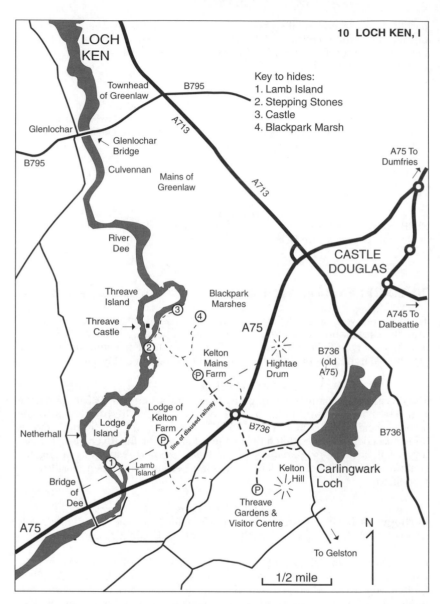

10 LOCH KEN, I

Key to hides:
1. Lamb Island
2. Stepping Stones
3. Castle
4. Blackpark Marsh

Greenland White-fronts), and Whooper Swan favour the farmland, while ducks, including Goosander, Red-breasted Merganser and Shoveler, use the river, which is also frequented by Kingfisher, and Hen Harrier is occasionally seen. There is a visitor centre at Threave Gardens (closed in winter), from which information is available and where a way-marked estate walk also accesses the disused railway line and hides.

West side of Loch Ken The south section of the Loch is visible by leaving the A713 west at Townhead of Greenlaw. Cross the river on the B795 over Glenlochar Bridge, and immediately turn right. This unclassified road gives good views of

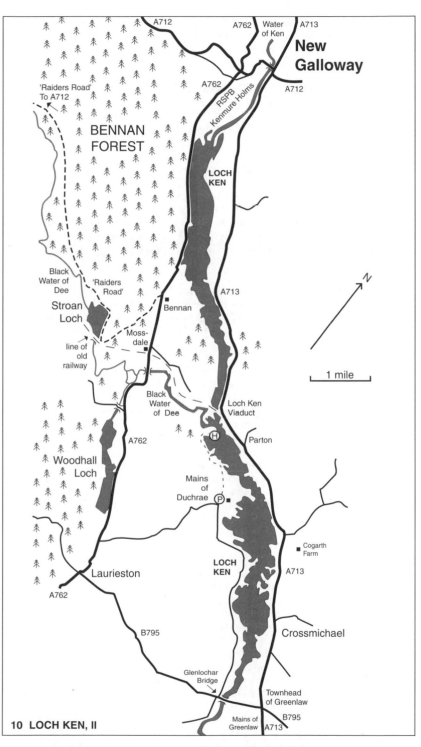

10 LOCH KEN, II

the Loch as far as Mains of Duchrae, and this is the best area for geese. Greenland White-fronts favour the rough grazing immediately south of Mains of Duchrae. Be careful not to block the road with your car. Whooper Swan favours the area south of Glenlochar.

East shore of Loch Ken The A713 between New Galloway and Crossmichael gives views of the entire east shore of the loch. Greenland White-fronts favour the permanent pasture southwest of Cogarth Farm. A large herd of Whooper Swans is sometimes found west of the A713 and south of the B795 at Culvennan/Mains of Greenlaw.

RSPB Ken–Dee Marshes This RSPB reserve comprises five separate parcels of land, the largest consisting of water meadows and freshwater marshes at Kenmure Holms near New Galloway and between Black Water of Dee and Mains of Duchrae. There is access only to the latter. A car park is sited off the minor road at Mains of Duchrae, from where it is possible to walk to the hide on the Loch shore (a 3-mile return trip through farmland, scrub, woodland and marshes). Look for Hen Harrier and Barn Owl in winter and Pied Flycatcher in summer, while Willow Tit is resident.

Bennan Forest The conifer woods west of Loch Ken are worth exploring. Following the disused railway line that runs west from Mossdale, there is a roost of Hen Harrier around Stroan Loch (best in early winter, with few after January), and it is also good for Crossbill, Siskin, Redpoll and, in summer, Nightjar. Continuing along the railway, you reach Loch Skerrow. Black Grouse can be seen here but there is little else en route to compensate for the 4-mile walk from the main road. The 'Raiders Road' forest drive also passes Stroan Loch. This leaves the A762 at Bennan, 1 mile north of Mossdale, and passes through Cairn Edward Forest to emerge on the A712 at Clatteringshaws Loch. There are three forest walks. The road is open late May–October (toll). A thorough search of the area around Clatteringshaws Loch may also produce Black Grouse.

Birds

Winter brings up to 120 Whooper Swans and 750–1,000 Greylag, both favouring the Threave Estate, where they are joined by Pink-footed Geese in the New Year. Around 300 Greenland White-fronts occur around Loch Ken, but Bean Goose, once regular in some numbers at Threave, now occurs only very irregularly in hard weather in the New Year. Ducks include Goldeneye, Goosander, Pintail (around Mains of Duchrae) and Shoveler (early winter only). Hen Harrier, Buzzard, Sparrowhawk, Merlin, Peregrine and Barn Owl are regular, with Great Grey Shrike occasional.

In summer, the marshes, loch and river hold breeding Great Crested Grebe, Teal, Shoveler, Oystercatcher, Redshank, Curlew, a handful of Common Terns, and Sedge and a few Grasshopper Warblers. Summer also brings Tree Pipit, Redstart, Wood Warbler and a few Pied Flycatchers.

On passage, almost any species of wader can occur, and Osprey is reasonably regular, as are terns.

Residents include Goosander, Peregrine, Buzzard and Barn Owl, with Willow Tit in areas of damp scrub, Great Spotted Woodpecker and a very few Green Woodpeckers in mature deciduous woodland, and Siskin and Crossbill around conifer plantations. Black Grouse also favours the conifers, but has fallen markedly in numbers and is hard to find.

Information

RSPB Warden: Paul Collin, Gairland, Old Edinburgh Road, Minnigaff, Newton Stewart, Wigtownshire DG8 6PL. Tel: 01671 402861.

NTS Dumfries & Galloway Ranger Service, Ranger Office, Threave Garden & Estate, Castle Douglas, Dumfries & Galloway DG7 1RX. Tel: 01556 502575.

11 AUCHENREOCH AND MILTON LOCHS
(Dumfries & Galloway)   OS Landranger 84

Eight miles northeast of Castle Douglas, these two lochs are particularly attractive to diving duck, and are best visited in winter.

Access
Auchenreoch Loch Lies alongside the A75 immediately west of Crocketford and is viewable from the road.

Milton Loch Leave the A75 just west of Crocketford on the minor road south to Milton. The Loch is north of the road, and again is viewable from the roadside or better, by pulling into a small turning area among the trees and then walking to the shore.

Birds
Wintering wildfowl include Goosander, Goldeneye and Pochard. Smew is fairly regular from December, and the area has also attracted rarities such as Lesser Scaup and Ring-necked Duck.

12 SOUTHERNESS POINT AND CAERLAVEROCK
(Dumfries & Galloway)   OS Landranger 84 and 85

On the north shore of the Solway Firth, this area holds thousands of wintering Barnacle and Pink-footed Geese. Caerlaverock NNR covers 13,593 acres of saltmarsh and mudflats along 6 miles of coast between the mouths of the River Nith and Lochar Water. Eastpark WWT Refuge covers 1,495 acres, with excellent viewing facilities. The whole area provides superb birdwatching in winter, especially for those who are deprived of the spectacle of large numbers of geese nearer home.

Habitat
There are five main habitats for birds in the area. The sea, extensive mudflats, saltmarsh or merse (especially at Caerlaverock), rocky coastline (from Carsethorn to Southerness), and finally farmland, both arable and pasture.

Access (see map)

Kirkconnell Merse and the north section of Caerlaverock NNR The B725 from Dumfries to Caerlaverock Castle gives views, firstly of Kirkconnell Merse, a good area for Whooper Swan, and secondly of the mudflats and merse in the north of the NNR. Pink-footed Geese are often visible from the road near the Castle.

Eastpark WWT Refuge Take the signed turning from the B725 1 mile south of Bankend to the WWT Refuge. There are 20 hides, a heated observatory and three observation towers. The pond in front of the observatory holds up to 17 species of wildfowl in winter. Open daily 10.00–17.00 (except Christmas Day), there is an admission charge for non-members of the WWT and visitors should report to reception on arrival.

Islesteps The fields around Islesteps, beside the A710 just south of Dumfries, are good for Whooper Swan.

Drummains Reedbed This small Scottish Wildlife Trust reserve overlooks the west shore of the Nith estuary, giving views of a typical range of wildfowl and waders. Park just east of the A710 at Drum-Mains and follow the footpath east for 300 yards to the hide.

Carsethorn On the A710 12 miles south of Dumfries, take the turning at Kirkbean to Carsethorn and drive to the waterfront. Check the sea and rocky coastline, especially for Scaup, which sometimes occurs in significant numbers.

Southerness Point Leave the A710 south on an unclassified road 1 mile southwest of Kirkbean and park at the end of the road. Divers (mainly Red-throated), Scaup, scoter, auks and the occasional skua occur off the point, with Purple Sandpiper and Turnstone on the rocks. There is a wader roost, often holding Grey Plover and Greenshank (on passage and in winter), as well as many Bar-tailed Godwits, and the area is generally very good for waders. It is worth exploring the mudflats and sandbanks east and west of the point, and the fields here sometimes hold Pink-footed and Barnacle Geese, especially in late winter.

Birds

Red-throated and sometimes Black-throated Divers winter offshore, together with Cormorant and Shag. Up to 350 Whooper Swans use the area in late September–April, and are joined by smaller numbers of Bewick's in late October. Both Pink-footed and Barnacle Geese arrive in late September–early October and depart in mid-April. Barnacles can peak at 13,700, this being the entire Svalbard breeding population (note that in late winter they often move to Rockcliffe Marsh in Cumbria, and can then be seen from minor roads west of Rockcliffe Cross). Pink-feet peak late in the season; numbers depend on the severity of the weather in the rest of Scotland—they reached 35,000 during the severe winter of 1984, but generally peak at around 5,000. Barnacles favour the merse, while the Pink-feet and several hundred Greylag use the surrounding farmland. In many years there are one or more Snow Geese, though these are likely to be feral birds, perhaps those that breed near Stranraer. Confusingly, there are also often several albino Barnacle Geese. In 1991–1994 a Red-breasted Goose also wintered at Caerlaverock. Other wildfowl include large numbers of Wigeon, Teal, Pintail (up to 2,500 in autumn—Carse Bay is especially good), and small numbers of Shoveler and Gadwall. Up to 1,000 Scaup (exceptionally 4,500) winter in the Inner Solway between the River Nith and Blackshaw Bank, and are best seen off Carsethorn and at Southerness Point (in late winter Powfoot, south off the B724, 3 miles west of Annan, may be a better bet); they are joined by smaller numbers of Red-breasted Mergansers. The sea formerly held thousands of Common Scoter at Southerness, but only a handful is seen now. Raptors in winter include Hen Harrier, Sparrowhawk, Peregrine, Merlin and Short-eared Owl. Waders are plentiful on the mudflats, especially Oystercatcher and Bar-tailed Godwit, and there are thousands of Golden Plover, Curlew and Lapwing in the fields. Purple Sandpiper and Turnstone occur on rocky coasts, especially at Southerness Point.

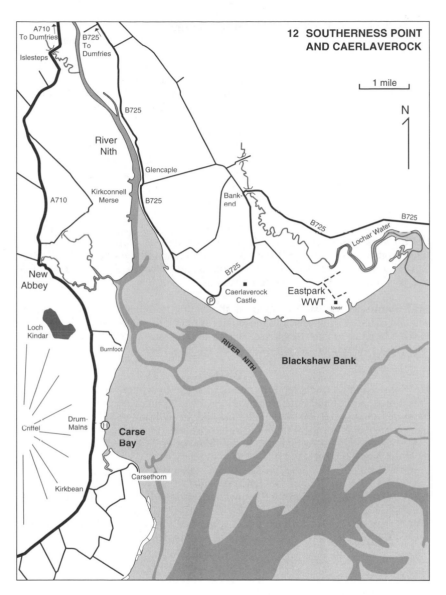

Passage brings a greater variety of waders. Large numbers of Sanderlings pass through in May, and in autumn they may be joined by Little Stint, Curlew Sandpiper, Black-tailed Godwit, Whimbrel and Spotted Redshank. Breeders include Shelduck, sometimes Pintail or Wigeon, Lapwing, Redshank and Oystercatcher, with Common Tern and gulls on the saltmarsh.

Information

SNH Warden: Wally Wright, SNH Reserve Office, Hollands Farm Road, Caerlaverock, Dumfries DG1 4RS. Tel: 01387 770275.

WWT Centre Manager: John Doherty, WWT, Eastpark Farm, Caerlaverock, Dumfries DG1 4RS. Tel: 01387 770200.

13 MERSEHEAD AND SOUTHWICK COAST

(Dumfries & Galloway)

This area lies west of Southerness Point, forming a narrow strip between the A710 and Mersehead Sands, and sharing a large population of geese and ducks with the better known Caerlaverock. Part of the area forms the RSPB Mersehead Reserve and the Southwick Coast Scottish Wildlife Trust (SWT) reserve.

Habitat

The coast is bordered in succession by inter-tidal mudflats, merse (saltmarsh), wet grassland and arable farmland, while just inland at the Southwick Coast reserve cliffs rise to c.130 feet and support Heughwood, an intriguing stand of ancient woodland. Notable features include a rock stack, Lot's Wife, and a natural arch, the Needle's Eye, lying isolated in the marsh.

Access

RSPB Mersehead Approximately 18 miles south of Dumfries, just east of Caulkerbush, turn off the A710 at the first turning south after Southwick Home Farm. There are two trails, covering 1½ miles and 3½ miles, a hide and an information centre. The reserve is open at all times.

SWT Southwick Coast Turn south off the A710 c.1½ miles west of the junction with the B793 at Caulkerbush to the small car park. From here follow the track to the Needle's Eye to view the merse. Slightly to the east (beyond Boneland Burn), the fields at Mersehead are attractive to Barnacle Goose.

Birds

The Solway Firth attracts large numbers of geese in winter, including Greylag, Pink-footed and, notably, Barnacle Geese, which may commute here from Caerlaverock; up to 9,500 of the latter may be present on the RSPB reserve. Also present are large numbers of wildfowl and waders, including up to 4,000 Teal, 2,000 Wigeon and 1,000 Pintail. See Southerness Point and Caerlaverock for a more detailed account (p.503).

Information

RSPB Mersehead: Eric Nielson, Southwick, Mersehead, Dumfries DG2 8AH. Tel: 01387 780298.

SWT, Cramond House, Kirk Cramond, Cramond Glebe Road, Edinburgh EH4 6NS. Tel: 0131 312 7765. E-mail: enquiries@swt.org.uk

14 BARONS HAUGH (Clyde)

Situated in the Clyde Valley, 1 mile south of Motherwell, this RSPB reserve attracts a variety of waders and wildfowl and is worth visiting in autumn and, more especially, in winter.

Habitat

The reserve is centred on an area of wet meadows ('haugh', with some permanently flooded areas as well as parts prone to winter flooding), alongside the River Clyde. Other habitats include woodland, parkland and scrub. A notable feature is the upwelling of tepid water around Marsh hide, keeping the area open even in freezing conditions in winter, resulting in concentrations of waterbirds in such conditions.

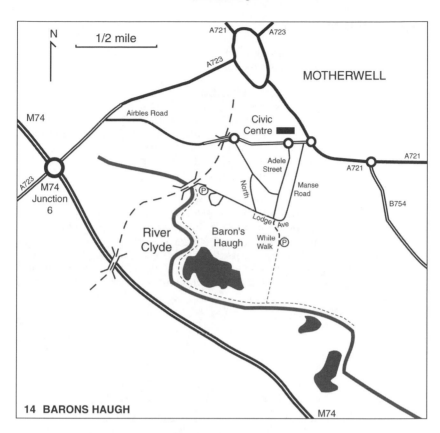

14 BARONS HAUGH

Access (see map)

From the centre of Motherwell (access from the M74, junction 6, or the M8, junction 6) take Adele Street, opposite the Civic Centre, south for ½ mile to North Lodge Avenue. Continue straight ahead along White Walk to the reserve entrance. Alternatively, turn right (west) along North Lodge Avenue and the west entrance is reached after c.½ mile. The reserve is open at all times, and there are two trails (½ mile and 2 miles) and four hides.

Birds

Residents include Little Grebe, Grey Heron, Teal, Shoveler, Gadwall, Ruddy Duck, Water Rail, Redshank, Kingfisher and Grey Wagtail. Willow Tit also occurs and, at the northernmost limits of its range here, is something of a speciality.

Breeding summer visitors include Common Sandpiper, Sand Martin, Whinchat, and Grasshopper, Sedge and Garden Warblers.

On autumn passage an excellent variety of waders can occur, with Ruff, Black-tailed Godwit, Spotted Redshank and Green Sandpiper possible. There is a late-summer concentration of up to 1,000 Lapwing.

Wintering wildfowl include up to 50 Whooper Swans, as well as numbers of Wigeon, Teal, Shoveler, Pochard and Goldeneye.

Information

RSPB Nature Centre, Largs Road, Lochwinnoch, Strathclyde PA12 4JF. Tel: 01505 842663. E-mail: lochwinnoch@rspb.org.uk

15 LOCHWINNOCH (Clyde)   OS Landranger 63

Lying 18 miles southwest of Glasgow, the best times to visit are autumn–winter for wildfowl and spring–early summer for breeding species.

Habitat

The reserve comprises two sections, Aird Meadow to the north and Barr Loch to the south, separated by the A760. Aird Meadow has some lily-covered ponds surrounded by sedge beds as well as wet meadows, areas of willow scrub and some small deciduous woodlands. Barr Loch was drained for a time to form farmland but the drainage system fell into disrepair in the 1950s and the area re-flooded to form firstly a marsh and now a large shallow loch.

Access (see map)

Turn west off the A737 towards Lochwinnoch on the A760. After ½ mile, having crossed the railway bridge, the reserve entrance is on the north (right). (Lochwinnoch station is 200 yards from the reserve entrance.) The reserve centre is open daily (except the Christmas and New Year Bank Holidays), 10.00–17.00, and has an observation tower affording views of Aird Meadows and the surrounding farmland. The nature trails and four hides are open at all times.

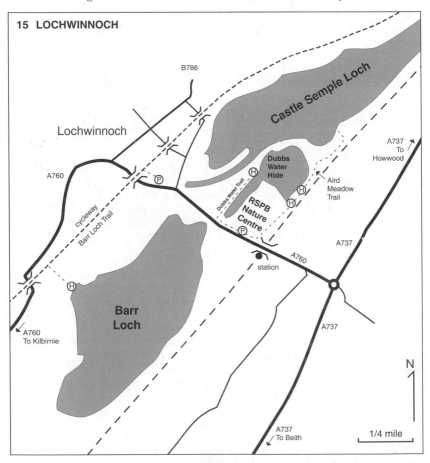

Birds

Great Crested Grebe, Teal, Pochard, Sparrowhawk, Water Rail, Black-headed Gull, Dipper (on the River Calder) and Redpoll are resident, and Cormorant, Grey Heron and Raven frequently visit. Buzzard occasionally appears throughout the year.

Wintering wildfowl include up to 50 Whooper Swan, 700 Greylag Geese, Wigeon, c.90 Goosander, Goldeneye and a handful of Pintail and Smew. Raptors may include Hen Harrier and Peregrine. Numbers of gulls roost on Barr Loch, and sometimes include Glaucous or Iceland. Other winter visitors include Jack Snipe, Kingfisher and sometimes Brambling.

Breeding summer visitors include Common Sandpiper, large numbers of Sedge Warblers, Grasshopper and Garden Warblers and Spotted Flycatcher.

On passage Slavonian Grebe may occur, as well as White-fronted and Pink-footed Geese, Garganey, Osprey, Marsh Harrier, Little Gull and Common Tern. From early August into autumn there is a large roost of Swallows and Starlings.

Information

RSPB Nature Reserve, Largs Road, Lochwinnoch, Strathclyde PA12 4JF. Tel: 01505 842663. E-mail: lochwinnoch@rspb.org.uk

16 MACHRIHANISH SEABIRD OBSERVATORY
(Argyll) OS Landranger 68

Situated at Uisaed Point, on the west coast of the Kintyre Peninsula, and overlooking Machrihanish Bay, this site has gained prominence in recent years as the premier seawatching site on the west coast of Scotland. It is most productive in September–October.

Habitat

The rocky coastline is bordered by areas of rough grazing, giving way to upland areas.

Access

The Observatory is accessed from the B843 just west of Machrihanish village, taking the track west off the road. There is parking for three vehicles only. The seawatching hide is open daily from dawn, May–October.

Birds

In autumn, during appropriate weather conditions, usually strong westerlies combined with poor visibility, the regular Gannet and Great and Arctic Skuas may be joined by Manx, Sooty and sometimes Balearic Shearwaters, Sabine's Gull or Long-tailed and Pomarine Skuas. Storm Petrel is regular, especially on days with poor visibility, while Leach's Petrel usually occurs after a deep depression has passed culminating in a severe northwest gale. From July to September, there is also a strong early-morning passage of waders. Golden Eagle and Twite are resident in the hinterland.

Information

Eddie Maguire, 25b Albyn Avenue, Campbeltown, Argyll PA28 6LX. Tel: 01586 554823 (mobile 07979 395269).

17 AVON PLATEAU AND FANNYSIDE PLATEAU
(Forth and Clyde)   OS Landranger 65

A relatively large flock of Bean Geese winters in this corner of central Scotland between Glasgow and Edinburgh.

Access
The Bean Geese tend to be very elusive and sightings cannot be guaranteed. Do not leave the roads or enter fields and moorland ('muirs'). The geese may roost on Fannyside Lochs (south of Cumbernauld), often on the smaller, east loch (even when it is almost completely frozen over). Park at the lay-by near the boating club. They arrive to roost very late and views are limited to calling silhouettes and a splash. Otherwise, their habits are in some ways unusual (often loafing on heather for hours at a time—a habitat in which they are almost invisible).

Birds
The Bean Geese usually arrive in mid-September, sometimes as early as 3 September. Up to 140 may winter, and the flock originates in central Sweden. Otherwise, the area holds very few birds indeed.

18 ST ABB'S HEAD (Borders)   OS Landranger 67

Twelve miles north of Berwick-upon-Tweed, St Abb's Head has 60,000 breeding seabirds, is a fine seawatching station, and, during passage periods, numbers of migrants are recorded. The best time for breeding seabirds is May to mid-July, and for migrants April–early June and mid-August–October. The coast between St Abbs village and Pettico Wick is a NNR, owned by the NTS and managed in cooperation with the Scottish Wildlife Trust.

Habitat
The cliffs rise to 300 feet, and immediately behind the Head is a man-made freshwater pool, Mire Loch, surrounded by dense gorse bushes and birch trees that are attractive to migrants. Otherwise the hinterland is largely pasture.

Access (see map)
Leave the A1 on the A1107 at Burnmouth (or, approaching from the north, at Cockburnspath), and from Coldingham take the B6438 to St Abb's Head NR. Park on the right at Northfield Farm, where there is a visitor centre (open daily 10.00–17.00, April–October), and from here take the footpath east for 300 yards to the track to the lighthouse and Head. This skirts the cliff and has seabirds en route, and it is possible to return via inland paths to complete a 3-mile circuit. There is a very small car park (fee) at the Head. Seawatch from Black Gable (the lowest point on the cliffs between the lighthouse and Kirk Hill), and during passage periods explore the cover around the loch and at Coldingham Bay.

Birds
The 60,000 breeding seabirds include Fulmar, Shag, Kittiwake, Herring Gull, Guillemot, Razorbill and a very few Puffins. Other breeders are Rock Pipit, Wheatear, Lesser Whitethroat and Raven, while Turnstone and Purple Sandpiper haunt the rocks for much of the year. Offshore there are always Gannet and Fulmar, but seawatching is most productive in autumn, when Manx and some-

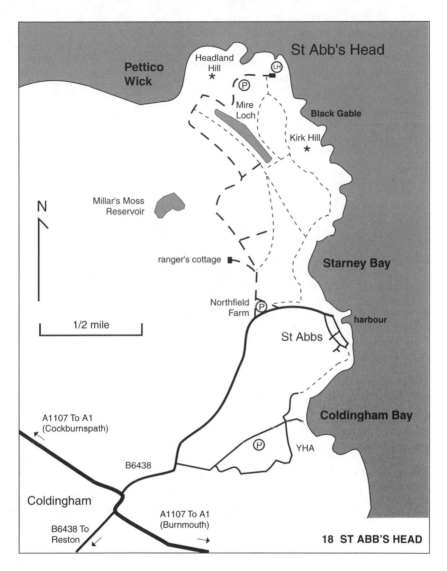

St Abb's Head

Pettico Wick

Headland Hill *

Mire Loch

Black Gable

Kirk Hill *

Millar's Moss Reservoir

N

ranger's cottage

Starney Bay

1/2 mile

Northfield Farm

harbour

St Abbs

Coldingham Bay

A1107 To A1 (Cockburnspath)

B6438

YHA

Coldingham

A1107 To A1 (Burnmouth)

B6438 To Reston

18 ST ABB'S HEAD

times Sooty Shearwaters, Arctic and a few Great Skuas, Little Gull and Black Tern are regular, and there are occasionally Mediterranean Shearwater and Pomarine or Long-tailed Skuas; strong winds between north and east are most productive. In late autumn and winter Little Auk occasionally occurs, but Red-throated Diver is regular, with the occasional Great Northern and Black-throated and small numbers of Common Scoter and Eider, the last especially at Starney Bay and Pettico Wick. In winter Goldeneye and Wigeon occur on the loch (and dabbling duck also on nearby Millar's Moss Reservoir) and Sparrowhawk, Peregrine and Merlin hunt the area.

As well as the commoner chats, flycatchers and warblers, scarce migrants are recorded annually on passage. Any wind from the east is good, but southeast is best, especially if coupled with rain or drizzle. Wryneck, Black Redstart, Bluethroat and Red-backed Shrike are annual in spring, and Wryneck, Barred and

Yellow-browed Warblers, Firecrest, Red-breasted Flycatcher and Red-backed Shrike equally frequent in autumn.

Information

Warden: Kevin Rideout, Ranger's Cottage, Northfield, St Abbs, Eyemouth, Berwickshire TD14 5QF. Tel: 01890 771443. E-mail: krideout@nts.org.uk

19 BARNS NESS (Lothian)   OS Landranger 67

This migration watchpoint at the southern entrance to the Firth of Forth has, over the years, produced a number of interesting birds.

Habitat and Access (see map)

Turn north off the A1 just east of Dunbar on the minor road to Oxwell Mains and, after ½ mile, turn right at the T-junction to East Barns. From here a minor road

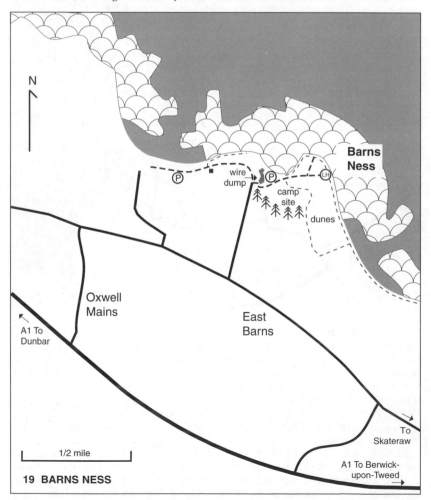

Slavonian Grebe

This beautiful grebe is restricted to the Scottish Highlands as a breeding bird, where around 40 pairs occupy various well-vegetated inland lochs. In winter it becomes much less attractively plumaged but a lot more widespread, making regular appearances on coastal lakes and sheltered offshore areas throughout Britain. It may also winter on inland lakes, although less frequently than the similar Black-necked Grebe.

Key sites: Loch Ruthven, Cairngorms and Speyside, Orkney (winter), Dungeness (winter), Old Hall Marshes and Tollesbury Wick (winter).

Dotterel

In summer, the Dotterel is a rare bird of the northern uplands – it reaches the southern limit of its breeding range in Scotland. To see these waders in their splendid summer plumage, a mountain hike is necessary. Birds can turn up on passage (spring and autumn) on open ground almost anywhere in Britain, but certain sites are more reliable than others; there are a few traditional sites that have been in use for many years.

Key sites: Cairngorms, Deeside, Donna Nook (spring passage), St Margaret's Bay (autumn passage).

Crested Tit

A resident speciality of the magnificent Caledonian pine forests that once covered much of the Highlands, this species is easily found if you are searching in the right habitat. Like the other members of the family, it is an active and lively bird, often travelling in groups, and draws attention to itself with frequent calls and energetic exploration of the lichen-covered twigs.

Key sites: Abernethy Forest and other Speyside pine forests.

Hen Harrier

The Hen Harrier breeds mainly on moorland in the north and west of Britain, but most disperse to lowland and coastal areas in the winter. It is still persecuted by gamekeepers across much of its range. Some of the Scottish islands hold good numbers, but on the mainland it is more thinly distributed. In autumn and winter, communal roosts occur at certain traditional sites.

Key sites: Orkney, Cairngorms, Sutherland, West Freugh Airfield (winter), Insh Marshes (winter), Horsey Mere (winter), Elmley (winter).

leads north to the beach car park (and from there a track leads to the lighthouse). The best spot for seawatching is just north of the lighthouse, although in the roughest conditions the higher ground by the wire dump is better. Good areas to search for passerine migrants include the lighthouse gardens, the wire dump and the campsite (access only possible October–March), with trees and scrub near its entrance and a belt of trees along the southwest perimeter.

Birds
Spring migrants can include White Wagtail, Black Redstart, and sometimes Bluethroat, Pied Flycatcher and Red-backed Shrike.

Autumn seawatching can be good, especially in NE winds. Manx and sometimes Sooty Shearwaters, sea ducks, Arctic and Great Skuas, Black and other terns and, especially in late autumn, Pomarine Skua and Little Gull, are possible, together with Gannet and Kittiwake. Passerine migrants are also weather-dependent, and as at all east coast migration watchpoints, winds from the east, combined with rain or drizzle, are the classic conditions for a fall. Among the scarcer species, Richard's Pipit, Icterine, Barred and Yellow-browed Warblers, Firecrest and Red-breasted Flycatcher have been recorded.

In winter, the sea is worth a look, especially after north or east gales, for divers, Glaucous Gull and Little Auk Turnstone and Purple Sandpiper may be found on the rocks.

20 JOHN MUIR COUNTRY PARK, TYNINGHAME (Lothian)

OS Landranger 67

Just west of Dunbar, the Country Park holds an excellent range of wildfowl and waders, with some notably wintering passerines, sometimes including Lapland Bunting.

Habitat
The Country Park comprises the estuary of the River Tyne with associated mudflats and saltmarsh, bordered to the north by a rocky headland known as St Baldred's Cradle and a narrow sandy spit (Sandy Hirst), and to the south by the dunes of Spike Island. The hinterland is grassland and scrub, with a plantation of Scots pine to the south of Spike Island.

Access (see map)
John Muir Country Park Leave the A1 northeast on the A1087 c.1 mile west of Dunbar. After ¼ mile turn north on a minor road to Linkfield car park. Another car park is reached by continuing on the A1087 and turning north as you enter Dunbar into Shore Road. There are information boards at both car parks and a footpath links them (passing Seafield Pond), continuing west along the south shore of the estuary to Ware Road and the A198. The inner estuary and Spike Island are best in the period two hours either side of high tide, with waders roosting on Spike Island on 'spring' tides and on the north part of the inner estuary on neap tides. Passage waders also favour the north end of Spike Island. For seawatching, St Baldred's Cradle is the best vantage point.

Tyninghame Estate Although private, access is allowed to certain routes through the estate. Turn north off the A1 onto the A198 towards North Berwick and, after 1¾ miles turn east into Limetree Walk, parking at the end by Tyninghame Links. From here, footpaths lead to St Baldred's Cradle.

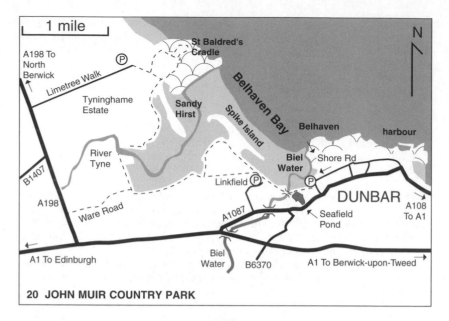

20 JOHN MUIR COUNTRY PARK

Birds

Wintering wildfowl include many Wigeon as well as Shelduck, Teal, Goldeneye, Eider and Common Scoter, and a few Velvet Scoter, Long-tailed Duck and Red-breasted Merganser. A flock of c.25 Whooper Swan frequents the fields west of the estuary, together with up to 500 Greylag and small numbers of Pink-footed Geese. The usual waders are present in winter, including Grey Plover, Knot, Bar-tailed Godwit and notably, 2–3 Greenshank, with Turnstone and Purple Sandpiper below the cliffs at Belhaven and Dunbar. The concentration of potential prey attracts Peregrine, Merlin, Sparrowhawk and occasionally Hen Harrier. Look for Red-throated Diver, Shag and Cormorant offshore. Wintering passerines are interesting, and may include Rock Pipit, Twite, and Snow and sometimes Lapland Buntings on the Spike Island saltmarsh. In some years, Shore Lark is also present. Dipper can be found wintering nearby on Biel Water.

On spring passage, migrants include Gadwall, Shoveler, Pintail, Sanderling, White Wagtail, Ring Ouzel, Wheatear, Whinchat, Redstart, and a few Spotted Redshank and Whimbrel. In autumn a few Barnacle and Brent Geese pass through, and a greater variety of waders is noted, with Whimbrel, Green Sandpiper, Greenshank, Spotted Redshank, Black-tailed Godwit, Ruff, Little Stint and Curlew Sandpiper worth searching for. Seawatching in autumn may produce Manx Shearwater, Kittiwake, and Great and Arctic Skuas.

Breeders include a few Eider, Shelduck and Ringed Plover, with over 200 pairs of Kittiwake nearby at Dunbar harbour. Little Grebe and Sedge Warbler breed at Seafield Pond. The Estate woodland holds Green and Great Spotted Woodpeckers and possibly breeding Hawfinch. Look also for passage Tree Pipit, Siskin and Crossbill. Several hundred Eider oversummer, and in late summer a moult gathering of up to 80 Goosanders is a feature, as is the number of Gannets offshore.

21 BASS ROCK (Lothian)

Probably the most accessible large gannetry in Britain, the Bass Rock is only 3 miles off North Berwick.

Access and Birds

During the breeding season there are regular boat trips around the island from North Berwick—contact the boatman for details. Over 21,000 pairs of Gannets are joined by Shag, Guillemot, Razorbill, a few Puffin, and Kittiwake.

Information

Fred Marr, Bass Rock boatman. Tel: 01620 892838.

22 GOSFORD, ABERLADY AND GULLANE BAYS
(Lothian)

This section of the Firth of Forth attracts a wide variety of species and is worth a visit year-round. In winter sea duck, divers, and grebes are prominent, and a speciality is Red-necked Grebe, which may appear as early as July. Aberlady Bay is a reserve of East Lothian District Council.

Habitat

Aberlady and Gosford Bays possess an extensive foreshore, with rocky areas at Port Seton and Gullane Point, but Gullane Bay has a relatively narrow foreshore. The beach is backed by areas of dunes and patches of sea buckthorn, most extensive in Gullane Bay, with a small freshwater loch (Marl Loch).

Access (see map)

Gosford Bay Can be viewed from the road. The B1348 runs east from Port Seton, joining the A198 just before Ferny Ness, and continues along the shore of the Bay. The best spot is Ferny Ness, where you can park.

Aberlady Bay, southwest shore A footpath, accessible from the A198, follows the coast from Gosford Bay to Aberlady village, running along the south shore of Aberlady Bay and passing a hide midway along the shore. At low tide it is best to watch Aberlady Bay from this footpath or from the A198 just east of Aberlady village. The key for the hide can be obtained from the warden by prior arrangement.

Aberlady Bay, east shore On a rising tide the east shore of Aberlady Bay is best. Leave Aberlady on the A198 and after ½ mile there is a small car park. From here a track crosses the stream via a footbridge and Gullane Point is then signposted. To reach the shore, fork left just after the sewage farm; there is no general access away from the paths.

Gullane Point This is an excellent seawatching spot, accessed via the footpath from Aberlady Bay or via a footpath from the car park in Gullane Bay.

Gullane Bay A footpath follows the shore of the bay from Gullane Point northeast to Black Rocks, accessed from the car park near the shore (accessible north off the A198 along Sandy Loan through Gullane). The bay often has an evening roost of up to 150 Red-throated Diver.

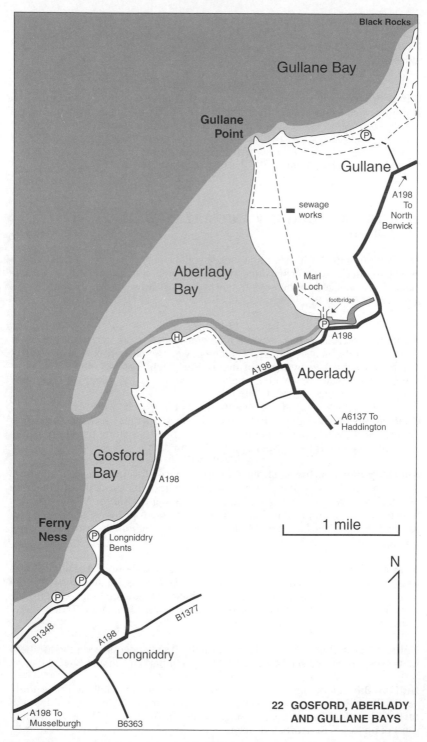

22 GOSFORD, ABERLADY AND GULLANE BAYS

Birds

Red-necked and Slavonian Grebes, as well as Red-throated Diver occur offshore and there can be as many as 160 Slavonian wintering along this stretch of coast. Great Northern and Black-throated Divers are infrequent. A small flock of Whooper Swan winters, together with up to 17,500 Pink-footed Geese (peaking in early winter). The swans and geese feed inland, usually on the fields around Fenton Barns and Drem, and roost in Aberlady Bay. Sea duck occur mainly in Gullane and Gosford Bays, with smaller numbers in Aberlady Bay. Up to 7,000 Eider and 6,000 Common Scoter are present, with up to 600 Velvet Scoter (both eiders and scoters peak in spring and autumn), 100 Long-tailed Duck, and a few Goldeneye and Red-breasted Merganser. Waders include Grey Plover, Sanderling, Turnstone and Purple Sandpiper, and sometimes Ruff in the Port Seton and Aberlady areas. Redwing, Fieldfare and Blackcap favour the sea buckthorn. Raptors may include Merlin, Peregrine, and Long-eared and Short-eared Owls. Finch flocks on the saltmarsh and nearby stubble fields may hold Tree Sparrow, Twite, Brambling and Snow Bunting, and also occasionally Lapland Bunting or even Shore Lark.

A variety of waders occurs on passage. Whimbrel, Black-tailed Godwit, Spotted Redshank, Greenshank, and Wood and Green Sandpipers are regular, with Little Stint and Curlew Sandpiper annual, and the best variety in autumn. The area has attracted a truly outstanding list of rare waders.

Breeders include 200 pairs of Eider, Shelduck, Ringed Plover, Snipe, Redshank, Common, Arctic and Little Terns, Sedge and Garden Warblers and Lesser Whitethroat, with Sparrowhawk in the area. Numbers of non-breeding Eider, and Common and Velvet Scoters are also present, as well as summering Grey Plover, Knot, Sanderling, Guillemot, Razorbill, and very occasionally Black Guillemot or Puffin. Fulmar, Gannet, and sometimes Manx Shearwaters can be seen offshore during the summer. Late summer and autumn is the peak period for Red-necked Grebe, with usually c.50 present. The best spot is around Ferny Ness. Late-summer gatherings of terns, especially Sandwich, are a feature, while Arctic Skua regularly occurs offshore at this time, and more irregularly, Great and Pomarine Skuas.

Information

Aberlady Warden: Ian Thomson, 4 Craigielaw Cottages, Longniddry, East Lothian EH32 0PY. Tel: 01875 870588.

23 MUSSELBURGH (Lothian)   OS Landranger 65

Situated on the east fringe of Edinburgh, this area attracts an excellent range of sea duck, waders, gulls and terns, and a visit is worthwhile at any time of year, although autumn and winter are probably best.

Habitat

A series of specially constructed lagoons east of the mouth of the River Esk have been filled with ash from nearby Cockenzie power station, and the remaining shallow pools attract large numbers of roosting waders, gulls and terns, with passerines in the rough grassland. Offshore, the waters of the Firth of Forth attract a range of waterfowl.

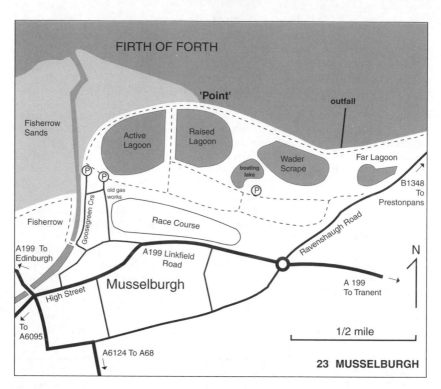

FIRTH OF FORTH

'Point'

outfall

Fisherrow
Sands

Active
Lagoon

Raised
Lagoon

boating
lake

Wader
Scrape

Far Lagoon

B1348
To
Prestonpans

old gas
works

Fisherrow

Race Course

Goosegreen Crs

Ravenshaugh Road

A199 To
Edinburgh

A199 Linkfield
Road

Musselburgh

A 199
To Tranent

N

High Street

To
A6095

1/2 mile

A6124 To A68

23 MUSSELBURGH

Access (see map)

Leave the A199 Linkfield Road at Musselburgh, forking right (west) at the race-course, and take the third right (Goosegreen Crescent), parking at the end by the seawall. (Alternatively, turn first right and park at the end of Balcarres Road, just beyond the old gas works.) View the river mouth from here or follow the seawall east for 1 mile to the sewage outfall to watch the sea (the 'Point' being one of the best viewpoints) and lagoons, returning along paths behind the lagoons. The river mouth is usually the most productive area at low water, while a visit in the three hours before high water is best for sea duck, and roosting waders, gulls and terns on the lagoons. Access on foot is permitted to most areas, except the active lagoons.

Birds

In winter there are Great Crested and Slavonian Grebes and Red-throated Diver offshore, with occasional Red-necked Grebe, Black-throated and Great Northern Divers (the divers most frequent in late winter). The Firth of Forth once held huge concentrations of Scaup (peaking at 30,000–40,000 in 1968–69), but now counts seldom exceed 25. Other sea duck include up to 1,000 Eider, 100 Red-breasted Merganser, 250 Common and 50 Velvet Scoters, 100 Long-tailed Duck and 500 Goldeneye. A few Guillemot and Razorbill are usually present, and occasionally Black Guillemot or Little Auk Wintering waders include large numbers of Oystercatcher, Knot and Bar-tailed Godwit, with lesser totals of Ringed and Grey Plovers, Curlew, Redshank, Dunlin and Turnstone. These may attract a Peregrine or Merlin. The rough ground and lagoon edges hold finches and buntings, includ-ing Snow Bunting and sometimes also small numbers of Lapland Bunting, Twite and occasionally Shore Lark, the last especially in cold weather.

A broad variety of waders and terns occurs on passage, including Golden Plover, Ruff, Whimbrel, Black-tailed Godwit, Greenshank, Common Sandpiper and Sanderling, with Little Stint and Curlew Sandpiper also possible, especially in autumn. Passage waders often feed near the river mouth. Migrant passerines may include Wheatear and White Wagtail. Large numbers of the commoner gulls frequent the area, often loafing at the river mouth. Mediterranean Gull is possible in spring, Little Gull in late autumn and Glaucous and Iceland in winter. Terns include a notable roost of up to 1,000 Sandwich and smaller numbers of Common. Seawatching can at times be productive, especially in late summer–autumn. north or east winds may bring numbers of Gannet, Manx Shearwater, Kittiwake and Arctic and Great Skuas inshore.

24 HOUND POINT (Lothian)   OS Landranger 65

Immediately west of Edinburgh, in recent years this seawatching station has established itself among the most reliable autumn sites for Long-tailed and Pomarine Skuas.

Habitat
The Point projects into the Firth of Forth on the south shore, just east of the Forth Road Bridge.

Access
Leave South Queensferry east on the B924 and park just before the Forth Railway Bridge. From here it a 2-mile walk along the coast to the Point. The period August–October is most productive (though spring can be good too), and light winds from northwest through north to southeast are best; south and west winds are usually poor. The passing of a front or clearance of sea fog may prompt a passage of skuas. Though birds can appear from any direction (and often overhead), the north and east quadrants are usually the most productive.

Birds
Passing seabirds generally include Fulmar, Manx Shearwater, Gannet, Kittiwake, Arctic Skua, Sandwich Tern and Guillemot. Large numbers of Long-tailed and Pomarine Skuas may occur in the correct conditions, and Pomarine Skua is regular in October–November; Great Skua is the rarest of the four skuas. Passing skuas often occur in flocks and move west along the Firth of Forth, gaining height to pass over the Forth bridges. They presumably make the short overland crossing to the Firth of Clyde. Other scarce visitors may include Black Tern and Little Gull, with Little Auk possible in late autumn.

25 LOCH LEVEN (Perth & Kinross)   OS Landranger 58

East of Kinross, Loch Leven attracts large numbers of wintering wildfowl, especially Pink-footed Goose. The Loch is an NNR and the RSPB has a large reserve at Vane Farm. The best time for geese is October–March.

Habitat
The Loch covers c.3,900 acres and has seven islands, which hold the highest concentration of breeding ducks in Britain, with over 1,100 pairs. Surrounded by

farmland, the fields provide feeding areas for the thousands of geese that roost on the loch. At Vane Farm there are areas of marsh, lagoons and a scrape on the shore, while farmland, birch woods and heather moor cloak the slopes of the Vane, a 824-foot high hill.

Access (see map)

Loch Leven NNR Access to the shore is permitted at three places: Kirkgate Park (April–September boat trips from the jetty to Loch Leven Castle), Burleigh Sands and Findatie. All are well signposted, with information boards at the car parks. Wildfowl, however, are best seen at Vane Farm.

Vane Farm RSPB Leave the M90 at junction 5 (signed RSPB) and take the B9097 Glenrothes road (turning sharp left, then right where the road crosses the B996) for 2 miles to the RSPB car park and visitor centre, which are south of the road. The reserve is open all year, and access is possible at all times to the car park, the woodland trails (which stretch for 1 mile from the car park to the top of the Vane), the Gillman hide (overlooking a small scrape on the Loch's shore, this is reached via a tunnel under the B9097 from the car park) and the adjacent Wetland Trail which extends west for ½ mile taking in the Waterston and Carden hides and more scrapes. The visitor centre with a coffee shop and comfortable observation room overlooking the loch and best geese fields is open daily 10.00–17.00 (10.00–16.00 January–March; closed New Year's Day and Christmas Day).

Birds

Numbers of Pink-footed Geese peak in late autumn and March, when up to 25,000 have been counted. Lower numbers winter. They are joined by 1,000–5,000 Greylag, c.100 Whooper and up to 10 Bewick's Swans; these favour Vane Farm. Occasional parties of Canada, Brent, Barnacle and White-fronted Geese are often found in the goose flocks, and Bean Goose may occur February–April. There are often ten species of duck wintering on the loch, including Goosander, Goldeneye, Wigeon, Shoveler, Gadwall, Ruddy Duck and occasionally Smew or Pintail. Other waterbirds include Great Crested Grebe, a few Slavonian Grebes, Cormorant, Golden Plover and Ruff. Buzzard, Sparrowhawk and Peregrine are resident in the area and may be joined in winter by Short-eared Owl, Hen Harrier, Goshawk and

Red Grouse

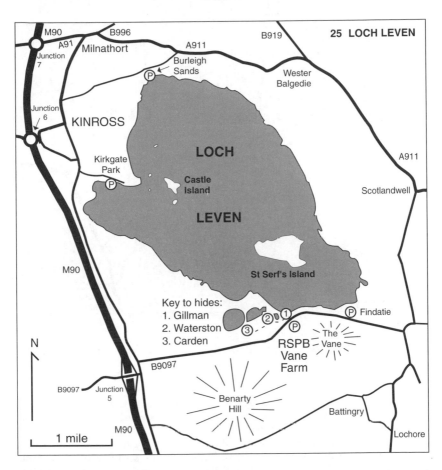

Merlin. There are often Siskin and Redpoll in areas of birch, and Long-eared Owl is occasionally recorded.

On passage the Loch shore at Vane Farm attracts waders, sometimes including Black-tailed Godwit, Ruff, Spotted Redshank, Greenshank, and Green and Wood Sandpipers. Both Black-necked and Slavonian Grebes occur on migration, as do Osprey and Marsh Harrier.

Over 1,000 pairs of ducks nest on St Serf's Island. Mostly Mallard and Tufted Duck, they also include Shelduck, Gadwall, Wigeon, Shoveler and Pochard. There are breeding Black-headed Gull (c.8,000 pairs) and a few pairs of Common Tern, as well as Oystercatcher, Ringed Plover, Common Sandpiper, Snipe and Redshank. Grasshopper Warbler sometimes breeds. The surrounding moorland has Red Grouse, Curlew, Whinchat and Raven, with Crossbill, Redpoll and Tree Pipit in the woods. An unusual sight is the handful of Fulmars that breed on nearby crags (8 miles from the sea).

Information

SNH: Paul Brooks (Reserve Manager), Loch Leven Laboratory, The Pier, Kinross KY13 8UF. Tel: 01577 864439.

RSPB: Ken Shaw, Senior Site Manager, Vane Farm Nature Centre, by Loch Leven, Kinross KY13 9LX. Tel: 01577 862355. E-mail: vanefarm@rspb.org.uk

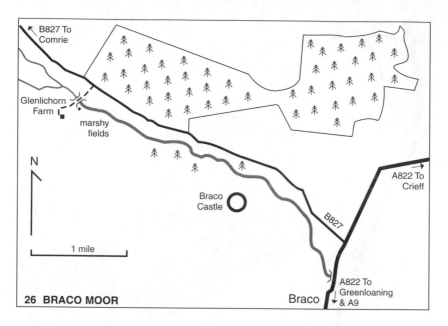

26 BRACO MOOR

---

26 BRACO MOOR (Perth & Kinross)   OS Landranger 57

This area, convenient for the A9, is a good one for lekking Black Grouse.

Access (see map)

Turn north off the A9 at Greenloaning onto the A822 towards Crieff and, ⅔ mile north of Braco, turn northwest on the B827 towards Comrie. Proceed along this narrow road for 3 miles until the steep valley on the left begins to open out, where the grouse favour the marshy fields just before the track to Glenlichorn Farm. Dawn is best, but stay in your car until the birds have dispersed of their own accord. Away from the lek, Black Grouse can sometimes be seen in the extensive plantations north of the road.

Birds

Up to ten Blackcocks may be present (though numbers have been lower in recent years, perhaps due to disturbance; remain in your car!). Other species include Buzzard, Red Grouse, Woodcock, Curlew, Short-eared Owl, Tree Pipit, Whinchat and sometimes Crossbill, with Common Sandpiper and Grey Wagtail on the River Knaik (and look for Dipper at the bridge on the edge of Braco). Occasionally, lone male Capercaillies may visit the stands of old pines along the river c.2 miles from the junction.

27 ISLE OF MAY (Fife)   OS Landranger 59

The Isle of May lies at the entrance to the Firth of Forth. It has colonies of seabirds, but the main attraction is migrants. The May rose to fame through the work of Evelyn Baxter and Leonora Rintoul between 1907 and 1933, and the Bird Observatory was established in 1934. The island is now a NNR, and the best times to visit are late spring and autumn.

Habitat

The island covers just 141 acres and there is little vegetation; most of the cover is concentrated in the Observatory garden. The coastline varies from low on the east shore to cliffs topping 180 feet on the west.

Access

Basic self-catering accommodation is available for up to six people, April–October (normally weekly), at the Observatory. The crossing from Anstruther on the Fife coast takes c.1 hour, and is organised when booking; delays are possible in bad weather. Day trips can also be organised from Anstruther or Crail by visiting parties.

Birds

Small movements of diurnal migrants occur in spring and autumn, but potentially more interesting are the falls of night migrants in east or southeast winds during poor weather. These often include scarcer species: Wryneck, Bluethroat, Icterine, Barred and Yellow-browed Warblers, Red-breasted Flycatcher, Great Grey and Red-backed Shrikes, Common Rosefinch, and Lapland and Ortolan Buntings are almost annual, mainly in autumn. There are also large falls of birds destined to winter in Britain and Ireland, especially thrushes. These can be spectacular, for example there were 15,000 Goldcrest on one day in October 1982. The May has an excellent list of rarities.

Seawatching can be interesting. Gannet is almost always present offshore, and divers, Manx and Sooty Shearwaters, ducks, Arctic and Great Skuas, and Common, Arctic and Sandwich Terns are all regular. Few birds use the island in winter, most notable is a flock of several hundred Purple Sandpipers and Turnstones, and there are sometimes Black Guillemot or Little Auk offshore.

Breeding seabirds include Fulmar, Shag (c.1,000 pairs), Puffin (c.20,000 pairs), Guillemot (c.12,000 pairs), Razorbill (c.2,000 pairs), Kittiwake (c.8,000 pairs), Herring and Lesser Black-backed Gulls, a few Common and Arctic Terns, as well as Eider (c.500 pairs), Oystercatcher, Swallow and Rock Pipit.

Information

Isle of May Bird observatory (bookings): Mike Martin, 2 Manse Park, Uphall, West Lothian EH52 6NX. Tel: 01506 855285. E-mail: mwa.martin@virgin.net
Day trips: Ian Gatherum, 27 Glenogil Gardens, Anstruther. Tel: 01333 310860 or Jim Reaper 01333 310103.
SNH: Caroline Gallacher, 46 Crossgate, Cupar, Fife KY15 5HS. Tel: 01334 54038.

28 LARGO BAY (Fife) OS Landranger 59

Largo Bay attracts large numbers of wintering sea duck, notably including regular Surf Scoter, and other interesting species include Black-throated Diver and Red-necked and Slavonian Grebes.

Habitat

The Bay extends for c.3½ miles and comprises sand and mud, with some rocky patches at Lower Largo. It is backed by sand dunes and urban and industrial development.

Access (see map)

Levenmouth A good area for sea duck. Park in the car park on the northeast side of the River Leven, just over the river from Methil power station, and look

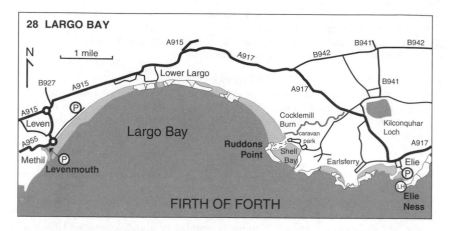

28 LARGO BAY

over the seawall. Low tide is best for gulls. It is possible to walk along the shore for c.4 miles from Leven to Ruddons Point, though Cocklemill Burn is difficult to cross at high tide.

Lower Largo Probably better for sea duck. View from the car park at the east end of the village.

Ruddons Point and Shell Bay Another excellent spot for sea duck, especially around high tide, and Black-throated Diver. Leave the A917 c.1 mile northwest of Elie and drive southwest through Shell Bay caravan park for c.2 miles to the end, from where it is a short walk to the Point (note that in October–March the gate is only open 09.00–16.00, outside these hours it is necessary to walk). For waders, walk from the Point along the east shore of Shell Bay.

Elie In winter there is occasionally Glaucous Gull in Elie harbour. Elie Ness, a small promontory, is the best place for seawatching around the Bay. Little Gull sometimes occurs on passage, as well as divers, Shag, auks and terns. There is direct access from the east side of Elie to the coastguards' lookout and lighthouse.

Birds

On the sea, wintering Red-throated Diver are usually joined by up to ten Black-throated Divers and sometimes Great Northern, and there are usually also Great Crested, Red-necked and Slavonian Grebes. There are many Common Scoter and Eider, and up to 300 Scaup, 300 Long-tailed Duck (favouring the waters off Methil Docks) and 200 Velvet Scoter, as well as Goldeneye. Surf Scoter is annual, with up to eight present October–May, often just west of Ruddons Point. For divers, grebes and sea duck, calm conditions are best. On the beaches and rocks there are usually Grey Plover, Knot, Sanderling and Purple Sandpiper. Glaucous and Iceland Gulls are occasional, favouring Levenmouth. January–March sometimes produces records of Little Gull.

On passage there are numbers of Common, Arctic and Sandwich Terns, often a few Roseate, which can be seen on the beach almost anywhere in the bay, and sometimes Little Gull. Small numbers of Eiders and scoters remain all summer, with a large concentration of moulting birds in late summer.

29 KILCONQUHAR LOCH (Fife) OS Landranger 59

This small loch is famous for concentrations of Little Gulls in July–August, as well as holding many wintering and breeding wildfowl.

Habitat
The loch covers c.135 acres. Shallow and fertile, it is largely surrounded by trees and, to the north, gardens.

Access (see map on p.524)
Leave the A917 north of Elie on the B941 to Kilconquhar. Park in the village and proceed to the churchyard, from where the loch can be viewed.

Birds
Kilconquhar Loch holds wintering duck though, being shallow, it freezes quite quickly in hard weather. Notable are large numbers of Goldeneyes, immatures often staying into late spring and summer. Others include small numbers of Gadwall and Shoveler. Greylag Geese roost on the loch, and there are occasionally parties of Barnacle Geese.

Numbers of Little Gulls visiting Kilconquhar Loch on passage in late July–August vary greatly. Only a few occur in some years and over 500 at once in others. The largest numbers generally occur when evening coincides with a high tide.

Breeders on the loch include Great Crested and Little Grebes and numbers of duck, including Gadwall and Shoveler.

Little Gull

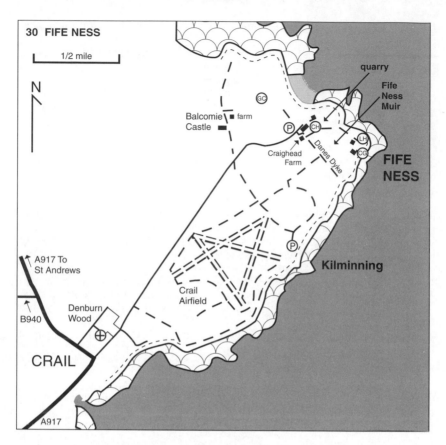

30 FIFE NESS (Fife)

OS Landranger 59

Fife Ness forms the east tip of the Fife peninsula, which explains its attractiveness to migrants. Both on land and sea, interesting birds can be seen. The Ness is worth visiting during spring and autumn, but only in a northeast, east, southeast or southwest wind, being otherwise usually very quiet. Part of the Kilminning coast and Fife Ness Muir are a reserve of the Scottish Wildlife Trust.

Habitat

The area is a mosaic of farmland, small woods, a golf course and coastal scrub, bounded by a rocky coastline. As at any migration watchpoint, any patch of cover is worth checking. Particularly good areas are Denburn Wood, the walled garden and large trees at Balcomie Castle, the quarry below the golf club, and Fife Ness Muir, the last-mentioned being the best, containing several artificial pools. Also below the golf club there is a small beach and pool, both of which attract waders. Inland of the Ness, Crail Airfield is worth a look for pipits, larks, thrushes, buntings etc.

Access (see map)

Please behave with the greatest consideration; in the past relations between locals and birders have been strained. Park only at Kilminning or in the car park

Pallas's Warbler

near the golf club. Around the golf course, keep to the road or coastal footpath. Always ask permission before entering private property, notably at Balcomie and Craighead Farms. When inspecting areas of cover around houses, respect peoples' privacy, especially in the early morning.

Denburn Wood This mature wood lies adjacent to the churchyard on the outskirts of Crail, and attracts migrant passerines filtering inland from the coast. There are a number of paths in the wood with free access from the road.

Crail Airfield Leave Crail northeast on the minor road to Balcomie golf course (a continuation of the main street), turning south after c.1 mile onto the road for the go-karts, and follow the signs over the abandoned airfield to park at Kilminning. The old airfield may attract waders, pipits, larks, thrushes and buntings.

Kilminning coast Park as for Crail Airfield. The Fife long-distance coastal path runs from Crail to Fife Ness, and from the car park you can follow it northeast for c.½ mile to the coastguards (the best seawatching point).

Balcomie Castle and Farm. Access on foot from either Fife Ness or Kilminning. Seek permission before entering the land around Balcomie Farm.

Fife Ness Take the minor road from Crail to Balcomie golf course where, just before the entrance, there is a car park (fee) on the left. Park and walk through the gate to the right of the road and then immediately left towards the sea. An overgrown quarry lies on the left immediately below the club house, while Fife Ness Muir is the gorse patch on the hill to the right (approach the latter *only* from the east, via the cottage on the shore). Note, the land around Craighead Farm is extremely sensitive.

Birds

On passage, the usual chats, thrushes, warblers and flycatchers are sometimes joined by scarce migrants. In spring, Long-eared Owl, Wryneck, Ring Ouzel, Black Redstart, Bluethroat, Firecrest and Red-backed Shrike are possible. Additional possibilities in autumn are Icterine, Barred, Pallas's and Yellow-browed Warblers,

Red-breasted Flycatcher and Great Grey Shrike. Occasionally Snow or even Lapland Buntings join regular Golden Plover and Lapwing on the airfield in late autumn–winter.

Seawatching can be productive: Gannet and Shag are almost always present off-shore, but in spring and autumn E–NE winds are best, though too strong a northeast wind in spring may delay the passage of terns, which should include Common, Arctic, Sandwich and sometimes Little. Autumn brings Manx and (regularly) Sooty Shearwaters, Little Gull, terns and skuas – mostly Arctic, with some Great and small numbers of Pomarines. The small beach and pool attract passage waders.

In winter seawatching can produce all three divers, auks and sea duck. There are Purple Sandpiper and Turnstone on the rocks and large numbers of Golden Plovers on the airfield.

Summer is quieter, but large numbers of Eiders can still be seen, as well as some of the seabirds that breed locally – Gannet, auks, Kittiwake and terns. Sedge Warbler and Corn Bunting are fairly common breeders but Stonechat only sporadic.

31 EDEN ESTUARY (Fife)   OS Landranger 59

Good numbers of sea ducks occur offshore at St Andrews, while the adjacent Eden estuary is easy to work and holds, for Scotland, an excellent selection of waders, plus internationally important numbers of Shelduck and Red-breasted Merganser. The entire area is good in winter and passage periods. Over 2,000 acres of the estuary are a LNR.

Habitat

The Eden estuary is relatively small and is flanked at the mouth by areas of dunes. By contrast, the shore at St Andrews is very rocky.

Access (see map)

St Andrews Straightforward access to the seafront. A good place to watch from is the Castle.

Out Head Follow signs in St Andrews along the shore road to West Sands. Continue to the road's end near Out Head and park. From here view the sea and it is a short walk to the Head to view the lower reaches of the estuary. Tracks off this road access Balgove Bay (the key for the hide is available from the ranger service).

Coble Shore Turn north off the A91 c.3½ miles west of St Andrews to Coble Shore, parking at the end of the short track. A footpath along the disused railway overlooks the estuary, while the Fife Bird Club has a hide at Edenside Stables. Waders roost on the saltmarshes in the area of the stables. A rising or high tide is best here.

Guardbridge The main concentration of birds in the estuary can be seen from Guardbridge, where the A91 crosses the River Eden. Park in the large lay-by just east of the bridge and view from there. There is a visitor centre (open daily 09.00–17.00, except Christmas and New Year's Days and the day of the Leuchars airshow), just north of the bridge, by the paper mill.

Kincaple Den Wintering Greenshank, Black-tailed Godwit and Goosander are

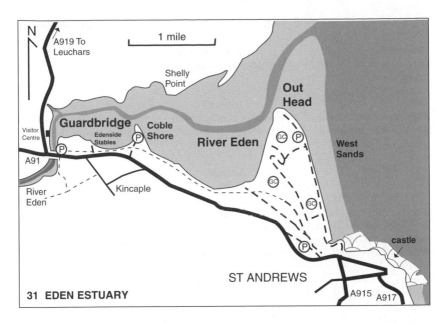

N

A919 To Leuchars

1 mile

Shelly Point

Out Head

Visitor Centre

Guardbridge Coble Shore

Edenside Stables

River Eden

West Sands

A91

River Eden

Kincaple

castle

ST ANDREWS

31 EDEN ESTUARY

A915 A917

sometimes seen upriver of Guardbridge. Take the footpath signposted Kincaple Den to the river south off the A91.

Birds

In winter, Red-throated and sometimes Black-throated and Great Northern Divers occur on the sea, together with Great Crested and occasionally Slavonian and Red-necked Grebes. There are large numbers of Eider and Common and Velvet Scoters, Long-tailed Duck and Scaup, while Surf Scoter is regular in late autumn–early winter. Other sea duck include Goldeneye, and the best area is often off the mouth of the estuary or occasionally off the Sea Life Centre at West Beach. The estuary shelters Wigeon, Teal, a few Pintail and large numbers of roosting Greylag Geese, with Goosander on the river. Waders such as Oystercatcher, Knot, Bar-tailed Godwit, Dunlin and Redshank are abundant, and there are up to 500 Grey Plover (a scarce bird in Scotland), Sanderling around the estuary mouth, up to 100 Black-tailed Godwit, and a few Ruff and Greenshank. The rocky coast at St Andrews is frequented by Purple Sandpiper and Turnstone. There are generally few raptors in the area, but Short-eared Owl, Merlin or Peregrine may be present, while Snow Bunting may be found in the dunes.

On passage, Little Ringed Plover may occur in spring in Balgove Bay, while Grey Plover, Black-tailed Godwit and Greenshank occur in larger numbers, and Little Stint, Curlew Sandpiper, Ruff and Spotted Redshank are usually seen a few times each autumn. There is a late-summer gathering of terns at Eden Mouth, and in early autumn these attract skuas, mostly Arctic. In late autumn, a few Barnacle Geese may pass through the area.

In summer, numbers of Eider and scoter remain offshore, as well as a few waders.

Information

Fife Ranger Service, Les Hatton, Silverburn House, Largo Road, By Leven, Fife KY8 5PU. Tel: 01333 429785. E-mail: refrs@craigtoun.freeserve.co.uk

Scottish Wildlife Trust, Cramond House, off Cramond Glebe Road, Edinburgh EH4 6NS. Tel: 0131 312 7765. E-mail: enquiries@swt.org.uk

32 CAMERON RESERVOIR (Fife)   OS Landranger 59

Around 4 miles southwest of St Andrews this water attracts wildfowl in winter, notably including both Pink-footed and Greylag Geese, while on passage a variety of waders has occurred.

Habitat
The reservoir covers c.100 acres and is bordered in several places by stands of willows. To the south there is a narrow belt of conifers, while to the north lies grassland.

Access
Leave the A915 4 miles south of St Andrews west along a minor road to Cameron Kirk, turning south after ½ mile to the car park at the water bailiff's house. The dams at the east and west ends provide good vantage points and it is possible to walk around the reservoir, though the south shore is rather marshy. There is a hide on the north shore, but this is locked and keys are available only to Scottish Wildlife Trust (SWT) and Scottish Ornithologists' Club members.

Birds
Winter wildfowl include Whooper Swan, Wigeon, Pochard, and sometimes Gadwall, Goldeneye and Ruddy Duck. Around 6,000 (occasionally up to 13,000) Pink-footed Geese roost at the reservoir in October–November. Numbers of Greylag Geese (up to 1,000) are also present. The geese are best viewed in the hour before sunset from the hide (to reduce disturbance). Other possibilities in winter are Sparrowhawk and Short-eared Owl.

On passage a variety of waders may occur, including Common, Green and sometimes Wood Sandpipers, Greenshank and Spotted Redshank.

Residents include Great Crested and Little Grebes, and Sedge Warbler breeds.

Information
SWT keys: Ian Cumming, 11 Canongate, St Andrews, Fife. Tel: 01334 473773.

33 LOCH OF LOWES (Perth & Kinross)   OS Landranger 53

Loch of Lowes was the first Scottish Osprey eyrie away from Loch Garten to be widely publicised, and the birds can be seen between early April and August. The Loch is a Scottish Wildlife Trust (SWT) reserve.

Habitat
The Loch of Lowes and adjacent Loch of Craiglush (connected by a canal) are shallow and very fertile, and the margins have areas of reed-grass, sedge and water-lily. They are surrounded by mixed woodland.

Access
Leave the A9 at Dunkeld on the A923 towards Blairgowrie and, after 1½ miles, take the minor road on the right. The Loch is immediately north of this road, and access is restricted to the south shore adjacent to the road, where there are a number of lay-bys, and to the hide, visitor centre and car park at the west end. The visitor centre is open 10.00–17.00 April–September (10.00–18.00 mid-July to mid-August). The hide is always open.

Birds

Apart from the Ospreys (present since 1969, but absent 1983–1991), raptors in the area include Sparrowhawk and Buzzard. Little and Great Crested Grebes, Teal, Common Sandpiper and Sedge Warbler breed around the Loch, and Slavonian Grebe has nested once. The surrounding woodland has Capercaillie and Black Grouse, though due to the restricted access these are unlikely to be seen. Resident Goshawk, Sparrowhawk, Woodcock, Green and Great Spotted Woodpeckers, Treecreeper, Redpoll, Siskin and Crossbill are joined in summer by Tree Pipit, Redstart, Garden Warbler and Spotted Flycatcher. In autumn over 1,000 Greylag Geese roost on the Loch and in winter, if not frozen, the Loch attracts Goosander, Goldeneye and Wigeon.

Information

SWT, Uwe Stoneman (Site Manager), Loch of the Lowes Visitor Centre, Dunkeld, Perthshire PH8 0HH. Tel: 01350 727337.

34 LOCH OF KINNORDY (Angus & Dundee)   OS Landranger 54

This RSPB reserve is a well-publicised site for breeding Black-necked Grebe, but can also hold a selection of passage waders and wintering wildfowl.

Habitat

Set in rolling farmland, this small, partially drained and very shallow, nutrient-rich loch is surrounded by marsh, willow and alder scrub, with Scots pine on higher ground.

Access

Leave Kirriemuir west on the B951 towards Glen Isla. The Loch is immediately north of the road after 1½ miles, and paths lead from the car park to three hides a short distance away, with a boardwalk through areas of marsh and willow carr. The reserve is open daily 09.00–21.00 (or sunset if earlier) except Christmas and New Year's Days.

Birds

Breeders include Black-necked (since 1989, with 11 pairs in 1994), Great Crested and Little Grebes, and eight species of duck, including Wigeon, Gadwall, Shoveler, Pochard and, since 1979, up to ten pairs of Ruddy Ducks (the species' first breeding locale in Scotland). Around 7,000 pairs of Black-headed Gull nest on the floating mats of vegetation, while the surrounding marshes hold Water Rail, Snipe, Curlew, Redshank and Sedge Warbler. The woodland has Sparrowhawk, Great Spotted and Green Woodpeckers.

On passage, waders such as Greenshank, Spotted Redshank, Ruff and Black-tailed and Bar-tailed Godwits may pass through. Marsh Harrier often summers, Osprey often visits to fish in mid–late summer, and Peregrine may also visit.

From October up to 5,000 Greylag Geese use the Loch as a roost, together with small numbers of Pink-footed and occasionally also Barnacle Geese. The surrounding rough ground attracts hunting Hen Harrier and Short-eared Owl.

Information

RSPB: Alan Leitch, 1 Atholl Crescent, Perth PH1 5NG. Tel: 01738 639783. E-mail: alan.leitch@rspb.org.uk

35 KILLIECRANKIE (Perth & Kinross)   OS Landranger 43

Lying close to the A9 between Pitlochry and Blair Atholl, on the west bank of the River Garry, this area holds an excellent selection of woodland species as well as some moorland birds. It is best in spring–early summer.

Habitat
Climbing from the dramatic narrow gorge of the River Garry, habitats include Sessile oak woods, which rise to a plateau of pastureland, and then birch woods that climb further to expanses of moorland (up to 1,300 feet in altitude) with some crags.

Access
From the A9 just north of Pitlochry, take the B8079 to Killiecrankie and, in the village, take the minor road (signed) southwest to Balrobbie Farm and the reserve, which is open at all times. There are two nature trails, 1½ and 3 miles long.

Birds
Residents include Buzzard, Sparrowhawk, Red Grouse, Black Grouse (ever-elusive, and best looked for in the mosaic of open ground and trees along wood and moorland edges), Woodcock, Green and Great Spotted Woodpeckers, Crossbill and Raven. In summer these are joined by Curlew, Snipe, Tree Pipit, Wheatear, Whinchat, Redstart, Wood and Garden Warblers and occasionally Pied Flycatcher. Common Sandpiper, Grey Wagtail and Dipper occur along the river. Golden Eagle and Peregrine are occasional visitors.

Information
RSPB: Alan Leitch, 1 Atholl Crescent, Perth PH1 5NG. Tel: 01738 639783. E-mail: alan.leitch@rspb.org.uk

36 INSH MARSHES (Highland)   OS Landranger 35

This RSPB reserve protects 5 miles of the floodplain of the River Spey between Kingussie and Loch Insh, attracting wintering wildfowl (notably Whooper Swan) and harbouring a number of interesting breeding species.

Habitat
The reserve comprises fen, rough pasture, willow carr and pools, with stands of birch and juniper on higher ground. In winter the whole area may flood, sometimes to a depth of 8 feet!

Access (see map)
Stopping places on the B970 and B9152 afford views of the Marshes and Loch Insh, and this should be adequate in winter.

The reception centre and car park are on the B970 just east of the ruins of Ruthven Barracks, 1½ miles southeast of Kingussie; two hides nearby overlook the west section of the Marshes, while the Invertromie trail permits a c.2-mile circuit of the west end of the reserve through birch woods, meadows and heather. The Lynachlaggan trail, in the northeast sector of the reserve, is reached from the lay-by by the pylon just north of Insh village and accesses a stand of birch and juniper woodland. The reserve is open daily, 09.00–21.00 (or dusk if earlier).

Birds

The entire area regularly floods in winter and attracts Greylag Goose, up to 200 Whooper Swans and a variety of ducks. There is a Hen Harrier roost (5–15 birds), and Peregrine is regular, while wandering Red Kite from the re-introduction programme on the Black Isle may winter, and White-tailed Eagle is rare.

Breeders include feral Greylag Goose, Wigeon, Teal, Shoveler, Tufted Duck, Goldeneye (in nest boxes), Oystercatcher, Snipe, Curlew, Redshank, Common Sandpiper, Black-headed Gulls and Grasshopper and Sedge Warblers. Pochard, Red-breasted Merganser and Goosander nest occasionally. Water Rail breeds and Spotted Crake is usually present in summer and up to five can be heard calling, but are impossible to see. Listen at night mid-May to mid-June for the abrupt *whip* call, from the B9152 between Loch Insh and Lynchat, especially in the area opposite the Highland Wildlife Park. Wood Sandpiper also breeds nearby and sometimes feeds on the reserve. In 1968 a female Bluethroat with a nest and eggs was found, while in 1985 a pair reared five young, the first successful British breeding record. Wooded areas have Tree Pipit, Redstart, Wood Warbler, Spotted Flycatcher and a few Pied Flycatchers. Osprey is a regular visitor in spring and summer; and up to ten species of raptor may be present in early autumn, including Hen Harrier. On passage good numbers of Greylag and Pink-footed Geese pass through in early autumn, and Marsh Harrier is occasionally noted in spring.

Information

RSPB Warden: Pete Moore, Ivy Cottage, Insh, Kingussie, Inverness-shire PH21 1NT. Tel: 01540 661518. E-mail: pete.moore@rspb.org.uk

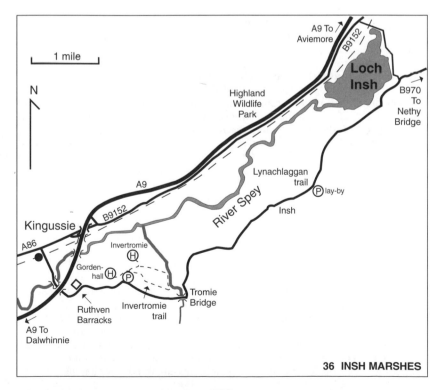

36 INSH MARSHES

37 CAIRNGORMS AND SPEYSIDE

(Highland)

OS Landranger 36 and 35
Outdoor Leisure Map 3

The range of habitats and birds in this area is reminiscent of the high arctic and boreal forests of north Eurasia, and supports all of the Scottish specialities. The best time to visit is April–July, though some of the more interesting species (e.g. Dotterel) do not arrive until May. There are three NNRs, including the giant Cairngorm reserve at 64,000 acres (mostly privately owned), while the RSPB owns the huge Abernethy Forest Reserve, comprising 30,895 acres.

Habitat

The region offers the exciting combination of three principal habitat types. Firstly the high peaks of the Cairngorms, some topping 4,000 feet (and including four of the five highest mountains in Britain), with their distinctive 'whaleback' profile. The bare, windswept summit plateau above 3,000 feet supports an arctic–alpine flora, and snow can lie in some of the high corries all year, while the lower slopes have extensive tracts of heather moorland. This wilderness is difficult to penetrate, except via the new Cairsgorm Mountain Railway (which has replaced the old ski-lift). Secondly, some of the best remnants of native Caledonian pine woodland, relics of the primeval wildwood that once covered much of Scotland, are important for breeding birds. Stands of Scots pine, some trees over 300 years old, shade a mixture of juniper, bilberry and heather, and support Britain's only endemic bird, the Scottish Crossbill. Although not as unique as the pine woods, the native birch woods are equally attractive, and there are also plantations of both native and introduced conifers. The third major habitat is the valley of the River Spey and its associated lochs and marshes.

Access (see map)

An OS map is almost essential to navigate the many minor roads and forest tracks in the area.

Carrbridge Landmark Centre At the south end of the village of Carrbridge on the B9153, the woodland to the rear of the centre often holds Crested Tit and Scottish Crossbill. Take the trail west from the north end of the car park. (The Centre offers audio-visual shows, outdoor exhibitions, a shop and restaurant.) At the north end of the village, where the River Dulnain is bridged by the B9153 is a good spot for Dipper.

Duthil Burn This is an area for lekking Black Grouse, but it is essential to *view from the car*. Leave the A938 c.2 miles east of Carrbridge north on the B9007. After c.1 mile scan the lush area west of the road.

Grantown-on-Spey The woodlands east of the town hold Capercaillie, as well as Crested Tit and Scottish Crossbill. Leave Grantown northeast on the B9102 towards Lettoch and park on the roadside by the gate after c.½ mile (just past the golf course), taking the track south into the forest.

Loch Garten Enclosed within the RSPB's Abernethy Forest Reserve, Loch Garten is sometimes visited by fishing Osprey, and holds breeding Goldeneye, a late-autumn roost of Goosander and a winter roost of up to 1,500 Greylag. The surrounding woodland has Crested Tit and Scottish Crossbill. From the B970 just northeast of Boat of Garten, turn right signed RSPB, parking on the right after c.1 mile. The road continues along the northwest shore of Loch Garten and from the car park a track leads on an interesting circular walk to Loch Mallachie. Crested

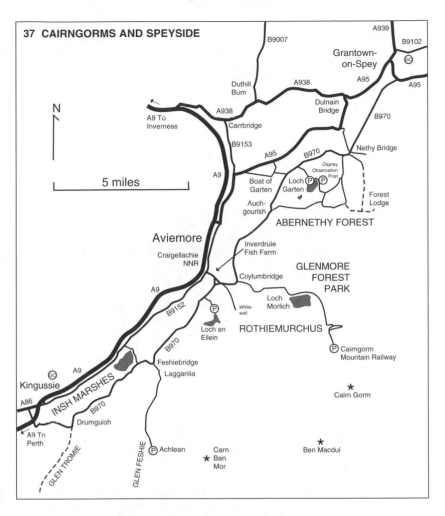

37 CAIRNGORMS AND SPEYSIDE

Tit is often around the car park or along the road. There is access to the reserve tracks at all times, except for the large sanctuary area around the Osprey nest. In recent seasons Capercaillie has been regular in front of the Osprey observation hides, especially in the early mornings.

Osprey Observation Post The Ospreys breed some distance from Loch Garten within a statutory bird sanctuary and can be seen from the Observation Post, open 10.00–18.00 April–late August. From the B970 just northeast of Boat of Garten, turn right signed RSPB. The Observation Post car park lies on the left after 1¼ miles. As well as Osprey, Capercaillie is often seen from the hide in spring (indeed, this is now one of the best sites in Britain for this declining species), and there may be Crested Tit and Scottish Crossbill around the car park and access track.

Forest Lodge, Abernethy Forest Lies in the southeast quadrant of Abernethy RSPB Forest Reserve, and is a good area for Capercaillie, Crested Tit and Scottish Crossbill. The area can be accessed from Auchgourish, Boat of Garten or Nethy

Bridge (all on the B970) via unclassified roads, taking the road east at NH 998167 to the car park at the Lodge. Explore the track north from the Lodge to the River Nethy, and the circular route south via Rynettin (leading to the right just before the car park), and also, a little to the west, the long forest road north to Dell Lodge. Visitors should stay on the tracks.

Aviemore Peregrine can often be seen on the high cliffs of Craigellachie Rock, easily viewed from the car park behind the Badenoch and Stakis Four Seasons hotels. Craigellachie NNR covers the birch woods on the Rock's lower slopes and entrance is from the footpath at the south end of the car park (or the footpath between the youth hostel and tourist office), via the underpass under the main A9. There is a signposted nature trail. At the south end of the town, the B970 bridge over the River Spey is a good bet for Dipper.

Inverdruie Fish Farm Offers the best chance in the region of seeing an Osprey fishing. Leave Aviemore east towards Coylumbridge on the B970 and turn left into the car park just after crossing the River Spey. There are two hides, and an entrance fee is payable. Mornings and evenings are best.

Rothiemurchus Estate Situated on the road between Aviemore and the Cairngorm Mountain Railway, there is a visitor centre just east of Loch Morlich and marked trails through a variety of habitats. The Moormore picnic site just south of the funicular road c.2 miles east of Coylumbridge is a favoured spot for Crested Tit and Scottish Crossbill. The quieter southwest section of the forest may produce Capercaillie and Black Grouse. Take the minor road from Inverdruie to Blackpark and on to Whitewell, following footpaths from here to the Cairngorm Club footbridge (NH 926078) and to the woodland between the confluence of the Am Beanaidh and Allt Druidh (a long walk).

Loch an Eilein Lies within Rothiemurchus Estate. Leave the B970 1 mile south of Inverdruie at Doune, turning southeast onto a minor road and continuing to the car park (fee) at the north end of the Loch, which holds Goldeneye and occasionally divers. Crested Tit and Scottish Crossbill may be seen on the forest trail encircling the Loch.

Glenmore Forest Park This large area (6,535 acres) of state-owned forest adjacent to Rothiemurchus Estate includes Loch Morlich, which although disturbed by watersports holds small numbers of wildfowl and is sometimes visited by Osprey, with Dipper on the Loch and its tributary streams. Crested Tit and, with luck and perseverance, Scottish Crossbill, can be seen around the Loch. A map/guide and booklet for the Park is available from Aviemore Tourist Office or the Glenmore Visitor Centre (on the road between Aviemore and the Cairngorm Mountain Railway, open 09.00–17.00 daily).

Cairn Gorm Take a minor road off the B970 at Coylumbridge and follow it for c.8 miles, past Loch Morlich, to the car park at the foot of the ski-lift (the *second*, upper, car park at Coire Cas). In the summer season (1 May–30 Nov) visitors can only reach the re-built Ptarmigan building near the top via the new funicular railway – and are not permitted to leave the top station. To access the high plateau it is now necessary to walk from Coire Cas. It is a steep 1½–2-hour walk on the well-marked path to the summit of Cairn Gorm. In winter the funicular gives easy access to the top for everyone. Ptarmigan, Dotterel and sometimes Snow Bunting occur on the summit plateau in summer, but due to disturbance are often difficult to find. Try walking south along the ridge path towards Ben Macdui; the further from the most accessible areas, the better the birds. In winter there is often Snow Bunting around the car park, while Ptarmigan descend to lower altitudes and, together with Red Grouse, may occur near the level of the car park; good areas to look are the valleys of Coire an t-Sneachda and Coire an Lochain south of the ski-tows. Access to Cairngorm NNR is unrestricted, except some areas in the deer-stalking season, August–October. Note, however, that the vegetation is very fragile and it is best to stay on the well-marked trails and paths, scanning carefully with binoculars and listening for calls. The weather on the high tops is very changeable, and walkers should be properly equipped and leave notice of their intended route (even a note on the car windscreen) if they stray far from the populous areas.

Carn Ban Mor An excellent, comparatively undisturbed, yet relatively accessible area for most of the upland specialities, peaking at 3,451 feet. From Feshiebridge on the B970 follow minor roads to Achlean, where there is limited parking at the end of the road. From here it is a steep but steady 2–3-hour walk to the summit on a broad, very well-marked track. Once on the tops it is best to remain on the track and scan carefully for Ptarmigan and Dotterel, which can be very easily overlooked. Part of the Cairngorm NNR (see Cairn Gorm above).

Glen Feshie A good area for raptors, while the woods hold Crested Tit and Scottish Crossbill, and the lower slopes Ring Ouzel. Follow directions to Achlean as for Carn Ban Mor, taking the path up the glen, which follows the river.

Moor of Feshie A woodland area that may produce Capercaillie. Access is from Feshiebridge or Lagganlia, or park by the B970 c.1¼ miles north of Feshiebridge (at NH 860060) and follow the tracks south into the woods.

Glen Tromie Running south from Drumguish on the B970, this has Black Grouse and sometimes Peregrine, Merlin, Golden Eagle and Hen Harrier, with Dipper on the river. A track runs up the glen from near Tromie Bridge on the B970.

Kingussie golf course Another area for lekking Black Grouse, the east end of the golf course is favoured.

Birds

Residents include Sparrowhawk, tiny numbers of Goshawk, Hen Harrier, Buzzard and Peregrine. There are a few Golden Eagles in the region, and these are occasionally encountered on the high tops, but by far the best area for the species is the Findhorn Valley (see p.539). Red Grouse breeds on the moors up to c.3,000 feet while Ptarmigan are on the high tops in summer, though they may move downslope in winter, often to below the snowline (when they overlap with Red Grouse). Black Grouse favour the forest edge and areas of scattered trees, as well as birch woods. They are most easily seen when lekking in late March–early June. As they are prone to disturbance, lekking Black Grouse should be watched from some distance or from a car. Capercaillie also prefers more open, heathery woodland and displaying males can sometimes be found on quiet forest roads in the early morning (and again in the evening) March to mid-April; as with Black Grouse, you should remain *in* the car. Occasionally 'rogue' male Capercaillies stake a territory and become fearless, attacking birdwatchers and even knocking them to the ground (the most notorious was a bird at Forest Lodge in the early 1990s). Both these species of grouse become very hard to find in summer when incubating and moulting, becoming more conspicuous again from September. Note that following successful management by the RSPB, their Abernethy Reserve has seen a four-fold increase in Black Grouse in the early 1990s, and now holds more than the rest of Strathspey (with two enormous spring leks of 177 and 190 birds in 1997!). Capercaillie numbers are stable there too, unlike the catastrophic declines reported from most other areas.

Long-eared Owl is resident, but hard to find. Not so Woodcock, which can be very conspicuous in early spring when roding. Crested Tit is quite common and often located by call; it tends to move into more open areas of long heather adjacent to woods in winter. Other small woodland passerines are Siskin, Redpoll and Scottish Crossbill; the last can be scarce one year and abundant the next, but tend to be most obvious April–July. Note that Common and even Parrot Crossbills also nest in these woods, so identification is critical for the purist! Snow Bunting occurs all year, though it is much commoner in winter when it can be found around the ski-tow car parks. A few pairs breed on the tops, favouring corries, boulder fields, scree slopes and the vicinity of snow fields. In open areas, both Carrion and Hooded Crows (and their hybrids) and sometimes Raven can be found.

Summer visitors include Slavonian Grebe in small numbers to several forest lochs. They are present early April–August. A few pairs of Red-throated and Black-throated Divers also breed, and occasionally visit some of the larger lochs. Breeding ducks include Wigeon, Teal, a few Shovelers, Tufted Duck, Red-breasted Merganser and Goosander. Goldeneye is a recent colonist, and has dramatically increased, due to the provision of nest boxes, to over 100 pairs since the first breeding record in 1970. On hatching, most ducklings and their parents transfer to the River Spey. Feral Greylag Goose is a scarce but increasing breeder in the region. Osprey is present early April–August, and is most reliably seen at the Osprey Observation Post at the RSPB's Abernethy Reserve, although Inverdruie Fish Farm often attracts fishing birds, and the species may put in an appearance at any loch or river. Other raptors include a few Merlins on the heather moors, and tiny numbers of Honey Buzzards. A few Water Rails breed, for example at Loch Garten. Waders include Golden Plover and Dunlin on the moors and tops, and Dotterel, which favours short grass, moss and lichen heath on the flat summit plateaux of the mountains above 2,600 feet. Oystercatcher, Common Sandpiper, a few Ringed Plovers, Common Gull, Dipper and Grey Wagtail haunt the streams and rivers, and Greenshank and Wood Sandpiper inhabit the forest bogs in very small numbers. Temminck's Stint, Green Sandpiper and Red-necked Phalarope have all bred in the past, and should be watched for. Great Spotted Woodpecker is joined by a few Green Woodpeckers and a handful of Wrynecks in open pine and birch woodland, although these are very difficult to find, with the best chance in early spring, when newly arrived birds are calling. Tree Pipit favours woodland clearings and areas of scattered trees, with Whinchat and Wheatear on open ground and Ring Ouzel around rocky valleys and scree slopes high in the hills. Around the woods, Redstart and Wood Warbler are reasonably common, with the occasional Pied Flycatcher (primarily in riverine woodland along the Spey). Areas of marsh and farmland support Lapwing, Redshank, Snipe, Curlew, Black-headed Gull and Grasshopper and Sedge Warblers.

In the last 20 years several species, presumably of Scandinavian origin, have colonised Scotland, and there is potential for others to do so. On the tops Snowy Owl, Purple Sandpiper, Sanderling, Shore Lark and Lapland Bunting are all slight possibilities, with Fieldfare, Redwing, Icterine Warbler, Red-backed Shrike, Common Rosefinch and Brambling a little more likely in the valleys, although the attempts by Shore Lark, Red-backed Shrike and Lapland Bunting to colonise may well have failed.

Large numbers of Pink-footed and Greylag Geese occur on passage, and there are sometimes Waxwings in autumn. Smaller numbers of Greylag winter, usually on farmland between Aviemore and Grantown-on-Spey, roosting at Loch Garten, as well as Whooper Swan (mainly around Boat of Garten–Nethy Bridge), and other wildfowl include Wigeon, Teal and Goldeneye. Wandering Red Kites from the re-introduction programme on the Black Isle may winter in the area, and rarely a White-tailed Eagle visits. Like many resident raptors, Hen Harrier moves to lower ground in winter. Occasionally a Great Grey Shrike appears, although you are more likely to see the much commoner Brambling.

Information

Aviemore Tourist Office, Main Road, Aviemore, Inverness-shire PH22 1PP. Tel: 01479 810363.

RSPB Abernethy Forest Reserve Warden, R. W. Thaxton, Guianan, Tulloch, Nethy Bridge, Inverness-shire PH25 3EF. Tel: 01479 831694 (office hours).

SNH, Sub-regional Office, Achantoul, Aviemore, Inverness-shire PH22 1QD Tel: 01479 810477.

Rothiemurchus Estate Visitor Centre. Tel: 01479 810858.

Forest Enterprise, Glenmore Visitor Centre. Tel: 01479 861220.

38 FINDHORN VALLEY (Highland)   OS Landranger 35

This remote valley is one of the best places in the east highlands to see Golden Eagle.

Habitat

A large area of primarily open hillsides grazed by sheep and Red Deer.

Access

From the main A9, 12 miles north of Aviemore, turn west on minor roads to Tomatin Services and, just west of the old Findhorn bridge, turn south to Garbole and Coignafearn on the single-track road which parallels the north bank of the River Findhorn. Stop and scan for eagles over the surrounding ridges as the Valley becomes precipitous after c.7 miles, continuing as necessary to the no entry sign at the road's end at Coignafearn Old Lodge, 10 miles from the junction (it is possible to continue on foot).

The road from Garbole, c.4 miles from the Findhorn Bridge, which meets the B851 at Farr, may produce a similar range of raptors, and may be a better bet for Hen Harrier.

Birds

Buzzard, Peregrine and, in summer, Osprey also occur, with the occasional Raven. Very occasionally, White-tailed Eagle may visit. The river has Goosander, Common Sandpiper, Grey Wagtail and Dipper, while the moors hold Red Grouse and Golden Plover, with Ring Ouzel on the rockier sections.

39 LOCH RUTHVEN (Highland)   OS Landranger 35

This loch, lying just east of Loch Ness, is a well-publicised site for breeding Slavonian Grebe and is also a good area for Black Grouse.

Habitat

Along the north shore of the loch are stands of birch woodland, otherwise the surrounding area is largely moorland, with some farmland around Tullich in the east.

Access

Leave the A9 c.6 miles south of Inverness south on the B851. After 8 miles, turn right on the minor road towards Tullich and Dalcrombie. (Alternatively, from Inverness take the B862 southwest and, after 12 miles or just past Loch Duntelchaig, turn southeast on the minor road to Dalcrombie and Tullich.) There is a car park at the east end of the Loch near Tullich and access is restricted to the 1½ mile trail along the southeast shore, leading to the hide. A warden is present April–August.

Birds

Up to ten pairs of Slavonian Grebe breed here, and are present late April–early September. Other breeders include Common and Black-headed Gulls, and Red-throated Diver may visit. Whinchat and Sedge Warbler nest in the surrounding vegetation, with Siskin and Redpoll in the woods and Twite in more open areas. The surrounding moorland has Peregrine, Hen Harrier and Raven. This is a good area for Black Grouse, which can be watched lekking in the early morning on the fields and moorland just northeast of Tullich. View from the RSPB car park, and take great care not to disturb lekking birds until they have dispersed of their own accord. During the rest of the day they can often be seen in the scrub on the surrounding hillsides.

In winter Goldeneye and occasionally Smew are recorded.

Information

RSPB North Scotland Office, Etvie House, Beechwood Park, Inverness IV2 3BW. Tel: 01463 715000.

40 DEESIDE (Northeast Scotland)   OS Landranger 37, 43 and 44

The River Dee drains the south flank of the Cairngorm massif, and the forests and mountains of upper Deeside have a similar range of birds to Speyside with the notable exception of Crested Tit. They are, however, less disturbed and more convenient for the visitor to east Aberdeenshire, and probably a better bet for the elusive Capercaillie. The best times to visit are March–April for residents and May–June for summer visitors.

Habitat

The Dee's wooded valley has areas of relict Scots pine and birch woods. The surrounding slopes are bog and moorland, and as the river winds west the hills rise higher and eventually reach 3,924 feet at Beinn A Bhuird. In the valley bottom are Lochs Davan and Kinord.

Access (see map)

Glen Tanar is a NNR, and west from Braemar parts of the area lie within Cairngorm NNR, and in these, as on the other estates, there are restrictions on access in the deer-stalking season, July–February. Exploration with the appropriate OS map is recommended.

Glen Tanar (OS Landranger 44) Leave the B976 at Bridge o'Ess (just southwest of Aboyne) and follow the minor road for 1½ miles to the car park at Braeloine. Continue on foot to Glen Tanar House, checking the river for Dipper, and from there follow any of the tracks into the forest. There is often Scottish Crossbill in the woods immediately beyond Glen Tanar House or on the hillock in the angle

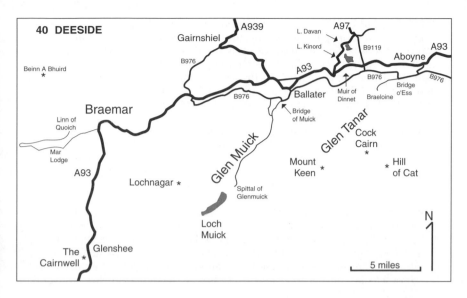

between the confluence of Water of Tanar and Water of Allachy. Capercaillie is reasonably common, a favoured area being the woods on the banks of Water of Tanar for up to 2 miles upstream of Glen Tanar House, with Black Grouse in the more open woodland and scattered pines. Goshawk and Sparrowhawk can be seen over the woods, with Hen Harrier and Merlin in the open areas above the forest and Golden Eagle over surrounding ridges and summits. Mount Keen lies at the head of Glen Tanar and holds Ptarmigan. Follow the old high-level drove-road to the summit or, perhaps better, the Firmounth Road along the valley of Water of Allachy towards the high ground around Hill of Cat or Cock Cairn. Note that excursions on foot to the high tops are arduous and require proper preparation. There is a visitor centre across the Water of Tanar from Braeloine, open April–September, providing information on the NNR and advice on access, particularly relevant in the grouse-shooting/deer-stalking seasons. Otherwise, visitors are requested to keep to the tracks, especially in May–June.

Muir of Dinnet NNR (OS Landranger 37 and 44) Covers c.3,500 acres of woodland, bog and moorland surrounding Lochs Kinord and Davan, which hold Goosander and sometimes summering Goldeneye. In late autumn–winter Whooper Swan and up to 2,000 Pink-footed and 8,000 Greylag Geese use the lochs. Access is from the A93, B9119 and A97 at Dinnet, and visitors should keep to the marked footpaths.

Gairnshiel (OS Landranger 37) A good area for Black Grouse. Leave the A93 just west of Ballater north on the A939 and, after c.5 miles, park just after the road crosses the River Gairn near Gairnshiel Lodge. The grouse may be seen lekking in the fields northeast of the river.

Glen Muick and Lochnagar (OS Landranger 44) Leave the B976 just south of Ballater at Bridge of Muick and follow the road to the car park at Spittal of Glenmuick, 8 miles from the junction. From here you can walk to Lochnagar (a fairly arduous climb) where there are Ptarmigan, Red Grouse, Dotterel, Peregrine, Merlin, Hen Harrier and Golden Eagle. Glen Muick is an excellent area. Black Grouse is relatively numerous and, if you are very lucky, you may see

Honey Buzzard or Wryneck in late spring. A good walk is to cross the River Muick northwest of Spittal to Allt-na-giubhsaich and follow tracks through the wood on the west bank of the river, this being a good area for Black Grouse. Another worthwhile route with fairly easy gradients is the old drove-road east of Loch Muick running south to Glen Clova. Over 6,000 acres of the area is a reserve of the Scottish Wildlife Trust by agreement with the Royal Estate. There is a visitor centre at Spittal of Glenmuick. Visitors should keep to the paths.

Glenshee (OS Landranger 43) Leave Braemar south on the A93 Old Military Road and park after c.7 miles at the car park near the foot of the ski-tows. This is an excellent site for Ptarmigan in winter, which can be seen with a telescope to the west on the slopes of The Cairnwell. In cold weather, they may descend and can then be seen close to the car park (sometimes from the car!).

Mar Lodge (OS Landranger 43) Leave Braemar west on the minor road paralleling the River Dee on the south shore. Park along the road or after 3½ miles cross the river at Victoria Bridge and park at Mar Lodge. Re-crossing the river on foot, Linn of Corriemulzie to the east is good for Capercaillie and Craig an Fhithich to the west for Peregrine. Scottish Crossbill can be found anywhere from Victoria Bridge west to the Linn of Dee in areas of Scots pine, and is often quite easy to find.

Beinn A Bhuird (OS Landranger 43) From Mar Lodge drive east for 1½ miles to Linn of Quoich and park at the Punch Bowl. There is usually a barrier across the road here, but you can walk west and north along the track to the foot of the mountain. Black Grouse occur on both sides (especially the northeast) of Glen Quoich, and there is also Capercaillie. Continue (well prepared) to the tops for Golden Eagle, Ptarmigan and Dotterel.

Birds

The high tops support Ptarmigan, which is often found around corries and moves lower in winter. It is joined in summer by Dotterel, which may be relatively numerous, and other breeding waders here and on the surrounding moorland include Golden Plover and a few Dunlin. Wheatear is widespread and Ring Ouzel quite common, but Snow Bunting is very rare—Beinn A Bhuird is probably the likeliest peak to support one. Raptors in the area include Golden Eagle, which prefers the more rugged and remote areas, Buzzard, Goshawk, Sparrowhawk, Hen Harrier and Peregrine are resident, and in summer there may be a Honey Buzzard and more regularly Merlin. Forest areas support Capercaillie and Black Grouse, and Woodcock is quite common. Among passerines, Siskin and Scottish Crossbill are resident, and Crossbill may breed in the conifer plantations. In summer there are also Tree Pipit, Redstart, Wood Warbler, Spotted Flycatcher and perhaps Wryneck or even a migrant Red-backed Shrike. In the forest meadows are a few pairs of Greenshanks, and along the river and its tributaries Goosander, Common Sandpiper, Grey Wagtail and Dipper, and these may also be seen on the lochs.

Information

Tourist Information Office, 45 Station Road, Banchory, Grampian. Tel: 01330 822000. Seasonal offices at Braemar (tel: 013397 41600) and Ballater (tel: 013397 55306).

SNH, Northeast Scotland Region, Wynne Edwards House, 17 Rubislow Terrace, Aberdeen AS1 1XE.

SNH, Muir of Dinnet, New Kinord House, Dinnet. Tel: 013398 810 022.

41 FOWLSHEUGH (Northeast Scotland)   OS Landranger 45

Fowlsheugh holds one of the largest seabird colonies in the country and is readily accessible. The best time to visit is April to mid-July, and 1½ miles of cliff are an RSPB reserve.

Habitat
The grass-topped sandstone cliffs reach over 200 feet high in places.

Access
Fowlsheugh is signposted east off the A92 at the Crawton turning, 4 miles south of Stonehaven. Park in the car park at Crawton at the end of the road and walk north along the footpath to the cliffs, with good views of the colonies at several points.

Birds
Fulmar, Shag and Eider are joined by nearly 30,000 pairs of Guillemot, 5,000 pairs of Razorbill and small numbers of Puffins. The 30,000 pairs of Kittiwake vastly outnumber the few Herring Gulls. Outside the breeding season there is little of special interest.

Information
RSPB Warden, Starnafin, Crimond, Fraserburgh, Aberdeenshire AB43 8QN. Tel: 01346 532017. E-mail: esro@rspb.org.uk

42 GIRDLE NESS (Northeast Scotland)   OS Landranger 38

This promontory, south of the mouth of the River Dee and immediately east of the conurbation of Aberdeen, is a useful seawatching station and also attracts a wide range of passerine migrants, regularly including rarities.

Habitat
Most of the promontory is a golf course with some areas of gorse scrub, flanked allotments and gardens, all of which are bounded by rocky cliffs.

Access (see map)
From Aberdeen city centre, take the A956 Market Street south and cross the River Dee via Victoria Bridge, continuing into Victoria Road and then turning left at the T-junction into St Fitticks Road and right into Greyhope Road, following this along the edge of the golf course to the lighthouse. There are two car parks on the Ness, both of which can be used for seawatching.

Birds
Seawatching in autumn can be good. Manx and Sooty Shearwaters are frequent offshore, especially in onshore (northeast) winds. Great and Arctic Skuas are common, and there are regularly Pomarine and occasionally also Long-tailed. Passage waders may include Ruff, Black-tailed Godwit and Curlew Sandpiper, and Barnacle Goose may pass through in October. In late autumn–winter divers and numbers of sea ducks, particularly Goldeneye and Eider, are usual. Glaucous Gull is regular and Iceland Gull occasional, as well as Little Auk, with Purple Sandpiper and Turnstone on the rocks.

In spring and autumn there may be many Wheatear on the golf course, and

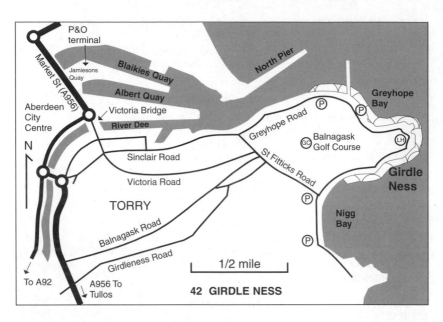

interesting migrants can occur among the commoner species: Wryneck, Bluethroat and Red-backed Shrike are near annual at both seasons, with Yellow-browed, Barred and Icterine Warblers and Common Rosefinch possible in autumn.

43 BRIDGE OF DON (Northeast Scotland)   OS Landranger 38

This area, just north of Aberdeen, attracts numbers of diving and sea duck in winter and concentrations of feeding and loafing terns in summer. As with any site on this east-facing coast, it can also hold passerine migrants in spring and autumn.

Habitat

Sandy beaches and low dunes.

Access

Don Mouth, north bank A minor road runs alongside the north bank of the river from the A92 immediately north of the bridge, with a car park at its east end giving views of the River Mouth.

Don Mouth, south bank A minor road (Beach Esplanade) runs alongside the south bank of the river from the A92 immediately south of the bridge, with plenty of roadside parking. From here, you can walk to the river mouth or follow the foreshore south to Aberdeen beach. Inland of the Don Bridge the high embankment bordering Seaton Park (accessed off the A92, c.⅓ mile south of the Don Bridge, via Harrow Road and Don Street) offers a good viewpoint over the inner estuary for ducks and waders.

Mains of Murcar Turn east off the A92, 300 yards north of the Don Bridge, direct-

Waxwing

The gorgeous Waxwing is a bird of Scandinavia and Siberia, which reaches Britain in varying numbers during the winter. Severe weather may herald spectacular influxes. Many flocks favour urban areas – systematically stripping berries from fruiting trees and bushes in supermarket car parks and on traffic islands. It is most likely to be encountered close to the coast, in north-east England and Scotland, only rarely penetrating southern England.

Key sites: Lindisfarne, Cairngorms and Speyside, Gibraltar Point – but probably more likely in 'non-birdy' settings.

Purple Sandpiper

This dumpy little wader is a fairly widespread non-breeding visitor to much of Britain, especially the north. It favours rocky coastlines, where it often associates with Turnstones. It has occasionally bred in the Scottish Highlands, but trying to find them here would probably end in disappointment – stick to the shoreline, where non-breeders can usually be found throughout the year.

Key sites: Fife Ness, St Abb's Head, Hilbre and Red Rocks, Oxwich, Mounts Bay.

Puffin

Britain's smallest breeding auk is also one of the most instantly recognisable of all British birds. Puffins nest in disused rabbit burrows, often at the tops of seabird cliffs, and winter at sea. The bulk of Britain's population is in the north, particularly Scotland, and the largest colonies are found in Sutherland and on the offshore islands, especially the Orkneys and Shetland, but the Pembrokeshire islands also hold good numbers.

Key sites: Sule Skerry, Handa, Clo Mor, Skokholm, Skomer, Bempton Cliffs.

Red-necked Phalarope

This charming aquatic wader is a very scarce Scottish breeder, easiest to find in the Shetlands. Breeding birds occupy small freshwater pools, where they can be watched swimming and spinning around at high speed on the water, snapping up small insects. On passage, it is rare but most frequent on the east coast of Britain, where it may appear on small freshwater or brackish ponds.

Key sites: Fetlar, Unst, North Uist.

ly opposite its junction with the B997, fork left to the golf course, and follow the track for 1⅓ miles to its end, proceeding to the shore.

Birds

In winter off the Don Mouth many Goldeneyes and Goosanders are present, and sometimes up to 15 Scaup and a few Long-tailed Ducks. Red-throated Diver is also numerous offshore, and the river mouth is a likely spot for Glaucous Gull and sometimes also Iceland Gull in late winter. To the north, at Mains of Murcar, numbers of scoters and eiders may be found (as at Blackdog, see below).

In summer there are concentrations of Common, Arctic and Sandwich Terns, and in late summer these attract Arctic and Great Skuas. Offshore in autumn, winds between the north and east may prompt a passage of Manx Shearwater, Gannet, Kittiwake and skuas.

During passage periods numbers of migrants can sometimes be found in the riverside bushes. Waders too can be interesting at the river mouth.

44 BLACKDOG (Northeast Scotland) OS Landranger 38

This area, just a few miles north of Aberdeen, holds good numbers of moulting sea duck in late summer and autumn, often including a King Eider or Surf Scoter. At this time of year, it is better for these species than the Ythan estuary to the north.

Habitat

A sandy shore backed by dunes and a golf course.

Access

Blackdog lies east of the A92 5 miles north of Aberdeen, and a track runs from the main road (just north of Blackdog Burn) east towards the shore, with limited parking around the houses at the end. It is then a short walk to the beach.

Birds

This is an excellent area for concentrations of moulting sea duck late June–early September, when there are up to 10,000 Eider, 2,000 Common Scoter and 250 Velvet Scoter, also regularly at least one King Eider and sometimes 1–2 Surf Scoters. Small numbers of Scaup occur in autumn, and the concentrations of loafing terns attract Arctic and Great Skuas.

Numbers of sea duck are much lower in winter, but the commoner species are still present, together with large numbers of Red-throated Diver, Red-breasted Merganser and Long tailed Duck. On the shore, look for Sanderling, with Snow Bunting in the dunes.

45 YTHAN ESTUARY AND THE SANDS
OF FORVIE (Northeast Scotland) OS Landranger 30 and 38

The Ythan lies 12 miles north of Aberdeen, and together with the sea and adjacent Sands of Forvie, is an excellent area for large numbers of wildfowl, waders and terns, with the largest colony of breeding Eider in Britain. Notably, at least one male King Eider has been present here April–June (sometimes from November; they move to Blackdog in late summer to moult, see above) most years since 1974 until the present. The area is worth a visit at any time of year, and much of the area is part of a NNR.

Habitat

The estuary is c.5 miles long but only a few hundred yards wide. Flanked for half its length by the A975, it is surprisingly undisturbed and very good views are possible. The extensive mussel beds at the mouth provide food for the hordes of Eider, while there are small saltmarshes in the middle reaches. The Sands of Forvie, an area of dunes and moorland, lie between the river and the sea. North of Rockend the coast is flanked by cliffs, rising to 130 feet at Collieston. Four small lochs, Meikle, Little, Cotehill and Sand, lie in the north of the area.

Access (see map)

There is open access to the NNR, apart from the ternery and moorland areas in April–August, and you should keep to the paths. The period two hours either side of high water (but not high tide itself, which is an hour later at Waterside Bridge than at the estuary mouth), is best for waders, while low tide is best for eiders.

Ythan Estuary, south shore Access to the south side of the estuary is from Newburgh. Turn off the A975 just south of the village by the Ythan Hotel (signed to the beach) and continue to the car park near the golf course. Walk over the dunes to the mouth of the river, from where you can view the terneries in summer, while in winter this is an excellent spot to see divers and sea duck at sea. This a good spot for the King Eider around high water, and is favoured by Snow Bunting in winter. Areas of bushes, which attract passage migrants, lie around the car park and golf course, in the dunes at the estuary mouth and further south on Foveran Links.

Inches Point, Newburgh The drake King Eider, if present, can often be seen in the area north of Inches Point around low water, which is reached via Inches Road off the A975 in Newburgh. Alternatively, view from the footpath on the opposite side of the estuary, running south from Waterside Bridge.

Waterside Bridge There are good views of the estuary from the A975. Heading north from Newburgh, park at the west end of Waterside Bridge to view the Sleek of Tarty and Inch Geck, which is used by roosting waders. A track follows the shore of the Sleek west from the bridge, giving the best chance of interesting waders. Continuing north there are more parking places affording views of the upper estuary.

Waulkmill Hide Turn northwest off the A975 c.2 miles north of Waterside Bridge (opposite the B9003 turning) and after c.1½ miles turn left on a track along the east side of the Burn of Forvie, reaching the car park and hide after 200 yards, with good views over the inner estuary.

Logie Buchan Bridge Accessible on minor roads off the A975, this is a good spot for wintering Water Rail.

Sands of Forvie, north section Turn off the A975 on the B9003 to Collieston. Cotehill Loch is adjacent to the road soon after the turn and is good for ducks and, if the water level is low, passage waders. Nearer Collieston, Forvie Centre, the NNR HQ, has a car park. A path leads from here past Sand Loch to the coast and Rockend Track. Sand Loch often has breeding Great Crested Grebe.

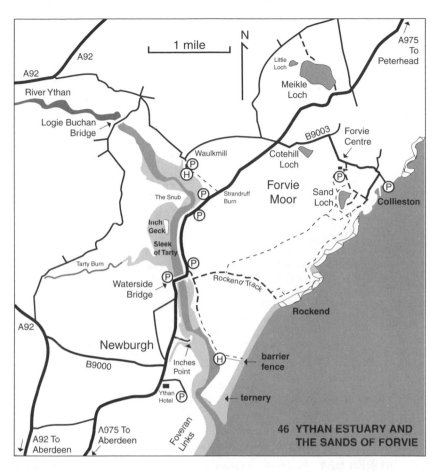

46 YTHAN ESTUARY AND THE SANDS OF FORVIE

Sands of Forvie, ternery April–August the south end of the NNR is fenced-off to protect breeding terns. These can be watched from a hide, reached by walking south from Waterside Bridge.

Collieston Take the B9003 to Collieston. The village gardens, allotments and coastal scrub can attract migrants, and the height of the cliffs make this a good spot to seawatch from.

Meikle Loch This is the main goose roost, and is also good for ducks. Continue on the A975 for 1 mile past the B9003 turning and take a track on the left just before the crossroads. To avoid disturbing the geese, stay on this track. Small numbers of passage waders regularly include Ruff and Green Sandpiper, and there is further access via the track along the east shore.

Birds

Wintering wildfowl include up to 250 Whooper Swan, which feed on the estuary and surrounding fields. Tens of thousands of Pink-footed Geese occur in autumn, together with large numbers of Greylag (the latter peak in spring); most geese roost on Meikle Loch. Passage geese may include a few Brent, Barnacle, White-fronted and occasionally a Snow Goose. And, although there are far fewer geese in winter, the numbers of both Greylag and Pink-feet around the estuary and fields are still significant. Other wildfowl include Teal and Wigeon, and sometimes Gadwall, Shoveler and Ruddy Duck on the lochs. Offshore, there are small numbers of Long-tailed Duck, Common and Velvet Scoters, Goldeneye and Red-breasted Merganser, and the 1,000 Eider in early winter reach the full summer strength of over 6,000 by February. Red-throated Diver is also present. Waders include Sanderling and sometimes small numbers of wintering Ruff and Jack Snipe. On the beach and dunes there are often Snow Bunting, and raptors may include Short-eared Owl, Peregrine and Merlin.

In summer there may still be several hundred Common Scoter offshore, often joined by Velvets, and occasionally a King Eider is found (usually in spring or early summer). Over 2,000 Eider breed on Forvie Moor, and feeding and loafing eiders concentrate on the mussel beds of the lower estuary. Common, Arctic, Little and c.1,500 pairs of Sandwich Terns breed, together with Black-headed Gull. The terns attract skuas, and both Great and Arctic are frequently present in small numbers. On the cliffs to the north there are small numbers of Fulmar, Kittiwake, Herring Gull and a few Razorbills, with Shelduck, Oystercatcher, Ringed Plover and Curlew on the dunes and moorland, and Red Grouse are resident on the moor.

A variety of waders is recorded in spring and autumn, including Greenshank and Ruff, and occasionally Little Stint, Curlew Sandpiper, Black-tailed Godwit, Spotted Redshank and Green Sandpiper, but by English standards the variety is usually quite poor. Occasionally Garganey is recorded in spring, especially on Cotehill Loch. Little Gull and Black Tern, which favour Meikle Loch, are also possibilities. In late spring and autumn, southeast winds, especially if combined with rain or poor visibility, may bring falls of migrants, which occasionally include some of the scarcer species.

Information

SNH Warden, Alison Matheson, Stevenson Forvie Centre, Little Collieston Croft, Collieston, Ellon, Aberdeenshire AB41 8RU. Tel: 01358 751330.

46 CRUDEN BAY (Northeast Scotland)   OS Landranger 30

This area regularly attracts interesting passerine migrants.

Access

The small wood along the stream near the harbour attracts birds, as do the gardens in the village. Access to the wood is from the village (park at the first car park) or on a track south off the A975 just north of Cruden Bay, immediately beyond a sharp right-hand bend (difficult to find).

Birds

The sheltered wooded valley acts as a migrant trap in spring and autumn, and is one of the best places to see migrant passerines at both seasons. In addition to common species such as Redstart, Ring Ouzel and Pied Flycatcher, a number of scarce migrants may be found in the area including Wryneck, Richard's Pipit, Bluethroat, Barred, Pallas's and Yellow-browed Warblers (the latter is regular), Firecrest, and Red-backed and Great Grey Shrikes. National rarities are also seen from time to time. In summer Tree Sparrows have been recorded breeding.

47 BULLERS OF BUCHAN (Northeast Scotland)   OS Landranger 30

The cliffs on this stretch of the north Aberdeen coast hold some notable colonies of breeding seabirds.

Access
Around 1 mile north of Cruden Bay on the A975, take a short track east off the main road to the cliffs at Robie's Haven.

Birds
Around 23,000 breeding seabirds of nine species include Fulmar, Shag, Kittiwake, Guillemot, Razorbill and Puffin.

48 LOCH OF STRATHBEG (Northeast Scotland)   OS Landranger 30

Midway between Fraserburgh and Peterhead, the Loch of Strathbeg is Britain's largest dune-slack lake and forms part of a large RSPB reserve. Only ½ mile from the sea, it is used by a variety of wintering wildfowl and is excellent for passage waders. Adjacent Rattray Head is a good spot in winter for all three divers, and in spring and autumn the area attracts small numbers of migrants.

Habitat
The Loch covers c.550 acres and is very shallow, a small rise in the water level can flood the surrounding marshes and farmland. Around it are areas of freshwater marsh, large stands of reed-grass, some reeds and scattered patches of willow carr and fen woodland. To the seaward, the dunes of Back Bar lead to the low-lying Rattray Head.

Access (see map)
RSPB Starnafin Farm The Loch lies northeast of the A952 and the reserve centre is signed off the A952 in Crimond (take the minor road north, just south of the church, turn left at the T-junction and then turn first right). The visitor centre is open daily from dawn until dusk, and there are purpose-built wader scrapes.

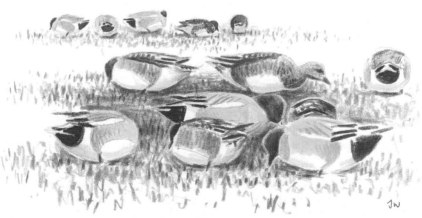

Wigeon

549

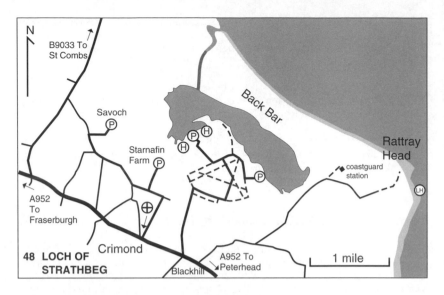

48 LOCH OF STRATHBEG

RSPB Savoch Continue past Starnafin Farm to the car park at Savoch.

Loch of Strathbeg, Loch hides For access to the loch-side hides (members and permit holders only) turn north off the A952 ½ mile southeast of Crimond church and follow the RSPB signs across Crimond Airfield to either of the two car parks (access across the airfield may be restricted at times). Do not stop or deviate from the route. There are four hides and a loch-side boardwalk.

Loch of Strathbeg, south sector The south of the Loch can be viewed from the unclassified road that leaves the A952 northeast between Blackhill and Crimond, a short track leads towards the south corner.

Rattray Head coastguard station The coastguard's cottages have small areas of cover, which should be checked for migrants after southeast winds in spring and autumn, preferably in the early morning. Except during foggy weather, migrants tend to disperse quickly.

Rattray Head Continue to the lighthouse and Rattray Head, and walk either north or south along the shore, looking out to sea for divers.

Birds

Several hundred Whooper Swans use the Loch in winter, peak numbers occurring in November; sometimes there are also a few Bewick's in early winter. Large numbers of grey geese roost at Strathbeg and, again, numbers peak during passage, late September–November and again late March–April: up to 10,000 Greylag and 28,000 Pink-feet may be present, small numbers of Barnacle Geese also pass through in early October and some winter, while one or two Snow Geese are regular. A few Brent and White-fronted Geese also appear on passage. Eider is resident and up to 500 Goldeneye winter, together with large numbers of Wigeon. Goosander occur for much of the year, with Red breasted Merganser on passage, a few Gadwall are regular, and there are occasionally Smew in late winter. Sparrowhawk, Merlin and Short-eared Owl are sometimes seen. All three divers winter off Rattray Head, as well as Eider and Long-tailed Duck, and there are frequently Snow Bunting on the shore and dunes.

Breeders include Fulmar in the dunes, Eider, Shelduck, Shoveler, Teal and, in 1984, Ruddy Duck, while Garganey has also bred. Others are Water Rail at the reserve, Common Tern and (irregularly) large numbers of Sandwich Terns. Sedge and Willow Warblers frequent the surrounding marsh and carr. Both Black-tailed Godwit and Marsh Harrier are regular in summer, and Osprey annual on passage. A variety of waders occurs on passage, notably large numbers of Ruff and Black-tailed Godwit, as well as Spotted Redshank, Greenshank, Green and Curlew Sandpipers and Little Stint, while Wood Sandpiper and Temminck's Stint are annual, and Pectoral Sandpiper nearly so. Spoonbills are regular visitors in summer, and other migrants can include Little Gull and Black Tern, the latter scarce in northeast Scotland. At Rattray Head a NW–SE wind may produce Sooty Shearwater and skuas in August–September.

Information
RSPB Warden, Starnafin Farm, Crimond, Fraserburgh, Aberdeenshire AB43 4YN. Tel: 01346 532017. E-mail: esro@rspb.org.uk

49 FRASERBURGH AND KINNAIRD HEAD
(Northeast Scotland)   OS Landranger 30

This area of northeast Scotland is excellent for white-winged gulls, and has great potential as a seawatching station in autumn.

Access
Fraserburgh Explore the coast from Fraserburgh harbour west to Broadsea, where the two fish factories and sewage outfall are especially attractive to gulls. Access is along a maze of roads north off the A98 in the town.

Kinnaird Head This, the north tip of Fraserburgh, is a good spot to seawatch from in NW–SE winds.

Birds
In winter Fraserburgh attracts wintering Glaucous and Iceland Gulls, sometimes in numbers. There is usually Black Guillemot on the sea and lots of Purple Sandpipers. At Kinnaird Head there are divers, often including Great Northern and Black-throated, and Black Guillemot among the masses of Guillemots and Razorbills.

In autumn Sooty Shearwater is seen regularly off the Head, and the large shearwaters and rarer skuas should also be possible.

50 BANFFF/MACDUFF HARBOUR
(Northeast Scotland)   OS Landranger 29

Situated on the north coast of Aberdeenshire, this is a good site in winter for gulls and sea duck.

Access
The harbour and adjacent rocky coast are easily accessed north off the A98.

Birds

In winter and on passage Red-throated Diver, Common and Velvet Scoters, and Eider are present offshore and may enter the harbours, and there are sometimes Great Northern and Black-throated Divers. Both Glaucous and Iceland Gulls are regular, and a Kumlien's Gull from North America wintered here for some years. Purple Sandpiper and Turnstone are common on the rocks.

On autumn passage skuas may occur offshore, and Little Auk may be present in large numbers in late autumn–early winter.

51 PORTGORDON—PORTKNOCKIE (Moray & Nairn)   OS Landranger 28

The small harbours along this coast may hold white-winged gulls, as well as sheltering sea duck.

Habitat

From Portgordon east to Portknockie the coast is rocky.

Access

The A990 follows the coast from Portgordon to Portknockie with straightforward access to the coast and harbours.

Birds

Large numbers of Purple Sandpiper and Turnstone winter along this coast, and offshore there may be Red-throated Diver and occasionally also Black-throated and Great Northern. Common and Velvet Scoters, Long-tailed Duck, Eider and Red-breasted Merganser may also be seen offshore. In rough weather, divers, sea duck, Guillemot, Razorbill and occasionally even Little Auk may seek shelter in the harbours. There are sometimes Glaucous and occasionally Iceland Gulls among the commoner gulls around the harbours. In autumn, especially given a strong northeast wind, Manx and Sooty Shearwaters, Gannet, and Great, Arctic and (occasionally) Pomarine Skuas may also be seen offshore, especially from Portknockie.

52 SPEY BAY AND LOSSIEMOUTH (Moray & Nairn)   OS Landranger 28

This area holds large numbers of sea ducks, and up to eight Surf Scoters have been recorded. Winter and spring are the best times to visit, though sea duck are present all year.

Habitat

The Rivers Lossie and Spey discharge into a long shallow bay. There are no large tidal flats, rather a sand and shingle beach between Lossiemouth and Portgordon, backed by plantations of Scots and Corsican pines at Lossie Forest.

Access (see map)

Lossiemouth Take the A941 from Elgin north to Lossiemouth and follow the road until it ends at Branderburgh pier and harbour. This is a good place to look for sea duck in the bay. Surf Scoter has been seen quite frequently. It is possible to cross the River Lossie on foot via a wooden bridge to work the river mouth and shore to the east. Low tide is best for waders.

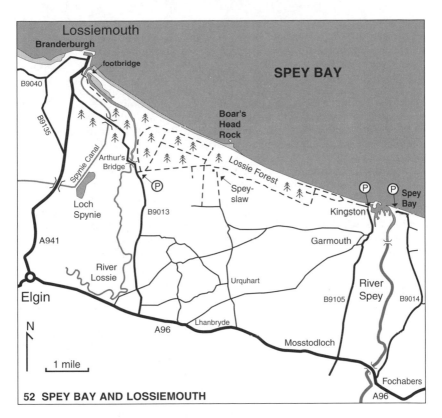

52 SPEY BAY AND LOSSIEMOUTH

Boar's Head Rock The best access to the middle of the bay; sea duck and, in autumn, divers are often numerous offshore. Turn north off the A96 on the B9013 and, after 3½ miles, park just before Arthur's Bridge over the River Lossie. From here it is a 2-mile walk through Lossie Forest to the rock (the route can be confusing, but the OS is of some help). Alternatively, follow minor roads north off the A96 to Speyslaw and walk north from here for 1 mile to the Rock.

Kingston Take the B9015 off the A96 north to Kingston and on to the picnic site by the river mouth. View the mouth of the river for waders at low tide or take the track west along the beach for sea duck, which may be numerous.

Speymouth Take the B9104 off the A96 at Fochabers, and drive to the coast at Spey Bay. The river mouth is good for waders at low water, and for sea duck scan the bay to locate the flocks.

Lossie Forest This is owned by the FC, and access is from the beach west of Kingston or along several tracks north off the A96. Cars are not allowed into the forest, and entry may be restricted because of activity on the firing range. The forest may be closed at times of severe fire-risk.

Birds

Red-throated Diver can be abundant offshore, especially in autumn but wintering Black-throated and Great Northern are only present in small numbers, although with persistence both may be seen. Common Scoter and Long-tailed Duck may peak at 1,000 (occasionally as many as 5,000 scoters), and Velvet Scoter can reach 500 (and in good years 1,000). A few hundred Eiders are joined by small numbers of Scaup and Red-breasted Merganser, and quite often Surf Scoter. As always, the duck can be well offshore at times. The fields between Elgin and Lossiemouth may hold Greylag Goose and sometimes Whooper Swan. Waders include large numbers of Purple Sandpiper and Turnstone at Branderburgh, otherwise the mouth of the Lossie holds numbers of the commoner species. There are sometimes Glaucous and occasionally Iceland Gulls along the beach, especially at Lossiemouth, and large flocks of Snow Bunting winter here, especially towards the west end. In Lossie Forest, Crested Tit and Scottish Crossbill are resident, though neither is numerous.

Small numbers of Common and Velvet Scoters oversummer, together with Goosander and sometimes Surf Scoter. A few Common and Arctic Terns breed, usually on islands in the lower reaches of the Spey. In autumn there are small numbers of passage waders and Sandwich Tern may be abundant. Especially in a strong N–E wind, Manx and Sooty Shearwaters, Gannet, and Great, Arctic and (occasionally) Pomarine Skuas may also be seen offshore.

53 FINDHORN BAY AND CULBIN BAR
(Moray & Nairn)   OS Landranger 27

This area is excellent in winter. Within a short distance there are concentrations of sea duck and waders and all three Scottish specialities. During summer there is less to see on the coast, but in April–June the forest is at its best. The east end of Culbin Sands is an RSPB reserve of over 2,000 acres.

Habitat
Culbin Sands is the largest dune system in Britain and has been extensively planted with Corsican and Scots pines, resulting in a large stand of monotonous woodland. Sandbars totalling nearly 5 miles border the coast, with some areas of saltmarsh. Findhorn Bay is an almost completely enclosed tidal basin, attractive to wildfowl and waders.

Access (see map)
Culbin Sands RSPB reserve Leave Nairn on the A96 and turn east just before the railway bridge to Kingsteps. Take the unsigned track from here to the shore, park and walk east along the coast. There is no warden and access is possible at all times.

Loch Loy and Cran Loch Accessible on tracks north off the minor road past Kingsteps. They attract wildfowl, including wintering Whooper Swan.

Culbin Forest Owned by the FC, this can only be entered on foot, from either Wellhill or Cloddymoss. These are accessible along a maze of lanes north off the A96. Tracks lead from the car parks through the forest to the shore and bar.

Findhorn Bay View the east shore from the B9011 Findhorn–Kinloss road. The west side can be seen by taking a minor road north off the A96, just west of the Findhorn bridge, and following this (without turning) for 2½ miles to Kincorth House and Wellside Farm. Park carefully and follow tracks along the edge of the forest to the Bay. Access to the south side is more complicated, with several minor roads leaving Forres north to the shore.

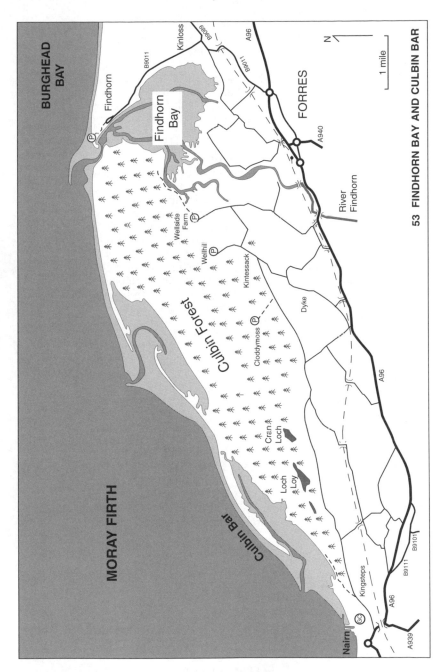

Findhorn village A viewpoint for sea duck in winter and terns in summer off-shore in Burghead Bay.

Burghead harbour (OS Landranger 28) On the B9089 north off the A96 north-east of Kinloss, the harbour often has Eider, Long-tailed Duck, Black Guillemot and Purple Sandpiper, and occasionally holds Little Auk in winter. The resident gulls may be joined by a Glaucous or Iceland. Divers and sea duck may be seen at sea from the harbour or headland.

Roseisle Forest Near Burghead, Crested Tit can be found in Roseisle Forest. Leave Burghead south on the B9089 and, after c.3 miles, turn north in Lower Hempriggs, following the track north for c.1 mile to the picnic site near the beach. In winter the birds can be around the car park, but in summer may be more dispersed.

Birds

On the sea, all three divers are regular in winter, though Red-throated far outnumber Black-throated and Great Northern. Large numbers of Common and Velvet Scoters and Long-tailed Duck join the local Red-breasted Merganser, and Black Guillemot is reasonably frequent. Greylag Goose and Whooper Swan favour the fields. Waders involve the usual species, including Knot and Bar-tailed Godwit. There may be flocks of Snow Bunting along the foreshore and in the dunes.

Breeding birds include small numbers of Eiders, Oystercatchers and Ringed Plovers, as well as a few Common and Arctic Terns at Culbin and in Findhorn Bay (joined by non-breeding Sandwich Tern). Ospreys quite often fish in Findhorn Bay in summer. In the plantations Buzzard, Sparrowhawk, dwindling numbers of Capercaillies, Long-eared Owl, Crested Tit, Scottish Crossbill and Siskin are resident. Crossbill may appear in late summer, especially in invasion years.

Passage brings some interesting waders, including Whimbrel and Greenshank, and less frequently Curlew Sandpiper, Black-tailed Godwit, Spotted Redshank and Little Stint. Findhorn Bay is the best place for these. Offshore there are often Gannet and Common, Arctic and Sandwich Terns. Skuas may appear, especially in northeast winds.

54 GOLSPIE, LOCH FLEET AND EMBO (Highland)   OS Landranger 21

North of the Dornoch Firth, this area holds large numbers of sea duck and often offers exceptional views of Eider and Long-tailed Duck. The best time to visit is probably late March–early May, when numbers peak.

Habitat

The coast is sandy towards Golspie, with dunes along the shore. About 3 miles long, the shallow saltwater basin of Loch Fleet is almost completely enclosed. An attempt to drain it resulted in the development of an extensive alder carr at the head of the Loch beyond the Mound (the embanked A9), and there are areas of both semi-natural and planted pines adjacent to the shore. The Loch and its north shore are a Scottish Wildlife Trust reserve, and a summer warden is present April–August.

Access (see map)

Golspie The sea and beach here are of straightforward access from the A9.

Loch Fleet, Littleferry Most sea duck congregate north of the Loch's mouth. Access is along the beach, either walking south from Golspie or, better, taking Ferry Road off the A9 at the south edge of Golspie, past the golf course and Ferry

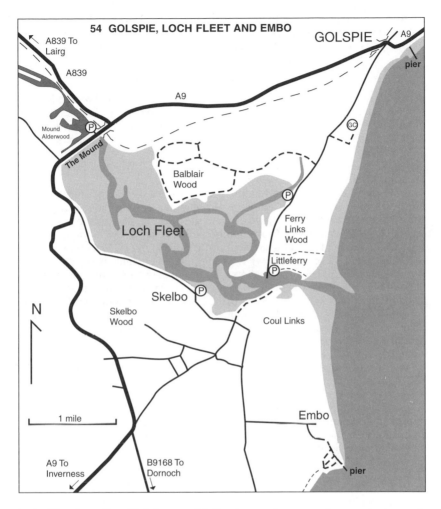

54 GOLSPIE, LOCH FLEET AND EMBO

Links Wood, south to Littleferry and following tracks east to the mouth. A permit is necessary to leave the tracks in Ferry Links and Balblair Woods.

Loch Fleet, Balblair Follow directions as for Littleferry but park where the minor road first meets the estuary at Balblair Wood to view the estuary.

Loch Fleet, The Mound The upper part of Loch Fleet, together with the fresh-water pools and carr beyond the Mound are visible from the A9, with a car park at the north end of the causeway.

Loch Fleet, Skelbo The Loch can also be viewed from the minor road to Skelbo off the A9. This skirts the south shore, with a car park and information board at Skelbo.

Coul Links Carry on the minor road past Skelbo and, after ½ mile, park by the right-angle bend.

Embo Continue past Skelbo to the shore at Embo, a collection of caravans and chalets. There are usually sea duck off the makeshift pier (with Purple Sandpiper on the rocks) and this is a good area for Common, Velvet and sometimes Surf Scoters; if not, walk north along the beach to the mouth of Loch Fleet.

Birds

In winter all three divers occur in small numbers, though Red-throated is commonest. There are also Slavonian and sometimes Red-necked Grebes. Variable numbers of Eider winter, sometimes as many as 2,000, together with several hundred Long-tailed Duck, Common Scoter and Red-breasted Merganser. Many Eider loaf around the Loch. Velvet Scoter and Goldeneye occur in smaller numbers, and other wintering wildfowl include up to 2,000 Wigeon, Teal and very occasionally Surf Scoter.

Sea duck peak in spring and autumn, with up to 2,000 Long-tailed Ducks in April–May, but only Eider is numerous in summer. A King Eider was present 1973–1993, with occasionally up to three in the area, but none has been seen in recent years. There are significant numbers of Greylag Geese in the area, with 400–500 in late winter, and a flock of up to 60 Whooper Swans uses the surrounding fields. Short-eared Owl is seen quite frequently, Hen Harrier and Peregrine less often. The usual waders are present in winter, with good numbers of Oystercatcher, Redshank, Dunlin, Knot and Bar-tailed Godwit; these roost at Skelbo Point, the beach at the mouth of the Loch and Balblair saltmarsh. Notable are small numbers of Purple Sandpipers, especially at Embo. One or two Glaucous Gulls are regular, and there are sometimes Iceland as well. Small numbers of Snow Bunting and, irregularly, Twite may be found in the dunes and along the shore.

On passage a few interesting waders occur, but are generally few and far between. In autumn, northwest or north winds, especially if it is misty or hazy, can push seabirds onto the coast, and Sooty Shearwater and skuas may occur.

Breeding birds include Fulmar, Shelduck, Eider and Arctic Tern. The surrounding woodland has resident Buzzard, Sparrowhawk, Siskin and Scottish Crossbill (at Balblair), and these are joined in summer by Redstart. Osprey is quite often seen fishing in Loch Fleet in summer.

Information

Scottish Wildlife Trust, Cramond House, Kirk Cramond, Cramond Glebe Road, Edinburgh EH4 6NS. Tel: 0131 312 7765. E-mail: enquiries@swt.org.uk

55 DORNOCH (Highland)   OS Landranger 21

The Dornoch Firth holds large numbers of sea duck and other wildfowl, including Scaup. The populations of Loch Fleet/Embo and the Firth are closely linked and both King Eider and Black and Surf Scoter can find their way here.

Access

Dornoch Take the B9168 or A949 east off the A9 to Dornoch, where several tracks lead to the shore. The best area for scoter.

Dornoch Point Reached on foot along a track south past the small airstrip.

A9 roadbridge This gives good views of the central part of the Firth.

Edderton Sands and Cambuscurrie Bay Leave the A9 at the roundabout at the south end of the A9 roadbridge on the minor road to Meikle Ferry. A good area for Pintail and up to 400 Scaup.

Birds
Wintering wildfowl include thousands of Wigeon, Teal, Shelduck, Pintail, Scaup and Common and Velvet Scoters. Waders include the usual species, notably small numbers of Turnstone and Sanderling.

On passage a variety of waders may occur, including small numbers of Grey Plover, Knot and Bar-tailed Godwit, and a few Greenshank. Osprey can be seen fishing in the Firth in summer.

56 TARBAT NESS (Highland)
OS Landranger 21

This promontory is quite good for seawatching.

Access
Take the B9165 to Portmahomack from the A9 3 miles south of Tain, and continue on a minor road to the lighthouse.

Birds
In autumn, quite large numbers of Sooty Shearwater, as well as skuas, auks and terns are seen.

57 FORSINARD (Caithness)
OS Landranger 10

This vast, new (purchased 1996) RSPB reserve covers 17,752 acres and protects an important area of deep peatland in the 'Flow Country' of Sutherland and Caithness. It is best visited in May–June.

Habitat
The 'Flow Country' consists of a vast expanse of more or less flat blanket bog interspersed by a mosaic of small pools and lochans. It is internationally important for both its flora and fauna, yet, in the 1980s, ill-designed government subsidies and tax incentives led to large areas being damaged or destroyed by plantations of coniferous trees. Fortunately the subsidies have been removed but, as in the case of Forsinard, the only sure protection is ownership.

Access
Reached along the A897, and 24 miles from Helmsdale on the A9 and 14 miles from Melvich on the north coast, the reserve is served by a railway station, with services from Inverness. The reserve is open at all times, and there is a visitor centre at Forsinard Station, open daily 09.00–18.00, Easter–late October. A mile-long trail passes a series of bog pools, and there are regular guided walks. Otherwise, access is restricted to the paths and roads to avoid disturbance between April and late June.

Birds
Breeders include Red-throated and Black-throated Divers, Greylag Goose (truly wild birds), Hen Harrier, Buzzard, Merlin, Short-eared Owl, Golden Plover, Greenshank and Dunlin. Golden Eagle may visit.

Greenshank

Information

RSPB Warden: Norrie Russell, Forsinard Station, Forsinard, Sutherland KW13 6YT. Tel: 01641 571225. E-mail: forsinard@rspb.org.uk

58 ARDNAMURCHAN (Highland)   OS Landranger 40 and 47

The rugged Ardnamurchan Peninsula is the most westerly land in mainland Scotland, and holds a wide range of breeding species. It is best visited May–October.

Habitat

The peninsula is c.17 miles long by c.7 miles at its widest point, and rises to 1,731 feet at Ben Hiant and 1,679 at Ben Laga. The varied habitats include heather moorland with many pools and lochans, and some very extensive conifer plantations in the inland areas, as well as stands of relict semi-natural oak woodland around the coast, bounded in many places by sandy beaches and bays.

Access

This vast wild area could justify many days exploration, especially for the serious walker. The following is a selection of the more interesting and accessible points.

Glenborrodale RSPB Reserve This 250-acre reserve comprises oak woodland, conifers, scrub, moorland and a section of rocky coast. The reserve is west of Glenborrodale village, immediately west of the black railings surrounding the grounds of Glenborrodale Castle, and a path starts west of this, where the stream crosses the road, re-joining the B8007 at the northwest tip of the reserve. Regular walks are organised (information from the RSPB's North Scotland Office or the Glenmore Natural History Centre).

Kentra Bay A good area for wildfowl and waders in winter and on passage. Leave the A861 in Acharacle (just north of the church) west on the B8044 towards Kentra. After c.½ mile turn left at the crossroads and follow the road to the small parking area at the end. Continue on foot along the track on the south side of the bay, which reaches Camas an Lighe after 1 mile. The north side of the bay can be viewed from the B8044 beyond Kentra.

Ben Hiant A car park by the B8007 affords good views of the mountain, and persistent scanning may produce raptors, including Golden Eagle.

Loch Mudle Viewable from the B8007, this water often has Red-throated Diver.

Point of Ardnamurchan From the B8007 at Achosnich a minor road leads to the Point. Seawatch from the vicinity of the lighthouse, or walk south along the cliffs to search for Peregrine and Raven.

Birds

Breeders include Great Spotted Woodpecker, Wood and Willow Warblers and Spotted Flycatcher in the oak woodlands, with Tree Pipit and Redstart on their periphery and on the more open slopes. Dipper occurs on streams and rivers, and conifer stands have Siskin and Redpoll. Areas of moorland hold Red Grouse, Golden Plover, Greenshank, Ring Ouzel. Wheatear, Stonechat, Whinchat and Twite, and the entire area is a good one for raptors including Golden Eagle, Buzzard, Hen Harrier, Short-eared Owl (the last two often around young conifer plantations) and Merlin, with Peregrine especially frequent along the coast. Raven should also be seen. Smaller lochans have breeding Red-throated Diver, which may visit the sea to feed, and around the coast look for Eider, Common Sandpiper, Common and Arctic Terns, and Gannet offshore.

On passage a wide variety of species may be present. Seawatching from the Point of Ardnamurchan may produce all three divers, Manx and sometimes Sooty Shearwaters, Storm and Leach's Petrels, Gannet, skuas, gulls and terns. Wildfowl may include Whooper Swan and Greylag, White-fronted and Barnacle Geese, and waders Golden Plover, Bar-tailed Godwit, Greenshank and less frequently Grey Plover, Knot, Sanderling, Green Sandpiper and Whimbrel.

In winter there are small numbers of Great Northern Divers as well as Goldeneye on the sea, and other wintering wildfowl around the coast include Wigeon, Teal and Greenland White-fronted Geese (the last in the area south of Loch Sheil). Wintering waders may include a few Greenshank.

Information

RSPB North Scotland Office, Etive House, Beechwood Park, Inverness IV2 3BW. Tel: 01463 715000.
Glenmore Natural History Centre. Tel: 01540 661518.

59 UDALE BAY (Highland) OS Landranger 21 and 27

Lying on the south shore of the Cromarty Firth, this area holds large numbers of wildfowl and waders from late summer until April, and is also visited by foraging Osprey.

Habitat

An extensive area of intertidal mudflats with large stands of eelgrass *Zostera*, backed by saltmarsh and wet grassland.

Access

Udale Bay RSPB reserve The B9163 skirts the entire south shore of the bay, with parking areas just west of, and c.1 mile east of, Jemimaville. The entrance to the reserve is 1 mile west of Jemimaville (NH 712651). Wildfowl and waders are best viewed in the hour either side of high water. The reserve is open at all times, and there is a hide.

Balblair The main channel of the Firth, good for divers, grebes and sea ducks, can be viewed from the minor road, which leaves the B9163 on the west side of Udale Bay for Balblair.

Birds

Wintering wildfowl include up to 5,000 Wigeon, as well as Teal and Shelduck, and large numbers of Greylag Geese may visit around high tide. In the deeper waters of the main channel, Red-throated Diver, Slavonian Grebe, Long-tailed Duck and Scaup can be seen. Waders include Oystercatcher, a few Grey Plover, Knot and Bar-tailed Godwit. These attract Sparrowhawk, Peregrine and sometimes Merlin.

In late summer look for Common and Arctic Terns, and also Osprey, which visit to fish.

Information

RSPB North Scotland Office, Etive House, Beechwood Park, Inverness IV2 3BW. Tel: 01463 715000.

60 CORRIMONY (Highland)   OS Landranger 26

Lying southwest of Inverness and west of Loch Ness, between Glen Urquhart and Cannich, and adjacent to the better known Glen Affric, this recent RSPB acquisition represents a long-term experiment in the restoration of semi-natural habitats from plantation woodlands.

Habitat

Covering 3,780 acres, the reserve comprises moorland and plantations bisected by the Allt Feith Riabhachain River, with areas of boggy land in the valley. There is a small patch of semi-natural Scots pine and birch near Corrimony Falls on the slopes of Carn Bingally, but most woodland consists of plantations of Scots and Lodgepole pines and Sitka spruce.

Access

Access is from the A831, east of Cannich. At Drumnadrochit on the west side of Loch Ness, leave the A82 and head west on the A831. A minor road on the left leads to Corrimony after 8 miles. Park in the Corrimony Cairns car park, and a way-marked trail leads to Loch Cromhnard.

Birds

Breeding raptors include Hen Harrier and Merlin, with Teal and Greenshank in wetter areas and Great Spotted Woodpecker and crossbills in the woodlands. Red-throated Diver may visit to feed. Both Black and Red Grouse breed, and it is hoped to increase their numbers by reducing grazing and removing deer fences, and to re-attract Capercaillie, which is now seriously reduced in numbers.

61 GLEN AFFRIC (Highland)   OS Landranger 25

This large and very scenic glen lies southwest of Inverness and is one of the richest and most diverse Scottish glens in all aspects of its fauna and flora. Over 3,000 acres are operated as a Caledonian Woodland Reserve by the FC.

Habitat

The Glen contains relicts of the once extensive Forest of Caledon, though heavy grazing pressure has prevented regeneration of native Scots pine, leaving ancient twisted 'granny pines' with an understorey of heather and blaeberry (the most natural pine woods, mixed with birch and rowan, are near Dog Falls and at Pollan Buide, between Loch Benevean and Affric). Restoration is underway, and away from the woodland areas there are open hillsides, a number of lochs and lochans, and the River Affric.

Access

Access is from the A831 at Cannich. From here a minor road reaches 11 miles along the glen, with various parking points en route. From the road a number of paths lead into the surrounding area (try the trails to Coire Loch or Dog Falls). Longer routes include a circuit of Loch Affric (11 miles) or a track along the south shore of Loch Beinn a' Mheadhoin (7 miles each way).

Birds

Small numbers of Black Grouse and Capercaillie persist in the Glen, but are difficult to locate. Late winter–early spring is the best period to look, but birdwatchers should be mindful that both have undergone serious declines in recent years and are particularly prone to disturbance in the breeding season. Crested Tit is common in the pines and generally easy to find, and Scottish Crossbill, at least in some years, is also numerous. Stands of conifers also hold Siskin and Redpoll, and small numbers of Redwing are present in summer. In more open areas look for Tree Pipit, Whinchat, Stonechat and Redstart. Along rivers and loch-sides search for Oystercatcher, Common Sandpiper, Dipper and Grey Wagtail, with Red-throated Diver, Red-breasted Merganser, Goosander and occasionally Black-throated Diver on areas of open water. Sparrowhawk, Buzzard, Golden Eagle and occasionally Merlin or Osprey can also be seen (though raptors are not prominent in this area).

Information

A detailed guide is available from the FC or Inverness Tourist Office.

62 DUNNET HEAD AND THURSO (Caithness)   OS Landranger 12

Dunnet Head marks the most northerly extent of the Scottish mainland and holds good seabird colonies; it is best visited in May to mid-July. Nearby Thurso harbour regularly attracts white-winged gulls in winter–early spring, and, together with Dunnet Bay, a variety of divers and sea duck.

Habitat

Dunnet Head is topped by moorland with a few small lochs, and there are cliffs, especially on the north and east flanks. St John's Loch and Loch of Mey at the base of the Head attract waterfowl, and, to the west, Dunnet Bay is sandy, with a rocky stretch of coast between it and Thurso harbour.

Access (see map)

Dunnet Head Leave the A836 at Dunnet village north on the B855, which ends after 4½ miles at the car park at Easter Head.

St John's Loch Lies northeast of Dunnet village and can be viewed from the A836.

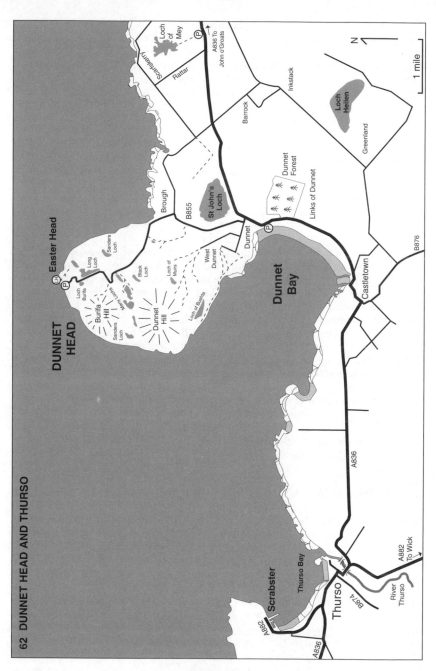

Loch of Mey Approximately 3 miles east of Dunnet village, access is either from
Scarfskerry (permission must be sought to cross the intervening crofts) or north
along an old peat track from the roadside pull-off on the A836. The water level
on the loch may be high and uninteresting, or low, attracting passage waders.

Loch Heilen This large loch can be viewed from surrounding minor roads, notably in the east at Lochend.

Dunnet Bay Castletown pier at the southwest corner of Dunnet Bay gives views of the bay, and the A836 parallels the shore from here to Dunnet, with a car park at the east end of the bay.

River Thurso In Thurso a track runs north from the A836 along the east bank of the River Thurso towards the ruined castle, and a footpath continues along the shore.

Thurso Harbour Access to the breakwater in Thurso harbour is straightforward from the town, and the A836 also affords views of the sea and shore.

Scrabster Harbour The departure point for the Orkney ferry, this sometimes holds a few divers, sea duck and gulls.

Birds

Breeding seabirds on Dunnet Head include Fulmar, Guillemot, Razorbill, Black Guillemot, Puffin and Kittiwake. Great Skua often attempts to breed on the moorland, especially on the west flank, but is usually thwarted by peat cutting and muir-burning. Rock Dove and Raven haunt the cliffs, and Twite can be found around crofts. Small numbers of Arctic Terns breed on Dunnet Links and may be seen fishing in the bay, where there are often summering Great Northern Divers.

In winter numbers of Red-throated and Great Northern Divers are present offshore at Thurso and Dunnet Bay, together with a few Black-throated Divers. Shag, Common Scoter, Long-tailed Duck, Goldeneye, Eider and Red-breasted Merganser are also frequent and are joined by Black Guillemot, Razorbill and Guillemot. In the area are small numbers of Whooper Swans, which together with a variety of wildfowl can be seen on St John's Loch. A flock of up to 100 Greenland White-fronted Geese regularly winters around Loch of Mey and Loch Heilen. Greylag Geese are also regular, and Brent Goose is occasional in Dunnet Bay. The few waders include Turnstone and Purple Sandpiper. Glaucous and Iceland Gulls are usually present, sometimes several of each. A Peregrine is often seen and, occasionally, large numbers of Snow Buntings.

Loch of Mey is attractive during passage periods and has held several rarities, and Dunnet Bay is also worth checking for migrant waders, but St John's Loch is disturbed by fishermen in summer.

Information

Thurso Tourist Centre. Tel (April–October): 01847 892371.

63 CLO MOR (Highland) OS Landranger 9

Mainland Britain's highest sea cliff, Clo Mor rises to 921 feet and lies c.3 miles southeast of Cape Wrath. It is truly spectacular and has huge seabird colonies. A visit between May and mid-July is recommended.

Habitat

The cliffs are backed by a typical Sutherland landscape of moors and hills.

Access

Leave the A838 at Kyle of Durness to Keoldale. From here a passenger ferry cross-es the Kyle, connecting with the road to Cape Wrath lighthouse. A minibus service runs to Cape Wrath several times daily in May–September. Ask to be dropped at the Kearvaig track, and then walk to Kearvaig, approaching Clo Mor from the west. Follow the cliffs east for c.3 miles and then cut inland along the east flanks of Sgribhis-bheinn to meet the minibus, by arrangement, at Inshore. This is a rough cross-country walk. Access is sometimes restricted because of activity on the firing range.

Birds

Breeding seabirds include Fulmar, Guillemot, Razorbill and Black Guillemot, with one of the largest British colonies of Puffin. Large numbers of Gannets are present offshore and Peregrine and Rock Dove nest on the sea cliffs. Ptarmigan occurs on rocky areas of adjacent hills, sometimes as low as 600 feet above sea level, together with Red Grouse and a few Golden Plovers. Greenshank is present along the river valleys, and there may be summering or even breeding Great Skua. Kyle of Durness holds Red-throated Diver, and wintering Great Northern Diver sometimes remain until late spring.

Information

Durness Tourist Information Centre. Tel. (April–October): 01971 511259.
Kyle of Durness Ferry (John Morrison). Tel: 01971 511376.
Minibus service to Cape Wrath (Iris Mackay). Tel: 01971 511343

64 FARAID HEAD (Highland)   OS Landranger 9

Smaller and less spectacular seabird colonies than Clo Mor, but easier to reach.

Access and Birds

From the A838 in Durness take the minor road northwest to Balnakeil. Park and walk along Balnakeil Sands to the Head. On the grassy east slopes there are Puffins, and other seabirds include Fulmar, Kittiwake, Black Guillemot, Guillemot and Razorbill. During late summer and autumn Sooty Shearwater may be seen offshore.

65 SUTHERLAND (Highland)   OS Landranger 9, 10 and 16

An area of sombre hills, vast expanses of moorland and flow country, this bleak but grand area is difficult to work. Distances are large and the going is rough, but the place has its own special attractions. The best time to visit is between the last week of May and early July; during the rest of the year there are few birds on the hills.

Habitat

The flow country of east Sutherland and Caithness is a mosaic of small lochans, peaty burns and blanket bogs. The stronghold of breeding Greenshank in Britain, it is threatened by forestation. One-third is owned by forestry interests and large areas have been planted with exotic species of conifer. There are small areas of native birch, mainly along watercourses, and other habitats include lochs, sea lochs and the high tops, with several 'arctic' species breeding and the potential for others to do so.

Access

In this vast area it is impossible to single out one place, because birds are scattered over the available habitat. It is more a question of convenient access. The following areas are suggested as a start.

Forsinard RSPB reserve See p.559.

Loch Eriboll (OS Landranger 9) The A838 parallels most of the shore, approaching closest on the east side.

Loch Hope (OS Landranger 9) A minor road runs along the east shore from Hope, on the A838.

Ben Hope (3,040 feet, OS Landranger 9) A minor road runs south, from the A838 at Hope, along the west flank of the mountain.

Kyle of Tongue (OS Landranger 10) A tidal inlet with extensive mudflats that attract passage waders. Tongue Pier is a good place to look from, while the A838 bisects the Kyle before paralleling the shore for a short distance and connecting with an unclassified road.

Loch Loyal (OS Landranger 10) East of the A836.

Ben Loyal (2,509 feet, OS Landranger 10) Access west from the A836.

Loch Naver (OS Landranger 16) The B873 runs along the north shore.

Ben Klibreck (3,157 feet, OS Landranger 16) East of the A836.

Loch Shin (OS Landranger 16) The A838 runs along the east shore and Lairg, on the A836, is at the south end.

Exploration away from the road is necessary to see at least some of the birds, and you should be properly equipped to deal with the sometimes harsh conditions. Though access is generally not problematic, grouse shooting and deer stalking take place in late summer and autumn; notices giving details of stalking are often posted at access points. You will be unwelcome if you disturb either the hunters or the hunted, and as a general rule you should keep off the moors from early July.

Birds

Larger lochs have nesting Black-throated Diver and sometimes Red-throated, though the latter tend to favour smaller, isolated pools and lochans, flying to bigger lochs and the sea to feed. Sea lochs hold Eider and Arctic Tern. Especially in the east, Hen Harrier and sometimes Short-eared Owl breed, favouring young conifer plantations, usually abandoning these once the trees are more than 6–8 feet high. Young plantations also attract Black Grouse, again mainly in the east, though it is a difficult bird to find. Siskin frequents older conifer woods. Buzzard is uncommon, but Golden Eagle, if not common, is widespread. The way to see one is to climb a mountain, though they can be seen from the roads. Peregrine is also widespread, favouring the vicinity of cliffs and crags, especially near woodland. Merlin is scattered over moorland areas in small numbers. Ptarmigan breeds on every hill above 2,500 feet, and may sometimes be seen at lower elevations. It prefers areas with rocks, scree or boulder piles, and overlaps altitudinally with Red Grouse. Rocky screes and corries also attract the rare Snow Bunting (around long-lasting summer snowfields with nearby rocks and boulders), and you may find Dotterel on the tops.

Greenshank breeds in broad marshy valleys within the moors, and often frequents the edges of freshwater lochs once the young have fledged; Dunlin is also scattered in marshy areas. Oystercatcher, Golden Plover, Curlew and Snipe are widespread, but Whimbrel, Wood Sandpiper and Red-necked Phalarope are rare and erratic breeders. Other species that may have nested and are worth searching for are Temminck's Stint, Sanderling, Green Sandpiper and Turnstone. Common Gull, Teal, Wigeon and sometimes Greylag Goose breed on scattered lochs on the moors and flows. Red-breasted Merganser is commonest near the coast, but may breed at the head of glens, while Goosander favours larger rivers and lochs. Common Scoter has bred on isolated small lochs in the moors, but there are few recent records. Common Sandpiper and Dipper occur on most streams and rivers.

The commonest passerines are Meadow Pipit and Skylark. Wheatear is widespread, but Whinchat more scattered. Ring Ouzel is found around crags and rocky gullies in the hills. In birch woods look for Woodcock, Tree Pipit, Wood and Willow Warblers, Redstart, Spotted Flycatcher and Redpoll. These, and areas of rhododendron (which are usually found around houses), also attract Redwing (Britain's first breeding record was in Sutherland in 1925). Brambling bred in 1920 and may do so again. Twite favours the vicinity of old buildings, rough pasture and moorland edge, especially on the coast. It particularly likes to feed on short grazed turf around crofts, cliffs and roadsides.

Information
Sutherland Tourist Board, The Square, Dornoch, Sutherland IV25 3SD. Tel: 01862 810400.

66 HANDA (Highland)   OS Landranger 9

This superb island off northwest Sutherland holds over 100,000 breeding seabirds and is easily accessed. The island is a reserve of the Scottish Wildlife Trust (SWT, previously the RSPB), and the best time to visit is May–early July.

Habitat
The island covers 766 acres and is only a few hundred yards offshore. On three coasts, cliffs rise to over 400 feet, but the south shore also has sandy beaches and dunes. Inland is rough sheep pasture and heather moor with six small lochans. There is a small plantation by the bothy.

Access
Handa is open 15 April–1 September, except Sundays. Boats leave from Tarbet, which is reached from the A894 by taking a minor road to the northwest c.3 miles northeast of Scourie. The first boat is usually at 09.30 and the last returns at 17.00. There is a shelter and display on the quay, and a warden is present in summer. Keep to the marked paths. Visitors may arrange to stay in a bothy on the island through the SWT.

Birds

Black-throated Diver is usually present offshore in summer, and wintering Great Northern sometimes stay until mid-May. Red-throated Diver, Eider and Shelduck breed and can be seen off the southeast coast. Approximately 100,000 pairs of Guillemot vastly outnumber the other seabirds, which include Razorbill (c.9,000 pairs) and Kittiwake (c.10,000 pairs) as well as Fulmar (c.3,000 pairs), Shag (c.200 pairs) and c.800 pairs of Puffin. Black Guillemot does not regularly breed, but is often seen on the boat crossing. Both Great and Arctic Skuas breed and are increasing, together with Great Black-backed and Herring Gulls. Peregrine and Buzzard visit, Oystercatcher and Ringed Plover breed on the beaches, Rock Dove nests on the cliffs, Common and Arctic Terns on the skerries in Port an Eilein (near the landing point), and Snipe, Stonechat and Wheatear on the grassland and moor, occasionally joined by Red Grouse and Golden Plover.

Passage periods bring small numbers of waders to shores, and there are occasionally movements of interesting seabirds offshore. Pomarine Skua is possible in early May, and Manx and Sooty Shearwaters in autumn.

Information

SWT Warden: Stephen MacLeod, 15 Scouriemore, Scourie, by Lairg, Sutherland IV27 4TG.

Conservation Manager: Mark Foxwell, Unit 4a, 3 Carsegate Road North, Inverness IV3 8PU. Tel: 01463 714746. E-mail: mfoxwell@swt.org.uk

Boatman: Charles Thomson, tel: 01971 502077.

67 TARBET (Highland)   OS Landranger 9

Tarbet lies on the mainland, opposite Handa (see p.568), and is worthy of exploration.

Access and Birds

The region south of Loch Laxford holds some of the typical Sutherland specialities—Black and Red-throated Divers, raptors and Greenshank. The A894 and A838 cross the area, as well as the minor roads to Tarbet. Be prepared for heavy going, and have an OS map to hand if you leave the road. Stalkers' paths and tracks are clearly marked, and there are few restrictions on access outside the deer-stalking season, which is from mid-August.

68 INVERPOLLY (Highland)   OS Landranger 15

Inverpolly is a true wilderness and magnificently scenic. A NNR covers 26,827 acres and holds the usual range of highland species. It is best in April–June.

Habitat

This remote, almost uninhabited area has a range of habitats. A rolling moorland plateau of heather and grass is interspersed with freshwater lochs (including the large Loch Sionascaig), lochans, streams and boggy hollows, and the impressive sandstone peaks of Stac Pollaidh, Cul Beag and Cul Mor, the latter reaching 2,787 feet. There are many small areas of remnant birch–hazel woodland, and the high tops form an arctic–alpine habitat. Sandy beaches and small islands flank the coast.

Access

The NNR covers a roughly rectangular area of land between Enard Bay in the northwest and the A835 between Drumrunie and Elphin in the southeast. It is managed by SNH in co-operation with the estate owners. Access is unrestricted (though permission is required from the Assynt Estate Office to visit Drumrunie, i.e. the area adjacent to the A835, between 15 July and 21 October, and during the stalking season, September–October, it is best to contact the SNH warden for advise on access to any area away from the road). The Knockan Information Centre, signposted on the A835 c.2½ miles southwest of Elphin, is open Monday–Friday, May to mid-September, and can provide information and leaflets for the adjacent Knockan Cliff Trail. No roads penetrate the reserve and there are few tracks; access is difficult and walkers should be experienced and properly equipped. Try walking the peripheral roads and the nature trail, and from the road on the west side of the reserve, just south of Inverkirkaig, walk along the north bank of the River Kirkaig to the falls. A variety of woodland species can be seen in the glen.

Birds

Breeders include Black-throated Diver, which favours the larger lochs, including Sionascaig, and may sometimes be seen on the lochs adjacent to the A835. Red-throated Diver, Red breasted Merganser, Goosander and Wigeon, with small numbers of Greylag Geese, also frequent the lochs, especially on the coast, where Fulmar, Shag, Eider and Black Guillemot breed. The high tops hold small numbers of Ptarmigan, with Red Grouse at lower elevations. Snow Bunting, which is a winter visitor to the area, may stay late in spring and perhaps even breed. Golden Eagle, Buzzard, Merlin and Peregrine occur, together with Raven. Though eagles may be seen from the road, exploration on foot is usually more productive. Golden Plover and Greenshank breed on the moors, with Stonechat, Wheatear and Ring Ouzel in higher, rockier gullies. Birch woodland has Woodcock, Wood Warbler, Spotted Flycatcher and sometimes Redwing. Twite occurs on the moorland edge and around crofts near the coast.

Information

SNH Warden: Knockan Cottage, Elphin, Lairg, Sutherland IV27 4H. Tel: 01854 666234.
Assynt Estate Office. Tel: 01571 844203.

69 BEINN EIGHE (Highland)   OS Landranger 19 and 25

Beinn Eighe was the first NNR to be declared in Britain and was established to protect remnant areas of Caledonian pinewood. The 11,757 acres also incorporate uplands, and is best visited May–early July.

Habitat

There are c.450 acres of natural pinewoods with an understorey of heather, as well as c.150 acres of birch. A further 1,200 acres have been re-planted with native tree species. Woodland is concentrated along the southwest shore of Loch Maree. The hills rise to over 3,000 feet; the highest Ruadh-stac Mor, which peaks at 3,313 feet, is just outside the reserve. Non-wooded areas mostly consist of heather and grass moorland and bog, but on the high tops this gives way to dwarf shrubs, which mix with mosses and liverworts to form an arctic–alpine heath.

Access

The SNH Aultroy Visitor Centre is at Kinlochewe, on the A832 1 mile north of the junction with the A896, and is open Easter–September (10.00–17.00). Information and advice are available as well as leaflets for two nature trails, which start at the car park at Glas Leitire (NH 000650) 1¾ miles further northwest. The Mountain Trail extends for 4 miles and rises above the treeline to c.1,800 feet, taking in moorland and mountain, and a second, shorter trail extends for 1 mile through typical woodland habitats. Otherwise, the Pony Trail, which runs west from the Visitor Centre (leaving the road at NH 022628), gives the best access to the highest ground.

There is unrestricted access to the hills in a large area south of Loch Maree and north of the A896, which includes the NNR; except for 1 September–21 November, which is the deer-stalking season, when permission must be sought from local estates to enter some areas. Birdwatchers, however, are unlikely to visit during this period. The A832 follows the southwest flank of Loch Maree, with several car parks along the shore. The reserve is bordered to the southeast by the A896, but within this area there are no roads and walkers should be properly equipped.

Birds

Areas of relict woodland hold resident Sparrowhawk, Woodcock and Great Spotted Woodpecker, while Tree Pipit, Redstart and Wood and Willow Warblers are summer visitors, and join Siskin and Redpoll. Both Common and Scottish Crossbills are sometimes seen, and fortunate observers may find breeding Redwing in the birches. Crested Tit has been recorded in the area, and may eventually expand its range to incorporate the reserve's pine forests. On lochs, streams and rivers are Red-throated and Black-throated Divers, Goosander, Red-breasted Merganser, Greylag Goose, Common Sandpiper and Dipper. Golden Eagle, Buzzard, Merlin, Peregrine and Short-eared Owl occur, as well as Raven. Probably the best chance to see an eagle is to regularly scan the hillsides. Common moorland birds are Skylark and Meadow Pipit, joined by smaller numbers of Golden Plover, Ring Ouzel, Wheatear, Whinchat and a few Twite. In wetter, boggier valley bottoms you may find Greenshank. Higher, Red Grouse is joined by Ptarmigan, and a thorough search of the tops may reveal summering Snow Bunting.

Information

SNH Aultroy Visitor Centre. Tel: 01445 760258.
SNH Reserve Manager: David Miller, Anancaun Field Centre, Kinlochewe, Ross-shire IV22 2PD. Tel: 01445 760254. E-mail: david.miller@snh.gov.uk
SNH, Dingwall Business Park, Strathpeffer Road, Dingwall, Ross-shire IV15 9QF. Tel: 01349 865333.

70 SKYE (Highland) OS Landranger 23, 32 and 33

Skye is the northernmost of the Inner Hebrides and is huge, nearly 50 miles long, with dramatic scenery. Mostly sheep-walk with some areas of forestry, no one site is outstanding. Divers, Peregrine, Golden Eagle, Ptarmigan, Black Grouse, Black Guillemot, Greenshank and Dipper all breed, and exploration on foot can be worthwhile in many places, though the Cuillin Hills in the south have Ptarmigan and eagles.

71 ISLE OF RHUM (Highland)

Rhum was the centre for the successful re-introduction of White-tailed Eagle into Britain. It has many other attractions, however, including numbers of breeding seabirds. The best time to visit is April–June. The island is a NNR covering 26,400 acres, managed by SNH.

Habitat

The basic habitats are the coast (with rugged cliffs, sandy bays and maritime grassland), moorland, the higher, more exposed hilltops, relict woodland, and, importantly, reforestation. SNH is trying to re-establish woodland and has planted extensive areas with native trees, notably in the east.

Access

A passenger ferry from Mallaig and run by Caledonian MacBrayne serves Rhum. It sails on Monday, Wednesday, Friday and Saturday, and the journey takes 3–4 hours. The boat returns the same day and day-trip landings are only possible on summer Saturdays. Occasionally, in June–September, day trips may be organised from Mallaig or Arisaig. These land at Loch Scresort and explore the area around Kinloch including the nature trails, without formalities. However, a day trip generally permits too little time ashore to be worthwhile (though the crossing has many birds: all three divers, Manx and sometimes Sooty Shearwaters, and Storm Petrel are possibilities). Prior permission is required for an overnight stay and all intending visitors should contact the warden. Full-board accommodation is available in Kinloch Castle, and there are also bothies and a campsite (but camping is uncomfortable July–October because of midges). Apply well in advance to the warden.

Birds

Breeders include Red-throated Diver, Fulmar, Shag, Common, Lesser and Great Black-backed and Herring Gulls, Kittiwake, Guillemot, Razorbill, Black Guillemot and Puffin, and occasionally Common or Arctic Terns. However, the Kittiwake and auk ledges are largely inaccessible, hidden at the base of the cliffs. There are c.100,000 pairs of Manx Shearwater, which breed on the tops in the centre of the island. Storm Petrel occurs offshore but there is no evidence of breeding. Small numbers of Greylag Geese nest, and the species is also regular on passage. Other wildfowl include Shelduck, Teal, Eider and Red-breasted Merganser. Two to five pairs of Golden Eagles are known, as well as Peregrine, Merlin and Sparrowhawk. A total of 82 White-tailed Eagles was released on Rhum between 1975 and 1985, but most have dispersed and can occur anywhere in the Inner Hebrides or, indeed, as far afield as Shetland, the Outer Hebrides and Northern Ireland. They may still be seen on Rhum, but are not guaranteed, and chances are currently better on some of the other Inner Hebrides. Red Grouse and Raven breed on the hills, and waders include Oystercatcher and Ringed and Golden Plovers, with Woodcock in the wooded areas, occasionally with Long-eared or Short-eared Owls. Common Sandpiper and Dipper nest along streams. Common open-ground birds are Meadow Pipit and Skylark, together with Stonechat, Whinchat and Wheatear, and Ring Ouzel in the hills. Whitethroat, Willow Warbler, Chiffchaff, a few pairs of Wood Warbler, and Siskin nest, and the number and variety of woodland birds should increase as the forest develops.

Offshore, especially in late summer, Sooty Shearwater, Gannet, and Great and Arctic Skuas are possible. On passage, Rhum holds a variety of waders and wildfowl, including Whooper Swan, Pink-footed, White-fronted and Barnacle Geese, Sanderling, Whimbrel, Greenshank and Turnstone, and numbers of common passerines. In winter there are Great Northern Diver and small numbers of sea ducks offshore.

Information
SNH Reserve Office, The White House, Kinloch, Isle of Rhum, Scotland PH43 4RR. Tel: 01687 462026.
Day trips from Arisaig (May–September), *MV Shearwater*: tel: 01687 5224. Day trips from Mallaig (occasional). Bruce Watt, tel: 01687 462320.

OUTER HEBRIDES

NORTH AND SOUTH UISTS
These islands are undoubtedly one of the most attractive parts of Britain. Supporting a range of raptors, wildfowl, and large numbers of breeding waders, the star bird is perhaps Corncrake, which maintains its British stronghold here. The best time to visit is May–July for breeding birds, but autumn could be productive for migrants. There are two large reserves, the Loch Druidibeg NNR and the RSPB's Balranald.

Habitat
The long sandy beaches of the Atlantic seaboard back onto the fertile machair, level grassland formed by a mixture of windblown shell-sand and peat, which supports the highest density of breeding waders in Britain. Often cultivated, the crops may still provide cover for nesting birds. In the machair and extending towards the east flank of the islands is a mosaic of lochs, marshes and wet grazing. The land becomes more acidic and peaty as it rises to the east hills, which peak at 2,033 feet on South Uist, but at only 1,139 feet on low-lying, watery North Uist. The islands are almost treeless, with only small, isolated stands.

Access
By Sea Caledonian MacBrayne operate car ferries to the islands from Skye (Uig) to North Uist (Lochmaddy), the voyage takes one hour direct (four hours via Harris), with sailings once or twice daily (except Sunday) from mid-May to September, less frequently during the rest of the year. From Oban to South Uist (Loch Boisdale) the journey takes 5–8 hours, with daily sailings (except Sunday) in summer, although less frequently in winter. Always book cars in advance. Both crossings are good for seabirds, with a good chance of Storm Petrel and shearwaters.

By Air British Airways has daily flights (except Sunday in winter) to Benbecula. Loganair operate a weekday service to Barra, but this connects with flights to Benbecula only a couple of times a week.

Accommodation For details of accommodation, contact the tourist board.

Note that crofting land in the Hebrides, as elsewhere in north and west Scotland, is often unfenced. Due care should be taken, and if in doubt concerning access to any area, please ask first.
North Uist, Benbecula and South Uist are connected by two causeways, and there are large areas of essentially similar habitat bisected by the main north–south road. The following areas deserve special mention, but are only representative of the entire area.

72 SOUTH UIST (Outer Hebrides)   OS Landranger 22 and 31

Lochboisdale harbour This attracts Glaucous and Iceland Gulls in winter, as well as divers and seabirds.

Loch Hallan at Daliburgh At the junction of the A865 and the B888, this often holds summering Whooper Swan. Take the road west at the crossroads in the village and after 1 mile follow a track north to view from the cemetery (which avoids disturbance). Do not approach the Loch over agricultural land.

The Rubha Ardvule peninsula This is a good spot for seawatching. Access is via a road and track from the main road. Visitors must keep clear of the point when in use by the military, but this is infrequently the case.

The Howmore area Formerly much visited because of the drake Steller's Eider that was resident in 1972–84, the area has a typical range of coast/machair/marshland species, with cheap accommodation at Howmore hostel.

Loch Druidibeg NNR View the loch from the main road and B890. Access away from these requires a permit during the breeding season. Birds include divers, breeding Greylag Goose, waders, and sometimes summering Whooper Swan. The trees around Grogarry Lodge provide some cover for migrants.

B890 Beside the B890 to Loch Skiport is a grove of rhododendrons and deciduous and coniferous trees that attract migrants and have breeding Long-eared Owl, Goldcrest and Greenfinch. It is a good spot to scan for eagles over the slopes of Hecla.

Hecla and Beinn Mhor These sombre peaks support Golden Eagle, Red Grouse, etc. Look for eagles from the main road or the road to Loch Skiport.

Loch Bee Excellent for wildfowl, with up to 500 Mute Swan. View from the main road crossing the loch.

Ardivachar Another good seawatching spot. Take the road west from the A865 in the north of the island to the peninsula. The best birdwatching is in North Bay.

73 BENBECULA (Outer Hebrides)   OS Landranger 22

Balivanich outfall The sewage outfall at Balivanich on the B892 attracts gulls, and is good for Glaucous and Iceland, even in midsummer. Waders frequent the adjacent foreshore and aerodrome (check with air traffic control before entering the latter).

The Benbecula–North Uist causeway This affords views of the intertidal flats for waders.

74 NORTH UIST (Outer Hebrides)   OS Landranger 18 and 22

Balranald RSPB reserve This has areas of beach, dunes, machair, pools and marshland, and is largely crofted. All three divers are often present in summer, and several species of raptor regularly visit. There is a dense population of breeding ducks and waders (and sometimes non-breeding Red-necked Phalarope) as well as 10–15 pairs of Corncrake. Arctic Tern breeds and an excellent seawatching spot is the headland of Aird an Runair, the most westerly spot in the Outer Hebrides. Turn west off the A865 2 miles northwest of Bayhead, signed Houghharry, and fork left to the reception cottage at Goular. The reserve is open at all times, and the visitor centre is open during the summer. Visitors should keep to the paths marked on the map at the cottage.

Loch Scadavay North of the A867, this is good for divers and Arctic Skua breeds in the vicinity.

Loch Skealtar North of the A867 just west of Lochmaddy, this is another good spot for divers; up to 21 Black-throated have been counted in August.

Lochmaddy harbour Worth checking for gulls, Black Guillemot and other seabirds, and eagles may be seen to the south over the Lees.

Newton House and Clachan The trees around Newton House and at Clachan attract migrants. Both are on the B893 in the northeast of the island. Permission to enter should be sought from Newton House and Clachan Farm respectively, but both can be seen well from the road. Other areas that have been productive in recent years are the conifer plantation on Ben Langass, south of the A867, and that on Ben Aulasary, just east of the minor road between Bayhead and Sollas.

Valley Strand and Vallaquie Strand On the north coast (off the A865), the extensive foreshore attracts waders.

Birds

Red-throated is the commonest diver and can often be seen flying between its tiny nesting pools and fishing grounds at sea. There are about five pairs of Black-throated Diver, almost all on North Uist. They breed and fish on the larger lochs and are less often seen in the air. Great Northern is present until June, almost always on the sea. Fulmar, Cormorant and Shag can be seen around the coast at any time, but most other seabirds are summer visitors. Arctic Skua breeds mainly in the centre of North Uist, with a few on Benbecula and South Uist. Five species of gull are joined offshore by non-breeding Kittiwake, as well as the occasional summering Glaucous or even Iceland Gull. Arctic, Common and Little Terns are widespread in that order of abundance, as is Black Guillemot. There are small numbers of Razorbill and Guillemot and these share the cliffs with Rock Dove.

A speciality is the several hundred pairs of Greylag Geese, deemed wild rather than feral. Their stronghold is Loch Druidibeg, which has 60–70 pairs. Outside the breeding season the flock grazes around Grogarry. Though several Whooper Swan may summer, the species has not been proved to nest since 1947. Shelduck, Teal, Shoveler, Eider and Red-breasted Merganser, and small numbers of Wigeon and Gadwall, are regular breeders. Raptors include Hen Harrier, with approximately a dozen nesting females, Buzzard, Golden Eagle, Kestrel, Merlin, Peregrine and Short-eared Owl. These may be seen hunting anywhere, though eagles favour the mountains, and harriers are best seen around Loch Hallan on South Uist and Loch Mor on Benbecula. Wandering White-tailed Eagles from Rhum are now a possibility on the east coast. Red Grouse occur at low density on the moorland, together with small numbers of Golden Plover and Greenshank. Commoner breeding waders are Oystercatcher, Ringed Plover, Lapwing, Dunlin, Snipe, Redshank and Common Sandpiper, and a few Red-necked Phalaropes still hang on. Corncrake arrives in mid-April and is best seen early in the season before the vegetation has grown. Rush, sedge and iris beds are favoured on arrival, and thereafter hay meadows. They call most frequently 00.00–04.00, and only irregularly during the day. The common passerines are Skylark, Meadow and Rock Pipits, Pied Wagtail, Wren (the Hebridean subspecies), Stonechat, Wheatear, Sedge Warbler, Hooded Crow, Raven, Starling (the Shetland subspecies), Twite, House Sparrow, and Reed and Corn Buntings. The Hebridean race of Song Thrush can be quite elusive, favouring heathery hill country as well as areas of shrubs, and Blackbird is also confined to gardens and pockets of woodland on the west coast, together with Long-eared Owl in the latter.

In spring, N–NW winds can prompt movements of skuas. Up to 271 Long-tailed and 436 Pomarine Skuas have been seen at Balranald in a day, as well as the more regular Great and Arctic. Every year since this skua passage was discovered (in 1971) and that observers have been present, Long-tailed and Pomarine have been seen, usually in the third week of May, though numbers are obviously weather-dependent. Manx Shearwater is sometimes seen in large numbers, April–August, as well as Sooty from June. Storm and sometimes Leach's Petrels occur off the west coast in strong onshore winds, but, like the shearwaters, the boat crossings are a better bet, especially for Storm Petrel. Gannet is common offshore March–November. Pink-footed, Brent and Barnacle Geese appear on passage, but rarely linger. Migrant waders may include Little Stint, Curlew Sandpiper, Black-tailed Godwit and Whimbrel, while Ruff favours the machair and crofts. Only small numbers of migrant passerines occur, notably the Greenland race of Redpoll and Snow Bunting, which may be abundant.

In winter, Great Northern Diver and Slavonian Grebe are widespread offshore, with just a few Red-throated Divers. Several hundred Whooper Swans winter, and Greenland White-fronted Goose is an erratic visitor in small numbers; Nunton on Benbecula, Loch Hallan and Loch Bee are the most regular areas. Other wildfowl include Scaup, Long-tailed Duck (especially between Rubha Ardvule and Grogarry on South Uist) and Goldeneye. There are internationally important populations of Ringed Plover, Sanderling and Turnstone, and smaller numbers of Knot and Purple Sandpiper are joined by a few Greenshanks and the occasional Grey Plover. Glaucous and Iceland Gulls are both regular, and after persistent northwest gales Iceland Gull may be relatively common. Small flocks of Rooks and Jackdaws winter.

Information
RSPB Balranald: Jamie Boyle, 9 Grenitoite, North Uist, Outer Hebrides HS6 5BP. Tel: 01876 560287. E-mail: james.boyle3@btinternet.com

SNH Area Officer, Stilligarry, South Uist, Outer Hebrides HS8 5RS. Tel. 01870 620238.

Caledonian MacBrayne, Ferry Terminal, Gourock PA19 1QP. Tel: 01475 650100; Lochboisdale, tel: 01878 700288; Lochmaddy, tel: 01876 500337.

Loganair Ltd, Glasgow Airport, Abbotsinch, Renfrewshire. Tel: 0141 848 7594; Stornoway, tel: 01851 703673.

British Airways, 134 Renfrew Street, Glasgow. Tel: 0141 332 9666; Benbecula, tel: 01870 602310.

Western Isles Tourist Board, 26 Cromwell Street, Stornoway, Isle of Lewis. Tel: 01851 703088. E-mail: stornowaytic@visitthehebrides.co.uk

ORKNEY

Orkney comprises 75 islands, 20 of them inhabited, and at the closest point is only 6 miles from mainland Scotland. Its attractions for the visiting birdwatcher are the vast numbers of breeding seabirds, the moorland specialties and passage migrants. The best time to visit for breeding birds is May–early July, and for migrants May–early June and late August–October.

Habitat
The islands, with the exception of Hoy, are rather low and fertile. In places the coasts have cliffs, sometimes spectacular, as at St John's Head on Hoy. Other parts have beaches and sheltered bays, while Deer Sound and Scapa Flow provide a haven for large numbers of divers and sea ducks. The original vegetation of Orkney was scrubby woodland but this was cleared by Neolithic and Viking settlers and replaced by moorland and bog. These form an invaluable habitat, but it would be a mistake to think that Orkney is cloaked in moorland. Since the early-18th century

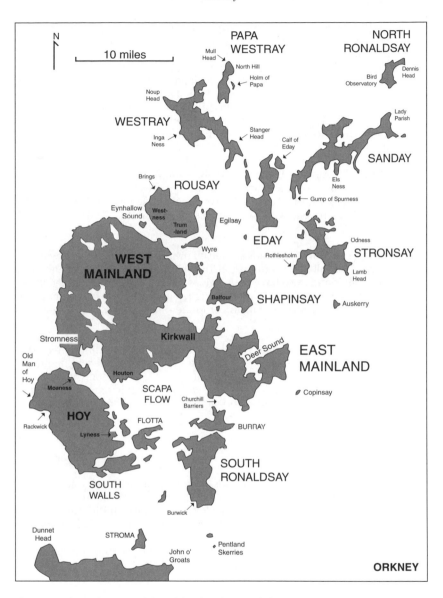

the moors have been reclaimed for farming, and the major land-use is now cattle pasture. Large areas of moorland do remain on Mainland and Hoy, often with scattered lochs, streams and marshes. Some of the smaller islands are still crofted and there are tracts of maritime heath, a habitat unique in Britain to Orkney and parts of Caithness. Exposure to the wind has produced dwarf shrubs of heather and crowberry, mixed with sedges and small herbs.

Access

Full details of all transport and accommodation are available from Orkney Tourist Board, 6 Broad Street, Kirkwall, Orkney KW15 1NX. Tel: 01856 872856.

By Sea (i) P&O Scottish Ferries ro-ro ferry *St Ola* sails daily (except Sunday) from Scrabster to Stromness on Mainland Orkney, with extra sailings April–October, including Sundays. The voyage takes one hour 45 minutes. Tel: 01856 850655. **(ii)** P&O Scottish Ferries ro-ro ferry *St Sunniva* sails from Aberdeen to Stromness twice weekly, continuing to Lerwick (Shetland) next day. The voyage from Aberdeen takes 8–14 hours, and to Lerwick eight hours. This service is less regular November–March. Tel: 01224 572615. **(iii)** In May–September John o' Groats Ferries operate a 45-minute passenger-only service from John o' Groats to Burwick on South Ronaldsay. There are two sailings daily, with extra services July–August. Tel: 01955 611353.

By Air (i) British Airways Express fly daily (except Sunday) to Kirkwall from Edinburgh, Glasgow, Inverness and Wick, with connections to the south. Tel: 01856 873457. **(ii)** British Airways operate daily (except Sunday) flights to Kirkwall from Aberdeen, with connections to the south. Reservations 0845 7733377.

Inter-island Transport All islands are served by ferries from Mainland, with bus services from Kirkwall to the terminals at Tingwall (for Rousay) and Houton (for Hoy). The north islands also have connections by air to Kirkwall. Full details are given under each island, but it is advisable to telephone for the latest timetables and prices, and if intending to take a car to the outer islands, it is essential to book in advance.

Throughout Orkney, care should be taken not to disturb breeding birds, especially divers, raptors and terns. Many of the sites described below are on private land and, if in doubt, seek permission before entering. In general you will get a very friendly reception. In addition, when searching for migrants, the nature of some of the habitats, such as crops and gardens, calls for extra discretion.

75 MAINLAND (Orkney)   OS Landranger 6

In winter there is an abundance of birds, with large numbers of waders, especially Curlew, throughout the whole island. Otherwise, Mainland can be conveniently divided into East and West along a line through Kirkwall, with the East mainly farmland, whilst the West still has considerable areas of moorland.

Stromness and Kirkwall harbours Both are worth a look in winter for Glaucous and Iceland Gulls, and at Kirkwall the abattoir on Hatston Industrial Estate west of the harbour also attracts gulls.

Scapa Flow and Deer Sound Outstanding areas for divers, grebes and sea duck, in winter they may each hold over 100 Great Northern Divers and 1,000 Long-tailed Ducks. Waders are also numerous. The Churchill Barriers, causeways that connect Mainland to Burray and South Ronaldsay, are good vantage points for Scapa Flow.

Binscarth Wood Near Finstown, this woodland holds a rookery as well as a variety of small passerines and, occasionally, wintering Long-eared Owl, but there is so much cover that it is difficult to work for migrants. A track through the wood leaves the A965 just west of Finstown.

Hobbister RSPB reserve Southwest of Kirkwall, this covers c.2,000 acres and includes areas of moorland as well as low cliffs and the large, sandy Waulkmill Bay. It lies between the coast, the A964 and Loch of Kirbister. Breeding birds include Red Grouse, Hen Harrier, Merlin, Black Guillemot, Short-eared Owl and Raven. Waulkmill Bay, which can be watched from the car, attracts passage waders and, in winter, Great Northern and Black-throated Divers and Slavonian Grebe are regular, as well as sea duck. The reserve lies 4 miles from Kirkwall on the A964. Access is only permitted to the area between the road and sea, and visitors should keep to paths. Enter via a track at HY 396070 or the minor road to Waulkmill Bay. A summer warden covers the Orkney Mainland reserves.

Birsay Moors and Cottascarth RSPB reserve Though much of West Mainland has been reclaimed for beef cattle farming, some large areas of moorland remain, especially around Orphir in the south, between Finstown and Kirkwall, and the area from Finstown north to the Loch of Swannay. A large part of the last is now the RSPB reserve of Birsay Moors and Cottascarth, which covers nearly 6,000 acres astride the B9057. Breeding species include Greylag Goose, Short-eared Owl, Hen Harrier, a few Merlin, Whimbrel, and Great and Arctic Skuas. There is a winter harrier roost at Durkadale on Birsay Moors. Access is at four points:
1. Lower Cottascarth. Turn west off the A966 on a minor road 3 miles north of Finstown (just north of Norseman Garage), and then right along the track to the hide at Lower Cottascarth.
2. A hide on Burgar Hill overlooks Lowrie's Water, which has breeding Red-throated Diver and other waterbirds. The entrance is signed from the A966 at Evie, ½ mile northwest of the B9057 turn-off, and the hide is near the wind generators.
3. View Birsay Moors from the B9057 between Evie and Dounby.
4. Dee of Durkadale. Turn south on a track off the minor road at the south end of Loch Hundland and follow this to the abandoned farm of Durkadale (HY 293252) or view from the road through the valley.

Loch of Banks This area has a winter Hen Harrier roost. View from the A967 or A986.

Loch of Harray This large loch may hold up to 10,000 wintering duck, mostly Wigeon, Tufted Duck and Pochard, while the adjacent tidal Loch of Stenness has Long-tailed Duck and Goldeneye. Between these lochs and around Loch of Skaill there are often several hundred Greylag in winter, together with Whooper Swan. The car park at the Ring of Brodgar on the B9055 provides a good viewpoint.

The Loons in Birsay RSPB reserve Of the marshes and lochans, one of the best is also an RSPB reserve, the Loons in Birsay, in northwest Mainland, which is a waterlogged basin with reed and sedge beds adjacent to Loch of Isbister. Breeders include Pintail, Wigeon, seven species of wader, Arctic Tern and Sedge Warbler. In winter up to 150 Greenland White-fronted Geese use the area, as well as waders and other wildfowl. The only access is to the hide at HY 246242: leave the A986, turning west at Twatt, 3 miles north of Dounby; the hide is off this minor road c.400 yards before the junction with the B9056, and the reserve can also be viewed from this road.

Marwick Head RSPB reserve On the northwest coast, this section of c.1 mile of cliffs rises to 280 feet. Breeding birds include over 30,000 Guillemot and 5,000 pairs of Kittiwake, while Peregrine is occasionally seen. Access is on foot from two points: either the end of the minor road off the B9056 to Mar Wick bay or the car park at Cumlaquoy (similarly off the B9056 north of the Mar Wick turning) from where it is a short walk to the cliffs.

East Mainland Largely farmland and, although there is some remaining moorland harbouring typical species, the main attraction is passage migrants. Any area of bushes, crops or other vegetation is worth checking in spring and autumn.

76 COPINSAY (Orkney)

This 375-acre island 1¾ miles off East Mainland was bought by the RSPB in memory of the late James Fisher. The grassy interior is bounded by cliffs that rise to 250 feet, and the entire southeast side is a large seabird colony. As well as the main island, Corn Holm, Black Holm and Ward Holm are accessible at low tide. Seabirds include 30,000 Guillemots and these are joined by Razorbills, Black Guillemots and a few pairs of Puffins, as well as 4,000 pairs of Kittiwakes, Shag, Fulmar and Arctic Tern. There are more Puffins on Corn Holm and Black Holm. Other species of note are Raven and Twite, and Copinsay also attracts passage migrants.

From Skaill in Deerness, at the terminus of the B9050, a small boat makes day trips to the island by arrangement. Contact S. Foubister, tel: 01856 741252. A converted farmhouse now serves as an information and display centre, and provides very basic self-catering accommodation for an overnight stay. Contact the RSPB Warden, Andy Knight, 12/14 North End Road, Stromness, Orkney KW16 3EQ (tel: 01856 850176 or e-mail: andy.knight@rspb.org.uk) for details.

77 HOY (Orkney)

This island is rather different in character to the rest of Orkney. Mainly rugged, bleak moorland, the Cuilags and Ward Hill, rising to 1,577 feet, are the highest points in Orkney. There are few people. The scenery is spectacular, and includes the sheer 1,100-foot cliffs of St John's Head and the Old Man of Hoy, which, at 450 feet, is the highest sea stack in Britain. There is a small colony of Manx Shearwaters on Hoy, and Storm Petrel may also breed. There are c.2,100 pairs of Great Skua and 100 pairs of Arctic Skua. Many are on North Hoy but the valleys on the west side of the island are also good, especially those around Heldale Water. The continual bombardment by skuas is something to consider in advance. As many as 1,500 pairs of Arctic Tern may nest but numbers have declined recently. Red-throated Diver, Buzzard, Hen Harrier, Peregrine, Merlin and Short-eared Owl all breed, though there are few harriers and owls because of the lack of voles. Golden Eagle formerly bred but has seldom been seen in recent years. Winter birds include up to 1,100 Barnacle Geese on South Walls.

North Hoy RSPB reserve This 9,700-acre reserve comprises most of the northwest of the island and includes Berriedale, Britain's most northerly natural woodland. It is otherwise moorland bounded by superb cliffs that are home to large numbers of seabirds (e.g. 22,500 pairs of Fulmar). There are no restrictions on access and the reserve can be explored via long footpaths from Rackwick on the west coast to the Old Man of Hoy, and north to Sandy Loch, while a footpath accesses the Old Man of Hoy.

There is a daily passenger service to Moaness on Hoy from Stromness (tel: 01856 850624/678); the journey takes 20 minutes. Ro-ro ferries, the *MVs*

Thorsvoe and *Hoy Head*, operated by Orkney Ferries, run from Houton on Mainland to Lyness (and to nearby Flotta; tel: 01856 811397). The voyage takes 35 minutes.

78 SOUTH RONALDSAY (Orkney)   OS Landranger 7

South Ronaldsay and Burray are connected by road to East Mainland by the Churchill Barriers. The east and west coasts of South Ronaldsay have colonies of seabirds, including small numbers of Puffins, and also Raven. Otherwise the islands are mainly farmed, with small areas of heath that support nesting gulls and a few skuas, and some lochans and marshes with breeding ducks and waders. Lying on the east side of the archipelago, the major attraction is passage migrants.

79 ROUSAY (Orkney)   OS Landranger 6

In contrast to South Ronaldsay, Rousay is predominantly moorland and has a fine range of breeding birds, including Red-throated Diver, Hen Harrier, Merlin, Short-eared Owl and Raven. Around Westness and Trumland House there are areas of trees with the common woodland species.

Trumland RSPB reserve This reserve in the south of the island comprises c.1,000 acres of dry moorland dissected by small valleys and wetter areas, with most of the moorland specialities. A nature trail through the reserve starts c.½ mile west of the ferry pier. There is open access but visitors should contact the summer warden at Trumland Mill Cottage.

Quandale and Brings Areas of maritime heath in the northwest support up to 1,000 pairs of Arctic Tern and 100 pairs of attendant Arctic Skua, as well as a few Great Skuas. The west cliffs have Guillemot, Razorbill, Kittiwake and Fulmar; the last also nests inland on scattered rocks in the moorland.

Eynhallow Sound Offshore, the sounds between Rousay, Egilsay and Wyre support numbers of wintering Great Northern Diver and Long-tailed Duck. View from the south coast, the Broch of Gurness on Mainland, or the inter-island ferry.

Rousay is served daily (including Sundays May–September) by the *MV Eynhallow* ro-ro ferry from Tingwall (off the A966) in northeast Mainland, with connections to Egilsay and Wyre, operated by Orkney Ferries (tel: 01856 751360). The voyage takes just 25 minutes.

80 EGILSAY (Orkney)   OS Landranger 5/6

A last refuge of the Corncrake, with four calling males in 1997, the RSPB has purchased Onziebust Farm in the hope of increasing the island's population to c.15 pairs. There are no access arrangements at present.

81 SHAPINSAY (Orkney)   OS Landranger 6

This island is almost entirely agricultural land, though in the southeast there is a small area of moorland with a few pairs of Arctic Skua. In winter up to 100 Whooper Swans may be seen around Mill Dam, which is now an RSPB reserve and also has significant populations of breeding waders and ducks, including Pintail. Woodland in the grounds of Balfour Castle supports a variety of small passerines. The island is connected by the *MV Shapinsay* ro-ro ferry to Kirkwall, operated by Orkney Ferries (tel: 01856 872044). The journey takes 20 minutes.

82 STRONSAY (Orkney)   OS Landranger 5

Mainly farmland, the east cliffs between Odness and Lamb Head hold seabirds and the small lochs have breeding wildfowl, including Pintail.

Rothiesholm This area of moorland on the southwest peninsula supports the best range of moorland birds in the north group of islands, including Red-throated Diver, large numbers of breeding gulls (five species, especially Great Black-backed), Arctic Tern, small numbers of Arctic and Great Skuas, and Twite. There is a small colony of seabirds on the coast. Leave the B9061 at the old school and ask for permission to proceed at Bu Farm. Park and follow the track east from the school for 400 yards to the moors.

Mill Bay Large numbers of sea duck and divers.

Meikle Water Large numbers of wintering wildfowl, including up to 100 Whooper Swans and 50 Greenland White-fronted Geese.

Stronsay Bird Observatory Well placed to receive migrants, Stronsay has produced some exciting birds, and a private Bird Observatory operates on the island. Contact John and Sue Holloway, 'Castle', Stronsay, Orkney, tel: 01857 616363, for details of accommodation, boat trips etc.

Whitehall on Stronsay is connected by ro-ro ferry from Kirkwall, operated by Orkney Ferries (tel: 01856 872044), the voyage taking c.95 minutes, and the island is also served by British Airways Express (tel: 01856 872494).

83 EDAY (Orkney)   OS Landranger 5

There is a large area of moorland on Eday supporting good numbers of Arctic Skuas, as well as a handful of Great Skuas and a few pairs of Whimbrel. Seabird colonies around the coast include the Calf of Eday (with large numbers of Great Black-backed Gull), Grey Head for auks, and the south cliffs, which have a large colony of Cormorants. Mill Loch in the north holds c.8 pairs of Red-throated Divers. Near Carrick House in the north are two small woods that attract migrants.

The island is connected by ro-ro ferry to Kirkwall, operated by Orkney Ferries (tel: 01856 872044), and the island is also served by British Airways Express (tel: 01856 872494).

84 SANDAY (Orkney) OS Landranger 5

There is almost no moorland on Sanday and the low-lying coast means that there are few cliff-nesting seabirds. There may, however, be large colonies of terns, mainly Arctic, at Westayre Loch, Start Point and Els Ness, as well as breeding Arctic Skua at Gump of Spurness in the extreme southwest. Raven regularly breeds and Short-eared Owl occasionally, while the island, with Stronsay, forms the last Orkney refuge for Corn Bunting. Sanday is ideally placed to receive migrants, especially Lady Parish in the northeast, and the extensive beaches hold large numbers of wintering waders.

Loth on Sanday is connected by ro-ro ferry to Kirkwall, operated by Orkney Ferries (tel: 01856 872044), and the island is also served by British Airways Express (tel. 01856 873457).

85 WESTRAY (Orkney) OS Landranger 5

The island's prime attraction is the spectacular numbers of seabirds breeding along 5 miles of the west coast between Noup Head and Inga Ness, including up to 20,000 pairs of Kittiwake and 60,000 Guillemot. There are several lochs with breeding waterbirds, the best probably being Loch of Burness (just west of Pierowall), which has Britain's most northerly Little Grebes. The island attracts migrants during passage periods, although being on the west side of the archipelago, it is not ideally placed.

Noup Cliffs RSPB reserve The north end of the seabird colony comprises the RSPB reserve of Noup Cliffs, straddling 1½ miles of cliffs and forming the northwest extremity of the island. Here, Peregrine and Raven haunt the cliffs and there may be several hundred pairs of Arctic Tern on the adjacent maritime heath, together with up to 100 pairs of Arctic Skua. Follow a minor road west from Pierowall to Noup Farm, and then the track northwest for 1½ miles to the lighthouse on Noup Head. There is no warden.

Stanger Head Puffins may be difficult to see at Noup Head, so it may be worth visiting Stanger Head in the southeast of the island. A track leads northeast to the Head from Clifton, which is just east of the B9066, c.6 miles south of Pierowall.

Rapness on Westray is connected by ro-ro ferry to Kirkwall, operated by Orkney Ferries (tel. 01856 872044), and the island is also served by British Airways Express (tel. 01856 872494).

86 PAPA WESTRAY (Orkney) OS Landranger 5

Known in Orkney as Papay, attention centres on the large tern colonies and, of course, migrants (any area of cover can produce birds). Most of the terns nest at North Hill, but there are other large colonies in the south at Sheepheight and Backaskaill, and there is a large colony of Black Guillemot on Holm of Papa, off the east coast; this island also has a small colony of Storm Petrel.

North Hill RSPB reserve This RSPB reserve covers the northern uncultivated quarter of the island. It includes an area of maritime heath, with one of the three largest colonies of Arctic Tern in Britain (over 2,000 pairs), together with up to 150 pairs of Arctic Skua. Visitors must not walk through the tern colonies. The coast has low cliffs with Kittiwake, Guillemot, Razorbill and Black Guillemot (and was the last breeding site in Orkney for Great Auk). The best area is in the southeast of the reserve at Fowl Craig. There is a summer warden at North Hill, based at Rose Cottage, 650 yards southeast of the reserve entrance (which is at the north end of the island's main road), and it is requested that he be contacted in advance to escort visitors around the colonies (tel: 01857 644240).

Mull Head This, the north tip of the island, offers excellent seawatching. Sooty Shearwater is regular in late summer, up to 1300 having been seen in a day. Other species include skuas and a notable day total of 40 Long-tailed Skua has been logged.

The island is connected by a daily vehicle ferry to Kirkwall, operated by Orkney Ferries (tel: 01856 872044) and by passenger ferry to Pierowall on Westray (tel: Mr T. Rendall, 01857 677216; with a private minibus service available between Rapness and Pierowall). The island is also served by British Airways Express (tel: 01856 872494).

87 NORTH RONALDSAY (Orkney) OS Landranger 5

This small island is the most northeasterly in the archipelago and is mostly crofted and very flat, with several small lochs and areas of marshland. The coastline is bounded by a dry stone wall, the 'Sheep Dyke', which restricts the kelp-eating North Ronaldsay sheep to the foreshore. This is mostly rocky, with some sandy beaches on the east and south coasts. There may be a few hundred pairs of Arctic Tern, erratically, Sandwich and Common Terns, and numbers of Black Guillemots. Other breeding birds include waders and ducks, notably Gadwall, Pintail and Raven.

The area between Orkney and Fair Isle is probably the main route for seabirds moving between the North Sea and Atlantic. North Ronaldsay, the northernmost of the Orkney archipelago, is well placed to witness these movements. Fulmar passes in vast numbers—up to 20,000 per hour. Sooty Shearwater regularly peaks at over 100 per hour, and Leach's Petrel also occurs. The best seawatching point is the old beacon at Dennis Head in the northeast corner of the island, and the best conditions are following a northwest gale when the wind returns to southeast at first light.

Following the establishment of a Bird Observatory in 1987 and the consequent intensive coverage of the island, many rarities have been found. Indeed, in several recent years North Ronaldsay has challenged Fair Isle's hitherto unquestioned supremacy as *the* rarity hotspot. The walled garden at Holland House with its fuchsias and sycamores is attractive but most migrants frequent the crops. Large falls of the commoner species occur, and annual scarce migrants include Wryneck, Short-toed Lark, Richard's Pipit, Bluethroat, Icterine, Marsh, Barred and Yellow-browed Warblers, Red-backed Shrike, Common Rosefinch, and Little and Rustic Buntings. A variety of passage waders and ducks includes large numbers of Whooper Swans and geese in late September–October, and among the numerous migrant Golden Plovers are regular rarities such as Pacific and American Golden Plovers, Buff-breasted and Pectoral Sandpipers.

North Ronaldsay Bird Observatory provides comfortable dormitory and guest-house accommodation in a wind- and solar-powered low-energy building (see Information).

The island is connected by weekly passenger ferry to Kirkwall, operated by Orkney Ferries (tel: 01856 872044, sailings are weather dependent) and is also served Monday–Saturday by British Airways Express (tel: 01856 873457).

88 OTHER ISLANDS (Orkney)   OS Landranger 5, 6 and 7

Four other islands are worthy of mention.

Sule Skerry This holds 44,000 pairs of Puffin, as well as breeding Storm Petrel, but is very difficult to reach, lying 37 miles west of Brough of Birsay (West Mainland).

Sule Stack Even more difficult to reach, it has 5,000 pairs of Gannets. It lies 41 miles west of Brough of Birsay, West Mainland).

Pentland Skerries Accessible from South Ronaldsay, these may have a large colony of Arctic Terns, along with Sandwich and Common Terns, and a small Storm Petrel colony.

Auskerry South of Stronsay, this was the site of some of Eagle Clark's pioneering studies of migration.

Birds

Fulmar, Cormorant, Shag, Kittiwake, Guillemot, Razorbill, Black Guillemot and Puffin are widespread on cliffs and small islands, which they share with Rock Dove and Raven. On moorland and heaths there are Arctic and Great Skuas, five species of gull, and Sandwich, Common and Arctic Terns, these last also favouring beaches. Gannet breeds on Sule Stack and is widespread offshore, but Manx Shearwater and Storm Petrel are rather elusive, although the latter is common.

Breeding ducks include Wigeon, Gadwall, Shoveler, Eider and Red-breasted Merganser, and a large proportion of Britain's Pintails. Scaup, Long-tailed Duck and Common Scoter have bred in the past. Wildfowl share the marshes and lochs with Red-throated Diver, of which there are c.125 pairs on the islands, half on Hoy. Waders include Golden Plover, Dunlin and a few Whimbrels on Eday and Mainland, but Curlew is the most conspicuous species, being abundant on

Bluethroat

the moors. Black-tailed Godwit and Red-necked Phalarope have bred. Passerines in the marshy areas include Sedge Warbler and Reed Bunting.

The moorland supports Red Grouse and ground-nesting Kestrel, Woodpigeon, Starling and Hooded Crow. Orkney was the last refuge for the Hen Harrier when persecution had all but eliminated it from the rest of the country. Now declining, up to 40 females of this polygamous species may attempt to breed (quite recently up to 100 females laid in a good year). Sparrowhawk, Buzzard, Peregrine and Short-eared Owl also breed, and since the mid-1980s low of six pairs, Merlin has recovered to c.20 pairs. Other birds on the moors, apart from the abundant Meadow Pipit and Skylark, are Stonechat and Wheatear. Twite is declining but widespread and can be found along roadside verges. Corncrake had declined to only six calling birds by 1993 but the instigation of the Corncrake Initiative increased numbers to 42 by 1996. Most are in West Mainland, the remainder being scattered across several islands, especially Egilsay (now an RSPB reserve). Areas of trees and plantations support Rook, Willow Warbler and occasionally other woodland passerines such as Spotted Flycatcher or Garden Warbler, and Fieldfare first nested in Britain in 1967 on Orkney. Redwing has also bred.

Offshore, wintering Great Northern Diver is common and there are much smaller numbers of Black-throated Divers, which probably most frequently occurs in late winter and spring. There is a significant winter population of Slavonian Grebe and small numbers of Little Auks around the islands. Wildfowl include Whooper Swan, though many or most of these move south after early winter, unless food remains available. Two hundred Greenland White-fronted Geese in three flocks are joined by much larger numbers of Greylag and Barnacle. These geese and swans occur more abundantly on passage, together with Pink-footed Goose. The breeding ducks are joined by several thousand Long-tailed Duck and a few hundred Scaup, Velvet Scoter and Goldeneye, but Common Scoter is scarce. As in summer, Curlew is abundant and Orkney supports a quarter of the British wintering population; though ubiquitous, it favours pastures and shores. Also notable are large numbers of Turnstone and Purple Sandpiper, as well as Knot, Sanderling and Grey Plover. Gulls in the harbours and along the coast should be carefully checked for Glaucous, Iceland and even Ring-billed. Other wintering species are Long-eared Owl and Snow Bunting.

In spring and autumn many of the breeding and wintering birds may be seen but there are several species which are more or less confined to these periods. A variety of waders occurs, Greenshank and Whimbrel being the most frequent, and these are joined by small numbers of Curlew Sandpiper, Black-tailed Godwit, Spotted Redshank and Green Sandpiper. Offshore there is a large, sometimes very large, autumn passage of Sooty Shearwater, especially off the northernmost isles. Pomarine and Long-tailed Skuas and Little Gull are also possible but distinctly uncommon. Other scarce migrants include Honey and Rough-legged Buzzards. A broad variety of passerines occurs; among the commonest are Robin, Blackbird, Fieldfare, Redwing, Blackcap, Willow Warbler, Chiffchaff, Goldcrest, Brambling, Chaffinch and Siskin, and with these there are small numbers of scarcer species—most regular are Wryneck, Richard's Pipit, Black Redstart, Bluethroat, Icterine, Barred and Yellow-browed Warblers, Red-breasted Flycatcher, Great Grey and Red-backed Shrikes, Common Rosefinch, and Ortolan and Lapland Buntings. The best conditions, in both spring and autumn, as on Fair Isle and Shetland, are southeast winds. As the cream on the cake, a wide variety of rarities has been recorded and, like Shetland, Orkney has immense potential for those who wish to find their own.

Information

RSPB Orkney Officer: Eric Meek, Smyril, Stenness, Stromness, Orkney KW16 3JX
  Tel: 01856 850176.

RSPB Orkney, Reserves Manager: Keith Fairclough, 12/14 North End Road, Stromness, Orkney KW16 3EQ. Tel: 01856 850176. E-mail: keith.fairclough@ rspb.org.uk

RSPB Hoy: Ley House, Hoy, Orkney KW16 3NJ. Tel: 01856 791298.

RSPB North Hill Summer Warden: c/o Rose Cottage, Papa Westray, Orkney KW17 2BU. Tel: 01857 644240.

RSPB Trumland Summer Warden: tel: 01856 821395.

North Ronaldsay Bird Observatory: Dr Kevin Woodbridge or Alison Duncan, NRBO, Twingness, North Ronaldsay, Orkney KW17 2BE. Tel: 01857 633200.

SHETLAND

Shetland has two major attractions for the birdwatcher: breeding seabirds and waders, and migrants, particularly rarities. There is immense potential for those who wish to discover their own birds. The best times to visit are late May to mid-July for breeding birds, and mid-May to early June and mid-August to late October for migrants.

Habitat

The Shetland archipelago consists of 117 islands, of which 13 are inhabited. At 60°N, or the same latitude as the south tip of Greenland, the islands have a land-scape of interlocking peninsulas and voes (inlets). The rolling, dark, peat-covered hills are bordered by a rocky coast. Indeed, with over 2,500 freshwater lochs as well as a labyrinthine coast, water forms a very important part of the Shetland environment. The sheltered voes often have sandy beaches but the outer coast-line consists of cliffs, occasionally rising to over 1,000 feet. The sun is above the horizon for nearly 19 hours a day in summer, and it is easy to read a book in the twilight at midnight, but its rays are not strong at these latitudes. In winter there are barely 5½ hours of daylight and Shetland can be very bleak indeed. There have been almost no indigenous trees on the islands for 2,000–3,000 years, apart from relict patches protected from sheep in steep valleys or on small islets. There are, however, small areas of planted woodland, the largest stand being at Kergord on Mainland. The lack of cover means that migrants must use what they can find, and any crops, trees or bushes are worth investigating. In particular, any and all areas of cover on the east coast can hold migrants; which you choose to work is a question of accessibility and convenience.

Access

Full details of all transport and accommodation are available from Shetland Islands Tourism, Market Cross, Lerwick, Shetland ZE1 0LU. Tel: 01595 693434.

By Sea P & O Scottish Ferries operate the ro-ro ferries *MV St Clair* and *St Sunniva* to the islands five times a week from Aberdeen, sailing overnight to Lerwick in Shetland. The voyage takes 14 hours. Additionally, the *St Sunniva* sails via Stromness in Orkney twice weekly in summer (the Aberdeen–Orkney voyage takes 8–14 hours, and Stromness–Lerwick eight hours). Advance booking is rec-ommended on all sailings, most especially for vehicles; contact P & O Scottish Ferries, PO Box 5, Jamieson's Quay, Aberdeen AB9 8DL. Tel: 01224 572 615.

By Air British Airways Express has scheduled flights from Aberdeen and most other Scottish airports to Sumburgh, some of which connect with flights from London Heathrow/Gatwick, Manchester etc. Full details are available from the operators: British Airways reservations 0845 7733377. British Airways Shetland: 01950 460345.

Ground Transportation Public transport on Shetland is very limited, so it is best to hire a car or bring your own. Most roads on Shetland are narrow and consideration should always be exercised when parking. In addition, many of the areas described below are private. Especially when searching for migrants, the nature of the habitat calls for discretion. *Do not enter gardens or crofts without permission*, and even when looking in from the outside remember that not everyone may appreciate you peeping over their garden wall. In general, however, you will receive a friendly reception if you ask first.

Inter-island All islands detailed below are accessible by ferry (details appear under each entry), though services are infrequent. Information on all inter-island ferries is available 24 hours a day, tel: 01426 986763. Foula, Papa Stour and Out Skerries are also served by British Airways Express from Tingwall (just north of Lerwick), tel: 01595 840246, while British Airways Express also fly to Unst from Sumburgh.

Accommodation Available on all islands detailed below (except Mousa), but away from Lerwick and Scalloway accommodation is limited. There is a youth hostel in Lerwick and cheap hostels at Cunningsburgh (South Mainland), Aith (West Mainland), Uyeasound (Unst) and on Foula. Camping is not discouraged, but ask permission before setting up. Official campsites are available on Fetlar, at Brae (North Mainland), Lerwick and Levenwick (South Mainland). There are camping beds in Mid Yell, Voe, Whiter and Sumburgh. Tel: 01595 694688 for details.

MAINLAND

89 SOUTH MAINLAND (Shetland) (see map)   OS Landranger 4

Sumburgh Head RSPB reserve Turn south off the A970 at Grutness, signed to the Head, and park in the main car park. The Head has significant colonies of seabirds (including Puffin) that are readily accessible, especially on the west side. In July–August up to 2,000 Eider gather to moult offshore, and occasionally a King Eider is found among them. The Head is also a good seawatching site, with Sooty Shearwater regular in late summer and autumn, when Storm Petrel and Pomarine and Long-tailed Skuas also occur, and Little Auk is regular in late autumn. Watch from just south of the lighthouse in south and west winds, and from the car park in east winds. The stone dykes and quarries around the Head often hold migrant passerines. West Voe of Sumburgh holds sea duck and Great Northern Diver in winter.

Sumburgh Hotel The gardens have some small trees and shrubs offering cover to migrants, and the tiny marsh behind the hotel is also worth checking (but beware disturbing breeding waders in summer).

Grutness Turn off the A970, just beyond the sign for Wilsness Terminal. Park near the beach or pier. The beach attracts waders and gulls, with breeding Arctic Tern north of the pier, while Grutness Voe has sea duck and Great Northern Diver in winter. There are areas of cover attractive to migrants around the gardens, but

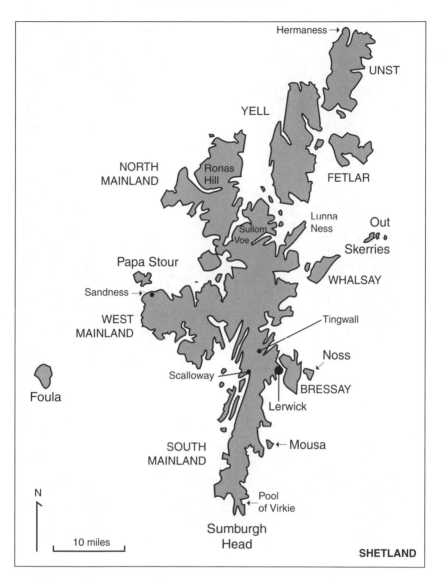

note that these are strictly private with no access. The *Good Shepherd* leaves for Fair Isle from the small harbour.

Scatness Loch Turn off the A970 at the sign to Scatness, parking carefully at the roadside after c.250 yards and walk south to the gate overlooking the pools. Access on foot from here is unrestricted. The Loch harbours wildfowl, gulls and waders (which may roost here at high tide or on the beach at the west end of the peninsula), and has breeding Arctic Tern, while the adjacent stone walls and gardens attract migrants.

Pool of Virkie One of Shetland's few tidal basins, usually holding a wider variety of waders than elsewhere, as well as gulls and terns. Turn east off the A970 to

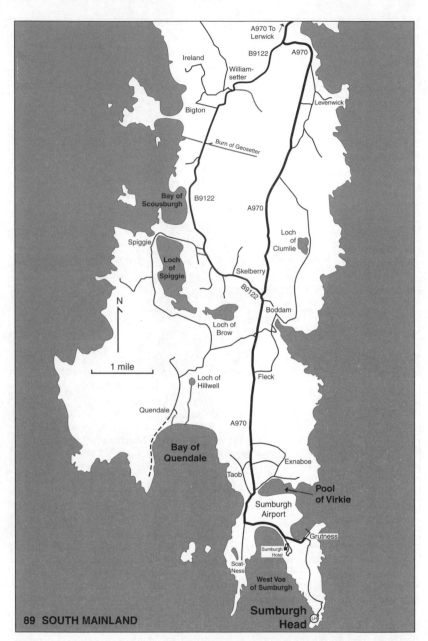

A970 To Lerwick

B9122

A970

Ireland

William-setter

Levenwick

Bigton

Burn of Geosetter

Bay of Scousburgh

B9122

A970

Loch of Clumlie

Spiggie

Loch of Spiggie

Skelberry

B9122

N

Boddam

Loch of Brow

1 mile

Loch of Hillwell

Fleck

Quendale

A970

Bay of Quendale

Exnaboe

Taob

Pool of Virkie

Sumburgh Airport

Grutness

Sumburgh Hotel

Scat-Ness

West Voe of Sumburgh

Sumburgh Head

LH

89 SOUTH MAINLAND

Eastshore (just north of the north set of airport warning lights) and view the pool from the road, preferably in the two hours before high water. The best site for Shelduck in the islands, there are also gardens on its north shore.

Toab Turn west off the A970 just north of the northern set of airport warning lights (or turn west off the A970 just north of the Exnaboe turning). The gardens and fields are productive areas for migrants.

Exnaboe Turn east off the A970 c.½ mile north of the Pool of Virkie turning. The gardens are good for migrants.

Bay of Quendale View from the road on the west side. Good for wintering sea duck and Great Northern Diver, which may linger into spring. The streams that run from Quendale and Loch of Hillwell to the sea attract migrants, and are favoured by Bluethroat and Marsh Warbler in spring.

Loch of Hillwell Turn west off the A970 to Quendale, just south of the G & S Mainland shop, and continue for 1¼ miles, parking carefully to view the Loch from the road. The only machair loch in Shetland, with marshy edges, it holds numbers of wildfowl, including Whooper Swan, Greylag Goose and occasionally Smew in winter, and attracts passage wildfowl, waders and passerines.

Loch of Spiggie A fertile eutrophic loch surrounded by areas of marsh, this is a RSPB reserve. Leave the A970 west on the B9122 at Skelberry and after c.1 mile turn west onto the minor road to Spiggie. There are good views from this road of the north, west and south shores. The Loch holds wintering wildfowl, including Greylag Goose and up to 400 Whooper Swans in late autumn/early winter, and small spring gatherings of Long-tailed Duck. Breeding birds include several duck species, while the Loch is used by bathing gulls and skuas, and waders occur on passage (favouring the northwest corner). In winter the dunes to the north hold Snow Bunting, and Bay of Scousburgh hosts sea duck and Great Northern Diver.

Boddam Turn east off the A970 just south of the B9122 near Skelberry or just south of the G & S Mainland shop, or at the turning to Fleck. The slaughterhouse here attracts many Great Skuas and Ravens, with sea duck, waders and gulls in the voe, while the gardens shelter migrants, especially around the voe and along the Fleck road.

Burn of Geosetter A very good area for migrants, park carefully by the B9122 and explore the patches of cover along the north side of the stream east of the road; the houses are strictly private.

Bigton and Ireland Access along minor roads off the B9122. The gardens and fields are attractive to migrants.

Levenwick Access from minor roads east off the A970. The many gardens attract migrants.

90 LERWICK AREA (Shetland) OS Landranger 4

Lerwick harbour Lerwick is the point of arrival for visitors coming by sea and the harbour is well worth a look, with resident Black Guillemot and gulls, including wintering Glaucous and Iceland. The *Shetland Catch* fish factory, just to the north at Gremista, is one of the best areas for white-winged gulls. Otherwise, the gulls often perch on warehouse roofs.

Sandy Loch Reservoir View from the A970 just south of Lerwick, and it is possible to walk around the reservoir. Loafing gulls and passage waders are the attraction.

Loch of Clickimin Gulls favours the sewage outfall directly south of Loch of Clickimin, and the short grass on the east shore is also frequented by loafing gulls. The Loch is used by diving duck in winter.

Helendale Immediately west of Loch of Clickimin at Helendale there are several large wooded gardens that attract migrants. Stay on the tarmac track.

Gremista Just north of Lerwick there are a few gardens and a dense sycamore copse west of the road along the North Burn of Gremista (just north of the A970) which holds migrants.

91 CENTRAL MAINLAND (Shetland)   OS Landranger 4

Scalloway This has similar attractions to Lerwick. The best area for gulls is the fish dock pier on the east side of the harbour near the castle and the adjacent fish factories. During westerly gales seabirds may seek shelter here, occasionally including Storm and Leach's Petrels and Pomarine Skua. Long-tailed Duck is present in winter, together with small numbers of auks, Tufted Duck and occasionally Scaup. The gardens in the town hold migrants, and formerly Long-eared Owl in winter.

Veensgarth Approximately 6 miles north of Lerwick turn south off the A971 (at HU 429446) and follow the road until it ends. Search the trees from the road for migrants and wintering Long-eared Owl.

Strand Plantation Around 6 miles north of Lerwick turn north off the A970 at the sign to Gott, parking by the small bridge. The plantation is owned by Shetland Bird Club, with open access, although best worked from the perimeter fence for migrants and wintering Long-eared Owl.

Lochs of Tingwall and Asta Adjacent to the B9074, these are good for diving ducks, passage Whooper Swans and passage waders, while Mute Swan has bred since 1992. The crofts on the west side of the B9074 may hold migrants.

92 WEST MAINLAND (Shetland)   OS Landranger 3 and 4

Tresta Voe, Sandsound Voe and Reawick Good for Great Northern Diver, Slavonian Grebe and sea ducks (often producing a King Eider, especially in Sand Voe and Kirka Ness), the area can be viewed from the A971 and B9071, with Reawick accessible via a minor road off the B9071). Weisdale Voe has a similar range of birds.

Tresta A good area for migrants, the village is on the A971 and has gardens and sycamore trees by the chapel.

Sandness Mainland's westernmost village, the nearby Loch of Norby and Loch of Melby (view from the track just northwest of Norby) and Loch of Collaster (view from the minor road to the north) have potential for vagrant American waders and ducks.

Ness of Melby At the terminus of the A971, this makes a good seawatching point, with the possibility of Pomarine or Long-tailed Skuas.

Wats Ness The most westerly point on Mainland. From Walls on the A971 take the minor road west to Dale and, after c.3½ miles, turn at the sign to Wats Ness. From the end of the road walk southwest to find a sheltered part of the cliff. The best seawatching station in spring in the entire archipelago, flocks of both Long-tailed and Pomarine Skuas are regular (in May 1992 Pomarine peaked at the astonishing day total of 2,093 birds). Strong west or northwest winds coupled with squalls are the best conditions, and May *the* month.

93 NORTH MAINLAND (Shetland)   OS Landranger 3

Kergord On the B9075 in the Weisdale Valley, this area has plantations of sycamore, larch and spruce, which support breeding Woodpigeon, Rook and sometimes Goldcrest or even Fieldfare. They also attract migrants but due to the extent of the cover are difficult to work. There is free access to the plantations but the walled garden at Kergord House is strictly private.

Voe The gardens at Voe, just off the A970 on the B9071, are very good. It is a large area with lots of houses.

Voxter and Sullom Plantations More good areas for migrants, the former north of the B9076 c.1 mile from its junction with the A970, the latter adjacent to the minor road to Sullom, c.2 miles from the A970.

Lunna Ness This peninsula in the northeast is an excellent area for migrants, especially Lunna itself with its line of sycamores (on the left of the road 300 yards before Lunna House). The gardens and stream at the head of Swining Voe, west of Lunna Ness, can also be productive.

Sullom Voe Wintering Great Northern Diver, Slavonian Grebe and sea duck, sometimes including Velvet Scoter. The sewage outfall just before the main gate of the oil terminal is good for gulls, and the Houb of Scatsta, north of the B9076 just beyond the airfield, attracts waders.

Ronas Hill In the far north of Mainland, this is the largest wilderness area in Shetland. The west flank has spectacular cliffs and, at 1,475 feet, is the archipelago's highest point, with areas of arctic/alpine habitats. The terrain is very rough and it is quite easy to get lost, especially in the very changeable weather. Snowy Owl has occasionally been seen, the best area being around Mid Field and Roga Field. Dotterel is irregular in spring and Snow Bunting has been seen in summer and may be numerous in autumn. Access is from the A970. The track west of the road just north of North Collafirth goes to Collafirth Hill, accessing Mid Field and Roga Field.

Ronas Voe This scenic fjord has the usual species, with King Eider a possibility. A minor road runs along the shore from the A970.

OTHER ISLANDS

94 MOUSA (Shetland)

OS Landranger 4

This 450-acre island is just over ½ mile off the east coast of Mainland, opposite Sandwick. It has the best Pictish broch in Britain and this archeological attraction is not without its birds—Storm Petrel nests in the walls as well as in the surrounding stone walls and on the boulder beaches. It is necessary to visit at night to see and hear the petrels, on one of the regular summer boat trips. The petrels are best viewed from the boulder beach just north of the broch; do not, however, lift rocks to look for nesting petrels! Ferries leave in summer from Leebotten (turn south off the A970 at the sign to Sandwick at Crossgerd and then follow signs to Leebotten; the crossing takes five minutes. Ring Tom Jamieson on 01950 431367 for details of ferries and nocturnal visits, or contact Shetland Islands Tourism. The island has several small pools that are good for migrant waders, and has breeding Arctic Tern and Arctic and Great Skuas.

95 BRESSAY (Shetland)

OS Landranger 4

Bressay lies immediately east of Lerwick and is accessible by frequent ro-ro ferry (five minutes). There are colonies of Great and Arctic Skuas on the southeast side of the island, but the main attraction is migrants. The best areas are the crofts on the west side. However, a lot of walking is required to cover them without a car.

96 NOSS (Shetland)

OS Landranger 4

A few hundred yards east of Bressay, Noss is a NNR covering nearly 1,000 acres and is open to visitors late May to late August, 10.00–17.00 daily except Tuesday and Friday. Follow signs to Noss and proceed to the end of the road, walking down the rough track to the 'wait here' sign. The resident wardens provide a ferry service using an inflatable dinghy from Bressay (two minutes) for a small fee, but in bad weather a red flag will fly on Noss indicating that the island is closed (it is worth checking with Shetland Islands Tourism (tel: 01595 693434) whether the ferry is operating. There is a visitor centre and toilets on the island.

This green and fertile island rises to 594 feet at the Noup. There are spectacular seabird colonies: over 100,000 individuals of 12 species breed, including 7,000 pairs of Gannets, 40,000 Guillemots, and Great and Arctic Skuas.

97 WHALSAY (Shetland)

OS Landranger 2

The Whalsay ro-ro ferry leaves Mainland from Laxo (30 minutes, though in some weathers it sails from Vidlin, the crossing taking 50 minutes; advance booking recommended, tel. 01806 566259).

Whalsay has breeding Red-throated Diver, Whimbrel (view from the road between Brough and Isbister) and Great and Arctic Skuas, but its main attraction is passage migrants. A large island, over 5 miles long, a certain amount of legwork is necessary to cover all of the better areas.

Dury Voe The ferry regularly passes small groups of Little Auks in winter, and a White-billed Diver wintered for 13 years in the Voe.

Symbister Bay Good for gulls in winter, attracted by the fish factory; the harbour is best viewed from the raised bank by the ferry terminal. The gardens and crops are also very attractive to migrants.

Skaw, Brough and Isbister Skaw in the far northeast of the island is where many of the most exciting migrants have been found, and all of the crofts should be checked, as well as the airfield (from the perimeter) and the close-copped grass of Skaw Taing. The gardens and crofts on the seaward side of Isbister and around Brough are also worth a look.

98 OUT SKERRIES (Shetland) OS Landranger 2

Skerries is a group of small, rocky islands. Their position at the easternmost point in Shetland and their ease of coverage has resulted in a list of rare birds unequalled in the archipelago away from Fair Isle. The *MV Fillia* ro-ro passenger ferry runs, weather permitting, from Lerwick (c.4 hours) and Vidlin (1½ hours); passengers and vehicles must be booked by 17.00 the previous day. For details ring G. W. Henderson, 01806 515226. Loganair operate flights from Tingwall. The best areas for migrants are the crops and gardens in Bruray and Housay.

99 PAPA STOUR (Shetland) OS Landranger 3

This small island off West Mainland has the largest Arctic Tern colony in Shetland, as well as Great and Arctic Skuas, seabird cliffs, spectacular coastal scenery and massive sea caves. Several small lochs are good for wildfowl and waders, and though under-watched it has great potential for interesting migrants. The *MV Westering Homewards* passenger ferry runs from West Burrafirth, weather permitting, the journey taking 35 minutes (advance booking essential; ring W. Clark, 01595 810460, for details of schedules and reservations). The island is also served by flights from Tingwall, operated by Loganair.

100 FOULA (Shetland) OS Landranger 4

Foula is one of the most isolated inhabited islands in Britain. Fourteen miles west of Mainland, it has a spectacular, precipitous coastline. At 1,220 feet the Kame is the second-highest sea cliff in Britain. The *MV Koada* passenger ferry sails, weather permitting (and it often doesn't), from Walls in West Mainland, the crossing taking 2½ hours. There is also a fortnightly ferry service from Scalloway, the voyage lasting 5½ hours (advance booking is essential for all ferries; enquiries to Mr R. Holbourn, tel: 01595 753232). In addition, Loganair operate weekly flights in summer from Lerwick (Tingwall). All accommodation must be booked in advance and sufficient provisions for the duration of the stay must be taken for self-catering, hostel or camping trips.

Foula's main attraction, apart from its splendid isolation and superb atmosphere, is the large number of breeding seabirds on the west cliffs, including Manx Shearwater, Storm and Leach's Petrels (the last almost impossible to see) and c.200 pairs of Gannets, while the moorland in the west of the island holds Britain's largest colony of Great Skuas, comprising over 2,000 pairs. Despite limited coverage Foula has produced many interesting migrants around the crofts and well-vegetated Ham Burn.

101 YELL (Shetland)

Yell is the second-largest island in Shetland and is predominantly covered by blanket-bogs on low, rounded hills. There are many areas of cover which are seldom visited by birdwatchers, and are thus fertile hunting grounds for more adventurous rarity hunters. Access is by ro-ro ferry across Yell Sound from Toft on Mainland (20 minutes), while to the north there are ferries to Unst and Fetlar.

Yell Sound Ramna Stacks and Gruney in the north of the Sound are managed by the RSPB and have breeding Storm and Leach's Petrels. There are, however, no visiting arrangements. In winter Great Northern Diver, Long-tailed Duck and, sometimes, Little Auk may be seen from the ferry between Yell and Mainland (but this route is poor compared to the Unst or Whalsay crossings).

Copister Broch Off the far south of the island, this holds a large colony of Storm Petrels.

Burravoe, Otterswick and Mid Yell There are good areas for migrants on Yell, including the gardens in Burravoe and Otterswick in the southeast, and Mid Yell in the centre of the island.

Lumbister RSPB reserve The RSPB has a reserve at Lumbister covering over 4,000 acres west of the A968 and northeast of Whale Firth. Moorland, several lochs and sea cliffs support breeding Red-throated Diver and both species of skua, as well as Merlin, seabirds and occasionally Whimbrel. Access is from the lay-by 4 miles north of Mid Yell. The reserve is always open, but contact the Fetlar warden for details.

102 FETLAR (Shetland) (see map)

Accessed by ro-ro ferry from either Gutcher on Yell or Belmont on Unst (sailing times 25 minutes; advance booking recommended, tel: 01957 722259/722268). The west of Fetlar, especially Lamb Hoga, is heather moorland and peat bog, while the east has grassy moorland and dry heath, all interspersed with lochs, pools, marshes and patches of cultivation. There is a fine coastline of cliffs and beaches, and seabirds breed in small numbers, the south tip of Lamb Hoga having a good selection.

Fetlar's specialities are Red-necked Phalarope (see below) and Whimbrel, which are quite widespread, good areas being the roadside moorland west of Loch of Funzie and moorland west of the airstrip and east of the school. With such rare birds, you should take special pains to avoid disturbance. Do not linger in Whimbrel territories and do not try to find phalarope breeding areas. Fetlar is also *the* place to see Manx Shearwater and Storm Petrel (see below), and there are large colonies of Arctic Terns, as well as Great and Arctic Skuas. Specific sites include:

Fetlar RSPB reserve Originally established to protect the Snowy Owl, the reserve extends over Vord Hill, Stackaberg and the surrounding slopes, and the coastline from East Neap to Urie Ness. Entrance is only by arrangement with the

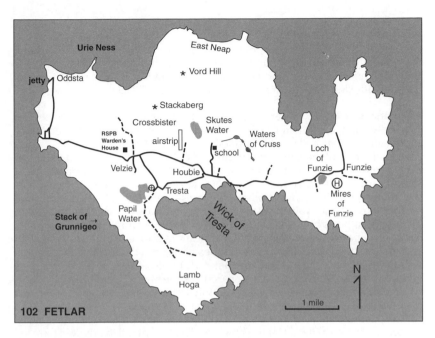

102 FETLAR

summer warden, whose house is signposted at Bealance, 2½ miles along the road from the pier (tel: 01957 733246 or e-mail: malcom.smith@rspb.org.uk), and Vord Hill is closed mid-May to late July. Snowy Owl no longer breeds (and is nowadays seldom present), but if there are owls on the reserve in summer the warden may escort visitors to see them.

Papil Water Used by large numbers of bathing seabirds in summer, notably Great Skua, and also Red-throated Diver. It attracts wildfowl in winter.

Wick of Tresta A few Manx Shearwaters breed on Lamb Hoga and a good place to watch the evening gatherings in the Wick of Tresta is the beach adjacent to Papil Water, especially the Tresta end.

Grunnigeo Storm Petrel cannot be seen in daylight but the colonies along the west slopes of Lamb Hoga are accessible with great care, especially at Stack of Grunnigeo. From Velzie walk past the north shore of Papil Water, directly over the saddle of the hills to Grunnigeo. Descend on the north side of Grunnigeo to the grassy ridge that connects the stack to the main slope. The ridge makes a good vantage and petrels can be seen and heard around midnight. They favour overcast nights, and in clear, bright conditions none may come ashore. A torch is essential.

Loch of Funzie Park carefully off the B9088 immediately east of Loch of Funzie. View the Loch only from the road and follow signs to the hide overlooking the Mires of Funzie. Almost 40 pairs of Red-necked Phalaropes breed on Fetlar, several of which are in the Mires of Funzie, though they are most easily viewed from the road along the north shore of the loch (the best tactic is to sit and wait for these confiding birds to come to you!). The Loch also holds Red-throated Diver.

Tresta, Houbie and Funzie Fetlar attracts its fair share of migrants and there are productive crofts in the south and east of the island.

103 UNST (Shetland)   OS Landranger 1

Unst is the third-largest and northernmost main island in Shetland. Loganair operate daily flights to Baltasound on Unst from Sumburgh. Access from Gutcher on Yell (ten minutes) and Oddsta on Fetlar (30 minutes) is by ro-ro car ferry but advance booking is recommended, tel: 01957 722259/722268.

Hermaness NNR Unst's star attraction is the magnificent seabird colony on Hermaness, at the northern tip of Unst. Here, the cliffs rise to 400 feet and overlook Muckle Flugga and Out Stack, Britain's most northerly point.

From the end of the B9086 at Burrafirth take the minor road north to the car park, where a visitor centre is sited in the old Muckle Flugga Shore Station; a summer warden is based here. From the car park a marked trail leads across the moor to the cliffs, and another path runs along the cliff edge from Saito north to the Greing. While crossing the moors, beware of dive-bombing skuas. They seldom press home an attack, but it is worth wearing a hat and taking a stick (or using your telescope and tripod) to hold above your head. Take great care on the steep and slippery grass slopes above the cliffs, especially when it is wet—there have been accidents here. Note also that the weather is very changeable and you should be prepared for the worst. Hermaness is a NNR with no restrictions on access except to the sensitive area.

Breeding seabirds include over 10,000 pairs of Gannet, 14,000 pairs of Fulmar, 25,000 pairs of Puffin, 20,000 pairs of Guillemot, and smaller numbers Shag, Razorbill, Black Guillemot and Kittiwake. The moorland holds Red-throated Diver, Golden Plover, and Arctic and Great Skuas (850 pairs). In 1972–1995 a solitary Black-browed Albatross (known affectionately as 'Albert') returned almost every year late March–August to build its nest among the Gannets (it could be seen well from the clifftop immediately above Saito, as well as from the Neap slightly to the north).

Burra Firth The beach at Burrafirth often holds Glaucous or Iceland Gulls, while to the south, Loch of Cliff attracts bathing seabirds and in winter may hold a few roosting white-winged gulls.

Northdale and Skaw Good spots for migrants in the extreme northeast of the island, access is off the B9087. Of note are the well-vegetated streams. Seek permission to venture off the road.

Haroldswick The village gardens attract migrants, the beach waders, and the bay wintering divers and sea duck. Between Norwick and Haroldswick there are marshy areas and several shallow pools by the roadside which sometimes attract migrant waders.

Baltasound This settlement on the east coast has some of the best areas of cover for passerine migrants, notably at the school and at Halligarth.

Uyeasound and Skuda Sound Access south off the A968 via the B9084 or the minor road to Uyeasound. The sounds hold sea duck and divers, with Great Northern Diver often staying late in spring. Nearby Easter Loch holds Whooper Swan and the village gardens at Uyeasound are attractive to passerine migrants.

Bluemull Sound This separates Unst from Yell. Large numbers of seabirds pass through the area on their way to and from the colonies. In winter there are large numbers of Eiders and Long-tailed Ducks as well as divers, Black Guillemot and sometimes Little Auk View from the ferry or from the ferry terminals on Unst, Yell and Fetlar.

Birds

Fulmars first bred on Foula in 1878 and now number over 150,000 pairs in Shetland; they include occasional 'blue' Fulmars. There are two known colonies of Manx Shearwater, Storm Petrel is widespread, and Leach's Petrel breeds on Foula and on Gruney in Yell Sound. The Gannet colonies at Noss and Hermaness are increasing, and Shag outnumbers Cormorant by 20 to 1. Guillemot, Razorbill and Puffin are all common (and easily seen at Sumburgh Head), with smaller numbers of Black Guillemot. Common and Arctic Terns, six species of gull, and Arctic and Great Skuas complete the complement of breeding seabirds.

Several hundred pairs of Red-throated Divers nest on the lochs and pools, and the marshes and wetlands also support Mute Swan, Greylag Goose, Teal, Tufted Duck and Red-breasted Merganser, with Eider on coastal moorland. There are also occasional pairs of Wigeon. Twelve species of wader breed, notably c.40 pairs of Red-necked Phalarope, 500 pairs of Whimbrel and often a few pairs of Black-tailed Godwit. The phalaropes usually arrive in late May and leave by early August. Corncrake has all but disappeared; few, if any, now breed on Shetland. Red Grouse has been introduced, and there are small numbers of Merlin and occasionally Peregrine. Skylark and Rock and Meadow Pipits are common, but Swallow breeds only in small numbers, House Martin only irregularly, and Pied and White Wagtails occasionally. Blackbird, Wheatear, Wren (the rather dark endemic Shetland form *zetlandicus*), Starling (subspecies *zetlandicus*, which also occurs on the Outer Hebrides), Raven and Hooded Crow are common, and Rook breeds at Kergord. Twite and House Sparrow are both common around crofts, and sometimes a few pairs of Reed Buntings nest.

Occasionally individuals of species that breed further north, in Iceland or Scandinavia, summer on Shetland. These include Great Northern Diver, Whooper Swan, Long-tailed Duck (believed to have bred three times in the 19th century), Common and Velvet Scoters, Purple Sandpiper, Turnstone, Glaucous Gull (has hybridised with Herring Gull), Snowy Owl (bred 1967–75 on Fetlar), Redwing (bred five times 1953–83), Fieldfare (bred most years 1968–73 and a few times since) and Snow Bunting.

Sooty Shearwater is regularly seen on passage in late summer/autumn, especially from Sumburgh Head. Other seabirds to look for include Pomarine and Long-tailed Skuas in both spring and autumn, and there is a notable late-autumn passage of 'blue' Fulmar. Flocks of Pink-footed, Greylag and Barnacle Geese occur, mainly in autumn, as well as Gadwall, Pintail and Shoveler. Migrant raptors include Long-eared and Short-eared Owls, and less often Honey Buzzard, Hen Harrier, Sparrowhawk, Buzzard, Rough-legged Buzzard and Osprey. Grey Plover, Sanderling, Bar-tailed Godwit and Knot occur almost exclusively on passage, joining the usual array of migrant waders. Woodcock, thrushes, chats, Blackcap, Willow Warbler, Goldcrest, Pied Flycatcher etc. all occur in quite large numbers given suitable weather. The best conditions are southeast winds. Among scarcer migrants, those usually more frequent in spring than autumn are Short-toed Lark, Bluethroat, Marsh Warbler, Golden Oriole and Red-backed Shrike. Icterine Warbler, Lapland, Ortolan and Little Buntings and Common Rosefinch are much more frequent in autumn, though they do occur in spring, but Richard's Pipit, Barred and Yellow-browed Warblers, Red-breasted Flycatcher and Yellow-breasted Bunting are virtually unknown in spring. Wryneck is recorded equally at both seasons, and Waxwing can also put in one of its erratic appearances at either season.

True rarities recorded with some regularity in spring include Thrush Nightingale,

Subalpine Warbler and Rustic Bunting, while in autumn Olive-backed Pipit, Arctic and Greenish Warblers and Rustic Bunting are annual. More erratic specialities include Great Snipe, Pechora Pipit, Citrine Wagtail and Lanceolated Warbler.

Some species common on the mainland but rare or absent as breeding birds on Shetland occur on migration. These include Dunnock, Robin and finches (apart from Twite), while Great Spotted Woodpecker, tits and northern Bullfinches are rare and erratic visitors. South Mainland and Out Skerries are probably the most productive areas for migrants, but birds can, and are, found almost anywhere.

A total of 500–600 Great Northern Divers winter around the islands, with many fewer Red-throated. Slavonian Grebe occurs in small numbers, especially in Tresta Voe. Up to 400 Whooper Swans pass through on migration, but in general there are few in winter unless it is very mild. They, like most of the duck (with the exception of Eider and Long-tailed Duck) move south early in the season. King Eider is seen most winters, with records widely scattered around the islands. Large numbers of Turnstone and Purple Sandpiper winter on shores, and away from the coast there may be Golden Plover, Curlew, Snipe and Jack Snipe and sometimes numbers of Woodcocks in late autumn. Small flocks of Little Auks can occur October–February, and Glaucous and Iceland Gulls are regular visitors, especially to fishing harbours. A few Long-eared Owls may winter, mainly in the Tingwall Valley, and small numbers of Snow Buntings sometimes remain and may be found almost anywhere.

Information

RSPB Shetland Officer: Peter Ellis, East House, Sumburgh Head Lighthouse, Virkie, Shetland ZE3 9JN. Tel: 01950 460800.

RSPB Fetlar (North Isles Shetland Officer): Bealance, Fetlar, Shetland ZE2 9DJ. Tel: 01957 733246. E-mail: malcolm.smith@rspb.org.uk

SNH Shetland: Ground Floor, Stewart Building, Alexandra Wharf, Lerwick, Shetland ZE1 0LL. Tel: 01595 693345.

104 FAIR ISLE (Shetland)   OS Landranger 4

Fair Isle is justifiably famous for the number of rare and unusual birds that appear annually, and an additional attraction in spring and summer are the excellent seabird colonies. Following the pioneering studies of Eagle Clark in the early years of the 20th century, George Waterston bought the island and established a Bird Observatory in 1948; the island now belongs to the NTS.

Habitat

The island is c.3 miles long and covers 1,890 acres. The cliffs of the magnificent coastline reach c.500 feet. The south of the island is crofted, while the north is mostly heather moor, rising to 712 feet at Ward Hill, and has nesting skuas. Migrants can occur anywhere but generally favour the crops, ditches and a tiny area of trees, as well as the geos (inlets) on the coast, which can be very good.

Access

By Air Loganair fly Shetland (Tingwall) to Fair Isle on Monday, Wednesday, Friday and Saturday, May–October, and Monday, Wednesday and Friday only for the rest of the year. These flights connect with Shetland–Aberdeen services. In summer Loganair operates a Glasgow–Kirkwall–Fair Isle–Tingwall service on Saturdays. For full details tel: Loganair (Tingwall), 01595 840246.

By Sea The *MV Good Shepherd IV* mail boat, operated by Shetland Islands Council, sails between Fair Isle and Shetland (Grutness) on Tuesday, Thursday and Saturday, May–September, Tuesdays only during the rest of the year. The voyage takes c.2½ hours and there is a nominal charge. Alternate Thursdays in summer the *Good Shepherd* sails between Lerwick and Fair Isle, the trip taking 4½ hours. Bookings are essential (Mr J. W. Stout, Fair Isle, Shetland, tel: 01595 760222), and sailings are affected by bad weather (this crossing is *definitely to be avoided* if you are a bad sailor). For details of transport to Shetland, see p.587.

Accommodation Available at Fair Isle Lodge and Bird Observatory mid-April to late October; by observatory standards, Fair Isle Lodge is luxurious. Bookings: Hollie Shaw, Fair Isle Lodge and Bird Observatory, Fair Isle, Shetland ZE2 9JU. Tel: 01595 760258. E-mail: fairisle.birdobs@zetnet.co.uk

Birds
Spring migration begins in March, but despite the occurrence of several outstanding rarities in early spring, it is in late May–early June that the most exciting range of species has been recorded. Golden Oriole, Bluethroat, Icterine and Marsh Warblers, Red-backed Shrike, Common Rosefinch, and Ortolan and Lapland Buntings are annual, and sometimes occur in comparatively large numbers. Thrush Nightingale is something of a specialty in the last week of May, and Red-throated Pipit, Short-toed Lark, Subalpine Warbler and Rustic Bunting are regularly recorded, though perhaps not annually.

Breeding seabirds include a few pairs of Storm Petrels, and many more non-breeders come ashore at night. There are c.43,000 pairs of Fulmar and 1,000+ pairs of Gannet. Shag, Kittiwake, four other species of gull, c.1,250 pairs of Arctic Tern (1996), a few pairs of Common Tern and all four auks also breed. There are c.120 pairs of Great and c.85 pairs of Arctic Skuas, and in midsummer single Long-tailed Skuas are occasionally seen in the colonies. The commonest breeding landbirds are Skylark, Meadow and Rock Pipits, and Wheatear, while the Fair Isle subspecies of Wren (*fridariensis*) is reasonably ubiquitous, with c.35 pairs on the island.

Corncrake, Wryneck, Richard's Pipit, Bluethroat, Icterine, Barred and Yellow-browed Warblers, Red-breasted Flycatcher, Red-backed and Great Grey Shrikes, Common Rosefinch and Lapland Bunting are annual in autumn, and several rarities are nearly annual. Aquatic Warbler and Black-headed Bunting have appeared several times in August–early September, and there has also been several Booted Warblers during this period. Arctic and Greenish Warblers and Red-throated Pipit can be seen from early September, but it is in the second half of September that interest usually peaks. However, the quality of birds is very weather-dependent. Just a hint of a southeast wind can, and does, produce rarities, and Yellow-breasted Bunting is almost guaranteed. West or southwest winds may spell disaster for the visiting rarity hunter, with very few birds at all. It is a risk you must take. Given favourable winds regulars include Great Snipe, Short-toed Lark, Olive-backed and Pechora Pipits, Citrine Wagtail, Siberian Stonechat, Lanceolated Warbler, and Little and (more erratically) Rustic Buntings. If these are not sufficient, the most sought-after species, for example Siberian Rubythroat, Red-flanked Bluetail, Pallas's Grasshopper Warbler, and Pallas's Reed and Yellow-browed Buntings have also occurred, some more than once. There are common migrants too, and sometimes large numbers of Woodcock, Redwing and Fieldfare. Others include Pink-footed and Greylag Geese, Whooper Swan, a trickle of Merlins, and some interesting subspecies, e.g. Greenland Redpoll and northern Bullfinch.

Seawatching is best from the *Good Shepherd* and South Light. Storm Petrel is regular from the boat in summer, and Manx Shearwater is joined in autumn by Sooty Shearwater and, occasionally, Leach's Petrel. Sea duck may also be interesting.

INDEX OF BIRDS BY SITE NUMBER

S3, 6, 10, 12, 20, 22, 23,
31, 36, 37, 44, 45, 48, 51,
52, 53, 54, 61, 62, 65, 68,
69, 71, 72-74, 75-88, 89-
103
Merlin: SW1-6, 8-10, 18, 24,
26, 27, 30, 31, 32, 33, 34,
43, 47, SE2-6, 7, 19-21,
30, 35, 42, 47-49, 50, 51-
53, 54-58, EA1, 3, 5, 6,
17, 18, 20, 22, 23, 24, 25,
28, 29, 31, 32, 33, 34, 35,
47, 50, 51, 52, CE2, 3, 4,
5, 6, 7, 10, 11, 18, 35, 36,
43, 47, 49, 51, W2, 4, 10,
11, 14, 18, 23, 24, 27, 32,
34, 37, 38, 40, 42, 49, 50,
51, 52, NE1, 2, 4, 7, 8, 9,
10, 11, 13, 17, 19, 20, 21,
22, 23, 24, 25, 27, 28, 36,
38, 39, 40, 41, 43, 44, 45,
46, 47, 48, 49, 51, S1, 3,
7, 10, 12, 18, 20, 22, 23,
25, 31, 37, 40, 45, 48, 57,
58, 59, 60, 61, 65, 68, 69,
71, 72-74, 75, 77, 79, 75-
88, 101, 89-103, 104
Murrelet, Ancient: SW31
Nightingale: SW43, 47,
SE19-21, 23, 24, 31, 54-
58, 60, EA2, 4, 6, 9, 11,
14, 15, 16, 17, 18, 28, 35,
38, 40-46, 48, 49, CE1, 3,
11, 12, 25, 31, 43, 45, 49,
51, 55
Nightingale, Thrush: S89-
103, 104
Nightjar: SW42, 52-57, SE2-
6, 19-21, 23, 33, 60, EA9,
16, 17, 28, 42, 44, 40-46,
CE12, 40, 42, W1, NE23,
36, S10
Nightjar, Egyptian: SW51
Nutcracker: SE40
Nuthatch: SE2-6, 25, 59,
EA32, CE5, W3, 8, 23,
24, 31, 32, 46, NE10, 38,
CE12, 21, 25, 39, 40, 42,
57
Oriole, Golden: SW1-6, 31,
SE40, 41, EA40-46, S89-
103, 104
Osprey: SW1-6, 22, 29, 37-
41, 45, SE1, 7, 10, 31, 32,

40, 42, 43-46, 59, EA4, 7,
9, 10, 17, 21, 23, 48, 49,
CE3, 7, 10, 12, 15, 16,
17, 22, 24, 25, 26, 27, 28,
35, 48, 49, 52, 55, 58,
W2, 8, 11, 21, 31, 32, 47,
NE1, 6, 10, 19, 20, 21,
22, 23, 24, 25, 29, 30, 39,
46, 48, 49, S10, 15, 25,
33, 34, 36, 37, 38, 48, 53,
54, 55, 59, 61, 89-103
Ouzel, Ring: SW1-6, 8-10,
18, 31, 34, 51, SE7, 10,
17, 22, 31, 37, 39, 40,
EA3, 5, 19, 25, 29, 32,
35, 36, 37, CE2, 3, 4, 5,
7, 11, 18, 27, 47, 52,
W28, 32, 34, 36, 40, 46,
49, 50, NE1, 3, 8, 9, 14,
16, 32, 37, 38, 39, 40, 41,
42, 43, 45, 46, S20, 30,
37, 38, 40, 46, 58, 65, 68,
69, 71
Owl, Barn: SW33, SE16,
30, EA1, 6, 15, 17, 20,
21, 23, 28, 29, 35, 47, 52,
CE2, 3, 4, 7, 15, 49, W11,
21, 24, 27, 37, 41, 42,
NE7, 10, 14, 17, 23, 24,
39, 48, S9, 10
Owl, Little: SW34, 51,
SE16, 54-58, EA47,
CE12, 15, 16, 17, 24, 35,
36, 47, 49, 51, 58, W14,
35, 36, 37, 40, 48, NE15,
19, 20, 22, 23, 24, 29, 39,
41, 47
Owl, Long-eared: SW1-6,
SE30, 54-58, EA21, 25,
29, 35, 44, 40-46, 50,
CE2, 3, 5, 8, 10, 11, 14,
25, 32, 34, 47, W49,
NE6, 7, 19, 22, 23, 28,
29, 41, 44, 45, 48, 49, 51,
S22, 25, 30, 37, 53, 71,
72, 72-74, 75, 75-88, 91,
89-103
Owl, Short-eared: SW1-6,
8-10, 26, 31, 32, 33, 37-
41, 43, 47, SE1, 7, 12-15,
16, 19-21, 22, 30, 35, 41,
42, 47-49, 50, 54-58, EA1,
3, 5, 6, 14, 17, 18, 20, 22,
23, 24, 25, 28, 29, 31, 32,

33, 34, 47, 51, 52, CE2,
3, 4, 5, 7, 8, 9, 11, 14, 25,
33, 34, 35, 43, 47, 49, 51,
52, W4, 10, 11, 14, 18,
24, 32, 34, 37, 38, 40, 42,
49, 50, NE1, 4, 7, 8, 9,
11, 13, 17, 19, 22, 23, 24,
25, 28, 29, 37, 38, 39, 40,
41, 43, 44, 45, 46, 48, 49,
51, S1, 3, 7, 12, 22, 25,
26, 31, 32, 34, 45, 48, 54,
57, 58, 65, 69, 71, 72-74,
75, 77, 79, 84, 75-88, 89-
103
Owl, Snowy: S37, 93, 102,
89-103
Owl, Tawny: EA32, CE12,
57, W3, 32, NE29
Oystercatcher: SW23, 32,
47, SE12-15, 16, 22, 38,
EA2, 3, 5, 13, 14, 15, 28,
30, 34, 35, 37, CE1, 3, 5,
6, 8, 10, 11, 13, 17, 23,
25, 29, 30, 31, 35, 37, 45,
52, W2, 4, 6, 10, 11, 13,
14, 21, 27, 31, 35, 37, 38,
41, 42, 45, 47, 50, 51,
NE1, 2, 4, 5, 6, 7, 10, 11,
13, 14, 17, 19, 37, 38, 40,
41, 44, 46, 47, 49, 50, 51,
S3, 9, 10, 12, 23, 25, 27,
31, 36, 37, 45, 53, 54, 59,
31, 65, 66, 71, 72-74
Parakeet, Ring-necked:
SE16, 27, 42
Partridge, Grey: CE15, 16,
47
Partridge, Red-legged:
SE37, CE47
Peregrine: SW1-6, 8-10, 13,
17, 18, 22, 24, 27, 30, 32,
33, 35, 37-41, 43, 47,
SE1, 7, 30, 31, 34, 35, 39,
47-49, EA3, 17, 18, 20,
30, 31, 32, 47, 51, CE2,
3, 4, 5, 6, 10, 12, 18, 22,
24, 25, 26, 36, 41, 43, 44,
W2, 4, 6, 7, 9, 10, 11, 12,
13, 14, 16, 18, 19, 20, 21,
22, 23, 24, 27, 30, 32, 33,
34, 35, 36, 37, 38, 40, 41,
42, 44, 45, 46, 47, 48, 49,
50, 51, 52, NE1, 2, 4, 7,
8, 9, 10, 11, 13, 14, 15,

38, 51-53, 54-58, EA4, 7,
9, 16, 17, 28, 29, 34, 47,
48, 49, CE1, 2, 3, 5, 10,
11, 13, 16, 20, 22, 23, 24,
25, 27, 28, 29, 30, 31, 32,
33, 35, 38, 43, 45, 48, 49,
51, 52, 54, 55, 58, W4, 7,
20, 50, NE1, 4, 5, 6, 7,
10, 11, 12, 14, 17, 18, 20,
21, 22, 23, 25, 28, 30, 39,
41, 43, 44, 45, 46, 47, 48,
S18, 24, 45, 48

Tern, Common: SW1-6, 8-
10, 12, 32, 37-41, 45, 46,
52-57, SE12-15, 16, 18,
26, 28, 30, 32, 37, 47-49,
50, 51-53, EA1, 4, 7, 13,
14, 16, 17, 18, 20, 23, 28,
29, 30, 37, 48, 49, CE1,
2, 3, 4, 5, 6, 9, 10, 11, 13,
14, 15, 16, 17, 20, 22, 23,
24, 25, 26, 27, 28, 29, 30,
31, 32, 33, 34, 35, 36, 37,
38, 43, 45, 48, 49, 52, 54,
55, 56, 58, 59, W4, 5, 8,
11, 40, 41, 42, 45, 47, 50,
NE1, 4, 5, 6, 7, 8, 10, 11,
13, 14, 15, 18, 20, 21, 22,
23, 28, 41, 43, 45, 46, 47,
49, 50, S1, 3, 10, 12, 15,
22, 23, 25, 27, 28, 43, 45,
48, 52, 58, 59, 66, 71, 72-
74, 87, 75-88, 104

Tern, Lesser Crested: NE50

Tern, Little: SW12, 13, 32,
37-41, SE12-15, 16, 30,
37, 41, 47-49, 51-53, EA3,
5, 12, 13, 14, 16, 18, 20,
23, 28, 29, 30, 32, 35,
CE2, 3, 4, 5, 6, W4, 7, 29,
31, 41, 50, NE2, 5, 11,
13, 14, 28, 43, 44, 45, 51,
S1, 3, 22, 45, 72-74

Tern, Roseate: SW1-6, 12,
13, 37-41, SE30, 31, 37,
EA17, 20, 29, 30, W41,
50, NE2, 39, 41, 42, 43,
44, 45, 50, 51, S28

Tern, Sandwich: SW8-10,
12, 21, 32, 36, 37-41, 52-
57, SE12-15, 16, 30, 37,
41, 47-49, 51-53, EA14,
16, 28, 29, 30, CE3, 4, 5,
6, W4, 8, 11, 31, 41, 45,

47, 50, NE5, 11, 13, 14,
15, 21, 29, 39, 41, 43, 45,
50, S23, 24, 27, 28, 43,
45, 48, 52, 53, 87, 75-88

Tern, White-winged Black:
SW44, SE37, CE58, NE44

Thrush, Grey-cheeked:
SW6

Thrush, Siberian: SW6

Thrush, Song: S72-74

Thrush, White's: SW6

Tit, Bearded: SW36, 44, 48-
49, 49, 50, 52-57, SE11,
16, 36, 43-46, 50, EA16,
17, 18, 21, 23, 29, 31, 32,
34, 47, 50, 52, CE4, 5, 8,
9, 25, 34, 56, 58, W8, 21,
NE10, 22, 24, 25, 29, 30

Tit, Coal: W37, NE21

Tit, Crested: S37, 40, 52,
53, 61, 69

Tit, Marsh: SW57, SE2-6,
19-21, 25, 59, EA17, 21,
32, CE12, 13, 15, 26, 39,
40, 42, W8, 23, NE10, 38

Tit, Willow: SW30, 33, SE2-
6, 19-21, EA17, 21, 39,
52, CE1, 12, 13, 16, 23,
26, 30, 35, 38, 40, 42, 51,
56, 58, W8, 23, 24, 27,
32, 33, 46, NE6, 19, 48,
49, S9, 10, 14

Treecreeper: SE2-6, 59,
EA32, CE12, 21, 42, W3,
8, 23, 24, 31, 32, 46,
NE30, S33

Turnstone: SW23, 37-41,
SE51-53, EA2, 4, 6, 14,
15, 28, 36, 37, 48, CE2,
6, 7, 13, 14, 22, 25, 29,
31, 35, 38, 45, 52, 56,
W4, 6, 8, 9, 10, 17, 31,
37, 41, 45, 48, 50, 51,
NE2, 3, 4, 5, 6, 11, 14,
17, 21, 24, 31, 35, 39, 40,
41, S3, 12, 18, 19, 20, 22,
23, 27, 30, 31, 42, 50, 51,
52, 55, 62, 65, 71, 72-74,
75-88, 89-103

Twite: SW32, SE16, 30, 34,
41, 47-49, 50, EA1, 3, 5,
6, 16, 17, 20, 30, 32, 34,
35, 47, CE2, 3, 4, 5, 6, 9,
16, 19, W45, 47, 50, 51,

52, NE1, 3, 4, 8, 9, 11,
17, 24, 28, 38, 39, 41, 43,
44, 51, S1, 3, 5, 6, 16, 20,
22, 23, 39, 54, 58, 62, 65,
68, 69, 72-74, 76, 82, 75-
88, 89-103

Vireo, Red-eyed: SW1-6,
18

Wagtail, Blue-headed:
CE36

Wagtail, Citrine: S89-103,
104

Wagtail, Grey: SE1, 17,
CE7, 11, 13, 17, 18, 23,
26, 30, 38, 40, 41, 42, 50,
56, 59, W3, 8, 21, 23, 25,
27, 31, 32, 33, 34, 46, 47,
49, NE9, 16, 17, 22, 35,
36, 37, 38, 47, 51, S9, 14,
26, 35, 37, 38, 40, 61

Wagtail, Pied: SW23, 49,
NE28, 50, S72-74, 89-103

Wagtail, White: SW46,
CE16, 23, 24, 29, 31, 52,
56, 58, W47, 50, NE1, 2,
3, 4, 5, 6, 7, 8, 14, 29,
S19, 20, 23, 89-103

Wagtail, Yellow: SW23, 34,
35, 43, 47, 49, 51, SE16,
17, 19-21, 26, 30, 35, 47-
49, EA1, 3, 4, 7, 13, 15,
21, 28, 47, 48, 49, CE4,
6, 10, 11, 12, 13, 14, 15,
16, 23, 29, 36, 37, 48, 51,
52, 54, 55, 56, 58, 59,
W2, 41, 47, 50, NE1, 2,
3, 4, 5, 6, 7, 9, 23, 28, 29,
39, 44

Warbler, Aquatic: SW15,
18, 36, 47, 49, SE47-49,
W4, S104

Warbler, Arctic: SW1-6, 35,
S89-103, 104

Warbler, Barred: SW1-6, 8-
10, 31, 51, SE31, 37,
EA3, 12, 15, 17, 18, 25,
28, 29, 30, 32, 35, CE3,
4, 5, W13, NE28, 34, 39,
40, 41, 42, 43, 45, 51,
S18, 19, 27, 30, 42, 46,
87, 75-88, 89-103, 104

Warbler, Black-and-white:
SW34

Warbler, Bonelli's: SW6

INDEX OF SITES